Competition Law and Policy in
Latin America

Competition Law and Policy in Latin America

Recent Developments

Edited by

Paulo Burnier da Silveira

Published by:
Kluwer Law International B.V.
PO Box 316
2400 AH Alphen aan den Rijn
The Netherlands
Website: www.wolterskluwerlr.com

Sold and distributed in North, Central and South America by:
Wolters Kluwer Legal & Regulatory U.S.
7201 McKinney Circle
Frederick, MD 21704
United States of America
Email: customer.service@wolterskluwer.com

Sold and distributed in all other countries by:
Quadrant
Rockwood House
Haywards Heath
West Sussex
RH16 3DH
United Kingdom
Email: international-customerservice@wolterskluwer.com

MIX
FSC® C103993

Printed on acid-free paper.

ISBN 978-90-411-6047-8

e-Book: ISBN 978-90-411-8688-1
web-PDF: ISBN 978-90-411-8689-8

© 2017 Kluwer Law International BV, The Netherlands

All rights reserved. No part of this publication may be reproduced, stored in a retrieval system, or transmitted in any form or by any means, electronic, mechanical, photocopying, recording, or otherwise, without written permission from the publisher.

Permission to use this content must be obtained from the copyright owner. Please apply to: Permissions Department, Wolters Kluwer Legal & Regulatory U.S., 76 Ninth Avenue, 7th Floor, New York, NY 10011-5201, USA. Website: www.wolterskluwerlr.com

Printed in the United Kingdom.

Editor and Contributors

Paulo Burnier da Silveira is Commissioner at the Brazilian Competition Authority (CADE) and Associate Law Professor at the University of Brasilia (UnB). He holds a PhD in International Law from the University of Paris II and the University of São Paulo (USP), a LLM from the Catholic University of Lisbon and a BA from the Catholic University of Rio de Janeiro. The views hereby expressed are personal and do not necessarily reflect those of the organizations involved.

Aldo Henrique Cáder Camilot holds a Law degree, is notary, Salvadoran and Italian national, with over ten years of experience in Competition Law; since 2009, and is the head of investigations for the Superintendence of Competition from El Salvador. In addition, he is Professor of Civil and Commercial Law at the Higher School of Economics and Business (ESEN). He has been juridical assistant, coordinator and secretary in the Salvadoran Constitutional Chamber of the Supreme Court of Justice.

Alejandro Lucero is a Lawyer graduated from Mar del Plata University, Argentina and Licenciado en Derecho in Spain. He holds a Specialist in Regulation of Public Services degree from Austral University, Argentina and a LLM in European Law from Radboud University, The Netherlands. He worked in Utilities Companies and in the National Competition Authority of Argentina. Currently is an International Independent Consultant in Competition Law and works in International Projects for UNCTAD.

Amanda Athayde is Head of the Leniency Unit at CADE. She holds a PhD in Commercial Law from the University of São Paulo (USP), a BA in Law from the Federal University of Minas Gerais (UFMG) and a BA in Business Administration in the UNA Centre. She is a Professor of Economic and Competition Law at the Public Law Institute (IDP) and a volunteer Professor of Commercial Law at the University of Brasilia (UnB). E-mail: amandathayde@gmail.com.

Ana Frazão is a Law Professor at the UnB. She holds a PhD in Law from the Pontifical Catholic of São Paulo, a LLM from the UnB and a BA from the UnB. She is a private attorney and was a Commissioner at the CADE from 2012 to 2015. E-mail: frazao@unb.br.

Editor and Contributors

Angelo Gamba Prata de Carvalho is a Law student at the UnB and former trainee at the CADE.

Ania Thiemann is the Head of Global Relations at the OECD's Competition Division. She is also in charge of the OECD Competition Committee's Working Party N°2 on Competition and Regulation. Before joining the OECD in 2009, she was Senior Economist at the Economist Intelligence Unit in London from 2000–2009. Ania holds an MSc in Economics from Birkbeck College, University of London; an MPhil in International Relations and Strategy from the Panthéon Sorbonne, Paris I; and an MSc in European Studies and International Relations from the London School of Economics. Ania.Thiemann@oecd.org.

Antonio Gomes is Head of the Competition Division at the OECD since November 2016. He has been President of the Portuguese Competition Authority (2013-2016), having previously served as a Senior Competition Expert in the OECD's Competition Division in 2013. Prior to joining the OECD in 2013, he was Director of the Merger Department of the Portuguese Competition Authority. Since 2005, he has been an Assistant Professor at the Universidade de Aveiro, Portugal. Antonio Gomes holds a Doctorate Degree in Economics from the University of York, United Kingdom, and Master's Degrees in Economics from the University of York and the Universidade Nova de Lisboa.

Carlos Mena Labarthe is Head of the Investigation Authority in the Federal Economic Competition Commission and university professor. The following opinions are expressed in a personal capacity and with the freedom that an academic discussion allows. As former Head of the Planning, Institutional Relations and International Affairs Unit, and former Director General for Cartels, comments may reflect such experience.

Cynthia Andino is of-counsel at AntiTrust Consultores & Abogados®, Quito-Ecuador. She holds a Master in Droit des Affaires from the University of Strasbourg 14', a European Master in Transnational Trade Law and Finance from the University of Deusto and the University of Tilburg 13'. She also has an International Commerce degree from the Universidad Americana of Asunción 09'. Mrs. Andino participated in the Commission that drafted Paraguay's Competition Law. The author thanks the contribution of Charles Reeves and David Sperber. The views hereby expressed are exclusively of the author and do not necessarily reflect those of the aforementioned organizations.

David A. Sperber is a Partner at AntiTrust Consultores & Abogados, Quito – Ecuador www.antitrust.ec. He holds a Juris Doctor from the Pontificia Universidad Católica del Ecuador '01, an LLM from Harvard Law School '02, and a PhD from Universidad de Barcelona '12. He teaches law at the Universidad Internacional del Ecuador.

Eduardo Caminati Anders is the Partner at Lino, Beraldi, Belluzzo and Caminati Advogados, Head of the Antitrust area. He is the Chairman of the Board of Directors of

Brazilian Institute of Studies of Competition, Consumer and International Trade – IBRAC and a member of the Applied Corporate Law Institute – IDSA. He was Chairman of the Commission on Competition Studies and Economic Regulation (CECORE) of the Brazilian Bars Association – Sao Paulo Section (OAB-SP) (2010/2012). He graduated from the Faculty of Law of the USP in 1999.

Eugênia Cristina Nilsen Ribeiro Barza is Associate Professor at Recife Law School of the Federal University of Pernambuco, where she teaches Private International Law, International Trade Law and Latin American Integration Law. She holds a PhD, a LLM and a Law degree from the Federal University of Pernambuco. She leads the research group Regional Integration, Globalization and International Law.

Fabián Pettigrew is economist from Mar del Plata University, Argentina. Member of the Board of the *Comisión Nacional de Defensa de la Competencia*. Argentina. During his mandate he was in charge of this investigation. Currently, he is an independent consultant in competition issues.

Francisco Javier Núñez Melgoza worked for more than twenty-two years in the antitrust agency of the Mexican government. He was Director General of Mergers of the former Federal Competition Commission (CFC) and Commissioner of the Federal Economic Competition Commission (COFECE). He is currently economic consultant and university professor.

Germán Enrique Bacca Medina is currently a Comisioner of the Communications Regulation Commission of Colombia. He is a lawyer from Universidad Externado de Colombia and holds a Specialist Diploma in Finance and Securities Law from the same University, an LLM degree in Communications and Computer Law from Queen Mary University of London and a Postgraduate Diploma in Economics for Competition Law from King's College University of London. Prior to his current position, he served as Deputy Superintendent for Antitrust at the Superintendence of Industry and Commerce and Deputy Superintendent for Data Protection at the same entity. He has also worked as Senior Competition Associate at the law firm Philippi Prietocarrizosa Ferrero DU & Uría in Bogotá.

Graciela Miralles is a Competition Specialist at the Trade and Competitiveness Global Practice of the World Bank Group. In this function, she has been involved in a wide variety of operational and analytical projects to promote competition policy reforms across countries in Latin America, East Asia Pacific, Europe and Central Asia, Middle East and North Africa. Graciela holds a PhD from the European University Institute (Florence, Italy), an LLM in European Community Law from the College of Europe (Bruges, Belgium); and an LLM in Comparative, European, and International Laws from the European University Institute. Dr. Miralles is a member of the Academic Society for Competition law (ASCOLA) and a qualified lawyer since 2003.

Guilherme de Aguiar Falco is a Competition lawyer and Economist with extensive experience in international antitrust cases, especially focusing on the Latin America region. Guilherme holds graduate degrees from Columbia University (LLM) and the Universidade Federal de Sao Carlos (MA in Applied Economics) as well as bachelor degrees in Law (Pontificia Universidade Catolica de Sao Paulo) and Economics (Universidade de Sao Paulo). Guilherme is currently working as a consultant for the World Bank Group.

Guilherme Teno Castilho Missali is a Senior Associate at Lino, Beraldi, Belluzzo and Caminati Advogados, focusing its activities on the Antitrust front. He is a member of the Brazilian Institute of Studies of Competition, Consumer and International Trade – IBRAC and a member of the CECORE of the Brazilian Bars Association – Sao Paulo Section (OAB-SP). He is currently attending Master Degree in Commercial Law at Faculty of Law of the USP. He is specialized in Compliance by Getúlio Vargas Foundation (FGV) and graduated from the Faculty of Law of the USP in 2011. He is the cofounder of the study group called "NECSO" at Faculty of Law of the USP that studies the interplay between sociology and competition.

James Mancini is an Analyst in the OECD's Competition Division. James has previously worked as an Economist specializing in competition litigation and policy analysis at PricewaterhouseCoopers Canada as well as NERA Economic Consulting. He has also served as an Economist at the Canadian federal Department of Finance and at a provincial utilities regulator. James holds an MSc in Economics from the London School of Economics.

Javier Tapia is currently Judge of the Chilean Competition Tribunal (Tribunal de Defensa de la Libre Competencia de Chile or TDLC) and academic of the Postgraduate School at the Universidad de Chile, School of Law. He also teaches in other universities in Chile and abroad. Javier holds a Law degree from Universidad de Chile, School of Law; a PhD from University College of London, U.K.; an MSc. in Regulation from The London School of Economics and Political Sciences, U.K.; and a Diploma in Torts from Universidad de Chile. Javier is the corresponding author: jtapia02@gmail.com

Julián Peña is a partner at Allende & Brea since 2004. He graduated as a lawyer from the Universidad Católica Argentina in 1995. He was legal adviser to the Ministry of Economy (1996/2004), having advised different Ministers and Secretaries of Trade. He has also worked at the Argentine Antitrust Commission (1999/2001). He is Professor of Competition Law at Universidad de Buenos Aires and was Visiting Professor at the University of Florida (2009). Mr. Peña is founder and moderator of ForoCompetencia, an antitrust community with more than 550 members from more than twenty countries. Peña is also officer of the IBA's Antitrust Committee; a member of the International Task Force of the ABA's Section of Antitrust Law; and an international advisor of the American Antitrust Institute. He co-edited the book "Competition Law in Latin America. A Practical Guide" (with Marcelo Calliari, 2016) and is the author of "Control de Concentraciones Económicas" (2002) and of numerous articles, chapters and columns on antitrust and trade law. He has lectured on antitrust and trade issues at various universities and conferences.

Editor and Contributors

Lucia Villarán Elias is a competition lawyer at the Competition Policy Cluster at the Trade and Competitiveness Global Practice of the World Bank Group. Lucia has extensive and applied experience on antitrust and regulatory sectoral frameworks worldwide, with focus on the Latin America region. Education: University of Michigan and Pontifícia Universidad Católica del Perú.

Marcelo Cesar Guimarães is currently a LLM candidate at Recife Law School of the Federal University of Pernambuco, specializing in International Competition Law. He holds a law degree from the same institution. In 2016 he was visiting researcher at the Centre d'études sur l'intégration et la mondialisation of the Université du Québec à Montréal.

Martha Martinez Licetti is the Lead Economist and Global Lead of the Competition Policy Cluster for the Trade and Competitiveness Global Practice at the World Bank Group, where she oversees a portfolio of more than fifty countries. She has more than fifteen years of experience in industrial organization, economic regulation and competition policy. She has held leading positions in the private and public sectors, including at the competition authority and the telecommunications regulator in her native Peru. She has lectured in industrial organization, network regulation, antitrust and economic analysis of law. Education: Northeastern University in Boston (Massachusetts), University of Austin (Texas) and Pontificia Universidad Catolica del Peru.

Marcela Mattiuzzo was Advisor and Chief of Staff at the Office of the Presidency at CADE (2015-2016). She is a Master's of Laws Candidate at the University of São Paulo, from were she holds a Law degree, and was a Visiting Researcher at Yale Law School (2016-2017). She is also a researcher at ITS Rio, with work focused on privacy and personal data regulation, and a partner at VMCA, a consultancy firm specialized in competition policy, compliance, and regulatory advocacy.

Pablo Márquez is a partner at Márquez, Barrera, Castañeda & Ramirez. Before joining the firm, Pablo served as Chairman of the Commission for the Regulation of Communications and Superintendent for Antitrust in Colombia. He holds a PhD in Competition Law for the University of Oxford, an LLM in Law from Harvard, an MSc in Economics, a BPhil and a BA in Law from Universidad Javeriana.

Pablo Reja Sánchez is a former UNPD Consultant at the CADE, University Professor and PhD student in International Law from the UnB, Master in International Relations at the State University of Paraiba/UnB and BA from the University of Granada. Erasmus exchange at University of Paris II Panthéon-Assas (2010/2011).

Pierre Horna is responsible for the design, formulation and implementation of technical assistance and capacity building programs on competition and consumer protection laws and policies for selected developing countries in the ASEAN, Balkan, CIS and Latin American regions. He is the legal affairs official at the Competition and Consumer Policies Branch at UNCTAD Mr. Horna has doctorate studies in International Competition Law at the University of Geneva, Switzerland. Master of

Editor and Contributors

Laws in International Business Law from Leiden University, The Netherlands with thesis on the developmental dimension of expanding WTO covered agreements into Competition Policy (2002) and studies on E-commerce and consumer protection at the Buckingham University, England (2001). Visiting research fellow at Oxford's Centre for Competition Law and Policy and Senior Associate at Pembroke College, University of Oxford.

Rosana Aragón Plaza is a Policy Analyst at the OECD's Competition Division. She is based at the OECD Mexico Center. Before joining the OECD in 2016, Rosana was a competition counsel at a major Brussels law firm. She holds an LLM from Harvard Law School and an LLM in EU law and economic analysis from the College of Europe; she obtained degrees in law and international relations from Universidad Pontificia Comillas de Madrid (ICADE).

Tanja Goodwin is an Economist in the Trade and Competitiveness Global Practice of the World Bank Group. She focuses on analytics and technical assistance in pro-competition sectoral regulation and on the implementation of competition policy. Before joining the World Bank Group, Tanja worked at private and public research institutes in Germany and in Latin America. Education: New York University and University of Tuebingen.

Vanessa Facuse is former Head of the Litigation Division at the Chilean Competition Agency (Fiscalía Nacional Económica or FNE). She teaches competition law in the MBA program at Universidad Diego Portales. Vanessa holds a law degree from Universidad de Chile, School of Law, a Master in IT Law and Telecommunications from Universidad de Chile, and a Diploma in Administrative Law from the same university.

Vinicius Marques de Carvalho was President of the CADE from 2012 till 2016. He is also Professor of Law at the USP and holds a PhD in Law from both the USP and the University Paris I (Panthéon-Sorbonne). After leaving the authority, Vinicius was a Yale Greenberg World Fellow and is now the managing partner at VMCA, a consultancy firm specialized in competition policy, compliance, and regulatory advocacy.

Summary of Contents

Editor and Contributors	v
Foreword *António Gomes*	xxv
Presentation *Vinícius Marques de Carvalho*	xxvii
PART I Institutional Setups and Advocacy Efforts	1
CHAPTER 1 New Competition Policy in Mexico *Carlos Mena Labarthe*	3
CHAPTER 2 New Competition Policy in Argentina *Julián Peña*	37
CHAPTER 3 New Competition Policy in Paraguay *Cynthia Andino*	45
CHAPTER 4 Antitrust Compliance Programs – The Brazilian Experience *Marcela Mattiuzzo*	59

Summary of Contents

CHAPTER 5
The Dissemination of the Competition Culture in Brazil: The Role Played by Civil Associations
Eduardo Caminati Anders & Guilherme Teno Castilho Missali   73

CHAPTER 6
Trends and Developments in Competition Advocacy in Latin America
Martha Martínez Licetti, Lucía Villarán & Tanja Goodwin   85

CHAPTER 7
Pro-competitive Regulatory Assessment in Latin America
Ania Thiemann, James Mancini & Rosana Aragón Plaza   111

PART II
Enforcement Experiences: Anticompetitive Practices and Merger Control   133

CHAPTER 8
Bid Rigging in Public Procurement in Colombia: Evolution and Challenges
Germán Enrique Bacca Medina   135

CHAPTER 9
Predatory Pricing Policy for Latin American Emerging Economies
Pablo Márquez   151

CHAPTER 10
Bid Rigging in Ecuador
David A. Sperber   187

CHAPTER 11
The Case of Automotive Market in a Special Customs Area of Argentina
Alejandro Lucero & Fabián Pettigrew   197

CHAPTER 12
Exchanges of Information in Competition Law: The Chilean (Incipient) Experience
Javier Tapia & Vanessa Facuse   205

CHAPTER 13
Ten Years Fighting Cartels: The Case of El Salvador
Aldo Henrique Cáder Camilot   227

CHAPTER 14
The Use of Indirect Evidences in the Fight Against Cartels in Brazil
Paulo Burnier da Silveira & Pablo Reja Sánchez   233

CHAPTER 15
Shareholders' Damage Claims Against Company Directors for Antitrust Violations? The Japanese Experience and Possible Lessons to Brazil and Latin America
Amanda Athayde 239

CHAPTER 16
The Relation Between Antitrust and Intellectual Property Law on CADE's Case Law
Ana Frazão & Angelo Gamba Prata de Carvalho 255

CHAPTER 17
Merger Control in Mexico: Development and Outlook
Francisco Javier Núñez Melgoza 269

PART III
International Cooperation 283

CHAPTER 18
Regional Coordination in Cartel Investigations: The Liquid Oxygen Case
Pierre Horna 285

CHAPTER 19
The Defense of Competition in Mercosur
Eugênia Cristina Nilsen Ribeiro Barza & Marcelo Cesar Guimarães 315

CHAPTER 20
Implications of the Trans-Pacific Partnership for Competition Policy
Martha Martínez Licetti, Graciela Miralles Murciego & Guilherme de Aguiar Falco 329

Index 361

Table of Contents

Editor and Contributors	v
Foreword *António Gomes*	xxv
Presentation *Vinícius Marques de Carvalho*	xxvii

PART I
Institutional Setups and Advocacy Efforts 25

CHAPTER 1
New Competition Policy in Mexico
Carlos Mena Labarthe 3

§1.01	Introduction		3
§1.02	Overview of the Evolution of Competition Law in Mexico		4
	[A]	First Competition Provisions	4
	[B]	First Competition Law. The Real Emergence of a Competition Law	4
	[C]	The Strengthening of Competition Law	6
		[1] Public Opinion as a Factor for Change	6
		[2] Relevant Cases	7
	[D]	Transformation Factors That Became Amendments	11
		[1] The 2006 Legal Reform	11
		[2] The 2011 Legal Reform	13
§1.03	Paradigm Shift in Competition Law		14
	[A]	Political Context of the 2013 Constitutional Reform	14
	[B]	The 2013 Constitutional Reform	15
		[1] Incremental Powers	17

Table of Contents

		[2]	Institutional Design of Checks and Balances	17
		[a]	Autonomy Between the Investigative and the Decision-Making Authorities	17
		[b]	More Accountability Obligations	19
		[c]	Creation of Specialized Courts	20
	[C]	The New Federal Law of Economic Competition		21
§1.04	Challenges and a New Competition Framework			22
	[A]	Institutional Arrangements		26
	[B]	Fight Against Cartels		27
	[C]	Coordination with the IFT		30
	[D]	Application of the New Powers of COFECE to Conduct Market Investigations		31
	[E]	Market Studies		32
	[F]	Mergers		33
	[G]	Advocacy		33
§1.05	Conclusion			34

CHAPTER 2
New Competition Policy in Argentina
Julián Peña 37

§2.01	Introduction	37
§2.02	Background	37
§2.03	New Developments	38
§2.04	Conclusions	42

CHAPTER 3
New Competition Policy in Paraguay
Cynthia Andino 45

§3.01	Introduction		45
§3.02	Legal Framework		46
	[A]	Law No. 4956 (Competition Law)	47
	[B]	Rules to Law No. 4956	47
§3.03	Illegal Conducts Established in Law No. 4956		47
	[A]	Anticompetitive Agreements	48
	[B]	Abuse of Dominant Position	49
	[C]	Merger Control	50
§3.04	Relevant Conducts Not Classified in the Competition Law		51
	[A]	Unfair Competition	51
	[B]	State Aid	51
§3.05	CONACOM: Paraguayan Competition Authority		52
	[A]	CONACOM's Powers	52
	[B]	Board of Qualifications	53

§3.06	Procedure to Investigate and Punish Illegal Acts Defined in Law No. 4956	54
	[A] Anticompetitive Agreements and Abuse of Dominant Position Procedure	55
	[B] Concentrations and Merger Control	55
	[C] The Administrative Sanctioning Procedure	55
§3.07	Conclusions	57
§3.08	Recommendations	57
Bibliography		58

CHAPTER 4
Antitrust Compliance Programs – The Brazilian Experience
Marcela Mattiuzzo 59

§4.01	Introduction	59
§4.02	Compliance Programs in the Brazilian Context	59
	[A] The Rise of Antitrust Compliance in Brazil – Enforcement by the New BCDS	60
	[B] Antitrust and Anticorruption	63
	[C] The Current Status of the Regulation	66
	[1] Case Law – HSBC/Bradesco	68
§4.03	Antitrust Compliance in Other Latin American Countries	69
	[A] Chile	69
	[B] Mexico	70
§4.04	Final remarks	71

CHAPTER 5
The Dissemination of the Competition Culture in Brazil: The Role Played by Civil Associations
Eduardo Caminati Anders & Guilherme Teno Castilho Missali 73

§5.01	Introduction	73
§5.02	Antitrust Compliance Initiatives: A Brief Outline	75
§5.03	Perceptions of the Competition Law in Brazil and Challenges Ahead	76
§5.04	Case analysis: an example of civil association (IBRAC)	79
§5.05	Conclusions	84

CHAPTER 6
Trends and Developments in Competition Advocacy in Latin America
Martha Martínez Licetti, Lucía Villarán & Tanja Goodwin 85

§6.01	Introduction	85
§6.02	Why Advocacy Efforts Are Relevant in the Context of Latin America	86
§6.03	What is the Status of Competition Advocacy in Latin America?	88

Table of Contents

§6.04	What Lies Behind the Successful Advocacy Initiatives in Latin America?		94
	[A]	Mexico	95
	[B]	Peru	97
	[C]	Colombia	101
	[D]	El Salvador	102
	[E]	Other Advocacy Strategies Conducted by Competition Agencies	104
§6.05	What Lessons Can Be Drawn from Recent Advocacy in Latin America and the Useful Activities for the Future?		107

CHAPTER 7
Pro-competitive Regulatory Assessment in Latin America
Ania Thiemann, James Mancini & Rosana Aragón Plaza   111

§7.01	Introduction		111
§7.02	Why Are Pro-competitive Regulatory Frameworks Good for Latin American Economies?		113
	[A]	Competition is Beneficial to Consumers	113
	[B]	Competition Enhances Productivity	114
	[C]	Regulatory Restrictions on Competition Harm Growth	115
	[D]	Latin America Faces a High Regulatory Burden	118
§7.03	What Is Competition Assessment of Regulations?		119
§7.04	Recent Experience of Competition Assessment in Latin America		121
	[A]	Assessments That Found Limitations to the Number or Range of Suppliers	123
	[B]	Assessments That Found Limitations to the Ability of Suppliers to Compete	126
	[C]	Assessments That Found Limitations to Incentives of Suppliers to Compete	126
	[D]	Assessments That Found Limitations to the Choices and Information Available to Consumers	128
§7.05	Emerging Opportunities for Competition Assessment in Latin America		128
	[A]	*Ex post* Assessment	128
	[B]	Digital Economy Innovations	130
§7.06	Conclusion		131

PART II
Enforcement Experiences: Anticompetitive Practices and Merger Control   133

CHAPTER 8
Bid Rigging in Public Procurement in Colombia: Evolution and Challenges
Germán Enrique Bacca Medina   135

§8.01	Introduction	135

§8.02	Bid Rigging in Public Procurement Evolution in Colombia			136
	[A]	Brief Historical Review Prior to Law 1340 of 2009		136
	[B]	Modernization of the Colombian Regime and Change in the Strategy Against Bid Rigging in Public Procurement		138
	[C]	Most Relevant Cases Following Law 1340 of 2009		145
		[1]	COMSAT INTERNATIONAL (2010) Case	145
		[2]	INPEC (2012) Case	145
		[3]	RAPISCAN (2012) Case	146
		[4]	VALME (2013) Case	146
		[5]	CORMAGDALENA (2013) Case	147
		[6]	NULE BIENESTARINA GROUP (2013) Case	147
		[7]	NULE HOGARES (2013) Case	148
		[8]	IDIPRON (2013) Case	148
		[9]	PAVIGAS (2014) Case	149
		[10]	VIGILANCIA (2015) Case	149
§8.03	Conclusions			149

CHAPTER 9
Predatory Pricing Policy for Latin American Emerging Economies
Pablo Márquez   151

§9.01	Introduction			151
§9.02	The Economics of Price Predation			152
	[A]	Exclusionary Pricing and Abusive Pricing Policy		152
	[B]	Market Power, Exclusionary Behavior and Price Predation		154
§9.03	Mainstream Standards for Predatory Pricing			157
	[A]	Per Se Legal Below Cost Selling		158
	[B]	Per Se Illegal Price Predation		160
		[1]	Below Marginal Cost Predation	161
		[2]	Below Average Variable Cost Predation	162
		[3]	Above-Cost Predation	165
§9.04	Predatory Pricing in Latin America			168
	[A]	Illegal Per Se Predatory Pricing		169
	[B]	Rule-of-Reason Approach to Predatory Pricing		171
§9.05	A Rule for Predatory Pricing Enforcement in Latin American Emerging Economies			176
	[A]	Justification for a Different Approach to Price Predation in Emerging Latin American Economies		176
		[1]	An Effect-Based Price Predation Standard for Emerging Economies	179
			[a] Dominance	180
			[b] Pro-competitive effects	180
			[c] Profits Sacrifice	180
		[2]	Administrability of a Below and Above-Cost Predation Standard	181

Table of Contents

		[a]	Below and Above-Cost Predation in Latin American Emerging Economies	182
§9.06	Conclusions			183

CHAPTER 10
Bid Rigging in Ecuador
David A. Sperber — 187

§10.01 Introduction — 187
§10.02 Legal Framework — 189
    [A] Public Procurement Legislation — 189
    [B] Competition Legislation — 190
    [C] Anticompetitive Agreements — 191
    [D] Public Procurement and Competition Law — 191
§10.03 An Overview of International Bid Rigging Cases — 191
    [A] United States of America: Multiple Listing Service, Inc. — 191
    [B] United Kingdom: Cirrus and Others — 192
    [C] Australia: Marine Hoses — 192
§10.04 Ecuador Bid Rigging Cases — 193
    [A] TUBOS Case (Ministry of Industry and Productivity) — 193
    [B] CRONIX Case (Superintendence of Control of Market Power) — 194
§10.05 Conclusions — 195

CHAPTER 11
The Case of Automotive Market in a Special Customs Area of Argentina
Alejandro Lucero & Fabián Pettigrew — 197

§11.01 Introduction — 197
§11.02 The Special Customs Area Created by Law 19.640 and the Automotive Regime — 198
§11.03 The Investigation Carried Out by the CNDC — 199
    [A] The Legal Frame of the Investigation — 200
    [B] The Fine — 201
    [C] The Judgment of the Cámara Federal de Apelaciones de Comodoro Rivadavia — 202

CHAPTER 12
Exchanges of Information in Competition Law: The Chilean (Incipient) Experience
Javier Tapia & Vanessa Facuse — 205

§12.01 Introduction — 205
§12.02 The Institutional and Substantive Framework — 208
    [A] The Institutional Framework — 208
    [B] The Main Substantive Provisions — 210

	[C] The Concept of Agreement in Chilean Competition Law	211
§12.03	Exchanges of Information as Support for Cartel Behavior	212
	[A] Exchanges of Information on Quantity	213
	[B] Exchanges of Information on Prices	214
	[C] Multimarket Contacts	215
§12.04	"Residual" Exchanges of Information	215
	[A] Market Structures and Characteristics of the Information	217
	[B] General Guidance by Chilean Authorities	222
§12.05	Summing Up	224

CHAPTER 13
Ten Years Fighting Cartels: The Case of El Salvador
Aldo Henrique Cáder Camilot   227

CHAPTER 14
The Use of Indirect Evidences in the Fight Against Cartels in Brazil
Paulo Burnier da Silveira & Pablo Reja Sánchez   233

§14.01	Introduction	233
§14.02	Types of Bid-Rigging	234
§14.03	Cartel of Solar Heaters in Brazil	235
§14.04	International Trend	236
§14.05	Final Remarks	237

CHAPTER 15
Shareholders' Damage Claims Against Company Directors for
Antitrust Violations? The Japanese Experience and Possible Lessons
to Brazil and Latin America
Amanda Athayde   239

§15.01	Introduction	239
§15.02	The Japanese Experience on Shareholder Derivative Actions Against Officers and Directors in the Antitrust Context	240
§15.03	Are Shareholder Derivative Suits Against Officers and Directors for Antitrust Violations a Possible Reality in Brazil?	243
§15.04	Conclusion	250

CHAPTER 16
The Relation Between Antitrust and Intellectual Property Law on
CADE's Case Law
Ana Frazão & Angelo Gamba Prata de Carvalho   255

§16.01	Introduction	255
§16.02	The Complex Relation Between IP Rights and Antitrust Law	256
§16.03	Legitimacy of Antitrust Intervention over IP rights: The ANFAPE Case	259

Table of Contents

§16.04	CADE's View on Standard-Essential Patents and License Agreements	262
§16.05	Sham Litigation and Intellectual Property	264
§16.06	Final Remarks	266

CHAPTER 17
Merger Control in Mexico: Development and Outlook
Francisco Javier Núñez Melgoza 269

§17.01	General Overview		269
§17.02	Evolution of the Regulatory Framework, 1993–2014		270
	[A]	Merger Control in the 1993 FLEC	270
	[B]	Changes to the FLEC in 2006	271
	[C]	Changes to the FLEC in 2011	272
	[D]	The Current Legal Framework	273
§17.03	Brief Review of Some Relevant Cases		274
	[A]	Mexicana/Aeromexico	274
	[B]	Coca-Cola/Jugos del Valle	276
	[C]	Mexichem	276
	[D]	Televisa/GSF Telecom Holdings	278
	[E]	Nestle/Pfizer	279
	[F]	Cinemex/Cinemark	280
	[G]	Comex/Sherwin Williams	280
§17.04	Conclusions		281

PART III
International Cooperation 283

CHAPTER 18
Regional Coordination in Cartel Investigations: The Liquid Oxygen Case
Pierre Horna 285

§18.01	Introduction		285
§18.02	Reviewing the Facts of Liquid Oxygen Cartel Cases in Panama (2001), Argentina (2005), Chile (2007), Peru, Brazil and Colombia (2010) and Mexico (2011)		288
§18.03	Reviewing Cooperation Agreements in Some of the Jurisdictions of the Liquid Oxygen Cartel Cases: Brazil, Chile, Colombia and Peru		293
§18.04	Challenges in Strengthening Cooperation in Cartel Cases for the Selected Jurisdictions		298
	[A]	Low Levels of Cooperation Between Competition Agencies	298
	[B]	Prohibition to Exchange Information in Open Cartel Investigations	300
	[C]	Modest Developments in Implementing Leniency Programs in the Seven Jurisdictions, with the Exception of Brazil and Chile	302

	[D] Proper Recognition of the Evidence Gathered Abroad	302
§18.05	Some Recommendations to Improve Coordination Between Cartel Enforcers in Latin America	303
	[A] Improving the Level of Cooperation and Coordination Between Agencies	303
§18.06	Steps Towards Effective Exchange of Information in Parallel Investigations	305
§18.07	Improving the Request of Evidence Abroad and Recognition: Establishing Ideas for a Victim of an International/Regional Cartel to Claim Private/Civil Damages Locally	308
§18.08	Final Remarks	311
Bibliography		313

CHAPTER 19
The Defense of Competition in Mercosur
Eugênia Cristina Nilsen Ribeiro Barza & Marcelo Cesar Guimarães   315

§19.01	Introduction	315
§19.02	The Treaty of Asunción and the Provisional Regulation of Competition Law	316
§19.03	The Protocol for the Defense of Competition of MERCOSUR (Fortaleza Protocol)	317
§19.04	New Directions for the MERCOSUR Antitrust Policy	319
	[A] The Antecedents	319
	[B] The Agreement for the Defense of Competition of MERCOSUR	321
	[C] A Review of the Agreement for the Defense of Competition of MERCOSUR and the Challenges of Cooperation Within the Bloc	324
§19.05	Conclusion	326
Bibliography		327

CHAPTER 20
Implications of the Trans-Pacific Partnership for Competition Policy
Martha Martínez Licetti, Graciela Miralles Murciego &
Guilherme de Aguiar Falco   329

§20.01	Introduction	329
§20.02	The Competition Chapter	334
§20.03	The SOE Chapter	339
§20.04	Vertical Dimension of Competition-Related Commitments	353
§20.05	Final Remarks	358
Index		361

Foreword

António Gomes

Competition Policy, Enforcement and Welfare in Latin America

Several countries in Latin America have undergone important economic and social transformation in the past two decades, engaging in reforms to favour open market economies which included the adoption of competition laws.

In the 90s and the 2000s, countries such as Argentina, Mexico, Brazil, Chile and Colombia, which have had competition laws for decades, have significantly modernized their competition laws whilst several countries introduced modern competition laws. More recently, further improvements based on national experience and international best practices were introduced, as is the case of the reforms of 2011 in Brazil or 2013 and 2014 in Mexico.

Effective competition is critical to guarantee a dynamic business environment and to deliver consumer welfare through lower prices, better quality and greater choice.

Competition among businesses can deliver efficiency improvements and brings newer and better products to consumers through innovation, leading to gains in productivity, competitiveness and economic growth. But a competitive environment with adequate competition rules and robust institutions also contributes to improve business confidence or to reduce the risk of corruption. Competition benefits not only consumers, but also firms, the State and taxpayers.

The OECD has been engaged in the development of competition law and policy in the region for many years. This has taken several forms. First, in partnership with the Inter-American Development Bank (IDB), the OECD has established, in 2003, the Latin American and Caribbean Competition Forum (LACCF). This Forum has been contributing to stronger and more effective competition law enforcers and advocates for pro-competitive reform, through the sharing of experiences and establishment of best practices in the region. The success of the LACCF also shows the growing importance of regional cooperation as the economies in the region become more and more interdependent.

Second, the OECD has supported several countries in identifying scope for improvement in their competition frameworks, through reviews which have often served as guidance for implemented reforms (Argentina, 2009; Brazil, 2005 and 2010; Chile, 2004, 2010, 2014; Colombia, 2009, 2016; Costa Rica, 2014; El Salvador, 2008; Honduras, 2011; Mexico, 2004; Panama, 2010; Peru, 2004; as well as follow up, in 2007 and 2012, of the recommendations in previous peer reviews in Latin America).

Lastly, in many countries in the region, the OECD has been providing capacity building in competition policy and enforcement, promoting the fight against bid-rigging, and also developing competition assessment of legislation and regulation which may unduly restrict competition.

This book brings together authors with extensive experience in Latin America, who bring their first hand experience and insight on the developments in competition law and policy in the region. It will serve as a testament to the impressive changes that have strengthened competition laws and institutions in recent years to the benefit of consumers and the economies of the majority of countries in Latin America. By doing so, this book will certainly contribute to shaping our views on how competition law and policy will, or should, evolve in the years to come.

Presentation

Vinícius Marques de Carvalho

A New Era for Competition Policy in Latin America

The new competition legislation in place in Brazil since 2012 significantly changed the structure of the Administrative Council for Economic Defense (CADE) in its capacity of watchdog for competition law, including merger control, unilateral conduct and antitrust sanctions. The overall numbers are quite impressive: CADE has drastically reduced the average time analysis for merger review and has exponentially increased the number of anticompetitive practices condemnations. The new legal framework enabled CADE to become one of the most important competition authorities in the world.

Nevertheless, the Brazilian experience is not a sole man journey in the region. This trend of boosting competition enforcement may be noticed thorough Latin America. The Mexican recent reform is surely an interesting example, as the new institutional setup allows for greater competition enforcement policy in line with what was experienced in Brazil.

This book sheds light on the increasing role of competition law and policy in Latin America. In twenty chapters, including contributions from Argentina, Brazil, Chile, Colombia, Ecuador, El Salvador, Mexico and Paraguay, the readers will have the chance to confirm the trend mentioned above, which became a reality in a very short time. In addition, contributions from experts with great experience from international organizations, such as the OECD, UNCTAD and the World Bank, complements the national experiences shared by local competition experts. In total, thirty-one competition experts participated in the endeavor.

The book is divided into three sections: (i) Institutional setups and advocacy efforts; (ii) Enforcement experiences, including anticompetitive practices and merger control; and (iii) International cooperation.

In a first section, new Latin American setups for competition policy are presented, including the recent legislation changes in Mexico and Paraguay. Some

Presentation

different advocacy initiatives are also addressed in other contributions, for instance those related to compliance in Brazil as well as efforts lead by the World Bank and the OECD in the region. The section reflects the constant effort to improve the governing rules about competition protection in the Latin America.

A second section focus on the analysis of concrete enforcement experiences in Latin America. It includes chapters covering predatory pricing, the use of indirect evidences, liability of company directors, bid-rigging, among others. The authors did not hesitate to put forward some difficult issues in the daily life of a competition authority, which may assist other competition authorities in the region to seek for solutions to similar challenges.

Finally, a third section will serve to illustrate international cooperation efforts in the region. It demonstrates the importance of international cooperation for competition protection, as well as ways to improve international cooperation among Latin American countries. Cooperation in enforcement activities, future of competition policy within Mercour and Trans-Pacific Partnership are topics addressed in this section

In a nutshell, competition law and policy in Latin America have taken huge steps towards development in the last decade, which enables us to speak of a "New Era" for competition enforcement in the region. Companies should be aware of this trend in order to increase efforts to comply with competition legislation, which are subject to modern investigation techniques and heavy fines.

PART I Institutional Setups and Advocacy Efforts

CHAPTER 1
New Competition Policy in Mexico[*]

Carlos Mena Labarthe

> Prediction is very difficult,
> especially if it is about the future
> Niels Bohr

§1.01 INTRODUCTION

In Mexico, we have experienced major changes to the competition regime in a very short period. From 2006 to 2016, things have changed dramatically every four or five years with a major overhaul to the system in 2013 and 2014.

From 1993 to 2013, the competition authority of Mexico, the Federal Competition Commission (CFC by its Spanish acronym) went from a somehow tortuous stage of "birth by C-section" to a stage of "relative maturity" which allowed stability and consolidation between 2007 and 2012.

The competition law of 1992 and the CFC were a result of important institutional reforms that began in 1988. It took a long time to modernize and adjust the system. The new law is the result of the modernization of the Mexican economy that matured between 2013 and 2014.

This paper aims to critically analyze these great institutional developments, enjoying the freedom that an academic discussion allows. Here, I try to identify some successes and failures of the Mexican competition policy that occurred during the past years, as well as the implications of the huge whirlwind of changes and reforms.

---

[*] This article is based on a previous Art. I published in Mena-Labarthe, Méndez-Rodríguez and Roldán-Xopa, Derecho de la Competencia en México, (Mexico City: Porrúa, 2015), 1–40. I appreciate the help of Ivonne Maricela Santillán García to translate and adapt some parts of such paper for this one. I also thank Victor Meyer, Daniela Barrón, Laura Méndez and Karen Ortiz for their research for this and the previous papers.

Controversial cases, innovative institutional reforms and a new institutional context will be key evidence to consider that we are now facing a "New Competition Policy Era" in Mexico.

§1.02 OVERVIEW OF THE EVOLUTION OF COMPETITION LAW IN MEXICO

[A] First Competition Provisions

Most of the Competition Law scholars in Mexico consider the 1857 Constitution as the origin of this subject. Said Constitution established for the first time the prohibition of monopolies in Mexico. Even though this constitutional provisional was a substantial achievement at that time, it has been largely ignored by scholars when they refer to the origins of competition and antitrust laws – literature normally addresses the United States' Sherman Act, or its Canadian predecessor, which appeared one year earlier. This might be due to the fact, that the prohibition of monopolies contained in the 1857 Constitution was never enforced.

In Mexico, the 1917 Constitution references the previous 1857 constitutional provision and makes Article 28 the cornerstone of the competition and free market participation system in our country.

In 1983, an amendment to this constitutional article was passed, introducing many of the concepts that to this day guide in our competition law. These are: (1) the confirmation of the prohibition of monopolies and "monopolistic practices"; (2) the creation of legislative obligations to maintain laws that "severely" sanction any concentration, in one or several individuals, of basic consumption goods which seeks to increase prices; (3) the mandate to pursue and punish any agreement or practice carried out by economic agents that aims to restrict competition and free market participation, as well as *"everything that constitutes an undue exclusive advantage in favor of one or several individuals and at the cost of the general public or of a social class"*; and, finally, (4) the power of empowered authorities to effectively pursue such practices.

Unfortunately, this constitutional provision was not effectively enforced or regulated until the establishment of the first Federal Law of Economic Competition (Competition Law) published in December 24, 1992 in the Federal Official Gazette (FOG) and which entered into force in June 22, 1993.

[B] First Competition Law. The Real Emergence of a Competition Law

The 1992 Competition Law abrogated several laws on economic regulation which allowed the Executive Branch to set price controls and establish other direct controls that mainly responded to interventionist policies. From its origins, Competition Law promoted economic modernization, competitiveness, as well as the promotion and strengthening of international trade. The law was oriented to reduce negative effects of abusive conducts from monopolies and anticompetitive practices. This sought to benefit not just initial buyers, but also final consumers, employment, competitiveness and income distribution. For that purpose, the CFC was created in order to enforce the law.

The creation of the Federal Competition Commission

With the entry into force of the Competition Law in 1993, the CFC was created as a federal regulatory agency dependent of the Ministry of Trade and Industrial Development (SECOFI by its Spanish acronym). Even under this legal structure, the CFC enjoyed technical and operational autonomy established by the law.[1]

The creation of the first competition authority in Mexico was a consequence of several factors, such as:[2] (1) personal convictions of some liberal public servants, with background in modern economic schools during the emergence of the regulatory State;[3] (2) the negotiation of a free trade agreement for North America; (3) the influence of international organizations, such as the Organisation for Economic Co-operation and Development (OECD) or the International Monetary Fund (IMF); and (4) the pressure from new market competitors, such as international firms and corporate bodies.

Each of these elements called for a counterweight against firms with wide market power that showed a clear proclivity towards monopolistic activities in the country. At the moment of its creation, the CFC was entrusted with the following powers: (1) investigate and sanction the existence of absolute monopolistic practices (cartels); (2) investigate and sanction the existence of relative monopolistic practices (vertical agreements and unilateral conduct cases); (3) review mergers; and (4) issue opinions on laws, bylaws, orders, circulars and administrative acts. These opinions had no legal effects and the Commission was not compelled to issue its opinion.

For the first time, a law in Mexico established the possibility to sanction monopolistic practices, which, in a very Mexican language, were named "absolute" and "relative." On one hand, "per se" violations, referring to clearly anticompetitive practices which accepted no justification, were baptized under the concept of "absolute monopolistic practices." On the other, conducts that were to be evaluated under the "rule of reason" were named "relative monopolistic practices."

---

1. The truth of this independence had highs and lows, but it was during the administration of Eduardo Pérez Motta when the CFC clearly demonstrated such independence from the Federal Government. For instance, the opinion issued on the assignation of slots in Mexico's City International Airport; or its opposition expressed through a binding opinion in order to avoid a designation of origin in the mezcal case, as well as other positions adopted by the CFC.
2. Carlos Mena Labarthe, "Biography of a Competition Commission," *Economic Competition and Law, Economics and Politics Studies*, Mexico, Porrúa, 2007, p. 30.
3. Majone Giandomenico, "The Rise of the Regulatory State in Europe," *West European Politics* 17, No. 3 (1994):77-10, accessed July 6, 2015. http://www.tandfonline.com/doi/abs/10.1080/0140 2389408425031?journalCode=fwep20; Majone Giandomenico, "From the Positive to the Regulatory State: Causes and Consequences of Changes in the Mode of Governance," *Journal of Public Policy*, No. 17 (1997):139-167, accessed July 6, 2015. http://www.jstor.org/stable/4007608 and; David Levi Faur and Jacint Jordana, "The Rise of the Regulatory Sate in Latin America," No. 61 (2004):1-18, accessed July 6, 2015. *http://papers.ssrn.com/sol3/papers.cfm?abstract_id=1750 251*.

In spite of the new competences and the recognition of its technical autonomy, the CFC was not perceived by public opinion as influential or even important. As a result, its first steps were rather weak.

The CFC was born with a team of barely ten professionals. In order to strengthen the technical abilities of the institution, there was an interest to select respected professionals with a highly regarded professional record as the first Commissioners. This was especially true of its president, Dr. Santiago Levy Algazi, who was a key piece in several economic modernization projects in Mexico, and demonstrated an enormous intellectual capacity.

Dr. Levy recently mentioned in the *Commissioners Meeting, 20 years encouraging Economic Competition Policy in Mexico*, that in that time there was a general understanding that macroeconomic stabilization would not be able to impulse the expected economic growth by itself and that it was necessary to foster a series of changes. He also considered that pressure from international companies alone would hardly generate competition in the Mexican economy, and thus, it was necessary to couple it with internal institutions that would promote it. This perspective deeply influenced how Competition Law in Mexico was first understood.[4]

[C] The Strengthening of Competition Law

[1] Public Opinion as a Factor for Change

After several years of the CFC's operation, Competition Law in Mexico gained ground in national and international agendas. Likewise, since 2000, Competition Law achieved the support of different government bodies, which began to recognize the importance of this topic in Mexico focusing the discussion in the creation of mechanisms for its efficient development.

Thanks to the significant efforts of important actors, such as commentators, scholars, international organizations, businessmen, public authorities and society in general, all of which were influential from their different trenches, it was possible to begin demonstrating the need for increased competition in the markets. This, because competition was identified as a central policy element to boost the competitiveness of the economy and economic growth in Mexico.

Certainly the most import example these efforts is the work led by Eduardo Pérez Motta, Chairman of the CFC (2004–2013) in order to "preach" the benefits of economic competition and the urgency to improve the regulatory framework not only in terms of the implementation of competition law, but also to identify regulation that prevented the access to markets and that had an impact in the lack of competition. This eventually led to the identification of a huge backlog that existed in the area, as there was an unclear idea of the competition regime in Mexico. Additionally, in a wise way, emphasis was made on the potential influence of competition policy in the solution of

---

4. Mexico, Federal Commission of Economic Competition, "Commissioners Reunion, 20 Years Strengthening Economic Competition Policies in Mexico," September 22, 2014.

problems such as: (1) low economic growth, (2) insufficient competitiveness in the markets, and (3) income inequality.

The topic became increasingly relevant between 2006 and 2008, as was it mentioned as a key factor for economic development in the reports issued by various national and international agencies, such as IMF, OECD, the World Economic Forum (WEF), the Bank of Mexico (BANXICO) and the Mexican Institute for Competitiveness (IMCO). The reports stressed the growing need to introduce greater competitive pressure in the Mexican markets. They identified a considerable lack of competition, excessive regulation and some economic sectors that were foreclosed. It was explained that the lack of competition resulted in a poor performance of the economy, thus, emphasis was made on the need to eliminate barriers to entry in the markets. Moreover, the reports identified the potential impact of increased competition on productivity, growth and income distribution.

Foreign and national commentators identified a problem that had been growing in the past years, but that had not had social or political resonance so far. At that time, the CFC embarked on a crusade to promote competition and place in the national agenda.

An important milestone in this effort was a study generated with the auspices of the OECD and the CFC, which identified the negative impact of lack of competition in the Mexican population; especially in the poorest families. In this study, which was titled "Assessment of the distributional and spatial impact of firms with market power in Mexico"[5] and published in August 6, 2008 by Carlos M. Urzúa, empirical evidence showed social losses deriving from the exercise of monopolistic power in Mexico. Moreover, it offered evidence that these social losses were not only significant but also regressive, because as I mentioned, they affected the less privileged.[6]

[2] Relevant Cases

In the early years of the CFC, its Presidents Santiago Levy and Fernando Sánchez Ugarte focused on some important cases, some of them dealing with the sale of some

---

5. Carlos M. Urzúa, *Evaluation of the Distributive and Spatial Effects in Companies with Market Power in Mexico*, Tecnológico de Monterrey, August 2008, accessed July 7, 2015. http://www.oecd.org/daf/competition/45047597.pdf.
6. To prove the aforementioned, this work was based in theoretical models about market behavior in light of the existence of monopolies and oligopolies (particularly Cournot's). Through these models, consumers welfare loses were estimated through the demand price elasticity concerning certain important goods, such as: corn tortilla, processed meat, cow milk, egg, chicken, sodas, packaged juices, bottled water, beers and drugs. Some other methodological aspects may be criticized, but it should be recognized that the analysis had such impact, that it eventually became one of the arguments used by the President Felipe Calderón to propose a series of legal reforms in 2011. *Vid.* President Felipe Calderón Speech during the presentation of the *Iniciativa de Decreto por el que se Reforman, Adicionan y Derogan Diversas Disposiciones de la Ley Federal de Competencia Económica, del Código Penal Federal y del Código Fiscal de la Federación*, which took place at the Manuel Ávila Camacho Hall, in the Official Residency of Los Pinos, accessed January 6, 2015. http://www.agendadeldesarrollosocial.com/index.php/lo-importante/24-ley-antimonopolios.

Mexican airlines and their holding company CINTRA,[7] cases related to Mexlub,[8] the College of Notaries of the Federal District,[9] the merger of Kimberly Clark of Mexico,[10] and Warner Lambert.[11]

In the later era, cases started to become more high-profile thanks to that knowledge that the CFC acquired from the first cases and their judicial resolutions. Some the most important resolutions of this period and the evidence they revealed about the effect of the CFC on the behavior of companies can be summed up in the following relevant examples:

(1) *Coca-Cola:* In June 2005, the Coca-Cola system, consisting of different enterprises of the same economic group, was fined with MXN 157 million after the accreditation of relative monopolistic practices. The case derived from a series of complaints filed by natural persons and the company Ajemex, which commercialized Big Cola products. This case represented a major success for the Commission since it was upheld at courts, creating an important precedent in the competition field. This case contrasted with a previous one, where Pepsi Cola also accused Coca-Cola and its bottling company, and in which legal protection (amparo proceedings[12]) was granted for the defendants, because of a deficient investigation from the CFC.

(2) *GRUMA:* In 2005, the Commission rejected the acquisition of Maseca Group – of the firm Agroimsa– by GRUMA, a corn and flour tortilla producer. The transaction was prohibited because the CFC considered there were very few companies participating in the industrialized flour industry. This case was eventually lost at the judicial stage because of an issue that arose in the notification of the resolution. Nevertheless, this resolution brought important

---

7. Mexico, Federal Competition Commission Press Release, *Federal Competition Commission Decision Concerning CINTRA selling,* October 2000, accessed September 4, 2006. http://www.cfc.gob.mx/contenedor.asp?P = Results.asp?txtDir = http://xeon2/cfc01/Documentos/Esp/Comunicaci%C3%B3nhttp://www.cfc.gob.mx/contenedor.asp?P = Results.asp?txtDir = http://xeon2/cfc01/Documentos/Esp/Comunicación.
8. Mexico, CFC File DE-024-2010, accessed January 5, 2015. http://www.cofece.mx:8080/cfcresoluciones/docs/Asuntos%20Juridicos/V75/9/1761112.pdf.
9. Mexico, Supreme Court, Complaint regarding to the File DE-14-95, October 23, 1997 resolution and Amparo Revision Procedure 761/1999.
10. The Federal Commission of Competition approved the operation between Kimberly Clark de México, S.A. de C.V. and Copamex Industrias, S. A. de C. V., and foresaw its compliance with a scheme of divestiture of assets that was imposed as main condition to authorize the Kimberly Clark merger with Compañía Industrial de San Cristóbal, S.A. de C.V. *See* Javier Aguilar Álvarez, *Glosa de la Concentración entre Kimberly Clark México y Compañía Industrial de San Cristóbal,* Federal Commission of Competition, 1996, accessed January 5, 2015. http://www.juridicas.unam.mx/publica/librev/rev/arsiu/cont/17/efo/efo24.pdf.
11. Mexico, Plenum of the Federal Commission of Competition, File DE-11-94, solved on February 8, 1996, *Chicles Canels, S.A. de C.V. v. Chicle Adams, S.A. de C.V,* https://www.cofece.mx:4443/cfcresoluciones/DOCS/Asuntos%20Juridicos/V45/6/1522970.pdf, accessed June 30, 2015; and Mexico, Federal Commission of Competition Ex officio Investigation to Warner Lambert, File IO-16-96, June 2, 2002. Accessed June 30, 2015. http://189.206.114.203/docs/pdf/ra-04-98.pdf.
12. Amparo proceedings are a Mexican legal institution (federal trial) that grants relief from authorities' actions that breach the complainants' constitutional rights.

lessons to the competition authority in terms of the formalities of the procedures, especially in the notification process.

(3) *Bid rigging in the pharmaceutical sector:* One of the most significant cases was file IO-003-2006[13] in which a fine of MXN 151,679,345.00 was imposed on six pharmaceutical companies that coordinated their positions in a public bid carried out by the Mexican Social Security Institute (IMSS)[14] with the clear intention to eliminate competition among them, and which forced the IMSS to pay higher prices for the treatments of its right holders. In this case, the CFC also sanctioned individuals who participated in the cartel representing the pharmaceutical companies. The CFC's resolution was challenged before the courts, and due to its relevance it reached the Supreme Court of Justice (Supreme Court). The Court determined the legality of the CFC's Plenum resolution on April 8, 2015. The cornerstone evidence used by the CFC consisted of an economic analysis of public bids for serums and human insulin made by these six pharmaceutical companies in public procurement processes carried out between 2002 and 2006. The Supreme Court recognized the Commission's economic analysis as an indirect valid proof to detect collusion cases and ruled that said economic analysis "was useful to evaluate if the conducts of competitors restrict free supply and demand operations in order for the price to reach the competitive equilibrium, or if the restrictions imposed by the companies with market power impeded the efficient operation of the market or maintain prices above the competition level, as was observed in the resolved files."[15]

It was determined that the economic analysis demonstrated not only that there was a clear pattern regarding the winning and losing bids, but also that prices that were offered in the bids maintained a certain similarity, whether they were the winner or losers bids. These actions had really no logic in a bid dynamic, in which an economic agent's main objective is to win.

Due to the use of economic analysis as a means – recognized by the Courts – to prove the existence of a cartel, this case set a fundamental precedent for ulterior cartel investigations.

(4) *Transportation sector:* In 2006, the merger between *Ferromex*, of *Grupo México*, and *Ferrosur* was rejected as the Commission considered that the railway transport sector would be left in the hands of only two firms. Grupo México's lawyers challenged the decision. In 2011, after five years of litigation, a Court cleared the merger. It is worth noting that several analysts agree that the merger has had negative effects in the market.

---

13. Mexico, Plenum of the Federal Commission of Competition, File IO-003-2006 of March 11, 2006. Accessed July, 5, 2015. https://www.cofece.mx:4443/cfcresoluciones/Docs/Asuntos%20Juridicos/V39/3/1371186.pdf.
14. COFECE, *Absolute Monopolistic Practice Analysis: Collusion in Public Tenders Concerning IMSS Drugs' Purchasing*, accessed July 14, 2015. https://www.cofece.mx/cofece/images/Promocion/Historias/HISTORIA_IMSS_080415.pdf.
15. Mexico, Federal Commission of Economic Competition, Press Release, accessed April 10, 2015. https://www.cofece.mx/cofece/images/Comunicados/Boletines_2015/COFECE-009-2015.pdf.

(5) *Breweries:* Miller Trading Company, a subsidiary of SAB Miller in Mexico, filed a complaint against *Grupo Modelo* and *Cervecería Cuauhtémoc-Moctezuma* because of possible vertical restrictions. The CFC's resolution of June, 2013 accepted a series of unilateral commitments from both dominant breweries which would limit their exclusivities and allow the entry of competitors. This case represents a challenge in the analysis of remedies for conduct cases that will be worth studying in the future.

(6) *Grupo Televisa:* the CFC fined *Televisa* because the firm did not allow a cable operator to transmit its open television channels. Later, the CFC sanctioned TV stations for fixing agreements between the 175 shareholders of *Productora y Comercializadora de Televisión por Cable S.A. de C.V.* aiming to allocate or distribute segments of the actual market and of the cable television potential sector.[16]

(7) *Telcel*: This investigation arose from the many complaints against *Telcel* for abuse of dominance in the interconnection services for the finalization of calls in mobile networks. In this regard, the CFC's Plenum considered that *Telcel* had imposed tariffs on third concessionaries for the service of finalization of calls in its public network that were higher than the cost *Telcel* charged itself for the cost of *on-net* calls, and even higher than the price for providing the mobile STL to its final users for the same service. Such conduct raised *Telcel*'s competitor's costs and a consequent reduction in their margin of gains. As a result, the Plenum imposed a fine of USD 11,989,653,276.40,[17] arguing that through this abusive conduct *Telcel* had used an essential input for the finalization of calls as a means to unduly displace its competitors in the market and establish exclusive advantages in favor of its economic interest group.

(8) *Televisa-Iusacell Merger:* Originally, the CFC rejected such transaction, arguing that the company GSF (shareholder of *Iusasell*'s actions) could be a vehicle for its members to coordinate and cooperate in the related markets of contents/programing and advertising. Even though such markets were out of GSF co-investment, the former CFC estimated that the effects of the merger would substantially change the way in which *Televisa* and *Grupo Salinas* interacted, favoring their coordinated behavior in the contents/programing and publicity markets.[18] Nevertheless, in the motion for reconsideration

---

16. Mexico, Plenum of the Federal Commission of Competition, File DE-022-2007 solved on April 25, 2013. Accessed, December 10, 2014. http://www.cfc.gob.mx:8080/cfcresoluciones/.
17. Mexico, Plenum of the Federal Commission of Competition, file DE-037-2006, solved in April, 2011. http://www.cofece.mx:8080/cfcresoluciones/docs/Asuntos%20Juridicos/V100/0/2073 266.pdf The fine was suspended latter during the motion for reconsideration filed by the telephonic firm, subject to commitments. Given that Cablemás and other companies filed an amparo procedure, IFT was ordered to investigate and process the complaints. The fine was revoked by IFT on June, 2015 for having complied with the commitments presented to the extinct CFC.
18. Mexico, Plenum of the Federal Commission of Competition, file CNT-031-2011, solved on January 24, 2012. Accessed, December 10, 2014. http://base.crcal.org/documentos/0f452dfa-3 fc3-4004-a9e6-e600c61084a0/MEXICO-CNT-TELEVISA-IUSACELL-2012.pdf.

RA-043-2012 the case was settled through a series of commitments: (a) the divestiture of TotalPlay in favor of *Grupo Salinas*; (b) the commitment not to tie television publicity sales to GSF services, and; (c) the commitment to offer publicity spaces in market terms and conditions to any person in possession of a concession.

Regardless of the efforts carried out by the Commission to detect and sanction anticompetitive conducts, the aforementioned examples reveal that the maximum penalties imposed during several years were very low in terms of the possible benefit that economic agents could gain as a result of an anticompetitive conduct. This situation lessened the efficiency of the Commission's attributions, given that it was more beneficial to pay the fines, rather than to comply with the law.

Nevertheless, during this evolution period, defined by reactive reforms to the successes and limitations of the Commission, an increase of 600% in fines' amounts was achieved during the former CFC's last year of operations; mainly in absolute monopolistic practices.

[D] Transformation Factors That Became Amendments

[1] The 2006 Legal Reform

The 2006 Reform was certainly one of the most relevant transformations of our competition law. This project was originally designed by the CFC and later supported in Congress. The project rested on two main axes: (1) remedying those deficiencies that the Judiciary had ruled as unconstitutional, and, at the same time; (2) giving the Commission greater powers and faculties for all types of sectors, especially those of sectoral regulation.

This reform significantly broadened the CFC's powers by clarifying the definition of some competition law concepts, such as "economic agent," and by adjusting the wording of certain articles that enriched the relative monopolistic practices chapter.

Likewise, the regulatory body was empowered to carry out verification visits (on site searches) in order to obtain information related to the investigated cases. Furthermore, adjustments were made to different articles and some precepts that had proven to be unconstitutional were eliminated. It also amended the mergers' chapter with the purpose of clarifying the criteria under which the notification should be made and of proposing more expeditious forms for the review of mergers.

The previously mentioned reform increased the amount of administrative penalties and created the "divestiture" concept, considered the most serious and important sanction, providing the Commission with a tool that would allow it to break up a recidivist company.

Additionally, the introduction of a leniency program finally allowed economic agents to recognize their participation in cartels and, in doing so, to qualify for the benefit of the reduction of sanctions. This mechanism sought to incentivize the members of a cartel to provide information that would be difficult for the Commission to obtain otherwise.[19]

Finally, the reform empowered the Senate to challenge the designation of Commissioners, appointed by the Head of the Executive Branch.

As a result of this reform, in 2007 a new internal regulation established a novel institutional arrangement for the Commission. New administrative units were created and a redistribution of functions was also put in place. These actions allowed the CFC to exercise its new powers with renewed energies.

Despite the great achievements of the 2006 reform, they turned out to be insufficient and inadequate according to the Unconstitutional Action 33/2006,[20] in which the Supreme Court referred to the following aspects:

- *CFC's legal nature:* In order to define it, the Supreme Court considered necessary to establish the difference between the two existing forms that Mexico's federal Constitution foresees for federal public administration: centralized and government-controlled. In this sense, the Supreme Court concluded that the CFC was as a federal regulatory agency de-concentrated from the Ministry of Economy for the efficient and effective attention of the matters within the jurisdiction of the Ministry. For this reason, the federal legislator granted the Commission with specific faculties to comply with the objectives of the respective law, such as the prevention, sanction and detection of the mentioned practices as a way to protect the general interest, incentivizing national economic development.[21]
- *Invalidation of the Commissioners' appointment procedure:* The Supreme Court estimated that an ordinary law cannot empower the Congress Chambers to intervene in the appointment of public servants of a body pertaining to the federal public administration because the Chambers only had the attributions explicitly provided by the Constitution itself. To do otherwise would a represent a violation of the principle of separation of powers.
- *Illegality of the requirement to obtain a judicial warrant in order to carry out verification visits:* the Supreme Court concluded that the power conferred to the administrative authority is autonomous and inherent to the faculties granted by the Constitution, and cannot, therefore, be exclusively limited to its physical or material execution; it rather implies also the faculty to issue the corresponding order.

---

19. *See* the work Carlos Mena Labarthe and Laura Méndez, "Leniency Program in Mexico: An International Perspective," *Política de Competencia en México*, Mexico, Porrúa, 2015, pp. 501–526.
20. Mexico, Federal Official Gazette, Supreme Court of Justice, Unconstitutional Action 33/2006 filed by the General Prosecutor, solved on May 10, 2007 and published in the on July 12, 2007. Accessed January 7, 2015. http://www.dof.gob.mx/nota_detalle.php?codigo=5381615&fecha=11/02/2015.
21. *Vid*, at: http://www.competenciaeconomica.com.mx/ley/lfce_capitulo_4.pdf, accessed on February 20, 2015.

The Supreme Court's resolution and several issues that became evident once the reform started to be implemented evidenced the need for a new reform, which would be especially oriented to address fines and verification visits.

[2] The 2011 Legal Reform

This reform was created with three main objectives:

(a) Facilitate compliance: (1) it contained the possibility of settlements to cease relative monopolistic practices or unlawful mergers; (2) the establishment of hearings with the Plenum of the CFC, to allow economic agents to exercise their right of defense in the trial-like procedure, and (3) the flexibilization of the notifications for mergers by exempting economic agents from notifying mergers to the CFC when they do not pose harm to competition.

(b) Improve effectiveness, efficiency and transparency in the CFC activities: (1) the incorporation of the "collective dominance" concept which allows to investigate markets where there is not a clearly dominant agent, but, instead, there is a joint exercise of market power; (2) empower the Commission to request information in order to elaborate market studies and opinions; (3) give the Plenum faculties to issue guidelines for other government authorities regarding concessions, acquisitions, leases and public work, and finally (4) create specialized courts in competition.

(c) Enhance competition policy through effective instruments for the investigation and sanction of anticompetitive practices. This area includes: (1) the increase of applicable sanctions according to the economic agent's capacity; (2) the acceleration of verification visits by eliminating the obligation to obtain a court order and the requirement to previously notify said order; (3) the possibility of the Commission to apply interim measures, and; (4) the more expedite implementation of the resolution's by clarifying that its enforcement and execution will be processed through the incidental way.

Thus, the 2011 reform brought substantial procedural adjustments to the law as it introduced a sanction's scheme, consistent with best international practices, in order to discourage anticompetitive conducts, strengthen the CFC, as well as to improve transparency and due process. It also gave content to some provisions that will be mentioned below.

In sum, the 2006 and 2011 reforms were critical for competition policy enforcement in Mexico. On one hand, international best practices were introduced to discourage and combat relative monopolistic practices. On the other, provisions were established to ensure due process within the proceedings.

Despite this, in 2013 there remained great slopes in this matter, although it could be argued that not enough time was given time to the 2011 reform in order to demonstrate its usefulness. As noted above, the concentration of markets, their low competitiveness, and the importance of the competition to attract investment were some of the main reasons that led to a new constitutional reform and to promote a new law which would change the paradigm of competition policy in the country. In doing so, it was necessary to introduce a new institutional arrangement and grant new powers to the respective regulatory bodies with the clear objective to ensure, in the most effective manner, an efficient performance of the markets.

§1.03 PARADIGM SHIFT IN COMPETITION LAW

[A] Political Context of the 2013 Constitutional Reform

Following the election of President Enrique Peña Nieto, the main political forces signed an agreement which was called the "Pact for Mexico." [22] This agreement entailed specific commitments[23] regarding competition policy enforcement:

> 2.1. [...]
> Economic competition in all sectors of the economy will be intensified, with special emphasis on strategic sectors such as telecommunications, transportation, financial services and energy, this is fundamental since the competition allows the generation of products and best quality services at lower prices, which encourages the growth of the economy, helps to reduce inequality and poverty, as it also triggers innovation processes that foster the economic, social and cultural dynamism of nations. To deepen economic competition in Mexico, a State policy will be established based on an institutional arrangement that gives it strength and permanence.

Various social actors were surprised that a political agreement without precedent devoted such important lines and commitments to the competition issue. This revealed that the economic competition agenda was not a topic of interest only for one political party; on the contrary, the main political forces in the country shared the sense of urgency and the need to introduce drastic changes to modify the institutional arrangement and the laws of the competition system in Mexico.

Consequently, the elements mentioned in the "Pact for Mexico" were echoed in the National Development Plan (2013–2018), which established as general objective to: "lead Mexico to its full potential." In this Plan, one of the main axis was to have a "Prosperous Mexico" that:

> promotes the sustained growth of productivity, in a climate of economic stability through the generation of equal of opportunities. This, considering that an appropriate infrastructure and access to strategic inputs foster competition and allow greater flows of capital and knowledge for individuals and companies with the greatest potential to take advantage of it.

---

22. The "Pact for Mexico" was signed on December 2, 2012 by national leaders of the three main political parties in the country.
23. *Pact for Mexico*, accessed December 28, 2014. http://www.foroconsultivo.org.mx/documentos/politicas_publicas/pacto_por_mexico.pdf.

[B] The 2013 Constitutional Reform

In this context, a great constitutional reform of economic competition was passed in June 2013.

This reform sought to combat the inefficiencies of the regulation and competition system, which was fundamentally manifested in the telecommunications sector, and to generate a new institutional organization that would allow a rearrangement of faculties and powers in the pro-market regulation.

To the surprise of many, the constitutional reform included a great level of detail and a broad scope. We could argue that much of what is included in this reform, and of that added to the Constitution, should be content of a law or even a bylaw. It would seem that the level of detail is due, mainly, to the mistrust regulatory and judiciary organs would change or render them ineffective to benefit economic agents. This distrust is illustrative of the little credibility that this entities had to deal with economic agents of enormous power, given the history of inefficiency during the implementation of the regulation; once again, especially in telecommunications. The abovementioned provides a possible explanation for the establishment of numerous "locks" at the constitutional level. The reform also sought to prevent deviations from the political parties that signed the pact when designing and approving the laws and bylaws, that is, opposition parties sought to ensure the achievements that derived from the original political negotiation of the Pact of Mexico.

Considering this background, the reform was mainly aimed at: (a) the creation of a new national agency of economic competition, the Federal Commission of Economic Competition (COFECE by its Spanish acronym), with autonomy and constitutional independence; (b) the strengthening of the COFECE through new powers such as: the elimination of barriers to competition, the regulation of access to essential inputs, and the possibility of ordering the divestiture of economic agents' goods to correct market failures; (c) the establishment of an institutional design with a checks and balances scheme, mainly with the separation of the investigation areas and the Plenum, and (d) an agency to regulate telecommunications and radiobroadcasting which would be also the competition authority in these sectors. These topics will be detailed below.

The creation of new autonomous agencies

The constitutional reform granted the competition agencies – the COFECE and the Federal Institute of Telecommunications – autonomy at a constitutional level, as well as their own legal personality and patrimony. This autonomy represented a gigantic step in the construction of a new Mexican regulatory framework for competition.

These agencies, COFECE and IFT, altered the order of interaction with the Executive, Legislative and Judicial Branches. In addition, the relationship with other regulators has also been overhauled.

In this sense, the Constitution provides that the State will have a Federal Economic Competition Commission, aimed at ensuring competition and free market participation, as well as preventing, investigating and prosecuting monopolies, monopolistic practices, unlawful mergers and other restrictions to the efficient operation of markets.

Both authorities are "independent in its decision making and operation, professional in its performance, impartial in its actions, and shall exercise its budget autonomously." Likewise, they issue their own organizational charters, as well as their own general provisions; as such, their governing bodies must fulfill the principles of transparency and access to information.

For their resolutions, COFECE and IFT collegiate plenary bodies deliberate in a democratic manner, requiring a voting majority to decide cases. Their sessions, decrees and resolutions are public, with some exemptions provided by the law (confidentiality).

Concerning the appointment of the Commissioners and the President Commissioner of the agencies, there were major reforms. The Constitution establishes that the governing bodies of COFECE and IFT are integrated by seven Commissioners, including the President Commissioner. The Commissioners' selection is defined by an Evaluation Committee (integrated by the Heads of the Central Bank, the National Institute for Education Assessment and the National Institute of Statistics and Geography), responsible of publishing the vacancy notice, verifying that the applicants fill all the requirements established in the Constitution,[24] and applying a knowledge test to evaluate their specialty degree and the command of concepts. Upon the conclusion of this process, the Committee sends to the President a list of the applicants who have obtained the highest approbatory grade, and it is his responsibility to nominate the potential Commissioner(s) from the most outstanding. The elected candidate(s) is submitted for the consideration of the Senate, in order to ratify the appointment. Such appointment has to be ratified by the approving vote of two-thirds of the Senate. Commissioners have a nine-year mandate and cannot be reappointed.

In light of the recent creation of the regulatory agencies, the Sixth Transitory article of the 2013 Constitutional Reform establishes that, in order to assure the tiered succession of Commissioners, the first members of the Board of Commissioners would one by one conclude their mandates on the last day of February of each year between 2016 and 2022. Therefore, on September 10, 2013, the Senate ratified the appointment of six Commissioners, and on November 7 of the same year, the last Commissioner was ratified. Likewise, on September 10, the IFT Board of Commissioners was established.

---

24. Such requirements are being a Mexican citizen by birth and in full enjoyment of their civil and political rights; being at least 35 years old; having a good reputation; having fulfilled at least three years of outstanding professional activities in the public or academic sector substantially related with economic competition, radiobroadcasting and telecommunications; proving the required knowledge and not having served as: Minister of the Supreme Court, Federal Attorney General, Senator, Federal or Local Representative, Governor of any state or Mayor of the Federal District during the previous year to nomination. Also, not having occupied, during the previous three years, any position in firms that have been subject to a sanctioning procedure conducted by COFECE.

[1] Incremental Powers

A second element of major relevance is the introduction of new powers granted to COFECE and IFT to efficiently fulfill their duties and achieve their objectives. Among such new powers are the authority to order measures for the elimination of barriers to competition and free market participation, to regulate the access to essential facilities, as well as the authority to order the divesting of assets, rights, partnership interests or stocks in the necessary proportions as to eliminate anticompetitive effects.

In order to exercise these new powers, the competition law establishes a special investigation procedure to detect the existence of essential facilities or barriers to competition. In case that the Commission finds the existence of a restriction to an essential facility or a barrier to competition, by means of a resolution, it has the authority to impose remedies. These remedies may consist of recommendations to public authorities, an order to the corresponding economic agent(s) to eliminate a barrier that unduly affects the competition process, the issuance of guidelines to regulate essential facilities or, as a last resort measure, the divestiture of assets, rights, partnership interests or stocks, in the necessary proportions to eliminate the anticompetitive effects. It is important to note that this procedure is different from the one established for monopolistic practices and unlawful mergers, in that it does not seek to sanction illegal conducts, but rather to solve structural and behavioral problems in a market.

Moreover, it should be pointed out that one of the most noteworthy changes of the 2013 constitutional reform is the reconfiguration of the appeal procedure by which the general rules, acts or omissions of the COFECE or the IFT may be challenged. Such acts or omissions can only be contested through an appeal procedure known as "indirect amparo," and will not be subject to suspension, except in cases where the COFECE (or IFT) impose fines or the divestiture of assets, rights, partnership interests or stocks. Otherwise, suspensions can only be implemented until the "amparo" trial is resolved, if any.

[2] Institutional Design of Checks and Balances

The stronger institutional design brought about an increase in the obligations and locks that maintain balance of the performance of the Commission before the citizenship and even before other authorities. This is displayed through three main aspects.

[a] Autonomy Between the Investigative and the Decision-Making Authorities

The Constitution establishes that, within COFECE, there must be a separation between the investigative body and the one in charge of conducting the trial-like procedure that follows the investigation. In this sense, the amended Constitution seeks to overcome some of the old criticisms to the CFC regarding the fact that the same body was prosecutor and jury. Such arguments and criticisms were brought up in many appeal proceedings during the early years of the CFC. In this regard, it seemed that the problems had already been addressed and resolved in the Amparo Proceeding 554/2011, where the Supreme Court affirmed that:

> the procedure followed by the Cofeco [CFC] progresses in the course of two independent phases: the first one, which can be initiated ex officio or per request of an interested party, is aimed at verifying if the economic agents' conducts comply with the competition provisions and, if considered otherwise, gather evidence to prove it and to allow the establishment of a presumptive responsibility of the economic agent or agents. The second phase initiates with the determination of the presumptive responsibility and seeks to allow the defendant to be heard by the authority and to refute the accusations made, as well as offer and introduce the evidence it deems necessary to defend itself. Subsequently, the Commission will set a timeframe to offer arguments, after which it shall dictate the corresponding resolution. Therefore, it is possible to draw the conclusion that *the investigation phase, in charge of Cofeco, constitutes a different, autonomous, and independent action from the second stage of the process*, which begins with the determination of the presumptive responsibility. Hence, during the execution of the investigative faculty, that is to say during the investigation phase, the activity of the Commission is mainly orientated towards the collection of reports and documents from economic agents. Thus, at this stage, the Commission is not acting as a decision-making entity; but rather investigating, with the scope of its powers, suspected monopolistic practices. The decision-making activity of the Commission begins in the next phase when the Commission subpoenas the accused economic agents to the trial-like proceedings. Hence, it can be argued that *the resolutions of the Cofeco do not breach the principle of impartiality, because in their issuance the Cofeco does not play a role as judge and jury. This, because the faculties granted to the Commission are not of a jurisdictional nature, but rather administrative, aimed at the designed to conduct an investigation, prior to the decision-making trial-type procedure, substantiated before the same Commission.*[25] [Emphasis added]

All that notwithstanding, the discussion of the constitutional reform reopened the debate, which ended with a sui generis model rather difficult to implement (as we will see in the final legislated design).

It is important to stress that in the institutional design, legislators looked at the international experience, where two main models prevail: (1) the prosecutor-court system and; (2) the agency which embodies both the investigative and decision-making powers.

Under the first model, the competition agency carries out the investigation, but in order to prosecute and sanction violations to the law, it must present its case before a Court, that might be specialized or not. Chile, the United States (in some cases), Canada and South Africa follow this model, for example.

---

25. Mexico, Second Chamber of the Supreme Court, Amparo Revision Procedure 554/2011, approved on August 31, 2011, accessed February 4, 2016. http://www2.scjn.gob.mx/ConsultaTematica/PaginasPub/DetallePub.aspx?AsuntoID=129388.

The second model, however, involves a single agency that investigates, judges and sanctions. Nevertheless, in some cases there are internal nuances. Some jurisdictions that function this way are the European Union, Japan, China and Peru.[26]

The Mexican case is actually a hybrid of these two models. The constitutional reform resulted in the new competition law that created the Investigative Authority, a body of the COFECE granted with technical and administrative autonomy, thus ensuring an autonomous and objective investigation, without interference from the decision-making body. The same if true about the Plenum's resolutions; this model ensures that they remain objective, impartial and uninfluenced, considering that the Plenum was impeded from participating in decisions concerning the initiation of new investigations and strategies to be following during these procedures.

In this way, the COFECE model is special because it consists of: (1) a body in charge of the investigation, and (2) a body in charge of deciding cases; both operating separately but coexisting within the Commission's structure. This seeks to promote a system of checks and balances in every step of the procedure, allowing each body to conduct itself with independence and impartiality.

It is worth noting that this is a big distinctive feature *vis-à-vis* other economic competition agencies worldwide that have sanctioning powers, since the same body that investigates, resolves the cases.

[b]   More Accountability Obligations

The autonomy involves entails more transparency and accountability obligations for COFECE and IFT. Among them, the Head of each agency must present their annual working plan before the Executive and Legislative Branches. Likewise, they also have a duty to present quarterly reports to both branches, and they are compelled to appear before the Senate on an annual basis. Finally, there is an obligation to appear before either Chamber of Congress (Senators or Deputies) when required or when their presence is necessary in the discussion of a law or of any issue related to their activities. The Executive may also request either Chamber of Congress the appearance of the Heads of these agencies.

The Constitution prescribes that bylaws shall foster governmental transparency under the principles of open government. As a result, COFECE publishes the stenographic version of the Plenum's sessions, agreements and resolutions on its website, always protecting information that could be considered confidential. However, it is paramount to mention that COFECE (and the Investigative Authority) must maintain the utmost secrecy of a case during the investigative stage.

Congress also decreed that greater transparency was required for any contact between COFECE's public servants and economic agents, in order to generate greater credibility and confidence among society. Among other provisions, the regulatory

---

26. Eleanor M Fox and Michael J. Treibilcok, "The Design of Competition Law Institutions and the Global Convergence of Process Norms: The GAL Competition Project," *New York University Law and Economics Working Papers*, No. 304 (2012):9, accessed December 10, 2014. http://lsr.nellco.org/nyu_lewp/304.

framework prescribes certain formalities that must be followed when Commissioners come in contact with economic agents, some of which consist in keeping a record of the topics addressed, as well as the name of the attendees. This information is disclosed in the Commission's website. In order to comply with its transparency obligations, all of these interviews are recorded and stored in electronic, optical or any another technology, maintaining these as reserved information. In similar fashion, the Regulatory Provisions (the bylaws) establish rules of contact to be followed by the Investigative Authority.

To improve accountability, Congress created an Internal Comptroller, whose Head will be appointed by two-thirds of the members of the Chamber of Deputies. Such appointment however has not taken place. In the meantime, employees from the former Internal Control body have been carrying out the audit and supervision work.

[c]   Creation of Specialized Courts

The constitutional reform also addressed the judicial principle of specialization by ordering the creation of specialized courts and judges in economic competition and telecommunications within the sixty calendar days following the publication and entry into effect of the Constitutional Amendment. Accordingly, on August 10, 2013,[27] two district courts, and two administrative Collegiate Circuit Courts specialized in Economic Competition, Radiobroadcasting and Telecommunications commenced their activities.

This step was very welcomed. Not only are competition cases highly technical, but they are also solved within a very particular and complex legal framework (both the investigative stage and the trial-like proceedings), which includes concepts and procedures not found in any other law. Even though in recent decades, federal courts had issued resolutions that helped to route and enrich the economic competition policy, their decisions did not live up to the challenge. It is required that judicial challenges to these cases are handled with the highest degree of professionalism and expertise, so as not to render the Commission's powers completely ineffective; not to mentioned within a reasonable timely period, which is why the creation of the specialized courts was considered as a truly positive step.

The first appointed specialized judges and magistrates are notable legal experts with outstanding technical capacities and a great degree of professionalism. These

---

27. Federal Official Gazette publication on August 9, 2013: General Order 22/2013 of the Plenary of the Federal Judiciary Council, related to the closure of functions of the Fourth and Fifth District Courts of the Auxiliary Center of the First Region (Centro Auxiliar de la Primera Región) and its transformation to First and Second District courts in Administrative Matters Specialized in Economic Competition, Radiobroadcasting and Telecommunications, with residence in Mexico City and territorial jurisdiction in all the country. Also, its address, initial operating date, reception and distribution system of affairs among the Jurisdictional bodies indicated. And the change of name of the common mail office of the Auxiliary Center of the First Region. Accessed February, 5, 2014. http://www.dof.gob.mx/nota_detalle.php?codigo = 5309912&fecha = 09/08/2013.

experts have been pioneers in the judicialization of economic competition and telecommunications in Mexico, establishing technical criteria.

[C] The New Federal Law of Economic Competition

Because of the constitutional reform of 2013, it was necessary to pass a new law which would follow and expand upon the principles prescribed at constitutional level, in order to make them fully applicable. The new law would not to aim to review the results obtained through previous legislations in order to improve upon them, but rather it would push for a real paradigm shift regarding the importance of competition in Mexico and the role COFECE would play in securing it. This explains why it was determined by both the President and Congress that a new law was needed; reforming the exiting law would not have the desired effect.

As it happens in every legislative process, this one required to conciliate different interests, including those of the Executive, the regulatory body, the private sector and the different political parties.

Accordingly, the new LFCE, was published in the FOG on May 23, 2014, abrogation the 1992 competition law.

Among some of the most relevant features of this law that helped to outline the new design and structure of COFECE, are: (1) the regulation of the so-called incremental faculties: (a) the power to order measures for the elimination of barriers to competition and to promote free market participation, (b) to determine the existence of essential inputs and issue guidelines to regulate its access, and (c) to order the divestiture of assets, rights, partnership interest or stocks, in the necessary proportions to eliminate the anticompetitive effects, through a new special procedure of investigation established in Article 94 of the law; (2) the faculty of the Executive, directly or through the Ministry of Economy or through the Federal Consumer Attorney's Office, to file complaints before COFECE with a preferential status; (3) the establishment of several transparency and accountability provisions, which have already been explained; (4) the shift to an "authorization" system for mergers and creating the possibility that economic agents have to present commitments before the Commission that reduce or nullify the anticompetitive effects of a merger; (5) the obligation that COFECE has to issue guidelines for the implementation of its attributions; and (6) the establishment of a mechanism to request formal opinions to COFECE regarding novel cases.

Additionally, two new relative monopolistic practices were included: refusing or discriminating access to essential facilities and margin squeeze. The elements to be considered for when determining the existing of an essential facility were prescribed in Article 60 of the LFCE.

Regarding cartels, the new law penalized any exchange of information between competitors which has either the objective or the effect of manipulating prices, restricting supply, allocating markets or rigging bids. It is worth recalling that according to the former legislation, information exchanges could only be considered anticompetitive when they referred to price manipulation.

Regarding advocacy, the Competition Law continued recognizing the faculty of the COFECE to issue opinions on regulation, even though now they are non-binding. Perhaps this was influenced by the fact that this faculty was only used once by the CFC and by the fact that Article 94 contains provisions that could counter anticompetitive regulation.

Since ensuring competition in the telecommunications sector was entrusted to IFT, new law had to determine a way to settle disputes between the two agencies concerning which one is competent to analyze a certain case. The LFCE provides that in case such conflict arose, it will be resolved by specialized courts.

In addition, the LFCE recognizes COFECE's faculty to file constitutional controversies (a judicial review procedure) before the Supreme Court. This procedure allows COFECE to defend the powers which it was entrusted with, avoiding interference from other authorities. COFECE has also the power to ask the competent agency to exercise action before the Supreme Court of Justice to declare as unconstitutional barriers to competition established by the States.

Furthermore, the sanctions framework was strengthened. There was an increase in the criminal penalties for cartels. Another major addition was turning and the obstruction in verification visits into a crime, punishable by prison. In addition, the new Competition Law establishes the Commission may impose as a sanction to individuals who participate in the commission of monopolistic practices or unlawful mergers, during a maximum five-year period, the ineligibility to act as a board member, manager, director, executive, agent, representative or legal representative of any company.

§1.04   CHALLENGES AND A NEW COMPETITION FRAMEWORK

In previous studies I published, I mentioned three specific challenges that the CFC faced in its quest of trying to be a creative regulator. The CFC it was a regulator constrained by its legal and social environment, and therefore it was forced to find creative ways to not only comply with the demands and meet the established restrictions, but at the same time to achieve its regulatory objectives.

Between the most specific and urgent challenges, I identified: (1) the monitoring and assessment of the markets, especially those where the CFC had intervened, I previously mentioned as examples the studies carried out by the Office of Fair Trading in the United Kingdom; (2) the necessity to create interpretative communities in order to generate understanding bridges between the agency and the main actors of the regulatory framework, promote competition culture and establish a competition language in public policies and in society, and (3) the intersection between specific-sector regulation and competition regulation. This last, is the one I considered the most important, mainly in economic sectors such as financial, telecommunications, energy and transportation. Not only because of their privatization history, but also because of the existent commercial practices, their enormous structural problems and the specific-sector regulations sometimes produced adverse effects on competition.

Chapter 1: New Competition Policy in Mexico §1.04

The experience concerning these challenges has been mixed. In all fronts, the CFC attempted to move forward during its last years, but given the interconnection between the different aspects and challenges that interacted and were mutually reinforcing, the Commission "could not afford to choose which challenge to take up first and which was left for later. The only path left, from the beginning, was to try to make progress simultaneously in every front."[28]

The CFC got many significant things[29] right but there are also issues that received significant criticisms, such as the infamous case in which the Plenum ended up revoking a *Telcel*'s[30] fine.

In this sense, the new administration of COFECE inherited some of these difficulties, and it also faced new challenges regarding the novel institutional arrangement, new faculties and the new obligations established in the Constitution and the law. As a starting point, the new institution has set forth a clear path and an agreement between the members of its governing body. Thus, the COFECE, for the first time in the history of a competition agency in our country, and according to international best practices, has adopted a Strategic plan 2014–2017 that facilitates and guides this evolution process.[31]

With this Strategic Plan 2014–2017, COFECE shared with society its mission, values, objectives, priorities and strategic lines that will guide and drive its actions. There, the mission that the COFECE has is made clear:

guarantee free market participation and economic competition, as well as to prevent, investigate, and combat monopolistic practices and unlawful mergers; regulate essential inputs and barriers to competition, as well as any other restriction to the

---

28. Eduardo Pérez Motta, "La maduración de la política de competencia en México, en: La política de competencia en el umbral de la consolidación," Mexico, Porrúa, 2013, pp. 83–93.
29. He was one of the most insistent promoters of the creation of Specialized Courts because of its expertise level, profound analysis and agility with which these cases could be conducted; nevertheless, perhaps the most important legacy of the last CFC's president was the human capital a with highly specialized profile and with the abilities to face the upcoming challenges of the regulator agency.
30. *Vid.* Mexico, Plenum of the Federal Commission of Competition, motion for reconsideration RA-039-2012. File DE-066-2011 solved on May 3, 2012, accessed January 10, 2015. http://base.crcal.org/documentos/0f452dfa-3fc3-4004-a9e6-e600c61084a0/MEXICO-CNT-TELEVISA-IUSACELL-2012.pdf. In this case a TELCEL's fine was condoned, in exchange of five commitments, among them, the reduction of interconnection tariffs.
31. Article 28 of the Mexican federal Constitution obliges COFECE to present quarterly reports before the Executive and Legislative branches. In doing so, it ensures transparency in the developments and results of competition policy implementation before society. The Commission took up a new working framework based on the objectives and lines of action mentioned in the Strategic Plan (SP) 2014–2017. The SP was submitted for a new public consultation process (created by the new Law) and includes immediate projects, as well as indicators to monitor the implementation of the institutional objectives. Likewise, and with the purpose to assure compliance with the Strategic Plan, COFECE elaborated an Annual Work Program for 2014 and established seven follow-up Committees. Here, there is detail about the action and projects aimed at the achievement of every objective in the Plan, while the Committees are in charge of monitoring the developments and goals.

efficient functioning of the markets, in the terms established by the Constitution, the treaties and the laws.[32]

To do this, the same document includes a diagnosis of the status of competition policy in the country, recognizing that it is a key factor for economic growth, competitiveness and social welfare; considering that the promotion of competition among companies brings along lower prices, better quality in goods and services, greater efficiency, and innovation in markets. To accomplish its mission, within the framework of such Plan, the COFECE set forth four main objectives: (1) comply with the constitutional and legal mandate regarding economic competition; (2) promote the benefits and the culture of competition among economic actors and society at large; (3) contribute to economic growth and social welfare through the promotion of competition in the markets, and (4) be an institution of excellence, recognized for its compliance with legality, impartiality, objectivity, transparency and professionalism.

Furthermore, as an unprecedented fact, the COFECE established in its Plan a prioritization approach in order to focus on economic sectors that would enable the Commission to maximize the effectiveness of its interventions. Consequently, the Commission defined six criteria by means of which priority sectors would be established for the period 2014-2017: (1) economic growth; (2) widespread consumption; (3) transverse impact; (4) lowest income households; (5) regulated sectors, and (6) regulations that can facilitate collusive agreements and abuse of market power. This prioritization is essential as it recognizes that the agency cannot count on unlimited resources, and should, therefore, make a more efficient use of them, particularly regarding the powers it exercises proactively in an *ex officio* manner.

Finally, with the purpose of evaluating institutional performance, and in order to monitor and assess the implementation of COFECE's objectives, indicators have also been established to measure management and results.

So far, the results are few, but the steps that have been made seem to be in the right direction. The creation of the Investigative Authority and the Technical Secretariat as new areas of COFECE have posed a challenge for the Commission and its crew considering that, unlike what happened in the United Kingdom with the creation of the new competition agency –the *Competition and Markets Authority* (which merged the *Office of Fair Trading* and the *Competition Commission*) –, the COFECE was not born as a parallel institution to the CFC. Instead, in Mexico, practically overnight, all human and material resources of the former CFC were transferred to the new COFECE. This involved huge complexities in terms of regulation and reallocation of functions. Of course, during this adjustment period, the COFECE continued analyzing and solving a great number of cases. For example, 2014 alone[33] saw the process of more than 270 mergers, monopolistic practices and opinions on bids, permits and concessions; concluding more than 80% of these procedures.

---

32. COFECE, *Strategic Plan 2014-2017*, accessed February 20, 2015. http://www.cofece.mx/attachments/article/37/PE_COFECE_2014-2017_0.pdf.
33. COFECE, *Cierre 2014 y Proyectos para 2015*, accessed March 10, 2015. https://www.cofece.mx/cofece/index.php/prensa/presentaciones?download = 715:cierre-2014-y-proyectos-para-2015.

Over its short existence, the COFECE has already conditioned some major merger operations. For instance, the purchase of Walmex's restaurants by Alsea[34] was subject to the elimination of exclusivities in the lease contracts. Similarly, in the merger of Continental and Veyance Technologies,[35] the Commission conditioned the authorization of the merger to the sale of assets in San Luis Potosi. Also, as a result of its investigation, COFECE conditioned the merger between Soriana Organization (Soriana) and Mexican Commercial Controller (CCM) considering that its clearance in the terms proposed by the economic agents would damage the competition process in twenty-seven retail locations. The Plenum agreed to clear the merger conditioned to the divestiture of twenty-seven CCM stores located in critical areas.

Likewise, in the analysis of the Aeromexico/Delta merger, the Commission concluded that in the terms it was proposed by said airlines, the merger would threaten competition in the market of regular passenger air transportation between Mexico and the United States of America (U.S.), in both direct and connecting routes. To keep the competitive pressure that Delta currently holds in the cross-border flights between Mexico and the U.S. market, as well as to prevent the increase of the barriers that could limit the development of networks of competing airlines, COFECE determined that the operation would only be authorized if both airlines accepted the imposed conditions, that included divesting a certain number of slots in the International Airport of Mexico City to other competitors that provide or may provide regular passenger air transportation services between Mexico and the U.S., and not maintaining their overlapping routes.

Regarding sanctions for monopolistic practices, the COFECE sanctioned Whirlpool, Panasonic and five other companies with a fine of MXN 223 million[36] for fixing the price of hermetic compressors used as inputs for devices of refrigeration and air conditioning, which were exported, imported and commercialized in Mexico between 2004 and 2008. In a cartel case resolved in 2015, COFECE sanctioned seven companies in the market of terrestrial passenger transportation in the state of Chiapas. As a result, the Plenum imposed a fine of USD 1.5 million. This case was critical considering that Chiapas is one of the states with the poorest population in Mexico. In fact, according to CONEVAL (National Council to Evaluate Development Policy), Chiapas population in poverty conditions is equivalent to 74% of the total State's population.

In 2015, the Commission also published the beginning of several new investigations in different markets, including the first investigation for the determination of essential inputs in the market of provision of aerial transportation services that use the

---

34. Mexico, Plenum of the Federal Commission of Economic Competition, File CNT-095-2013, solved on February 21, 2014, accessed February 5, 2015. http://www.cofece.mx:8080/cfcresoluciones/docs/Concentraciones/V539/55/1797956.pdf.
35. Mexico, Plenum of the Federal Commission of Economic Competition, File CNT-084-2014, solved on December 16, 2014, accessed January 8, 2015. http://www.cofece.mx:8080/cfcresoluciones/docs/Concentraciones/V591/88/1883446.pdf.
36. Mexico, Federal Economic Competition Commission, File IO-002-2009, solved on February 25, 2014, accessed January 8, 2015. http://www.cofece.mx:8080/cfcresoluciones/docs/Asuntos%20Juridicos/V85/19/1797812.pdf.

International Airport of Mexico City for landing and/or takeoff procedures.[37] During this investigation, the Investigative Authority determined that certain infrastructure within the Mexico City International Airport (runways, taxiways, platforms and visual aids) is an essential input for the transportation market. Therefore, it was found that access to the essential facility generates a series of anticompetitive effects in the investigated market, such as high concentration and low availability of slots for takeoff and landing procedures, which in turn hinder other companies' entry or expansion, and contribute to low route innovation and to the existence of high prices. As a result, the Investigative Authority proposed suitable and economically feasible measures to eliminate the identified problems and to generate efficiency gains in the market; such as: (a) facilitate access to information and establish clear criteria regarding access to the market, in order to promote competition; and (b) create a Reserve Fund of schedules that would reduce entry barriers to the essential input.

It is now time for the Plenum of the Commission to resolve such investigation and mandate the corresponding remedies.

In spite of the significant progress that competition policy has made in Mexico during the last years, there are still various issues pending in order to complete the strengthening of this policy, which is vital for the growth and economic development of the country. Success will not only lie in the actions of the competition authority during the forthcoming years, which by the way are critical, but it will also depend on other political and social actors, who should assume their responsibility in developing more efficient markets that will translate into greater benefits for consumers. Support from public authorities and regulators will be also be fundamental in effectively implementing competition policy in Mexico. Likewise, and considering that we live in a world of global trade, it will be very important for the COFECE to strengthen its ties with competition agencies of other jurisdictions, not only to learn from their best practices, but also to expand the scope of its actions, thus, facilitating the work of the Commission and generating confidence towards its peers. Some of the challenges that I believe must be faced in the short and medium term are listed below.

[A]   Institutional Arrangements

The new powers conferred to the "Investigative Authority" guarantee independent investigations and prevent the Plenum from prejudging on them. Moreover, the new Technical Secretariat, as the "executive arm" of the Plenum, will be responsible for serving process on economic agents identified as probably responsible and for carrying out the trial-like procedure. Consequently, the new institutional arrangement will seek to ensure that the decisions adopted by the Commissioners are objective, impartial and professional.

In addition, the Commission has been granted with important tools to meet its goals. Compared to the previous period, Congress increased by more than 60% the

---

37. Mexico, Federal Official Gazette, File IEBC-001-2015, with the Initiation Decision issued in the on February 16, 2015, accessed January 8, 2015. http://www.dof.gob.mx/nota_detalle.php?codigo=5382063&fecha=16/02/2015.

Commission's budget for 2015. As long as the new professionals of the regulatory entity become more involved and specialized in the field of economic competition, efficiency in the investigations will increase, technical support for the application of sanctions will be strengthened and the COFECE will be positioned as a leading international agency. However, the exercise of those resources also entails a great responsibility as it must be transparent, efficient and aimed at the fulfillment of the objectives of the COFECE.

All this has represented and will continue to represent a huge challenge of organizational adjustment, management of expectations, and creation of human capabilities, both within and outside the authority. William E. Kovacic in his work *Competition Agency Design: What's on the Menu?*[38] highlights the importance of competition agencies' "engineering" and design in order to achieve the implementation of an effective competition policy. According to Kovacic, innovation in the design of the agency involves three stages: (1) the identification of insufficiencies in the existing agreements; (2) the development of a proposal for reform; and (3) a battle about whether to adopt the said proposal. However, Kovacic argues that the only way to know how the prototype will turn out is putting it in place.

Thus, in the case of the COFECE, the agency has undergone these three stages, since starting up the machinery and observing the way it works. Definitely, the only way to understand the effectiveness of a competition system design is implementing it. Then, it will be the time to evaluate it and see if it meets society's expectations. The challenge to evaluate, evaluate and evaluate remains.

[B]   Fight Against Cartels

Cartels are the most harmful behaviors for competition. It is estimated that they cause billions of dollars of damage to consumers each year around the world. Although it was one of the priorities for the CFC and now for the COFECE, it is necessary to work more on the strengthening of the anti-cartel policy. For this purpose, the COFECE must put special emphasis on these areas:

(1) *Leniency program:* the COFECE shall promote with greater effort the leniency program,[39] which allows any person or company that has participated or is participating in unlawful agreements with its competitors, to receive a total or partial reduction of the sanctions that would apply, in exchange for its cooperation with the authority. This program allows a discouragement, detection and sanction of absolute monopolistic practices in a more efficient manner.[40] The Commission already published its Guidelines for Leniency

---

38. William E Kovacic and David A. Hyman, "Competition Agency Design: What's on the Menu?" *GWU Legal Studies Research Paper* No. 135(2012), accessed October 20, 2014. http://ssrn.com/abstract=2179279 or http://dx.doi.org/10.2139/ssrn.2179279.
39. Established in the Art. 103 of the FLEC, related to the Arts. 114 through 116 of the Regulatory Provisions.
40. *Supra*, Mena Labarthe, Mendez, pp. 501–527.

Program, and is currently working in an Advocacy Document for foreign companies and lawyers regarding this program.

(2) *Verification visits*: undoubtedly one of the greatest achievements of competition reforms consists of the possibility to carry out unannounced verification visits. Although verification visits were also referred in 2006 reforms, they had huge problems. These were somehow solved when the law was amended in the 2011 reform, but one key feature stopped them from being as effective as they could: under the previous law, the CFC was compelled to publish the initiation of an investigation Federal Official Gazette in order to gain use of its powers, thus alerting economic agents of an impending visit to their offices and headquarters. This situation not only delayed the conduction of proceedings, but it also allowed the economic agents to hide or destroy evidence that could prove the existence of a monopolistic practice. As result of the aforementioned, the visits were not very fruitful.

The obligation to immediately publish the initiation of an investigation was eliminated in the new LFCE. Now, the COFECE can wait 120 days to go public, but during those days it can carry out verification visits and use its other investigative tools.

In this sense, the challenge for the COFECE consists in taking advantage of this new verification visits model, which is more expedite and effective to collect the necessary evidence for the conduction of a procedure. However, this scheme is also subject to complications and challenges, among them, the duty of properly establishing the legal grounds and reasoning for each of the actions of the authority in such a way that will not violate the rights of the governed. In the absence of clear legal criteria on how to perform verification visits that comply with that provided by constitutional Articles 14 and 16, it will be experience and the Courts' decisions that will set forth the standards in the use of this critical attribution.

(3) *International cooperation*: it is important to highlight the enormous role that international cooperation will play for the timely detection and sanction of cartels. There is no doubt that facing the consolidation of a globalization model shaped by transnational corporations, the COFECE should strengthen ties with other economic competition agencies to apply the Competition Law and allow sanctioning those companies that committed collusive acts abroad with an impact in the national market.[41] Additionally, international cooperation will enable a greater acknowledgement of the experiences of other jurisdictions, and the increased effectiveness of the investigative tools.

(4) *Information exchange between competitors*: the new Competition Law prescribes in its Article 53, that absolute monopolistic practices (prohibited per se) are contracts, agreements, arrangements or combinations amongst competing economic agents, which have as their purpose or effect, among others,

---

41. David Gomez, "Extraterritoriality in Competition Law and Globalization: Square Peg in a Round Hole," University Of Northumbria, accessed January 8, 2015. http://www.launchpadbz.com/resourcesmodule/download_resource/id/14/src/@random4bc9dace55ec3/.

the information exchange with any of the objects or effects referred to in the subsections of said article (fix prices, restrict supply, allocate markets or manipulate tenders). Also, the Federal Criminal Code establishes in its Article 254*bis* that, among others, the information exchange with some of the objects referred to in the subsections of Article 53 of the competition law shall be punished with five to ten years of jail time, and with 10,000 days of fine.

Information exchange between competitors (direct or indirect) is present in a considerable number of markets. It is often pro-competitive and increases the efficiency in the market; for this reason COFECE does not intend to discourage pro-competitive information exchange. The main problem with exchanging information between companies from a competition point of view, is that it can artificially increase transparency in the market, allowing coordination of strategies, without the need to establish pricing fixing or other monopolistic behavior. Likewise, there are some situations such as the information exchange that occurs in the context of a merger's planning process, or within associations or business and commerce chambers where it is necessary to grant certainty on the criteria that the authority uses to classify these as legal or unlawful practices. Considering these issues, the Commission issued Guidelines for the Exchange of Information between Competitors.

These guidelines were issued on December 10, 2015 and contain: (1) purpose and scope; (2) the elements of the exchange of information to be taken into consideration to determine if they pose a risk to competition and its possible effects on the markets, according to the nature of the information, the market conditions and the mechanisms for the exchange; and, (3) some recommendations in terms of exchanges of information for economic agents who are in a situation of contact with competitors, when this might generate risks to competition, such as pre-concentration activities, collaboration between competitors, price signaling, discussions in professional and trade associations and chambers of commerce and cross board directories.

(5) *Enforcement of criminal penalties*: as noted before, Article 254*bis* of the Federal Criminal Code establishes that the commission of absolute monopolistic practices established in Article 53 of the law will be sanctioned with five to ten years of jail time, and with 10,000 days of fine. Investigations in criminal matters will be initiated per request of the Investigative Authority, upon the issuance of the statement of objections. Those economic agents that are part of the leniency program will not face criminal responsibility.

It is important to point out that the criminalization of absolute monopolistic practices was already established in the 2011 reform, however, to date no case has been prosecuted under criminal legislation, partly due to the fact that any cartel conduct committed before the amendment could not be sanctioned with prison. Is not surprising that the implementation of criminal sanctions has not been easy, as international experience has shown that it is difficult to apply criminal sanctions in the field of competition; it is difficult at least before considering adjustments in the systems in order to make them truly functional. I consider that the new legal framework will allow the Commission to start the first criminal prosecutions of cartel conducts, despite of the important challenges that both the Commission and the Office of General Attorney will have to face. Undoubtedly, it would have a great deterrent effect on this type of behavior as it has happened in other jurisdictions such as the United States and Brazil.

[C]   Coordination with the IFT

Arising from the new institutional design, the coordination between the COFECE and the IFT must be close in the study and resolution of cases where they have coincident powers. The IFT was established as the economic competition authority in the sectors of radiobroadcasting and telecommunications. In accordance with the law, at the time when one of these entities, the COFECE or the IFT, has information that its counterpart is processing a matter of its jurisdiction, it shall require the submission of the corresponding file. In addition, if the requested entity acknowledges its own lack of jurisdiction to resolve in a given case, it shall submit the file, within the following five days after receiving the request. On the contrary, if the entity considers that it has jurisdiction in a given case, it shall notify the requesting entity of its resolution in the same period, suspending the procedure and submitting the file to the specialized Court in economic competition, radiobroadcasting and telecommunications, which shall resolve on the jurisdictional issue within a period of ten days.

In case one of these entities is processing a matter and considers it lacks the jurisdiction to resolve it, such entity shall submit the corresponding file to the other entity within the following five days. If the latter accepts it has jurisdiction, it shall further undertake the procedure of the case. On the contrary, within the following five days, it shall notify the entity that it has declined jurisdiction of the case and submit the file to the specialized Court in economic competition, broadcasting and telecommunications, which shall resolve on the jurisdiction issue in a period of ten days.

The system outlined in the law to resolve over issues where it is estimated that one of the entities has full jurisdiction on a subject, does not foresee cases in which the powers can be coincident. Also, cases that will undoubtedly pose a challenge are those related to technological convergence. In this regard, as it has happened in other jurisdictions, multimedia mergers, as well as exclusive content and platforms could pose problems to competition, and will therefore be topics in which both authorities will have to coordinate to determine their jurisdiction.

On October 24, 2013, the IFT and the COFECE signed a collaboration agreement, with the aim of carrying out actions of training, promotion and protection of competition, exchange of information and technology, legal and economic research, development of internal policies, and any other joint activity that facilitates the timely implementation of their powers on competition within the scope of their respective faculties, in order to promote economic efficiency in the markets of goods and services in our country. This was a necessary step and it will be essential for both institutions to work closely in order to achieve an effective implementation.

[D] Application of the New Powers of COFECE to Conduct Market Investigations

Derived from the constitutional reform and the new law, the COFECE, by means of the Investigative Authority, may initiate investigations to determine the existence of essential inputs or barriers competition and free market participation (in terms of Article 94 of the law). As a result of these investigations, the COFECE may issue recommendations to public authorities, guidelines to regulate essential inputs, orders to eliminate barriers to competition and free market participation and, if necessary, order divestiture of the involved economic agent's assets, rights, partnership interest or stocks, in the necessary proportions to eliminate the anticompetitive effects.

In this sense, one of the most important challenges for the COFECE is to conduct these investigations under the principles laid down in the law, as follows:

(1) The publication of a summary of the investigation's initiation decision in the Federal Official Gazette.
(2.) The accreditation of the absence of effective competition conditions and the absence of a better solution in the given market, as a prerequisite for the determination of divestiture of assets.
(3) Respect the economic agents' right to a hearing, so that within a forty-five days period upon the notification of the preliminary investigative opinion, they reply and thereby assert their rights, bring forth any documentary evidence at its disposal; as well as introduce the evidentiary elements estimated relevant.
(4) The right of the economic agent to propose suitable and economically feasible measures to eliminate the competition problems identified.

On the other hand, it is important to mention that this innovative model was inspired by jurisdictions like the United Kingdom or Australia;[42] however, Article 94 of the LFCE is not a faithful copy of such systems as it rather presents two significant features the COFECE shall face in an efficient and, I would dare to say, even creative (but responsible) way. First, there is a problem resulting from a shortening in the deadlines for these proceedings, because in Mexico, unlike other countries, the Investigative Authority works with short deadlines for the conduction of the investigations. This means that the Investigative Authority must comply with the criteria of appropriateness, necessity and proportionality in each of its actions, with the intention to make the most out of them.

---

42. B. Marshall, "Regulating Access to Essential Facilities in Australia: Review and Reform of Part III of the Trade Practices Act" (PhD Dissertation Queensland University of Technology, 2004), accessed January 10, 2015. http://eprints.qut.edu.au/15912/1/Brenda_Marshall_Thesis.pdf.

Second, it is possible to face difficulties as a result of the adoption of models from other countries. The challenge in this field is not minor, as the emergence and development of the essential inputs' concept is very complex. The content and scope of the term widely varies in each country. While in the United States its application is limited to inputs that are part of natural monopolies, in the European Union it has a more extensive use and has even been applied to agro products[43] and inputs protected by intellectual property.[44]

[E]   Market Studies

The COFECE has the express authority to carry out market studies. These studies play an important advocacy role in various jurisdictions around the world. In this sense, the study of the financial market is one of the most important among those published by COFECE throughout its history. The financial reform issued on February 9, 2014, provided that the COFECE would have a period of 120 calendar days upon its issuance to carry out a research on the conditions of competition in the financial system and its markets. COFECE handed the study to the Mexico's federal Congress in July, 2014. The study warns that users of the Mexican financial system have only a few options to access better quality products and services that offer higher yields and lower costs as consequence of the low competitive pressure that exists in the sector and its markets. Moreover, thirty-six recommendations were issued in order to encourage competition in the sector and to reduce the restrictions that prevent access for other participants.

The study identified some problems which derived from a possible lack of competition in the ATM infrastructure, branches and technology; credit information; unfavorable terms of engagement, and obstacles to transfer the balances in mobile payments. Additionally, a possible risk of discrimination in access was also considered.

The COFECE is currently following up on the recommendations that it issued to several sectorial regulators, thus, in the months and years to come it will be possible to assess their impact in the financial markets. Additionally, in December 15, 2015 the COFECE unveiled the report on the conditions of competition in the food sector, which allowed the COFECE to gather information on the characteristics of the markets, as well as an analysis of the cross-cutting aspects that affect a large number of markets that integrate the food sector, such as gathering, subsidies, storage and wholesale as well as retail commercialization activities. As a result of the analysis, the report includes a series of recommendations to promote, along with other government agencies, a greater rivalry between producers and traders, with the aim to generate more competition and to benefit consumers.

A challenge for the COFECE in this area will be to link market studies with the investigation of monopolistic practices, barriers to competition and free market participation, as well as essential inputs. It will be in the forthcoming years when such

---

43. OCDE, "The Essential Facilities Concept," OCDE Policy Roundtables 1996, accessed January 10, 2015. http://www.oecd.org/competition/abuse/1920021.pdf.
44. European Union, UE Court of Justice, Oscar Bronner *GMBH &CO. KG v. Mediaprint*, accessed February 2, 2016, http://curia.europa.eu/juris/liste.jsf?language=en&num=C-7/97.

relationship will begin to be defined and elucidated, as it has happened in other jurisdictions.

[F] Mergers

International literature recognizes that mergers may increase companies' efficiencies and positively impact the market. However, there are mergers that may have negative effects. The law establishes the cases in which mergers must be "authorized" or rejected by the COFECE, granting the Commission a period of sixty days for its analysis; which is greater than the forty-five business days provided before. Despite this, the COFECE is committed to reduce as much as possible its analysis timeframe. This analysis should assess the implications of the proposed merger and evaluate the consequences of such process in the market.

Therefore, one of the greatest challenges for the COFECE is the clearance of mergers with the maximum technical thoroughness and the highest level of expertise within a reasonable time and consistent with the complexity of the operation. The ultimate goal is to ensure that resolutions are expeditious, in compliance with the law and if necessary, to impose commitments, or otherwise refuse them in those cases where clear risks to competition are identified. The shift to become a "suspensive jurisdiction" involves huge responsibilities that the COFECE must look at. The COFECE should seek to be transparent, predictable, and open to dialogue within the applicable legal framework. Especially when the merger poses major risks, the parties must have a safe interlocutor to achieve the best results in the conditions that could be imposed, if any.

[G] Advocacy

In order to meet its objectives, the COFECE must strengthen the communication channels with the three branches of the government, to accompany and participate in bills and reform proposals or amendments to laws or regulatory instruments. The objective overall is to build pro-competitive regulation.

Similarly, a challenge that the COFECE will face ahead is the development of a communication strategy to disseminate the benefits of economic competition and to create incentives so that more Mexicans are interested in these topics.

Another challenge for the COFECE is to promote spaces for discussion with sectoral regulators and to foster common criteria in the application of economic competition principles. Also, emphasis must be made on the strengthening of linkages with businesses, bars, economists associations, consumers, think tanks, universities, representatives of the three levels of government, and society at large. This, aiming to promote principles and the advantages of economic competition, disseminate studies, resolutions and share guidelines, so as to spread the best practices and facilitate compliance with the law.

Derived from the energy reform, the COFECE has been devoting resources to the analysis of competition conditions in this sector. The possibility of having a pro-competitive impact directly or by means of recommendations in the markets within the energy sector will certainly allow to improve the quality of goods and services, and make energy prices competitive and accessible for both companies and for Mexican households.

§1.05 CONCLUSION

Competition law in Mexico had a clear evolution from its origins until the constitutional reform of 2013 and the new law of 2014, which allows us to say that we stand before a "new competition law" and a new era in Mexican competition policy.

The participation of several actors, coupled with the economic factors of Mexico's reality, will lead to a new institutional and policy design for competition in our country. The reforms of 2006 and 2011 were fundamental to advance the construction of a Mexican competition law aligned with international best practices. However, the constitutional reform of 2013 was the first time that the Executive and Legislative Branches, as well as the political forces, sought to create a truly effective competition law, in order to solve the special and profound issues that had plagued the markets in our country for many years.

The reform arose from the need to create the best conditions that would establish an even floor for all competitors, in order to encourage and attract investment in several sectors of the country and trigger economic growth. The reform granted the new COFECE with powers uncommonly found in the rest of the world, so that it could deal with the structural problems that markets are facing. These new powers have been embraced by the COFECE as a great responsibility, and I believe that the checks and balances system that was put in place as part of the amendment, will ensure that the powers of this renewed Commission are exercised in strict compliance with the law, with impartiality and with professionalism. The arsenal of weapons is enormous, thus, the responsibility of using them should be equally huge.

Moreover, competition culture has been evolving rapidly. Apart from the enactment of a new Competition Law, the Commission has issued relevant regulatory provisions as well as innovative Guidelines and Criteria to provide legal certainty and facilitate the implementation of the law. Moreover, the Commission has launched a major Advocacy Program, which has included the diffusion of the importance of compliance, opinions to regulators, among other actions that are transforming the competition culture in our country.

In the past two years, COFECE has been actively using its new powers, always acting with great responsibility.

The Commission is aware of the challenges that globalization and the liberalization of the energy markets pose for competition policy, and is ready to face them.

Now it will be up to the Judicial Branch, litigants, business chambers and scholars, to responsibly assume their own roles as part of the Mexican competition system. I am convinced that during the next years, competition law in Mexico will develop in an exponential way. This has placed and will continue to place Mexico in the eye of many countries around the world. It will depend on all the actors of this system to become an "exemplary" system and, above all, that competition in Mexico becomes a reality and that we can have efficient markets for the benefit of all.

CHAPTER 2
New Competition Policy in Argentina

Julián Peña

§2.01 INTRODUCTION

Competition law in Argentina is going through times of deep transformation since the beginning of 2016 and in less than one year, the scenario is very different than the one found until the end of 2015. After many years, Argentina is working hard to return to mainstream with regard to competition enforcement and these changes can be perceived in different fronts.

The change of government in Argentina in December 2015 was a turning point regarding the paradigm of State intervention in the markets and this was translated, among other changes, in the prioritization of competition law enforcement in order to force business to compete more.

These changes have been taken with an unprecedented speed thanks to the combination of various factors, including political will and an existing antitrust community and background which has been forged over many years at the public, private and academic sectors.

§2.02 BACKGROUND

Argentina is one of the first countries in Latin America to have competition laws. In fact, ever since 1923 Argentina has had anti-monopoly laws (a reform took place in 1943). However, it was in 1980 when Argentina introduced its first comprehensive and modern antitrust regulation (Law No. 22,262). Law No. 22,262 took a less repressive approach and introduced new features, such as the creation of the *Comisión Nacional de Defensa de la Competencia* (*"CNDC"*), the rule of reason approach to anticompetitive conducts, and the concept of abuse of dominant position.

Since the enactment of Law No. 22,262 until its major reform in September 1999, antitrust enforcement in Argentina was focused exclusively on anticompetitive conducts. With the introduction of merger control regulations in Law No. 25,156 of 1999, the CNDC shifted antitrust enforcement mainly towards merger control, with a limited and sporadic cartel activity.

In the meantime, competition law acquired constitutional status through the 1994 amendment to the Argentine Constitution, which in its section 42 states that the federal authorities shall provide for "the defense of competition against any kind of market distortions," and "the control of natural and legal monopolies."

Today, Law No. 25,156 governs all competition matters (i.e., cartels, unilateral conducts and merger control) and its enforcement is vested in the Secretariat of Trade of the Ministry of Production, which is assisted by the CNDC.

During the first thirty-five years of modern competition law enforcement, but mainly since the 1999 reform, a vast antitrust community of lawyers and economists has been developed at the private, public and academic sectors. Although after the Argentine economic and political crisis of 2002, competition law enforcement was relegated as a political priority and sometimes even strongly misinterpreted, the antitrust community not only survived but it has also grown and strengthened in all areas. The development of this community has been pivotal for the changes that are currently taking place to succeed mainly because his antitrust community has provided many critical human resources for the new government to be able to implement its decision to have a world-class competition regime.

§2.03 NEW DEVELOPMENTS

The new government that took office in Argentina in December 2015 from the very beginning made it clear that a sound competition law enforcement was going to be one of its political priorities. Since then various new developments have taken place in the first months of the new administration.

Competition enforcement as a political priority

For the first time ever, a President of Argentina announced in its annual speech to Congress that competition law enforcement was going to be one of the political priorities of his administration. When the President of Argentina opened the Congressional sessions on March 1, 2016, he said that one of the goals of the new administration was to "strengthen competition law enforcement."[1]

Additionally, in another symbolic gesture, when he appointed the new President of the CNDC there was an oath-taking ceremony at the main saloon of the Presidential Palace that was transmitted live on TV and that was witnessed by the entire Cabinet of Ministers and the heads of the Senate and of the Supreme Court. Such a privilege is

---

1. http://www.casarosada.gob.ar/informacion/discursos/35651-palabras-del-presidente-mauricio-macri-en-la-134-apertura-de-sesiones-ordinarias-del-congreso.

normally granted only to new ministers and very exceptionally has a lower rank government official received such treatment.

The new government has as its main goal to prioritize the defense of competition as "an instrument to promote consumer welfare and, at the same time, improve productivity and opportunities to enhance economic development ... through the triple P rule: penalize, prevent and promote."[2] The three P's stand for: penalizing anticompetitive behaviors, preventing concentration, and promoting competition by fostering a competition culture and for establishing pro-competitive regulations.

Strengthening of the CNDC

In February 2016, Esteban Greco was appointed as the new President of the CNDC. For the first time in over a decade, the appointed President has previous antitrust experience and knowledge. Esteban Greco had previously worked at the CNDC first as the Chief Economist and later as Commissioner. Since he left the CNDC, he has been a consultant for public and private organizations on competition policy, economic regulation and energy economics. This background allowed him to start the necessary reforms from day one.

Along with him, new commissioners have been appointed. The new CNDC commissioners were chosen by his experience either on the public, private or academic sectors in antitrust or law and economics. The fact that the new team of commissioners were appointed within a very short time frame was helpful in setting up the new team.

In July 2016, a new administrative structure was created by Administrative Decision No. 756/2016 of the Chief of Staff of Ministers of Argentina. This new structure included the creation of directorates for anticompetitive conducts, economic concentrations, legal and economic studies and competition advocacy. The latter is a position that has never existed in Argentina before and it has the challenge of helping create a competition culture in Argentina, among other goals.

The CNDC was also empowered to carry-on investigations. By the enactment of Law No. 26,993 in September 2014, the CNDC was totally cleaned of any powers which were totally transferred to the Secretariat of Trade. The CNDC was reduced only to a mere assistant to the Secretariat of Trade with powers only to issue recommendations, opinions, studies and reports, but with no binding effects. Since then, and given that this reform had turned the CNDC into an inoperative body, the Secretariat of Trade issued its Resolution No. 359/2015 granting the CNDC certain investigative powers, though much less powers than the CNDC had before the legal reform of 2014. In July 2016, the Secretariat of Trade issued its Resolution No. 190/2016 replacing Resolution No. 359/2015 and re-established the CNDC with the different powers it historically had.

Lastly, the CNDC also has went through a major internal restructuring of its human resources, hiring new junior and senior economists and lawyers and training them. The training of the new professionals has been handled both internally by senior

---

2. Greco, Esteban M. and Quesada, Lucía – "Argentina: Competition Authority," The Antitrust Review of the Americas 2017, Global Competition Review, London, 2016, pg. 107.

professionals with strong academic background and also externally through training programs given by either foreign antitrust agencies such as the Federal Trade Commission and the U.S. Department of Justice, or by international organizations such as the World Bank.

Greater international approach

The CNDC has substantially changed its international approach in the first months of the new administration. This change reflects the greater government policy of reinserting Argentina in the global scene after years of isolation.

The objective of the CNDC is "to reactivate and increase our links with other agencies as a way to improve our practice and learn from the international experience" since "we can only benefit from sharing methodologies and information with our colleagues around the world, especially as competition cases become increasingly international."[3]

Within the first months of the new administration, the CNDC has established contacts with its Latin American counter parts, as well as with the agencies of the United States (Federal Trade Commission and Department of Justice), Canada and the European Commission.

The international outreach of the CNDC also included strengthening its relations with different international organizations such as the World Bank, the Inter-American Development Bank, UNCTAD and the OECD. This has included, for instance, a training program given by the World Bank to the staff of the CNDC on cartel prosecution in May 2016. In October 2016, the President of the CNDC presided the Group of Experts Meeting organized by UNCTAD in Geneva and in November 2016, the OECD (organization to which Argentina started the negotiations in order to become an active participant of its Competition Committee), held a training program on competition and public procurement.

The CNDC has also actively participated during 2016 in conferences organized by the Section of Antitrust of the American Bar Association ("ABA") and by the International Bar Association ("IBA"), events where the CNDC had not participated for many years. Furthermore, the CNDC has expressly requested both organizations for comments to the draft bill reforming the current competition law, even translating the draft bill into English in order to facilitate those comments. In October 2016, both the ABA and the IBA made comments and recommendations for the first time ever to an Argentine antitrust initiative.

New draft bill

In an unprecedented action, on August 30, 2016, the Argentine Antitrust Commission ("CNDC") opened a public consultation process for its draft bill reforming its competition law.

The main characteristics of the draft bill include:

---

3. Greco et al., *supra*, p. 108.

- *Per se hard core cartels* – The draft bill establishes that hard core cartels are to be considered per se unlawful creating an exception to the general *rule of reason* regime. These conducts would also be considered null.
- *Reform to the institutional framework* – The creation of an independent agency, the National Competition Authority (the "ANC"), as a decentralized and independent agency within the sphere of the Argentine Government. The ANC's five members would be a President and four commissioners, all of them requiring technical background and suitability. They would have five-year terms and can only be removed with certain proper justification.
- *Greater sanctions for anticompetitive conducts* – The implementation of new criteria for the determination of fines, implementing a system based on the business volume of the affected markets, multiplied by the number of years of the duration of the conduct. There would be a limit based on the economic group's international business volume, taking into account the previous financial year. Second offences will be subject to a duplication of the fine. The draft bill also eliminates the requirement introduced in 2014 by which the parties had to pay the fines in order to have the right to appeal a fine.
- *Introduction of a Leniency Program* – The creation of a Leniency Program which would fully exempt from any sanction to the first party that applies for leniency and meets the requirements, and would reduce the fines to those who file later but meet the requirements and provide useful information. The draft bill also contemplates the introduction of a Leniency Plus mechanism by which a party could be benefited in case it provides useful information about another cartel.
- *Changes in merger control* – The draft bill introduces various changes to the existing merger control system, including the implementation of a pre-merger control regime; the update and modification of the notification thresholds which were established in pesos in the 1999 reform (since then the peso was devaluated more than fifteen times vis-à-vis the U.S. dollar) and the methods used for their calculation; and the introduction of a fast track mechanism for certain transactions.
- *Damages actions* – The draft bill allows for damages suits as a consequence of infringements to the competition regulations.
- *Judicial review* – The draft bill would create the National Antitrust Court of Appeals, which would act as the competent court in matters regarding appeals to the ANC's decisions.

On September 27, 2016, the government announced that it would merge its draft bill with the ones prepared by two deputies of the ruling coalition *Cambiemos* (Mario Negri and Elisa Carrió). A new version of the draft bill, which includes many of the suggestions received from the various organizations, was circulated in Congress at the end of 2016.

Competition advocacy

In April 2016, the CNDC launched eleven market investigations with the objective of assessing the competitiveness conditions in sectors highly concentrated and with significant impact on production and consumption. Markets under investigation included that of milk; meat; laundry detergent; cooking oil; mobile communications; credit cards; air and ground passenger transportation; steel, aluminum; and petrochemicals.

On August 29, 2016, the CNDC released the results of the credit cards and electronic payment methods market investigation (the "CNDC Report"). The CNDC concluded that in the investigated market there is a lack of competition and transparency, with high commissions, a technological delay, and a dominant position held by Prisma Medios de Pago S.A. (Visa Argentina).

As result of the investigation, the CNDC Report issued regulatory recommendations to the Central Bank of Argentina and the Secretary of Trade, including the proposal of some amendments to the current Credit Cards Law, in order to guarantee competition and enhance the alternatives of financing commerce and consumers. Additionally, the CNDC Report recommended the Secretary of Trade to initiate an antitrust investigation against Prisma for alleged abuse of dominant position and to its shareholders (fourteen banks, both private and public) for the existence of an alleged cartel.

According to the CNDC Report, credit cards and electronic payment methods market shows certain concerns as lack of competition in consumption financing, lack of transparency (closured financing cost), high commissions for big shops and technological retardation, as there is an evidenced delay in the introduction of electronic payment methods.

With that purpose, the CNDC Report recommended the Central Bank of Argentina to generate competition in the card acquisition market; to eradicate the restriction to commission differentiation; to promote competition in consumption financing; and to make product prices and financing conditions more transparent.

§2.04 CONCLUSIONS

Since the change of government of Argentina in December 2015, there have been many new developments in the area of competition. Competition enforcement has received political support from the highest government officials; the CNDC was completely renovated with professionals with experience in the areas of antitrust or law and economics in the private, public and academic sectors while also receiving back the powers that were taken away in 2014; a more international approach has been taken by the authorities; competition advocacy was introduced in the agenda; and a draft bill reforming the law in order to modernize it was launched.

It is still early to make a proper assessment as to how antitrust enforcement in Argentina will evolve with respect to anticompetitive conducts and merger cases.

However, the many steps already taken on the right direction help foresee the future evolution in an optimistic manner. The new changes added to the vast experience and the existence of a strong antitrust community, is a good combination that will help Argentina to be back as a prominent player in the global competition map sooner than later.

CHAPTER 3
New Competition Policy in Paraguay

*Cynthia Andino**

§3.01 INTRODUCTION

New competition laws, because of their economic importance, are been enacted around the world. In 2013 Paraguay, for its part, passed its first competition law – Law No. 4956, "*Defensa de la Competencia*" (hereinafter "Law No. 4956" or "Competition Law"). Previously Guatemala and Paraguay were the only two countries in Latin America that did not have competition regulation.

Even though the Republic of Paraguay now has a basic tool to protect the market economy, it lacks essential aspects, which are discussed in this study. Notably, at the genesis of Law No. 4956 is unusual because it was drafted by the private sector as represented by the Federation of Production, Industry and Commerce (hereinafter FEPRINCO)[1] and then enacted by Congress. FEPRINCO also provided commentary on the Rules of Law No. 4956.

This paper analyzes the substantive aspects of the Competition Law, especially the anticompetitive conduct it covers as well as significant elements that were omitted from the law. It also examines the organizational and functional structure of Paraguay's Competition Authority – the National Competition Commission (hereinafter "CONACOM"). Moreover, this article reviews and discusses the general aspects of how CONACOM investigates and sanctions anticompetitive agreements and abuse of dominant position, as well as how it controls mergers. We also provide a brief

---

* The author thanks the contribution of Charles Reeves and David Sperber. The views hereby expressed are exclusively of the author and do not necessarily reflect those of the aforementioned organizations.
1. ABC newspaper of Paraguay. "Empresarios presentan anteproyecto de Ley de Defensa de la Competencia". April 19, 2010. *http://www.abc.com.py/edicion-impresa/economia/feprinco-presento-propuesta-sobre-ley-de-competencia-92122.html*. Vid. Diario ABC. Paraguay. *http://www.abc.com.py/edicion-impresa/economia/reglamentaran-ley-de-competencia-604126.html*.

comparison of other countries' competition law regulations. It should be noted that this paper will not discuss other related laws such as intellectual property, consumer protection, *inter alia*. It will also not comment the various prior drafts of the Competition Law that were discussed by the Paraguayan Congress or MERCOSUR's regional regulations.

Paraguay's Congress nominally initiated discussions of the need for an antitrust law in 2003, but it did not really take the issue seriously until 2010 when a controversial article for published in the newspaper of the wholesaler-retailer "Casa Grutter." This article issued a clarion call for competition regulation in Paraguay as Casa Grutter exposed the pressure it had received from a group of suppliers to trade-up their prices because other customers (supermarkets) were going to boycott if the suppliers continued to sell to Casa Grutter, which retailed goods at lower prices than the other supermarkets. This newspaper article confirmed that thirty-five companies had stopped supplying to Casa Grutter.[2]

It should also be noted that while the Competition Law was enacted nearly three years ago, it has not yet been implemented. Thus, no national case law exists. Also, Paraguay's Ministry of Finance has provided limited financial resources to CONACOM: USD 712,000 in 2015,[3] and approximately USD 858,000 in 2016.[4] CONACOM publicly announced in a March 18, 2016 hearing before Congress that it could not implement or enforce the Competition Law because of these limited resources.

Paraguay's President appointed CONACOM's three Commissioners on July 31, 2015 though Presidential Decree No. 3842. To date, however, they are still in the process of forming the Agency's other dependencies, and the institution still does not have either a physical space or a website.[5]

Finally, we emphasize that we have not found a previous analysis of Law No. 4956; therefore, this papers seeks to provide helpful commentary about the Paraguay's new Competition Law.

§3.02 LEGAL FRAMEWORK

Article 107 of Paraguay's Constitution of 1992 establishes the legal framework for competition regulation.[6]

---

2. ABC newspaper of Paraguay. *http://www.abc.com.py/edicion-impresa/economia/proveedores-presionan-a-un-centro--comercial-para-que-suba-sus-precios-88926.html*.
3. The equivalent of 3,947,411,100 and 4,754,734,058 Paraguayan Guarani (PYG), respectively.
4. *http://www.congreso.gov.py/index.php/noticias-2/173652-evaluan-implementacion-de-la-ley-de-competencia-2016-03-18-13-11-56*.
5. Verified until April of 2016.
6. Constitution of the Republic of Paraguay of 1992. Article 107. "Free Competition: Everyone has the right to engage in lawful economic activity of their choice, within a regime of equal opportunities. Competition in the market is guaranteed. It will not be allowed the creation of monopolies and the artificial rise or fall of prices or breach of free competition. Usury and unauthorized trade in harmful items will be sanctioned by the Criminal Law."

[A] Law No. 4956 (Competition Law)

On June 21, 2013, after more than a decade of debates, the Paraguayan Congress enacted the Competition Law. It was published in the Official Gazette on June 25, 2013. The law applies to national and foreign economic agents, whether public or private, even when its object or effect is performed outside the country where all or part of its impact is in Paraguay. Significantly, it also applies to "central government entities and decentralized entities exercising a state monopoly" and those authorized by law (Article 3).

Law No. 4956 did not adhere to the model of a specific country. Rather it is a combination of several laws and includes some unique features. As for its legislative technical standards, the law has relevant deficiencies and omits important elements that limit its effectiveness.

[B] Rules to Law No. 4956

Paraguay's president issued Decree No. 1490 (hereinafter the "Rules"[7]) regulating Law No. 4956 on April 14, 2014.

The Rules' purpose is to facilitate the application of the law and to complement it. According to the principle of hierarchy, the Rules shall not change the law. This paper, however, addresses several inconsistencies between Law No. 4956 and the Rules that create legal uncertainty.

Some relevant aspects omitted in the law are covered by the Rules. In regards to merger control, for example, the law provides for an *ex post* control while the Rules include a non-compulsory *ex ante* notification. An inconsistency pertains to investigation procedures. Whereas the law does not give CONACOM with the power to do dawn raids (also known as "unexpected inspections"),[8] the Rules state this power that was not included in the Law; as otherwise they could be considered to be possible violations of the right to private property that the Constitution enshrines.

§3.03 ILLEGAL CONDUCTS ESTABLISHED IN LAW NO. 4956

This section discusses the classifications of conduct that Law No. 4956 prohibits: (a) anticompetitive agreements; (b) abuse of dominant position; and, (c) merger control. We emphasize that the legislation uses the *rule of reason* criteria in all cases and not the per se rule. Notwithstanding, the recommendations urges the new competition

---

7. *Decreto No. 1490 por el cual se Reglamenta la Ley No. 4956/2013 "Defensa de la Competencia"*.
8. As per inspections, it should be noted that the last amendment to Brazil's Competition Act, which was passed in November 2011, and entered into force on May 29, 2012, modified this point. These surprise searches can be carried out by the Authority without judicial authorization.

agencies to use of the per se rule for collusions and price fixing, since the institutions do not have enough experience to deal with certain cases.[9]

[A] Anticompetitive Agreements

Anticompetitive agreements are prohibited when they limit or affect competition. These agreements, also called collusive practices, are generally secret arrangements between companies where they collude to affect a third party or to not compete. These agreements are classified as "horizontal" (between competitors in the same level of the goods or services they provide) or "vertical" (different levels of the production or commercialization chain).

Law No. 4956 prohibits the following (not exhaustive) as anticompetitive agreements. Those that:

(a) Establish, impose or recommend, directly or indirectly, purchase or sales prices, or other trade conditions.
(b) Limit or control unjustifiably the market, the production, the distribution, technical development or investments in detriment of competitors or consumers.
(c) To deal out or divide the market, customers or supply sources.
(d) Apply unjustifiably dissimilar conditions to equivalent transactions placing a person in competitive disadvantage.
(e) Subordinate the acceptance of supplementary obligations which by its nature or commercial usage has no connection with the subject of such contracts.
(f) Collusive tendering.
(g) Restraints on production or sales, in particular through market quotas.
(h) Concerted refusal to acquire.
(i) Collective unjustified denial to participate in an agreement or the admission to an association, which is crucial to competition.

The list of anticompetitive conducts is positive. However, one type of conduct (boycotting) that should have been included explicitly is only implicitly covered under the umbrella of the general prohibition clause in first paragraph of Article 8.

One erroneous component of the Competition Law is found in the last paragraph of Article 8, which requires the authority to, "analyze the efficiency gains arising from the conduct" before making a determination whether a specific conduct in anticompetitive. This should not be compulsory since in some cases the collusive purpose may not be profit or prohibiting entry to an association. Thus, this requirement should be eliminated.

---

9. Honduras' competition law (Decree No. 357-2005) uses the per se rule for cases of hard cartels. OECD's *Peer Review of Law and Competition Policy in Honduras* (2011, p. 64) regards this as one of the standard's strengths.

[B] Abuse of Dominant Position

Article 9 of the Competition Law prohibits, "The abuse of dominant position in all or part of the relevant market by one or more natural or legal persons contained in Article 3 of this Law."

The doctrine classifies abuse of dominant position as exploitative abuse and exclusionary abuse.[10] Moreover, the abuse of dominant position can be horizontal or vertical. Having a dominant position is not per se violation of the Law; the element of "abuse" of this dominant position is required.

Law No. 4956 classifies (but does not limit) unilateral or joint abuse of a dominant position in the relevant market as:

> The imposition, directly or indirectly, of prices, other trade conditions or inequitable services.
> The unjustified limitation of production, distribution or technical development to prejudice companies or consumers.
> The unjustified refusal to meet the demand of purchase of products or services.
> The unjustified application of unequal conditions in equivalent commercial relations placing competitors at disadvantage.
> The subordination of contracts subject to the acceptance of supplementary obligations which, by their nature or commercial usage, has no connection with the subject matter of such contracts.
> Obtain or attempt to obtain, under the threat of disruption of commercial relations, prices and payment terms, sales terms, payment of fees or other commercial terms not included in the general sale conditions previously agreed upon.

For example, an error in the wording of this article was not to determine in paragraph (c) the unjustified refusal to meet the demands of purchase also applies to the sale of such products or services, since it can occur both ways.

Another aspect to note is the inclusion of a specific article on predatory pricing (Article 10). It can only be penalized if the economic operator has a dominant position in the relevant market, otherwise it should correspond to unfair competition. In most laws, predatory pricing is listed in the article of abuse of dominance position. Also, paragraph (a) of Article 10 refers only to the purpose of excluding competitors from the market; we consider that this behavior can also be penalized based on the effect of the conduct.

Furthermore, as a legislative technique, Article 10 has a defect because it exposes an assortment of prohibitions and definitions. So, when the law and rules are next

---

10. Are those in which the company's dominant position hinders the competitive process through the elimination of current rivals (or by deterring the entry of new competitors), such as the use of essential facilities, among others.

reformed, certain paragraphs should be moved to the glossary of definitions in order to separate the illegal conducts and the definitions.

[C] Merger Control

The structure of enterprises plays a fundamental role in the economy, so some mergers or concentrations may affect the market. This is the reason why *ex ante* merger control is a vital as part of antitrust rules.

Paraguay's Competition Law contemplates an *ex post* merger control. Article 14.1 requires the acquirer to notify CONACOM of a concentration within ten days after the conclusion of the agreement. There is no provision requiring the suspension of the operation until CONACOM has issued its authorization. This *ex post* authentication has proven to be a negative for competition. Even Decree 1490 seeks to repair this to some degree by noting that "previous or *ex ante* filing" can be done,[11] the Rules do not expressly make the *ex ante* procedure mandatory. This leaves the decision to provide prior notification to the economic agents.

The non-cumulative requirements to file an economic concentration under Article 14 of the Competition Law are:

(a) Purchase or increase of quota equal to or greater than 45% of the national or defined geographic market of a particular product or service.
(b) The overall gross turnover in the Republic of Paraguay of all participants subject to the merger that exceeds, in the last fiscal year, the amount of 100,000 workers minimum monthly salary, or USD 32,364,000.[12]

In this sense, we believe that paragraph (a) represents a high threshold and thus only a few concentrations are going to be subject to control in the Paraguayan market. As a reference, we point out that the thresholds in Ecuador and Argentina are 30% and 25%, respectively. While Uruguay's 50% threshold intentionally seeks to avoid the regulation of concentrations, or to do it only in exceptional circumstances.

Paragraph (a) should be more categorical and determine that the 45% is of the relevant market. As currently written it only considers the product or service without taking into account its substitutes – which is the intent of the global rules of economic competition. As a result, many concentrations are going to be subject to CONACOM verification even though it will not affect 45% or more of the relevant market. Article 16(k) of Decree 1490 provides that the filing must point out the competitors in the relevant market; it therefore constitutes a contradiction.

Some experts and countries consider that establishing market share as a criteria for an antitrust filing is obsolete because it is difficult to establish – especially in

---

11. Rules. Article 14. "The natural or legal persons may request prior authorization of the merger. In that case, the rules on notification, assessment and the decision of the CONACOM on the merger shall apply as established in the Law and its Rules."
12. The monthly salary to January 2016 is PYG 1,824,055; equivalent to USD 323.64 (approximately).

countries were no significant or accurate market statistics and data exist.[13] The inclusion of this criterion only hinders the work of the respective competition authority because they must allocate adequate technical capacity to identify the market share.

The second requirement for filing a notification of a concentration refers to the overall gross turnover only in Paraguayan territory equivalent (as of April 2016) to approximately USD 30,800,000, which is a low threshold.

Significantly, worldwide merger control remedies are behavioral and/or structural. Since the purpose of the control is to prevent potentially harmful effects on competition in a timely manner. In that sense, the trend of current regulations is to use *ex ante* notification because in some cases once the transaction has been completed it is difficult and costly to reverse the transaction in order to correct the affected market.

§3.04 RELEVANT CONDUCTS NOT CLASSIFIED IN THE COMPETITION LAW

This section will focus on the exempted conducts that the Competition Law has not incorporated and were intentionally and/or wrongfully omitted by its drafters.

[A] Unfair Competition

Sometimes unfair competition is confused with competition or antitrust as both have similar scopes and pursue like objectives in order to correct the market. Both are necessary to protect competition and consumers. Unfair competition, however, is dissimilar to collusive practices and abuse of dominant position. So despite their differences they can be investigated and sanctioned by a competition authority (e.g., Colombia, Nicaragua and Peru.)

Paraguay did not include a section for unfair competition in the new Competition Law because there was a relevant provision in Article 108 of the Mercantile Law (No. 1034/1983). But Law No. 1034 is obsolete with no reforms having been made to it since its enactment. In that sense, the Mercantile Law also has a section on trade competition that contradicts the new Competition Law on the matter. The later did not foresee the repeal of existing rules that contravene the purpose of the antimonopoly rule. Ecuador, in contrast, provided a chapter on unfair competition in its Competition Law of 2011 that updates its rules and fines.

[B] State Aid

State aids are subsidies or benefits of any kind or nature that the State or public entity (at any level) grants to certain economic sector including State-owned or private corporations pursuant to its economic sovereignty.[14]

---

13. The market share criterion is no longer applicable in Brazil under the latest amendment to the Competition Act, passed in November 2011 and in force as of May 29, 2012.
14. Gutierrez, Gilberto; Sperber, David. "Manual de Competencia Económica Para Empresarios. Ley Antimonopolio". Quito, 2012, p. 27.

State aid regime has gained great importance in recent years and is an integral part of competition policy because of the markets distortions that these measures can create. The absence of market distortion regulations for public economic actors is notable. That said, many Latin American jurisdictions have not included them in their competition laws for political considerations and because some governments do not want another authority to review and potentially limit their economic and political decisions – even those that alter competition.

The new Paraguayan Competition Law does not regulated public aid activity. The next reform should incorporate corresponding regulations to do so.

§3.05 CONACOM: PARAGUAYAN COMPETITION AUTHORITY

CONACOM, the national competition authority, has investigative and sanctioning powers. Its jurisdiction is nationwide, and it is autonomous and independent. Although, the Ministry of Industry and Commerce (MIC) is the liaison between the CONACOM and the Executive Branch.

CONACOM has a vertical structure and is integrated in two separate bodies: the Commission and the Investigations Bureau. Each has different functions and attributions that are coordinated by CONACOM's president. These bodies will rely on different departments detailed in the Rules of the Competition Law (Decree No. 1490).

The Commission (*Directorio*) has three members. They must be lawyers, economists, accountants or business managers.[15] The Commissioners are appointed by the country's president from three-person shortlist proposed by MIC. They serve a six-year term and can be reelected once.

The Investigations Bureau is the technical body that investigates abuse of dominant position, anticompetitive conduct, and controls concentrations. It is managed by a director show is appointed through the same procedure as that for the Commissioners. He or she serves for period of five years and can be reappointed indefinitely.

We approve of the separation of CONACOM's two bodies. Since one investigates and the other imposes sanctions and remedies, the author believes that the division of powers promotes regulatory transparency in antitrust matter proceedings.

[A] CONACOM's Powers

The Commission has the following powers:

(a) Acknowledge and resolve procedures within its competence.
(b) Order the initiation of an investigation.
(c) Authorize, place conditions on, or deny economic concentrations.
(d) Sanction economic operators that breach Law No. 4956.

---

15. This requirement is limiting. It is advisable to open this requirement to a broader range of professionals with knowledge or experience relevant to free competition matters.

CONACOM can act ex officio or pursuant to a legal proceeding or lawsuit brought by a legitimate party (Article 45). We believe the Rules requirements for filing a lawsuit are excessive and inconsistent with Article 47 of the Competition Law, since the Rules cannot impose more requirements. Also for example, Article 83 of the Rules requires the claimant to present evidence of abuse of dominant position and show that the accused has profited from the arrangement. This is inconsistent with the investigative duty that the Competition Law allocates solely to CONACOM.

Another weak point is that it does not allow consumers (who often suffer from the indirect effects of abuse of dominant position or anticompetitive agreements) to file an antitrust action unless they prove direct legitimate interest. We recommend that CONACOM issue a clarification that would include consumers in the definition of an "interested party" even if they have no direct interest.

[B] Board of Qualifications

The Paraguayan law has an unusual figure – the so called the Board of Qualifications (*Junta de Calificaciones*) – that was created during the debate of the law between the public and private sector. It arose out of private sector's reluctance at (and mistrust of) having the government control competition matters. This body was proposed by the private sector through FEPRINCO.

The main and unique function of to the Board of Qualifications is to call for a competitive merit-based contest to determine the three shortlists for the president's appointment of the CONACOM commissioners. As indicated above, the law requires the president of Paraguay to shall appoint the three commissioners (and one alternate) as well as the Director of Investigations from the Board's shortlist.

The Board of Qualifications has eight *ad-honorem* members. They serve a three-year term. FEPRINCO (representing the private sector: production, industry, trade and services) appoints four members of the Board. The public sector appoints the other four members. For this purpose the president, the Consumers Protection Department of the MIC, the Paraguayan Congress, and the Paraguayan Senate each appoint one member to the Board.

When the bill for initially discussed the MIC offered counter-proposal that would have allowed a representative from academia to be represented on the Board of Qualifications. FEPRINCO, however, rejected this idea for the sole reason of avoiding the dilution of its voting quota on the Board.

The above mechanism is unique as in most Latin American countries it is the executive and legislative branches exclusive domain to appoint members of their competition authorities without any direct private sector participation. We note, moreover, that although Law No. 4956 does not specify that the President of the Republic may reject the shortlists, it may occur.

Nevertheless, Paraguay's Competition Law, according to the NGO Social Research Foundation, was prepared by FEPRINCO (with a few modifications) to ensure that it was more palpable for the private sector.[16] Referring to the Board of Qualifications they affirmed, "Even agreeing all public sector representatives, they could not include a single candidate in the shortlists without the agreement of the representatives of FEPRINCO, since the shortlist requires simple majority of the Board, or 5 out of 8 votes."

On this matter, Nicaragua has a similar procedure as Paraguay where its Directors/Commissioners are appointed by the country's president and ratified by the National Assembly (Congress) from three shortlists proposed by the Superior Council of Private Enterprises (COSEP), the Nicaraguan Council of Micro, Small and Medium Enterprises (CONIMIPYME), and the Ministry of Development, Industry and Trade (MIFIC).[17]

As previously mentioned, most South American competition officials are appointed by the respective president and ratified the country's congress. This is the case in Argentina, Brazil, Uruguay, *inter alia*. Paraguay's decision to appoint their antitrust commissioners from a shortlist provided by the private sector goes against the grain of international competition policy doctrine. This establishes a negative standard for Paraguay.

§3.06 PROCEDURE TO INVESTIGATE AND PUNISH ILLEGAL ACTS DEFINED IN LAW NO. 4956

CONACOM investigation and sanctioning actions are classified as administrative sanctioning procedures.

The starting point for analyzing the practices stipulated in Law 4956 is the definition of relevant market contained in Article 6.[18] It draws the attention to the phrase regarding "significant price increase,"[19] because some anticompetitive agreements or abuse of dominant position conduct do not necessarily have a single or direct impact on prices. For example, Article 8(j) sanctions the unjustified collective denial of an admission of an association.

---

16. For further information *http://www.baseis.org.py/proyecto-de-ley-de-defensa-de-la-competencia-en-realidad-defiende-a-las-corporaciones/*.
17. According to the Voluntary Peer Review Law and Competition Policy in Nicaragua made in 2013 by the UNCTAD (DITC / CLP / 2013/2), on this point it was mentioned that "The fact that Council members represent private sector groups and the government, in principle could compromise the independence of the body or be a source of conflict of interest ... ". Also in the recommendations they said, it would be worth reconsidering the appointment of members of the Board of Procompetencia start from lists proposed by the aforementioned bodies."
18. Article 6 states:

    For the purposes of this Act, the term relevant market the field of economic activity and the geographical area defined in such a way that covers all goods or substitutable services, and all nearby competitors, that consumers could turn in the short term, if a restriction or abuse would result in a significant increase in prices. The Enforcement Authority shall establish the criteria for determining the relevant market.

19. Other examples of abuse not based on the price are boycotting, contractual tying, exclusive purchasing, and refusals to supply, et al.

Thus, the wording in the relevant market definition is mistaken. This may affect the proper implementation of the Competition Law because it is essential in determining whether or not a violation of Law 4956 exists.

[A] Anticompetitive Agreements and Abuse of Dominant Position Procedure

The law provides a ninety-day investigative phase. Investigations may be extended for an additional 90 days, for a total of 180 days. The author believes that this is too short of a period given that these are complex cases that typically require a longer time to be properly investigated and resolved. The Commission cannot suspend this time limit even in cases where it requests additional information.

The Competition Law allows any person to file a commitment-to-cease an anticompetitive conduct where he/she commits to cease the practice under investigation. The law, however, does not impose fines on the person that confesses the unlawful practice through an approved commitment-to-cease.[20] In Ecuador, in contrast, the Superintendence of Control of Market Power can impose a corrective sum, which they normally do.

[B] Concentrations and Merger Control

The Competition Commission has ninety days to approve, condition, or reject a concentrations filing. Law 4956 does not stipulate a possibility of extending this deadline, except where the Merger Control Division requests additional information, providing fifteen to thirty days to supply the information. In this case, it can suspend the procedure once. It may also do so at the request of the acquirer for thirty days. Thus, the filing procedure could be extended from 90 to 150 days.

The Rules divide the filing assessment in two stages. This is positive for the purpose of alacrity. At the first stage, CONACOM may approve simple concentrations that do not pose a threat to competition within thirty days. The second stage is for notifications that require further analysis. This stage has a sixty-day time period (plus the thirty days of the first stage). Significantly, the European Commission also uses the two-phase merger control procedure, which we believe is positive.

[C] The Administrative Sanctioning Procedure

As per the government's sanctioning power, Article 63(c) of the Competition Law allows for fines up to 150% of the profits obtained from the illegal practice, or 20% of the gross income from products sold pursuant to the infringing practice in the affected relevant market in the past twelve months. This term runs from the initiation of

---

20. It is unclear since the Competition Law contemplates a fine for the "cessation breach of the undertaking." Article 63(h).

administrative proceedings. These fines exclude taxes. The fine also cannot be less than the advantage gained (if quantifiable).

Determining the profit obtained from certain behaviors is complex and difficult to establish. The legislators recognized this when it used the language, "when it is quantifiable." Second, competition law doctrine considers the alternative of applying the fine on the gross sales of the "products" covered by the illegal practice to be insufficient because some companies can infringe using a minor product but use this practice to create leverage for its leading product.

Moreover, it should be emphasized that it is not the product that committed the infringement but rather the economic actor. So it would have been preferable to have the fine was calculated based on the economic actor's overall gross turnover. This is what most competition laws worldwide do. Without out it the law does not have sufficient teeth to deter anticompetitive conduct and enforcement efforts are weakened.

Paraguay's antitrust deterrence and enforcement efforts are also hampered because the Competition Law does not provide for non-monetary sanctions, only fines. Other South American countries competition laws, for example, Brazil's and Uruguay's, contain behavioral measure sanctions and injunctions to stop practicing the anticompetitive conduct. They include publication of the sanction in the media[21] and issuing personal fines to participants in the cartels. Moreover, Law 4956 fails to categorize fines on different levels (e.g., minor, severe or very severe).

Ad avizandum: The second paragraph of the Rules' Article 77 sanctions the submission of false information or the failure to comply with information requirements. Nonetheless, we believe that it was mistake that this fine was established in the Rules – but not in the Law. Thus, there is a risk that it may be declared void for breaching of the principle of legality because there seems to be a contradiction between Article 79 and Article 90(c) of the Rules. The first set fines for failure to provide information (which is not stipulated in the law) and the second refers to the principle of legality.

Another debatable issue is destination of the fines that CONACOM issues. The Competition Law provides that 50% of the fines will go to the National Treasury and the remaining 50% to CONACOM's treasury. The trend in most jurisdictions is to designate all revenue from fines to the National Treasury and not to the government body that issues them. This is to avoid giving an authority an incentive (real or perceived) for imposing fines in order to raise income the institution.[22] FEPRINCO

---

21. *Ibid.* Uruguay. Article 17 Penalties B); Ecuador. Article 87. Advertising sanctions. It is worth noting, the corporate image and goodwill is very important for companies, thus the reputation that they hold on consumers plays a significant role.
22. On this matter the conclusions of the Peer Review of law and competition policy in Colombia, published by the OECD in 2009, test the problem that the fines imposed by the agency goes to its own treasure and expressed in its budget, as this could be a clear incentive for increasing fines for the agency. It was also recommended that fines are intended for the general fund of the Government, i.e., the National Treasury and the agency is financed by the state budget. *See* p. 66 *https://www.oecd.org/daf/competition/44111213.pdf.*

lawyers initially proposed assigning 100% of the fines to the competition authority, but the MIC convinced them that this had to be modified.

§3.07 CONCLUSIONS

The new Paraguayan Competition Law is an important step to promote and protect competition in the country.

We noticed that it reflects a combination of different legislations that have been adapted to what the drafters' deemed relevant to Paraguay.

The following are what we believe to be the Competition Law's main strengths and weaknesses:

(1) *Strengths:*
   (a) The investigative and resolution bodies are separate and independent.
   (b) Concentration filings are decided in two stages.
   (c) Precautionary measures.
   (d) The existence of pecuniary fines.
(2) *Weaknesses:*
   (a) The definition of relevant market.
   (b) The direct involvement of the private sector participating in the shortlists for the election of CONACOM Commissioners and the Director of Investigations.
   (c) The *ex post* control of concentrations and high thresholds.
   (d) Insufficient time periods for investigations.
   (e) Meager fines and mild sanctions.
   (f) The allocation of revenues from fines to CONACOM.
   (g) No provisions for unfair competition practices.
   (h) Failure to repeal legal provisions that conflict with the Competition Law.
   (i) The absence of State aid control.
   (j) The nonattendance of leniency programs.
   (k) Contradictions between the Law and its Rules.

§3.08 RECOMMENDATIONS

The author recommends that the following modifications and additions be made to Law No. 4956 to ensure more vigorous promotion of fair competition and effective consumer protection in Paraguay;

(a) Modify the control of concentrations to *ex ante* review.
(b) Correct the current thresholds in concentrations by eliminating the market share criteria and modifying the total turnover element.
(c) Extend the time periods for control of concentrations, abuse of dominant position, and anticompetitive practice proceedings.

(d) Adjust the definition of relevant market as the current description could generate problems in the implementation of the law.
(e) Remove the Board of Qualification to appoint CONACOM Commissioners and Directors. They should instead be appointed by Paraguay's president of and ratified by the Senate.
(f) Include a chapter on unfair competition and repeal the relevant provisions currently in force.
(g) Incorporate rules on state aid because of the importance of public economic actors in Paraguay's economy.
(h) Amend the Competition Law to include the leniency program of the type that exist in Brazil, Canada, European Commission, USA, United Kingdom, et al. Leniency programs represent one of the most important and effective measures for fighting cartels that are so harmful to free competition and consumers.
(i) Establish activities for the advocacy of fair competition.

BIBLIOGRAPHY

Decreto Ejecutivo 1152, Reglamento a la Ley Orgánica de Regulación y Control del Poder de Mercado, República del Ecuador, 2012.
Decreto N° 357-2005 "Ley para la Defensa y Promoción de la Competencia", República de Honduras, 2005.
Decreto N° 1490, Por el cual se reglamenta la Ley N° 4956/2013 "Defensa de la Competencia", República del Paraguay, 2014.
Gutierrez Perdomo, Gilberto y Sperber Vilhelm, David "Manual de Competencia Económica para Empresarios. Ley Antimonopolio, Crecer en Competencia". Antitrust Consultores, Quito, 2011.
Ley N° 25.156 "Defensa de la Competencia". Argentina.
Ley N° 8.884/94 "Lei Antitruste". República Federativa del Brasil.
Ley N° 601 "Ley de Promoción de la Competencia". Nicaragua.
Ley N° 4956 "Defensa de la Competencia". República del Paraguay, 2013.
"Ley Orgánica de Regulación y Control del Poder de Mercado". República del Ecuador, 2011.
Ley N° 18.159 "Promoción y Defensa de la Competencia". República Oriental del Uruguay, 2007.
OCDE. "Derecho y Política de la Competencia en Honduras". Examen inter-pares. 2011.
UNCTAD. "Examen Voluntario entre Homólogos del Derecho y la Política de Competencia: Nicaragua". UNCTAD/DITC/CLP/2013/2.

CHAPTER 4
Antitrust Compliance Programs – The Brazilian Experience

Marcela Mattiuzzo

§4.01 INTRODUCTION

Antitrust Compliance programs are today among the most discussed topics on the vast range of competition enforcement issues. Whether the debate regards the need for clearer and more consistent directives from authorities, or the challenges faced by companies in implementing the programs, the topic is ever present in high-level analysis of competition policy.

The goal of this chapter is to shed some light on the Latin American experience regarding antitrust compliance, with a strong focus on the Brazilian example. To do so, I will first shortly present the motives which led to the rise of corporate compliance – and particularly antitrust compliance – in Brazil and the current status of the regulation put forward by the Brazilian antitrust authority, the Administrative Council for Economic Defense, CADE. The intertwining of antitrust and anticorruption will also be analyzed, as this is an especially significant development which will clarify the path followed by the Brazilian authorities and the incentives the private sector received for implementing and updating compliance programs. Finally, I will present brief overviews of how antitrust compliance is understood and dealt with in other Latin American countries, namely Chile and Mexico.

§4.02 COMPLIANCE PROGRAMS IN THE BRAZILIAN CONTEXT

To better understand the reasons which led to the current paradigm for antitrust compliance in Brazil, two aspects must be explored. First, the restructuring of the Brazilian Competition Defense System (BCDS) by means of Law 12,529/2011 and the subsequent changes in competition policy put forward by CADE. Second, the strengthening of anticorruption regulation, notably by Law 12,846/2013 and Decree 8,420/2015, and its effects on corporate compliance as a whole.

[A] The Rise of Antitrust Compliance in Brazil – Enforcement by the New BCDS

In 2011, after being ruled by Law 8,884/1994 for over fifteen years, the BCDS was modified by the Brazilian Congress with the approval of Law 12,529/2011. This change had several impacts in competition policy covering many areas, but the focus here will be on how it allowed for the rise of antitrust compliance. Since the law itself does not utter a word on compliance programs, it is necessary to more closely verify why it cleared the path for this agenda.

When the new law unified the previous three-fold enforcement structure – formed by the Secretariat of Economic Law from the Ministry of Justice, the Secretariat for Economic Monitoring from the Ministry of Finance, and the Administrative Council for Economic Defense – in a single two-fold authority, much changed in Brazil. CADE is now an agency formed by two main bodies: the General Superintendence, responsible for investigations, and the Administrative Tribunal, the decision-making branch. When this model was set forth by Congress, there was need for a full reorganization of internal structures within the authority, which subsequently entailed a more efficient flow of proceedings.[1]

Notably, the new law established an *ex ante* notification system for mergers, according to which the General Superintendence is responsible for ruling on the majority of notified operations.[2] Consequently, the number of mergers judged by the Administrative Tribunal was severely reduced, opening up room for decisions on conducts – or as the Brazilian legislation calls them, the administrative proceedings.

---

1. Specificities on how such remodeling was possible and what changed from the previous to the current system can be found in CARVALHO, Vinicius Marques de (org.). A Lei 12.529/2011 e a Nova Política de Defesa da Concorrência, 1 ed., São Paulo: Editora Singular, 2015.
2. Article 88 of Law 12,29/2011 and Resolution n. 2/2012 put forward a difference between ordinary and summary mergers. As a general rule, only ordinary mergers are forwarded to the Tribunal. All others are directly decided on by the General Superintendence.

Chapter 4: Antitrust Compliance Programs – The Brazilian Experience   §4.02[A]

Figure 4.1   Administrative Proceedings Decided by the Administrative Tribunal

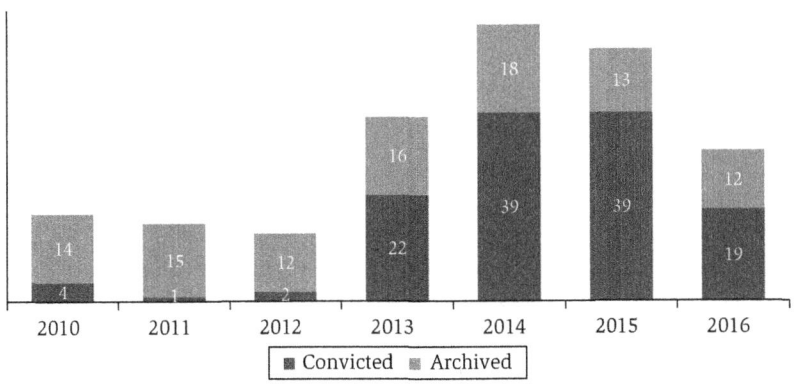

Source: CADE

Such rise in enforcement was paralleled by the establishment of a new settlement policy through Resolution n. 5/2013,[3] one that drastically increased the number of leniencies and Cease and Desist Agreements (also known as TCC, for their Portuguese acronym)[4] signed with CADE.[5]

---

3. The Resolution was responsible for some important modifications. It established new, stricter criteria for settlements in cartel cases, including: (i) the need for pecuniary contributions in all cartel cases, (ii) the mandatory collaboration with the authority with the investigations, and (iii) the recognition of participation in the illicit conduct. The full content of the Resolution is available in Portuguese at: http://www.cade.gov.br/assuntos/normas-e-legislacao/resolucao/resolucao-5_2013.pdf/view.
4. In cartel cases, the Termos de Cessação de Conduta are available to those who are no longer able to sign a leniency but still wish to negotiate with the authority. More on TCCs can be found at CADE's Guidelines for Cease and Desist Agreement for cartel cases, available at: http://www.cade.gov.br/acesso-a-informacao/publicacoes-institucionais/guias_do_Cade/guidelines_tcc-1.pdf
5. Data can be retrieved at: http://www.cade.gov.br/servicos/imprensa/balancos-e-apresentacoes/balanco-4-anos-nova-lei-1.pdf.

Figure 4.2 Settlements Signed with the BCDS

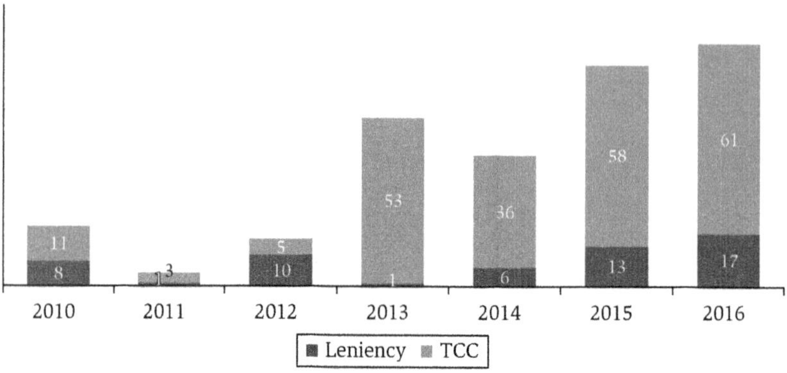

[Bar chart showing Leniency and TCC settlements by year:
2010: Leniency 8, TCC 11
2011: Leniency 1, TCC 3
2012: Leniency 10, TCC 5
2013: Leniency 1, TCC 53
2014: Leniency 6, TCC 36
2015: Leniency 13, TCC 58
2016: Leniency 17, TCC 61]

■ Leniency ■ TCC

Source: CADE

This process showed companies how serious Brazil is about competition enforcement and how prepared the authority is to apply heavy penalties. By broadening the investigations and rulings on anticompetitive conducts, as well as setting strict fines[6] in its convictions, CADE made it clear that the private sector should be concerned with antitrust violations and take measures to prevent them. One of such measures is precisely the establishment of effective compliance programs, which the authority later started promoting.

The process of promoting compliance was kicked off with the organization of an international seminar in 2014. In collaboration with other Brazilian institutions, such as the Association of Federal Judges (AJUFE) and the Center for Economic and Social Law (CEDES), CADE brought together academics, private sector specialists and authorities from around the world to discuss the issue and offer an insight into the Brazilian legal system. This process later developed into the Antitrust Compliance Guidelines issued by the authority, which will be further assessed in item 1.3 below. Before doing so, I will describe some of the interplay between antitrust and anticorruption in the Brazilian legal system and how the process of strengthening one policy impacted the other.

---

6. Several condemnations have set this standard, but some were significant in giving antitrust violations more visibility. One of such was the cement cartel in 2014. The total penalty was of more than BRL 3 billion. Votorantim alone, one of the convicted companies, had to pay over BRL 1 billion: http://www.valor.com.br/international/news/4155252/cade-upholds-r3bn-fine-cement-cartel.

[B] Antitrust and Anticorruption

Corruption is a long-standing issue in Brazil. The problem dates back to the very founding of the country, and some claim the structures that support it were build long before that, during the colonial period.[7] Studies by non-governmental organizations (NGOs) such as Transparency International have shown that both individuals and companies view Brazil as a fairly corrupt nation. The Corruption Perceptions Index elaborated by this NGO analyzes the perceived levels of public sector corruption and puts Brazil in line with countries such as Zambia, Egypt, India, China and Mexico.[8]

Figure 4.3 Corruption Perceptions Index over the Years

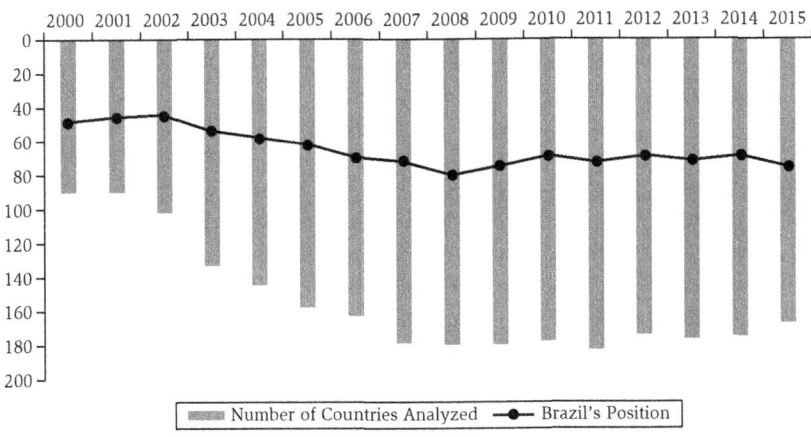

Source: Transparency International

Globally, a trend towards the stricter persecution of corrupt practices has been established ever since the enactment of the Foreign Corrupt Practices Act by the United States (U.S.) in 1977. With the institutional reform that emerged since the end of the military dictatorship and the promulgation of the current Brazilian Constitution in 1988, efforts have been made to change that reality within the country, among which are the signing of the Convention on Combating Bribery of Foreign Officials in International Business Transactions from the Organisation for Economic Co-operation and Development (OECD) in 2000,[9] and the passing of national legislation prohibiting and condemning corrupt practices.[10]

---

7. One such references is Celso Furtado's work on the Brazilian economic formation. FURTADO, C. Formação Econômica do Brasil, 22 ed., São Paulo: Editora Nacional, 1987.
8. Available at: http://www.transparency.org/cpi2015.
9. Brazil ratified the Convention on August 24, 2000, but its entry into force happened in October of the same year and the legislation which effectively implements the Convention was enacted in 2002.
10. Such as Law 8,429/1992, which criminalized the conducts of public officials involved in corrupt practices.

The latest international developments on this front include changes in French legislation, German and Japanese regulations, and famously the edition of the U.K. Bribery Act in 2010. In Latin America, significant reforms have been announced in Chile, including the creation of the Consejo Asesor Presidencial Contra los Conflictos de Interés, el Tráfico de Influencias y la Corrupción,[11] and in Mexico, with the establishment of the Sistema Nacional Anticorrupción (SNA).[12] In Brazil, the most relevant progress was the enactment of Law 12,846/2013, also known as the Clean Company Act, and of Decree 8,420/2015.[13]

The Act establishes a series of innovations for the fight against corruption in Brazil, including the administrative persecution of corrupt practices by the hands of the Office of the Comptroller General (CGU).[14] One of the mechanisms introduced by the legislation is the so-called integrity program. This is but a different terminology for the anticorruption compliance program and it received striking attention from companies, as both the Act and the Decree are clear in stating that the existence and robustness of an integrity program may come to represent discounts for the prosecuted entities.[15]

With this signal from the government, as well as with the ongoing (and ever growing) investigations on Brazilian corruption schemes – the most notable of which is the Car Wash Operation, that already arrested several CEOs, politicians, and led to fines of up to BRL 1 billion – the private sector was pushed towards compliance.

But why – other than through the general admission that competition and corruption are somewhat intertwined in the sense that less competition tends to lead to the spreading of corrupt practices – would this development in anticorruption legislation be at all relevant for antitrust compliance? Simply put, because the Clean Company Act was influenced by provisions from the antitrust law, namely in regards to the leniency program, and because the BSCD identified the compliance trend promoted by the new legislation and inserted antitrust compliance in companies' agenda, alongside the fight against corruption.[16]

---

11. The Final Report from the Council on Conflict of Interests, Influence Peddling, and Corruption is available in Spanish at: http://consejoanticorrupcion.cl/wp-content/uploads/2015/06/2015.06.05-consejo_anticorrupcion.pdf.
12. The Law governing the National Anticorruption System can be found in Spanish here: http://www.senado.gob.mx/comisiones/anticorrupcion/docs/corrupcion/MMH.pdf.
13. Both the Act and the Decree can be found in English at: http://www.merrillbrink.com/?LeadSource=Public_Relations&CampaignID=701C0000000jOY4 and http://www.merrillbrink.com/translation-of-Brazil-decree-Clean-Company-Act-04062015.htm.
14. The Office of the Comptroller General (CGU for the Portuguese acronym) was transformed into the Ministry of Transparency, Inspection, and Control with the enactment of Provisional Measure n. 726/2016.
15. Article 18 of Decree 8,420/2015 states that "the values corresponding to the following percentages of the gross earnings of the legal entity in the year prior to the opening of the proceedings, excluding tributes, will be subtracted from the result of the sum of the factors in Article 17: V – one percent till four percent if the legal entity possesses and applies an integrity program, according to the parameters set forward in Chapter IV."
16. The former President of CADE, Vinicius Marques de Carvalho, explicitly stated this intention at the Fundação Getúlio Vargas Seminar on Competition Law. Videos for the full seminar, which was held in Portuguese, are available at: http://epge.fgv.br/conferencias/seminario-topicos-do-direito-da-concorrencia-2015/video.html.

Chapter 4: Antitrust Compliance Programs – The Brazilian Experience   §4.02[B]

After Law 12,846/2013 was enacted in 2013 and the compliance strategy had been discussed at the antitrust authority for some time, came the turning point for antitrust compliance in Brazil: the issuance of CADE's Draft Compliance Guidelines in 2015. The initiative materialized the efforts and the intention of the authority to take the agenda seriously and grabbed the private sector's attention. The document was made available even before CGU issued its own guidelines on integrity programs and as such helped frame the corporate compliance debate.[17]

CADE decided to translate the Guidelines into English, in order to receive comments on its draft both from national and international organizations. The strategy was fruitful, as several relevant actors took part in the discussion: the American Bar Association, the International Bar Association, the U.S. Chamber of Commerce, the Brazilian Bar – OAB, the IBRAC (Instituto Brasileiro de Estudos de Concorrência, Consumo e Comércio Internacional, Brazil's main private institute for the discussion of competition law), as well as several companies – Alstom, Fibria, Siemens – and world-renowned specialists such as Joseph Murphy.[18]

In addition to taking effective measures by providing guidance on how compliance would be addressed by the authorities, CADE, CGU and other public bodies such as the Ministry of Planning effectively collaborated in raising awareness about compliance in different ways, mainly by strengthening enforcement in regard to bid rigging.

They signed cooperation agreements among themselves, establishing ways by which information and experience can be exchanged, thereby providing more efficiency for the persecution of illegal activities.[19] One of such exchanges is the Public Expenditure Observatory (or Observatório da Despesa Pública, for its Portuguese equivalent), which collects and concentrates data from public bids all around the country. By analyzing such data, CADE and CGU have been able to identify suspicious patterns that suggest bids have been rigged, and therefore to further investigate such practices.[20] The experience has proven fruitful in providing a tool to identify cartels that does not depend on leniencies, a goal that has been at the center of antitrust authorities concerns all over the world.

---

17. On September 2015, CGU issued the Directives for Private Companies on Integrity Programs, available in Portuguese at: http://www.cgu.gov.br/Publicacoes/etica-e-integridade/arquivos/programa-de-integridade-diretrizes-para-empresas-privadas.pdf.
18. CADE registered all contributions in a public proceeding available at its electronic system under number 08700.008222/2015-80. The guidelines themselves are available at: http://www.cade.gov.br/acesso-a-informacao/publicacoes-institucionais/guias_do_Cade/compliance-guidelines-final-version.pdf.
19. The functioning of the cooperation agreement between CADE and CGU was discussed in more detail in Brazil's submission to the OECD: http://www.cade.gov.br/assuntos/internacional/publicacoes-anexos/5.pdf/view.
20. According to CGU and CADE, the ODP is a unit that aims to "combine the practical knowledge and experiences of auditors with the use of advanced tools of information technology to speedily process an enormous volume of data." The overall objective of the ODP is to foresee fraud-risk situations. This knowledge-building exercise is quite useful in designing public policies aimed at preventing and combating corruption. Based on systematic information and periodic updates, the ODP provides CGU and some other government agencies with elaborated knowledge, analytical statements about the quantity and quality of public spending as well as with indications of sensitive areas of public spending, in terms of corruption risk."

Other than emphasizing enforcement, the focus on advocacy was equally crucial in bringing compliance, antitrust, and anticorruption to the forefront of both the public and private sectors' agenda. The participation of international organizations such as the OECD and the International Competition Network (ICN) in this agenda has been active. In 2015, for instance, CADE promoted the "OECD-CADE Competition Summit: Public Procurement & Fighting Bid Rigging," which also counted with the participation of members from the CGU and discussed strategies to tackle bid rigging.[21] Nationally, CADE and CGU are active in discussing compliance and public procurement at the ENCCLA – the National Strategy for Fighting Corruption and Money Laundering. For the past two years, the authorities have been involved in debates regarding how to analyze the effectiveness of compliance programs and also on how to create mechanisms to provide companies which do have robust compliance programs with some advantage in public procurement.[22]

[C]   **The Current Status of the Regulation**

Even though the recent compliance wave in Brazil took corporate integrity to a whole new level, this is not the first time antitrust compliance has been the focus of discussion in the BCDS. Back in 2004, still under Law 8,884/1994, the then Secretariat of Economic Law from the Ministry of Justice issued Decree n. 14, introducing the Program for the Prevention of Economic Order Infractions (PPI, for the Portuguese acronym). The decree was aimed at providing entities with a certificate declaring the PPI's fulfillment of all requirements set forth by the legislation. The certificate was valid for a period of two years and entitled the company to the reduction in penalties, under the circumstances specified in Article 9.[23]

The PPI was not very successful in engaging the private sector and as such the adhesion to the program was not particularly effective, but it still posed an important effort in bringing attention to compliance programs. The initiative was resumed recently, with the issuance of CADE's Compliance Guidelines. The Guidelines took a different approach to antitrust compliance when compared to the PPI and also to the anticorruption program. While the PPI relied upon a certification method and Decree 8,420/2015 decided to specify fixed criteria for the analysis of the programs, the Guidelines are more open-ended. The document puts forward two circumstances in which compliance may be taken into account: in setting fines and in establishing pecuniary contributions. The fines are due when there is a condemnation, while the contributions must be collected in case of settlement agreements.

It should be noted that CADE's Guidelines on Cease and Desist Agreements gives detailed information on how antitrust compliance programs will be taken into consideration when setting pecuniary contributions. They are not relevant in determining the

---

21. More details on the event can be found at OECD's website: http://www.oecd.org/brazil/oecd-in-brazil-november-2015.htm.
22. More information on the activities of the ENCCLA can be found in Portuguese at: http://enccla.camara.leg.br.
23. http://www.deloitte.com.br/publicacoes/2004all/042004/diversos/Por14.pdf.

discount slots, but in attesting the percentage of the calculation base for the expected fine,[24] and they are analyzed in terms of their relevance for the decision to file for a TCC.[25]

Figure 4.4 Mitigating Circumstances

Severity of the violation

Having been coerced to participate in the conduct

Peripheral / occasional participation in the conduct

Extremely short duration (up to six months), as long as this circumstance does not result from the actions of public authorities to interrupt the conduct

Good faith of violator

Previous suggestion of adoption of the conduct by a public entity (e.g., terms of commitment with Public Prosecutors or other bodies, court decisions, decisions of regulatory agencies, bylaws, etc.)

Existence of compliance programs that relate directly to the decision to file for TCC and/or resulting from cooperation presented within the TCC

Financial standing of the violator

Proven low financial capability or inability to pay

Source: CADE's Guidelines on Cease and Desist Agreement for cartel cases

The Guidelines understand that the antitrust compliance programs may be taken into consideration because they embody one of the sentencing criteria of Article 45, the good faith of the violator. They however do not provide any binding specifications that the programs must follow, only indications and suggestions for private entities.

First and foremost, the authority more than once states that compliance is heavily dependent on a company's own characteristics, meaning there is no "one size fits all" program. Still, it brings about four general criteria that should be somehow verified in every case: commitment – mainly through the so-called tone from the top, which entails an assertive position from the company's high-level personnel ensuring the importance of compliance; risk analysis – which takes into consideration the characteristics of the company and determines its main competitive hazards; risk mitigation – after identifying problematic areas, the entity should minimize risks by effectively training its employees and monitoring its program; and review – it is essential to adapt the program to new directives and understandings from the authorities. CADE also emphasizes some particularities from individual cases that should be taken into

---

24. The pecuniary contribution is determined following a two-step process: first it is necessary to determine the applicable law – if for some reason Law 8,884/1994 is more beneficial to the defendant and the conduct took place before Law 12,529/2011 came into force, the previous law should be applied; second, the calculation of the pecuniary contribution. In order to calculate the pecuniary contribution, three further steps are analyzed: setting the calculation basis, updating such basis, determining the percentage of the expected fine, and then the applicable discount slot.
25. *See* footnote 4.

consideration when designing a program, namely the risk of collusion, of bid rigging, and of unilateral violations.

In any such cases, the burden of proof lies with the private parties, meaning it is the parties' responsibility to prove that the implemented antitrust compliance program is robust and effective.

It is interesting to note that the analysis of the anticorruption compliance program follows a rather different methodology. Other than entailing sixteen fixed criteria according to which the evaluation must be carried on, the CGU issued an Executive Order which determines steps that any entity must follow in order to have its program analyzed[26] and also promotes the Pró-Ética Program, an initiative aimed at giving companies public recognition for its efforts in preventing corrupt practices.[27]

[1] Case Law – HSBC/Bradesco

Decisions by CADE over the past year have stressed the importance of the compliance agenda. Other than allowing for the signing of leniency and cease and desist agreements, one of the largest mergers analyzed in 2016, the acquisition of HSBC by Bradesco, strongly emphasized the need for effective compliance programs.

The HSBC/Bradesco case, submitted to the antitrust authority in October 2015, was a significant merger in the Brazilian banking sector.[28] HSBC announced its intention to leave Brazil in June 2015 and a run for its business was immediately set off among the biggest banks in the country. In August, Bradesco was announced as the buyer. The merger analysis then started at the General Superintendence and moved on to the Administrative Tribunal, which approved it in May 2016, but imposed restrictions and conditions for its completion. Among such conditions, the Merger Control Agreement (or Acordo em Controle de Concentrações, ACC) established compromises from the parties in six different areas: communication and transparency, incentives to credit portability, training, quality indicators, restriction on the acquisition of financial institutions and compliance.

An entire section of the ACC is dedicated to compliance, in the following terms:

> *2.7 Compliance:*
> 2.7.1 The Promisee commits to revising the internal governance structure, improving and/or implementing policies and provisions specific for anticompetitive practices, adhering to CADE's Antitrust Compliance Guidelines, whose documents shall be delivered to CADE separately from the Annual Report, in no later than 12 months from the date of closing. The execution of the compliance program shall be delegated

---

26. Full text of the Executive Order: http://www.cgu.gov.br/sobre/legislacao/arquivos/portarias/portaria_cgu_909_2015.pdf.
27. Though the Pró-Ética does not equate an immediate reduction in fines, it gives the company a status of compliance with the legislation. More details on the program can be found in Portuguese at: http://www.cgu.gov.br/assuntos/etica-e-integridade/empresa-pro-etica.
28. AC 08700.010790/2015-41, press release available at: http://en.cade.gov.br/press-releases/cade-authorizes-hsbc2019s-acquisition-by-bradesco.

Chapter 4: Antitrust Compliance Programs – The Brazilian Experience   §4.03[A]

>> to an agent external to the Bradesco Group, of the highest repute on the market and approved by CADE.
>> i) The Promisee will have 30 continuous days, counted from the date of closing, to present to CADE the office/company hired for the elaboration of the program. The failure to do so in the stipulated deadline under no circumstances modifies the schedule for the fulfilling of the conditions and its respective confirmation, and, if applicable, the penalties set forward in this ACC will be observed nonetheless.
>> ii) CADE may, in up to 10 (ten) days, speak in favor or against the chosen office/company. If it disagrees with the choice of the Promisee, the Promisee shall present another office/company for CADE's approval. Under no circumstances will the deadlines for the fulfilment of the agreed upon conditions be postponed owing to the delay in hiring the person responsible for the design of the compliance program.
> 2.7.2 The parameters, goals, and implementation methods of the measures put forward in Provision 2.7.1 are described in Annex 2.7 of this ACC.[29]

The commitment is intended to be long-term, as CADE established a five-year period for its fulfillment. Moreover, since Bradesco already counts with a Code of Conduct, as well as with committees and commissions dedicated to internal control, the ACC highlights the need for the compliance program to specifically address competition concerns, following the Guidelines issued by the authority, and stresses that its design and implementation must be supervised by a third party.

This decision is the latest and perhaps most eloquent position established by the Brazilian authority in regards to compliance and strengthened the need for companies to not only implement effective programs, but specially for antitrust and competition to be a central concern within corporate compliance. Such understanding is in line with positions from other authorities and organizations around the world, and sets a tendency for upcoming manifestations from CADE.

§4.03 ANTITRUST COMPLIANCE IN OTHER LATIN AMERICAN COUNTRIES

Initiatives to promote corporate compliance are naturally not exclusive of Brazil. Recently, other Latin American countries gave emphasis to this agenda. The efforts of two of them will be further assessed: Chile and Mexico, nations that have strengthened the focus on antitrust enforcement and advocacy over the past decade.

[A] Chile

Chile is seen as a case of success in the promotion of free market in Latin America. Much like in Brazil, the effective application of competition law started after the end of the military dictatorship in the 1990s, though official legislation on the topic existed

---

29. Translation from the original Portuguese version.

years before.[30] Since then, the Office of the National Economic Prosecutor (Fiscalía Nacional Económica, FNE) has been active in engaging the private sector in discussions and actions on how to avoid anticompetitive practices. One such initiatives was carried out in 2012, when the FNE issued its Guidelines for Competition Law Compliance Programs.

Other than establishing the essential requisites for an antitrust compliance program (real commitment in complying with the legislation, risk identification, internal procedures, and participation from the high administration) and mechanisms that a program may wish to incorporate (such as an internal guideline, the training of employees, the monitoring and auditing of the program, and disciplinary measures for those who transgress the program), FNE dedicates a section of the document solely to the benefits that may run from the program.

Naturally, the more immediate benefit from any compliance program is the avoidance of infractions. However, the authority goes further and stresses that the penalties may be reduced owing to compliance, so long as the determinations of both the Guidelines and of Article 26 of Decree n. 211/1973 are met.[31]

[B]   Mexico

Mexico has recently devoted much effort into the promotion of competition. The Comissión Federal de Competencia Económica, COFECE (or Federal Commission for Competition) was created in 2013 after a modification of the Mexican Constitution, and the competition system was reformed in 2014 with the new Federal Economic Competition Law,[32] giving COFECE more powers and its penalties, more severity. Despite being a young body, the authority has achieved important accomplishments, such as the nomination as vice-chair at the ICN in 2016.

As part of its efforts to bring competition policy to the forefront of the economic discussion, COFECE issued a comprehensive booklet on the activities of the authority, its benefits for the economic agents, and the means by which competition can be promoted in the private sector.[33] Among such methods of promotion are the compliance programs. The document covers in detail how to generate a corporate culture of effective commitment to the legislation, indicating the need to: (i) nominate a chief compliance officer – or person responsible for the program, (ii) carry on risk evaluation, (iii) elaborate codes or guidelines in order to train employees, (iv) monitor, audit,

---

30. Decree n. 211 of 1973 established the current system and is available at: http://www.fne.gob.cl/marco-normativo/marco-normativo/.
31. The Article states that: "Para la determinación de las multas se considerarán, entro otras, las siguientes circunstancias: el beneficio económico obtenido con motivo de la infracción, la gravedad de la conducta, la calidad de reincidente del infractor y, para efectos de disminuir la multa, la colaboración que éste haya prestado a la Fiscalía antes o durante la investigación."
32. The full text is available in English at: https://www.cofece.mx/cofece/images/Documentos_Micrositios/Federal_Economic_Competition_Law.pdf.
33. Available in Spanish at: https://www.cofece.mx/cofece/images/Documentos_Micrositios/SDO_Cumplimiento250815.pdf.

and provide mechanisms to report illicit behavior, (v) determine internal disciplinary actions, and (vi) constantly evaluate and improve the program.

COFECE, much like the FNE and CADE, highlights the importance of compliance programs to prevent infractions and to help companies benefit from leniency programs. Nevertheless, there is no indication that the authority will take compliance into consideration for reducing the applicable penalties.

§4.04 FINAL REMARKS

As competition policy evolved and conquered jurisdictions, so did its implementation. Nations devoted more and more efforts to enforcement and lately have also invested time on advocacy and on the spreading of competition culture. The debate regarding compliance is part of that agenda.

Antitrust compliance programs have generated a lot of buzz recently, specially in Latin America. With the recent corruption scandals in the region and the public's attention turned to anticompetitive practices such as cartels, antitrust authorities have taken the opportunity to foster competition. Time will tell whether this initiative will last and be fruitful or if it will be a transitory and passing trend. Everything indicates compliance is here to stay.

CHAPTER 5
The Dissemination of the Competition Culture in Brazil: The Role Played by Civil Associations

Eduardo Caminati Anders & Guilherme Teno Castilho Missali[*]

§5.01 INTRODUCTION

This chapter summarizes the role of civil associations and non-governmental organizations in addressing competition/antitrust law matters in Brazil. We understand that the role played by such players is pivotal to leverage the competition culture within the Brazilian legal framework. More specifically, we will draw attention to some of the main activities performed by the Brazilian Institute of Studies on Competition, Consumer Affairs and International Trade (IBRAC), geared to disseminate the competition culture in Brazil.

In line with the international landscape,[1] there are consolidated players in Brazil that have long been encouraging in-depth debates on antitrust matters so as to organize studies and researches, promote events and conferences, nurture work groups and stimulate groundbreaking discussions with the academy and the civil society, with a view to collaborate in a comprehensive fashion for the refinement of the competition agenda in Brazil. It is possible to notice a genuine engagement to this end, striving for

---

[*] The authors would like to thank Jessica W. Olivieri and Gabriella Dochnal for their invaluable review. Any inaccuracies should be considered authors' oversights only.
1. Under a broad standpoint, we make reference to international institutions, organizations and international bodies, such as (i) Organisation for Economic Co-operation and Development (OECD) - Competition; (ii) International Chamber of Commerce (ICC) - Competition; (iii) International Competition Network (ICN); (iv) American Bar Association (ABA) - Antitrust Section etc. For more information on those entities, please see the following websites, respectively: < http://www.oecd.org/competition/ > ; < http://www.iccwbo.org/advocacy-codes-and-rules/areas-of-work/competition/ > ; < http://www.internationalcompetitionnetwork.org/ > ; and < http://www.americanbar.org/groups/antitrust_law.html > . Accessed on: August 7, 2016.

the exchange of ideas and viewpoints in a way to promote an open and constructive dialogue.

In that vein, there is an outstanding work being performed by a multitude of organizations, whose critical mass is mirrored through a variety of initiatives aimed at achieving a common goal of strengthening the competition culture in Brazil, intertwining it in the society's daily routines. Still, there is a role of competition advocacy played by such players when leading discussions for purposes of defending and promoting some legal actions that are beneficial to the society. This practice covers a dialogue with the competent authorities and yields immensurable outcomes; in fact, it is a highly desirable action in order to boost the antitrust culture within the business environment.

Undeniably, the role of those institutions and organizations is added to the efforts forged by the authorities in the sense of strengthening the competition culture, given rise to a fertile ground for collective empowerment on the matter. In this regard, one should bear in mind that in developing economies such as the Brazilian, a mindset oriented to disseminate compliance within laws is crucial, particularly in light of competition rules. In other words, when one looks back to the past and sees a history characterized by a strong State intervention in the economy, it makes perfect sense to stimulate a culture that values true competition.

In addition, when considering the role of advocacy, from a general perspective, an interesting step towards it would be some private sector's initiatives. For instance, the economic agents could implement Antitrust Compliance Programs (from an autoregulation approach) and debate practical improvements in its features with the competent authorities to achieve a common understand in that regard. All in all, compliance measures are crucial to encourage free enterprise and competition *vis-à-vis* an economy marked by a bureaucratic tradition. As a result, favorable conditions are forged in that structure in order to set a healthy and balanced competitive environment, with markets and players that are adherent to the premise of "competition matters."

Based on this quick outlook, the following topics depict: (i) a summary of certain compliance initiatives within the Brazilian competition framework which, in turn, will address; (ii) questions that are likely to challenge (or are indeed challenging) the Brazilian antitrust authority in the near future, demanding a clear-cutting and savvy position to maintain a balanced antitrust atmosphere. Thereafter, under a standpoint that seeks to highlight the pivotal role of civil associations and non-governmental organizations in weighing on antitrust issues, this chapter[2] will shed (iii) a vivid light on IBRAC, as a way to illustrate the successful role it has been playing since its creation, besides determining its goals and challenges. In the end, the chapter presents the epitome of the review.

---

2. As a reference, even though they do not constitute the primary focus of this chapter, it is important to signalize other important entities, with whom the IBRAC interact so as to enrich the opinions. In this regard, it is worth mentioning: (i) the Commission on Competition Studies and Economic Regulation (CECORE) of the Brazilian Bar Association - São Paulo Section (OAB-SP); (ii) Center of Studies of Law Firms (CESA), Competition and Consumer Relations Committee, São Paulo Section; (iii) Center of Studies on Economic and Social Law (CEDES); (iv) Economy Group of Infrastructure & Environmental Solutions of Fundação Getúlio Vargas etc.

§5.02 ANTITRUST COMPLIANCE INITIATIVES: A BRIEF OUTLINE

Firstly, it is important to explain the legal milestone that contributed to honing the role of civil associations within the scope of the Brazilian competition system. That is, if from the outset of Law No. 8,884/1994 (Revoked Competition law) the said associations had started working on ways to promote the assimilation of the mentioned law within the society in terms of knowledge, upon enactment of Law No. 12,529/2011, on May 29, 2012, one can infer a remarkable advance in this regard, that is due to a solid and committed work for perfecting the awareness of competition in Brazil.

In particular, such advance stems from a new institutional setting that has encouraged detailed discussions on compliance matters – it is undoubted that the experience amassed over years was a keystone to reach the current level of understanding on competition – thus propitiating a development of the discussions over the matter. In that context, the civil associations have taken a leading position in the interaction with the competent authorities, economic agents, academia etc.

Therefore, in harmony with the spirit that illuminates the Law No. 12,529/2011, a myriad of initiatives was introduced by the Administrative Council for Economic Defense (CADE) under the rational of compliance. It is worth mentioning, for example, the publication of guidelines concerning relevant competition matters that function as important tools to instruct the parties on day-to-day subjects, hence improving the level of transparency, predictability and legal certainty.[3]

Considering the positive outcomes arising from such guidelines, one may assert that new guidelines are expected to be issued in the future. Without hesitation, guidelines are desirable and very much welcomed, mirroring a movement that can be clearly noticed in mature jurisdictions overseas.

Furthermore, as to compliance initiatives from the *lato sensu* scope, one can cite underlying actions when observing the resolution that governs the consultation procedure (Resolution No. 12, of March 11, 2015). This is a mechanism made available to the consulting party that is intended to grasp the CADE's Tribunal position on the antitrust legislation in light of a specific situation based on parameters set forth in such resolution.

Specifically, it is worth noting that during the preparation of the guidelines already issued by CADE and the aforementioned resolution, as will be pointed in this chapter, a constructive dialogue between civil associations was CADE was perceived, yielding contributions extremely appreciated by the authority. Moreover, the prolific work that has been performed by the Department of Economic Studies (DEE) should be mention when it comes to compliance in general. This body has been producing

---

3. In this regard, up to the date hereof, CADE has already issued the following guidelines: Guidelines for the Analysis of Previous Consummation of Merger Transactions (Gun Jumping Guideline); Guidelines for Competition Compliance Programs (Compliance Guideline); Guidelines for Cease and Desist Agreement for cartel cases (TCC Guideline); Guidelines for CADE's Antitrust Leniency Program (Leniency Guideline); and Guidelines for Analysis of Horizontal Mergers (Horizontal Merger Guideline). Such guidelines are available for consultation at the following website: <http://www.cade.gov.br/acesso-a-informacao/publicacoes-institucionais/guias_do_Cade/capa-interna>. Accessed on August 7, 2016.

important material to enlighten the competition analysis, thus assisting under the case review.[4]

§5.03 PERCEPTIONS OF THE COMPETITION LAW IN BRAZIL AND CHALLENGES AHEAD

More recently, in light of rigorous decisions handed down by the CADE in addition to sensitive ongoing investigations, in particular those involving alleged cartels, the importance of complying with the antitrust legislation seems to have become more supported subject under the standpoint of the parties. In any event, the "mere" compliance with the laws may not be sufficient, meaning that the economic agents should genuinely engage themselves in the debates through a sense that goes beyond the automatic spirit of "following the rules otherwise there will be penalty."

In essence, the ultimate approach should be to understand the real meaning behind the law so as to truly engage in debates in a proactive and cooperative fashion. To put it simply, it means understanding compliance in a holistic perspective, so as to infer that compliance does not encompass the adhesion to the laws only, but also it implies a structured set of actions, such as advocacy, educational initiatives and awareness techniques, etc., to spread out the spirit of law inside the company. For example, one may point insightful debates with regulators aiming at honing the law when it comes to the real life and practical issues experienced on a daily basis.

On top of that, one may add that there has been a prominent improvement in the antitrust strand in Brazil by virtue of more robust dissuasion instruments (e.g., the Cease and Desist Agreement (TCC) and the Leniency Program).

Under this perspective, in order to genuinely instill the antitrust compliance within the business community, one should recall a number of tasks that some institutions have been developing. In that regard, the encouragement of a transparent and constructive atmosphere for discussions by promoting events that enable the participation of the public and private players is a loadstar for the construction of a rich, harmonic and integrated competition environment. In doing so, one can perceive a ripple effect that is beneficial to leverage transparency, predictability and legal certainty.

Furthermore, as anticipated, the discussions within the antitrust scope have been continuously requiring deeper reflections given the new challenges posed in the market. In this particular, an interdisciplinary and multifocal analysis is certainly welcomed. Beyond the economic rationale embedded in antitrust reflections, competition law has currently become more puzzling and complex, entailing a clear need to pay close attention to variables from other areas (e.g., IP, anti-corruption, arbitration,

---

4. The DEE was created upon enactment of Law No. 12,529/2011. To date the DEE has already published the following studies (CADE Books): (i) Fuel Retail – 2014; (ii) Mercado Supplementary Health Market: Conducts – 2015; and (iii) Mergers in the higher education service market. Such books are available for consultation at the following website: < http://www.cade.gov.br/acesso-a-informacao/publicacoes-institucionais/publicacoes-dee/Cadernos%20do%20Cade >. Accessed on: August 7, 2016.

consumer etc.), in order to promote a holistic view when scrutinizing a given case. The current business *demarché* is characterized by peculiarities and implications that, if not consider thoroughly, may raise serious risks to the market, meaning that the analysis could be affected by a short-sighted review, so as to weaken the proposal of remedies and alternatives, for example.

That said, taking into account academic discussions and practical reflections, we envision that a myriad of dilemmas are yet to be faced. Without prejudice to other challenges that are continuously raised, it is worthwhile to point out, in summary, the intersection between antitrust law and intellectual property rules, primary due to a scenario of technological features and modernization, whose innovative and fast paced dynamic, at times disruptive and/or reactive, is not on the same wavelength that the lawmakers, mentioning, for instance, the matter of the licensing commitments (RAND or FRAND) and the standard of essential patents.

Moreover, one can state cross-border discussions between the thin lines of antitrust and anti-corruption strands. For sure there is a sensitive matter with a plethora of implications in such frontier. As a result, one should encourage a responsive attitude, bearing in mind certain circumstances permeated by cronyism conducts that ultimately may facilitate *rent-seeking* practices. As noted, considering that some wrongdoing may be twofold, that is, triggering antitrust and anti-corruption concerns at the very same moment, it might be useful to encourage interconnected actions between the competent regulatory bodies in order to achieve a more coherent and consistent outcome when it comes to investigations and decisions. In reality, the discussions involving antitrust and anti-corruption matters may seem tangled at first time, which means that the matter is not trivial and may influence the rules to be formulated by the policymakers.

In addition, one would also underline the interface between the antitrust and corporate law, which is not a recent phenomenon, yet still has been acquiring a more vibrant shape. Corporate engineering and transactions have been rebuilding themselves under a much more creative perspective, in a way that antitrust is compelled to review certain traditional standards of analysis. To put it simply, antitrust authorities have been encouraged to rethink the effectiveness of some of its rules in order capture all the nuances of high-level transactions and complex arrangements. Corporate transactions are likely to become increasingly refined, many of them with bold structures that may give rise to some concerns, pointing out the need of a reasonable scrutiny and, when needed, credible remedies to mitigate issues. Indeed, a thought-provoking subject concerns the dosage of remedies (and the proper combination) within the scope of merger control when a transaction is labelled as "problematic" from the competition viewpoint.

Still, it is worth mentioning a growing movement in Brazil when it comes to the intervention of third parties in the ongoing fact-finding stage of administrative proceedings before CADE (under a general scope). For instance, it is legitimate that third parties are qualified to submit their opinions under a grounded basis, expressing the way they (and the market) can be affected by the transaction so as to, presumably, help the completeness of the review.

By way of additional reference, other subjects that intertwine with antitrust matters are bankruptcy and arbitration affairs. With respect to the latter, notwithstanding the fact that it has not yet been subject to a detailed analysis in Brazil from the antitrust strand, one could not neglect its effects and should consider delving deep into it. What is more, the interplay between competition law and consumer law requires a modern angle of thinking, considering practices that are likely to generate antitrust effects on the economic order and that, concurrently, can impair consumer relations. Additionally, it is worth mentioning the challenges posed by the advance of internet and data, underscoring potential vertical practices that may arise in such space. In that line, one can see the interaction amongst antitrust, big data and privacy that requires meticulous studies and tests to apprehend the effects arising from such strands. Yet, the sharing economy model should not be disregarded when it comes to the actual puzzles in the center of the debate.

Further, a subject that has the strong potential to evolve in Brazil in the medium term is the one related to the private actions in the context of anticompetitive practices (notably, the cartel). Although actions of such nature are set forth in the Brazilian competition law, to this date it has been used way too mildly[5] when compared to the dynamic of mature jurisdictions, where private actions are a fierce reality.Nonetheless, with the hope of gradual internalization of the antitrust culture in Brazil and the incentive to this type of action – as well as considering a series of condemnations for cartel practices –, at first it would be possible to infer a fertile ground to develop such topic. Moreover, the damage quantification in light of cartels cases comprises a matter of controversial and heated debates in Brazil, which had recently started.

In view of this succinct outline, one may summarize with the capillarity need, that is, the interdisciplinary approach that matters when it comes to the antitrust discussion. Within such context, it is vital to pinpoint the role of civil associations, so as to analyze and reflect on subjects involving antitrust matters in a critical and constructive manner. Accordingly, we believe that disseminating competition values is the cornerstone to reap the benefits of such culture. As such, a number of initiatives are carried out by the said associations, such as workshops, seminars, study groups etc. aiming at discussing hot topics in the antitrust environment, analyzing and commenting the CADE's public consultations, exchanging views with related areas so as to achieve richer inputs and contributions and so on. Those institutions also foster courses, contests, academic publications etc., with a view to build a fine-tuned critical mass. Ultimately, the goal is to instruct the civil society under the premises of the competition law. We regard this as a useful and important approach to encourage the dialogue and to make antitrust reflections easier to be comprehended taking into account a certain portion of the audience that may not be completely familiar and

---

5. The CADE has recently put into public consultation a resolution that provides for procedures for access to documents arising from antitrust investigations, which, theoretically, could help leveraging the private actions. For more information, see the following website: < http://www.cade.gov.br/noticias/cade-submete-a-consulta-publica-resolucao-sobre-procedimentos-de-acesso-a-documentos-provenientes-de-investigacoes-antitruste > . Accessed on: February 6, 2017.

specialized with antitrust.⁶ By doing so, we envision enrichment in terms of a notion of competition by the society, once the economic agents become more realistically inserted under the antitrust environment.

Thus, the empowerment provided by such institutions and organizations to the society, alongside with the educational role promoted by the authority itself, are crucial tools for the antitrust awareness to reach a substantive maturity.

§5.04 CASE ANALYSIS: AN EXAMPLE OF CIVIL ASSOCIATION (IBRAC)

The IBRAC is a non-profit civil association, founded in 1992.⁷ Amongst the IBRAC's objectives, in line with the description in the previous chapter, is the conduction of researches, studies and discussions so as to promote the development of a free competition regime within a market economy policy in Brazil.

It should be emphasized that the IBRAC's activities goes beyond antitrust affairs. In other words, apart from the antitrust front, the IBRAC also carries out researches, studies and debates aiming at exploring discussions in connection with consumer affairs and international trade. As such, in order to fulfill its objectives,⁸ the IBRAC carries out a number of programs and activities. Amongst the IBRAC's initiatives the following examples are worth mentioning:

(i) release of studies, encouraging debates and exchanging different viewpoints by means of publications, news, magazines and others;
(ii) permanent and efficient work with the governmental bodies, taking the lead concerning topics relating to the professional practice, best practices, institutional improvements, bills of law and any initiatives related to competition, consumer affairs and international trade, by offering to the official specialized bodies the contributions achieved from its initiatives;
(iii) periodic meetings, seminars and symposiums to discuss all matters included within its basic objectives, including by identifying controversial topics and matters, proposing its studies and suggesting solutions;
(iv) incentive to lectures and qualification courses targeted at class entities, companies and practitioners, Law, Administration and Economy students,

---

6. Since it refers to a non-trivial matter, it is not unreasonable to believe that many lay people in antitrust law would think that "competition law" would be a comprised to a single rule book. As stated by Richard Posner in the beginning of his work: "To the layperson a 'law' is a rule written down in a book somewhere. The lawyer realizes that the matter is often a good deal more complicated." (POSNER, Richard A. *Competition law*. 2 ed. The University of Chicago Press. 2001. p. 1).
7. The IBRAC was founded shortly before the enactment of the Revoked Competition Law, therefore it has followed the entire evolutionary nature of such Law during its 18 years in effect, and it follows *pari passu* Law No. 12,529/2011. Hence, as antitrust legislation matured, the IBRAC has also enhanced its organization. The experience amassed over such period is IBRAC's major differential – there is a prolific institutional memory, a legacy that serves both for learning and reflection to address the coming challenges.
8. For a full view of the objectives of the IBRAC, as well as related matters, consult the IBRAC's Bylaws, available at the following website: < http://www.ibrac.org.br/template.aspx?id = 2 >. Accessed on: August 7, 2016.

among other people interested in competition matters, consumer affairs and international trade;

(v) sponsorship to scholarships for the development and enhancement of professionals from the competition, consumer and international trade areas;

(vi) creation of a contest open to students, other awards and incentives to those who prepare papers and studies on the matters comprised by IBRAC's objectives;

(vii) encourage and support to the academia (universities) with respect to the implementation of courses specialized in the matters comprising its basic objectives;

(viii) promote clarification campaigns to class entities, governmental bodies and the society in general about the advantages of the free enterprise system – the free market – and the appropriate conduction of competition, consumer and international trade matters, identifying possible detours by the state, bodies and entities when addressing propositions contrary to such principles.

In short, these are some general activities performed by the IBRAC, corroborating the relevant role of such association so as to seek to achieve a fruitful environment under the free competition regime within a context of market economy. As noted above, the IBRAC's activities are not restricted to competition subjects only, as it equally addresses consumer and international trade affairs, with noteworthy synergies arising from this multifocal performance.[9]

In order to focus on sound discussions and to better divide the fields of investigation, the IBRAC is internally organized by means of Thematic Committees that meet on a regular basis. The following committees are currently operating: (i) Competition Committee; (ii) Consumer Affairs Committee; (iii) International Trade Committee; (iv) Regulation Committee; (v) Economic Affairs Committee; (vi) Compliance Committee; and (vii) Economic Litigation Committee.

The IBRAC's activities unfold in meetings held in the cities of São Paulo, Rio de Janeiro and Brasília.

As a practical example of the activities and initiatives performed by the IBRAC, it is illustrative to briefly synthesize the agenda of the events held in 2016. The schedule is characterized by prominent events that, first and foremost, seek quality and excellence, with renowned specialists, practitioners, scholars, authorities and so on, gathering top-notch lecturers, seminars etc. from the public and private sectors, in order to promote a rich and amplified experience. The IBRAC's events are acknowledged in the market by their high-level discussions, welcoming guests so as to enlighten the debates and different viewpoints.

---

9. Notwithstanding, given this chapter's main focus, we aimed our attention at considerations of IBRAC's antitrust agenda, addressing the other IBRAC's other themes *en passant*.

The 2016 IBRAC's schedule consolidated the success of its initiatives, besides breaking frontiers, as shown below: (i) 22nd International Competition Defense Seminar;[10] (ii) AWARD IBRAC-TIM 2016; (iii) 16th Seminar on International Trade; (iv) IBRAC Meetings on International Trade; (v) IBRAC Meetings on Consumer Affairs; (vi) Microeconomy Course Applied to Antitrust for Lawyers; (vii) BRAC Course on Competition law Theory and Practice: Cartels; (viii) Updates and Challenges to Competition Defense in the European Union;[11] (ix) IDP São Paulo – Course for Specialization in Regulation and Competition; (x) Course on Politics and Regulation of International Trade; (xi) USP/IBRAC Tables – Challenges of Telecommunication Regulation: The Case of Reversible Assets; (xii) 1st IBRAC Workshop of Antitrust Compliance Anticorruption; (xiii) Balance and Perspectives of the Competition Defense in Brazil; (xiv) IBRAC Meetings | Impact of the New CPC in the Administrative Proceedings of CADE; and (xv) Program of Supplementary Qualification and Research in International Trade –Brazil Team at the WTO and other Economic Organizations in Geneva.

Aside from the foregoing, it is relevant to mention the two annual editions of the IBRAC's Magazine, a traditional publication respected in the legal sphere due to its academic seriousness and technical quality of the articles.

In addition, IBRAC's view in favor of the extraterritorial expansion of its operation must also be pointed out. In this respect, institutional publications depicting up-to-date and challenging issues are being encouraged among its international associates and partners. A successful example in this sense was the publication of the Overview of Competition Law in Brazil[12] and Overview of Competition Law in Latin America,[13] in 2015 and 2016, respectively.

Furthermore, it is opportune to stress the contribution of the IBRAC to CADE in a variety of instances. In fact, a focal point for the IBRAC is the monitoring of public consultations so as to heavily study and discuss projects and drafts and, accordingly, effectively contribute to the regulatory improvement, in a participative spirit amongst all associates and the civil society. Within such context, the IBRAC has cooperated in

---

10. This seminar constitutes an event of outstanding repercussion given the quality of the debates. It takes place on an annual basis and comprises discussions about controversial issues in antitrust law, trends and cross-border perspectives, hot topics and so on, attended by national and international audiences. The 22nd seminar took place in the city of Campos do Jordão – São Paulo and broke records in terms of audience. The 23rd seminar is also expected to be held in the city of Campos do Jordão – São Paulo.
11. Event held by Emeritus Professor Law from King's College of London, Richard Whish.
12. ZARZUR, Cristianne; KATONA, Krisztian; VILLELA, Mariana (Coord.). *Overview of competition law in Brazil*. São Paulo: IBRAC/Editora Singular, 2015. 448 p. Available at the following website:
    < http://www.ibrac.org.br/Downloads/Overview_of_Competition_Law_in_Brazil. pdf >. Accessed on: August 7, 2016.
13. ANDERS, Eduardo Caminati; DEL PINO, Miguel; RIBAS, Guilherme F. C. *Overview of competition law in Latin America*. São Paulo: IBRAC, 2016. 266 p.

all last public consultations released by CADE in the past ten years, either within the scope of guidelines or within the scope of resolutions, including by addressing contributions arising from those interested parties located overseas.

Besides public consultations, the IBRAC also organizes itself so as to address to CADE studies on specific topics (sometimes the request is made by the authority itself, which reflects the trust the authority envisages in such association), so as to contribute to indicate the views of the practitioners and also to explain the dilemmas faced by the economic agents, outlining to CADE a realistic portrait of business atmosphere. The meetings and debates organized by the IBRAC are so to help in that regard: usually the meetings seek to combine the viewpoints of the public and private sectors, on which circumstance CADE's representatives usually accept invitations and discuss with attorneys, economists, scholars and the civil society on matters of sensitive relevance to the antitrust agenda. As referred above, we understand that such approach is of utmost importance to align expectations, collaborating to a synergy in terms of understandings so as to favor the legal certainty.

Still, one should bear in mind that the IBRAC has actively engaged itself with respect to the creation of CADE's structured career plan. Practically speaking, the IBRAC has institutionally mobilized itself and contacted the Civil Affairs Office to explain its position about the need to create an effective career plan for CADE's servants *vis-à-vis* the current personnel organizational structure of the antitrust authority, its annual budget etc., everything that would be expected so that an authority could exercise its function on full and effective manner. And notwithstanding the lack of personnel and shortage of budget currently existing at CADE, the authority successfully overcomes such limitations and has been performing its activity in stark success, leaving an important legacy which – not by chance – is clearly recognized worldwide.

That being said, in prospective terms with respect to the IBRAC's operation, under the assumption of a constant enhancement for the organization of its committees, activities and events, and always attentive and open to new proposals and ideas so as to strengthen its objectives, there are daily goals that the IBRAC calls to challenge itself in a way to evaluate its initiatives, in a self-critical perspective. When it comes to the objectives, some of them seem more trivial, such as strategies to expand its penetration in other Brazilian states, ways to attract more associates etc. Nevertheless, there are other goals of bolder nature. As a quick reference, it is worth stressing some of them, even if they are in the hypothetical context and in an initial stage thus far. In other words, the goals/challenges to follow might be translated into opportune initiatives to stimulate in a profound way the compliance to the competition legislation.

In that vein, based on the incentive pointed out by the CADE in the scope of the implementation of effective Compliance Programs, at a first glance, the IBRAC could structure a technical committee that would create a type of indicator for the economic agent (voluntary measure), so as to illustrate how solid its Compliance Program would be considering parameters normally established by the authority, as well as in light of other evidence and documentation submitted, all in line with the particularities and risk profile of each economic agent. The better the indicator, in theory, the better the exposure for the agents (i.e., positive screening) in the market would be. As a result, the indicator could signalize a good reputation to the market, thus sending a positive message to the stakeholders and to the authorities.

It must be clarified that the purpose under the reflection above would not be to elect the IBRAC to a condition similar to a "certification body"; instead, the idea would be to advise the economic agents as to the implementation of a genuine Compliance Program, hence designing thresholds to measure the supposed level of conformity of the Compliance Program to the general premises that is usually accepted when it comes to best practices in this kind of program.

The mentioned idea, on a plain manner, could work as that system existing in the context of the Ministry of Transparency, Inspection and Control. In particular, the analogy intended interacts with the Pro-Ethical Company Record (Cadastro Empresa Pró-Ética),[14] a commendable initiative implemented in 2010 by the then Federal General Controllership Office and Instituto Ethos de Empresas e Responsabilidade Social, so as to promote with the corporate sector the voluntary adoption of integrity and corruption prevention measures, encouraging the creation of a corporate environment with more integrity, ethics and transparency. Accordingly, for purposes of competition defense, in specific under the angle of Compliance Programs, the IBRAC could have a role similar to the one played by Instituto Ethos.

Also inserted in the prophylactic-guidance strand, it could eventually make sense if the IBRAC issues straightforward instructions to the economic agents encompassing tips and functional ways to establish the Antitrust Protocol for handling competitively sensitive information within the context of merger filings, in which one could face grey zones that at the end of the day may hamper the clarity in terms of acts allowed or not allowed under the gun jumping rules, for instance. Therefore, the main objective would be to avoid incurring in gun jumping violation, that is, the prior consummation of the transaction. Under such perspective, the exchange of competitively sensitive information between the counterparties before the antitrust authority hands down its final decision, in theory, would raise concerns so as to triggering gun jumping rules.

In light of the above, IBRAC could propose and design an Antitrust Protocol that would function as a main pattern to the agents that, in turn, would shape a document in view of their specific reality/transaction.

In sum, IBRAC's tasks would complement even more the SBDC's actions and initiatives by means of publications of educative guidelines with a view to inform the civil society, on didactic manner, about the competition legislation, focusing on antitrust wrongdoing, implications of non-compliance, appealing case studies etc. In that elucidative spirit, IBRAC would also consider disseminating such guidelines within schools, from the outset of students' academic education. In connection to this point and to bring more leverage and visibility to its roles, IBRAC would consider invest funds in digital media, strengthening its footprint in the antitrust strand on a worldwide basis (in addition to consumer and international trade affairs).

---

14. For details about the Pro-Ethics Company Record, *see* the following website: < http://www.cgu .gov.br/assuntos/etica-e-integridade/empresa-pro-etica > . Accessed on: August 7, 2016.

§5.05 CONCLUSIONS

All in all, if in the current context the perils inherent to the price fixing between competitors may sound like a truism to the eyes of an increasing number of economic agents (and that is a laudable fact in terms of achievement, corroborating the rise of antitrust awareness within the society), such apparent obviousness was not built by chance. In fact, the awareness on antitrust matters is an ongoing (and sometimes not smooth) and permanent process. In this strand, the progress has stemmed from a mix of actions, and we underscored in this chapter the role of the IBRAC to that aim, spurring a myriad of events that show the core benefits of a true competition culture.

Given the current scenario in Brazil, we argue that we are in the correct direction to foster the consolidation of the competition culture. Of course, in order to achieve a high-level understanding of antitrust law before the society (which, in fact, is not a trivial matter), the rule of thumb should be the constant discussions on competition under a variety of ways, so as to inculcate the advantages of the competition in the market (and ultimately the compliance and non-compliance) so as to become logical to the society seeing the right path to follow. In that respect, we truly foresee a fertile space for the role of civil associations, and firmly believe that IBRAC has been contributing to the propagation of the competition culture in Brazil, as evidenced throughout this chapter.

Clearly, the articulated and transparent work among SBDC's authorities, civil associations and organizations, practitioners, academy and economic agents is critical to sediment the competition culture. Therefore, the cooperation amongst those involved parties by means of thoughtful dialogues is of utmost importance to beef up the awareness as regards competition culture.

That being stated, IBRAC has been leading a number of initiatives and the outcomes have been fruitful. With the reinvigorated waves in the context of Law No. 12,529/2011, new initiatives are expected and encouraged within IBRAC's agenda, whose commitment and seriousness is unanimously recognized by the civil society and regulatory authorities (including the CADE).

In conclusion, taking into account all the foregoing, we contend that in a country marked by a background of interventionist state tradition, it makes total sense to encourage compliance with competition rules. As such, one can see IBRAC as a key institution in the society, whose contributions to leverage the competition culture in Brazil is praiseworthy.

The so-called mantra of "competition matters" should gear the society in a way to promote a healthy environment that facilitate the genuine compliance with the rules, not due to the fear of being punished in case of an eventual breach, but rather because being compliant with the rules (and also helping the counterparties fully engage in the compliance) is the right thing to do. In summary, the compliance with the rules must be the gold premise to the economic agents in a way to contribute to the development of the whole country.

CHAPTER 6
Trends and Developments in Competition Advocacy in Latin America

Martha Martínez Licetti, Lucía Villarán & Tanja Goodwin

§6.01 INTRODUCTION

This chapter examines new trends and developments in competition advocacy in Latin America associated with the recent notable successes in the region and offers an outlook on the role that competition policy and advocacy may play in the future in the design of economic policies.

Competition policy is commonly defined as a "set of policies and laws that ensure competition in the marketplace is not restricted in such a way as to reduce economic welfare."[1] The World Bank Group's (WBG's) view is that a strong Competition Policy Framework involves rules that prevent anticompetitive business practices, as well as policies that ensure open markets, a business environment with low barriers to entry and low operational risks, and enhanced private sector participation in commercial activities.

Countries often establish public competition authorities in order to track down and punish those in violation of the Competition Law. In practice, however, the national entities entrusted with the enforcement seldom have powers to issue policies – even if directly set up under a ministerial body. This implies that in order to best implement the Competition Policy Framework, competition agencies must interact with other public bodies that issue and implement policies and regulations that have direct or indirect consequences for competition in the marketplace, and therefore need to make use of non-enforcement methods in order to better encourage competition.

Competition advocacy is one such method a competition authority may use to cultivate a competitive environment. *Competition advocacy* was defined by the

---

1. Massimo Motta. 2004. *Competition Policy*. Cambridge Books, Cambridge University Press, p. 30.

International Competition Network (ICN) in 2009 as "all activities conducted by a competition agency related to the promotion of a competitive environment by means of non-enforcement mechanisms, mainly through its relationships with other governmental agencies and by increasing public awareness of the benefits of competition."[2]

Advocacy efforts have become a critical function of competition agencies worldwide and complement enforcement. Given competition's positive impact on productivity, enhancing trade and reducing poverty, these efforts also leverage the role of competition policies for the broader policy agenda and development priorities.

This chapter presents the practical experience of several competition agencies in Latin America that have been successful in combining common advocacy tools with the strategic use of other tools available in their legal frameworks to promote a competition culture and transform markets in their countries. These stories are contextualized by the conceptual framework developed by the WBG for classifying advocacy activities based on their goals, scope and tools used. This framework builds on the experience gained by countries worldwide with practical implementation of advocacy strategies.

Between 2013 and 2016, six competition authorities in Latin American received awards for ten out of forty-two successful advocacy initiatives honored under the annual Competition Advocacy Contest. This Contest is jointly hosted by the ICN and the WBG and has so far received close to one hundred submissions from competition authorities in developing and since 2014 also advanced economies.[3] The award-winning model initiatives in Latin America, which boosted competition with non-enforcement means, are representative of a broader evolution of competition advocacy in the region.

§6.02 WHY ADVOCACY EFFORTS ARE RELEVANT IN THE CONTEXT OF LATIN AMERICA

First, WBG studies in Latin America highlight that in critical sectors of the economy, lack of competition is associated with government interventions in markets[4] that are not conducive to competition.[5] These interventions may be as harmful to competition as anticompetitive private practices. New data from a joint dataset by WBG and the

---

2. As defined by the International Competition Network (ICN).
3. Winners and Honorable Mentions of the Competition Advocacy Contest in Latin America in the respective contest rounds: Brazil (2015/16), Chile (2013/14), Colombia (2013/14), El Salvador (2013/14, 2014/15), Honduras (2015/16), Mexico (2013/14, 2014/15, 2015/16), available at https://www.wbginvestmentclimate.org/advisory-services/cross-cutting-issues/competition-policy/winners-2013-competition-advocacy-contest.cfm; http://www.worldbank.org/en/events/2014/11/26/2014-competition-advocacy-contest; http://www.worldbank.org/en/events/2015/10/30/the-2015---2016-competition-advocacy-contest-how-to-build-a-culture-of-competition-for-private-sector-development-and-economic-growth#5.
4. Following the World Bank Group Markets and Competition Policy Assessment (MCPAT), government interventions include direct government participation in markets as a supplier or buyer of foods and services as well as indirect participation in markets through government policies, regulations, rules, procedures and actions of government officials that affect decisions made by market players regarding economic matters.
5. World Bank (2015); Vostroknutova et al. (2015).

Organisation for Economic Co-operation and Development (OECD) on Product Market Regulation (PMR) in thirteen Latin American countries quantifies the degree of restrictiveness of such public barriers to competition. It reveals that in Latin America, PMR is on average 54% more restrictive to competition than in European, North American and Asian OECD countries.[6] Based on simulations conducted for Peru and Brazil, removing anticompetitive provisions only in professional licensing, pricing rules and other self-regulatory measures would yield spillover effects on the broader economy that constitute between 0.1 and 0.2% additional growth of GDP.[7]

Second, even in comparatively open market economies, digital and disruptive innovations arrive with new challenges for competition policy and regulatory frameworks. In general, larger and more advanced economies in Latin America introduced regulatory reform starting in the 1990s. Today, the Pacific Alliance Member States, for example, have regulatory frameworks in place that are only 22% more restrictive than those in the rest of the OECD, according to the WBG-OECD PMR Indicators. The advance of the digital economy has the potential to transform markets in public transport, financial, communication and many others services sectors, and reignite much-needed productivity growth in Latin America in order to close the 30% gap in total factor productivity with the United States.[8] These benefits will materialize faster if competition and regulatory frameworks allow and provide the right incentives to innovate and compete.

Third, evidence suggests that anticompetitive private practices are prevalent in Latin America and that the parties involved, in particular Trade and Business Associations, are often either unaware of the applicability of the law or perceive a low risk of the Competition Authority detecting and sanctioning the infringement. At least 220 cartels have been detected in ten Latin American countries over ten years, which is likely just the tip of the iceberg given that Competition Agencies in this region rarely handle more than a few cases of anticompetitive practices per year.[9] One out of three cartel cases involved trade or business associations. One out of four cartels was detected in local markets, and some have been shown to be particularly harmful for local economies. A cartel in bus transport in Chiapas, one of the poorest Mexican States, forced consumers to pay a total of USD 2.5 million more on a single route.[10] A much larger share of such local cartels are likely escaping the view of the competition authorities. Targeted advocacy may be essential to prevent cartels, especially those that form due to ignorance of the law or the rigor of its enforcement.

---

6. The WBG-OECD Product Market Regulation database captures the government's direct participation in commercial activities and State influence in markets through rules that affect market outcomes (State control); rules that limit market entry and reduce the intensity of rivalry among competitors (barriers to entrepreneurship) and barriers to trade and investment.
7. World Bank (forthcoming); Vostroknutova et al. (2015).
8. Fernández-Arias and Rodríguez-Apolinar (2016).
9. Data from World Bank Group Antitrust Enforcement Database, as of March 2016, for Latin America in collaboration with the Regional Competition Center for Latin America.
10. *See Resolución del expediente IO-004-2012*, available at https://www.cofece.mx/cofece/index.php/prensa/historico-de-noticias/sanciona-cofece-a-empresas-de-transporte-de-pasajeros-del-estado-de-chiapas-por-incurrir-en-practicas-monopolicas-absolutas.

Fourth, in Latin America, several countries show a high degree of government intervention in the economy, and critical sectors seem to be dominated by vested interests. Hence, there is a clear rationale for competition agencies to develop advocacy strategies that embed competition principles in broader public policies and progressively build a competition culture in the country. But competition agencies should be strategic in doing so. Even when they have gained the legal mandate to enforce competition principles in other policies and regulations, these authorities usually have limited resources for conducting advocacy activities, both human and monetary. Furthermore, because aligning government interventions with competition principles requires public momentum, it is key to select sectors and markets that are relevant to the country's economy, and where implementing pro-competitive reforms or removing anticompetitive government interventions can have the greatest impact. Therefore, competition authorities require tools that allow them to prioritize not only sectors but also the most relevant reforms, as well as a sound strategy for making their recommendations relevant and actionable. Finally, it is critical for the agencies to understand how to strategically combine the different instruments they have at hand to achieve more impactful results in their advocacy strategies, and at the same time enhance their enforcement activity.

The degree of development of a competition agency's advocacy mandate, and in general, the level of its maturity, varies significantly across Latin American countries. These differences are explained not only by the number of years that the competition authorities and their competition legal frameworks have been in place, but also by their available resources and in some cases, by the scope of their legal mandate. But regardless the level of development of the agencies, at any stage of maturity, enforcement activities have to be complemented by and articulated jointly with advocacy strategies.

§6.03   WHAT IS THE STATUS OF COMPETITION ADVOCACY IN LATIN AMERICA?

Based on a comprehensive review of worldwide examples of competition advocacy, in 2016 the WBG proposed a systematic framework for the multi-faceted means of promoting competition through advocacy.[11] The following segment summarizes and visualizes this overarching framework for advocacy initiatives: (a) the objectives of competition advocacy; (b) the various areas of analysis on which advocacy initiatives are based; (c) examples of tools employed to implement advocacy (further detailed in Figure 6.2) to achieve the initial objectives; (d) the sets of mandates that competition authorities hold across the globe with varying degree of specificity and compulsion in their terms; and finally (e) the advocacy strategies that make a difference in whether or not a tool or mandate is well implemented to achieve the initial objective.

---

11. Adapted from Goodwin and Martínez Licetti (2016).

Figure 6.1 Framework for Advocacy Initiatives

Advocacy objectives	General areas of analysis for advocacy	Advocacy tools (Examples)	Advocacy mandate	Advocacy strategies
Advocating for a change in the way that governments intervene in the markets	Regulatory reform and economic policies	Competition impact assessment of regulations and government policies	Explicit mandate to issue opinions	Technological solutions
	Investment incentives and public aid	Assessment of potential effects of privatization itself and/or design of privatization conditions	Binding opinions	Early engagement/ Anticipation
Conducting activities that increase knowledge of key stakeholders about the rationale and benefits of competition policy	Deregulation or proposals for regulation	Subsidiarity/competitive neutrality analysis prior to change in SOE mandate	Provision obliging public body to justify deviation from opinion	Take advantage of country's economic/political trends
	Privatization, SOEs and competitive neutrality	Guidelines for trade, professional and business associations	Non-binding opinion	Limiting the scope of market to be addressed
	Competition policy in regulated sectors		Non-binding opinion (only on existing regulation)	Focus on reform feasibility
Advocating for a change in private companies' behavior in the market and compliance	Compliance (both public and private sector)	... (see full list in Fig.2)	Explicit mandate to conduct market studies or sector inquiries	Independent panel to receive and evaluate the information
			Explicit mandate to prior opinion in decisions and administrative procedures regarding privatization, price control, public aid, (de-) regulation, SOE-mandates; concessions, licenses and tenders in regulated sectors	Inter-agency cooperation

← Compulsory power of opinion

Source: WBG. 2016. Transforming Markets through Competition. Book, available at: http://www-wds.worldbank.org/external/default/WDSContentServer/WDSP/IB/2016/05/09/090224b08431052f/2_0/Rendered/PDF/Transforming0m0competition0advocacy.pdf.

Framework for Promoting Competition through Advocacy:

(1) *Advocating for a change in the way that governments intervene in the markets, which may imply:*
   (a) modifying a (proposed or existing) regulation or economic policy that: (i) reinforces dominance or limits entry, (ii) is conducive to collusive outcomes or increases costs to compete in the market, (iii) discriminates and protects vested interests;
   (b) minimizing distortions caused by selective industrial policies investment incentives and public aid;
   (c) supporting decisions as to when competition conditions call for regulation/de-regulation;
   (d) providing mechanisms to establish a level playing field between competing private and State-Owned Enterprises (SOEs);
   (e) guaranteeing competitive conditions for auctions and public private partnerships and/or privatizations;
   (f) clarifying and delineating the reach of respective legal mandates of competition authorities and sector regulators as well as other agencies regarding the promotion of competition principles, and collaborating across these institutions to implement competition policies in regulated sectors;
   (g) embedding competition principles in broader economic policies (trade, business environment and regulatory reform, sectoral policies, incentives and investment policy, among others).
(2) *Conducting activities that increase knowledge of key stakeholders (e.g., civil society, media, judges and policy makers), about the rationale for and benefits of competition policy which may include:*
   (a) increasing awareness of the ways that incorporating competition principles in regulatory and broader economic policies can promote and protect the consumer benefits associated with vigorous competition;
   (b) providing technical expertise regarding particular industries or markets to other policy makers;
   (c) increasing awareness of the impact of competition enforcement on citizens and business.
(3) *Advocating for a change in private companies' behavior in the market and compliance, which may include:*
   (a) clarifying applicability of competition law to conduct or self-regulation under Trade and Business Associations;
   (b) promoting compliance with the law and/or voluntary cessation of anti-competitive practices through special programs with grace periods;
   (c) promote compliance in public procurement through certificates of Independent Bid Determination.

Competition authorities have developed a variety of tools to advocate and address potential or existing obstacles to effective competition in the market. Figure 6.2 lists the advocacy tools that have been applied by Competition Authorities in the ICN-WBG Advocacy Contest and in WBG projects. The graph further maps the tools to their general area of competition analysis (such as regulatory reform), the element that it addresses (such as a particular regulation that inhibits competition) and the timing of when the advocacy tool is used (when the measure is under discussion, i.e., *ex ante*, or already in place, i.e., *ex post*). Not only can several tools be used simultaneously and in a complementary fashion, they may address several issues in the market and be *ex post* (with respect to the existing framework) and *ex ante* (of the proposed new framework) at the same time.

Figure 6.2 Advocacy Tools

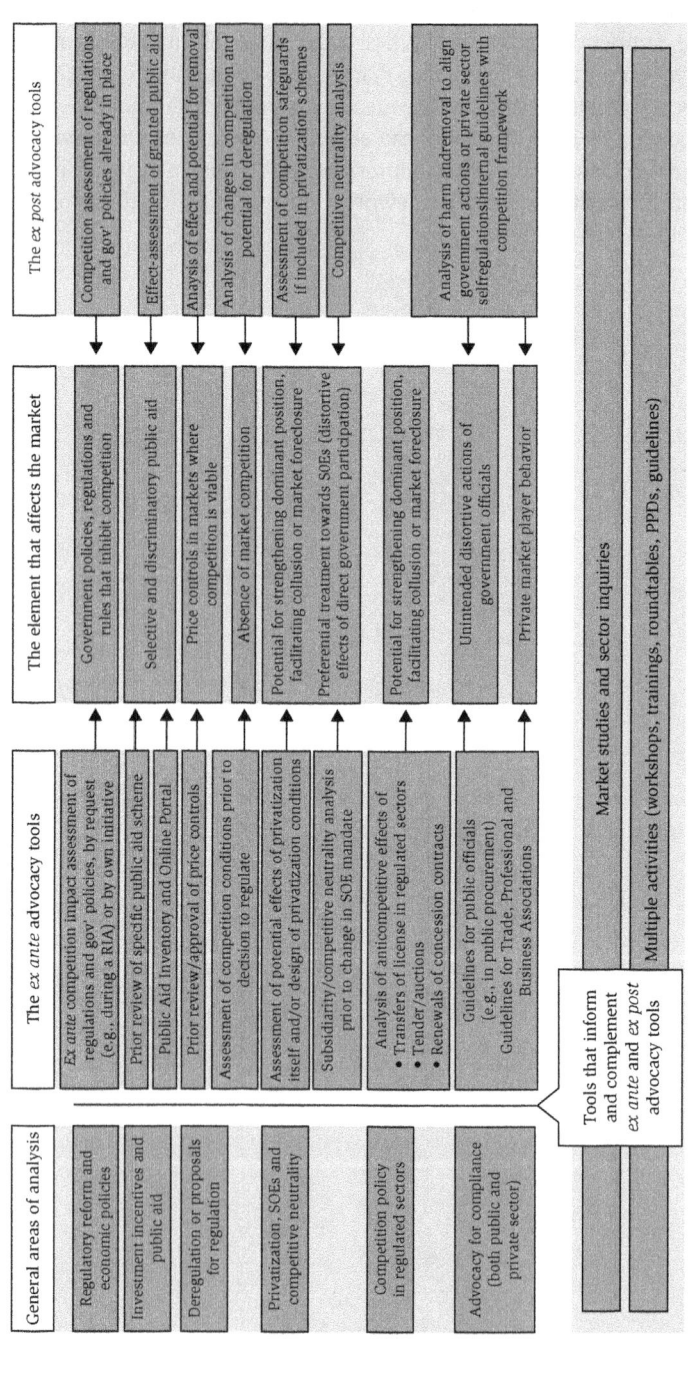

Source: WBG. 2016. Transforming Markets through Competition. Book, available at: http://www-wds.worldbank.org/external/default/WDSContentServer/WDSP/IB/2016/05/09/090224b08431052f/2_0/Rendered/PDF/Transforming0m0competition0advocacy.pdf.

The majority of the competition agencies in the LAC region have an advocacy mandate within their legal framework. The scope of this mandate, however, varies across countries and in several cases has been expanded over time as a result of consistent implementation of the mandate by the competition agencies. It is worth noting that several authorities in Latin America with successful advocacy initiatives did not hold a specific advocacy mandate, which highlights that an explicit legal mandate is not necessarily sufficient for success.

In general, for many competition agencies in Latin America, conducting market studies, issuing opinions on anticompetitive regulations and general information material and activities about competition law have been the focus of advocacy efforts. For instance, in Central America, three countries have produced a total of fifty-five market studies in total.[12]

Figure 6.3 Competition Authority's Advocacy Mandate

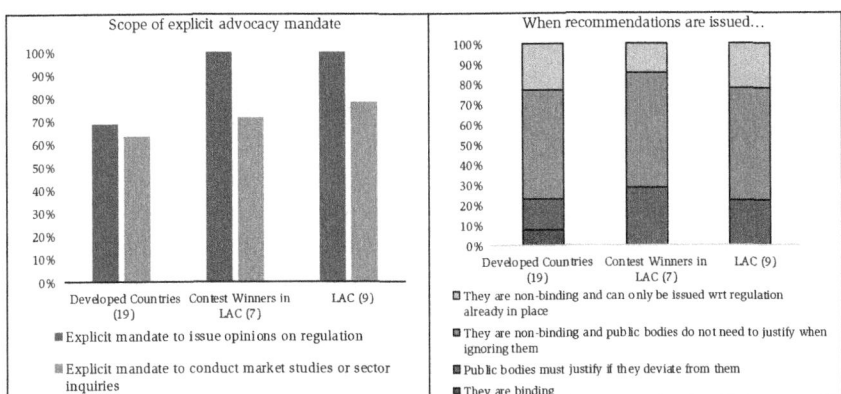

Source: WBG analysis based on publicly available legislative frameworks and secondary reports or questionnaires.

On the other hand, some competition legal frameworks in the region have provided the competition agencies with complementary tools that have allowed them to enhance and expand their advocacy activities. For instance, Mexico has a mandatory system for *ex ante* assessment of impact on competition of proposed regulations at the federal level. In Chile, the agency has issued several opinions on privatizations, and the Peruvian competition agency has assessed, through enforcement procedures and special examinations, whether SOEs breached the rule of the subsidiarity role of the State (as set forth in the Constitution) by competing with private enterprises in markets where private initiative exists or is feasible.

---

12. Honduras: 25 (2007–2014) Correa Yanez, E., "Estudios de Mercado: La Experiencia de Honduras" (Presentation at Market Study Workshop in Santiago de Chile, March 18–19, 2015); El Salvador: 23 (2006–2016); *see* M. Tobar *"Ten Years of the Competition Superintendence – Past, Present, and Future,"* Developing World Antitrust Blog, May 2016 *(www.developingworldantitrust.com)*; Costa Rica: 7 (2010–2016).

In other cases, given their limited advocacy mandate, competition agencies in Latin America have developed strategies that have allowed them to be more effective in advocating for changes in other public policies, such as the signing of a Memorandum of Understandings (MoU) with key government institutions. This is the case in El Salvador, where the competition authority has been very strategic in signing MoU's, empowering the agency to review a significant amount of regulatory proposals which otherwise might not have been within the scope of the advocacy role of the agency.

Another advocacy strategy developed by competition authorities in the Latin America region is the issuing of guidelines for business associations aiming at raising awareness of and promoting compliance with antitrust rules. Chile has issued such guidelines, along with a media campaign that enhanced the impact of this strategy. Honduras is in the process of issuing similar guidelines. This is also an example of the high potential for replicability of these initiatives within the region.

Finally, several competition agencies have been very active in developing advocacy strategies through informing policy makers and the wider public about competition principles and the law. In at least six Competition Authorities in the region, outreach activities include a high-profile "National Competition Day."[13]

§6.04 WHAT LIES BEHIND THE SUCCESSFUL ADVOCACY INITIATIVES IN LATIN AMERICA?

This section presents the experiences of several competition authorities in the region that have used their advocacy mandates for changing the way that governments intervene in markets, increasing knowledge among stakeholders about the rationale for and benefits of competition, and promoting compliance by private companies with the competition framework. As shown, these authorities have followed different patterns, reflecting the varying scope of their legal mandates and the advocacy instruments available. However, these experiences have as a common denominator the strategic use of instruments and the sequencing of interventions, resulting in successful and impactful outcomes, and in some cases leading to an expansion of their explicit legal mandate afterwards. At the same time, these stories point out that successful results are not necessarily a direct consequence of a broader mandate but rather of a wise use and combination of instruments. Finally, some of the stories show how competition authorities have been able to learn from "mistakes" and refocus and better target their advocacy efforts, achieving notable effects in markets and enhancing their enforcement activities.

Although there are significant differences among countries within the region in terms of the level of experience that competition authorities exhibit, both in conducting advocacy activities and implementing their enforcement mandate, countries in Latin American have a similar cultural and political background and face broadly similar development challenges. In addition, firms tend to operate in several markets within the region and government interventions tend to follow similar patterns in critical

---

13. Colombia, Honduras, Peru, El Salvador, Chile, Brazil.

sectors for their economies. Therefore, the lessons extracted from this set of experience in terms of the common elements behind success can be helpful for other agencies in implementing similar strategies in the future.

Finally, in some cases decisions by competition authorities with respect to governments' interventions can be seen as mandatory exertion of their mandate. However, the timing, sequencing, degree and scope of the use of different advocacy instruments, and particularly, the decision on how they complement enforcement activities, are within the discretion of the competition agency. Hence, the competition agency's vision is crucial in order to take full advantage of the interplay among these tools, broaden the scope of the advocacy agenda and build more impactful competition advocacy.

[A]   Mexico

The Mexican competition agency has a strong record of advocacy activities and has further leveraged the use of several instruments to infusing competition principles in public policies.

The use of competition-specific Impact Assessment as an advocacy tool

Mexico is the only country in the region that has a formal Regulatory Impact Assessment (RIA) system in place. Furthermore, the competition agency has been innovative in embedding a specific competition assessment, thereby amplifying its advocacy powers. Competition impact assessment can be considered a new advocacy tool.[14] RIA is a tool for improving the quality of new regulations by assessing regulatory objectives, identifying alternative policy options and benefits and costs associated with each alternative. Thus, the competition assessment complements the RIA, enhancing regulatory quality by assessing potential impact of proposed regulations on the dynamics on the market. Mexico's Federal Economic Competition Commission (COFECE), in collaboration with the Federal Commission for Regulatory Improvement (COFEMER), set up the substantial competition analysis as part of the framework for regulatory impact analysis. Through this instrument, COFECE has been able to review *ex ante* a significant number of regulatory proposals and highlight their potentially adverse impact on competition, progressively infusing competition principles in the rule-making process of a wide array of public entities. This ex ante tool complements the role that COFECE has played in issuing opinions and conducting market studies in several markets, not only at the federal level but also highlighting the anticompetitive effects of regulations and decisions issued by subnational authorities.

Opinions on regulations at both the federal and subnational level broadened the scope of typical advocacy activities

The Mexican competition authority has held a mandate to comment on federal public administration programs and policies since 1992 and may comment when requested on

---

14. Competition Law and regulation, Drexl, 2015.

the amendments to the drafts of laws and regulations. Despite the lack of statutory requirements for consultations, COFECE has been routinely invited to participate in reviewing proposals that originated in both Congress and the executive branch agencies. In 1998, the authority's mandate was extended. The new mandate specified that when legal or regulatory provisions expressly provided for competition concerns to be resolved, it would be the responsibility of the COFECE to issue the corresponding judgment. From 1998 until 2004, the authority issued non-binding recommendations to State and local governments in at least twenty cases in matters relating to the sale of pharmaceutical products, taxi services, beer, funeral services, tortillas, telecommunication and others. In 2006, competition law reform provided for a lengthy set of detailed powers regarding ex officio opinions on policies, regulations and legislation and promotion of market inquiries. By then, the Authority had established a track record for judging the need for regulatory intervention to achieve policy objectives in very specific market segments. In 2014, COFECE issued a total of 103 opinions: fifty-four opinions addressed competition issues with respect to proposed regulation, and the remaining forty-nine regarding tenders and the granting of governmental licenses, concessions, and permits. COFECE has also published studies on agriculture and food sector and financial services.

COFECE's assessment of distortive effects of regulations at the subnational level has been complemented by COFEMER's strong record of implementing reforms at the subnational level. This enabled a fruitful collaboration between agencies in tackling competition barriers at the subnational level. Finding synergies with other institutions that have a strong record with practical implementation of policy and reform proposals can leverage the technical knowledge of the agency for a more effective role in promoting the alignment of subnational regulations with competition principles. In Mexico, this strategy was granted political recognition: The presidential decree that establishes the Integral Better Regulation Strategy in Mexico covering both federal and subnational entities foresees the use of the WBG's analytical tool – already deployed jointly with COFEMER in three States – to assess the impact on competition of administrative procedures.[15]

Strategic opinions and interventions have shaped the design of regulatory policies for key markets and for disruptive innovations

COFECE engaged with the Mexican Institute of Social Security (IMSS by its Spanish acronym), an institution serving nearly half of Mexico's population and its third largest public purchaser, to promote competition. COFECE began working with IMSS as part of a broader effort to take on the problem of bid rigging in public procurement. In particular, the agency worked with IMSS on its tender design and procurement processes to reduce the risk of bid rigging. In this intervention, COFECE combined enforcement actions with advocacy, since one of the main goals of the activity was to reduce companies' incentives to engage in collusive conducts in the public

---

15. http://dof.gob.mx/nota_detalle.php?codigo=5378008&fecha=05/01/2015.

Chapter 6: Trends and Developments in Competition Advocacy §6.04[B]

procurement process. It has been estimated that this intervention saved consumers USD 4.5 billion between 2006 and 2011.[16]

In addition, as a result of the advocacy opinion by Mexico's competition authority, Mexico City's Department of Transportation was the first local government in Latin America to issue a specific regulation allowing Transportation Network Companies (TNCs), such as Uber and Cabify, to operate fully. The Federal Economic Competition Commission (COFECE) had issued an opinion recommending that local governments formally recognize the services provided by TNCs, and avoid imposing regulations that would restrict their ability to compete. Furthermore, spillover effects were substantial, with other local governments following Mexico City's lead.

[B] Peru

In the case of Peru, the competition authority (INDECOPI) was granted a legal mandate that expanded beyond the more common advocacy powers of conducting market studies and issuing opinions on regulations that may have an adverse impact competition. This broader set of instruments has allowed Peru's competition authority to exert direct control over several government interventions that restrict competition and to progressively instill pro-competition principles within the rule-making process of other government entities and the direct market participation of SOEs. Another unique feature of the Peruvian framework is that these tools have empowered the competition agency to oversee the alignment of the decisions of subnational authorities with competition principles, even though these decisions are typically outside of the scope of the advocacy role of competition agencies.

Enforcement of the subsidiarity principle to guarantee competitive neutrality

INDECOPI enforces the alignment of commercial activities conducted by SOEs with the constitutional subsidiarity principle. This principle indicates that State participation in the economy should be subsidiary to private sector participation and guided by clear policy objectives.

The economic activity (directly or indirectly) of the State is constitutionally legitimate only when the following circumstances are met: (a) State participation in business activities should be authorized by a special law; (b) State participation in business activities should be subsidiary to private businesses; i.e., the State intervention should not foreclose private businesses from the market or should be only implemented in cases where private supply is insufficient; (c) State participation in business activities can only occur for reasons of overriding public interest or manifest national benefit.

INDECOPI is in charge of assessing whether a specific State intervention in the economy is consistent with the aforementioned subsidiarity principle. In evaluating a case, INDECOPI defines relevant markets in which State and private enterprises are competing, as well as the rationale for State intervention. Currently, INDECOPI has

---

16. https://www.wbginvestmentclimate.org/publications/upload/Competition-Policy-Advocacy-Awards.pdf.

assessed several cases in which it has determined that the activity of SOEs in the market was not in alignment with the subsidiary principle and has therefore sanctioned the SOEs for conducting unfair competition activities. Between 2010 and 2015, twenty cases on this subject were decided by the INDECOPI's Tribunal.[17] INDECOPI's oversight on the SOEs' activities in markets where they compete with private firms or where private initiative could be viable contributes to preserve competitive neutrality and sends a strong signal to private enterprises that the constitutional principles protecting private initiative on a level playing field will be enforced.

The removal of bureaucratic barriers as a tool to reduce illegal and unreasonable government interventions that can harm competition

The competition agency has a special division in charge of declaring reported or self-identified norms or administrative acts as an "illegal or unreasonable bureaucratic barrier" to market entry.

Within its legal mandate, the Commission for Elimination of Bureaucratic Barriers *(CEBB for its initials in Spanish)* is entitled to: (a) remove the legal effect of any illegal or unreasonable action or regulation issued by national, regional or local entities, such as supreme decrees or local decrees, among others. (The laws issued by Congress are out of the scope of its mandate.); (b) impose fines on public officials in certain cases, such as the failure to remove barriers previously declared as illegal and/or unreasonable, which aims at dissuading the repeated application of regulations that have already been declared illegal or unreasonable; (c) promote constitutional actions to expel from the legal system regulations (supreme decrees and local/regional decrees) ex officio declared as bureaucratic barriers.

The CEBB has developed a technical methodology for assessing whether administrative decisions or regulations could be deemed as illegal or unreasonable bureaucratic barriers. This two-step methodology the first defines legality of the measure, meaning whether the decision or rule was issued by the authority within its legal mandate, following the legal procedures and requirements. If the regulation passes the first step of the assessment, the second step evaluates its reasonableness, meaning whether the measure is justified by public interest, whether the restriction or burden imposed by the measure is proportional to the benefit, and finally whether there are other less restrictive alternatives to achieve the same regulatory objective.

In applying this tool, INDECOPI has determined that numerous regulations have adverse effects on competition in key markets. In fact, some estimations suggest that 70% of the restrictions to competition imposed by those barriers affect competition in critical sectors for development of local markets such as transport, telecommunication, retail, construction/real estate or tourism. The following graph illustrates how INDECOPI has been increasingly effective in sanctioning and removing these barriers. Between 1993 and 2008, the CEBB analyzed 1403 alleged barriers to market access. CEBB analyzed another 2052 alleged cases of undue bureaucratic barriers between 2009 and 2014 – almost four times more cases per year in relation to the first sixteen years of the commission.

---

17. *Source:* Tribunal de Defensa de la Competencia INDECOPI.

Figure 6.4   Commission for Elimination of Bureaucratic Barriers (CEBB)

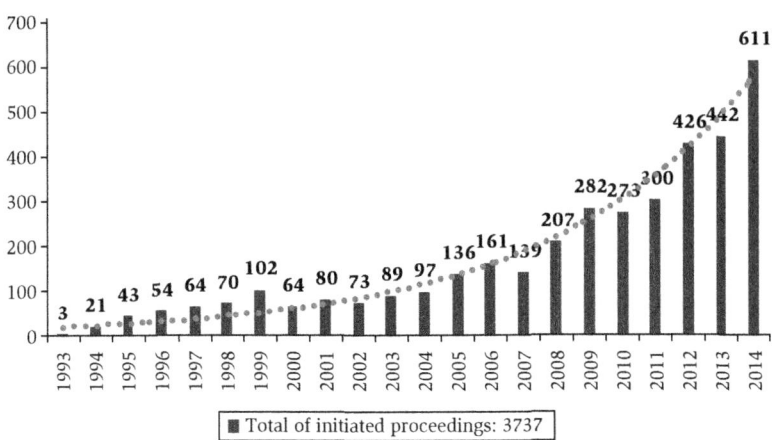

Source: INDECOPI. 2014. "Propuesta para Mejorar la Competitividad del País." Press Conference, November 25, Lima, Peru, available at http://agenciaorbita.org/indecopipresenta-conjunto-de-medidas-para-mejorar-lacompetitividad-del-pais/.

It is important to highlight that although the majority of cases ruled upon by INDECOPI were triggered by private complaints, the competition agency has also steadily increased the number of cases initiated *ex officio*. These ex officio rulings demonstrate strategic considerations on when and in which sectors the use of this tool could be more effective in discouraging government interventions that not only increase costs for doing business but could also adversely impact competition dynamics in key sectors.

Figure 6.5   Eliminated Bureaucratic Barriers

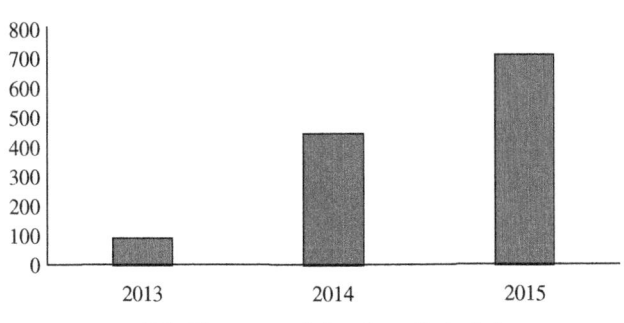

Source: INDECOPI. 2013–2014. "Estadísticas sobre identificación y eliminación de barreras burocráticas a nivel nacional." Economic Studies Unit. Available at: file:///C:/Users/Usuario/Downloads/Reporte%20estad%C3%ADstico%202013%20(1).pdf.

A reform of the bureaucratic barriers system in 2015 enhanced INDECOPI's power to effectively eliminate undue regulatory barriers and enable competition by providing that any mode of proceedings by any entity of the public administration may constitute a bureaucratic barrier. Before this change, only administrative actions could be sanctioned. Now the scope has been widened to include "de facto" practices by officials. It is important to notice that the legal mandate of INDECOPI for declaring and eliminating bureaucratic barriers has been progressively enhanced to increase its scope and effectiveness.

INDECOPI's CEBB has been awarded at the ICN Annual Conference in 2016 for its track record in addressing barriers that do not only raise the cost of entering a market or doing business but in numerous instances directly inhibit competition in the marketplace.

Reinforced mandate to conduct market studies as a result of consistent content-driven advocacy and enforcement activity

The first Competition Law in Peru did not include an express mandate for competition advocacy. Nevertheless, INDECOPI regularly published market studies and "observatories" to develop public recommendations. During the late 1990s and 2000s, it also issued several opinions to infuse competition principles in government policies such as Special Economic Zones as well as tax and incentives policies.

The 2008 competition law reform introduced competition advocacy provisions and by 2014, the commission had published studies on notary, health insurance and driver's licensing services.

Further reforms in 2015 strengthened INDECOPI's advocacy mandate by requiring institutions to respond to recommendations set forth by the Competition Commission on how to promote competition, increasing its ability to require public bodies to align their policies and regulations with competition principles. The following graph shows how INDECOPI has progressively become more active in issuing opinions and conducting market studies using a reinforced legal mandate.[18]

Figure 6.6   Issued Market Studies

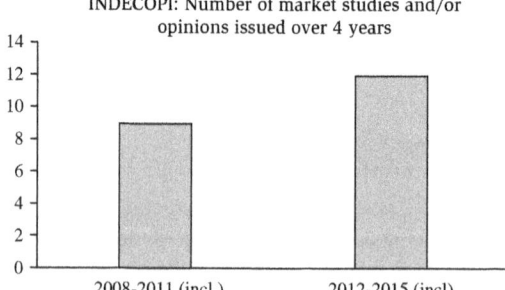

Source: INDECOPI.

---

18. Data for 2007 to 2013 reflects "estudios de mercado" issued by the *Gerencia de Estudios Economicos*. (Source: INDECOPI). Data for 2014 reflects "advocacy efforts," "opinions on

[C] Colombia

Strong record of opinions allowed the competition agency to strengthen its advocacy mandate

In 2009, Colombia's competition agency, the Superintendence of Industry and Commerce, (SIC) gained formal powers to issue opinions on draft regulation that had the potential to affect competition. These opinions would be binding for the recipient authority, which henceforth needed to expressly justify any deviation. In the same year, the Agency issued opinions and reports on postal, freight, private security and telecommunications services. In 2010, the legislation introduced an obligation for administrative bodies to report drafts and acts with the potential to affect competition to the competition agency (the *ex ante* competition assessment system in place today). Between July 24, 2009, and December 31, 2014, the SIC issued 158 advocacy opinions to twenty-two agencies. As shown in the figure 6.7 below, the SIC has issued opinions in key sectors of the Colombian economy, reaching out to both regulated and unregulated markets.

During 2014, the SIC issued fifty-one advocacy opinions. The most relevant opinions were issued regarding the sugar market, transportation network platforms, long-term gas contracts, asymmetric mobile termination rates.

Figure 6.7   Advocacy Cases Addressed by the SIC

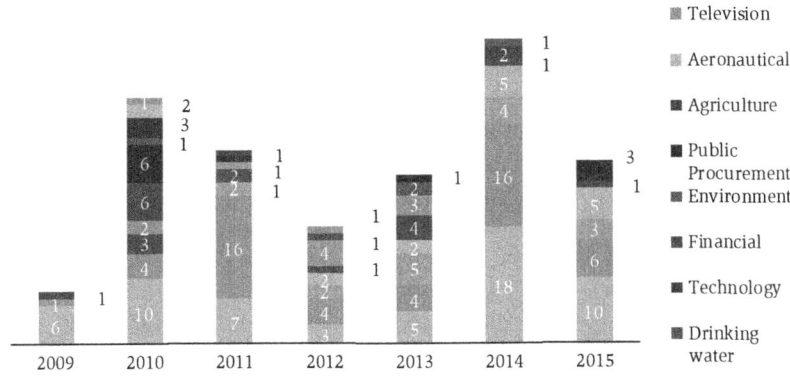

Source: SIC. 2016. "Base de Datos de Conceptos Emitidos." Available at: http://www.sic.gov.co/drupal/abogacia-de-la-competencia.

Strategic opinions and interventions that have shaped the design of regulatory policies for key emerging markets

The Colombian government has prioritized mobile Internet as an emerging, important market for growth. In response to a proposed public auction of 4G LTE spectrum, the

---

congress bills" in sectors, and "competition condition reports" (Source: OECD Annual Reports by Competition Authorities). Data for 2015 reflects "sector inquiries" defined as "investigations/information requirements regarding an economic sector or a particular industry" (Source: INDECOPI).

SIC acted quickly at a strategic moment to inform a decision by means beyond its usual regulatory comments. SIC conducted an economic analysis of the country's mobile voice and Internet market, including simulations of post-auction market scenarios. The study identified risks in the plan to assign the spectrum that could prevent new entrants from participating in the auction. These findings prompted SIC to recommend a reconsideration of the auction design. The government adapted the auction process and promoted regulations on infrastructure sharing and network access (roaming) to encourage at least one entrant in the market. The SIC advised the national government's regulatory agencies on the protection of competition in the allocation of spectrum and participated in congressional discussions on the importance of competition in the telecommunications sector.

The process involved collaboration among several branches of government: the National Spectrum Agency (ANE), the Communication Regulatory Commission (CRC), the Ministry of Information Technology (MinTIC), the military, and the academy, the General Prosecutor Office, the Comptroller General, and the National Planning Department. During the process, SIC kept in close contact with the ANE, CRC, and MinTIC and presented their points of view on various adjudication process drafts for the Congress and other stakeholders. Private institutions and firms, including current providers, had the opportunity to provide comments, which were received and considered.[19]

Two new operators entered the mobile communications market in the new spectrum auction design with pro-competitive considerations in line with the advocacy initiative by SIC. According to the estimate of a 2015 study by the competition authority, consumers should benefit considerably from price reductions with up to USD 56 million savings on mobile internet charges. Moreover, in 2014 the overall number of mobile internet users increased by 22% and the two new market entrants have gained increasing numbers of subscribers.

The SIC has further complemented individual and highly technical opinions with seminars and events aiming at increasing broader awareness and competition culture at the highest political level. In the midst of a heated debate about the largest (collective) fine imposed in Colombia against a sugar-cartel, the Superintendence staged a high-profile event around the National Competition Day with participation of the Nation's President, who noted in his speech that competition was a necessary condition for a more equitable Colombia and affirmed his support for more effective cartel enforcement.[20]

[D] El Salvador

Although El Salvador's Superintendencia de Competencia (SC) does not have an explicit set of legal powers and tools for exerting its advocacy role, the fact that it has

---

19. https://www.wbginvestmentclimate.org/publications/upload/Competition-Policy-Advocacy-Awards.pdf.
20. http://wp.presidencia.gov.co/Noticias/2015/Octubre/Paginas/20151021_08-Palabras-del-Presidente-Juan-Manuel-Santos-en-el-III-Congreso-Internacional-de-Libre-Competencia-Economica.aspx.

a dedicated advocacy division – unlike the majority of competition agencies in LAC- has allowed the SC to strategically broaden the scope of their advocacy activities for achieving more impactful interventions in critical markets for its economy. The SC complements these specific activities in the regulatory production process with strategies to increase the effectiveness of its advocacy role.

Inter-institutional collaboration mechanisms have enabled SC to prevent and remove anticompetitive product market regulation in key sectors

SC had accumulated significant knowledge on competition assessments of existing laws and new proposals through dozens of market studies since its set up in 2006. In 2012, it signed MoUs with high-level public entities that are in charge of reviewing important economic and trade legislation so that these units would flag potentially anticompetitive legislative proposals. The MoUs were signed with the Presidency's Secretariat for Legislative and Legal issues, its Technical Secretariat, as well as with the Ministry of Foreign Affairs. Virtually all important economic and trade legislation passes through one or more of these institutions. The SC provided these institutions with guidelines that would help government officials assess the impact of various policy options on competition, thus embedding competition principles at a high institutional level.

Now, the SC saves time on monitoring the issuance of reform proposals, and dedicates its resources instead to reviewing those that are "flagged" and ensuring that recommendations are heard.

In 2013, the competition authority in El Salvador had already issued a total of twenty opinions on various draft regulations that had been flagged for potential anticompetitive effects through the MoUs with presidential and ministerial technical secretariats. Ten of these, ranging in subject area from civil aviation to health registrations to energy efficiency and consumer protections, received favorable reviews. Five, covering such issues as public purchasing, food safety, and micro, small, and medium enterprises, were partially accepted. As a result of this targeted advocacy, incumbent airlines are no longer exempt from financial guarantee requirements and scheduled flight operators can no longer block permits for charter flights. This may allow smaller airline operators to enter the market in El Salvador and build up business in the regional market with smaller aircraft but high frequency services.[21] Foreign sanitary registrations from countries with high sanitary standards are now acknowledged and raise competitive pressures on the incumbent agents in the domestic market. The SC also prevented a subjective "professional aptitude" clause in the licensing process of public accountants.

The graph below shows that although the SC has been very active in issuing recommendations in important markets under the authoritative environment provided by the MoUs signed with key institutions, the number of recommendations accepted by policy marker is still low. This highlights the potential that a stronger advocacy legal

---

21. *See* Superintendencia de Competencia de El Salvador (2013), *Estudio de Transporte Aéreo*, available at http://app.sc.gob.sv/estudio.php?id = 153.

mandate could have in ensuring more effective incorporation of pro-competition proposals in the design of regulations in several markets.

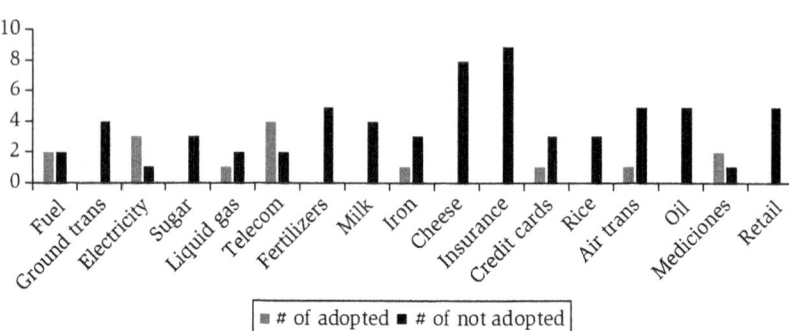

Figure 6.8 Issued Recommendations by the SC

Source: SC. 2016. "Estudios de Caso." Available at: http://app.sc.gob.sv/estudio.php?id = 153.

The SC is using outreach platforms with specific objectives to raise pressure on judicial bodies to resolve antitrust cases and on legislative bodies to consider its recommendations

The SC has created an "App" with the specific purpose of raising awareness of judicial delays in resolving appeals of antitrust cases. The online platform allows users to track, share and comment on antitrust enforcement cases. To do so, the user locates a card with the case's most relevant information; the current status of the fine imposed [paid, not paid, or temporarily suspended]; a brief summary of the case; the key number; public comments made on social networks and a chronology of the case. In its second phase, the authority has published all market studies to disseminate its findings and recommendations. With a user-friendly checklist, any interested party can quickly identify which of the recommendations have been taken up and implemented by the respective public entities and which ones have not yet been considered. This uniquely focused social media strategy ensures that the civil society is engaged for a targeted objective.

Again, given the lack of legal powers to impose compulsory adoption of its recommendation, the SC has used alternative means to raise awareness among the public entities and civil society not only of the content of its recommendations but also of the degree of adoption by public entities.

[E] Other Advocacy Strategies Conducted by Competition Agencies

Honduras

The initial focus of the advocacy activities of the *Comisión para la Defensa de la Competencia* (CDPC) was narrowly focused on conducting market studies. Between

2007 and 2014, the CDPC produced twenty-five market studies. Although specific recommendations were provided in these studies, the CDPC's efforts to reach out and effectively advocate to other government agencies for the adoption of these recommendations were too timid to yield widespread effects.

However, more recently, the CDPC has recognized the necessity of building on these market studies with adequate strategies to deliver the recommendations or specific goals in order to effectively achieve the changes in public or private practices.

Therefore, the CDPC has become more strategic in leveraging the knowledge gained as a result of its market studies to target specific sectors that are also the focus of its enforcement activities.

In fact, the CDPC has recently reinforced the findings of a particular market study in the context of an enforcement case. In 2012, a market study by the CDPC in Honduras identified that the Honduran Pharmacist Association required a 250-meter minimum distance to the nearest pharmacy in order to grant a solicitor a license for a new outlet or location change certificate for an existing one. In 2014, an economic actor filed a complaint about having being denied the necessary license from the Pharmacist Association, and the authority took advantage in issuing a resolution that contained a "provisional measure" to grant the economic actor access to the market and officially deemed the self-regulatory measure by the association as anticompetitive. It actively sought the dialogue with the association to explain the rationale behind its opinion and persuade the association to removing the provision.

Following the removal of the minimum distance restriction in late 2015, sixty-seven pharmacy outlets were opened in thirty-three different cities across Honduras and in particular in strategic locations close to medical facilities and shopping centers. Pharmacy storeowners have further estimated that consumer prices may decline by 5–10%, which according to the competition authority could results in USD 4–6 million in annual savings.[22] With lower entry barriers, it will also presumably become less viable to sustain anticompetitive agreements among competitors such as those detected in 2008 among pharmacies.[23]

Chile

The Chilean competition agency succeeded in changing behavior by private trade and business associations.

The Competition Authority in Chile recognized the role of trade associations in the formation and stability of anticompetitive practices. Over time the *Fiscalía Nacional Económica* had found evidence of associations of electricians fixing services fees, an association of manufacturers dividing urban zones into exclusive supply areas, an organization of bus companies penalizing one of its members for charging a price lower than that of all other members; and the president of a bakers' association even

---

22. Information provided as part of the submission by the *Comisión Nacional de la Defensa de la Competencia* for the Competition Advocacy Contest 2015–2016.
23. *See* Resolución Número 004-CDPC-2008-Año-III, available at http://base.crcal.org/documentos/3dc560ca-598a-44f5-8c43-071339dc046a/Honduras-Cartel-2012-Farmacias.pdf.

announced a bread price increase of 17% in the newspaper. In response, the authorities published guidelines for associations that focused on the relationship between information-sharing practices and competition law. This not only triggered a prolonged public debate, but also prompted the Chilean Chamber of Construction and Mining Council to develop their own compliance guidelines to further raise the awareness among private firms about the risk of incurring infringements. An association of executives that oversees business ethics, the Confederation of Production and Trade, and the leading Chilean newspaper likewise joined forces in publishing competition guidelines. According to an outsourced impact study, three out of four antitrust lawyers in the country reported that trade associations were changing formal or informal procedures as a result of the campaign.[24]

Brazil

The Brazilian competition authority has been advising local authorities on how to handle new passenger transport services emerging through digital platforms.

The Council for Economic Defense (CADE) issued two studies concluding that ridesharing applications can result in several benefits for consumers – these platforms have the potential to serve as a substitute for private cars for one group of consumers, and as a substitute for taxis for another group. Since releasing these studies, local governments, such as the executive government of the city of São Paulo, have been consulting with CADE on the regulation of ridesharing platforms and the market for individual passenger transportation services.

Furthermore, SEAE (Secretariat of Economic Monitoring of the Ministry of Finance) has issued several technical opinions on the potential anticompetitive effect of legislations and regulations, at both the local and national levels. In 2015 alone, for example, it issued over 300 opinions on public hearings about regulatory rules.[25]

At the local level, there is a recurrent demand for evaluating regulatory barriers in the market of transport licensing (mostly driver's licenses) in several States affecting different market dimensions.[26] In 2014, for example, one State regulator prohibited providers of driving lessons from selling their services through websites for group deals. According to the regulator, several providers were offering prices that were too low (below their cost) and consequently failing to fulfill their commitments with

---

24. See *The Competition Policy Advocacy Awards: Changing Mindsets to Transform Markets: Lessons Learned from the First Annual Awards on Competition Policy Advocacy*, World Bank Group (2014), available at https://www.wbginvestmentclimate.org/publications/the-competition-policy-advocacy-awards.cfm.
25. OECD (2016), "ANNUAL REPORT ON COMPETITION POLICY DEVELOPMENTS IN BRAZIL – 2015," DAF/COMP/AR(2016)10, p. 12, available at http://www.oecd.org/officialdocuments/publicdisplaydocumentpdf/?cote=DAF/COMP/AR(2016)10&docLanguage=En.
26. Only in 2016, for example, SEAE issued reports on the potential anticompetitive effects of regulations of traffic Alagoas and Pernambuco, two States in the Northeast region. Since 2010, SEAE has issued similar analysis for other States as Tocantins and Santa Catarina (2010), Rondônia and Paraná (2012), Piauí and Paraíba (2013), Epírito Santo, Mato Grosso do Sul, Mato Grosso and Maranhão (2014). *See* reports in the official SEAE's website, available at http://www.seae.fazenda.gov.br/assuntos/advocacia-da-concorrencia/notas-tecnicas/2016/notas-tecnicas-advocacia-da-concorrencia-2016.

consumers. The prohibition was intended to avoid consumers from being harmed by unrealistic promotions. SEAE issued an opinion pointing out the potential anticompetitive effects of prohibiting market players to freely access these platforms of electronic sales and advertising due to isolated problems caused by individual companies.[27]

§6.05 WHAT LESSONS CAN BE DRAWN FROM RECENT ADVOCACY IN LATIN AMERICA AND THE USEFUL ACTIVITIES FOR THE FUTURE?

The examples presented in this chapter highlight several successful advocacy strategies that other competition authorities in the region may want to adopt to achieve more tangible outcomes. The cases have shown that success was not only reflected in reforms, but also in raising awareness of the benefits of including pro-competition principles within public policies and in contributing to a culture of competition in the country. This section extracts common elements behind the success. It aims to go one-step further, and in extrapolating the lessons learned along with a set of best practices in advocacy around the world, provide a medium-term vision and practical strategies to provide advocacy with an even more important role in Latin America.

The success of advocacy initiatives is often precursor to a broader scope and more explicit mandate. The experience of countries such Colombia and Peru demonstrate that agencies have been able to actively advocate for competition without the explicit mandate gained later on. In the case of Colombia, the agency chose strategic markets to implement their advocacy efforts, while in the case of Peru the agency has been able to combine several tools to send a strong signal about the anticompetitive effects that government interventions can have in several dimensions. These activities were undertaken not only through specific opinions and market studies, but also using mechanisms such as ex officio procedures declaring bureaucratic barriers illegal or assessing government intervention in markets through SOEs. At the beginning, these authorities did not have systematic or mandatory mechanisms to persuade other government institutions to adopt their recommendations. Moreover, the language of these early advocacy mandates was typically vague. Nevertheless, these agencies were able to build a reputation strategically using the tools available and creating the authoritative environment to broaden the scope of their legal mandate later on.

The success of competition advocacy strategies is not necessarily related to resources or the scope of a legal mandate, but may instead be related to strategic development of both. The data does not suggest that successful advocacy requires a high level of staff or monetary resources dedicated to advocacy. For instance, those with impactful initiatives honored by the ICN-WBG Advocacy Contest spent between almost zero and 18% of their budget on advocacy, and dedicated between three and eighty-three staff to advocacy efforts. However, dedicated units for competition advocacy, as in the case of El Salvador, may ensure specialization of a cadre of officials with a solid understanding not only of the economic impact of various policies on

---

27. *See* Nota Técnica from 2014, n.° 06254/2014/DF COGUN/SEAE/MF, available at http://www.seae.fazenda.gov.br/assuntos/advocacia-da-concorrencia/notas-tecnicas/2014/notas-tecnicas-2014/NT-06254-2014_DETRAN-ES.pdf.

competition but also the advocacy tools and strategies that are most likely to achieve results in each case.

Competition authorities achieve results when selecting the right tool for the market problem at hand. For example, the Mexican competition authority, COFECE, understood the relevance of disruptive innovations, which can significantly increase competition, in the key market of transport. It chose to steer the policy discussion early on with an impactful technical opinion that – once put into action – resulted in effects that opened up high replicability potential at the subnational level. These interventions reflect an understanding of how opening markets, designing tenders competitively or – as in the case of Chile – informing business associations about illegal practices can lower the likelihood of anticompetitive practices arising in the first place, to the benefit of the consumer.

Selecting markets and sectors with spillover effects and those at a crossroads for competition dynamics in the medium-term makes for a powerful advocacy target. Colombia's competition agency has been particularly strategic in selecting markets such as telecommunications, with significant spillover effects. Colombia's *ex ante* intervention was strategic in terms of allowing the agency to participate in the future design of the market and ensuring the embedding of pro-competition principles in the future development of the industry. Moreover, the notable effects of these advocacy initiatives reflect the fact that they focused on the critical constraints for these markets.

Strategic partnerships are frequently essential to putting knowledge into action. In the case of El Salvador, MoUs signed with precisely those institutions in charge of reviewing regulations at a central and strategic instance empowered the agency to expand its advocacy activities to a broader universe of government decisions. In the case of Mexico, the collaboration between the competition agency and the regulatory improvement agency has leveraged unexploited synergies among these agencies to work on a common agenda for removing competition barriers at the subnational level, strategy that has become a priority for the government and will be systematically implemented across the thirty-one States in Mexico following a presidential initiative.

Carefully selected media tools and communication strategies are particularly relevant for mobilizing larger constituencies and an incipient competition culture. Chile and El Salvador have been creative in using social media platforms to generate a stronger impact from their advocacy activities, to raise social awareness among stakeholders on the benefits of competition, and to exert pressure to other governmental bodies to take into account the opinions issues by the agency.

There are some useful strategies that can be adopted by competition agencies, building on a set of best practices in advocacy that have been identified by the World Bank Group in several countries around the world.[28]

Resources to conduct advocacy activities are limited and agencies have competing needs. Additionally, effective advocacy requires political capital. Therefore, the selection of the market and sector to be targeted, the activity and intervention to focus on, and the tools must align with the ultimately desired effect in the market.

---

28. http://documents.worldbank.org/curated/en/2016/04/26220953/transforming-markets-through-competition-new-developments-recent-trends-competition-advocacy.

The first decision in an advocacy strategy will be about the sector on which to focus the advocacy activities. Several criteria have been developed within best international practices to guide competition authorities to make this decision strategically. A first set of criteria involve whether the sector contributes significantly to GDP, productivity, or investment; whether it is a source of essential inputs with spillover effects on other sectors; or, whether through its improvement, it would contribute to alleviating poverty. A second set of criteria includes whether the sector presents economic characteristics that generally determine that markets are more concentrated or where collusion is more feasible; or whether the sectors presents significant market deficiencies resulting from low productivity, insufficient, or an excessive number of firms.[29]

In the particular case of Latin America, as the experiences presented highlight, markets that are subject to disruptive innovations can be a strategic target of advocacy efforts given that these innovations occur in markets that are usually protected by vested interests that stand to lose from the disruptions. Therefore, advocating for the right framework that ensures the incentives to innovate and compete in these markets will immediately produce positive changes in the competition dynamics in the sector. Another strategy to be considered is a focus on markets in which recommendations or advocacy activities can have a potential for replicability. This can be the case, for instance, for the activities related to subnational government interventions, given that the rationale and scope of these interventions is usually similar. Therefore, one intervention can impact several subnational markets and be successfully replicated without investing much effort and resources.

Advocacy is more likely to achieve a goal if the goal is narrowly defined in the first place. Interventions should be aimed at tangible and actionable results, so that the agency can better target the audiences to reach and the political economy considerations to face.

The *selection of advocacy tools* is a key step. Advocacy is often understood as an activity associated mainly with conducting market studies or with general awareness raising seminars. As evidenced by the stories presented in this chapter, market studies without a strategy, actionable recommendations, a targeted audience and an analysis of the feasibility of the recommendations – both in terms of content and political economy challenges involved – will likely remain a fruitless endeavor. Awareness raising seminars that explain the law and the benefits of competition in a very broad sense are unlikely to change behaviors of market actors or policy makers. Again, it is critical to clearly set out the behavioral changes that the advocacy activity intends to achieve. Furthermore, the agency's creativity is critical at this stage in order to assess which tools that they have at hand, beyond one-size-fits-all market studies, and which combination of tools could be more effective. Combining advocacy tools with specific objectives such as compliance has been proven a very successful strategy for several countries in Latin America.

The *sequencing of advocacy efforts* is another critical factor behind success. Given the lack of resources and experience of some agencies in Latin America, embarking on

---

29. World Bank Group Markets and Competition Policy Assessment (MCPAT), 2016.

comprehensive and simultaneous competition sectors assessments from the very start without any specific recommendations has not shown to been effective. Instead, young agencies cam start with a targeted advocacy activity with impactful effects, allowing the agency to build credibility based on the effectiveness of its recommendations. Advocacy activities can progressively expand without losing focus on tangible results and feasible recommendations. Media campaigns and social media platforms have proven to be useful complementary strategies to such focused activities.

Additionally, *the engagement with stakeholders early on is key for assuring* the effectiveness of advocacy activities. Raising awareness among citizens and civil society on the benefits of competition should be a priority of advocacy efforts. Moreover, building productive relationships with public stakeholders that will implement reforms should be a critical goal for the competition agencies. The stories presented underscore that several different strategies can be used with this aim, by means of engaging with key policymakers or agencies that centralize the review of significant amount of regulations to then progressively expand the collaboration with regulatory agencies in key markets.

Finally, conducting *ex ante impact assessments and ex post analysis* of advocacy activities, as well as disseminating the results, make these initiatives more tangible and accountable, and helps the agency to make a stronger case among stakeholders for the potential effects of reform. Quantifying the effects of lack of competition in a particular sector and presenting estimates of the prospective benefits of pro-competitive reforms for consumers and business is an effective catalyst for reform momentum. Furthermore, conducting ex post assessments of the reforms that are the result of advocacy activities helps agencies gain credibility and support for further advocacy efforts.

Over the last decade, competition advocacy in Latin America has had a more central role in the rule-making process, mobilizing broader parts of civil society and increasingly embedding competition principles in sectoral policies. This trend is likely to continue as the challenges at the micro-level – such as lack of competition in the markets – are more than ever a burden to macro-economic performance. Some of the competition advocacy initiatives presented in this chapter are already beginning to resemble characteristics and achieve objectives that would be expected from and would correspond to a formal recognition of Competition Policy as a National State Policy.[30] Taking these examples and extrapolating the lessons learned and the common factors behind success can help to set out the foundations for a national competition policy (NCP). Indeed, the growing understanding of the relevance of competition principles as cornerstone to effective economic policies and regulations, and the integration of competition analysis into centrally managed inter-institutional coordination mechanisms could eventually become an effective means to implement more comprehensive and ambitious NCP Plans across Latin America.

---

30. Worldwide, there have been few instances in which a central and high-level public entity has been formally entrusted with an explicit National Competition Policy or Competition Plan that institutes competition principles as a systematic, overarching, priority and long-term central State objective. In 1995, the Australian State and Territory Governments agreed to implement a National Competition Policy (NCP), under the guiding principle that policies that restrict competition should be kept only if they were proven to be in the public interest.

CHAPTER 7
Pro-competitive Regulatory Assessment in Latin America

Ania Thiemann, James Mancini & Rosana Aragón Plaza

§7.01 INTRODUCTION

Policy makers can make use of new policy tools to boost economic growth. Latin American economies tend to be highly regulated and can benefit from more competition in product markets to stimulate growth and job creation in a context of sluggish growth. Regulatory barriers to competition can hamper economic growth by preventing new entry into markets, thereby harming consumers and businesses alike. Competition assessment is a powerful tool to remove such obstacles through identifying and assessing the impact of regulation. Some competition authorities in the region have already started using competition assessment to lift regulatory barriers to competition. There is scope to continue the work, using the OECD's Competition Assessment Toolkit to achieve results and to persuade policy makers to undertake structural reform that may encounter entrenched resistance from incumbents and vested interests. Recent work by competition authorities has demonstrated the benefits to consumers, including in the digital economy.

So, at a time of stagnant global economic growth and an ever-delayed recovery, policymakers are in desperate search of reliable measures to boost employment and innovation, and to address inequality. Competition policy is often an overlooked tool when it comes to growth-boosting policies. While it is a diverse region, Latin American economies[1] share many common features, including historically and culturally, and this communality also stretches to the structure of their economies. As such, the

---

1. While there are indications that Caribbean economies could also benefit from pro-competitive regulatory assessment, they are not discussed here due to limitations on data and the availability of relevant case studies.

policymakers in the region also share the same opportunity to take advantage of the current economic climate to enact structural reform: the promotion of competition through regulatory assessment.[2] Reviewing regulation in order to remove barriers to competition is an activity that helps stimulate productivity growth and supports consumer welfare, and has already been employed with success by a number of competition authorities and sector regulators in the region.

Competition in markets for goods and services incentivizes firms to become more efficient and to cut costs. It spurs the development of new or improved products and services through innovation of production techniques, products and services. It allows consumer preference to play a significant role in determining market composition, while promoting lower prices and greater choice. It helps prevent the accumulation of rents that lead to social inequality. In sum, competition when properly implemented is a productive force that considerably improves market outcomes where it is permitted, and able, to materialize.

Despite its benefits, competition is often forgotten when policymakers look for instruments to stimulate growth and lay the foundations for dynamic markets. Moreover, in economies with a history of strong, centralized governments, there is often a legacy of rigid market regulation or a tendency to turn to regulation first as a policy solution. There are many valid reasons for imposing market regulation that sets limits on firm behavior, especially when market failures[3] arise from situations such as natural monopolies, where efficient market outcomes cannot be attained without a degree of intervention. Regulation may also be needed to protect consumers or the environment. Much too often, however, market regulations meant to achieve these objectives create unnecessary market inefficiencies by inhibiting competition, and therefore result in sub-optimal economic outcomes. Further, those standing to benefit from a limitation of competitive pressures can be strong advocates for competition-distorting regulations, while the original aims, such as protecting consumers, are not achieved. In this context, competition assessment of regulations (identifying and removing regulatory barriers to competition) can provide an objective tool to substantially improve regulation and market outcomes.

This chapter will provide a brief overview of the use of competition assessment in Latin America. It begins by setting out the broad base of evidence in favor of pro-competitive regulatory frameworks. Next, it describes the broad parameters of a regulatory competition assessment, and presents cases in which this tool has been applied in Latin America. Finally, future opportunities for expanding on experience in the region will be identified.

---

2. In this chapter, "competition assessment of regulations" and "competition assessment" are used interchangeably.
3. "Market failure occurs when there are too few markets, non-competitive behaviour, or non-existence, leading to inefficient allocations" (Ledyard, 2008).

§7.02 WHY ARE PRO-COMPETITIVE REGULATORY FRAMEWORKS GOOD FOR LATIN AMERICAN ECONOMIES?

We begin by summarizing the case for competition as a positive economic force. The research briefly summarized below demonstrates why competition assessment of regulation is necessary. First, we discuss how competition has a beneficial impact on consumers and on productivity, as well as on economic growth generally. We will then review how regulatory barriers to competition can harm productivity, job growth and equality, with a particular focus on Latin America.

[A] Competition is Beneficial to Consumers

Consumers have much to gain from competitive markets. The ability to choose between producers and products allows them to select the product or service that best suits their needs at the price and quality that they prefer. Inefficient or unresponsive firms will be pressured to exit the market, while firms with a better price or quality proposition will be incentivized to enter. Competition in upstream markets can also improve prices and quality for consumers throughout the value-chain.

The OECD has collected a wide range of studies which make it clear that consumers stand to benefit from competition, at a minimum through lower prices. For example:

- Pro-competitive deregulation of the U.S. airline industry was estimated to have caused airfares to be 20% lower on average than they would have otherwise been (Morrison and Winston, 1999).
- A study of bus route competition in Ireland found that routes not subject to competition (because they were exempted from competition policy) had prices between 109% and 122% above those on routes subject to competition (Barrett, 2004).
- Permitting the entry of a new firm into Singapore's mobile telephone market in 1996 caused prices to drop by 50%–70% within one year (Singh, 1998).
- The removal of restrictions on the road-freight sector in Mexico beginning in 1989 was estimated to have led to a 30% decrease in prices (Dutz, Hayri and Ibarra, 1999).
- Commission rates on transactions on the Toronto Stock Exchange in Canada dropped by 25% after rate competition was introduced in 1983 (Krinsky and Rotenberg, 1989).
- Deregulation of road freight in France between 1987 and 1990 was estimated to have caused prices to drop by 15% (McKinnon, 1996).
- Quantitative limits on steel imports imposed by the U.S. have been estimated to increase steel prices by approximately 7% (Tarr, 1989).
- Restrictions on the establishment of new automobile dealerships near existing dealers adopted by thirty-six U.S. states between 1963 and 1984 were found to have increased the price of some models by approximately 8% (Rogers, 1986).

- Restrictions to trade in professional services (legal, accountancy, architectural and engineering services) were estimated to have led to prices being between 10%–15% higher than what they would have been in Austria, Mexico, Malaysia, Indonesia and Germany in 2000 (Nguyen-Hong, 2000).
- Regulatory reform in Japan that boosted competition in the electricity sector resulted in prices falling by more than 12% (OECD, 1997).

These studies are just a sample of the overwhelming evidence showing a clear link between allowing competition in a market or sector, and lower consumer prices, improved quality and choice for consumers.

[B] Competition Enhances Productivity

Competitive pressures act as an effective discipline on firm costs and prices while a providing a strong incentive to innovate. The broader economic benefits from this have been well documented, and the evidence makes a convincing case for the promotion or protection of competition in policy design. In particular, competition can be a driver of productivity growth, which is a primary determinant of per capita GDP growth.

The economic evidence that competition drives productivity growth is vast. The relationship is borne out in empirical analyzes of firm-level data[4] and sector-level studies.[5] The mechanisms through which competition improves productivity include both a reallocation of market share from less productive to more productive firms and an improvement of efficiency within firms.[6] The introduction of competition laws that ban cartels, and that therefore promote competition, provides an ideal natural experiment. Studies have confirmed that the adoption of these laws has been followed by increased productivity growth.[7]

Importantly, these results are not confined to high-income countries. As noted by the OECD (2015a), the "link between competition and firm productivity arises in advanced OECD economies as well as in fast-growing emerging economies, especially in Asia, that are often held to exemplify an alternative growth model based on state protection." For those who point to the rapid growth of emerging economies without fully competitive markets and, at the time, without the laws and institutions required to enforce market competition, OECD (2015a, 230–231) notes:

> policymakers in emerging economies sometimes [ask]: if China, India and others grew so fast before introducing competition law, how is it possible to state the importance of competition policy for growth? One answer is that very rapid growth in very low income economies is possible as long as basic conditions for business success – such as reasonable protection of property rights – are in place. Rural

---

4. *See*, for instance, Nickell (1996), Disney, Haskell and Heden (2003), Blundell, Griffith and Van Reenen (1999), Januszewski (2002), Symeonidis (2008), Syverson (2004a), Ahn (2002), and Bourles et al. (2013).
5. *See*, for instance, Sakakibara and Porter (2001), Baek, Kim and Kwon (2009) and Andrews, Criscuolo and Gal (2015).
6. Arnold et al., 2011; Schmidt, 1997; Nalebuff and Stiglitz, 1983.
7. *See*, for instance, Symeonidis (2008).

exodus allows industries to expand rapidly taking on low-skilled labour. Such industries, typically in manufacturing, may have rather low productivity but nonetheless contribute substantially to GDP growth. However, later on the presence of numerous inefficient firms in the sector can become a significant drag on the economy. Then in order to move to the next level of economic development, effective competition is needed. In other words, putting in place effective competition policies, including a well-designed and appropriately enforced competition law, could be an important part of avoiding the middle-income trap and moving to the next phase of development, when the easy gains available to low-income economies have been exhausted.

The relationship between competition and productivity also holds in international trade. That is, foreign competition can have a positive impact on domestic productivity. Aghion et al. (2004 and 2009), for instance, found that reforms in the U.K. during the 1980s, which liberalized several markets to allow foreign firm entry, led to greater innovation and faster total-factor productivity growth of domestic incumbents. Aggregate productivity consequently grew as well. Further, Griffith (2006) finds positive productivity effects from the creation of the EU's Single Market. Sakakibara and Porter (2001) demonstrated that the sectors in Japan that have been the most exposed to foreign competition (through fewer trade barriers) were successful competitors on world markets, while protected sectors (such as aircraft manufacturing) did not reach similar levels of productivity.

Thus, exposure to competition from both foreign and domestic sources has been demonstrated in a variety of contexts to lead to productivity growth, and therefore economic growth.

[C] Regulatory Restrictions on Competition Harm Growth

An absence of competitive pressures in a market harms growth and productivity. One of the most common reasons for weak competition is over-regulation. Regulations, such as norms, safety standards and operation licenses that restrict market entry and competition are often defended on the grounds that they protect jobs. However, there is a substantial body of evidence on the benefits of eliminating such regulatory restrictions.

Using the OECD's Product Market Regulation indicator, OECD research demonstrates that the degree of regulatory restrictiveness in a market in a country is negatively correlated with productivity growth (Arnold, Nicoletti and Scarpetta, 2011). Box 7.1 describes research by Cole et al. which demonstrates that competition can be a particularly effective tool in Latin America to promote productivity and therefore economic growth.

> **Box 7.1 Cole, Ohanian, Riascos and Schmitz on competition restrictions and competition in Latin America**
>
> In a 2004 paper called "Latin America in the Rear View Mirror," Cole et al. compare Latin American economic growth with Western and "successful" East Asian countries. Using a neoclassical growth model, the authors find that Latin America's relatively slow historical growth could be attributed to differences in productivity levels, rather than human capital, relative to the other countries studied.
>
> Next, the authors examined barriers to competition in Latin America relative to the Western and East Asian comparator countries. They found that Latin America exhibited "many more international and domestic competitive barriers." These barriers included high international trade barriers and high barriers to entry for domestic firms (in the form of firm registration, access to capital, job security measures and political influence in access to funding). As a result, the authors conclude that "competitive barriers are a promising channel for understanding low Latin [productivity]."
>
> To further substantiate these findings with a micro-level approach, Cole et al. consider the productivity impacts of the addition or removal of barriers to competition in several industries. Specifically, they find that the reversal of import bans on foreign-produced computers in Brazil, privatization of Brazilian iron ore enterprises, opening the copper industry to new entrants in Chile and the privatization of Argentinian and Mexican SOEs resulted in significant productivity improvements in each case.

The conclusions of Cole et al. remain highly relevant today: OECD statistics indicate that productivity levels in Latin America continue to fall behind many other regions. For example, 2014 average labor productivity in Latin America countries was at least 50% lower than the upper-half of OECD countries in Argentina, Brazil, Colombia, Costa Rica, Chile, Mexico and Peru, as shown in the figure 7.2 (OECD, 2016).

Source: OECD, 2016, Figure 1.2.

Figure 7.1 Gap in 2014 Labor Productivity Relative to the Upper-Half of OECD Countries

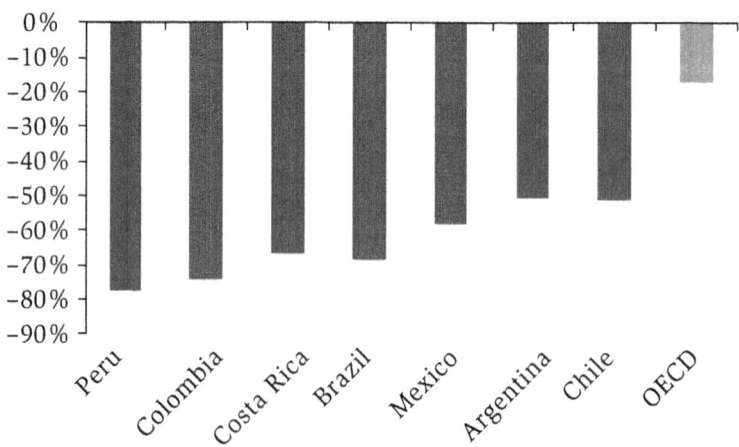

Source: OECD Economic Outlook 2013, Volume 1, Figure 4.6.

In addition to productivity, regulatory barriers to competition can have a negative impact on aggregate job growth. Regulation that restricts competition, whether by limiting the entry of potential competitors into a market or by limiting the intensity of competition between firms, is sometimes defended on the grounds that competition would result in job losses. However, research conducted by the OECD and others[8] indicates that pro-competitive regulatory reform in product markets can lead to both short- and long-term job growth. In cases where competition is followed by short-term job losses, research suggests that these losses are transitory at worst and the long-term impact of competition remains positive.

Further, measures to protect firms from competition lead to the accumulation of rents, which have a negative impact on growth. Schwab and Werker (2014) find that countries where the manufacturing sector earns high rents (due in part to high tariffs and anticompetitive regulation) grow more slowly. The effect can be strong enough to overcome the "catch up" advantages of poorer countries, leading to slower growth than what it would be in a more liberalized economy. This suggests that when emerging economies liberalize and open up their industries, there is scope for (even) faster economic growth.

The impact of regulatory restrictions on competition is highly significant. In particular, the removal of restrictions in product markets has the potential to raise GDP by more than 10% in some large emerging economies, as shown in figure 7.2.

Figure 7.2 Potential GDP Gain from Attaining Product Market Regulation Best Practice in Selected Countries in 2060

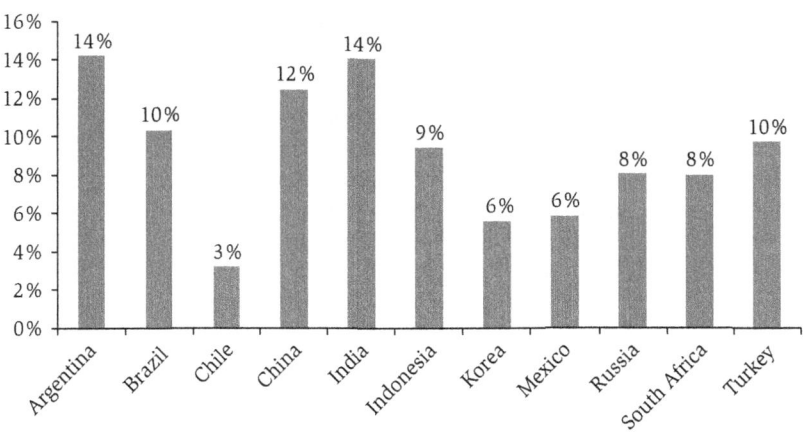

Source: Egert, B. and P. Gal (2016), "The Quantification of Structural Reforms: A New Framework," *OECD Economics Department Working Paper*, forthcoming.

---

8. *See*, OECD (2015a, p. 231); Cacciatore et al., (2012).

Finally, the removal of regulatory barriers to competition can make economic growth more equal. Recent OECD studies (Causa et al., 2014; OECD, 2015b) have found, using both micro- and macro-level data, that pro-competitive measures (including reductions in the barriers to competition) narrow income inequality. Properly enforced competition law helps prevent inefficiency and favoritism, and contributes to keeping both businesses and governments alike accountable and transparent. Thus, sound competition policies and the proper enforcement of competition law also favor inclusive growth, by ensuring that economic growth is accompanied by policies that support access to markets by companies, and to goods and services by consumers, including the poorest.

[D]   Latin America Faces a High Regulatory Burden

There is strong evidence to suggest that Latin American economies are highly regulated. Figure 2 shows that there would be substantial economic benefits for emerging economies, including Latin American economies, if they removed regulatory restrictions in product market to stimulate competition. These findings have been echoed by the International Monetary Fund (2015), World Bank (2014) and the Inter-American Development Bank (Pages-Serra, 2010). The fact that Latin America appears to have a high regulatory burden is also reflected in the observations made by businesses themselves. For example, the World Bank Group's Enterprise Surveys observe that firms in Latin America and the Caribbean report "fac[ing] a greater regulatory burden than firms in the rest of the world," with 13% of senior management's time being spent on regulation, significantly greater than the time spent in East Asia and the Pacific (7%), South Asia (6%), Sub-Saharan Africa (8%), and Eastern Europe and Central Asia (11%) (World Bank, 2014).

There are preliminary indications that progress has been made in Chile and Mexico on reducing competition-limiting regulation, although the extent of product market regulation in Brazil and Mexico remains significantly above the OECD average (see Figure 3 below). Similar trends are evident in the OECD's regulation index for professional services and retail trade for Chile and Mexico between 1998 and 2013.

Chapter 7: Pro-competitive Regulatory Assessment in Latin America §7.03

Figure 7.3   Product Market Regulation Index in 2013 in Selected Countries

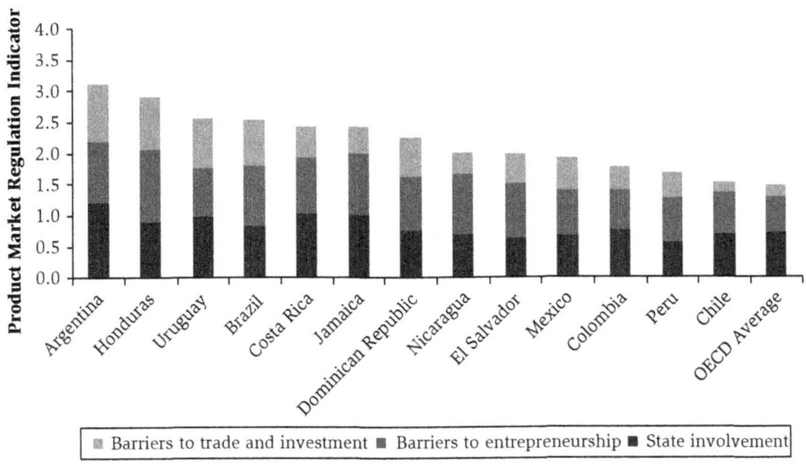

[Bar chart showing Product Market Regulation Indicator for: Argentina, Honduras, Uruguay, Brazil, Costa Rica, Jamaica, Dominican Republic, Nicaragua, El Salvador, Mexico, Colombia, Peru, Chile, OECD Average. Components: Barriers to trade and investment, Barriers to entrepreneurship, State involvement.]

Source: Chart from OECD (2016), p. 10.

Next, we will discuss competition assessment: how it works, how to perform it and what the expected benefits are. In the following section we then move on to discuss ways in which policymakers in Latin America use competition assessment to tackle competition-limiting regulation in order to unlock the benefits of competition.

§7.03   WHAT IS COMPETITION ASSESSMENT OF REGULATIONS?

Based on this evidence, what can policymakers in Latin America do to successfully promote competition? Recent experience in the region, as well as international best practice, suggest that two of the most effective measures are: (i) implementing regulatory reform that increase market competition through the examining of existing regulation, and (ii) maintaining a sound competitive framework through the careful *ex ante* analysis of prospective policies or regulations that may affect competition in a sector. However, assessing anticompetitive regulation and identifying alternatives can be challenging. For instance, there may be conflicting or competing policy goals motivating a particular law or regulation, or the incumbents are benefiting from the current regulatory regime and will resist any change. As such, a careful review of regulations, taking into account their initial policy objective and potential alternatives, is required to identify reforms that eliminate unnecessary barriers to competition.

Policymakers, including competition authorities performing a competition advocacy function, should therefore undertake competition assessment to achieve this goal. To do so, they should emphasize the use of a transparent and comprehensive methodology to enhance credibility. Sectors should be prioritized and selected for analysis based on factors including relative size in the economy, potential for driving future economic growth or other economic policy objectives, and the extensiveness of regulatory restrictions in the sector. The outcome will be an evaluation that can be used to make decisions taking into account the market impact of new or existing regulation. The OECD's Competition Assessment Toolkit[9] proposes a methodology for carrying out this analysis, and is described further in Box 7.2 below.

Box 7.2   OECD Competition Assessment Toolkit

The OECD Competition Toolkit was developed to assess and identify regulation that contains barriers to competition or that have anticompetitive effects. This includes analyzes of existing policies as well as regulation at the drafting stage. The Toolkit is designed for use by a wide range of policymakers, legislators, public officials and others seeking to implement and evaluate policy, and does not require economics or competition law expertise.

The Toolkit has been used by several governments, both OECD and non-OECD members. In addition, the OECD has applied the Toolkit to assess regulation for anticompetitive effects in Mexico,[10] in a sequence of projects from 2008; in Greece in three different projects since 2013, and most recently in Romania, in a project that was completed in May 2016.

Competition assessment based on the OECD Toolkit involves an initial screening using a checklist to identify regulations that may cause harm to competition.

The Checklist consists of a series of questions that provide an initial check on whether the regulation under analysis limits (Toolkit, Vol I., pp. 8–18):

- the number or range of suppliers;
- the ability of suppliers to compete;
- the incentive of suppliers to compete; and
- the choices and information available to consumers.

If the regulation is found to fall into any of these four categories, it means that there is a potential harm to competition form the restriction. The regulation is then subjected to an in-depth review of the impact on and possible harm to competition arising from the restriction. If there is sufficient data, the impact on consumer welfare or on the market can be quantified. If the impact is deemed harmful, the Toolkit provides a process for determining potential alternatives regulation (or for determining whether the regulation should be abolished altogether).

In addition to providing guidance, the Toolkit also helps the advocacy process in order to gain political support for reforms, as it contains analysis that quantifies the benefits of reforms, including several case studies from around the world, and empirical evidence from more than 200 studies collected by the OECD and hosted in a database.

Source: OECD Competition Assessment Toolkit.

---

9. Available for free download at www.oecd.org/competition/assessment-toolkit.htm.
10. *See* OECD (2011); OECD and Comisión Federal de Competencia, México (2010 and 2012).

> **Box 7.3 OECD Competition Assessment of Greece (2013)[11]**
>
> Over an eleven-month period in 2013, the OECD, in cooperation with the Government of Greece, conducted competition assessment of the food processing, retail trade, building materials and tourism sectors using the OECD Competition Assessment Toolkit. The review of 1,053 legal documents resulted in 555 restrictions on competition being identified, and 329 recommendations being formulated to remove restrictive legislation and regulations with a direct negative impact on competition. The principal issues identified in the regulations reviewed included obsolete legislative restrictions left over in the body of law for decades, numerous barriers to entry, price distortions and third-party levies. The scale of the impact to competition of these restrictions, and the economic benefit that would accrue as a result of their removal, were estimated, demonstrating the value that competition assessment can generate for economies. For example:
>
> - Consumers would gain an estimated EUR 33 million annually from the removal on restrictions with regard to the regulatory definition and sale of fresh milk;
> - Permitting Sunday trading would create an estimated 30,000 new jobs and generate EUR 2.5 billion in new annual retail expenditure;
> - Removing anticompetitive restrictions on cruises leaving Greek ports would result in an estimated increase in direct and indirect revenue of EUR 65 million per annum; and
> - Liberalizing advertising restrictions, including removing taxes on advertising, would generate an estimated EUR 1.8 billion in consumer benefits per year.
>
> *Source: OECD Competition Assessment of Greece (2014).*

§7.04 RECENT EXPERIENCE OF COMPETITION ASSESSMENT IN LATIN AMERICA

Competition assessment in Latin America is gaining a track record as a policy tool that has proven its worth in some jurisdictions. In particular, the results from regulatory competition assessment have been a clear voice in favor of competition in policy debates that have otherwise been blurred by competing interests. This has in many cases meant standing up for consumers whose perspective is often forgotten in such debates. The following section will discuss case studies of recent assessments completed by competition authorities in the region. We have organized the case studies according to the nature of limitations to competition they identified, based on the classification in the OECD Competition Assessment Toolkit as listed above. The assessments carried out relate to both existing and proposed (i.e., draft) regulations. The aim of discussing them here is in order for them to serve as an example for officials to consider when seeking to undertake exercises in similar sectors, or with respect to similar types of restrictions.

While the majority of the examples below were conducted by competition authorities, competition assessment can also be undertaken by sector regulators, or government officials in charge of drafting regulation. Indeed, the OECD Competition

---

11. Full report available at http://www.oecd.org/competition/greece-competition-review-2013.htm.

Assessment Toolkit was originally designed for government officials, and hence the methodology does not require an in-depth knowledge of competition law or economics in order to be effective. Ideally, however, any assessment should involve cooperation between all parties involved in the sector under scrutiny: the competition authority, the sector regulator (where applicable) and the government experts with responsibility for the sector.

Table 7.1 Summary of Selected Competition Assessments in Latin America

Assessment Subject and Author	Limitations on Competition Identified			
	Number or Range of Suppliers	Ability of Suppliers to Compete	Incentives of Suppliers to Compete	Choices and Information Available to Consumers
Agri-food sector COFECE (Mexico, 2016)	•	•	•	•
Banking COPROCOM (Costa Rica, 2007)	•	•	•	
Bureaucratic barriers to competition (various): INDECOPI (Peru)	•	•		
Construction: Fiscalía Nacional Económica (Chile, 2009)	•		•	
Consumer fuel stations: COFECE (Mexico, 2015)	•		•	•
Hydrocarbon policy: ACODECO (Panama, 2003)	•		•	
Iron and steel products: COFECE (Mexico, 2015)	•	•		
Pharmaceuticals: Inter-American Development Bank (Central America and Panama, 2011)	•			
Retail gasoline and diesel: COFECE (Mexico, 2016)		•	•	•
Rice: COPROCOM (Costa Rica, 2006)	•	•	•	•
Taxis: CADE (Brazil, 2015)	•	•		•
Taxis: COFECE (Mexico, 2015)	•	•		•

Assessment Subject and Author	Limitations on Competition Identified			
	Number or Range of Suppliers	Ability of Suppliers to Compete	Incentives of Suppliers to Compete	Choices and Information Available to Consumers
Telecommunications: Competition Regional Centre for Latin America (Latin America, 2013)	•		•	
Telecommunications: Fiscalía Nacional Económica (Chile, 2010)	•	•		

Table 7.1 shows that competition assessment has often been useful to identify a broad range of restrictions. The sections below will highlight some of the principal restrictions identified in a selection of these studies.

[A] Assessments That Found Limitations to the Number or Range of Suppliers

Limitations to the number or range of suppliers in a market (in other words, entry barriers) are among the most common barriers to competition identified in the competition assessments reviewed. These restrictions mean that firms already present in the market or sector under review are subject to less intense competition than would otherwise be the case, and therefore that there is less pressure on these firms to reduce costs and innovate in order to deliver cheaper or better products or services to consumers. For instance, limits to the number of suppliers in a market or stringent criteria for obtaining a permit or operation license effectively bar new firm entry, and thereby grant incumbents a greater market share than a competitive outcome would generate.

Licensing schemes are a common restriction to the range of permitted suppliers, for example in the passenger transportation market, which has occupied several Latin American competition authorities in recent years. The continuing rise of mobile car-hailing applications in the region, such as Uber and EasyTaxi, means that debates about these limitations are not likely to go away.

The Mexican competition authority (COFECE) issued an opinion on the passenger transportation market in June 2015. COFECE noted that the development of mobile applications for the transport of passengers offers a solution to information asymmetries and coordination deficiencies existing between clients and service providers, contributes to urban mobility, fosters innovation and offers efficient consumption options that increase societal welfare. Therefore, the authority recommended the legal recognition of this new type of service provision.

COFECE's competition assessment proposed that any new legal framework (including a licensing system) should be limited to safeguarding public and user safety, for instance by requiring drivers to prove possession of insurance, or by reviewing drivers' abilities and criminal records. The authority suggested that the verification of these requirements could be carried out by accredited third parties or by the companies themselves. Moreover, the authority noted that any new legal framework should avoid competitive restrictions, including prior authorization or registration of eligible vehicles, fee regulations and vehicle color requirements.

Similarly, a study of the individual passenger transportation market was published in 2015 by the Department of Economic Studies (DEE) of the Brazilian competition authority (CADE). DEE found that applications such as Uber:

- offer a satisfactory self-regulatory mechanism;
- cater to a demand heretofore unsatisfied by taxis (being a better alternative to car ownership for some consumers and to taxis for others); and
- increase competition in the market for individual passenger transportation.

Building on this positive assessment, the DEE also analyzed the potential for taxi market deregulation on the basis of empirical research. The DEE determined that entry deregulation in the form of the elimination of rules that limit market access, has the general effect of increasing supply. The study did not find any economic justification for a prohibition on new service providers entering the market given that the entrance of new agents in general tends to have a positive effect from the point of view of competition and consumers.

The competition authority in Panama, Acodeco (formerly known as Clicac), has also published a number of opinions on proposed regulatory changes that would have established new limitations on the range of suppliers in several sectors. For example, between 2003 and 2004 the authority analyzed a proposed draft regulation (and its subsequent modifications) establishing a national hydrocarbons policy. The competition assessment found both anticompetitive measures, such as entry requirements that unfairly favored existing companies in the market (including minimum financial or experience requirements), and pro-competitive measures.

COFECE (Mexico) issued an opinion in 2015 in response to proposed restrictions on market entry in the retail fuel market. The Coahuila State Congress United Commissions of Economic Development, Competitiveness and Tourism released a report on a draft bill to be passed in that State. The United Commissions' report advocated for the introduction of a mandatory minimum distance of 1,500 meters[12] between service stations for the direct sale of fuel to the general public. COFECE's assessment found that these limitations on the entry of new competitors were not justified by any legitimate public policy objectives, nor were they determined by market conditions. In particular, COFECE indicated that the proposed changes would benefit established service stations, whose turnover would be protected from competition, without delivering any efficiency gains in terms of price or quality improvements.

Regulatory barriers to competition need not be motivated by a desire to actually limit market entry in a specific market in order to have an impact on the number or

---

12. The minimum distance was 10,000 meters for rural areas with highways.

range of suppliers. Often, technical requirements for market participation that are motivated by consumer protection or other policy concerns (such as health and safety regulation) can be unnecessarily restrictive. Peru's competition authority, Indecopi, has a specific Commission (the "CEB") for the elimination of these sorts of restrictions, which it terms *bureaucratic barriers to competition* (Indecopi, 2016). In creating the CEB, Indecopi noted that, although bureaucratic barriers do not necessarily have a negative impact on society, they may restrict competition when they are illegal or unreasonable. The CEB evaluates governmental processes and rules (be they national, regional or local) in order to determine whether they impose illegal or unreasonable bureaucratic barriers, and if so, recommends their elimination. The CEB does not deal with requirements imposed by law.

The CEB has been highly active and, while its work is not expressly labeled as such, it has conducted a wide range of competition assessments which have identified restrictions on the range of suppliers in markets. For instance, in late 2014 and 2015 it issued a number of resolutions declaring administrative requirements and restrictions at the national level to be illegal including, among many others:

- the requirement to be in possession of a civil defense report in order to apply for authorization to operate as an educational institution;[13]
- requirements relating to the supply of individual personal safety services established by the Ministry for the Interior;[14]
- the refusal of a municipality to install radio electrical base stations and/or infrastructure for the supply of telecommunications services;[15] and
- the imposition of age limits for vehicles permitted to transport goods imposed by the Ministry of Transport and Communications.[16]

Multilateral studies have also uncovered restrictions of this nature. The Central American Competition Policy Group and the Inter-American Development Bank published, in January 2011, a report on the competition conditions in the pharmaceutical sector in Central America and Panama. The report recommended against certain policy measures on the grounds that they would limit new entry in the market, including the entry of the generic producers that are vital for access to pharmaceuticals for lower-income population groups in the region. The report made recommendations against rules or practices preventing laboratories from directly participating in tenders, or from directly selling to pharmacies, since this hindered competition at the distribution level.

---

13. *See* Resolution N° 0437-2015/CEB-INDECOPI.
14. *See* Resolution N° 0425-2015/CEB-INDECOPI.
15. *See* Resolution N° 0406-2015/CEB-INDECOPI.
16. *See* Resolution N°0584-2014/CEB-INDECOPI.

[B] Assessments That Found Limitations to the Ability of Suppliers to Compete

Limitations on the ability of suppliers to compete often involve measures that provide advantages to a particular group of suppliers (including incumbents), or otherwise prevent newcomers from exerting pressure on their competitors in all dimensions of competition (including price and quality).

Such measures may come in the form of import restrictions meant to protect domestic producers. For example, in its study of the Agri-food sector, COFECE (2016) identified health standards associated with farm product distribution and customs measures, particularly high most-favored nation (MFN) duties and phytosanitary measures, as unnecessarily restrictive limitations to foreign competition.

Technical regulations can also act as competitive barriers and disadvantage both foreign and domestic suppliers relative to competitors with more influence over the design of these regulations. COFECE issued an opinion in 2015 on proposed iron and steel product regulations. The proposed rules required iron and steel products manufactured or sold in Mexico to comply with certain standard specifications and test methods, on the grounds of user safety. COFECE determined that the proposal effectively made 104 voluntary Mexican Norms mandatory and potentially applicable to a broader range of products. The assessment considered the core objective of the regulation[17] (relative to the status quo), and found that there was no evidence suggesting that the existing regulatory framework was insufficient. Further, the negative impact of the proposed regulatory change included potentially reducing the import of foreign products and the imposition of additional costs on a sub-section of producers in the market.

A 2007 study of Costa Rica's banking sector identified similar issues. Specifically, Costa Rica's competition authority (COPROCOM) found that operating regulations differed between public and private banking, as did the regulatory and tax segmentation of offshore banking. Moreover, certain banks, created through specific laws, still benefitted from special treatment relative to their competitors. In both cases, some banks were rendered less able to compete than others, leading to distorted market outcomes.

[C] Assessments That Found Limitations to Incentives of Suppliers to Compete

When suppliers are protected from competition law, or if there are regulatory provisions that facilitate their cooperation (for instance, in setting prices and standards), the competitive potential of a market is limited. As with other limitations, the impact on consumers and productivity can be significant.

---

17. Competition assessment methodologies such as the OECD Competition Toolkit include seeking to identify the policy objective of the regulation, and to assess the proportionality of the objective against the effect of the regulation on the market.

For example, a competition assessment of regulation conducted by Fiscalía Nacional Económica (Fiscalía, 2014), governing the Chilean construction sector and its public tender procedures for work contracts found that public authorities may have been facilitating collusive agreements in public work tender procedures. In particular, the Ministry of Public Works could open what were termed "Special Registries" for tenders, inviting only certain contractors to bid. Further, Fiscalía drew attention to the fact that prices used in project budgets were established on a case-by-case basis, a level of discretion that could result in regulatory capture or collusive agreements.

In 2006, COPROCOM published a report on the competitive conditions of the rice sector in Costa Rica. This competitive assessment addressed the effects of regulation in the rice sector from a consumer welfare perspective. Specifically, the report reviewed the effects of the actions of Conarroz (the public entity responsible for regulating prices and determining when preferential import duties are required as a result of rice shortages) in light of its objectives to guarantee the rational and equitable participation of rice producers and agri-food businesses in the rice sector, while promoting competitiveness and development. Conarroz was responsible, *inter alia*, for setting the minimum prices that agri-businesses would be required to pay to rice producers, and for determining the amount of rice that should be imported in order to make up for shortages of domestic product. COPROCOM found that Conarroz did not meet its goals, and in fact harmed competition and consumer welfare through imposing regulatory restrictions that limited the incentives of producers to compete.

To alleviate these restrictions to competition, COPROCOM recommended the adoption of a number of measures: (i) the reduction of import duties on *pilado* (ready to consume) rice; (ii) the gradual deregulation of prices established along the supply chain, accompanied by the monitoring of price formation mechanisms; (iii) the substitution of the minimum price system for direct subsidies to farmers in order to support the profitability of rice agriculture; (iv) the substitution of the system of maximum prices with direct subsidies to ensure that the low-income population can have access to adequate rice consumption; and (v) improving the transparency of Conarroz's decision-making mechanisms.

Also in the agri-food sector, COFECE (2016) recommended the elimination of all legal provisions allowing producer associations and organizations to fix prices or quantities, share markets and exchange information for these purposes, and to eliminate the requirement to obtain the authorization of farmers' associations in order to transport animals.

The Competition Regional Centre for Latin America (CRCAL) published a report on the application of competition law in the Latin American telecommunications sector.[18] The report discusses some frequent competition issues that may stem from legal requirements in certain jurisdictions. For instance, mandated network sharing can increase the likelihood of anticompetitive agreements. The report includes a suggested checklist of elements that authorities must consider when assessing the legitimacy of these agreements.

---

18. The report formed part of a partnership program between the World Bank and the Bank of Netherlands, "Strengthening competition policy in Latin American Countries."

[D] Assessments That Found Limitations to the Choices and Information Available to Consumers

Finally, regulatory restrictions to the information or choices available to consumers can lessen the intensity of competition and create market distortions. These restrictions either bar consumers from purchasing certain products or limit their ability to make informed decisions.

COFECE's agri-food study identified restrictions of this type when it analyzed rules for the participation of farmers and ranchers in cooperative insurance funds. These rules prevented farmers participating in one fund from also contributing to another cooperative insurance fund. In fact, the membership of farmers or ranchers in a cooperative insurance fund could be suspended or terminated in the event they obtained insurance from another cooperative fund. COFECE indicated in its study that these restrictions were anticompetitive, and significantly narrowed the insurance options available to farmers and ranchers.

§7.05 EMERGING OPPORTUNITIES FOR COMPETITION ASSESSMENT IN LATIN AMERICA

The examples that we have discussed show that competition assessment is being employed with some frequency to evaluate potential and existing policies in Latin America. Competition authorities, regulators and policymakers should take inspiration from this tool, and its increasing use in certain jurisdictions, such as Mexico. Beyond more frequent use, there are specific areas in which Latin American policymakers have an opportunity to produce results that will yield real economic benefits through competition assessment. For instance, policymakers can conduct *ex post* analyzes of the impact of existing regulatory regimes, while competition authorities can carry out *ex post* assessment of past competition enforcement actions to constantly improve their advocacy efforts. Further, the competition assessment methodology can be used to analyze regulatory obstacles to innovation, for instance in the nascent digital economy. This is particularly important in light of the benefits such innovations can bring to consumers in emerging markets, and the conflict between certain market participants and regulators that such innovations may involve.

[A] *Ex post* Assessment

Competition assessment of regulatory restrictions can generate significant benefits for markets and consumers in the short run, and promote economic growth in the longer run by making markets more dynamic through the removal of barriers to competition. Attaining these benefits however depends on governments (including regulators) making available the resources necessary to conduct the assessments on the one hand, and on the other hand on the willingness of governments to accept the recommendations eventually emanating from the assessments, whether it is *ex post* or *ex ante*. To persuade governments to undertake such efforts, demonstrating the impact of regulations, whether through quantification or qualitatively assessment, is important in order to promote the continuing use of competition assessment, and to build awareness of the impact of regulatory limitations on competition, economic growth and consumer welfare. Advocacy of this kind has been supported in recent years by the World Bank Group which has conducted an "Advocacy contest," rewarding competition agencies that have demonstrated novel or innovative ways to use advocacy to promote competition, including the use of competition assessment. The Hellenic Competition Commission was rewarded in 2014 for its Competition Assessment project. Winners in the 2015–2016 contest included COFECE, Mexico, for issuing an opinion "recommending that local governments formally recognize the services provided by Transportation Network Companies (TNCs), such as Uber and Cabify, and *avoid imposing regulations that would restrict their ability to compete.*"[19] CADE, Brazil, received an honorable mention for issuing an opinion in favor of allowing ridesharing platforms after demonstrating consumer benefits from such applications.[20]

Recent competition assessments in Latin America have helped shape public policy. Several of the assessments described above resulted in, or at least contributed to, the modification or abandonment of proposed restrictions to competition, such as COFECE's studies and comments with respect to iron and steel, consumer fuel stations, retail gas and diesel, and passenger transportation markets, as well as ACODECO's comments on Panama's hydrocarbons policy. Others resulted in changes to existing policies or regulations, in particular, Fiscalía's competition analysis of the Chilean construction sector and INDECOPI's recommendations on the elimination of bureaucratic barriers to competition.

As such it is likely that that significant economic harm from regulatory barriers to competition has been prevented or alleviated thanks to the competition assessment exercises carried out. In an era of strong limits on public spending, however, users of competition assessment may need to go further to demonstrate their value. There will always be budget constraints, and a general reticence on the part of policymakers to challenge the status quo or indeed special interests. In the face of such resistance, even initial attempts at quantifying consumer and economic benefits from the removal of limitations to competition resulting from the adoption of competition assessment recommendations could go a long way in laying the foundations for a broader public discussion about the benefits of competition and the impact of regulations that limit it. Policymakers may find that such a discussion is necessary to overcome the intransigence of market participants who have a vested interest in perpetuating limitations to competition.

Opponents of competition in markets will point to the need to protect local jobs and businesses. *Ex post* evaluations of competition assessments, and of competition enforcement decisions, could be an effective answer to these critics. The OECD has

---

19. *See*: http://www.worldbank.org/en/events/2015/10/30/the-2015---2016-competition-advocacy-contest-how-to-build-a-culture-of-competition-for-private-sector-development-and-economic-growth#5 [emphasis added].
20. *Ibid.*

developed specific guidance on methodologies and approaches to conducting *ex post* assessment of competition interventions (including competition assessment).[21]

[B]   Digital Economy Innovations

Several markets in Latin America are evolving rapidly thanks to innovations enabled by new technology, broadly classified as the "digital economy." Prominent examples of these innovations have taken advantage of mobile technologies and increasing data processing power to offer new and easily scalable services to consumers. They may also rely on business models premised on the avoidance of regulation and unnecessary costs. In so doing, these innovations may offer significant benefits to consumers in the form of less expensive, better quality services (for instance in taxi services) that are more tailored to their preferences. However, as recent examples such as Uber show, these innovations can foster an atmosphere of acrimony among regulators and incumbents. There may be calls for the enforcement of existing regulations or the imposition of new regulations on digital economy innovations. In this challenging atmosphere, policymakers can use competition assessment to evaluate existing regulation, assess competing regulatory proposals and to promote the interests of consumers through competition.

Competition assessment is a valuable tool for approaching controversial issues using a transparent, reasoned approach. In these situations, it is first worth asking whether the rationale of current regulations is relevant in markets undergoing significant innovation, and whether the design of regulations limits competition and innovation. It may well be that regulations reflect established business models, obsolete technologies and consumer protection issues that may be irrelevant in today's market. As a result, digital innovations can be used as a valuable opportunity to assess existing regulations and ensure that they continue to achieve their goals while promoting innovation.

Policymakers should also use competition assessment to examine any new regulations that are proposed in response to digital economy innovations. These proposals may come from incumbents harmed from new digital innovations, or may reflect a desire to return to the status quo by expanding the scope of regulations to new market entrants. As demonstrated by CADE and COFECE's studies of the passenger transportation industry, however, such proposals can harm consumers despite their stated intention to protect them. Competition assessment can help identify pro-competitive alternatives to achieving legitimate policy goals, including consumer protection.

Competition authorities have a particular role in advocating for competition in the wake of controversial innovations. They can use competition assessment to identify proactive solutions to incumbent/innovator conflicts in regulated markets, bringing together regulators, disruptive innovators and incumbents before controversy

---

21. For more information, please visit: http://www.oecd.org/competition/evaluationofcompetitioninterventions.htm.

sets in. This could help prevent complete bans on innovations, as well as explicit regulatory non-compliance by innovators.[22]

§7.06 CONCLUSION

Competition is a powerful driver of productivity and economic growth, and it delivers substantial benefits to consumers. Restrictions on competition achieve the opposite, by for instance preventing the entry of new firms with fresh business models, ideas or processes that would put pressure on incumbent firms to better serve consumers. Regulation can also unfairly advantage certain firms over others, or enable firms to collude amongst themselves. It is not difficult to imagine how this can harm innovation, productivity and even income equality, since a protected few stand to gain from all consumers. Despite the likely voices of opposition from entrenched interests, policymakers would therefore be well-advised to identify ways to promote competition to achieve their economic objectives.

In so doing, policymakers should use competition assessment to ensure that the benefits of competition receive the attention they deserve. It has already been implemented by competition authorities across Latin America, but many opportunities remain, including for policymakers in government, seeking to understand the economic impacts of current or proposed regulations. *Ex post* evaluations of past assessments can help clarify these opportunities, and provide the basis for a public discussion about the benefits of competition. Such a discussion is needed now more than ever, as regulatory frameworks in several markets are being challenged by the wide range of new, competitive digital innovations that are being offered to consumers. Regulation can often achieve policymaker objectives without standing in the way of consumer benefits, and competition assessment is a valuable tool for pursuing this outcome.

---

22. The Latin American and Caribbean Competition Forum, organized by the Inter-American Development Bank OECD, discussed these issues and their particular implications for the region in April 2016. For more information, please visit: http://laccf2016mexico.com/en.

PART II   Enforcement Experiences:
          Anticompetitive Practices and
             Merger Control

CHAPTER 8
Bid Rigging in Public Procurement in Colombia: Evolution and Challenges

Germán Enrique Bacca Medina

§8.01 INTRODUCTION

Bid rigging in public procurement is perhaps the most deplorable of all anticompetitive conducts. With this behavior, not only the collective constitutional right of free economic competition is affected, but also the governmental resources that ultimately belong to all citizens. Agents that are involved in this type of cartelization arrange in an artificial way the conditions in which they apply to public selection processes, in order to be awarded with the respective contract by procurement entities.

When this behavior occurs, there is no genuine competition and bidders who are not part of the cartel are illegally obstructed. Moreover, one of the fundamental objectives of public procurement is to find better goods and services at lower prices, and such objective is directly affected with bid rigging practices, since the natural incentive of cartelized agents is to substantially increase the value of products and, in some cases, affect their quality. The conduct is so serious for the society that even in countries where anticompetitive agreements do not have criminal consequences, such behavior has been introduced as a crime. This is the Colombian case.

The forms of bid rigging are diverse, therefore two premises must be taken into account in order to combat this conduct. First, it is a dynamic conduct in terms of its modalities. Depending on the selection process in which it takes place it is possible to identify different strategies to collude, which vary to the extent that contract conditions are modified. Second, there is not perfect contracting model to prevent bid rigging. While it is possible to design processes with high security measures against possible infringers, it is difficult to ensure success on this goal.

Despite the above, competition authorities have identified several types of bid rigging practices in public procurement. Probably the most common one is the "complementary offer" or "kamikaze," where one of the cartelized agents offers very high or very low bids in order to manipulate the value on which the contracting entity qualifies proposals. This mode can also occur when the presentation of documents to participate in the selection process is incomplete or inadequate. Another type of collusion is the suppression of supply, where one of the cartelized bidders withdraws to give better options to another undertaking involved in the conduct. Bid rotation on the other hand, implicates several selection processes that are distributed by turns, depending on the illegal agreement. Finally, the distribution of markets geographically or by product is considered another option of cartelization against public procurement.[1]

However, as it will be noted later, Colombia has faced a different type of bid rigging based on the creation of economic groups that are not declared or legalized, in order to use controlled companies to make them appear as competitors before the procurement entities. *Nule Bienestarina* (2013) and *Nule Hogares* (2013) are two of the most important investigations carried out by the Superintendence of Industry and Commerce (hereinafter referred to as SIC) on bid rigging. Such cases represent the modality described where the State is doubly deceived, since on the one hand, a competitive environment is artificially created, and on the other, public contracts are awarded illegally.

This chapter seeks to make a journey through the evolution of the way in which the Colombian Competition Authority has handled bid rigging practices, and also seeks to identify the challenges that such entity faces today.

§8.02 BID RIGGING IN PUBLIC PROCUREMENT EVOLUTION IN COLOMBIA

[A] Brief Historical Review Prior to Law 1340 of 2009

The competition protection regime in Colombia has its origins in Law 155 of 1959. Its Article 1 establishes a general prohibition against all commercial practices that restrict competition. It is worth mentioning that this provision is now fully in force and has been applied by the SIC in recent and important cases, as in the investigation related to rubbish collection in Bogotá (2014).[2] However, when the Law was enacted no mention was made regarding the types of possible anticompetitive conducts that could be object of control.

Subsequent to the issuance of the referred provision, no significant development of competition law in the country occurred. The latter is explained in the fact that public economic policies during the next thirty years were structured under a protectionist model of import substitution, which hardly coexisted with free economic competition. Only until the expedition of 1991 Constitution, free competition was recognized as a collective right (Article 333), and after that, Decree 2153 of 1992 was

---

1. OCDE Guidelines for Fighting Bid Rigging in Public Procurement.
2. It was also applied in IBOPE case (2012) and in the recently opened investigation against General Motors (2015).

issued. This introduced a list of the anticompetitive conducts which is valid today. That was the introduction of bid rigging in Colombia:

> ARTICLE 47. AGREEMENTS CONTRARY TO FREE COMPETITION. In order to comply with the duties referred to in article 44 of this Decree, the following agreements, among others, are considered contrary to free competition:
> (...)
>
> 9. Those whose object is to collude in bids or contests or those whose effect is to allocate contracts' awards, distribute contests or fix the terms of proposals.

Despite having a specific provision on bid rigging since 1992, the first sanction reference that is found in Colombia's history is the *Informática y Tecnología Limitada* case (2004),[3] where it was determined that within the framework of the tender No. IDU[4]-CD-DTF-023-2002, individual tender offers submitted by the consortia IMPLEMENTACIÓN TÉCNICA and COMPUTADORES 2002 had been prepared by the same bidder: CONSORCIO IMPLEMENTACIÓN TÉCNICA. Bidders, like several individuals linked to them, were sanctioned with fines that did not exceed MXN 980 million (approximately USD 26,000).

A few years later, *Intersystem S.A* (2009)[5] was sanctioned. The existence of bid rigging was demonstrated in the tender processes conducted in 2006 by some educational institutions of the District of Bogotá, whose objective was to acquire systematization services for students' grading. The offense was based in two major actions: (i) increasing the possibility of being awarded a contract by the inscription in the contracting process, and, if one of the cartelized agents was designed as enable to make an offer, the other investigated parties who were also selected refrained from submitting their respective offers; and (ii) reducing the possibility of registered participants of being selected to make offers. It is also important to clarify that the omission in the submission of the offers by the cartelized agents prevented the educational institutions to have a larger number of bids to evaluate. This time the amount of the fine rose to MXN 5 million (approximately USD 1,700).

In *Consorcio de Oriente* (2011),[6] the conducts took place within the bidding process named IPG 2027-196076. Bid rigging practices were evidenced by the identification of several matches in the bids presented by CONSORCIO VIAL COLOMBIANO and CONSORCIO DE ORIENTE. The most outstanding of such matches were they payment of the participation rights of the consortia with checks from the same checkbook and the same bank account; and the texts of the consortia agreements, which were identical in structure, format, text, writing and lyrics. As for the total fines, it should be noted that the amount represented the highest fine imposed in that time on this type of behavior (approximately USD 880,000).

---

3. SIC Resolution No. 21822 of September 1, 2004, confirmed by SIC Resolution No. 2048 of November 22, 2004.
4. The IDU is the Institute of Urban Development of the Capital District.
5. SIC Resolution No. 1055 of January 19, 2009, confirmed by SIC Resolution No. 69716 of December 30, 2009.
6. SIC Resolution No. 64400 of November 16, 2011, confirmed by SIC Resolution No. 30 of January 5, 2012.

The previous cases have in common two fundamental aspects. On the one hand, it can be seen that qualitative analysis prevails over economic study. In fact, the evidence of the infringement is mainly extracted from the behavior performed by the investigated agents, without examining if such behaviors had a direct or indirect economic link with the contracts' awarding process. On the other hand, it is clear that the fines imposed were not related to the seriousness of the behavior. Probably, this has been one of the most relevant historical problems that bid rigging in public procurement has faced in Colombia. During the first years of law enforcement, the competition authority did not have as a strategic focus repression of these agreements. No dimension of their consequences for the economy were dimensioned.

[B] Modernization of the Colombian Regime and Change in the Strategy Against Bid Rigging in Public Procurement

Without doubt, the issuance of Law 1340 of 2009[7] marks a historic moment in the protection of free competition in Colombia. With this Law important tools needed for modernizing the regime and fighting cartelization were introduced. Without describing in detail each one of them, it is worth mentioning: (i) inclusion of the leniency program; (ii) establishment of the SIC as the unique competition authority; and (iii) some procedural adjustments. However, the most important modification under an enforcement point of view was the substantial increase on fines. Maximum fine for legal persons increased from 2000 CLMMW[8] (approximately USD 500,000) to 100,000 CLMMW (approximately USD 23 million); and for individuals, fines rose from 300 CLMMW (approximately USD 68,000) to 2000 CLMMW (approximately USD 500,000).

Under this new framework, the competition protection regime acquired a protagonist role that had not had until such moment. The business sector began to measure the importance of the control and the repression of anticompetitive behaviors within a free market structure, and the competition authority was provided with the most suitable mechanisms to exercise its function efficiently.

Despite the above, after the issuance of Law 1340, the country faced one of the most serious scandals in its history on corruption. In mid-2010, it was announced that the Nule Group, a conglomerate of companies led by Guido Nule Marino and his cousins, which were in charge of an important section of the construction of the Transmilenio transport system in Bogotá, was in serious financial problems that came from bad management.[9] Although the origin of the case were improper cross-financing operations among projects that involved the Nule Group, the situation drew the attention of the National Government and, of course, the competition authority. At that time, the complementarity relationship between corruption and bid rigging in public

---

7. Law 1340 of 2009 (July 24), whereby rules and regulations on competition protection are enacted. Official Gazette No. 47.420.
8. Current Legal Minimum Monthly Wages.
9. Read "Grupo Nule y la Caída de su Imperio." Available at: http://www.eltiempo.com/Multimedia/info grafia/nule/.

procurement began to have great importance,[10] and because of that, different measures to prevent and combat such offenses in a stronger way were implemented. Some of them intended to make the behaviors more burdensome conducts, and others looked for the redesign of the investigation strategies within the SIC.

Bid rigging as a crime

Law 1474 of 2011, "whereby provisions aimed at strengthening the mechanisms for the prevention, investigation and punishment of corruption acts, and for the effectiveness of governance, are dictated," modified the Colombian Penal Code by introducing in its Chapter II several measures to combat public and private corruption. Article 27 of such Law included a new criminal offense related to competition restrictive agreements:

> *Article 27. Competition restrictive agreements.* Law 599 of 2000 shall have an article 410A, which will state as follows:
> Who in a public procurement, auction, abbreviated selection or contest agrees with another to illegally alter the contractual process, will incur in imprisonment of six (6) to twelve (12) years and a fine of two hundred (200) to one thousand (1,000) monthly legal minimum wages, and inability to contract with government entities for eight (8) years.
> Paragraph. Who, as informer or lenient, obtains by firm resolution total exemption of the fine to be imposed by the Superintendence of Industry and Commerce in an investigation on anti-competitive agreements in procurement processes, will get the following benefits: reduction of the sanction in a third, 40% of the fine to be imposed and an inability to contract with government entities for five (5) years.

In Colombia, therefore, bid rigging in public procurement is the only anticompetitive conduct that has criminal consequences. Moreover, as observed in the referred article, a reference is made to the leniency policy of the competition regime, which is intended to find a meeting point between the administrative and criminal fields. However, it should be noted that, to date, no criminal sentences for competition restrictive agreements have been enacted.

In practice, the coexistence of criminal and administrative reproaches has allowed significant progresses on investigation and collaboration techniques between the SIC and the Attorney General's Office. In the development of this inter-institutional relationship, three possibilities of interaction has been developed, which depend on the case type and the moment when the infringement possibly takes place.

The first has to do with those cases in which the Attorney General's Office becomes aware of an alleged bid rigging behavior before the Anti-Corruption Statute entered into force, moment in which such body did not have faculties to undertake criminal investigations in this regard. In these cases, the information has been submitted to the SIC in order to begin an administrative investigation. An example of this type of interaction is the *Pavigas* (2014), where a prosecutor of the Anti-Corruption

---

10. Felipe Serrano Pinilla (2011), *El derecho de la competencia como mecanismo para garantizar rivalidad en las licitaciones públicas e impulsar el crecimiento económico*, 19 International Law, Revista Colombiana de Derecho Internacional, 147–182 (2011).

Unit of the Attorney General's Office closed the proceeding by non-criminality, although the case was related to the manipulation of bids within a selection process.[11] However, the prosecutor sent the case to the SIC in order to let this entity conduct the investigation, which, in fact, culminated in sanctions against the involved undertakings.

The opposite has also occurred: the SIC has known possible anticompetitive behaviors of this type, and has submitted the corresponding cases to the Attorney General's Office in order to allow the criminal authority to conduct the respective criminal investigations as well. It should be noted that, normally, the remission is made only when the competition authority decides to open a formal investigation. This happened in the *Corporación Melquiades* (2015),[12] which culminated with the imposition of fines by the SIC and currently is also being investigated by the Attorney General's Office.

Finally, cooperation has also been present under a coordinated action of the entities. Efforts and investigative experiences have been combined in some cases of high relevance for the country, in order to be more efficient when collecting evidence and understanding the behavior from a legal and economic point of view. Specifically, as part of the initiated strategy, SIC officials have been provided with judicial police powers by the Attorney General's Office, to support prosecutors who conduct investigations on bid rigging in public procurement.

In addition, in December 2015, an inter-administrative agreement between the Attorney General's Office and the SIC was signed, in order to intensify joint actions against cartels in public procurement.[13]

Among the most representative cases in which cooperation has taken place, *Vigilancia (2015)*[14] and *IDU (2012)*[15] stand out. Mutual training regarding procedures to be followed, as well as the exchange of collected evidence and relevant information in investigations, are essential to achieve the repression of anticompetitive conducts and corruption within the framework of public procurement. However, it is clear that the experience obtained so far has also led to the identification of some aspects that require review and the implementation of solutions.

In first place the experience has shown that existence of criminal consequences discourage the leniency program of Law 1340 of 2009. The reason is that so as to apply for the program, express recognition of the illegal conduct by the cartelized agent is

---

11. According to SIC Resolution No. 83037 of 2014, whereby sanctions were imposed in this case, "[t]he proceedings in the Attorney General's Office were closed because at the time the facts occurred, the crime of anticompetitive agreements was not punishable under the Penal Code, given that Law 1474 of 2011, which contains the Anticorruption Statute, had not been issued yet, from which the conduct represents a criminal offense against the public administration."
12. SIC Resolution No. 91235 of November 24, 2015, confirmed by SIC Resolution No. 10412 of March 7, 2016.
13. Press release of the Superintendence of Industry and Commerce dated December 5, 2015. Available at: http://www.sic.gov.co/drupal/noticias/fiscalia-y-superindustria-firman-convenio-para-fortalecer-la-lucha-contra-la-cartelizacion-empresarial-y-otras-formas-de-colusion-en-con trataciones-publicas.
14. The case was opened in 2015 by SIC Resolution No. 2065 of January 28.
15. The case was opened in 2012 by SIC Resolution No. 61497 of October 19. It is part of the cases that are related to the Nule Group and it is currently in formal investigation phase.

required. Thus, by giving such recognition a confession of a criminal and punishable offense is obtained. Moreover, the criminal law only provides up to a third reduction benefits to the informer, which prevents the presence of possible informers in the administrative investigation, because in any case they will be deprived of their liberty. In practice, the situation described has been considered as the main barrier for the leniency program effectiveness in the bid rigging field. The Bill that seeks to modify the current Competition Regime,[16] which was prepared by the SIC, modifies the mentioned article of the Criminal Code in order to grant the "opportunity principle" to anyone who has obtained total exemption under SIC's leniency program. Such principle consists in the suspension, interruption or renounce of the exercise of the criminal action by the Attorney General's Office.[17]

A second aspect regards to the difficulties that have arisen when converging criminal and administrative theories in the demonstration of the investigated behaviors. It is clear that in the criminal field the demonstration of an intention behind the offense is required, whereas for the competition authorities such evidence in not always required. A mutual understanding of priorities, procedures and analysis methods is needed to achieve synergies that enable greater efficiencies in the common tasks, and better investigations results. A practical example of this could be the joint preparation of dawn raids, where the legal faculties of both entities can be used to avoid dissuasive or obstructive actions by alleged infringers.

Creation of the Interdisciplinary Bid Rigging Working Group

By Resolution No. 22724 of April 18, 2012, the Interdisciplinary Bid Rigging Working Group was created within the Deputy Superintendence for Competition Protection of the SIC. This group is composed of lawyers, accountants, economists and experts in public procurement and competition, who are in charge of handling complaints, preliminary inquiries and investigations exclusively related to bid rigging practices. The group is also responsible for identifying warning signs and indications of alleged collusive conducts in different procurement processes that are conducted by procurement entities. The following table 8.1 shows investigation figures before and after the creation of this specialized group:

Table 8.1

Year	Number of Cases under Investigation
2002–2011	51
2012	53

---

16. Bill No. 038 of 2015, whereby amendments are made to the competition protection regime, to the functions of the Superintendence of Industry and Commerce, and other provisions are enacted. Available at: http://190.26.211.102/proyectos/index.php/textos-radicados-senado/pl-2015-2016/467-proyecto-de-ley-038-de-2015.
17. "Principio de Oportunidad. Bases Legales para su Aplicación. Fiscalía General de la Nación" (2010).

Year	Number of Cases under Investigation
2013	52
2014	51
2015	84

Source: SIC- Statistics obtained by the Interdisciplinary Bid Rigging Working Group.

One of the most significant findings is that the first year after the Working Group's creation the number of investigations in the SIC were more than in the whole decade between 2002 and 2011. Additionally, during the aforementioned decade fines for approximately USD 1,360,320.00[18] were imposed, while between 2012 and 2015 fines went up to USD 16,919,244.00[19] in total.

While it can be stated that the creation of the specialized group has been a success,[20] more efforts to fight bid rigging in public procurement are still required. It is estimated that in 2015 in Colombia, took place approximately 12,813 selection processes, from which 6,863 were performed.[21] This is a very broad universe of supervision in which the SIC, unfortunately, has to limit its action to cases of greater impact or to those who reach the eyes of authority by complaints. Therefore, the ex-officio action is very limited, which leads to an inevitable impunity in many cases.

Considering the above, the Superintendent of Industry and Commerce announced in November 2016, the intention to strengthen the Working Group in 2017. The Government, in the framework of its current policy against corruption, provided the SIC with significant resources aimed at the creation of an "elite" version of the Bid Rigging Working Group with sixty new officials specialized in law, public procurement, economics, accounting, engineering, administration and forensics.

However, although it is necessary to strengthen the institutional capacity, such measure must not be understood as the main solution to the problem. The creation of common awareness is also required, not only among the supervisory authorities, but also among procurement entities across the country, and, of course, within the business sector. The strategy should be based on three fundamental pillars:

(i) Efficient and coordinated supervision:
Several government entities have the power to fight bid rigging and / or corruption. Within the Presidency of the Republic, the Secretariat of Transparency is responsible for coordinating public policy against such conducts. Moreover, Colombian political structure has the Attorney General's Office, the Comptroller General's Office, the Public Prosecutor's Office and the SIC, which also have faculties in this regard. Legal

---

18. OECD Secretariat Report on Fighting Bid Rigging in Colombia (2013).
19. SIC – Statistics obtained by the Interdisciplinary Bid Rigging Working Group.
20. Almost simultaneously with the creation of the Interdisciplinary Bid Rigging Working Group, the SIC began an improvement strategy in research techniques, whose axis was the creation of the Computer Forensics Lab in 2014. Thanks to this project, the ability of acquisition, processing and making available digital evidence within investigations increased substantially.
21. Data obtained from SECOP (Electronic System for Public Procurement). Available at http://www.contratos.gov.co/consultas/montos.html#.

and – especially – punitive tools are given to such entities; however, the coordination among them is not effective and, therefore, it is difficult to send dissuasive messages to the market. Probably, the creation of an Elite Interagency Working Group could be the solution to the needs that have been identified so far. There is no need to make structural modifications of the entities to achieve such goal; the only aspect that is needed is the will of its directors to provide knowledge, information, technology and government officials to handle the most complex and representative cases in the country. The aim would be to show results in an accelerated way, and to take simultaneous decisions on criminal, administrative, disciplinary and political fields.

(ii) Involvement of the contracting entities:

Although contracting entities at all levels recognize the existence of difficulties faced in the fight of bid rigging and/or corruption, their role has been limited to the identification of themselves as "affected parties." To achieve a proper action level regarding the identification of alarms of possible anticompetitive or corruption behaviors, they must perform a role that goes beyond their functions as procurement entities; they must become the first supervisors of compliance. Unfortunately, the priority of the procurement entities is to achieve their budgetary goals, and for that reason, the control that must exist in each selection process is not considered as a priority.

It is not possible to make a comprehensive surveillance if there is no active collaboration from each contracting entity. This need was identified by the OECD in its Report on Fighting Bid Rigging in Colombia (2013). In this paper, more communication between the National Public Procurement Agency – Colombia Compra Eficiente – and the SIC is recommended, and it makes a specific reference to trainings for contracting entities across government:[22]

The training program should reflect lessons learned from previous initiatives and include case studies from SIC bid-rigging investigations. The training programs should have the active participation of the NPPA given their statutory responsibilities, knowledge and contacts with respect to government procurement in Colombia.

Although the OECD recommendation is addressed to the National Public Procurement Agency and the SIC, the responsibility of knowing, monitoring and reporting any illegal conduct is in charge of each and every one of the procurement entities across the country, including their directors and officials. In most cases, for instance, it is not very complex to identify hints or signs of possible bid rigging behaviors. A simple comparison between the bids that are submitted in a public procurement is enough to recognize if bidders have had previous and

---

22. OECD Secretariat Report on Fighting Bid Rigging in Colombia (2013), p. 26.

undue interactions, by identifying unusual similarities in the corresponding tender offers.

(iii) Change in the corporate culture:

An infallible contracting model to prevent bid rigging in public procurement does not exist. As in all forms of cartelization, it is possible to create strategies with a competitor to manipulate the market by giving simple data or exchanging just a number.[23] For this reason, joint action of the supervisory authorities and active intervention of the procurement entities are not enough. It is imperative that economic agents understand the illegality of their behavior, regardless of the cultural and historical acceptance that certain business sectors have given to such conducts.

In several cases of the SIC, a clear lack of knowledge about the illegality of the anticompetitive behavior has been identified. In some of them, investigated parties have deemed as normal conducts like sharing information and even preparing tender offers jointly.[24]

In this regard, probably the only alternatives available are to strengthen college education of the future professionals who will be contractors, and to implement coercive and dissuasive enforcement mechanisms, both in the design of tender offers and in the sanction of law infringers. In this respect, one of the recommendations made by the OECD in its Report refers to the signing of certificates by bidders, in which a declaration of knowledge of the competition regime is made.[25] Also, as a coercive mechanism, the Competition Bill that was prepared by the SIC[26] includes inability to participate in public contracting processes as a sanction for those who engage in bid rigging in public procurement.

Probably, with measures as the mentioned above, it would be possible to introduce the information and trainings that are necessary to make entrepreneurs understand the importance of this topic. Moreover, such measures would help to implement deterrent and dissuasive mechanisms, which, as inability, may raise awareness on the risks that are taken when incurring in bid rigging practices and / or corruption.

---

23. In Colombia, several cases involving tacit anticompetitive agreements have been sanctioned, where there is no direct evidence of the conduct but there is evidence of the concertation through improper exchanges of information. See Acemi (2012).
24. See Valme case (2013) and Melquiades case (2015).
25. OECD Secretariat Report on Fighting Bid Rigging in Colombia (2013), Annex 3.
26. Bill No. 038 of 2015, whereby amendments are made to the competition protection regime, to the functions of the Superintendency of Industry and Commerce, and other provisions are enacted. Available at: http://190.26.211.102/proyectos/index.php/textos-radicados-senado/pl-2015-201 6/467-proyecto-de-ley-038-de-2015.

[C] Most Relevant Cases Following Law 1340 of 2009

After the implementation of legal and strategic changes to the policy on fight bid rigging in public procurement, and specifically after to the issuance of Law 1340 of 2009, cases of great importance have been opened and decided in the framework of this offense. From a general analysis of such cases, two trends can be identified. The first is related to the increasing relevance of quantitative elements of the behaviors as part of the investigations. Initially, much of the evidence that was collected was quantitative ("bid rigging of guidelines");[27] however, the current trend of the SIC shows a greater role of the economic elements.

The second trend refers to the presence of a special and very frequent form of bid rigging in Colombia: the aforementioned strategy of creating undeclared groups of companies controlled by a same agent in order to manipulate procurement processes. In the cases described below it is possible to find at least one of the two aforementioned trends.

[1] COMSAT INTERNATIONAL (2010)[28] Case

An alleged cartelization was investigated in the selection process No. 2042-197032 IPG developed by FONADE,[29] whose purpose was to hire the phase III of the Compartel Program of Broadband Connectivity for Public Institutions. There were hints that investigated parties had manipulated the determination of the Efficient Foment Value understood in the process as an assessment factor of greater value for the selection of the contractor. The SIC determined at the end of the investigation that it was not possible to demonstrate an interaction between bidders from the qualitative point of view. The interesting thing about this case is the application of the game theory by the competition authority to demonstrate that the probability of bid rigging from a quantitative point of view was not clear, and to demonstrate as well that there could be different reasons that could explain the way the contract was assigned. Aspects such as the asymmetric costs structures of the companies and the lack of monitoring evidence when submitting bids were emphasized.

[2] INPEC (2012)[30] Case

The investigation began under the bidding process No. 001 of 2011 (LP-001-2011) of INPEC,[31] whose purpose was to hire feeding ration services for inmates of detention

---

27. Examples of this type of conduct are the following cases: (i) *INTERSYSTEM S.A. (2009)* sanctioned by SIC Resolution No. 1055 of January 19, 2009, confirmed by SIC Resolution No. 69716 of December 30, 2009, and *ML INGENIEROS (2010))* sanctioned by SIC Resolution No. 64400 of November 16, 2011, confirmed by SIC Resolution No. 30 of January 5, 2012.
28. SIC Resolution No. 47481 of September 1, 2010.
29. Financial Fund of Development Programs.
30. SIC Resolution No. 40901 of June 28, 2012, confirmed by SIC Resolution No. 30 of January 5, 2012.
31. National Penitentiary and Prison Institute.

centers of the national order. The Deputy Superintendence for Competition Protection found matches in the value of the tender offers that were submitted by the investigated parties. From the evidence that was collected during the investigation, it was established that the investigated parties altered the public procurement's competitive process, and by this, they secured the award of the contracts. Specifically, a mechanism was implemented to artificially alter down the average value of the tender offers in order to make it closer to the economic offer of one of the three investigated parties.

[3] RAPISCAN (2012)[32] Case

In this case, the investigated companies and individuals colluded in order to seek a contract award in the Abbreviated Selection Process No. 001 of 2008, in favor of the consortium named UNIÓN TEMPORAL SEGURIDAD CARCELARIA. It should be noted that the contract award was effectively achieved. It was established that the investigated parties implemented a coordinated mechanism, which was intended to influence the awarding process of a State contract, specifically of the Ministry of Justice. This case not only generated consequences on public spending, but also affected the provision of an important service within the prison system.

[4] VALME (2013)[33] Case

This precedent is related to the Abbreviated Selection Process of minor value No. SA-03-06-2010, conducted by the Government of Arauca, where similarities between tender offers of VALME LTDA. and CONSORCIO H & F were found (cellular and phone numbers were the same on several documents of the bidders; serial policies were consecutive; it was found that VALME LTDA. was the equipment supplier of CONSORTIUM H & F; among others). During the investigation, the economic rationality of the investigated parties was analyzed in order to determine if their behaviors were explainable in schemes of bid rigging, and it was concluded that there had been an undue interaction between them, which was permanent during the pre-contractual, contractual and post-contractual stages. Strong evidence showed that far from real competition, there had been an absolute cooperation that was convenient to the businesses purposes of the parties.

In addition, the economic analysis showed that the tender offer of CONSORCIO H & F was complementary or instrumental to the success of VALME LTDA. This case is of great importance because of the econometric exercise that was used to prove bid rigging. Specifically, a conceptual framework was created, "using tools provided by the game theory, by which a bidder has an incentive to instrument the tender offer of another bidder in order to achieve higher expected benefits (especially for the

---

32. SIC Resolution No. 53991 of September 14, 2012, confirmed by SIC Resolution No. 8917 of March 4, 2013.
33. SIC Resolution No. 40901 of June 28, 2012, confirmed by SIC Resolution No. 65842 of November 14, 2013.

elimination of the uncertainty that is generated under the equilibrium of free competition)."[34]

[5] CORMAGDALENA (2013)[35] Case

This investigation refers to bid rigging practices that allegedly took place within the tender LP-007 of 2010, opened by the Regional Autonomous Corporation of Rio Grande Magdalena (CORMAGDALENA). Tender offers showed various matches of formal nature, which could be the result of collusive behaviors intended to alter the normal result of the tender. Despite the signs, the SIC decided to close the investigation because from the assessment of the evidence gathered and the economic analysis of the facts, it was not possible to conclude the existence of a collusive agreement. The only facts that were proven in relation to the alleged bid rigging behavior were the coincidences on mere formalities that were not aimed at altering the competitive process; such matches simply represented an innocuous cooperation between the bidders. In this sense, no evidence proved that the conducts displayed by the investigated parties were suitable to reduce the level of competition in the tender. Thus, in cases like this, the proof of the economic nature is particularly important, because it is the only tool that helps to deduce, with clarity and certainty, the existence of a bid rigging cartel.[36]

[6] NULE BIENESTARINA GROUP (2013)[37] Case

The investigation refers to bid rigging practices within the Public Tender CP-ICBF-SN-005-2007, organized by the Colombian Family Welfare Institute (hereinafter referred to as ICBF). The object of this tender was to hire supervision services on a concession contract for the operation of food production plants of high nutritional value owned by the ICBF ("bienestarina").

Warning signs of bid rigging were noted in some formats of the items' values that formed the economic offer in the bids submitted by the consortia named CONSORCIO INTER ICBF 2007 and PROMESA DE SOCIEDAD FUTURA INTERVENTORÍA DE LA

---

34. See p. 57 of SIC Resolution No. 40875 of July 9, 2013.
35. SIC Resolution No. 40835 of 2013.
36. It is worth quoting the following section which summarizes the position of the competition authority regarding the value of qualitative and quantitative evidence:

    Given that the previous economic analysis does not show as a result apparent bid rigging practices between the investigated parties, this office cannot consider the structure of the economic offers as an indicator of the existence of a collusive agreement between them. On the contrary, economic analysis aims at undermining the realization of such agreement. If, in addition, it is taken into account that, in the opinion of this Office, documentary matches that were found in the tender offers of the investigated parties are not sufficient to conclude that they made a collusive agreement, we must state that there is not enough evidence to sanction them for the alleged conducts stablished in the Opening Resolution.

37. SIC Resolution No. 54693 of September 16, 2013.

CONCESIÓN DE PLANTAS DEL VALLE – ATLÁNTICO. The companies of NULE GROUP presented themselves independently, as members of two different consortia in the referred tender, as a strategy to implement bid rigging practices that would distort competition of other bidders.

By Resolution No. 54693 of September 16, 2013, the SIC decided that the members of the investigated parties, which were part of NULE GROUP and its controlling members, had made deceptive conducts which represented infringements to competition rules. The latter, because they misrepresented and distorted the competitive process by deploying a strategy that sought to achieve the illegal award of the contract in favor of GRUPO NULE, to the detriment of the other bidders.

[7]   NULE HOGARES (2013)[38] Case

Infringers in this case participated in a bid rigging agreement within the Public Tender ICBF SN-014-2007, conducted by the ICBF. This tender was intended to hire technical and administrative supervision services of various programs (which could be named altogether as "homes"). The selection process was divided into six different macro-regions that were awarded separately, so the bidders had the power to choose in which of them they would present their tender offer.

The companies of the NULE GROUP presented themselves separately as members of two different consortia in the tender, and warning signs were identified in the formats of the items' values and in the multiplier factor contained in the tender offers submitted by the consortia CONSORCIO SUPERVISORES INTER ICBF-2007 and PROMESA DE SOCIEDAD FUTURA "SUPERVISIONES DESARROLLO SOCIAL COLOMBIA S.A.

The SIC concluded that constant information exchanges found during the investigation and financial guarantees shared between the investigated parties showed an interdependent action of the companies, which de facto obeyed to the same head under the command of the NULE family. Thus, although they formally presented themselves as independent competitors, their purpose was to distort competition and increase the contract awarding possibilities within the public procurement, as effectively happened in this tender.

[8]   IDIPRON (2013)[39] Case

The Institute for the Protection of Children and Youth of the Capital District (IDIPRON) conducted the Abbreviated Selection Process SAS-8-2011, in the form of electronic reverse auction, whose object was to supply groceries for different projects of the entity. After making previous verifications of three bidders, only one was found as enable to submit tender offers, and therefore the contract was awarded to him. In the investigation, various similarities among the two other bidders were found, specifically

---

38. SIC Resolution No. 54695 of September 16, 2013.
39. SIC Resolution No. 53914 of September 9, 2013.

related to structures costs; quotation of products; names, formats and font size; margins on costs and administrative staff; among others. It was also possible to demonstrate that they shared a file called "Model of Auction Offers" with which it was possible to perform simulations discounts during the auction, sharing information such as prices and the total value of the contract.

[9]   PAVIGAS (2014) Case

The SIC fined the firms named INCOEQUIPOS INGENIERÍA CONSTRUCCIÓN Y EQUIPOS S.A., GISAICO S.A., ESTYMA S.A., and PAVIGAS S.A.S., as well as several of their legal representatives, for cartelization within a public tender conducted by INVÍAS[40] whose objective was the reconstruction and repaving of the road CIRCUN-VALAR GALERAS in the Department of Nariño. In this case it is important to mention that the competition authority declined to forward copies to the Attorney General's Office, because at the time of the facts (2009–2010), as already mentioned, bid rigging in public procurement had not been criminalized yet. From the evidence collected in the investigation, it was concluded that the companies involved agreed previously that GISAICO S.A. would be the winner of the contract, and implemented an anticompetitive strategy in which they presented tender offers that were previously agreed, in order to guarantee or make more likely to award the contract to GISAICO S.A. This situation was warned by the INVIAS, who declared void the public tender.

[10]   VIGILANCIA (2015)[41] Case

The proceeding began in 2011 by a complaint filed by the ICBF, according to which several companies that presented themselves as individual competitors were apparently acting in a coordinated manner when presenting their bids in a public tender. After conducting dawn raids, it was found that ICBF processes were part of a universe of 252 processes where apparently such behavior had also taken place. Resolution No. 2065 of January 28, 2015 formally opened the investigation, and it involved several companies for allegedly simulate to be independent competitors in tenders, when in fact they were acting in a coordinated and concerted way, apparently deceiving the various contracting public entities. According to the investigation, the agents involved participated in at least 100 public procurement processes and managed to win twenty-five of them for more than MXN 63 billion. Currently, this case is in the evidence collection stage, so the final decision of the SIC is still pending.

§8.03   CONCLUSIONS

From the considerations shared in this paper, it is possible to draw several conclusions on the history, the present and the future challenges on fighting bid rigging in public

---

40. National Roads Institute.
41. SIC Resolution No. 2065 of January 28, 2015.

procurement in Colombia. It is clear that in the last seven years there has been a significant evolution in relation to the powers of the competition authority, the tools available to face this conduct and the legal framework in general. However, it is crucial that the various bodies responsible for investigating and punishing this behavior from the administrative and criminal perspective, have more interaction among them and act together to block this conduct. In addition, considering the difficulty to cover potential risks in all selection processes that occur in the country, a strategy based on three pillars must be implemented: (i) efficient and coordinated supervision, (ii) involvement of the procurement entities, and (iii) change in the corporate culture.

As for the direct relationship between the SIC and the Attorney General's Office, greater interaction is required between their investigation teams, in order to promote a common language among them and use the research tools that each one has in a more effective way. A modification or adaptation in the application of the opportunity principle in cases where whistleblowers apply for benefits before the SIC should also be reviewed.

Moreover, when assessing trends in cases and positions of the SIC, it can be seen that the economic analysis of the behavior is involved increasingly, and a balance between quantitative and qualitative evidence is sought. In addition, it was identified that the most common and dangerous type of bid rigging in recent years consists in form undeclared business groups in order to deceive the contracting entities through strategies to simulate competition.

CHAPTER 9
Predatory Pricing Policy for Latin American Emerging Economies

Pablo Márquez

§9.01 INTRODUCTION

Price predation has traditionally been a controversial notion in competition law.[1] The current literature in developed economies shows that it still is a vague concept that does not yet have a set of clear and administrable rules.[2] Defining which policy to follow in Latin American emerging economies has not been the exception. The goal of this chapter is to establish whether the analysis and application of the prohibition on price predation in Latin America is appropriate for such emerging economies and whether, having regard to economic growth as competition law and policy's guiding principle, there is a superior standard and, therefore, a different approach is justified.

In simple words, price predation is an exclusionary abuse that has as its goal to drive competitors from the market by the direct use of market power to set prices that

---

1. *See* Blair and Harrison, "Airline Price Wars: Competition or Predation", p. 494. According to the authors the question is, if competition involves winners and losers and the sole extent of competition is to exclude, then what is unlawful exclusionary conduct? The authors show that most people would agree that predation and price predation are undesirable forms of exclusion, but price predation should be taken with caution, as there is also agreement that it should not be prohibited unless the form of competition that may replace it is fully understood.
2. *See* Roth, "Predation, Cost-Based Tests and Predatory Intent", pp. 35a–35b (stating that three recurring themes are still being discussed by the literature on predation: first, the notion of predatory pricing; second, the reliance on A–T's cost-based test; and third, the courts' failure to take into account the industrial organization literature). Miller III and Pautler, "Predation: The Changing View in Economics and the Law", p. 495 (stating that predation is among the most difficult problems in economics and the law, since it is one of those specific business practices that may undermine competition or be itself a part of the competitive process). Areeda and Hovenkamp, *Antitrust Law*, §7.23a (holding that there has been a relative failure to delineate appropriate rules due to an "exacerbated fear" that dominant undertakings will use predation as a means to exclude rivals).

are substantially different from competitive prices.[3] This definition includes not only excessively low prices but also excessively high prices that are used as a means to drive competitors from the market, and therefore, predatory pricing includes not only incumbents' low prices that attempt to encourage exit or discourage rivals' entry from the supply side but also incumbents' high prices that attempt to encourage exit or discourage entry of rivals in the purchasing side of the market. Both are predatory actions by dominant undertakings.

This chapter is structured as follows. First, in section §9.02, the economic analysis of price predation is presented and a definition of price predation as an exclusionary abuse is proposed. In section §9.03, the mainstream perspectives on price predation are described, showing the different standards used to enforce price predation providing the range of different approaches with different efficient rules. In section §9.04, a description and assessment of the Latin American emerging economies rules on price predation are presented, showing the different policies, rules and standards followed and adopted by such countries.

Finally, section §9.05 proposes economic growth as the guiding principle of price predation policy design in order to find a superior standard applicable to exclusionary predatory pricing in Latin American emerging economies. Following such principle, and acknowledging that Latin American emerging economies are characterized by high industrial and aggregate concentration, it is found that these emerging economies should design their abusive pricing policies using a rule that prohibits above and below cost price predation. This rule, in addition to be efficient, encourages investment and rapid economic growth and discourages strategic behavior by dominant undertakings.

§9.02   THE ECONOMICS OF PRICE PREDATION

In this section, the economics of price predation is analyzed. The aim of this section is to show the different mainstream economic analysis approaches regarding predatory pricing. In the first subsection, an introduction to the economics of exclusionary abuses will be presented and then a subsection on the economics of price predation will be explained.

[A]   Exclusionary Pricing and Abusive Pricing Policy

Abusive pricing is composed of a mixture of exploitative pricing, predatory pricing, and price discrimination.[4] All these acts are regularly defined by the literature as price–cost relations or as actual price and perfectly competitive price relations. Indeed, most pricing strategies, as shown before, are based on standards that structure undertakings' behavior as a result of pricing above or below what prices should be with regard to a perfectly competitive market structure. Such an assessment standard, as was stated in

---

3. *See* Edlin, "Above Cost Predatory Pricing", p. 952 (stating that price predation is achieved when firm charges abnormally low prices to drive or chasten rivals from the market, but those low prices are not the result of competition on merit but temporary until the rivals exit).
4. *See* Whish R, *Competition Law*... p. 6.

Chapter A, may not be best for market structures where aggregate market concentration simply makes a situation of perfect competition impossible.

Regarding exclusionary pricing, contrary to the case of exploitative excessive pricing, price predation is usually defined as an abuse whereby dominant undertakings, by using market strategies, unilaterally interfere with the normal process of competition.[5] Such a pricing strategy is usually referred to by the literature as exclusionary abuse,[6] since the predator's goal is to use its dominant position to exclude actual or potential rivals from a particular market by pricing excessively low.[7] Low pricing is usually regarded as detrimental to competition if prices are excessively low in favor of dominant purchasers. But low pricing is also taken as detrimental to competition when prices are so low that they induce market participants to exit the market or not to enter.[8] These prices are usually named predatory prices and are classified as predatory and exclusionary behavior.[9]

Exclusionary practices are considered important for economic policy, mostly for competition policy, because exclusionary acts destroy incentives to compete *ex ante*.[10] These practices are strategies "by which firms attempt to exclude a rival, other than by having lower costs and therefore lower prices."[11] Thus, an undertaking's exclusionary behavior is considered detrimental to competition in terms of welfare diminution.[12] Most high-income economies, when exploitative acts are employed by firms with

---

5. As explained below, the literature and the courts have qualified the process of competition.
6. Posner, "Exclusionary Practices and the Antitrust Laws", pp. 506–507.
7. *See* Manfred Neumann, *Competition Policy: History, Theory and Practice* (Edward Elgar 2001), Chapter 3, cited by Coloma, "The Argentine Competition Law and Its Enforcement", p. 97 (stating that exclusionary abuses under Argentinean competition law are those practices meant to hurt competitors and that exploitative abuses are those that are illegal due to the departure from the conditions of normal competition). With regard to exploitative pricing, on the other hand, there is an exploitation of market power by imposing prices on the demand side of the market, but not necessarily a displacement of actual or potential rivals. *See* Lyons, *The Paradox of the Exclusion of Exploitative Abuse* (arguing that there is an inner contradiction on the definition of exclusionary abuses, as hurting rivals is necessary for an exclusionary abuse, but it is not sufficient to be considered an abuse since exclusion requires an eventual or expected harm to consumers, or any other exploitation of market power. The author states, "it is good to prohibit only those exclusionary practices which can be expected to result (indirectly) in an exploitative abuse ... but at the same time it is bad to prohibit directly exploitative practices!").
8. Simon Bishop and Mike Walker, *The Economics of EC Competition Law: Concepts, Application and Measurement* (2nd edn, Sweet & Maxwell 2002), §6.68.
9. Predatory behavior includes a set of actions that a dominant undertaking may undertake to force exit or restrict entry, such as scheduling in transport industries, large introduction of brands in the market, or the use of excess capacity. See *Ibid.*, §§6.78–6.84.
10. Posner RA, "Exclusionary Practices and the Antitrust Laws" (1974) 43 The University of Chicago Law Review 506.
11. *See* Posner, "Exclusionary Practices and the Antitrust Laws", p. 506 (showing the difference between different exclusionary practices and explaining examples such as predatory prices, tying arrangements, vertical interaction, exclusive dealing, and group boycotts); Richard O. Zerbe Jr. and Donald S. Cooper, "An Empirical and Theoretical Comparison of Alternative Predation Rules" (1982) 61 Texas Law Review 655, p. 658 (showing the strategic perspective on exclusionary practices).
12. *See* Fox EM, "What is Harm to Competition - Exclusionary Practices and Anticompetitive Effect" (2002–2003) 70 Antitrust Law Journal 371; Whish R, *Competition Law* (6th edn, Oxford University Press 2009); Posner RA, "Exclusionary Practices and the Antitrust Laws" (1974) 43 The University of Chicago Law Review 506.

significant market power and market dominance, generally consider the effects of exclusionary practices on competition to be harmful for the economy.[13] Often exclusionary behavior is developed by commercial strategies that may or may not involve pricing. Those exclusionary abuses, which involve pricing strategies, price predation, and some forms of price discrimination, are considered exclusionary.[14]

[B]   Market Power, Exclusionary Behavior and Price Predation

One of the most commonly cited benefits of competition is its virtue to pressure prices downwards.[15] This is usually regarded as in the best interest of consumers and firms. However, economic analysis shows that there are certain circumstances where low prices are detrimental for consumers and the competition process in the long run;[16] therefore there should be intervention in order to prevent anticompetitive behavior.[17]

Exclusionary predatory behavior is a concept extensively studied in academic literature; yet there is not a single perspective regarding its welfare effects.[18] On the one side, part of the literature has qualified all predatory behavior as an irrational strategy that does not occur or exist in competitive markets,[19] and on the other side, another

---

13. *See* Simon Bishop and Mike Walker, The Economics of EC Competition Law: Concepts, Application and Measurement (2nd edn, Sweet & Maxwell 2002), §6.68.
14. The literature regularly states that tying and bundling, refusals to deal and exclusive agreements are non-pricing exclusionary abuses (*see* Whish, *Competition Law*; Ekaterina Rousseva, *Rethinking Exclusionary Abuses in EU Competition Law: Rethinking Article 82 of the EC Treaty* (Hart 2010); Bergh and Camesasca, *European Competition Law and Economics: a Comparative Perspective*).
15. Bishop and Walker, *The Economics of EC Competition Law: Concepts, Application and Measurement*, §6.68.
16. O'Donoghue and Padilla, *The Law and Economics of Article 82 EC*, pp. 235-236 (arguing that under Art. 82 EC (102 TFEU) not all forms of price competition are legitimate, since some of them as predation may harm consumers; however the authors reckon that consumers may also benefit from low prices in the short term); Hovenkamp, *Federal Antitrust Policy: The Law of Competition and Its Practice*, p. 340b (arguing that predatory pricing is a difficult antitrust allegation because "low prices are a principle if not the primary goal of antitrust policy", but showing that at the core of predation are not low prices but price cuts to chill competition); Phillip Areeda and Donald F. Turner, "Predatory Pricing and Related Practices under Section 2 of the Sherman Act" (1975) 88 Harvard Law Review 697, p. 697 (arguing that although antitrust law is not concerned with limiting price competition, low prices may have anticompetitive effects).
17. Bishop and Walker, *The Economics of EC Competition Law: Concepts, Application and Measurement*, §6.68; Areeda and Hovenkamp, *Antitrust Law*, §723a (arguing that a firm that is engaging in behavior that is predatory is not competing on the merits); Bergh and Camesasca, *European Competition Law and Economics: a Comparative Perspective*, p. 280, §7.5 (arguing that in price predation, prices are so low that the competitive process itself is damaged).
18. *See* Bishop and Walker, *The Economics of EC Competition Law: Concepts, Application and Measurement*, §6.70 (arguing that predation is "a deliberate sacrifice of profits in the short run in the expectation of earning more profits in the long run after rival has exited the market").
19. According to Bork (Robert H. Bork, *The Antitrust Paradox: a Policy at War with Itself* (Basic Books 1978), p. 155), "the theoretical argument presented here is that suggests that predatory price cutting is unlikely to exist and that attempts to outlaw it are likely to harm consumers more than would abandon the effort. The analysis also indicates that we should look for methods of predation which do not require the predator to expand output and incur disproportionately large costs." *See* Bergh and Camesasca, *European Competition Law and Economics: A Comparative*

part of the literature has considered that any price reaction by dominant undertakings should be stopped.[20] For those approaches that find predation a rationally workable strategy, predation has been defined in multiple ways, ranging from actions that are only profitable if competitors exit the market[21] to actions calculated to exclude as efficient rivals.[22] However, there is consensus that the likelihood of succeeding in predation is highly correlated to market concentration. Market structures where there are industries with single-firm dominant players or highly concentrated industries are therefore more likely to see predation happening.[23]

Predation, in simple words, is a market strategy directed to discipline other market participants. This strategy has the effect of driving out or excluding rivals, or of disciplining competitors by selling at non-remunerative prices.[24] Such a strategy can take different forms. On the one side, price predation is regularly seen as a type of abuse of a dominant position where dominant undertakings develop price reductions to levels below costs intended to harm competitors.[25] But also, other forms of pricing strategies are deemed predatory, such as dominant undertakings above cost and price cutting directed towards facing new entrants or existing competitors.[26] In addition, predation can happen on both sides of the equation.[27] Predatory buying happens when demand is composed by a single dominant firm or a monopsonist that, in order to drive from the market or discipline other market players, pays suppliers higher than competitive prices.[28] This behavior has as a consequence the denial of input to

---

Perspective, p. 281 (stating that under the Chicago school of law and economics, predatory pricing is irrational because any increase in prices will attract entry and any price cut made to disrupt entry will not have an opportunity to recoup losses).
20. See O'Donoghue and Padilla, *The Law and Economics of Article 82 EC*, p. 236, §5.2.
21. Bishop and Walker, *The Economics of EC Competition Law: Concepts, Application and Measurement*, §6.70.
22. Ibid., §6.70.
23. Areeda and Hovenkamp, *Antitrust Law*, §724a3.
24. Ibid., §7.23a. It also defined as a strategy "whereby a firm offers low prices in the short-term in order to induce competitors' market exit, followed by higher prices in the medium to long-term." See O'Donoghue and Padilla, *The Law and Economics of Article 82 EC*, p. 236 (the authors state that predation involves not only reduced short-term profits but also medium- to long-term additional profits granted by strengthened market power by a rival's exit).
25. Barry J. Rodger and Angus McCulloch, *Competition Law and Policy in the EC and UK* (4th edn, Rutledge-Cavendish 2009), p. 126 (arguing that predatory price reductions are "characterized by a selective price reduction which is intended to harm a competitor", and stating that under European law, even above-cost price reduction may be considered predatory under standards such as *Compagnie Maritime Belge* (Case C-395/96 [2000] ECR I-1365)).
26. Edlin, "Above Cost Predatory Pricing" (stating that above-cost price cutting is as harmful as predation; therefore strict measures should be taken). See Whish, *Competition Law*, pp. 730–731 (stating that the dominant firm that has been charging supra-competitive prices reduces its prices to loss-making levels below cost. The author argues, however, that price reductions by dominant firms may give such undertakings a reputation that prevents new entry). Hovenkamp, *Federal Antitrust Policy: The Law of Competition and Its Practice* (arguing that price predation is a practice of driving rivals out of business by selling at a price below cost).
27. Areeda and Hovenkamp, *Antitrust Law*, §747a.
28. Blair and Harrison, *Monopsony in Antitrust Law and Economics*, p. 73.

competitors, and once competitors are driven form the market, the undertaking recoups the investment made by paying lower-than-competitive prices to suppliers.[29]

The economics of monopolistic predation, on the one hand, state that a dominant undertaking on the supply side has the power to determine prices by increasing output. It predates when it prices its products below their marginal cost, or the cost per additional unit of output. Such irrational behavior would only be plausible if the revenues' loss is expected to be recovered in the future.[30] Monopsonistic predation, on the other hand, is based also on the market power of a dominant undertaking on the demand side, which allows the undertaking to increase purchasing in order to overpay for the input.[31] As in the case of monopolistic competition, the goal is to exclude competitors from access to the output.[32] There is overpay, theoretically, if the payment for inputs is higher than the input's marginal revenue or the additional revenue granted by increasing one unit of input.[33]

The literature has identified that predation is not only a pricing strategy.[34] Non-price predation might be an attractive policy in order to appease other market participants. Such a strategy is commonly seen as safer than price predation since it is much less expensive and does not require the sacrifice of short-run profits on a large volume of sales. Non-price predation, therefore, is effective for "creating and exploiting cost asymmetries *vis a vis* existing rivals, deterring entry or mobility by potential or fringe rivals ... [T]hus, non-price predation can be effective in a larger number of markets."[35]

Research has shown that non-price predation may be more serious than price predation.[36] In general, the authors consider any strategy that raises rivals' costs is likely to be preferable to predatory pricing because it "a) is less expensive, b) can be profitable even if it does not ultimately force the victim to exit, c) does not require the sacrifice of short-run profits ... e) is more likely to be credible,[37] and f) sunk costs and the perceived intensity of competition constitute a barrier to entry."[38] The effects of such strategies are questioned, or at least found to be very limited, by part of the

---

29. Roger D. Blair and Jeffrey L. Harrison, *Monopsony: Antitrust Law and Economics* (Princeton U Press 1993), p. 154.
30. Blair and Harrison, *Monopsony in Antitrust Law and Economics*, p. 74.
31. *Ibid.*, p. 74.
32. *Ibid.*, p. 39.
33. *Ibid.*, p. 39.
34. *See* Areeda and Hovenkamp, *Antitrust Law*, §747c–747e; Terry Calvani, "Non-Price Predation: A New Antitrust Horizon" (1985) 54 Antitrust Law Journal 409; Miller III and Pautler, "Predation: The Changing View in Economics and the Law."
35. Calvani, "Non-Price Predation: A New Antitrust Horizon", p. 409.
36. Non-price predation is any activity that is aimed at rising rival's costs. *See* Khemani RS and Shapiro DM, Glossary of Industrial Organisation Economics and Competition Law (Directorate for Financial Fiscal and Enterprise Affairs ed, OECD 1993); Calvani T, "Non-Price Predation: A New Antitrust Horizon" (1985) 54 Antitrust Law Journal 409.
37. Miller III and Pautler, "Predation: The Changing View in Economics and the Law", p. 500.
38. *See* Hal R. Arkes and Catherine Blumer, "The Psychology of Sunk Cost" (1985) 35 Organizational Behaviour and Human Decision Processes 124; Hal R. Arkes and Laura Hutzel, "The Role of Probability of Success Estimates in the Sunk Cost Effect" (2000) 13 Journal of Behavioural Decision Making 295 (stating that sunk costs have a larger effect to dissuade individuals than profits to incentivize individuals to entry).

literature. Posner, for example, questions the likelihood of price predation strategies to drive competitors from the market but finds that it is a perfect strategy to delay entry and is therefore profitable for the dominant undertaking.[39]

In summary, predation could be seen as an exclusionary strategy by a dominant undertaking aimed at driving competitors form the market. Having the last analysis in mind, now the mainstream proposals regarding price predation will be explained in order to show what the range of standards in the market that may influence policy design in Latin American emerging economies is.

§9.03 MAINSTREAM STANDARDS FOR PREDATORY PRICING

The economics of predatory pricing varies vastly depending on the definition given to the act of predation and the benchmark used to determine what acts constitute predatory behavior.[40] The design of competition policy rules related to predation involves at least the definition of: (i) an economic model that defines what prices variations are rational, and (ii) the legal rules that govern such model to determine whether the action is unlawful.[41] The problem in antitrust analysis of price predation is the determination of a guideline or a benchmark that allows the antitrust authority to distinguish between legitimate competition through pricing and pricing meant to unlawfully predate a rival's market share.

In order to solve that problem, the literature and competition authorities have developed a set of standards that aim to draw the line at what sort of predatory behavior may constitute an abuse. As explained before, price predation standards range from standards that consider all predatory behavior to be an irrational strategy that does not occur or exist[42] to standards where any prices downward reaction by dominant undertakings should be deemed predatory.[43] Then, price predation rules indicate that predatory pricing standards of analysis identify it either as a per se legal behavior or per se illegal behavior.

---

39. Posner, "Exclusionary Practices and the Antitrust Laws", p. 517 (stating that "to conclude that predatory pricing is never an effective exclusionary practice is unsupportable.... [H]owever, our analysis implies that predatory pricing at most is likely to delay, rather than prevent the entry of new competitors").
40. O'Donoghue and Padilla, *The Law and Economics of Article 82 EC*, pp. 236–237 (showing that there are at least two common agreements on predatory pricing literature: first, that cost benchmarks are useful objective tools to determine if a firm's prices are predatory or not, and second, that price predation is a strategic behavior that requires analysis of the context in which it takes place).
41. *Ibid.*, p. 236.
42. According to Bork (Bork, *The Antitrust Paradox: a Policy at War with Itself*, p. 155, "the theoretical argument presented here is that suggests that predatory price cutting is unlikely to exist and that attempts to outlaw it are likely to harm consumers more than would abandoning the effort. The analysis also indicates that we should look for methods of predation which do not require the predator to expand output and incur disproportionately large costs." Bergh and Camesasca, *European Competition Law and Economics: A Comparative Perspective*, p. 281 (stating that under the Chicago school of law and economics, predatory pricing is irrational because any increase in prices will attract entry and any price cut made to disrupt entry will not have an opportunity to recoup losses).
43. *See* O'Donoghue and Padilla, *The Law and Economics of Article 82 EC*, p. 236, §5.2.

In the background is a basic and recurrent question for those designing legal rules: whether to have bright-line rules or case-by-case inquiry? Bright-line, or clear-cut rules, have the advantage of clarity and legal predictability, but they may at the same time have the disadvantage of failing to take into account atypical cases that require individual consideration. At the other extreme, a case-by-case inquiry carries the advantage of allowing particular unusual circumstances to be explored in depth, while the disadvantage lies in the cost of the consequently unavoidable lack of certainty and predictability under such a model. Plainly, neither approach is right or wrong. The key insight is that a choice has to be made by law and by policymakers based on weighing the advantages and disadvantages and the goals of law and policy. In the case of emerging Latin American economies, the use of economic growth as the policy's guiding principle helps on choosing a legal design that privileges those institutions that might help economic growth. Price predation is one of those prohibitions that are very much affected by choice of the type of rule chosen.

[A] Per Se Legal Below Cost Selling

The first standard in the literature is Bork–Easterbrook's. According to Easterbrook,[44] Bork's thesis on the inexistence of price predation allows competition law to avoid the notion of price predation as an act of monopolization. Easterbrook elaborates Bork's assertion that "predatory pricing should not violate the antitrust laws."[45] The thesis as elaborated by Easterbrook is based on game theoretical and welfare analysis, and concludes that price predation would not occur, or if it occurs, it would only benefit consumers, since the costs of an anti-predation rule would be greater than any benefit it would create. Therefore, price cuts should be deemed per se legal.[46]

The same argument may apply to high-pricing predation that may arise in monopsonic or oligopsonic market structures pervasive in emerging markets. Successful monopsonic predation is also unlikely since the predator is required to buy all the input in the market at a high price, and the costs of extra input make recouping profits more difficult.[47]

This standard, in either fashion, is subject to strong criticism by the literature. Zerbe and Cooper, for example, state that Easterbrook's analysis fails to consider that: (a) price predation can be harmful to social welfare, (b) does not demonstrate that price predation cannot occur or will always fail, and (c) fails to recognize that even in the case that price predation fails, it may have welfare consequences among others.[48] In a

---

44. Frank H. Easterbrook, "Predatory Strategies and Counterstrategies" (1981) 48 The University of Chicago Law Review 263, p. 48.
45. Zerbe Jr. and Cooper, "An Empirical and Theoretical Comparison of Alternative Predation Rules", p. 697.
46. *Ibid.*, p. 697.
47. Blair and Harrison, *Monopsony in Antitrust Law and Economics*, pp. 74–75.
48. Zerbe Jr. and Cooper, "An Empirical and Theoretical Comparison of Alternative Predation Rules", p. 698.

phrase, Zerbe and Cooper state that Easterbrook "refuses to recognize that predatory pricing can injure consumer and social welfare."[49]

Not much case law has supported this approach. The European courts, for example, have not explicitly claimed that price cutting should be seen as legal per se. However, some courts in the United States have found that such pricing strategies are not feasible. For example, in *Matsushita Elce. Indus. v. Zenith Radio Corp.*,[50] the U.S. Supreme Court showed certain skepticism to the likelihood of a successful predatory pricing scheme. After citing Bork's argument, the Court stated that "the success of such [predatory] schemes is inherently uncertain: the short-run loss is definite, but the long-run gain depends on successfully neutralizing the competition."[51] Then, the Court concluded, showing the skepticism regarding the success of a predatory pricing scheme and saying that:

> predatory pricing schemes require conspirators to suffer losses in order eventually to realize their illegal gains; moreover, the gains depend on a host of uncertainties, making such schemes more likely to fail than to succeed. These economic realities tend to make predatory pricing conspiracies self-deterring: unlike most other conduct that violates the antitrust laws, failed predatory pricing schemes are costly to the conspirators.[52]

Similarly, in *Cargill Inc. v. Montfort of Colorado Inc.*,[53] the Supreme Court stated that "there is ample evidence to suggest the practice does not occur" and heavily relied on Bork's statements to conclude "although the commentators disagree as to whether it is ever rational for a firm to engage in such conduct, it is plain that the obstacles to the successful execution of a strategy of predation are manifold, and that the disincentives to engage in such a strategy are accordingly numerous."[54]

The most recent skeptic standard decided by the Supreme Court was *Weyerhaeuser Co. v. Ross-Simmons Hardwood Lumber Co., Inc.*,[55] where the Court considered whether Weyerhaeuser bid up the prices of sawlogs in order to drive an incumbent from the market.[56] The case is somewhat different from *Matsushita* and *Cargill* since Weyerhaeuser is a single dominant buyer of red alder sawlogs in the Pacific Northwest; therefore predation happens by increasing prices. The Supreme Court explained that "to engage in predatory bidding, a purchaser bids up the market price of an input so

---

49. Ibid., p. 697.
50. *Matsushita Elec. Indus. v. Zenith Radio Corp.* 475 U.S. 574 (1986).
51. Ibid., pp. 588–593.
52. Ibid., p. 595. *See also* Thomas J. Campbell, "Predation and Competition in Antitrust: The Case of Nonfungible Goods" (1987) 87 Columbia Law Review 1625, p. 1627, and Edlin, "Above Cost Predatory Pricing", p. 495.
53. *Cargill Inc. V. Monfort of Colorado Inc.* 107 S.Ct. 484 (1986), p. 495.
54. Ibid., fn. 16. The Court also highlighted the impact and effect of an error in the assessment of an anticompetitive conduct stating that "the mechanism by which a firm engages in predatory pricing – lowering prices – is the same mechanism by which a firm stimulates competition, and therefore, mistaken findings of liability would chill the very conduct the antitrust laws are designed to protect."
55. See *Weyerhaeuser Co. v. Ross-Simmons Hardwood Lumber Co., Inc.* 127 U.S. 1069 (2006); J. Thomas Rosch, "Monopsony and The Meaning of 'Consumer Welfare': A Closer Look at Weyerhaeuser" (Milton Handler Annual Antitrust Review).
56. *Weyerhaeuser Co. v. Ross-Simmons Hardwood Lumber Co., Inc.*, pp. 1076–1077.

high that rival buyers cannot survive, thus acquiring monopsony power."[57] However, the Court did not follow the predatory pricing precedent of the Brooke Group[58] or find that predatory buying is a strategy that is likely to succeed, despite finding that monopoly and monopsony are similar phenomena that provide agents identical economic incentives.[59] The Court stated that "the general theoretical similarities of monopoly and monopsony combined with the theoretical and practical similarities of predatory pricing and predatory bidding convince us that our two-pronged Brooke Group test should apply to predatory bidding claims."[60] However, the Court concludes oddly, saying that the predators' actions must cause exit not only in the market where the predator buys but also in the market where the predator sells its output. Thus, the Court sets as a standard of proof in predatory buying cases that "a plaintiff must prove that the alleged predatory bidding led to below cost pricing of the predator's outputs. That is, the predator's bidding on the buy side must have caused the cost of the relevant output to rise above the revenues generated in the sale of those outputs."[61]

In conclusion, according to the rules stating that price predation should be per se legal, there is neither a rational nor a reasonable strategy to drive rivals from the market that may lead one to think that predation constitutes an unlawful monopolization or it is an illegal use of a dominant position. The evidence of such is that such pricing schemes have no likelihood of succeeding.

[B] Per Se Illegal Price Predation

Contrary to the aforesaid standard, predation can be deemed illegal per se. Just as in the previous standard, predation can be considered unlawful in both its versions: first, by any undertaking's action to price below cost, and second, by any undertaking's action leading to a price cut. Such standards are aimed at determining that there are pricing strategies that, despite seeming to follow what competition law encourages (competitive prices), they are in the end meant to mitigate a market's intensity of competition.

Three different standards that may be used as a foundation for determining per se illegality of predation are studied: first, a cost-based standard founded on the concept of marginal cost; second, a cost-based benchmark based on the concept of average variable cost (AVC); and third, a price-cut standard that considers that either below or above cost price cuts are predatory and per se illegal.

---

57. *Ibid.*, pp. 1076–1077.
58. See *Brook Group Ltd. V. Brown & Williamson Tobacco Co.* 509 U.S. 209 (1993).
59. *See* Blair and Harrison, *Monopsony in Antitrust Law and Economics*, pp. 76–79 (showing the reluctance of the Supreme Court to set a standard for predatory buying similar to price predation despite finding monopoly was the "mirror image" of monopsony).
60. *Weyerhaeuser Co. v. Ross-Simmons Hardwood Lumber Co., Inc.*, p. IV(c).
61. *Ibid.*

[1] Below Marginal Cost Predation

The per se illegality of pricing below cost was long ago established by the literature. The difficulty was always determining what economic cost is low enough to be considered by itself as per se illegal. According to Posner, there are "two conventional approaches to the identification of predatory pricing, one through intent and the other through cost."[62] However, neither is the right approach, since intent may be impossible to prove and if price predation is defined by cost, the rule may forbid too much or too little.

Posner states that only two practices are per se predatory. First, it is predatory selling below "short-run marginal cost." Any sale below short-run marginal cost is only rational if it has the purpose and effect to exclude a rival.[63] Posner acknowledges that this may be very difficult to measure; therefore it is a standard of difficult administration. Second, according to Posner, it should also be forbidden to sell "below long-run marginal cost with the intent to exclude a competitor."[64] The author defines *long-run marginal cost* as what must be recovered to stay in business for an infinite future. If there is intent, says Posner, pricing below long-term marginal cost is/will have the purpose and likely effect of excluding an equally efficient rival. Moreover, says Posner, "the need to rely on evidence of intent is a disturbing feature of this approach, especially to economists, whose assumption is that people's actions yield better insight into their true purposes than they say."[65]

However, not every price below short- or long-run marginal cost should be deemed illegal. There are several pricing policies that, despite being below the abovementioned benchmarks, are pro-competitive. For example, in a promotional pricing scheme, a firm wants to attract some would-be customers by pricing a product very low for a short term.[66] Then, unless the conduct is held for a long period, it is a safe strategy that posits no long-term harm to competition.[67] It is also considered that pricing below short-term marginal cost is not illegal in cases where the dominant undertaking is solely meeting competition in order not to lose market share. However, part of the literature considers that, on the one hand, the monopolist cannot have a case for promotional pricing unless it is directed to new geographical markets or new customers.[68] On the other hand, dominant undertakings' pricing below cost to meet competition is not a valid defense, as the incumbent's response will destroy the rival's efforts to enter the market.[69]

---

62. Posner, "Exclusionary Practices and the Antitrust Laws", p. 518.
63. *Ibid.*, p. 519.
64. *Ibid.*, p. 519.
65. *Ibid.*, p. 520.
66. Areeda and Turner, "Predatory Pricing", p. 713.
67. See *Ibid.*, p. 713. New entrants or small firms without monopoly power create no harm or danger for competition as it might be and serve as purely informational advertising.
68. *Ibid.*, p. 714.
69. *Ibid.*, p. 715.

[2] Below Average Variable Cost Predation

Areeda and Turner devised the most cited standard on price predation.[70] According to the authors, administrative problems would make a standard based on short- or long-run marginal costs impracticable. With regard to such a problem, the authors suggested that an "average variable cost rule ... should be flexible enough to allow a defendant to demonstrate that its price was equal or above a reasonably anticipated average variable cost."[71]

Indeed, at any price that is below AVC, or the average cost per unit produced, the producing firm will necessarily earn no return on its investments and could incur fewer losses by ceasing operations.[72] The AVC is regularly lower than the short-run marginal cost; therefore, the AVC is a less strict standard.[73] However, it is due to its simplicity in being determined and its slight difference with marginal cost that AVC is not only considered a very useful surrogate for price predation analysis but also an administrable standard.[74]

This benchmark for predation analysis, as shown by the authors, leads to the conclusion that marginal cost data are regularly unavailable or difficult to measure, and therefore no administrable.[75] In addition, any price that is at or above AVC must be presumed lawful, but any price below AVC is per se illegal and predatory. According to the latter rules, with regard to the fact that AVC is regularly lower than marginal cost, then: (a) any short-run profit-maximizing price is non-predatory even though it is below average cost, (b) a price at or above average cost should be deemed no predatory even though it is not maximizing profit in the short run, and (c) a price at or above short-run marginal cost and AVC should be deemed non-predatory even though it is not minimizing loss in the short run, therefore, unless at or above average cost.[76]

Other non-pricing predation schemes are analyzed by Areeda and Turner, such as investments. The authors consider that an investment might be seen as predatory "if the firm knows that the revenues obtained from the investment over their useful life will not cover all costs, including a normal rate of return."[77] Nevertheless, the authors find it very unlikely to happen:[78] a rule prohibiting investment that may be deemed as predatory may impair good investments and may be a hurdle to risk-taking behavior by dominant firms. Not every investment is successful, and if, once done, an investment is considered predatory, there will be two restrictions to engage in probably pro-competitive, pro-consumer, and pro-growth investment.

---

70. See *Ibid.*; Areeda and Hovenkamp, *Antitrust Law*; Areeda and Turner, "Predatory Pricing"; Phillip Areeda and Donald F. Turner, "Williamson on Predatory Pricing" (1978) 87 The Yale Law Journal 1337.
71. Areeda and Turner, "Predatory Pricing", p. 716.
72. *Ibid.*, p. 717.
73. *Ibid.*, p. 718.
74. *Ibid.*, pp. 732–733.
75. *Ibid.*, pp. 732–733.
76. *Ibid.*, pp. 732–733.
77. *Ibid.*, p. 719.
78. *Ibid.*, p. 719.

It is important to distinguish the argument that predation does or does not happen and the argument regarding costs related to the identification of predation. That is why similar approaches have tried to improve the administrability of Areeda–Turner's AVC standard. For example, Zerbe and Cooper conclude that the best rule is one that prohibits pricing below average total cost at high production levels and below AVCs at lower production levels.[79] The rule developed by Zerbe and Cooper states that there must be a relationship between costs and the decision-making process. Therefore, the authors say that the rule they propose can be split into three statements: first, a price below average total cost is predatory when production is in the upward sloping part of the average total cost curve; second, any price below AVC is predatory; and third, both AVC and average total cost must be related to the decision-making process and are therefore opportunity costs.[80] The authors consider that in most cases this rule will promote social welfare by promoting desirable price cuts and prohibiting price cuts that are undesirable, thereby promoting social welfare better than other rules.[81] The authors conclude that "the modified A–T rule provides the most appropriate compromise between the dangers of prohibiting beneficial price cuts and allowing detrimental ones."[82]

EU case law has extensively shown a preference for the A–T test and the AVC cost standard.[83] The most important case is *AKZO Chemie BV v. Commission*,[84] where the Commission of the European Communities found that AKZO had prices below AVC in the organic peroxides market. The Court of Justice of the European Union (CJEU) found that predation is presumed in cases where a dominant undertaking's prices are below AVC.[85] The CJEU, however, found that prices above AVC but below average total cost may also be regarded as abusive "if they are determined as part of a plan for eliminating a competitor."[86] Unlike the U.S. Supreme Court in *Brook Group Ltd. v. Brown & Williamson Tobacco Co.*,[87] the CJEU stated a clear cost standard and the reasons for deeming such prices as predatory, stating that:

> prices below average variable cost (that is to say, those which vary depending on the quantities produced) by means of which a dominant undertaking seeks to eliminate a competitor must be regarded as abusive. An undertaking has no interest in applying such prices except that of eliminating competitors so as to

---

79. Zerbe Jr. and Cooper, "An Empirical and Theoretical Comparison of Alternative Predation Rules", p. 685.
80. *Ibid.*, p. 686.
81. *Ibid.*, pp. 686–687.
82. *Ibid.*, p. 657.
83. *In Re ITT* 104 F.T.C. 280 (1984) (following the orthodox AT Test stating that any price below AVC is presumed predatory and prices between AVC and ATC should be presumed legal and prices above ATC are legal per se); *Accord Stearns Airport Equipment Co. v. FMC Corp.* 170 F.3d 518 (5th Cir.1999) (suggesting the AVC cost standard cited by Hovenkamp, *Federal Antitrust Policy: The Law of Competition and Its Practice*, p. 342, n. 4).
84. AKZO.
85. *Ibid.*, §70–71.
86. *Ibid.*, §72.
87. See *Brook Group Ltd. v. Brown & Williamson Tobacco Co.*

enable it subsequently to raise its prices by taking advantage of its monopolistic position, since each sale generates a loss.[88]

The above standard has been regularly used by the Commission and the CJEU in the following cases. For example, in *Tetra Pak International SA v. Commission*,[89] the CJEU used the AVC cost standard defined in *AKZO* in order to determine that Tetra Pak had abused its dominant position by pricing substantially lower than its AVC in the non-aseptic cartons market in Italy during the years 1976 and 1981.[90] Also, in *France Télécom SA v. Commission*, both the Court of First Instance (CFI)[91] and the CJEU[92] found that Wanadoo (subsidiary of France Télécom SA) abused its dominant position by charging excessively low prices for its eXtense and ADSL Internet services.[93] Both the CFI and the CJEU found that the sole fact that prices were below AVC was enough to prove predation, rejecting the need to show an effect or the likelihood to recover or recoup losses.[94] As stated by the CFI:

> it is clear from the case law on predatory pricing that, first, prices below average variable cost give grounds for assuming that a pricing practice is eliminatory and that, if the prices are below average total cost but above average variable cost, those prices must be regarded as abusive if they are determined as part of a plan for eliminating a competitor.[95]

The U.S. Supreme Court's case law, on the other hand, as said before, has been reluctant to define a measure or standard of cost. For example, the leading price predation case in U.S. antitrust law is *Brooke Corp. Ltd. v. Brown and Williamson Tobacco Co.*[96] Brooke participated in the economy segment of the U.S. cigarette market and charged that Brown and Williamson (B&W) had cut its prices on "generic cigarettes below cost and offered discriminatory volume rebates to wholesalers" in order to discipline Brooke.[97] The Court held that a price predation claim could only be found if, in addition to the demonstration of a period of below cost pricing, there was a dangerous probability that the losses incurred by the dominant undertaking during the predation time could be recouped afterwards.[98] The Supreme Court however relied

---

88. *AKZO*, §71.
89. See *Tetra Pak II*.
90. *Ibid.*, §44.
91. *CFI France Télécom*.
92. Case C-202/07 *France Télécom SA v. Commission of the European Communities* [2009] 1 FLR 1149 European Court of Justice.
93. *CFI France Télécom*, §151–154.
94. *CJEU France Télécom*, §37.
95. *Ibid.*, §130.
96. *Brooke Group Ltd. v. Brown & Williamson Tobacco Corp.* 509 U.S. 209 (1993).
97. *Ibid.*, p. 213.
98. *Ibid.*, p. 224. The Supreme Court makes a strong effort to clarify what it means by "a dangerous probability" to recoup losses; however, it makes no clarification regarding the cost standard. The Court states that:

> [t]he second prerequisite to holding a competitor liable under the antitrust laws for charging low prices is a demonstration that the competitor had a reasonable prospect, or, under 2 of the Sherman Act, a dangerous probability, of recouping its investment in below cost prices .... Recoupment is the ultimate object of an unlawful predatory

on *Matshushita* and *Cargill* dicta, stating that the cost standard is "some measure of incremental cost."[99] Despite the Court's analysis, it based its arguments on the impossibility of evidencing the probability of recoupment.

[3] Above-Cost Predation

Price predation, as stated before, is generally an act directed at disciplining or driving rivals from the market through prices. Part of the literature has found that certain price cuts are per se illegal regardless of their relation with costs. For example, Edlin presents a model where an incumbent is sanctioned not for pricing below cost but for pricing to drive new entrants. According to Edlin, the law fails to recognize certain prices as predatory because they are above cost.[100] Edlin's model states that:

> in markets where an incumbent monopoly enjoys significant advantages over potential entrants, but another firm enters and provides buyers with a substantial discount, the monopoly should be prevented from responding ... by lowering or matching the entrant's prices or by making significant product enhancements until the entrant has had a reasonable time to recover its entry costs.[101]

According to Edlin, this rule, which prevents and freezes incumbents' prices, encourages the incumbent to charge low prices from the start in order to discourage entry.[102] Edlin finds this rule a better alternative to similar rules such as Williamson's and Baumol's. On the one hand, Williamson's rule states that the question for antitrust is whether competition law "should tolerate or acquiesce in responsive pricing by dominant firms confronted by the prospect or fact of new entry, subject only to the condition that prices exceed marginal cost."[103] Then, Williamson's approach states that price and quantity responses to entry by dominant firms are inherently suspect of predation; therefore changes in quantity by dominant undertakings should be deemed predatory.[104] On the other hand, Baumol's rule requires price reductions to be quasi-permanent to eliminate the high-price period of recoupment and such rule will

---

pricing scheme; it is the means by which a predator profits from predation. Without it, predatory pricing produces lower aggregate prices in the market, and consumer welfare is enhanced.

Regarding costs, it only states that "a plaintiff seeking to establish competitive injury resulting from a rival's low prices must prove that the prices complained of are below an appropriate measure of its rival's costs" (1 See, e.g., *Cargill, Inc. v. Monfort of Colorado, Inc.*, 479 U.S. 104, 117 (1986); [509 U.S. 209, 223] *Matsushita Elec. Industrial Co. v. Zenith Radio Corp.*, 475 U.S. 574, 585, n. 8 (1986); Utah Pie, 386 U.S., at 698, 701, 702–703, n. 14; In re E.I. DuPont de Nemours & Co., 96 F.T.C. 653, 749 (1980). Cf. *United States v. National Dairy Products Corp.*, 372 U.S. 29 (1963) (holding that below cost prices may constitute "unreasonably low" prices for purposes of 3 of the Robinson-Patman Act, 15 U.S.C. 13a).

99. *Ibid.*, quoting Cargill, at n. 12, quoting Matsushita at n. 9.
100. Edlin, "Above Cost Predatory Pricing", p. 495.
101. *Ibid.*, p. 495.
102. *Ibid.*, p. 496.
103. Oliver E. Williamson, "Predatory Pricing: A Strategic and Welfare Analysis" (1977) 87 The Yale Law Journal 284, p. 292.
104. *Ibid.*, p. 292.

not, in the words of Edlin, "provide any incentive to price low before entry because it creates no link between post-entry and pre-entry prices."[105]

For Edlin this rule makes the market more contestable. The model set by Edlin assumes that the incumbent has lower costs than the entrant, and as the entrant knows this fact, it will always fear predation. The author states that the entrant, having knowledge of the above fact, knows that the price charged before entry is "cognizant" of the rule regarding predation and it can be higher or lower if the incumbent know that price cuts are a tool to discipline new entrants or to drive entrants or other incumbents from the market. Thus, if an entrant decides to pay the sunk costs of entry and compete, the incumbent, in order to deter entry, may cut prices below marginal, average, or variable cost, or may cut prices above costs. Under Edlin's rule, both below and above cost price cuts are per se predatory since the price set is only concerned with discouraging the potential entrant from entering or with driving another incumbent from the market. Despite that the author denies there is short-term sacrifice,[106] the price cut may be also considered as a sacrifice on profits.

The above-cost predation standard is mostly concerned with *ex ante* rather than *ex post* incentives. Edlin's is defining a model where incentives to price low are given to market participants. Therefore, the author's approach is based on encouraging entry and low prices, rather than punishing predators. For that, Edlin uses the model to explain that incumbents have several advantages over entrants and need no price cuts to meet competition. Then, as the model shows, no matter what the size of the price cut is, since monopolies and dominant undertakings have other non-cost advantages as quality, advertising and branding that grant them the possibility to compete with an entrant at any given price.[107]

This approach to predation is tremendously different from the other definition where predation can only occur among equally efficient competitors. Theoretically, Edlin's standard cannot happen if the entrant is an as efficient firm. In fact, Edlin may not be having as an end protecting competitors but is indeed looking for a definition to protect less-efficient competitors from the abuse of market power granted by higher efficiencies and grant a certain right to entry to small and less-efficient firms.

The U.S. lower-court case law finds such an approach plausible. For example, in *Transamerica Computer Co. v. International Business Machines Corp.*,[108] the Court held that in some circumstances "price cuts" above average total cost might be predatory.[109] The Court was explicit about the cost standards, stating that there is predation when "a monopolist sets prices above average total cost but below the short-term profit-maximizing level" if such price cut is aimed at discouraging new entrants.[110] The Court concludes that there should not be a "free zone" in which monopolists can exploit their power without fear of scrutiny by the law and a rule based solely on costs might undermine considerations of "intent, market power, market structure, and long-run

---

105. Edlin, "Above Cost Predatory Pricing", p. 496.
106. *Ibid.*, p. 498.
107. *Ibid.*
108. *Transamerica Computer Co. v. International Business Machines Corp.* 698 F.2d 1377 (1983).
109. *Ibid.*, §50.
110. *Ibid.*, §50.

behaviour";[111] therefore, for above-price predation, a rule-of-reason approach may apply. A very similar, approach was held by the court in *CalComp*,[112] when the court stated that "limit pricing by a monopolist might, on a record which presented the issue, be held an impermissible predatory practice."[113]

However, the Supreme Court in *Brooke*, following *Atlantic Richfield Co. v. USA Petroleum Co.*,[114] stated that "when the pricing in question is above some measure of incremental cost," there is no doubt that "only below-cost prices should suffice" since "above-cost prices that are below general market levels or the costs of a firm's competitors inflict injury to competition cognizable under the antitrust laws." The Supreme Court in Atlantic Richfield stated that "[l]ow prices benefit consumers regardless of how those prices are set, and so long as they are above predatory levels, they do not threaten competition." Therefore, the Supreme Court held in Brooke that:

> [a]s a general rule, the exclusionary effect of prices above a relevant measure of cost either reflects the lower cost structure of the alleged predator, and so represents competition on the merits, or is beyond the practical ability of a judicial tribunal to control without courting intolerable risks of chilling legitimate price cutting .... To hold that the antitrust laws protect competitors from the loss of profits due to such price competition would, in effect, render illegal any decision by a firm to cut prices in order to increase market share. The antitrust laws require no such perverse result.[115]

European courts, on the other hand, have found above-cost predation as anticompetitive only exceptionally. The CGI and the CJEU found in *Compagnie Maritime Belge Transports and others v. Commission*[116] that certain selective price cuts may be exclusionary and anticompetitive. In this case, the Compagnie Maritime Belge and other members of a shipping conference line, Central and West African Conference, operating between Zaïre and certain Northern European ports, were found to be abusing of their collective dominant position by selectively cutting prices in order to deter entry of an undertaking in the market.[117] The CJEU considered that when "a liner conference in a dominant position selectively cuts its prices in order to deliberately to match those of a competitor, it derives a dual benefit. First, it eliminates the principal, and possibly the only, means of competition open to competing undertaking. Second, it can continue to require its users to pay higher prices for the services which are no threatened by that competition."[118]

Probably the best description of the problem was given by Attorney General Fennelly, who after explaining the similarities between this case and a price predation case, said that:

---

111. *Ibid.*, §53 and n. 17.
112. *California Computer Products and Century Data Systems v. IBM* 613 F.2d 727 (United States Court of Appeals, Ninth Circuit., 1979).
113. *Ibid.*, at 743.
114. *Atlantic Richfield Co. v. USA Petroleum Co.* 495 U.S. 328 (1990).
115. *Transamerica Computer*, §53 and n. 17.
116. Joined Cases C-395/96 P and C-396/96 P *Compagnie Maritime Belge Transports and others v. Commission* [2000] ECR I-01365 European Court of Justice.
117. *Ibid.*, §115.
118. *Ibid.*, §117.

normally, non-discriminatory price cuts by a dominant undertaking which do not entail below-cost sales should not be regarded as being anti-competitive .... Different considerations may, however, apply where an undertaking which enjoys a position of dominance approaching a monopoly, particularly on a market where price cuts can be implemented with relative autonomy from costs, implements a policy of selective price cutting with the demonstrable aim of eliminating all competition. In those circumstances, to accept that all selling above cost was automatically acceptable could enable the undertaking in question to eliminate all competition by pursuing a selective pricing policy which in the long run would permit it to increase prices and deter potential future entrants for fear of receiving the same targeted treatment.[119]

The conclusion of the case showed that the fact that CMB and others prices were not below total average costs does not render legitimate the application of a pricing policy that selectively cuts prices in order to deter entry or drive competitors from the market.[120]

§9.04 PREDATORY PRICING IN LATIN AMERICA

Price predation prosecution in emerging economies is certainly much more common than in developed economies.[121] In contrast with larger economies such as in the U.S. and the EU, which have had a very small number of prosecutions on price predation grounds, emerging markets regularly engage in investigations regarding price cuts that seem to be directed to produce rivals' exit. As said before, market structure makes price predation a highly likely strategy in emerging economies, since structural factors may rationally incentivize dominant undertakings to attempt to or to drive a rival from the market in order to gain additional monopoly power or to discipline rivals already incumbent in the market.[122]

With regard to structural factors that are regularly associated to successful predation, cost standards become the rule that differentiates the policy followed by competition agencies. Statutes in the countries reviewed have not been specific about the definition of what behavior constitutes price predation as an offence to free competition. In contrast with excessive pricing prohibitions, statutory language shows that most jurisdictions have had a similar approach to prohibit price predation with cost-based standards.

In contrast, prosecution of price predation and the cost standards defined by the competition authorities has been as asymmetrical and do not have a single coherent policy. Having in mind that price predation in these emerging economies has not been

---

119. *Opinion of AG Fennelly on Compagnie Maritime Belge Transports and others v. Commission* I-01365 European Court Reports 2000 I-01365 Attorney General Office, §132.
120. See *Ibid.*, §137; *Compagnie Maritime Belge*, §117.
121. *See* Pittman and Tineo, "Abuse of Dominance ..." in and Philippe Brusick and Simon Evenett, "Should Developing Countries Worry About Abuse of Dominant Power?" (2008) 2 Wisconsin Law Review 269.
122. Janusz A. Ordover and Robert D. Willing, "An Economic Definition of Predation: Pricing and Product Innovation" (1981) 91 The Yale Law Journal 8, p. 13; Rey, "Competition Policy ..." (showing that predatory strategies may present a real threat to competition in developing economies due to failure in other markets such as credit markets).

seen as legal per se, two enforcement standards on predatory pricing may be identified in these emerging Latin American economies: first, price predation considered as illegal per se, and second, price predation considered illegal under a rule-of-reason approach. Part of the literature has shown that, regarding predation, the task is to develop a cost rule that is consistent with economic efficiency and, in this thesis perspective, adequate with regard to economic, social and political values as justifications, such as economic growth.[123]

In this section, first, the statutes of the countries of the region and the most relevant cases of each jurisdiction are described, focusing on the legal standard of prosecution. Second, the explicit and implicit considerations of competition authorities regarding market structure and competition policy goals are described in order to show whether the analysis and application of the prohibition on price predation in Latin America is appropriate in order to later define whether a different approach is justified.

[A] Illegal Per Se Predatory Pricing

Brazil, Colombia and Mexico have stated in their statutes that price predation is prohibited. Colombian law considers it anticompetitive for a dominant undertaking to sell below cost.[124] The Brazilian statute prohibits sales below cost and sales below the price in the exporter country.[125] Finally, Mexico has stated that in certain circumstances, it is an anticompetitive "monopoly practice" to sell below average costs or AVC.[126]

Despite most Latin American countries have prosecuted predatory pricing, only the Colombian and the Mexican competition authorities have sanctioned it, in two occasions, both, surprisingly, in the chewing gum retail market. In *SIC v. Cadbury Adams*,[127] the Colombian competition authority found, first, that Adams was dominant in the retail chewing gum market with a market share of 80%, and second, that there were strong barriers to entry due to the low possibility of supply-side substitutability, high sunk costs, need for high investment in advertising, difficulty of access to distribution channels, and economies of scale in the production process, among others. Given these structural factors, the Competition Authority found that Adams sold chewing gum during the years 2002 and 2003 at prices lower than the AVC, and such a price drop was only aimed at preventing Tumix, a new national brand of chewing gum, from entering the national chewing gum market.[128] In Mexico, *CFC v. Warner Lambert*,[129] Warner Lambert, formerly known as Adams, is a group of undertakings participating in the Mexican chewing gum market. The Mexican Commission held that

---

123. Zerbe Jr. and Cooper, "An Empirical and Theoretical Comparison of Alternative Predation Rules", p. 681.
124. Decreto 2153, Art. 50(1).
125. Lei 8884, Art. 21(XVIII–XIX). The statute states that selling below cost in the origin country is only applicable for those countries that have not signed a GAAT agreement.
126. Ley Federal de Competencia, Art. 10.vii.
127. *Superintendencia de Industria y Comercio v. Cadbury Adams S.A.*
128. Ibid.
129. *Comisión Federal de Competencia v. Grupo Warner Lambert México.*

Warner Lambert had substantial market power in the market, which was reinforced by large barriers to entry. The Mexican Commission found also that Warner cut its prices between 42 and 46% below its competitors', Cannel's, price during the year of the investigation, and that during such period, the company priced the chewing gums below total average cost and the AVC.[130]

Several other cases have been prosecuted but no undertaking has been found to be predating by the Mexican, the Colombian or other Latin American authorities. For example, the Colombian authority also prosecuted *Setas Colombianas S.A.*,[131] a producer of mushrooms, for price predating in the Colombian geographic market. The Colombian competition authority held that Setas Colombianas S.A. did not predate in the market, since its prices were higher than the average total production and commercialization costs[132] except during one month when costs increased due to a problem in the production line.[133] It is also interesting in this case that the Authority found that the indictment made by the Superintendent for competition against Setas Colombianas[134] had no grounds since the cost measured used included all the costs, not only the costs associated with the production and commercialization of mushrooms.[135] The Mexican Commission also prosecuted several other cases, such as *Lineas Aereas Azteca*,[136] *Sepsa*,[137] and *Savi*,[138] finding no evidence of price predation. For example, in *Savi*,[139] the Mexican Competition Commission found no evidence of predation by Savi in the institutional insulin market. The Commission found that Savi was always distributing Novo's insulin product at prices above total average cost.[140]

Similarly, in *Nellitex Industria Textil Ltda v. Textil J. Serrano Ltda*,[141] the Brazilian Secretaria de Direito Econômico accused Textil J. Serrano of price predating in the 100% polypropylene textiles market.[142] According to the Brazilian Secretaria de Direito Econômico, the prices charged by Textil J. Serrano were in several types of 100% polypropylene products, not enough to cover either the AVC or the average total cost, and in some cases, the prices charged by Textil J. Serrano were between AVC and average total cost. The Tribunal, the Conselho Administrativo de Defesa Econômica, found that there were neither economic conditions nor structural restrictions that could make predation a rational pricing policy for the defendant.[143] According to the

---

130. *Ibid.*, pp. 9–12.
131. *Superintendencia de Industria y Comercio v. Setas Colombianas S.A.*
132. *Ibid.*, §4.3.
133. *Ibid.*, §4.3.
134. See *Ibid.*
135. *Ibid.*, §4.3.2.2.
136. See *Líneas Aéreas Azteca v. Volaris y Avolar.*
137. See *Matoh v. Sepsa.*
138. *Cryopharma v. Savi Distribuciones* Expediente No. DE-33-2006 Comisión Federal de Competencia, México.
139. *Ibid.*
140. *Ibid.*, p. 20.
141. *Nellitex Industria Textil Ltda v. Textil J. Serrano Ltda* Processo Administrativo No. 08012.007104/2002-98 Conselho Administrativo de Defesa Econômica, Brasil.
142. *Nellitex Industria Textil Ltda v. Textil J. Serrano Ltda* Processo Administrativo No. 08012.007104/2002-98 Secretaria de Direito Econômico, Brasil, §616.
143. *Nellitex Industria Textil Ltda v. Textil J. Serrano Ltda*, §35.

Brazilian Tribunal, the price–cost analysis made by the Brazilian Secretaria de Direito Econômico was biased in several ways, as the 100% polypropylene textiles included several products and references that were not comparable; therefore the costs determined by the Brazilian Secretaria de Direito Econômico were inaccurate.[144] Both the Brazilian Tribunal and the Brazilian Secretaria de Direito Econômico used as a cost standard the AVC and average total cost, finding that prices below AVC are per se predatory and prices above AVC and below average total cost are anticompetitive.[145]

In summary, both the Colombian and the Brazilian policies against price predation consider that any price below AVC is per se anticompetitive. Statutes, however, are much more open as they define predation as any price below cost. Such an open standard, as it is said by the SEAE, is considered by authorities as an over-inclusive definition that might have consequences harmful to consumer welfare by mistaking a predatory practice with vigorous competition and inhibiting or restricting it.[146]

[B] Rule-of-Reason Approach to Predatory Pricing

In contrast with the statutory language in the Mexican, Colombian, and the Brazilian regimes, the Chilean and Peruvian statutes do not have prohibitions of price predation but general prohibitions of abuse and predatory actions. For example, the Chilean law prohibits any exploitative and predatory practice carried on with the aim to obtain, maintain, or strengthen a dominant position.[147] The Peruvian statute simply considers restrictive any act that may impede or make difficult to enter or to remain in the market for reasons different than economic efficiency.[148] Both statutes do not condemn price predation by selling below cost or buying above marginal revenue but aim to drive competitors from the market or to monopolize the market.

On the other hand, the Argentinean law prohibits selling goods or services at prices lower than its cost without reasons regarding commercial uses and customs, with the aim to displace competition from the market or produce damages to the image, brands or assets of suppliers of goods and services.[149] These wide open approaches have led their competition authorities to set rule-of-reason standards while studying competition restrictions derived from low pricing.

---

144. Ibid., §38–30.
145. Ibid., §35. According to the Guidelines on Price Predation (Secretaria de Acompanhamento Econômico, *Guia para Análise Econômica da Prática de Preços Predatórios* (Diário Oficial da União No. 241, 2002), §36–41), the standard followed by the SADE states that prices are per se anticompetitive if they are below average variable cost or, being below average total cost, there are no contractions on demand or an industry's sudden excess capacity.
146. As stated by SIC (*Superintendencia de Industria y Comercio v. Setas Colombianas S.A.*, §4.3.2.1), "certain business practices recognized by the system and routine in the market, such as ... the penetration of markets, promotional events, the sale of seasonal inventories, rotation of inventories closer to an expiration date, could not be made punishable, as it is not the undertaking's intention [to predate] or it does not involve any grievance to the market, and rather, they can bring significant benefits for the company and consumers."
147. Ley 19911, Art. 3(c).
148. DL 25868, Art. 10(2)(h).
149. Ley 25156, Art. 2(m).

Regarding the standard to determine predation, such authorities have used from price comparisons to cost measures that depart from the Areeda-Turner Test, and the variable average cost standard. For example, in *CNDC v. YPF S.A. y YPF GAS S.A.*[150] the Argentinean Commission for the Defence of Competition (hereinafter CNDC) studied the pricing policy developed by YPF and YPF Gas in the retail market of bottled Liquefied Petroleum Gas (R-LPG). According to the complaint presented by Shell Gas S.A., YPF attempted to drive from the market several firms that participated in the downstream market of LPG packaging and distribution. The Argentinean Commission, to determine price predation, established what prices were charged for bottled LPG by YPF competitors and, through comparison, found that YPF charged the largest prices among the four market participants; charging prices above 13% and 14% the average charged by its competitors. The Competition Commission, after reviewing price information, found there was no merit to continue prosecuting the case.

Despite in the latter case, where the single variable studied by the Argentinean Commission was price and there were no cost studies involved to determine predation, in *Impsat S.A. v. Telefónica de Argentina S.A. et. al.*,[151] Impsat accused several companies in the market of data transmission in Argentina to be price predating. The Argentinean Commission, using the AVCs standard, stated that in these markets variable costs are so low that it will be very difficult to demonstrate that prices are lower than such.[152]

The Mexican Commission, using statutory provisions, has used two types of standards regarding predation. First, it has used the total average cost standard in cases in which it systematically sells or prices goods or services below such cost measures.[153] Second, it has used the Areeda–Turner test in cases in which the concerned undertaking occasionally sells or prices goods or services below the AVC.[154] For example, in *Warner Lamber*, the Mexican Commission found that the chewing gum produced by Warner Lambert was systematically priced below both average total cost and AVC.[155] Also, in *Savi*, the claimant's allegations were considered with no grounds, as all pricing made by Savi in the tenders it participated in were above both the average variable marginal cost and average total cost.[156]

Other cost standards were also used, mostly by the Chilean authority. For example, in *FNE v. Agmital*,[157] the Chilean National Prosecutor accused before the Chilean Tribunal the association of owners of minibuses, Agmital, of price fixing and price predating in the market of public transportation of passengers on the route Talca–Almendros–Queri–Buenos Aires. The Chilean National Prosecutor found that after the entry of a new competitor to the market, the Bus Azul company, Agmital,

---

150. *Autogas S.A.I.C. v. YPF S.A. y YPF Gas S.A.*
151. *Impsat v. Telefónica de Argentina S.A et. al.* Dictamen No. 442 Ministerio de Economía y Producción Comisión Nacional de Defensa de la Competencia, Argentina.
152. *Ibid.*, p. 121.
153. Ley Federal de Competencia, Art. 10.vii.
154. *Ibid.*, Art. 10.vii.
155. *Comisión Federal de Competencia v. Grupo Warner Lambert México*, p. 18.
156. *Savi*, pp. 19–20.
157. *Fiscalía Nacional Económica v. Asociación Gremial de Dueños de Mini Buses Agmital* Sentencia 102/2010 TDLC Tribunal de Defensa de la Libre Competencia, Chile.

started a price predating strategy that was exclusively aimed to discipline and drive such a company from the market. Agmital members started by cutting prices in schedules that coincided with the entrant's, first from CLP 600 to 500 per route[158] and after a while to CLP 200.[159] The Chilean Tribunal found that the entrant could not match the 200 charged by the incumbents, losing a large stake of passengers and substantial losses after entry. It also found that the CLP 200 tariff was excessively low since, once compared to other prices charged on similar routes, the price difference was excessively large.[160] The CLP 200 tariff was also found to be not enough to cover the AVCs of the service. The Tribunal, despite finding that the sole aim of the price cut was exclusionary,[161] found that using an average avoidable cost standard, it could not be assured with certainty that there was no predation; therefore the predation charges could not be held.[162] However, the Tribunal sanctioned the members of Agmital under price-fixing charges.

By the same token, in *Producción Química y Electrónica Quimel S.A. v. James Hardie Fibrocementos Ltda.*,[163] the Chilean Tribunal held that low prices are also explained by new entry; therefore not every low price is to be held anticompetitive or predatory. The company James Hardie Fibrocementos Ltda. (JHF) was accused by one of its competitors, Quimel, of setting excessively low prices in the market of fiber cement sheets.[164] The Chilean Tribunal developed a deep analysis regarding market power, entry barriers, prices, and cost dynamics, finding that JHF had no dominant position in the market for fiber cement sheets, barriers to entry to the market were low, and prices were not higher than costs. The Tribunal found that prices were lower than total average costs, but higher than average avoidable costs; therefore it held that there was no price predation.[165]

Regarding justifications of predation, the authorities have been much more creative than merely studying costs. As was shown by Coloma,[166] the case *Argentine Chamber of Stationer's Shops v. Supermercados Makro*,[167] ended with the opinion that the pricing practice of Makro was not anticompetitive, although it was clear that the product was sold below its marginal cost. The Argentinean Competition Commission understood, however, that no offense to the competition law existed, since the accused supermarket had a very small market share and had neither the intention nor the possibility to exclude competitors. Its practice of selling the product at a very low price

---

158. *Ibid.*, §35.
159. *Ibid.*, §41.
160. *Ibid.*, §42.
161. *Ibid.*, §48.
162. *Ibid.*, §46–47.
163. *Producción Química y Electrónica Quimel S.A. v. James Hardie Fibrocementos Ltda.* Sentencia 39/2006 TDLC Tribunal de Defensa de la Libre Competencia, Chile.
164. *Ibid.*, pp. 1–3.
165. *Ibid.*, §29–33.
166. German Coloma, *The Argentine Competition Law and Its Enforcement* (CEMA 2007), p. 13.
167. *Argentine Chamber of Stationer's Shops v. Supermercados Makro* Expediente N° 064-000962/97 CNDC Comisión Nacional de Defensa de la Competencia, Argentina.

was, therefore, part of a business strategy to attract customers to its outlets, aimed at selling all the other products that were offered by the supermarket.[168]

Similarly, in the Chilean case *Camera de Comercio de Tagua-Tagua v. Distribución y Servicios S.A.*,[169] the Chilean National Economic Prosecutor studied the sale of bread to the final consumers in order to determine if there was abuse of dominance by two supermarkets, Supermercados Mayorista 10 and Lider, in the retail market of products of periodical consumption at home in the municipality of Tagua-Tagua. According to the complainant, the Tagua-Tagua Chamber of Commerce, the prices charged by such supermarkets per kilo of bread in the town of San Vicente of Tagua-Tagua were below production cost, and such prices were not sporadic offers or a decline in the stock that justified those prices, but a strategy to prevent entry. According to the Chilean National prosecutor, the market of bread sales to final consumers is highly atomized, and such a structural fact prevents dominant companies from effectively blocking entry or disciplining market participants. The Chilean National prosecutor followed the precedent defined by the Tribunal, that there are prices that, despite being below cost, are not necessarily exclusionary or do not necessarily imply losses for the undertakings charging them, remarking "loss leading" as an example of such behavior.

The Tribunal's precedent was also held in *Arauco v. Distribución y Servicio S.A.*,[170] the company Arauco complained stating that *Distribución y Servicio S.A.* (D&S) was predating in the retail market of products of periodical consumption at home in the municipality of Valdivia. According to the plaintiff, D&S was advertising fifty PVC products that, after discounts, had excessively low prices. The Chilean Tribunal established that the plaintiff was accusing that D&S was selling and advertising known value items[171] at prices lower than the costs with the sole intent to drive from the market other participants. The Chilean Tribunal used the AVC standard in order to determine whether D&S was predating in the relevant market. The use of such a standard led the Tribunal to conclude that only four out of fifty products had prices under AVC, and that the margin (rate between the price charged and the AVC) of such products was around 4.5% while the average margin of the fifty products was 7%. The Chilean Tribunal held that the facts showed that the strategy followed by D&S seemed to be consistent with promotional loss leading, a subset of products of high awareness and sensitivity to price for consumers offered under the AVC, to increase the demand for other products that obtained sufficient margin to offset the losses.

The Tribunal said:

> as pointed out in judgment 9-2004, the Tribunal considers that, in principle, sales under cost that are carried out to promote a product and provided that they last a short period, are not *per se* contrary to free competition, however when these sales

---

168. Coloma, *Argentine Competition Law*, p. 13.
169. *Cámara de Comercio de Tagua-Tagua v. Supermercados Mayorista 10 y Líder* Rol 168210 FNE Fiscalía Nacional Económica, Chile.
170. *Comercial Arauco Ltda. v. Distribución y Servicio D&S S.A.*
171. According to the TLDC, known value items are goods, due to their importance on consumption, whose prices are regularly remembered/guessed by consumers.

are made persistent and are used as a means to exclude competitors, they may be a discretion to limit competition.[172]

The Court considers that such strategies do fall into the category of promotional prices to which reference was made in consideration thirty-third, are not necessarily contrary to free competition.[173]

This rule, according to which, promotional sales are not predatory, was also held by the Chilean prosecutor in *Compañía Frigoríficos de Magallanes S.A. v. Distribución y Servicio S.A.*,[174] where D&S was accused of price predating in the retail market of products of "frequent consumption at home" in the municipality of Punta Arenas. The Chilean National prosecutor found that D&S was using some hook products in order to promote sales.[175] Therefore, the Chilean prosecutor held that this was a legal pricing strategy that had only a promotional, aim not an exclusionary object.[176] In addition, in *CMET v. Compañía de Telecomunicaciones de Chile S.A.*,[177] CMET accused the Chilean Telecommunications Company (CTC) of price predating in the market of fixed telephony.[178] According to the Chilean National prosecutor, price predation could not occur, since the duration of the discount regarded as predatory was no longer than a month; therefore it did not have the likelihood of excluding or disciplining a well-established company from the market.[179]

Regarding structural factors, in *Argentine Chamber of Stationer's Shops v. Supermercados Makro*,[180] ended with the opinion that the pricing practice of Makro was not anticompetitive since Makro had a low market share of 9% that made it not dominant in the retail market.[181] Regarding barriers to entry, in *Universal Gas S.R.L. v. Repsol YPF Comercial del Perú*,[182] Universal Gas S.R.L. (hereinafter Universal) accused Repsol of price predation in the market of packed LPG in the province of San Martin. The Peruvian Competition Commission found that, despite that Repsol YPF did not have a dominant position,[183] the bottled LPG gas market structure showed no significant barriers to entry, due to the potential competition that is represented by agents that, once prices go up, will have an incentive to enter the market.[184]

In summary, Chile has been the fiercest prosecutor of price predation; however, the authorities have not been able to find it. Other countries have been more reluctant to stop predation, mostly with regard to the difficulties and problems with the

---

172. *Comercial Arauco Ltda. v. Distribución y Servicio D&S S.A.*, §33.
173. Ibid., §35.
174. *Compañía Frigoríficos de Magallanes S.A. v. Distribución y Servicio S.A.* Rol-807-06 FNE Fiscalía Nacional Económica, Chile.
175. Ibid.
176. Ibid.
177. *CMET v. Compañía de Telecomunicaciones de Chile S.A.* Rol N° 977-07 FNE, Fiscalía Nacional Económica, Chile.
178. Ibid., §4.
179. Ibid., §4.
180. *Argentine Chamber of Stationer's Shops v. Supermercados Makro*.
181. Coloma, *Argentine Competition Law*, p. 13.
182. *Universal Gas S.R.L. v. Repsol YPF Comercial del Perú* Expediente N° 013-2004/CLC Comisión de Libre Competencia, Perú.
183. Ibid., §65.
184. Ibid., §55–56.

administrability of the different standards. As shown before, price comparisons, average total cost, AVC, and average avoidable costs were used to determine whether there was predation, and most of them were not successful at it. Despite statutory provisions in Latin American countries have not been as asymmetrical as in the case of excessive pricing, the cases studied show that it has been inconsistent regarding the arguments to define what predation is, to justify predatory pricing, and, mostly, to envision a policy that is coherent with other abusive pricing standards and their aggregate market structure.

§9.05 A RULE FOR PREDATORY PRICING ENFORCEMENT IN LATIN AMERICAN EMERGING ECONOMIES

In this section, having regard to economic growth as the guiding principle of competition law and policy, the question about what is the superior standard for emerging Latin American economies will be replied. The last section shows that there is no single standard for predation enforcement in Latin American economies. As in the case regarding excessive pricing, for price predation cases, it is required to define not what rule to use, as there are several valid approaches to predation, but at least to define a coherent policy applicable for Latin American emerging economies.

It was established in a previous section on the economics of predation that there are always high risks of false positives or negatives in enforcing predation claims.[185] The question for developing a standard for Latin American emerging economies is, with regard to the harm and the likelihood of misapplying a predation prohibition, is there still reason to allow its enforcement? And what sort of enforcement is needed?[186] It is required, then, to determine what enforcement standard to choose, taking into account economic growth as the policy's guiding principle and a set of structural restrictions.

The purpose of this section is to show that, taking into account economic growth as the guiding principle for policy design, and acknowledging the aggregate market structure Latin American emerging economies, it can be concluded that a standard that enforces any kind of predatory strategy through pricing is the best standard to attain rapid economic growth and a sound competition policy. This last statement is further developed below.

[A] Justification for a Different Approach to Price Predation in Emerging Latin American Economies

A few words regarding the background economics of price predation are worthwhile in order to justify such a standard. It is explained above that several factors determine the

---

185. Hovenkamp, *Federal Antitrust Policy: the Law of Competition and its Practice*, p. 286a–b (stating that in a highly concentrated market with a dominant undertaking with market power, the costs of over-deterrence are relatively low, while the costs of under-deterrence are high).
186. Zerbe Jr. and Cooper, "An Empirical and Theoretical Comparison of Alternative Predation Rules", p. 657.

likelihood of a successful predation. Such factors are mainly structural ingredients that may determine successful predation, and the same are the factors that characterize most industries' structure in emerging economies. These are, first, high levels of horizontal concentration and/or superdominance,[187] and second, barriers to entry that determine the irreversibleness of entry sunk costs.[188]

The presence of such elements makes the likelihood of a successful predation higher.[189] Such, as was shown in the Introduction of this thesis, are pervasive characteristics of Latin American emerging economies. As indicated, emerging Latin American economies tend to be highly concentrated, both vertically and horizontally. Such market structure imposes a constraint on the design of competition policy and enforcement standards, since the rule regarding market structures in most emerging economies' industries is to have highly concentrated, single dominant undertakings. Therefore, if an enforcement standard for emerging Latin American economies is developed with the aim to follow economic growth as the lighthouse in the competition law and policy route, such should be designed in order to promote and provide incentives to invest and innovate.

Taking the latter into account, it is fair to state that in Latin American emerging economies, incumbent undertakings have a structural incentive to discipline, induce, or drive rivals from the market. Such incentive is exacerbated when rivals or entrants must face structural, technological, or legal entry hurdles[190] and when there are exit[191] or re-entry restrictions.[192] Where those barriers are inexistent, or minimized, the contestability of the market eases entry and promotes investments that lead to economic growth. Therefore, the legal rule or standard to define in Latin American emerging economies, as has been said, should be one that encourages investment and entry by discouraging predatory pricing strategies. Such a rule would comply also with the requirement to be the best option to increase market contestability and to provide incentives for investment and, therefore, the best path with short term economic growth.

Authors criticizing predatory behavior state that such predatory acts are not rational.[193] In addition, some authors state that, in the case of high income economies, there is an unclear definition of what the practices that may constitute price predation are. It is also highlighted that there may be exaggerated fears that large firms will price

---

187. Ordover and Willing, "An Economic ...", p. 11.
188. *Ibid.*, p. 11. *See* Baumol and Willing, "Fixed Costs, Sunk Costs, Entry Barriers, and Sustainability of Monopoly,"
189. Rey, "Competition Policy ..."
190. Ordover and Willing, "An Economic ...", pp. 11–12.
191. *See* David Harbord and Tom Hohen, "Barriers to Entry and Exit in European Competition Policy" (1994) International Review of Law and Economics 411, pp. 333–337 (concluding that there are no sufficient reasons to take seriously predation as an anticompetitive practice).
192. If an undertaking has the opportunity of facing predatory behavior by exiting and re-entering the market, the firm has no problem in gaining profits in the recoupment stage of the "predatory campaign," Therefore, it is also necessary that entry and re-entry are costly and the entry, exit and re-entry barriers are not necessarily correlated. *See* Ordover and Willing, "An Economic ...", p. 11.
193. *See* Easterbrook, "Predatory Strategies and Counterstrategies."

predate.[194] However, the unlikelihood of price predation is not a sufficient reason to assure that there should be no rules to prevent or sanction price predation; such rules must be carefully defined, though.[195] Yet, in the case of Latin American emerging economies, it is documented that the presence of strategic entry barriers presents a significant threat to competition.[196] In the case of predation, barriers to entry, market concentration, and capacity constraints, pervasive features of Latin American emerging economies, are considered anticompetitive behavior-triggering factors.[197] Barriers to entry, as shown in section §9.02, are a set of factors that impose greater costs to entrants in order to engage in competition regardless of market structure. These factors, which affect sunk costs and price competition, are used by incumbents in order to drive entrants out, in the case of price predation, by pricing at entry-discouraging levels.

The entry decision-making process has at least two clearly defined stages:[198] the first stage is characterized by a decision to invest where sunk costs play a major role.[199] Once an undertaking has made a decision to invest, pricing on the second stage will depend only indirectly on sunk costs by influencing the decision to enter, knowing that the sole entry might change the intensity of competition and, therefore, prices.[200] It is the intensity of competition[201] and its interplay with sunk costs in the relevant market that determines the decision to enter. As quoted in the previous chapter, "the greater the degree of price competition at the second stage, the lower the post-entry profits and the fewer the number of firms choosing to enter."[202]

This approach to entry, where entry is a forward and backward decision-making process determined by sunk costs and expected prices, is particularly applicable to understand predation in Latin American emerging economies since: (a) sunk costs are regularly higher than in developed economies and entry decisions are drastically reduced by the structural characteristics of industries, and (b) entry decisions are subject to the industry's intensity of competition, therefore, pricing power by an

---

194. Areeda and Turner, "Predatory Pricing", p. 698.
195. *Ibid.*, p. 699.
196. *See* Anusha Chari and Nandini Gupta, "Incumbents and protectionism: The political economy of foreign entry liberalization" 88 Journal of Financial Economics 633 (showing the firms in concentrated industries in emerging economies are successful at preventing entry); Laffont, *Regulation and Development*, pp. 34, 35–36 (arguing that entry barriers, capacity constraints, and market concentration are factors likely to be present in developing economies; therefore a U.S.-style competition policy is not achievable for these economies.
197. *See* Laffont, *Regulation and Development*, p. 34 (arguing that entry barriers, capacity constraints, and market concentration are factors likely to be present in developing economies).
198. A similar game is shown by Sutton in (Sutton, *Sunk Costs*), p. 28, and Sutton, *Technology and Market Structure: Theory and History*, p. 37; however in these models the author assumes that marginal costs at the second stage are similar for all.
199. Sutton, *Sunk Costs*, p. 28.
200. In a perfectly competitive market, this would not be the case, as entry has no effect on market prices. In this case, where the market is concentrated, entry by any kind of undertaking has a direct effect on the relevant market prices.
201. The degree of price competition.
202. Sutton, *Sunk Costs*, p. 29.

undertaking makes entry much more unlikely.[203] Such a model is also applicable to undertakings that already are incumbents in the market, as every expansion of output or other investment decision that affects its pricing policies is associated with an entry or sunk cost, an intensity of competition, and an expected price.

It has been stated that, in order to promote economic growth, Latin American emerging economies require competition rules that send the right signals to market participants regarding what to expect once they have entered a market. If the policy guiding principle of emerging economies is to attain rapid economic growth, then encouraging entry investment through competition law and policy is necessary. As shown, there is a relationship between competition intensity, post-entry profits, and entry levels, and the role of a competition law enforcement rules that aims to encourage entry. The rule that encourages entry is the one that prohibits above and below cost price predation.

This rule has two properties: first, as it will be shown in the next section, it encourages market participants to avoid pricing excessively and to price more efficiently once they are the sole incumbents in the market,[204] and second, it imposes on incumbents the restriction not to price based on strategic responses to competition aimed to drive out entrants or to discipline other market participants.

[1] An Effect-Based Price Predation Standard for Emerging Economies

Despite that the standard defined above seems to be quite restrictive for undertakings' pricing policy, in order minimize Type II errors and avoid over-deterrence caused by such standard, it is mandatory to set a rule-of-reason approach that grants the economy's authority with a sufficient margin not to punish pro-competitive behavior. The latter is based on the character of emerging economies. These economies are regularly at an early stage of development; therefore product demand is growing rapidly, technological improvements are being regularly implemented, and most incumbent undertakings are profitable but have not necessarily developed economies of scale.[205]

The aforementioned features impose a great burden on competition authorities to distinguish between behavior that is a consequence of early industry development and behavior that is a strategic response to new entry. This identification problem requires that a standard such as this should be grounded on an effects-based approach that helps to identify precompetitive behavior and reduce appreciation errors. Such an approach, therefore, should not consider every excessively low price – or excessively high price on monopsonic industries – as per se illegal but take into account the plausible pro-competitive effects of some low-pricing policies.[206] Such a standard

---

203. *See* Motta and Steel, "Excessive Prices" in; Geradin, *The Necessary Limits to the Control of "Excessive" Prices by Competition Authorities - A View from Europe*, p. 44.
204. Posner, "Exclusionary Practices and the Antitrust Laws", p. 518.
205. Williamson, "Predatory Pricing: A Strategic and Welfare Analysis", p. 323.
206. *See Drogheda Independent Case v. Ireland Competition Authority* Decision No. E/05/001 ICA Ireland Competition Authority. In Ireland's *Drogheda* case, the Competition Authority used the

should take into account at least three elements: (a) whether the conduct was developed by a dominant undertaking, (b) whether there are pro-competitive effects, and (c) whether there are profits sacrifices.

[a] Dominance

There is not much to add regarding dominance tests except that they are required in order to find the relationship between market power and strategic pricing. Some authors state that dominance is not required in predation allegations since the predator's goal is "to get a significant increase in market power" that is later translated into higher prices and profits.[207] However, it seems tremendously unlikely that an undertaking with small market power could get a significant increase in market power by predating, since its likelihood of excluding rivals or increasing prices to exploit consumers after predating is very low.

[b] Pro-competitive effects

Regarding pro-competitive effects, as was stated before, industries in Latin American emerging economies are in early stages and price cuts are a consequence of demand and scale economies. Therefore, simple price cuts by dominant undertakings should not be regarded as predatory. As the proposed standard is quite restrictive on strategic pricing and punishes even profit sacrifices above cost, there must be a mechanism for investigated undertakings to show that price cuts are pro-competitive and the result of regular competitive interaction or efficiencies, for example those derived from scale economies. Therefore, if such a course of action is used to face entry without sacrificing profits, the price cut may be understood as a consequence of entry if there is a business rationale behind it. For example, there are investments that require certain profit sacrifices that may be large enough to be considered anticompetitive; however some investments may enhance consumer welfare and be considered pro-competitive.[208]

[c] Profits Sacrifice

Finally it is required to show that there is a profits sacrifice. Evidently there are profits sacrifices when prices are below cost. Only certain profit sacrifices can happen above

---

standard formulated by Brodley et al. (Joseph F Brodley, Patrick Bolton and Michael Riordan, "Predatory Pricing: Strategic Theory and Legal Policy" (2000) 88 Georgetown Law Journal 2239) where a four-item standard is proposed, taking as elements the plausibility of alleged predation, a business justification, feasibility of recoupment, and below cost pricing as elements to determine whether or not there is predatory behavior.

207. Miguel De la Mano and Benoit Durand, *A Three-Step Structured Rule of Reason to Assess Predation under Article 82* (Office of the Chief Economist, DG Competition, European Commission 2005), p. 28.
208. *See* Einer Elhauge, "Why Above-Cost Price Cuts to Drive Out Entrants Do Not Signal Predation or Even Market Power - And the Implications for Defining Costs" (2003) 112 Yale Law Journal 681.

cost.[209] Such profit sacrifices regularly come from price cuts that are large enough to exclude or discipline rivals or deter entry, and therefore only have economic sense if they are meant to exclude rivals.[210] The literature has extensively shown the pros and cons of this approach, concluding that profits sacrifice must be assessed with reference to "competitive circumstances."[211] However, it is also acknowledged that monopoly power not only is enough to induce a rival to exit the market but also is necessary such that the market possesses several structural characteristics that favor successful predation.[212] This is a condition that most Latin American emerging economies hold; therefore the opposite should be proven.

[2]   *Administrability of a Below and Above-Cost Predation Standard*

Authors such as Williamson consider that in choosing among predatory pricing rules, an important consideration is the relative difficulty of enforcing such standards.[213] The author says that "rather than slip inadvertently into a regulatory posture – which, experience discloses, is typically hostile toward competition – antitrust is better advised to seek simple rules enforceable in court."[214] Despite the selection of this standard is based on its properties to provide incentives to investment, entry and innovation, Latin American emerging economies may also be benefited by enforcement standards that are administrable and efficient in achieving the desired result. The guiding principle of competition law and policy is to encourage economic growth by mitigating exclusionary price strategies. Then, a rule-of-reason approach based on measures such as profits sacrifice may help to reduce the costs of administering a standard that is based solely on costs.

There is always a risk in enforcing competition law in order to over-deter activity. As was shown above, price predation entails a great risk of over-deterring action by punishing competitive behavior or under-deterring action by not punishing uncompetitive behavior. The standard defined, however, should be flexible enough to allow the authority to avoid errors, but it should be simple enough not to be costly and unmanageable. This standard is indeed difficult to administer if the whole burden of proof is on the authority. However, it is always easier for a government agency to observe prices than to observe costs; therefore supervising price cuts requires fewer resources than determining marginal or average costs. Then, in addition to supervising prices instead of costs, imposing the burden of proof on the undertakings helps to presume that price cuts after entry are the result of predation, and it is undertaking's responsibility to show that its behavior was indeed precompetitive.

---

209. *See* Edlin, "Above Cost Predatory Pricing", pp. 495–496 (showing why the law fails to recognize certain low prices as predatory because they are above cost); De la Mano and Durand, *A Three-Step Structured Rule of Reason to Assess Predation under Article 82*, p. 29.
210. De la Mano and Durand, *A Three-Step Structured Rule of Reason to Assess Predation under Article 82*, pp. 36–37.
211. Ordover and Willing, "An Economic ...", p. 10.
212. *Ibid.*, p. 10.
213. Williamson, "Predatory Pricing: A Strategic and Welfare Analysis", p. 288.
214. *Ibid.*, p. 288.

[a]   *Below and Above-Cost Predation in Latin American Emerging Economies*

In this section, the rule proposed for predation analysis will be evaluated looking at the ability for Latin American competition authorities to adopt this new benchmark. Then, the purpose of this section is to show whether the benchmark can be adopted, or, if a new set of rules should be proposed in order to modify the current legal system in these countries.

As explained in section §9.04, there are two types of price predation rules in Latin American emerging economies. The first set of rules define a strict prohibition, where price predation is considered illegal per se under a below cost predation rule, where only pricing by dominant undertakings that is below a certain cost benchmark, regularly AVC, are considered anticompetitive. The statutes of Argentina, Mexico,[215] Colombia[216] and Brazil,[217] show this language that certainly limit the use of a rule such as the one proposed above. The Mexican regime considers that it is anticompetitive the systematic sale of goods or services at prices below their average total cost or their occasional sales below the AVC, not including a above-cost predation.[218] In similar terms, the Argentinean statute is concerned with the selling of goods or the provision of services at prices below their cost, without reasons based on business customs and aimed to displace the competition in the market or of damage to the image or the brand-value of their suppliers of goods or services'.[219] This rule, as in the Mexican case, does not grant any room to follow a above-price predation rule and a legislative reform should be proposed, despite the general principle for the authority's interventions allows a rule based on the exclusionary power of above-cost pricing.

On the other hand, the Brazilian regime defines predation as the unjustified sell of goods or services below cost, leaving no room to above-cost predation other than the use of the general prohibition in Article 36.I, where any action that may limit free competition is prohibited.[220] Similarly, under the Colombian Statute, despite the predation rule is attached to cost, the above-cost predation rule could be adopted using the general rule under which any practice, procedure or system that tends to limit free competition is prohibited.[221] Under this rule, as shown above, it could be held that above-cost price cutting that under a rule-of-reason approach might be anticompetitive is prohibited. This approach cannot be used in Mexico or Brazil, since their regulations define prohibitions that are explicit enough to avoid any interpretation of a predatory practice based on above-cost price cutting strategies, and therefore, a regulatory reform should be proposed in order to make this standard of predatory analysis workable.

The Peruvian and Chilean legislation define general prohibitions that might allow the use of an above-cost predation rule. As was shown before, the Chilean Statute

---

215. Ley Federal de Competencia, Art. 10.vii.
216. Decreto 2153, Art. 50(1).
217. Lei 8884, Art. 21(XVIII–XIX). The statute states that selling below cost in the origin country is only applicable for those countries that have not signed a GAAT agreement.
218. Ley Federal de Competencia, Art. 10.vii.
219. Ley Federal de Competencia, Art. 10.vii.
220. Lei 12529, Art. 36 (XV).
221. Ley 155 de 1959, Art. 1.

considers anticompetitive any "predatory, or unfair competition practices carried out in order to attain, maintain or enhance a dominant position."[222] This statutory language, in addition to the regular path followed by the Chilean case law, indicates that a rule that may consider predation not only selling below some standard of cost but also price cuts above costs that are aimed at disciplining rivals and maintaining a dominant position. Finally, the Peruvian regime considers that "behaviours that prevent or hinder access to or retention of current or potential competitors in the market for reasons other than economic efficiency" are prohibited and considered illegal. This prohibition could also grant the room for a standard on predation, which allows not only below cost predation but also above-cost predatory practices.

In summary, most emerging Latin American economies have a regime that would require a legislative reform in order to consider above cost-pricing and price cutting as a predatory practice. Other countries, such as Colombia and Chile, could use their current legislation and define a standard of analysis for predatory practices based on the rule proposed, which emerges having regard to economic growth as the guiding principle of competition policy.

§9.06 CONCLUSIONS

This Chapter's was aimed to define what rule or standard regarding price predation should be used in Latin American emerging economies if economic growth is seen as policy design guiding principle, and therefore, the guiding light of competition law design. Having this in mind, the standard proposed prohibits above and below cost price predation. This standard encourages market participants to price more efficiently once they are the sole incumbents in the market,[223] and imposes on incumbents the restriction not to price based on strategic responses to competition aimed at driving out entrants or disciplining other market participants. It also provided entrants and small incumbents in the market, the incentives to invest and innovate in order to enter or remain in the market.

A few more words may be useful, in order to show the importance of this standard from the perspective of emerging Latin American economies. As was explained, predatory pricing is the purest form of the exclusionary use of economic power. In this chapter, it has been shown that there are different understandings regarding the economic consequences of predatory pricing, but there is, however, no consensus regarding when there is economic predation or what the best policy is. It also has been shown that the mainstream approaches to predatory pricing, as well as the Latin American emerging economies' approaches to predation, are dissimilar in terms of normative grounds and goals. The Latin American emerging countries' competition laws studied regularly follow standards similar to the mainstream predatory pricing doctrines. These are not necessarily appropriate for such economies due to

---

222. Ley 211 de 1973, Art. 3.c.
223. Posner, "Exclusionary Practices and the Antitrust Laws", p. 518.

poor acknowledgement of Latin American emerging economies' goals and the industrial structure of their markets, and mostly, because the selection of the policy is not based.

As explained, in Latin American emerging economies, the likelihood of successful predation is higher due to the fact that the structural ingredients that may determine successful predation are the same factors that characterize most industries' structure in emerging economies. Such a market structure imposes a constraint on the design of competition policy and the enforcement of standards; therefore, enforcement standards developed for high income economies are not necessarily appropriate. Therefore, in Latin American emerging economies, incumbent undertakings have a structural incentive to discipline, induce or drive rivals from the market. Such incentive is exacerbated when rivals or entrants must face structural, technological or legal entry hurdles[224] and when there are exit[225] or re-entry restrictions.[226] Therefore, having economic growth as the policy's guiding principle, the legal standard to define in Latin American emerging economies, as has been said, should be one that encourages entry by discouraging predation.

In the general case of emerging economies, it has been documented that the presence of entry barriers presents a significant threat to competition.[227] In the case of predation, barriers to entry, market concentration, and capacity constraints, pervasive features of Latin American economies, are considered anticompetitive behavior-triggering factors.[228] The entry decision-making process has two defined stages: first, a party makes a decision to invest and sunk costs play a major role, and second, a decision regarding pricing on the second stage that will depend indirectly on sunk costs and directly on the intensity of competition.[229] Entry, seen as a backward decision-making process determined by sunk costs and competition intensity, is particularly applicable to understanding predation in emerging economies since it has been stated that emerging economies require competition rules that send the right signals to market participants regarding what to expect once they have entered a market. If the guiding

---

224. Ordover and Willing, "An Economic …", pp. 11–12.
225. *See* Harbord and Hohen, "Barriers to Entry and Exit in European Competition Policy", p. 333–337 (concluding that there are no sufficient reasons to take seriously predation as an anticompetitive practice).
226. If an undertaking has the opportunity to face predatory behavior by exiting and re-entering the market, the firm has no problem to gain in the profits recoupment stage of the "predatory campaign." Therefore, it is also necessary that entry and re-entry are costly, and these entry, exit, and re-entry barriers are not necessarily correlated. *See* Ordover and Willing, "An Economic …", p. 11.
227. *See* Chari and Gupta, "Incumbents and protectionism: The political economy of foreign entry liberalization" (showing the firms in concentrated industries in emerging economies are successful at preventing entry); Laffont, *Regulation and Development*, pp. 34, 35–36 (arguing that entry barriers, capacity constraints, and market concentration are factors likely to be present in developing economies; therefore a U.S.-style competition policy is not achievable for these economies).
228. *See* Laffont, *Regulation and Development*, p. 34 (arguing that entry barriers, capacity constraints, and market concentration are factors likely to be present in developing economies).
229. In a perfectly competitive market, this would not be the case, as entry has no effect on market prices. In this case, where the market is concentrated, entry by any kind of undertaking has a direct effect on the relevant market prices.

principle of policy design of Latin American emerging economies is economic growth, then encouraging entry through competition law and policy is necessary. As shown, there is a relationship between competition intensity, post-entry profits and entry levels, and the role of a competition law enforcement standard, that aims to encourage entry, is such that it guarantees undertakings that there will be no predation of profits through exclusionary acts before and after entry.

CHAPTER 10
Bid Rigging in Ecuador

David A. Sperber[*]

§10.01 INTRODUCTION

Bid rigging, in general terms, is an illegal *conspiracy* whereby *competitors* join to artificially increase the price of *goods* and/or *services* offered in *bids* to potential *customers*. It may also include carving up potential *business* between the conspirators. Economists, including those at the Organisation for Economic Co-operation and Development (OECD) have highlighted that bid rigging is, "particularly harmful if it affects public procurement as it takes resources from purchasers and taxpayers, it diminishes public confidence in the competitive process, and undermines the benefits of a competitive marketplace."[1]

Why do companies collude in public bidding? The main reason is that bidding for contracts demand time and high costs when only one winner can prevail. The lure to lessen these expenses by agreeing on which contracts to bid on (and predetermining the likely winning bidder) is high. Ecuador's Competition Law[2] (Law to Control Market Power (LORCPM)) prohibits these agreements and mandates that such cases be investigated by the Ecuadorian Competition Authority[3] (SCPM).

Bid rigging occurs in many forms. The following are the most commonly found bid rigging practices:

---

[*] dsperber@antitrust.ec; davidspeber@hotmail.com. Disclaimer: The views expressed herein are the author's and do not represent those of the aforementioned organizations.
1. Peter CURRAN, OECD Recommendation on Fighting Bid Rigging in Public Procurement, November 4, 2012. Cfr. OECD. Guidelines for Fighting Bid Rigging in Public Procurement in 2009.
2. *Ley Orgánica de Regulación y Control del Poder de Mercado* – LORCPM. R.O. S. 555 of October 13, 2011.
3. Ecuadorian Competition Authority. Superintendence for Control of Market Power. *Superintendencia de Control del Poder de Mercado.*

(a) Bid suppression: where Bidder A agrees to suppress his bid so that Bidder B can win the contract.
(b) Bid withdrawal: Bidder A withdraws its bid to leave Bidder B as the only bidder.
(c) Cover pricing: where Bidder A shares its proposed bid price so that Bidder B can bid a higher price to ensure that Bidder A wins the contract.
(d) Bid rotation: where Bidder A and Bidder B take turns being the designated successful bidder on certain contracts, alternating submissions of the lowest priced bid to win successive contracts.
(e) Non-conforming bids: Bidder A deliberately submits a bid that does not comply with the specifications of the tender requirements so that Bidder B prevails.

In these scenarios, the "losing" bidder may receive a compensatory payment, a sub-contract by the winning bidder, or the next bid.

Ecuador's Antitrust Law, which was enacted in 2011, aims to protect the competition process. By outlawing anticompetitive practices, it also seeks to ensure the well-being of the economy and consumers.[4]

This paper analyzes collusive agreements between economic actors to win contracts with public institutions for the purchase of goods or services and how Ecuador's antitrust legal framework applies.

Ecuadorian law as it pertains to bid rigging has not been discussed or studied before. I thus examine the administrative precedents in Ecuador and present future recommendations. To do so, I have analyzed the first cases in which the SCPM has ruled and issued sanctions in the *TUBES Case*[5] and *CRONIX v. SOLNET and IESS*.[6]

---

4. LORCPM, Art. 1.:

> The purpose of this Law is to avoid, prevent, correct, eliminate and sanction the abuse of economic agents with market power; the prevention, prohibition and sanction of collusive agreements and other restrictive practices; the control and regulation of concentrations; and, the prevention, prohibition and sanction of disloyal commercial practices, seeking market efficiency, fair commerce and the general well-being and that of consumers and users, for the establishment of a social, solidarity and sustainable economic system.

5. Ministry of Industry and Productivity- *Ministerio de Industria y Productividad*, Resolution No. MIPRO-003-2012, October 11, 2012.
6. *CRONIX Cia. Ltda. v. SOLNET S.A., RECAPT RECUPERACION DE CAPITAL CONTACT CENTER S.A. and Instituto Ecuatoriano de Seguridad Social (IESS)*.SCPM. September 7, 2015.

§10.02 LEGAL FRAMEWORK

[A] Public Procurement Legislation

The National Public Procurement System Act (LOSNCP)[7] establishes procurement procedures and rules for the acquisition, or lease of, goods and services (including consultancy and advisory services) by all State powers, agencies and entities. The National Public Procurement System (SNCP) is the governmental authority responsible the oversight and control of contracts and contractual standards while ensuring transparency and preventing illegal discretion in public procurement.

The following are the primary laws governing public procurement in Ecuador:

2.1.1. Constitution of Ecuador (2008).[8]
2.1.2. National Public Procurement System Act and its Regulations.

LOSNCP categorizes the different modalities that contracting institutions must follow based on the nature and amount of the goods or services in question. They are:

- Bidding.
- Quotation.
- Electronic Reverse Auction.
- Electronic Catalog.
- Small and Very Small Amounts.

In the *CRONIX v. SOLNET and IESS* case, the Ecuadorian Social Security Institute (IESS) required the purchase of "a comprehensive system for management, scheduling and interrelation with the intention of health and improvement of services provided by the IESS to its users" (or call center), under the electronic reverse auction modality.[9] This modality, as well as the others mentioned above, are governed by the principles of: legality, fairness, equality, quality, technological effectiveness, opportunity, competition, transparency, publicity and national participation.[10] Although these principles are closely related to competition law, there is no specific provision in the LOSNCP that sanctions or punishes collusion in public procurement – so only LORCPM applies in bid rigging cases.

This paper thus focuses on the analysis of the awarding of contracts by State institutions and how antitrust rules and regulations apply to big rigging practices.

---

7. National Public Procurement System Act or *Ley Orgánica del Sistema Nacional de Contratación Pública* (LOSNCP). R.O.S 395 of 29-II-2016.
8. Constitution of Ecuador R.O. 449, October 20, 2008.
9. Reverse Auction Electronics Modality – This procedure is viable when the following requirements and characteristics are met: (a) contracting entities purchase goods and/or standardized services which exceed the amount equivalent to 0.0000002 of the State's total Budget (approximately USD 54,000,00 in 2015); (b) cannot be contracted through electronic catalog shopping; and, (c) the suppliers of those goods and services bid the lower price offered by electronic means through the institutional portal (*www.compraspublicas.gov.ec*).
10. LOSNCP. Article 4.

[B] Competition Legislation

The following are Ecuador's main legislation applicable competition:

  2.2.1 Constitution of Ecuador (2008).[11]
  2.2.2 Andean Community Decision 608, "Rules for the Protection and Promotion of Competition within the Andean Community."[12] (Decision 608)
  2.2.3 Andean Community Decision 616, *"Entry into Force of Decision 608 for the Republic of Ecuador."* (Decision 616)
  2.2.4 Presidential Decree 1614 (repealed by LORCPM).[13]
  2.2.5 Ecuador's National Competition Law: Law to Control Market Power (LORCPM).[14]
  2.2.6 Ecuador's National Competition Law rules (RALORCPM).[15]

Presidential Decree 1614 enacted competition law procedures and established the Ministry of Industry and Productivity (MIPRO) as Ecuador's National Interim Competition Authority. This decree was necessitated by two factors. First, Ecuador did not have a competition law until 2011 despite the fact that Article 2 of Andean Decision 616 required, "Ecuador, by August 1, 2005, at the latest, shall name its interim National Competition Authority in charge of enforcing Andean Decision 608." Second, a petition for compliance was filed at the Secretariat-General of the Andean Community that alleged Ecuador had failed to comply with its obligation.[16] Beforehand Article 1 of Decision 616 allowed Ecuador to apply Decision 608 as a national law until it enacted its own national antitrust law.

LORCPM subsequently created the Superintendence of Control of Market Power (SCPM) in 2011. SCPM is the country's competition authority with broad investigatory and sanctioning powers. LORCPM, in turn, focuses on five areas[17] and classifies bid rigging as serious anticompetitive conduct.[18]

---

11. Constitution of Ecuador, Arts. 304, 335, 336, and 363.7.
12. CAN Decision 608, Art. 7. They are presumed to constitute restrictive to competition behaviors, among others, the agreements that have the purpose or effect of: (...) e) establishing, arranging or coordinating positions, abstentions or results in tenders, contests or public auctions.
13. Presidential Decree 1614, R.O. No. 558, March 27, 2009.
14. *Ley Orgánica de Regulación y Control de Poder de Mercado* – LORCPM.
15. *Reglamento de Aplicación a la Ley Orgánica de Regulación y Control de Poder de Mercado* – RALORCPM.
16. Petition for compliance presented by Alejandro Ponce V. and his legal procurator David A. Sperber. Cfr. Andean Community General Secretariat. Resolution 03-2009, G.O.A.C. Year XXVI, No. 1723, June 10, 2009.
17. LORCPM areas: (a) restrictive agreements; (b) abuse of market power; (c) merger control; (d) public aids; and, (e) unfair competition that affects competition.
18. Article 11 of LORCPM – Agreements and Prohibited Practices: All agreements, decisions or collective recommendations or concerted or consciously parallel practice, and in general all acts or conduct made by two or more economic actors of any manifested form, related to the production and exchange of goods or services, the object or effect is or may be to prevent, restrict, falsify or distort competition or adversely affect economic efficiency or general welfare are prohibited and shall be punished in accordance with the rules of this law. Article 79 of LORCPM – Sanctions: The Superintendence of Control of Market Power can impose on companies or economic actors, associations, unions or groups who intentionally or negligently, infringe the provisions of this Law, the following sanctions:

[C] Anticompetitive Agreements

Article 7 of the supranational Decision 608 outlines the anticompetitive agreements that are presumed to be illegal, although they are not deemed per se monopolistic agreements. LORCP's Article 11 accordingly defines (but does not limit) that restrictive practices to be any agreement, decision, collective recommendation, concerted decision or consciously parallel practice whose object or effect restricts, affects or distorts competition or adversely modifies economic efficiency or the general welfare.

LORCPM Article 11.6 and 11.21[19], in turn, classify bid rigging as illegal conduct.

[D] Public Procurement and Competition Law

LOSNCP governs public procurement procedures and LORCPM determines the collusion procedures, sanctions and competent authority to resolve bid rigging cases. Collusive agreements need not be formal agreements and can be sanctioned when the effect of them is anticompetitive, as bid rigging can take many forms. But one frequent modality is where competitors agree in advance which company will triumph in the bid.

§10.03 AN OVERVIEW OF INTERNATIONAL BID RIGGING CASES

[A] United States of America: Multiple Listing Service, Inc.

Multiple Listing Service, Inc. (MLS) was a joint venture private real estate association made of members to foster real estate brokerage services. The complaint[20] alleged that MLS acted anti-competitively by adopting rules and policies that limited the publication and marketing of certain sellers' properties. This limited the ability of real estate brokers to use Exclusive Agency Listings to offer unbundled brokerage services at a lower price compared to the full service package. The rule discriminated on the basis of lawful contractual terms between the listing real estate broker and the seller of the

---

a. Minor offenses with fines of up to 8% of total turnover of the company or operator economic offender in the immediately preceding the imposition of the fine exercise. b. Serious offenses with a fine of up to 10% of the total turnover of the company or operator economic offender. c. Very serious infringements with a fine of up to 12% of the total turnover of the company.

19. *Article 11.6. of LORCPM: Illegal agreement. Acts or omissions, agreements or concerted practices and generally all conduct of suppliers or bidders, whatever form they take, the object or effect the prevention, restriction, falsify or distort competition, either in the presentation of offers and positions or seeking to ensure the result to their advantage or another vendor or bidder in a tender, contests, auctions, public auctions or other established in the rules governing public procurement, or in processes of private recruitment open to public.*
    Article 11.21 of LORCPM: Illegal agreement. The agreements between suppliers and buyers, regardless of the provisions of the law, which can be given in public purchases and routed hiring to unfairly favor one or more economic actors.
20. United States of America before the Federal Trade Commission (2008), File Number 0610090.

property. The rule did not have any justification that it improved competitive efficiency.

The Federal Trade Commission (FTC) alleged that the rules were collusive and exclusionary and served to withhold the MLS's valuable benefits from brokers who did not use traditional listing contracts with their customers. The acts and practices of MLS, Inc. violated section 5 of the FTC Act, as amended, 15 U.S.C. § 45. Under the terms of the December 2007 consent, MLS is barred from adopting or enforcing any rule that treats one type of real estate listing agreement more advantageously than any other, and from interfering with the ability of its members to enter into any kind of lawful listing agreement with home sellers.

[B] United Kingdom: Cirrus and Others[21]

The Office of Fair Trading (OFT) issued an Infringement Decision finding that four suppliers of access control and alarm systems to retirement properties have breached competition law. The OFT found that, between 2005 and 2009, Cirrus Communication Systems Limited ("Cirrus"), Peter O'Rourke Electrical Limited ("O'Rourke"), Owens Installations Limited ("Owens") and Glyn Jackson Communications Limited ("Jackson") engaged in a number of collusive tendering arrangements in relation to the supply and installation of certain access control and alarm systems to retirement properties in the U.K. The infringements span different periods for different parties between 2005 and 2009.

The OFT found that each of CCSL, Jackson, O'Rourke and Owens committed the infringements either intentionally or at least negligently. Each of the infringements was aimed at misleading a potentially vulnerable consumer group as to the nature of the tendering process, in that the purpose of each of the arrangements was to eliminate competition in the tendering process.

The evidence indicated that the Contractors had gained or anticipated gaining as a result of the collusive tendering arrangement, in that the Contractors expected to be compensated through the provision of work on a contract, in the form of subcontracting work from Cirrus in the future.

[C] Australia: Marine Hoses[22]

The Marine Hoses Industry are used to load sweet or processed crude oil and other petroleum products from offshore onto vessels and to offload them back to offshore or onshore facilities. This case involved price fixing, bid rigging and market sharing by four foreign companies that supplied rubber hosing to transfer oil and gas from production and storage facilities to offshore tankers.

---

21. Office of Fair Trading (2013) *Collusive tendering in the supply and installation of certain access control and alarm systems to retirement properties*, CA98/03/2013 (CE/9248-10).
22. Commission of the European Communities (2009), *Marine Hoses*, Case COMP/39406.

Evidence uncovered revealed that, at least since 1986, members of the marine hoses cartel had been running a scheme to share out amongst themselves the tenders awarded by their customers. The four companies involved Dunlop Oil & Marine, Bridgestone Corp., Trelleborg Industrie SAS and Parker ITR each appointed members to a committee that allocated jobs and coordinated bidding and quoting for these jobs.

Under the scheme, any member of the cartel who received an inquiry from a customer would report it to the cartel coordinator, who, in turn, would allocate the customer to a "champion," which means the member of the cartel who was supposed to win the tender. To make sure that the tender was awarded to the "champion," in the tendering procedure the cartel agreed on the prices that each of them should quote so that all their bids would be above the price quoted by the champion.

The Australian Competition & Consumer Commission (ACCC) initiated court proceedings against the companies in June 2009, claiming they rigged bids to supply marine hose to customers in Australia from 2001 to 2006. They allege that between 2000 and 2007 Bridgestone (Japan), Dunlop Oil & Marine (U.K.), Parker ITR (Italy) and Trelleborg (France) engaged in price fixing, market sharing and other anticompetitive conduct when supplying marine hose in contravention of the Trade Practices Act 1974, in which, the Federal Court in Melbourne ordered to pay penalties. In 2010, the Federal Court of Australia made orders restraining the parties from repeating such conduct and imposed penalties exceeding USD 8 million.

§10.04 ECUADOR BID RIGGING CASES

Ecuador's competition authority has resolved only two cases regarding bid rigging:

    4.1. TUBOS
    4.2. CRONIX.

[A] TUBOS Case (Ministry of Industry and Productivity)[23]

The SNCP (formerly INCOP) filed a claim at the Ministry of Industry and Productivity for breach of Decision 608's Article 7(a)&(e). In this case, the Transition Commission of Guayas had initiated an electronic reverse auction to acquire specific steel and galvanized pipes. The four bidders submitted offers: Emilio Tuma-Cedeño, Alfredo Sevilla-Dalgo, IMPOSIDOF CÍA LTDA. and SICOMSE S.A.

The facts of the case showed that:

    4.1.1. None of the bidders had sufficient experience to participate in the electronic reverse auction;
    4.1.2. All of the bidders were authorized distributors of the same manufacturer and all four solicited identical certificates for the products to be offered on the same day.

---

23. Ministry of Industry and Productivity – *Ministerio de Industria y Productividad*, Resolution No. MIPRO-003-2012, October 11, 2012.

4.1.3. All of the bidders invited themselves to the bidding process.
4.1.4. The four bidders held a meeting to discuss the bidding and the contract process.
4.1.5. The day of the electronic reverse auction each party submitted only one bid.
4.1.6. The price of the "champion" was above normal market price.
4.1.7. The winner submitted the bid on his on behalf and as CEO of a bidding company.
4.1.8. Some of the bidders were related and/or neighbors.

The Ministry found that the four bidders had not acted independently and ruled that the their conduct fell within the prohibitions stipulated in Article 7(e) of Decision 608. The Ministry sanctioned the offenders with a penalty of 10% of the total turnover of each offender (a total of USD 132,940,22).

[B] CRONIX Case (Superintendence of Control of Market Power)

CRONIX, a call center company, filed a complaint with the Superintendence of Control of Market Power (SCPM) for breach of LORCPM's Article 11.6 and 11.21. This complaint alleged bid rigging against *SOLNET S.A.* (SOLNET), *RECAPT RECUPERACION DE CAPITAL CONTACT CENTER S.A.* (RECAPT) and *IESS*.

In this case, IESS had required the services of an independent company to "establish a comprehensive system for management, scheduling and interrelation with the attention of health and improvement of services provided to IESS's users." IESS initiated an electronic reverse auction for this public procurement contract. Six companies (including CRONIX, SOLNET and RECAPT) sought to participate in the process. Once the submitted offers were analyzed, IESS determined that only two of the companies (RECAPT and SOLNET) were qualified to participate in the process, and RECAPT was subsequently awarded the contract.

In this case, SCPM found that:

4.2.1. The Comptroller General's Office had conducted a special investigation into this reverse auction and determined that, "similarities and coincidences exist in the only two offers [that] qualified."
4.2.2. Both companies used the same personnel to prepare pre-contractual and contract documentation.
4.2.3. Neither "qualifying" company complied with all of the minimum participation requirements.
4.2.4. The IESS Technical Commission had not complied with the "*in-situ*" visit requirements and other prerequisites that the law imposes.
4.2.5. Both tenders exhibited false or irregular documentation regarding prior call center experience.
4.2.6. SOLNET's actual business was found to be the sale of electronic goods. It had never participated in call center related activities.
4.2.7. The same person filed the bidding documents for both companies.

In light of these findings, SCPM held that RECAPT and SOLNET had violated LORCPM's Article 11.6 and 11.21. Both companies were sanctioned with the maximum fine of 12% of each company's total turnover (a total of USD 2,344,140.04). As a corrective measure, the SCPM also submitted its resolution to a civil judge and sought to have the reverse auction process voided.

§10.05 CONCLUSIONS

Ecuador's competition laws and regulations were enacted in 2009 (Presidential Decree 1614) and 2011 (LORCPM). They aim to protect the competitive process and prohibit anticompetitive practices to protect the general welfare and consumers.

The country's public investment and procurement expanded significantly between 2007 to 2015. In the last five years, many sectors have been affected by bid rigging, making it necessary to investigate and fine important actors in the local economy. This is the reason why the government needs to protect the competitive process and outlaw anticompetitive practices in public procurement acquisitions by all State powers, agencies and entities.

The *CRONIX* case established an important precedent in Ecuador when it found that bid rigging had occurred and that such behavior constitutes anticompetitive practices. SCPM's imposition of the maximum fine of 12% of each company's total turnover for their illegal collusion also sent a strong message to potential bid riggers. These results, however, were tempered by the fact that a criminal prosecutor subsequently decided not to prosecute RECAPT and SOLNET, stating that his investigation did not find that a crime or felony had been committed. It should also be noted that despite its decision in the CRONIX Case sanctioning the bid riggers, an SCPM Commission also found that no evidence existed to sanction the procurement officials at the public acquiring institution (IESS) because they did not affect the relevant market.

We expect that in future cases SCPM will order, as a deterrent to collusion, the infringing party to publish an extract of its administrative decision in the country's mass media (e.g., newspaper, Internet).

In the meantime, the Ecuadorian government should assess its laws and public procurement practices at all levels of government in order to promote more effective recruitment and reduce bid rigging in public procurement.

CHAPTER 11
The Case of Automotive Market in a Special Customs Area of Argentina

Alejandro Lucero & Fabián Pettigrew

§11.01 INTRODUCTION

In 2008, a complaint was submitted to the Comision Nacional de Defensa de la Competencia (hereinafter CNDC), stating that the selling prices of automobiles in the Province of Tierra del Fuego was gradually assimilated to the selling prices in the rest of the territory of Argentina, in spite of the existence of a special promotion system which established a special customs area, Area Aduanera Especial (hereinafter AAE), in that Province. The case was considered as a tacit collusion by the Competition Authority in December 2014, but later was overturned in court.

So, in 2008 the CNDC, after the complaint of individual residents in the Province of Tierra del Fuego, began an investigation against the car dealers in that Province. The complaint stated that, despite the tax benefits which the Province has by the special regime established by Law 19640,[1] the selling price of cars in that Province was gradually increased up to be similar to the selling price of the same cars in the rest of the country since 2002.

The investigation carried out by the CNDC analyzed the performance of the automotive sector sales in that Province concluding the existence of a tacit collusion by the terminals that operated in the Argentina, bearing in mind the special customs regime area created by law 19640.

---

1. Argentina. Promotion to the National Territory of Tierra del Fuego. Official Bulletin. June 2, 1972. http://infoleg.mecon.gov.ar/infolegInternet/verNorma.do?id=28185.

The rationale used by the CNDC to concluded in the existence of an anticompetitive conduct and the imposition of the largest fine in its history, the legal frame that was determined in the light of competition law and the interpretation made by the Federal Court with territorial jurisdiction in the Province of Tierra del Fuego, about the evidentiary activity conducted by the CNDC will be analyzed in the present.

§11.02 THE SPECIAL CUSTOMS AREA CREATED BY LAW 19.640 AND THE AUTOMOTIVE REGIME

The law 19640 established a special tax and customs regime for the Territorio Nacional de Tierra del Fuego, Antártida e Islas del Atlántico Sud, today Province of Tierra del Fuego, Antártida e Islas del Atlántico Sud, through the creation of a special customs area.

The recitals of the law pointed out that the low volume of general activity in the geographic area, involved imperfections in the offer and in order to mitigate that circumstances was advisable to organize an open system that would facilitate competition and thus defend the local demand and their purchasing power.

From a tax and fiscal point of view the regime AAE establishes as a benefit an exemption for the payment of all national taxes, such as the value added tax, income tax, personal assets tax, import tariff, etc., to natural and legal persons that carry out activities or transactions relating to goods and services based or conducted in the abovementioned geographic area. For tax purposes, the AAE is considered a third country and any commercial transaction between this area and the rest of the country is considered a foreign trade transaction.

Mentioned some of the economic benefits of the law, it is important to mention that a car that is sold in the AAE does not have any taxes with exemption of those of provincial origin. Therefore, the importation of a vehicle to the AAE does not pay import tariff from ExtraMercosur – 35% –, or added value tax, that is currently 21%, or statistic tax that is a tax linked to the transaction of foreign trade.

In the case of the cars produced in Mexico or Mercosur,[2] they are exempted from the payment of the 35% fee which is the common external tariff. Additionally, vehicles produced in Argentina have imported components and some of that are considered from local origin and in these cases the automotive companies have a refund export by 6% over the national component on all shipments to external markets different from Mercosur, included the AAE.

On the other hand, it should be mentioned that AAE's residents are required not to selling the vehicles outside the AAE for a minimum period of three years for cars produced in Mercosur and of five years for cars considered ExtraMercosur, otherwise they must pay all taxes which are duty expected.

---

2. The importation of cars from Mexico has a similar treatment to Mercosur's regimen.

§11.03 THE INVESTIGATION CARRIED OUT BY THE CNDC

In 2008 began the procedure[3] because a complaint in which it was stated that since the repeal of the regime of convertibility of the peso/dollar, happened in 2001, the automotive sales market gradually suffered a mismatch that ended up the selling prices in similar values and even more expensive than their counterparts in the rest of the country, without any reasonable justification. Although the complaint was made against the dealerships based in the Province of Tierra del Fuego, the CNDC by virtue of the collected information decided to extend the investigation to the automotive terminals which operate in Argentina.

After analyzing the automotive market in Argentina,[4] the CNDC concluded that the domestic market is basically supplied in the small car sector for vehicles produced in Brazil, in the mid-range market by vehicles produced in Argentina and for the upper-range market by vehicles produced in ExtraMercosur markets.

The selling price of the cars in the AAE produced in Mercosur or Mexico was similar to the selling prices of those cars in the rest of the country, excluding the added value tax (IVA), 21%, while in the case of those cars imported from an ExtraMercosur area, the selling price was lower in percentage terms than those sold in the rest of the country.

The CNDC analyzed the information about dealers; final consumers; import invoices; export prices to regional and border markets for the periods 2002–2010 about all the automotive undertakings and concluded that those undertakings without any kind of production process in Argentina[5] sold their cars produced ExtraMercosur in prices considerably lower than the price they sold in the rest of the country. However, those automotive undertakings with production in Argentina or Brazil[6] sold their cars produced ExtraMercosur with slightly lower price than its correlate in the rest of the country.

For the CNDC it was clear that if those undertakings with production processes in the Mercosur sold their ExtraMercosur cars (upper-range cars) with a price that shows the tax benefits of the AAE regime (35% tariff ExtraMercosur plus 21% tariff added value tax), those cars might have a selling price similar to the more expensive vehicle produced in Mercosur or México and commercialized in the AAE regarding the most economic car produced in ExtraMercosur.

On other words, the CNDC concluded that analyzing the situation taking in mind a price perspective, certain cars produced ExtraMercosur might have gobble up certain cars produced IntraMercosur, making that the price of these last one tender to the low.

---

3. File S01:0000803/2008 of the Registry of ex Ministerio de Economía y Producción and current Ministerio de Economía y Finanzas Públicas "Hugo Atilio Riello Gasperini y José Luis Catalán Magni S/ Solicitud de Intervención Ley 25.156 -CNDC" (C. 1234).
4. The investigation was focused in cars for particular use, the sector of utility vehicles was not analyzed.
5. Like Mercedes Benz; Audi or BMW.
6. Like Toyota Argentina S.A.; Volkswagen Argentina S.A.; General Motors de Argentina S.A.; Renault de Argentina S.A.; Ford Argentina S.A.; Fiat Auto Argentina S.A.; Peugeot-Citroen Argentina S.A.; Honda Motor Argentina S.A.

If any of the automotive undertakings would have done this kind of transactions, they would have disciplined the Mercosur and Mexico car offer. However, any of the competitors adopted this commercial attitude and this is what made the CNDC stated that they had a concerted conduct expressed as selling prices in similar levels as the selling prices in the country in spite of the tax benefit of the AAE.[7]

[A] The Legal Frame of the Investigation

The Argentine Competition Law, 25.156[8] in its first article defined in a non-exhaustive way acts or behaviors that are considered anticompetitive, stating that acts or conducts in all manifested forms are prohibited when limit, restrict, or distort competition or access to the market or that constitute abuse of a dominant position, so that can be detrimental to the general economic interest.

The reading of Article 1, suggests that the regime has adopted the conditional illegality criteria, since acts or conducts would constitute restrictive practices once affect the general economic interest, economic concept of difficult application from a legal point of view.[9]

Article 2 of the law sets out a series of behaviors not exhaustively, which constitute violations of competition, whenever they are in line with the above-mentioned Article 1. In other words, the Argentine legislation does not consider anticompetitive practices illegal per se, the general rule in the Argentine competition law enforcement is the rule of reason.

Thus this article lists a number of behaviors which will constitute at the light of Article 1 restrictive practices of competition, such as set, arrange or handle directly or indirectly the price of sale or purchase of goods or services that are offered or demanded in the market as well as exchanging information with the same object or effect; distribute areas markets, customers and supply sources; arrange or coordinate stances in tenders or contests, conclude the limitation of technical development or investments to the production or marketing of goods and services; fix, impose or practice directly or indirectly, in agreement with competitors or individually, in any way prices and conditions of purchase or sale goods, provision of services or production or to regulate markets for goods and services, by means of agreements to limit or control the research and technological development, the production of goods or provision of services, or to hinder investment in the production of goods or services or its distribution.

The formal accusation stated by the CNDC in Resolution 42/2014 was defined as "realization of concerted practices in order to maintain the current prices in the AAE to levels similar to those prevailing on the continent since 2002 to at least 2010 inclusive,

---

7. The Final Opinion made by the CNDC in this file can be found in http://www2.mecon.gov.ar/cndc/archivos_d/865.pdf.
8. Argentina. Competition Law. Official Bulletin September 20, 1999. http://www.infoleg.gob.ar/infolegInternet/verNorma.do?id = 60016.
9. For further interpretation of the general economic interest can be consulted http://www.cndc.gov.ar/NOTA220116.pdf.

in order to restrict competition with potential harm the general economic interest as provided for in Article 1 and subparagraphs a)[10] and g)[11] of Article 2do. 25.156 law."

The legal framework of the behavior "realization of concerted practices" deserves some considerations with regards to different characterizations that emerge from the Resolution and that subsequently had incidence in the assessment of the evidence in court when it considered the direct appeal by the investigated undertakings.

In the case, the CNDC has not been able to determine the existence of an explicit cartel, because an agreement about prices, agreement on quotas or horizontal divisions of the market, which are considered typical behavior of a cartel actions have not been properly demonstrated. It is important to emphasize that in the case of express collusion in Argentine jurisprudence has been uniform in sanction this type of behavior as contrary to the general economic interest.

What the CNDC determined is a manifestation of homogeneous parallel conducts by competitors in the geographical market of the province of Tierra del Fuego, and considered that this behavior have responded to a concerted practice. Thus, the issue is to determine if the existence of a parallelism of conduct set up the existence of a cartel, question that can only be answered through a probative activity which allows it to demonstrate the existence of a concerted practice.

The CNDC in its Final Opinion, based on the economic analysis of the proof collected during the investigation concluded that was proved the existence of a tacit collusion expressed through a parallelism in selling prices.

[B]   The Fine

The CNDC in its Final Opinion[12] when analyzed the imposition of fines[13] stated that price agreements are considered not only by national legislation but for international legislation as serious law infringements and that the fines imposed in collusive cases must be established in an amount that allows compensate the damages that the undertakings caused with its anticompetitive conduct to the society.

The total amount of the fine imposed to the eight automotive terminals was approximately ARS 1 billon and became the largest fine imposed by the CNDC in its history.

While this large fine was widely covered by the media in Argentina, is important to point out that according with the recitals of the Final Opinion, that amount could be

---

10. Set, arrange or handle directly or indirectly the price of sale, or purchase of goods or services that are offered or demand in the market as well as exchanging information with the same object or effect.
11. Fix, impose or practice, directly or indirectly, in agreement with competitors or individually, in any way prices and conditions of purchase or sale goods, provision of services or production.
12. http://www2.mecon.gov.ar/cndc/archivos_d/865.pdf.
13. Article 46 of the Argentine Competition Law establishes the following limits in the imposition of fines: ARS 10,000 (USD 10,000) to ARS 150,000,000 (USD 150,000,000), which will be graduated based on: (1) the losses incurred by all persons affected by the prohibit activity; (2) the benefit obtained by all persons involved in the prohibited activity; (3) the value of the involved assets of persons indicated in point (2) above, at the time the infringement was committed, In the case of recurrence, the fine amounts will double.

larger than the one finally considered. Indeed, it is important to bear in mind that the amount limits stated in the competition law dated from 1999 and although the inflationary processes that Argentina suffered since that year, this limits have not been modified.

[C] The Judgment of the Cámara Federal de Apelaciones de Comodoro Rivadavia[14]

The Resolution 271/14 of the Secretary of Commerce[15] was subject to direct appeal which was analyzed by issues of territorial competence by the Federal Appeals Chamber of Comodoro Rivadavia. Although the Judgment of March 18, 2015 conducted a detailed analysis of several procedural issues, for the purposes of this chapter we only will highlight those issues related with the assessment of the probative activities that the CNDC carried on in order to demonstrate the collusive conduct.

The Federal Court stated that the CNDC had as demonstrated the unlawful conduct on the basis of a series of behaviors that were considered as indications of a collusive agreement, through which the automotive undertakings would concerted higher prices than that would be under conditions of free competition. It is in this point, when it pointed out that unlike that was verified in previous precedents in which different anticompetitive conducts were fined because of being proven the existence of a cartel, like the cases of cement or liquid oxygen[16] any direct evidence supports the CNDC accusation.

The approach taken by the Federal Court was that the indicative evidence must be confirmed by other direct proof. Therefore, who alleged the presumption, in this case the CNDC, must prove those signs which have been served as a starting point for its reasoning. Then and without ignoring that in administrative processes all test measures are admissible, the Federal Court stated that this does not preclude that the general principles of the weighting of the test are applicable. In conclusion, in order to have a particular fact proven in base of indicative proof, this must be clear, accurate, serious and concordant.

The Judgment added that when the analysis is about parallel conducts is not necessary that they were identical or of similar nature, but always is necessary to demonstrate or prove the existence of a subjacent concertation, a clear correlative conduct between the competitors. In particular, it stated that in the framework of competition law is necessary prove the concurrence of wills and the negative impact in the relevant market, i.e., a situation in which the undertakings had agreed to not compete between with the aim of increasing the joint profits of the whole group.

---

14. The Federal Appeals Court judged the Direct Appeal in interposed against Resolution 271/14 del Secretario de Comercio de la Nación, caratulado "HONDA MOTORS ARGENTINA S.A. Y OTROS c/ ESTADO NACIONAL- SECRETARÍA DE COMERCIO s/RECURSO DIRECTO LEY 25156." This according to Art. 52 of Competition Law 25.156. Court Case N° 81000803/2008/CA1.
15. http://www2.mecon.gov.ar/cndc/archivos_d/865.pdf.
16. "CNDC c/Loma Negra y otros"; "Oxígeno Líquido."

Therefore, the Federal Court decided to upheld the direct appeal brought by the automotive undertakings and revoked the Resolution of the Commerce Secretary, regarding the imposition of the fine based on an anticompetitive conduct.

Final comments

The investigation against the automotive industry carried on by the CNDC was an interesting case not only because of the amount of the fine that the Competition Authority suggested the Secretary of Commerce to imposed but also because of the analysis that can be done about how and what is necessary to demonstrate to state the existence of a tacit collusion that can establish a concerted practice.

In investigations on oligopoly markets, it is common find some kind of parallel conduct, but as the international and national doctrine and jurisprudence state the existence of that kind of behavior does not always constitute an anticompetitive conduct. Indeed, the European Court of Justice, stated that "a parallel behaviour may not by itself be identified with a concerted practice although it could provide strong evidence of such a practice if it leads to conditions of competition which do not correspond to the normal conditions of the market, having regard to the nature of the products, the size and number of the undertakings, and the volume of the market."[17] Criteria that was completed when it stated "parallel conduct cannot be regarded as furnishing proof of concertation unless concertation constitutes the only plausible explanation for such conduct."[18]

In so complex cases like the one of the automotive industry in the Province of Tierra del Fuego, would be difficult to find out direct evidence which confirmed the indicative and presumption proof that could be collected during the investigation, like the Judgment of the Federal Court stated. However, the challenge for the CNDC in future cases will be not only the evidential activity itself but the demonstration in case of the absence of a direct evidence, that the concertation constitutes the only valid explanation for the parallel behavior of the undertakings.

---

17. European Court of Justice. "*ICI v. Commission.*" Cases 48, 49 and 51-57/69. (1972). ECR 619, para. 66.
18. European Court of Justice. *Re Wood Pulp Cartel: Ahlström Oy v. Commission (Wood Pulp II)* Cases C-89, 104, 114, 116–117 and 125–129/85 (1993) ECR I-1 307.

CHAPTER 12
Exchanges of Information in Competition Law: The Chilean (Incipient) Experience

Javier Tapia & Vanessa Facuse[*]

§12.01 INTRODUCTION

This chapter describes exchanges of information between competitors in the Chilean case-law and practice. Its main aim is to describe the rules competition authorities have provided in the few cases that have dealt with this topic so far and sketch some possible conclusions for the future enforcement in the country and (possibly) other Latin American jurisdictions. Also, it gives a brief account on the relevance of different types of information and market structures for analyzing a case.

Information exchanges are ubiquitous in oligopolistic markets. It is very common that firms exchange data on prices, quantities, capacities of production, demand, costs and others – albeit not necessarily directly. This situation presents a potential dilemma for competition systems and authorities. For the lawfulness of an exchange depends on its purpose. Therefore, the scrutiny of information exchanges depends on the eye of the beholder.

On the one hand, exchanges of commercially sensitive information (first and foremost prices or quantity) can be functionally equivalent to a cartel. They lie at its heart, being its "operative part," even if there is no "promise" to act in certain way (Wagner-Von Papp, 2013). For instance, the mere knowledge of current or future prices may be a very good substitute for cartel conduct, since it allows to monitor deviations and apply punishments. In practice, most cartels include this kind of exchanges between their members. Indeed, they are illegal (per se illegal in those jurisdictions that

---

[*] The views presented in this chapter are the authors' solely and do not necessarily represent those of the TDLC, the FNE or the persons that work in them.
    All translations from Spanish texts, including official documents, have been done by the authors. In some cases, the actual text may have been slightly altered to keep its true meaning.

embrace such rule), because they are a mere support of illegal conduct.[1] On the other hand, "pure" exchanges of information about market conditions may even be beneficial if firms behave competitively. In fact, nearly every legitimate, pro-competitive cooperation agreement between competitors involves some level of sharing of key information. As Bennett & Collins (2010: 311) have stated, *"[m]any sectors of our economies now depend upon ready access to detailed information and some firms have made information their business"*. In these cases, the lawfulness of information exchanges should be out of question.

In the middle, the outcome is not clear at all –not even for experts.[2] In this grey area, "residual" exchanges of (certain) information have the potential for harm market outcomes *by themselves*, and are potentially anticompetitive regardless whether the participants in the exchange are deemed guilty of cartelization through direct means. The question is whether the fact that some information exchanges are a mere support of cartel conduct justifies a general hostile treatment towards most residual information exchanges – or the general perception of suspicion that seems to be common amongst authorities. The identification of licit and illicit exchanges of information is then crucial to combat collusion, but also essential to allow the normal functioning of business.

Competition authorities worldwide need to decide on the most suitable rules and guiding principles that allow discerning between lawful and unlawful conduct.[3] This objective is particularly relevant in Latin American, where exchanges of information between competitors are ubiquitous. This is due to several reasons. First, the degree of concentration in most industries remains high. Oligopolies are (or have been until fairly recently) largely dominant in many markets,[4] as a result of a long tradition of State-controlled economies combined with social conflicts and resentments[5] and/or various concerns about "too much competition." Second, there are powerful interests that have strong political power. It is extremely difficult to go against these ruling elites.

---

1. In this sense, *see* the EU Commission decisions in *Fasteners and Attaching Machines* (2007) (upheld in *Prym*, 2009) and *Gas Insulated Switchgear* (2007) (partially upheld on appeal in *Areva*, 2014). In the literature, *see* Whish (2009) and Posner (2001).
2. Quoting Bennett & Collins (2010: 312) again:

    Ask a consumer lawyer the main problem with information, and he or she might reply that firms do not disclose enough of it and there is often too little transparency in the market for consumers to make informed decisions. However, ask a competition lawyer the same question and he or she might reply that firms disclose too much of it, with too much transparency limiting competition and harming consumers. Then, of course, if you ask an economist, the answer is too often "it depends" – an answer that may be true, but not one that is particularly helpful for legal certainty of for business.

3. Many competition authorities have issued guidelines on the topic, including some in Latin America. *See*, e.g., COFECE's "Guía para el intercambio de información entre agentes económicos" (Mexico).
4. At least in principle, oligopolistic markets are more prone to cartelization. This insight began with Stigler (1964), but there is literature offering empirical support.
5. Gerber (2010).

Threat of entry is fairly limited in both tradable and non-tradable sectors.[6] Particularly in the latter, there is no credible threat, since financing is not readily available for new entrepreneurs outside these concentrated groups.[7] Third, with the exception of a few countries where competition policy has become an important part of the rules of the game, support for competition as a "value" is weak – particularly amongst governments and political leaders, but also amongst business communities. Competition is seldom seen as the best path to enhance productivity and achieve prosperity and economic progress. Conversely, ideological reasons and historical anti-market traditions still play a role, making industrial policy and control over the wider economy a favorite amongst many governments.[8]

Despite important macro- and microeconomic advances, Chile is not entirely exempt from this reality. Oligopolies and market concentration are still a significant source of concern. So it is information sharing. Auspiciously, authorities have started providing rules and guidance on the topic and thus providing helpful clarification on how firms should address the effects of their information sharing. But there is still a long way to go. As we will show, most cases are clear-cut: the exchange of information allows to support straight cartel behavior. Nonetheless, these type of cases have served for the purpose of drawing a line between lawful and unlawful conduct in a context of high skepticism of competition outcomes. At the same time, few cases and guidelines have allowed to sketch rules for dealing with residual exchanges of information. All in all, current Chilean stage of development seems appropriate to draw some lessons from this initial experience.

The remaining of the chapter is organized as follows. Part 2 describes the Chilean legal and institutional framework. Chile has a broad provision condemning anticompetitive conduct, with subsections giving some more detail as to the different types of conduct covered. Also, since the Chilean institutional structure is somewhat unusual within the international context (having a separate agency that investigates and prosecute, and a tribunal that makes actual decisions on cases), it is worth to give a quick reminder thereof before embarking in the analysis of the exchanges of information. Part 3 offers an account of the main cases where information exchanges have been a central part of cartels. Such exchanges have allowed to sustain collusive behavior and, therefore, have been an important part of the evidence taken into account to condemn. Part 4 refers to residual exchanges. Despite the fact that these exchanges have been at the center of only a handful of cases (mostly indirectly), both the tribunal and the agency have developed important rules and principles that now generally frame them. Part 5 summarizes the main ideas of the chapter.

---

6. Indeed, in some sectors the threat of entry may come from imports – especially in some countries with very open economies, such as Chile or Panama (on the latter, see OECD 2011, highlighting openness with respect to the Panamanian economy).
7. Khemani & Carrasco-Martin (2008).
8. Historically, import-substitution policies were common in Latin America between the 1950s and 1980s.

§12.02 THE INSTITUTIONAL AND SUBSTANTIVE FRAMEWORK

[A] The Institutional Framework

In Chile, rules and principles governing exchanges of information are given in an institutional structure that is somewhat unusual within the international context. Its most prominent feature is the presence of two completely separate institutions in charge of enforcing competition laws: an administrative body (the Fiscalía Nacional Económica (FNE)) that investigates and prosecutes, and a specialized judicial tribunal (the Tribunal de Defensa de la Libre Competencia de Chile (TDLC)) that makes decisions. The structure is summarized in Figure 1. Since the main characteristics of the system have been described in full detail in other accessible documents,[9] we only refer here to their most salient aspects.

Figure 12.1 Chilean Competition Defense System

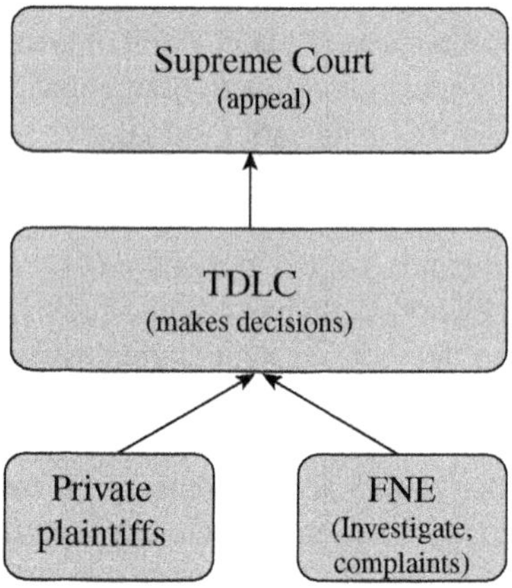

```
            ┌─────────────────────┐
            │   Supreme Court     │
            │      (appeal)       │
            └─────────────────────┘
                      ▲
                      │
            ┌─────────────────────┐
            │       TDLC          │
            │  (makes decisions)  │
            └─────────────────────┘
                ▲           ▲
               /             \
    ┌──────────────┐   ┌──────────────┐
    │   Private    │   │     FNE      │
    │  plaintiffs  │   │ (Investigate,│
    │              │   │  complaints) │
    └──────────────┘   └──────────────┘
```

Source: Authors' creation.

Both the FNE and the TDLC are independent. On the one hand, the FNE is headed by the National Economic Prosecutor, who must be a lawyer by profession and is appointed by the President of Chile after a public contest handled by the special State agency in charge of recruiting high-level public officials. The Economic Prosecutor may only be removed by cause and subject to a prior motion at the Supreme Court.[10] On the other hand, the TDLC is headed by a President (a lawyer with experience in competition law) and has another four expert members (two economists and two lawyers, also

---

9. *See*, e.g., OECD (2010) and Wise (2003).
10. According to the Competition Act, the FNE is *"a decentralised public service, with legal status and own assets, independent from any other agency or service"* and the Economic Prosecutor is directed by law to *"discharge his duties independently"*, to *"defend the interests entrusted to him [...] based on his own discretion"* and to represent *"the general economic interests of the community"*. Only for budget purposes, the FNE is part of the Ministry of the Economy.

experts on competition). The five members are appointed for fix six-year terms, renewable once. All the five members attend hearings and vote on decisions.

Investigations can begin either through receiving a complaint or through FNE's own initiation. After that, the FNE has extensive powers to investigate.[11] The FNE does not have a time limit to investigate, besides a somewhat similar rule stipulating a statute of limitations of five years for collusion cases and three years for other conducts. The results of an investigation may be an administrative decision closing the investigation; a report to the TDLC in a proceeding, in which the TDLC asks for the FNE's opinion; or an ex officio complaint (*requerimiento*) seeking a fine or other remedy.

Besides investigations, the FNE fulfills an important advocacy role, stated in the Competition Act[12] laconically as "promoting competition." Although the Act does not specify how this task should be accomplished, the common understanding is that the FNE may, among others, issue non-binding guidelines highlighting the benefits of competition in a specific area or market. Some of these guidelines, such as the "Trade Association Guidelines" or the "Guidelines for Compliance" have played a crucial role in developing rules and principles for exchanges of information –particularly since the TDLC started embracing them in cases.

Before the TDLC, there are two main procedures, adversarial (which ends by "Judgements") and non-adversarial (which ends by "Decisions"), both initiated when the FNE or a private party files a complaint.[13] Only adversarial procedures may lead to sanctions. Conversely, non-adversarial procedures may only lead to recommendations and the setting of some conditions for future acts or contracts. Regarding sanctions, the Competition Act allows the TDLC to impose fines and/or behavioral or structural remedies. Orders can amend or eliminate anticompetitive acts, contracts, agreements, schemes or arrangements in violation of the Act.[14] The TDLC can also order divestiture or dissolution of partnerships, corporations or business companies whose existence rests on anticompetitive arrangements. Administrative fines may be imposed upon the infringing legal entity and on its directors and managers and persons who participated in the infringement. According to the current version of the Competition Act,[15] the amount depends on the financial benefit received from the infringement, the severity of the breach and the offenders' recidivism. The maximum fine is 30,000 "annual tax

---

11. It can compel the production of documents and the cooperation of public agencies, State- owned companies, firms and individuals. It can also summon anyone with potential knowledge of an infringement to testify as a witness (including the defendant's representatives, managers and advisors); to inspect the premises of the investigated entities on a voluntary basis; to conduct search and seizure of company premises (so-called dawn raids); and do wiretapping. Dawn raids and wiretapping require authorization from the TDLC and the issuance of an order from a judge of the Court of Appeals.
12. D.L. N° 211/1973, as amended.
13. On abuses of dominance cases, antitrust private litigation has generally been more active than public litigation.
14. For example, mandatory requests to modify internal procedures were made to private dominant firms in *GTD/EFE* (Decision 76/2008) and *Atrex/SCL* (Decision 75/2008).
15. At the time of writing this chapter, the Act is about to be modified significantly. Among the main changes are the inclusion of incarceration for collusion and new fines. These will be either the double of the economic benefit of the offender, 30% of the sales, or up to 60,000 tax units when the previous two cannot be calculated.

units" (approx. USD 25 million) for cartel offenses and 20,000 annual tax units (approx. USD 20 million) for other infringements.[16] The Act also gives the TDLC the faculty to propose Executive amendments to the legislation.[17]

On top of the system lies the Supreme Court of Justice (the highest court in Chile). Final decisions of the TDLC are subject to its judicial oversight under a special recourse called "complaint recourse" (*recurso de reclamación*). The scope of the review is not defined in the act, but the Supreme Court has interpreted it in the broadest possible terms, comprising questions of law, policy or fact,[18] and, on occasions, even substituting its judgment for that of the TDLC.[19] That means the recourse has functioned in practice as an appellate review.

[B] The Main Substantive Provisions

Besides the institutional structure, legislation governing competition has its own particulars. As in other legislations, the Competition Act does not refer specifically to exchanges of information. However, the Act is unusually broad – both in terms of objectives and substantive provision.[20] On the one hand, Article 1 states that the purpose of the Act "[...] *is to advocate and defend free competition in the markets. Affronts to free competition in economic activities will be corrected, prohibited or repressed in the manner and with the sanctions provided in this law.*" This is supplemented in Article 2 by the mandate to competition authorities to "*to enforce the present law to safeguard free competition in the markets.*" Beyond these general statements, no explicit objectives are stipulated.[21]

On the other hand, the substantive provisions are contained in Article 3, which indicates that:

---

16. Tax units are a special monetary measure of value used by the legislation to keep the value of sanctions, exemptions, tax purposes and others, in line with inflation.
17. Chilean Competition Act, Art. 18.3. The TDLC has used this faculty in several cases. For example, in both *Transbank I* (Judgment 29/2005) and *CCS I* (Judgment 56/2007), the Chilean TDLC recommended the sectoral regulator (in both cases the financial authority) to apply the corresponding norms and regulations (!). Likewise, in *Lan Airlines* (Judgment 55/2007), the TDLC proposed "*the regulatory changes that were necessary and suitable to favour competition*" to be introduced by the customs agency; instructed the FNE "*to keep watch the functioning of the airfreight transport market and the custom warehousing market*"; and ordered the dominant firm "*to restructure its tariffs for airfreight transport*" (it also imposed several other regulatory measures to the dominant firm).
18. Commenting on the nature of the *reclamación*, the Supreme Court has stated that it has jurisdiction to "fully" review all the grounds considered by the TDLC, "*including the legal and economic analysis that allowed it to reach the decision it took*" (Supreme Court, *Consulta de Subtel sobre participación de concesionarios de telefonía móvil en concurso público de telefonía móvil digital avanzada*, Rol 4797-2008, Decision of January 27, 2009, C. 6°).
19. The most salient case on this is *Hardie*, where the Court sustain a textualist approach to Art. 3 "c" of the Chilean Competition Act (*see* Supreme Court, *Producción Química y Electrónica Quimel S.A. contra James Hardie Fibrocementos Limitada*, Rol 3449-2006, Decision of January 22, 2007).
20. OECD (2010).
21. As a consequence, for a number of years before the creation of the TDLC, freedom to compete was considered more important than efficiency (OECD, 2004). This may be explained by the

Any person that enters into or executes, individually or collectively, any action, act or convention that impedes, restricts or hinders competition, or sets out to produce said effects, will be sanctioned with the measures mentioned in article 26 of the present law, notwithstanding preventive, corrective or prohibitive measures that may be applied to said actions, acts or conventions in each case.

The following will be considered as, among others, actions, acts or conventions that impede, restrict or hinder competition or which set out to produce said effects:

a) Express or tacit agreements among competitors, or concerted practices between them, that confer them market power and consist of fixing sale or purchase prices or other marketing conditions, limit production, allow them to assign market zones or quotas, exclude competitors or affect the result of bidding processes.
b) The abusive exploitation on the part of an economic agent, or a group thereof, of a dominant position in the market, fixing sale or purchase prices, imposing on a sale of another product, assigning market zones or quotas or imposing other similar abuses.
c) Predatory practices, or unfair competition, carried out with the purpose of reaching, maintaining or increasing a dominant position.

As Article 1, Article 3 is general, broad and flexible. Its first paragraph generally provides that any deed, act or agreement (including a contract) that prevents, restricts or hinders free competition or tends to do so, is subject to sanctions under law. Although subsections in the second paragraph specifically refer to the traditional categories in competition law, they provide only illustrative detail.[22] For this reason, in practice many cases are brought by parties or the FNE under the first paragraph.[23] Indeed, direct ruling on information sharing may easily be framed within that paragraph.

[C] The Concept of Agreement in Chilean Competition Law

An important substantive aspect for the analysis of exchanges of information is the concept of agreement adopted in each legislation and/or the case-law. For there must always be an agreement to sanction collusion or equate an exchange of information to a collusive conduct. It is not enough that a firm obtain information – let us say – from the press or direct discussions with consumers or purchasers. Consequently, the

---

wording of the law and a formal approach to the conducts. However, although some commentators still advocate this or other objectives, the most recent case-law has explicitly mentioned consumer welfare in a number of particular decisions. This has been reflected in more efficiency-oriented decisions.

22. Note that the categories in the second paragraph are closer to the competition provisions of European Law than the Sherman Act. This fact, along with the existence of paragraph one, shows that despite its old American origins, Chilean competition law currently is far from being a mere "transplantation of American antitrust and Chicago School of Economics" adapted to the local context, as some have mistakenly argued (e.g., Bauer, 2011). Moreover, most substantive standards are far away from those proponents of the Chicago School.
23. This produces some important procedural differences (particularly in collusion cases) and, to some extent, has curbed more refined developments on the interpretation of the provision. These aspects, however, go beyond the scope of this work.

concept of agreement becomes crucial. That concept must be broad enough to include a broad range of practices that may not account for direct cartelization.

Although to some extent the Competition Act facilitates a wide approach to cartels – given the broadness of Article 3° and its reference to *"express or tacit agreements among competitors"*,[24] until fairly recent the TDLC had not ratified the broad understanding of the provision. This was done in *Ginecologos*,[25] in 2015. In that case, the Tribunal explicitly embraced – for the first time – a concept of agreement, and did it in a manner that allows the sanctioning of unlawful exchanges of information that goes beyond formal "legal" agreements. Citing Areeda and Hovenkamp (2003), the tribunal stated that:

> as it is known, in competition law the term "agreement" is considered in a very wide manner, including a multiplicity of contractual forms, conventions, mere preliminary discussions, promises, collaboration agreements, gentlemen agreements, conduct guidelines, memos, among others [...]. The agreement may be oral, or may manifest itself in one or more documents or even in a series of material acts. In general terms, the suppression of the individual will of two or more competitors and its change with a collective will that unifies their decisions is, in competition law, considered an "agreement," whatever the form it may take.[26]

§12.03 EXCHANGES OF INFORMATION AS SUPPORT FOR CARTEL BEHAVIOR

In Chile, there have been three recent and important adversarial cases where information sharing played a relevant role in allowing competitors to engage in –and sustain – explicit coordinated behavior. That is, information exchanges were part of hard-core cartels. In two cases the information was managed by a trade association, which was condemned along with the cartel members. Whereas the first case was based on information on quantities, the second one was centered on prices. In the third case, multimarket contacts between the firms facilitated the exchange of commercially sensitive information.

---

24. For this reason, the well-known "Turner-Posner debate" in the U.S. has not had echoes in Chile. *See also* Kaplow (2013).
25. *Ginecologos* (Judgment 145/2015). In this case, the TDLC declared that a local Gynaecologists' Trade Association and several of its members engaged in price fixing infringing the Competition Act. The case started by a complaint filed by the FNE, which provided evidence of an agreement among the doctors, through their professional association, to steadily increase the price of the gynaecologists' medical consultations and surgeries in the local geographic market. The cartel worked at least during the period January 2012 to October 2013. The TDLC fined both the doctors and the association, and ordered the latter to implement a compliance program following the FNE Guidelines on the topic. The FNE had requested the dissolution of the association, but the TDLC dismissed the request. However, on appeal, the Supreme Court ordered the dissolution.
26. *Ibíd.*, para. 5°.

[A] Exchanges of Information on Quantity

The first case was based upon information sharing of quantity. Information on quantity is highly sensitive for the competitiveness of the firms interacting in the market. For quantity may be indicative of a number of variables that, if known by competitors, may affect the commercial strategy of the firm. Among them are the rate of growth of the firm in the market (stagnation, moderate growth, rapid or aggressive growth, and so on); its targets of future growth; its capacity of production or storage; the amount of sales to third parties; and the product lines in which the firm may want to concentrate its production or sales (therefore its growth). Furthermore, depending on the amount information revealed, quantity may provide a fair account of the level of integration of the firm (therefore its level of production) or the actual purchases it makes to third parties (including imports). Likewise, information on quantity may be useful to infer or directly know the market share of the firm and possible that of its competitors – particularly if the estimated total sales in the market are also known.

In *Pollos*,[27] three producers of poultry meat (*Agrosuper*, *Ariztía* and *Don Pollo*) agreed on the tons of poultry meat to be produced and sale in the local market, and assigned markets shares to each of them in the market of production and commercialization of poultry. The three firms produced more than 80% of the poultry meat in Chile. The agreement was implemented through the Poultry Producers' Trade Association (APA, for its Spanish acronym), who acted as monitor and coordinator of the cartel. Notably, the association was formed exclusively by the firms involved in the cartel. The TDLC condemned *Agrosuper* and *Ariztía* to pay the maximum fine, whereas *Don Pollo* was fined nearly USD 10 million. The TDLC also ruled the dissolution of the APA, among other measures. The Supreme Court upheld the judgment.

The TDLC established the agreement through emails and other evidence of explicit coordination seized by the FNE. There was enough evidence in the process to prove that the firms were acting jointly to define certain level of production and, consequently, keep the prices of poultry meet within certain range agreed. The sharing of sensible information was crucial to keep the internal stability of the cartel. One of the main roles of the APA was to forecast future poultry demand and disseminate the results among the members. During the whole period of cartelization, the agreement was yearly controlled and adjusted by the APA, which "suggested" quantities, the killing of chickens, or other mechanisms to keep market shares within the commonly established levels. The TDLC recognized that all the process was done in an implicit and imperfect way, given the complexities for forecasting the demand function in the market. However, the cartel was successful for a long period of time – almost fifteen years. The role of the association was not only make the information verifiable, but also increase the level of trust necessary to sustain the collusive behavior.

---

27. *Pollos* (Judgment 139/2014).

[B] Exchanges of Information on Prices

In another cartel case the agreement was mostly based upon the direct sharing of information on prices. Generally, these types of exchanges are treated harshly, because they tend to produce uniformity or high interdependency of prices in the market. Note that it is not necessary that two firms expressly agree on prices. The sole fact of giving or acquiring information on prices is enough to equate the exchange to price fixing. This is certainly the case under U.S. antitrust laws. As the U.S. Supreme Court said in *Gypsum* (1978), the direct exchange of price information between competitors has the highest potential to generate anticompetitive effects –particularly if there are other suspicious circumstances.[28] In EU law, the tenet is that positive steps must be adopted in order to avoid engaging in such exchanges. It is not enough not to act according to an agreement or remain silent in a concerted practice. A firm must show "public distance" of the meetings leading to the agreement. Otherwise, other members might understand that it agrees with them and will participate in the agreement.

Two caveats apply: first, the per se rule does not apply against exchanges of price information (unlike cartels in many jurisdictions).[29] Despite the fact such exchanges can be considered unlawful even when only one firm provides the information, there must always be an effect on prices. However, the effect is presumed. The sole ability to produce such an effect is enough to condemn, unless the defendant is capable to rebut the presumption of illegality.

The second caveat is that direct exchanges of information on prices may refer to different contents. The main reason is that, as Lafontaine & Slate (2013: 958) indicate, "many market transactions do not take place in arm's-length spot markets but instead are governed by long- or short-term contracts," which can take innumerable forms. The clearest case is the sharing of the level of actual prices – that is, prices actually used between a seller and its purchasers. Since these prices are a significant element of the costs structure of the buyer and hence may reveal important information on its margins and costs, this kind of sharing is a main source of concern for competition. Also, actual prices are a central part of the competitive advantage of any firm. For depending on the level of known information, actual prices may show a low-cost strategy, one based on product-differentiation, or any other one chosen by the firm.

Another subset of exchanges of information on prices is the sharing of (contractual) pricing or tariff structures. For instance, the actual price in a contract may not be established in first place, but be dependent on the costs of the product plus certain mark-up. A rather similar structure may be based on margins or discounts. Conversely, the actual price in a contract may be based on a single, fix-price according to a pre-determined amount of product. In this case, the price is entirely independent of the cost. Other examples of pricing structures are the well-known contracts with two-part tariffs (generally, a fix amount plus an amount per unit) and the so-called shared-contracts. The specific structure varies on a case-by-case basis, depending on the level

---

28. *United States v. United States Gypsum Co.*, 438 U.S. 422 (1978).
29. In the U.S. law, *see Citizens & Southern National Bank* (1975) and *Gypsum* (1978). In EU law, *see UK Agricultural Tractor* (1992), affirmed by the ECJ (*John Deere*, 1998).

of risk each party must bear; the trust between the parties; asset-specificity; the level of the technology; and the incentives to control, among others. Pricing structure may be indicative of any of these variables.

[C] Multimarket Contacts

It may be the case that competitors have multimarket contacts, increasing the chances for sharing information and the possibilities of engaging in anticompetitive coordination. In *Asfaltos*[30] the FNE filed a complaint against four firms accusing them of bid-rigging public tenders and private requests for bids. The firms assigned contracts among themselves for the provision of asphalt and other derivative products for road construction. The firms were found guilty in some of the accused cases, but there was no proof to condemn in all of them. The TDLC fined three of the competitors (*ACH, Dynal* and *QLA*), and the fourth (*ENEX*) benefited from the leniency program. Also, the Tribunal imposed the obligation to each firm of implementing compliance programs.[31]

In its judgment, the TDLC acknowledged the possibilities for multimarket contacts between the firms. In paragraph 19 it stated that:

> along with the reduced number of competitors in the industry, it is not controversial that they have a number of commercial and property relations, which can be summarised as follow: i) ACH and ENEX jointly own Conosur, firm through which they control the port located in Ventanas, where they import asphalt as raw material; ii) Dynal and QLA own approximately 49% of ACH; iii) the four accused firms are, jointly with Probisa, owners in equal parts of DASA, firm through which they managed the supply of asphalt they obtain from ENAP [a Chilean producer]; iv) there are production agreements for specific products between the firms; and v) there are sales of raw materials between them.[32]

§12.04 "RESIDUAL" EXCHANGES OF INFORMATION

As mentioned, residual exchanges of information –those that are not part of a cartel or price agreements in themselves – are more complex to qualify. It is important to remark, once again, that in many contexts such exchanges are part of normal business relations.[33] They include sharing of accounting information (e.g., accounting methods or ways to keep the accounts of a firm), exchanges of technology, research and development, contractual aspects (e.g., standardization of contracting forms), credit

---

30. *Asfaltos* (Judgment 148/2015).
31. At the time of writing, an appeal was pending before the Supreme Court.
32. Also, the TDLC acknowledged that the numerous meeting the competitors in hotels, restaurant and cafes was an abnormal business situation, regardless the multiple commercial relations the parties had.
33. As Whish (2009: 525) indicates, benchmarking increases efficiency. Competitors cannot compete in a statistic vacuum. The more the information they have on market conditions, demand quantity, capacity levels and investments plans of rivals, the easier the taking of decisions on production and the adoption of rational and effective marketing strategies. This is particularly true in the case of firms producing homogeneous products.

information or historical information about consumers, among others. These exchanges may be beneficial for firms, particularly in markets where the nature and extension of publicly available information is limited.[34] Moreover, such exchanges may also be beneficial for consumers when they enhance transparency in the market. And they may even be positive for competition if they promote entrance of new firms to the market (Teece, 1993). However, residual information sharing does have a collusive potential. For it may act as platform for oligopolistic coordination.[35] Therefore, these exchanges must be judged in the context of a thorough market analysis, taking into account the specificities of the exchange and the type of information shared.[36]

All of the above necessarily implies a case-by-case analysis. In order to establish whether an exchange of information between competitors may affect competition, the sole analysis of the nature of the information is insufficient. For the information exchanged cannot be considered in vacuum. It is crucial to analyze it in a specific context – i.e., considering the structure and characteristics of the relevant market where the exchange takes place. Compare, for instance, the volume of information exchanged in stocks markets with the volume exchanged in the market for artworks. Also, as the literature has pointed out, there are some market structures that make collusive behavior and unlawful information sharing easier. The analysis therefore depends on a number of factors that interact with each other and vary on a case-by-case basis. For this reason, any general guidance is necessarily of limited value.

---

34. Between rivals, exchanges of information may, for instance, contribute to eliminate possible adverse selection and moral hazard concerns that may be present in some industries. Also, they may facilitate fast convergence to an equilibrium point in non-durable commodity markets.
35. For instance, see the European cases of the EU Commission *Re Cimbel* (1972) (condemning the obligation of informing plans of capacity enlargements to competitors); *Zinc Producer Group* (1984) (condemning the obligation to inform investment plans); *Steel Beams* (1994) (objecting exchanges of information on request and purchases); y *EATA* (1999) (objecting exchanges of information on capacity and percentages of use, and capacity forecasted).
36. As stated by the ECJ in *Asnef-Equifax* (2006):

> According to the case-law on agreements on the exchange of information, such agreements are incompatible with the rules on competition if they reduce or remove the degree of uncertainty as to the operation of the market in question with the result that competition between undertakings is restricted (*John Deere v. Commission*, paragraph 90, and Case C-194/99 P *Thyssen Stahl v. Commission* [2003] ECR I-10821, paragraph 81) (para. 51).
>
> [...] the compatibility of an information exchange system, such as the register, with the Community competition rules cannot be assessed in the abstract. It depends on the economic conditions on the relevant markets and on the specific characteristics of the system concerned, such as, in particular, its purpose and the conditions of access to it and participation in it, as well as the type of information exchanged — be that, for example, public or confidential, aggregated or detailed, historical or current — the periodicity of such information and its importance for the fixing of prices, volumes or conditions of service (para. 54).

Although the judgment refers to two previous cases: *John Deere* (1998) and *Thyseen Stahl* (2003), the first precedent in the subject is *Suiker Unie* (1975).

[A] Market Structures and Characteristics of the Information

The vast number of punishments as well as the variety of forms that cartel can take makes it easier for firms to collude in certain industries. The question is how easy collusion is. Unfortunately, there is scarce economic evidence (at least in our knowledge) clarifying the manner in which some industries will coordinate around a collusive equilibrium and which one this equilibrium shall be. The only aspects possible to analyze, as proxy, are the market characteristics that shall affect the probability of collusion in an industry. This one is associated to a relatively large number of factors affecting the sustainability of the coordination. Generally speaking, those factors may be structural, related to the demand, related to supply conditions, and other "unclassifiable."

Some structural features of market may facilitate anticompetitive coordination. First, *ceteris paribus*, the lesser the number of firms, the higher the probability of collusion –particularly tacit collusion.[37] This is not only due because it is easier for firms to coordinate behavior, but also because potential punishments for deviations become more credible and effective.[38] Conversely, as the number of firms increases, gains from collusion (in the long-run) decrease and gains from deviations (in the short-run) increase. Second, entry barriers are another relevant factor.[39] Coordination is more likely to occur when there is no entry of firms whose behavior is unknown by the incumbents (for instance, the risk of hit-and-run strategies is lower). However, entrance by itself is not a sufficient condition to break coordinated behavior, because this depends largely on the credibility of the incumbents' reaction.[40]

---

37. The idea is intuitive. However, some studies hold it. Huck et al. (2004) argue that anticompetitive effects are more likely in duopoly markets and less likely in oligopoly markets with more firms. In a study on the groceries market in the U.K. (CC, 2008), the former Competition Commission held that *"Increased concentration in the groceries supply chain may make collusion more likely. The exchange of information between retailers via their suppliers is simpler when there are fewer suppliers of a particular product or category [...]"* (¶8.10). Note that even though there is a legitimate objective in principle, the dangers for competition are still present:

    > This consolidation has been encouraged by grocery retailers to some extent which have sought to reduce costs by reducing the number of suppliers that are used in each product category [...]. If this continues, such consolidation may make collusion easier to undertake (¶8.12).

38. Nonetheless, the number of participant in the market is not relevant. There are "benign" oligopolies for competition. The center of the concern for competition remains market power. If prima facie few competitors facilitate coordination, the identification of such situation with market power is far from being a mere "accounting" exercise.
39. There is a longstanding debate in competition law regarding entry barriers. The main antagonistic positions are those of Bain (1954, 1956 y 1968 [1959]) and Stigler (1968).
40. Note that it is not necessary for the entrant to enter the market on equal terms with the incumbent. The sole entrance is relevant. As the then Court of First Instance said in *Airtours* (2002: ¶213–214), the issue is not whether a small player can reach the size necessary for it to compete effectively with an oligopoly by challenging the incumbent firms for their places as market leaders. Rather, it is a question of whether a number of small players already present on the market, taken as a whole, can respond effectively to a reduction in capacity put on to the market by the oligopoly to a level below estimated demand by increasing their capacity to take advantage of the opportunities inherent in a situation of overall under-supply.

A third structural factor is the degree and frequency of interactions between firms during a period of time.[41] Frequent interactions allow fast reactions to deviations. The same idea applies to the frequency of price adjustments: more frequent price adjustments allow a faster application of punishment. Hence no maverick firm can profit from deviations for a long time. Note that it is not relevant whether firms sell or produce the product in each period or in some of them, but the frequency of interactions and price adjustments. If firms do not interact or are not capable of adjusting their prices fast, collusion is improbable, because punishment is not credible.

Finally, transparency is another central structural feature that may facilitate anticompetitive coordination (Stigler, 1964; Green & Porter, 1984; Abreu et al., 1986). Transparency allows to identify deviations easier. If prices are not observable or cannot be inferred from market data, sustainability of coordination becomes difficult.[42] Lack of transparency makes difficult to monitor a cartel. In case of tacit collusion, it makes more difficult to figure out whether price adjustments are due to new market conditions or deviations. Therefore, it is crucial to analyze all the features from information sharing: its nature,[43] how easy is to obtain it, and so on.

A second group of factors that may facilitate coordination is related with demand conditions. Generally speaking, coordination is easier to hold if the market is growing – that is, if actual profits are lesser that future expected profits.[44] Conversely, in declining markets (or markets that are about to collapse) sustaining coordination is more difficult due to scarce expected profits. Indeed, this conclusion may sound counter-intuitive. Demand growing is commonly seen as a factor that makes collusion more difficult. However, this depends on entry barriers: if they are low, collusion is unlikely. But the isolated effect of the growth of the market is the aforesaid.

Second, demand fluctuations are also important. Generally speaking, a stable demand contributes to transparency, making deviations harder. Conversely, demand fluctuations make collusion more difficult, particularly if they are deterministic (for instance, because of stationary cycles) rather than random (Rotemberg & Saloner, 1986; Haltiwanger & Harrington, 1991). When markets are in their peak, gains from deviation are maximized and potential costs from punishments are minimized.[45] Hence if demand is unstable (in some period it is higher than average), incentives to deviate increase.

---

41. Interactions include minority shareholding between competitors and joint ventures. They decrease gains from deviation (Martin, 1995).
42. Notice that transparency does not prevent collusion, but makes it more difficult to sustain (and limits its reach). However, it is also possible that lack of transparency makes the formation of an agreement more difficult. That is, cartels might be hard to form, but once firms have reached an agreement, it might be hard to punish deviations. Unfortunately, the relation is not precise and there are no studies on the issue –at least in our knowledge.
43. Less aggregated information facilitates collusion (Kuhn, 2001).
44. As long as the number of players remain the same.
45. Indeed, collusion is facilitated when demand is in the lowest part of the cycle. Nevertheless, collusion is harder to hold in absence of fluctuations.

Finally, demand elasticity has no impact on coordination.[46] However, it does affect gains from coordination. If elasticity is low, firms may keep prices high without losing many consumers. In other words, the impact on welfare is bigger the more inelastic the demand is.

Other factors are related with the supply side. First, when firms are alike, collusion becomes easier. For instance, firms may be similar in cost structure (Bain, 1948). Conversely, a common price strategy may be difficult to adopt by firms with asymmetric costs. There are three main reasons. First, more efficient firms (with lower marginal costs) will prefer a price the others cannot, or does not, wish to hold. Second, it may become impossible to establish a focal point (Schelling, 1981 [1960]). Finally, technological reasons will push the transference of market shares to efficient firms, a situation that requires express agreements or monetary or non-monetary transferences (Schmalensee, 1987). But even if firms agree on a collusive price, those with lower costs have incentives to deviate, because threat of retaliation is less credible. Foreseeing this situation, firms may agree on sharing the benefits of collusion asymmetrically, with more benefits for firms with lower costs. They could also redistribute market shares asymmetrically (Harrington, 1989). However, since incentives of firms with higher costs are also affected, the outcome is unpredictable (Ivaldi et al., 2003). As a result, the analysis must be cautious.

Symmetry can be analyzed in term of capacity, plant size, market shares, range of production, and innovation,[47] among others. Generally speaking, the more asymmetry there is in the market, stronger the incentives to deviate –particularly if aggregate capacity is limited (Compte et al., 2002; Lambson, 1994). Conversely, the effects of symmetry are ambiguous (Abreu, 1986; Brock & Shainkman, 1985). If firms face capacity restrictions, gains from deviation decrease. At the same time, however, capacity to retaliate decreases.

The characteristic of the product is another factor to consider. The key here is "horizontal differentiation": different combinations of the same product, at comparable prices, being offered to different sets of consumers.[48] The objective of such an strategy is to create market segmentation, loyalty and increasing market power on a specific group of consumers. The effect on coordination is contradictory. On the one hand, horizontal differentiation limits gains from deviation, because it makes more difficult to attract new consumers. On the other hand, it limits price wars in case of deviations, making punishment less credible. The literature concludes that horizontal homogeneity or heterogeneity of the product has an ambiguous impact on collusive outcomes, depending on the nature of competition in the market (price competition

---

46. By contrast, Jones & Suffrin (2008) argue that firms would be capable to increase prices and profits only when demand is inelastic.
47. A variant of cost asymmetry is the idea that coordination is more difficult when innovation in the market is high. For innovation allows advantages over rivals, especially when it is disruptive. Note that it is irrelevant if the innovator is the incumbent or the maverick: if the market is dynamic in this sense, competition authorities should sleep better.
48. The opposite concept is "vertical differentiation", which refers to the development of better products –i.e., differences on quality. In this case, the situation is similar to cost asymmetry. Firms that can differentiate their products have more incentives to deviate. The magnitude of the incentives depends on the magnitude of the competitive advantage.

vis-a-vis competition on quantity) (Ross, 1992; Martin, 1993).[49] Notwithstanding this result, competition authorities normally consider product homogeneity as a factor that facilitates collusion.[50] For differentiation increases informational concerns in less transparent markets (Raith, 1996), whereas homogeneity makes it easier for a firm to infer information from its own prices and quantities.

Another supply factor is multimarket contacts. There is evidence that coordination becomes easier in presence of such contacts (Berheim & Whinston, 1990).[51] There are at least three reasons for this. First, frequency of interactions increases. Second, asymmetries decrease. Finally, firms may collude even in markets with characteristics that make collusion more difficult in principle.[52]

Finally, there are a number of other "unclassifiable" factors that should also be taken into account in a structural analysis. For instance, purchasing market power may stimulate competition under some conditions (Snyder, 1996). Conversely, high frequency of purchase orders may facilitate coordination because they help to impose credible punishments (Motta, 2004).

Once structural elements have been taken into account, the "inherent" characteristics of the information become relevant. By this we refer to a number of features such as the nature of the information exchanged (prices, quantities, sales, and so on); the time to which it refers (past, present or future information); its level of aggregation (disaggregated by players, aggregated anonymously, etc.); the form of delivery (directly between competitors, through third parties such as trade or professional associations, suppliers or others); and the frequency of the exchange (daily, weekly, monthly, etc.); among others. These features depend on market structure. For instance, what is "historic information" depends on interactions between competitors (including their contractual relations) and the nature of the market.

On this, despite the fact that, as mentioned, any general guidance is of limited value, it is still possible to sketch some general rules. First, as long as information is "farther" from prices, authorities should be reluctant to consider an exchange as anticompetitive.[53] This kind of information is normally expensive to produce, so they joint production may imply significant economies (Hovenkamp, 2005a). Second, the

---

49. The ambiguous effect is better illustrated with differentiated products. In principle these products do not facilitate collusion, due to the difficulties to apply punishments (demand will be positive even if rivals decrease prices). But they may also facilitate it for the same reason: deviation is less beneficial (price reductions must be considerable to gain a significant market share). Hence it is equally likely that collusion is produced between firms with homogeneous products – such as gasoline (e.g., as shown by Hosket et al., 2008) – than between firms producing heterogeneous products.
50. This seems to have been the implicit thinking of the TDLC in *D&S/Falabella* (Decision 24/2008). Applying a concept of "integrated retail", the TDLC expressly considered that the likelihood of collusion in the market was higher due to the homogeneity of products the only two integrated retailers produced (para. 225).
51. As seen, they played a crucial role in the *Asfaltos* cartel case. See above, __.
52. At a first glance, it may seem that multimarket contacts decrease sustainability of collusion, since they allow firms to apply punishments in different markets. However, as Motta (2004) explains, a firm can deviate in all those markets at the same time. The crucial point is the relation with asymmetries.
53. This was stated, for instance, by the U.S. Court of Appeal of the 9° Circuit in *Zozlaw* (1982).

timing of the exchange should also be considered (Posner, 2001). Third, duration matters. It is likely that a systematic exchange is indicative of or constitutes a concerted practice (Monti, 2008). The underlying idea is always that, despite the exchanges, each competitor establishes its own market strategy independently.

Another relevant aspect is the way of disseminating information between competitors. First, information may be shared in an ample way within the industry –for example, throughout a commercial association or another organization.[54] It is particularly relevant to consider the relationship between the domain in which the information is exchanged and the relevant market (Hovenkamp, 2005a).[55] As we have shown, in Chile trade associations have played a crucial role in sustaining cartels.[56] Also, most cases condemned by the *Comisión Resolutiva* or the *Comisión Preventiva Central* (the TLDC predecessors) were against associations or their members.[57]

Second, firms may provide unilateral price announcements or unilateral production announcements that may also contribute to collusion.[58] There have been no cases of this kind in Chile. Generally, the focus of the analysis should be on transparency. If the announcements are public (for instance, through commercial advertisements), they should not be considered prima facie anticompetitive.[59] Conversely, private announcements, directed exclusively to rivals, should be banned. For the efficiency of that communication is practically inexistent (Kühn, 2001). They are normally direct to avoid costly periods of price wars and price instability (Motta, 2004) and may be a strong inductor of price fixing. Finally, firms may obtain or provide information by

---

54. The two seminal cases in U.S. law are *Hardwood* (1921) and *Maple Flooring* (1925). A complete analysis of both cases can be found in Posner (2001: 159 et seq.). Fraas & Greer (1977) was one of the first empirical studies demonstrating the collusive potential of associations.
55. For instance, Posner (2001) note that in *American Column* (1921), the association condemned had 365 members that collectively controlled only one third of the U.S. market of hardwood. Therefore, even assuming express price fixing it would be hard to show how a cartel with so many members that control only a fraction of the market may have been affected prices substantially as the U.S. Supreme Court concluded. Conversely, in the Chilean *Pollos* case, the association was formed solely by the three cartelized firms.
56. See above, ___.
57. For example, see *Comisión Preventiva Central*, Ruling N° 1128/2002: "This Commission considers that announcements to increase prices [...] [made by] leaders of the association are a wrongful intervention in the market [...] and their statements may incite to price agreements", therefore "they should refrain from forecasting of price variations"; Ruling N° 589/1987:

> It cannot be said that [the statements of the leaders of the association] in the press are anticompetitive. However, they have been inconvenient, considering a price increase is coming. Even though the object of such statement is to make users and authorities conscious of the need of price increases, due to the increase on supplies [...] the sole fact of making the statement before the increase is materialized induce members to increase the price, either for mere parallelism or in a concerted manner.

> Ruling N° 365/1982: "associations cannot, in any event, suggest to their members nor to third parties, specific costs, prices or tariffs for goods and services, because it is anticompetitive."

58. The seminal study is Farrel (1987), who analyzed the influence of non-verifiable and non-compulsory communications (cheap talk) in agreements in a context of games with multiple equilibria. Later theoretical and empirical confirmed the collusive potential of unilateral announcements *See*, among others, Cooper et al. (1992), and Farrel & Rabin (1996).
59. If there are positive and negative effects, the former tend to take precedence over the latter.

direct contact to one or more competitors.[60] In such a case, potential benefits of information sharing disappear completely, and it is highly likely that the exchange is part of a mere price fixing. Conversely, if the exchange is indirect, the situation is less clear. However, this does not imply less risk.[61] Even though the form of the exchange is relevant for its qualification of lawfulness, it should not be too relevant for the analysis. For the election of certain form may depends on factors not related to the effects of the information exchange for competition (Posner, 2001).

[B] General Guidance by Chilean Authorities

Considering all of the aforementioned, both the FNE and the TDLC have issued rules that aim to provide clearer guidance to parties that wish to exchange information.

In *Dentistas*,[62] a non-adversarial case, a group of dentists part of a local Dentists' Trade Association requested the TDLC to clarify whether they could provide "pricing guidelines" (*arancel de referencia*) for its associated members. The association requested the Tribunal to establish the conditions under which such references could be less risky for competition. Considering the market structure, the TDLC ruled that prices references cannot be established in case of services with a reduced number of suppliers in the market. Also, it said that price references must not be based on estimations of the dentists' future incomes. However, the TDLC did not completely restricted price references. It ruled that in circumstances different than the mentioned, prices references should comply with the following rules:

(i) They must be based on historical variables, including prices, costs or others.
(ii) They must be determined by a third party (not the trade or professional association).
(iii) References should provide aggregate information, that is, suppliers should not be identifiable from the information.
(iv) Following the reference should be voluntary for associated members, and sanctions cannot be adopted in case a member does not follow the reference.
(v) References should be publicly available.

The Dentists' Trade Association also asked whether the estimation of costs or supplies the dentists would use, and the information on the criteria for adjustments of those costs, supplies or the valuation of the services related with the dentists' medical specialties, could be considered against the Competition Act. The TDLC stated that only the provision of information by the association to its members on the historical costs the treatments represent for the average of the members, based on surveys or studies, does not infringe the Act.

A slightly different case is *Lan/Tam*,[63] a review of the merger between a Chilean and a Brazilian airlines (*LAN Airlines S.A.* and *TAM Linhas Aéreas S.A.*, respectively).

---

60. The seminal case is *Container Corp.* (1969), ruled by the U.S. Supreme Court.
61. See above, note __.
62. *Dentistas* (Decision 45/2014).
63. *Lan/Tam* (Decision 37/2011).

Chapter 12: Exchanges of Information in Competition Law §12.04[B]

The TDLC decided to approve the operation subject to a number of remedies, including limitations on information sharing. Among the remedies was the elimination and review of the code sharing agreements with airlines that were not part to the same alliance as LATAM (as the merged entity was called), within the routes and intermediate sections indicated in the decision[64] – which were those that affected the Chilean market more directly. Note that code sharing agreements are commonly accepted and of intense use in the airline industry. The TDLC stated that the characteristics of these agreements imply high levels of coordination, because they consider the mutual access to information on public and private tariffs and availability of seats on each flight (i.e., prices and quantities). Also, code-sharing agreements are associated to the so-called *Special Prorate Agreements*, by which airlines directly agree on the price per seat for each section that the seller will pay to the operator, instead of distributing income proportionately. The Tribunal recognized that both in the literature and the case-law of other jurisdictions such level of coordination has been deemed as a mechanism with potentially anticompetitive effects.[65]

The TDLC acknowledged that the sharing-code agreements generated efficiencies and enhancement of quality of the supply,[66] but also risks for competition. Both must be counterbalanced. Among the main risks was the reduction in the intensity of competition between the airlines that subscribe the agreement. Also, it would be more difficult for new firms to enter the market, because an entrant should offer at least the same number of daily flights as the airlines that operate jointly. That is, its minimum efficient scale increases. Considering that the residual demand makes difficult to increase passenger, this risk was considered particularly important.

In parallel to the case-law, the FNE has fulfill an important role advocating best practices. Due to the lack of specific legal regulation, the FNE has provided some guidance, although not directed to address specifically exchanges of information, but only as a subsequent topic. Guidance has been given mainly in the FNE Guidelines on Trade Association and Guidelines on Interlocking –being the first one the most relevant in practice so far. Regarding exchanges of information between associated members, the Trade Associations guidelines state that:

(i) Only historical information should be compiled.
(ii) Frequency of the exchanges should be reduced.
(iii) Information to be disseminated among members should only be aggregated and refer to general topics.
(iv) Any request for information should be voluntary.
(v) The gathering and processing information should be externalized.

---

64. The TDLC also recommended to review the interline agreements.
65. The TDLC expressly stated that the lawfulness of a specific agreement from the competition law standpoint depends on the clauses it contains, the routes it covers and the manner in which it is complemented with other agreements subscribed by the same airlines. As a general rule, the TDLC affirmed, the more the coordination and the more the number of routes that overlap with each other, the riskier the agreement for competition.
66. The TDLC admitted the fragmentation in the aeronautic Latin American market, which makes competition between airlines from different countries more difficult. Alliances and sharing-code agreement are hence useful to facilitate competition.

The Guidelines also refers to recommendations made by trade associations to their members. They indicate that such recommendations should not make references to prices, quantities or commercial strategies, and should always be voluntary (no disciplinary action can be taken against members that do not adopt a recommendation).

Another important area is participation in meetings. On this, the Guidelines suggest that meetings should be registered and documents saved; that minutes of every meeting should be saved, detailing every subject of the meeting; and that specialized legal training may be required.

Finally, there are also a number of other topics expressly referred to by the Guidelines. Among them, collaboration between competitors, boycotts, membership conditions, services to non-affiliated members, self-regulation and codes of conduct, technical standards-setting, and publicity.

§12.05 SUMMING UP

What is it possible to conclude from this short review? First, the analysis of market structure is crucial to assess exchanges. As seen, the lawfulness of an exchange depends in an important part on how easy collusion may arise from such structure. The different structural factors that may affect coordination and their effect on the sustainability thereof are summarized in Table 12.1.

Table 12.1   Market Structure and Its Potential Influence on Collusive Behavior

Factors Affecting Anticompetitive Coordination			Effect on Sustainability of Coordination		
			Positive	Negative	Ambiguous
Structural factors	Number of participants in the market	High		x	
		Low	x		
	Entry barriers	Many	x		
		Few		x	
	Frequency of interactions and price adjustments	High	x		
		Low		x	
	Market transparency	High (stable market)	x		
		Low (unstable market)		x	

Factors Affecting Anticompetitive Coordination			Effect on Sustainability of Coordination		
			Positive	Negative	Ambiguous
Demand factors	Growth	Growing markets	x		
		Stable markets or shrinking		x	
	Fluctuations	High		x	
		Low	x		
	Elasticity	Elastic			x
		Inelastic			x
Supply factors	Characteristics of the firms	Cost symmetry	x		
		Cost asymmetry		x	
	Level of innovation	High		x	
		Low	x		
	Product-differentiation	Vertical	(similar to cost asymmetry)		
		Horizontal			x
	Contacts between firms	Multimarket	x		
		Single market		x	
Other factors	Purchasing power	High		x	
		Low	x		
	Maverick firm	-			x
	Inventory and excesses of capacity	-			x

Source: Authors' elaboration.

Second, aside the importance of market structures, it is possible to sketch a general view on the sharing of different types of information, "raking" it from exchanges that should in principle be banned (ranked number 1) to information that does not produce competition concerns (ranked 4). Most categories fall under number 3, which means that prima facie they should not produce competitive concerns, but they should be look with some care depending on the circumstances. This is summarized in Table 12.2 herein below.

Table 12.2   Characteristics of the Information

	Type of Information	Characteristics / Conditions	Information Exchange
Commercial information	(Actual) prices	Historic	3
		Present	1
		Future	1
		Aggregated	3
		Disaggregated	3
	Costs	Historic	3
		Present	3
		Future	3
		Aggregated	3
		Disaggregated	1
	Volume of production	Units	1
		Level of production (aggregated)	3
	Product quality	-	3
	Technology	-	3
	Security standards	-	3
	Other technical aspects	-	3
Strategic Information	Market studies	Positioning	2
		Market shares	2
	Pricing (models, strategies)	Prices (re)adjustments	2
		Prices by areas	2
		Minimum resale prices	2
		Discounts	2
	Commercialization strategies	Strategic stock	2
		Marketing strategies	2
		Commercialization plans	2
		Sales objectives	2
Non-strategic information	Regulations	-	4
	Inflation	Publicly available	4
	Exchange rate	-	4

Notation: 1–4: from prohibited to permitted under competition laws.
Source: Authors' elaboration.

A mix of a thorough market structure analysis and the inherent characteristics of the information should allow competition authorities make robust inferences on the lawfulness of a practice that is common in business and may even be beneficial when firms behave competitively. The emerging Chilean experience is proof.

CHAPTER 13
Ten Years Fighting Cartels: The Case of El Salvador

*Aldo Henrique Cáder Camilot**

The Competition Law (LC, by its Spanish acronyms) in El Salvador (ESV) and the authority on the matter, the Superintendence of Competition (SC) came into full force on January 1, 2006. The ten-year anniversary of having one competition law and an autonomous administrative institution that watches and protects the competition in El Salvador in support of the economic efficiency and the well-being of the consumers[1] was recently celebrated.

It is no surprise that before this date, the commercial and mercantile practices of various economic agents in El Salvador were based, among other things, on actions or omissions opposite to competition, or on the fact that current juridical norms were created to promote anticompetitive practices. Starting on January 2006, the companies had to do an official review of its commercial practices and self-assess their adherence to the new anti-trust regulation. It is highly likely that some economic agents have modified its way of doing business and left aside agreements between competitors or stop actions that constituted abuse of dominant position; nevertheless, it is also highly likely that others have maintained its way of acting on the market. The existence of a competition regulation does not ensure that agents would stop conducts opposite to free competition.

---

* The author acknowledges the assistance of Lic. Flor Alicia Calvo (economist at the Superintendencia de Competencia) and Flor Cortez (intern) in the review and translation of this document.
1. The objective of this law is to promote, protect and guarantee competition, by preventing and eliminating any anticompetitive practice, regardless of its nature, and that limits or restricts competition in any way, or that impedes the access of any economic agent to the market, in order to increase economic efficiency and consumer's welfare. Any agreement, pact, or contract among competitors and non- competitors is banned, as well as any action among competitors and non-competitors aimed to limit or restrict competition or impede the access of any economic agent to the market, under the terms and conditions established herein.

In effect, the cases developed in these ten years by the SC demonstrate that in El Salvador existed companies that operated in a way opposite to the stipulated by the institution. Moreover, some companies colluded or abused their dominant position on their relevant markets in spite of the law. This report tries to describe how the SC protects competition, particularly through investigation and dismantling of anticompetitive agreements between competitors (cartels); practices that have been recognized by the doctrine, national and international jurisprudence, like the most serious and harmful for competition.[2] The description of this fight will include a reference to quantitative aspects (information, statistics, etc.), and also to qualitative aspects that will help understand this fight: research tools, analysis rule, burden of proof, etc.

Since 2006, the SC investigated, either ex-officio or at the request of a third party, a total of twelve cartel cases. Of these, cartel existence could only be verified on seven cases. In the remaining five, the economic agents were absolved for lack of sufficient evidence.

At this point, before delving into the particularities of these cases, it is necessary to refer to certain important aspects related to the cartels' evidence and analysis.

According to the Salvadoran Competition Law[3] and the "jurisprudence" of the SC,[4] the cartels are analyzed under the per se rule, meaning that is enough to accredit cartel existence for them to punish economic agents, regardless of why the agreement was adopted, its consequences or effects on the market. To credit its existence, it is necessary to make use of the commonly used procedures in Competition Law (witnesses, declarations, documents, etc.) and of the recourses (inspection visit, records, raids, etc.) that the competition authorities possess. Also, it is necessary to use the applicable system for weighing evidence. Currently, this system (in El Salvador's case) is the "sana crítica ":[5] an evaluation done the authority, but motivated and reasoned,

---

2. Agreements between competitors are considered the most serious anticompetitive practices, due to the negative effects that these behaviors have on the functioning of markets "Flours Cartel" https://issuu.com/scompetencia/docs/sc-005-o-pa-nr-2008_040908_1200_har/0.
3. Article 25:

   Anticompetitive practices among competitors are prohibited, these practices include the following, amongst others:

   a) Establish agreements to fix prices or other purchase or sales conditions under any form whatsoever;
   b) Fixing or limiting quantity output;
   c) Fix or limit prices at auctions or in any other form bidding private or public, national or international, with the exception of the joint bids submitted by economic agents that are clearly identified as such in the documents submitted by the bidders.
   d) Market allocation; either by territory, volume of sales or purchases, by type of good sold, customer or seller, or by any other means.

4. In the record SC-005-O-NR-2008 (MOL, SA de CV and HARISA, SA de CV) contains what the directive board declared "in many jurisdictions, hard core cartels (anticompetitive practices between competitors) are per se illegal because of their pernicious effect on competition and lack of economic value redeemable," https://issuu.com/scompetencia/docs/sc-005-o-pa-nr-2008_04 0908_1200_har/0.
5. "In the system of sound judgment, the judge, court or authority, is not bound to certain rules, under this system, fail (solve) reasonably and within the period prescribed by law, according to the rules of logic, common sense and their own psychological assessment of the facts brought into

Chapter 13: Ten Years Fighting Cartels: The Case of El Salvador

declaring why certain means or tools verified the existence of the cartel, and why others have not managed to generate certainty for the "judge".

In effect, so that the SC proves an anticompetitive agreement between competitors (and ultimately punished, without making any further analysis: per se rule) requires proof of its existence which can be derived from any means or tools, or a combination of several.

Regardless if the test is qualified as best evidence, direct or circumstantial evidence, corroborating evidence, economic or judicial, etc., the main goal is to prove cartel existence. If an accredited research done is cataloged in the final analysis of the SC as *proof*, it is because it has been able to generate certainty for the authority, regardless of the categorization the evidence may receive. To summarize, the SC initiates an investigation whenever it has a hint of cartel existence, and in the development of this investigation evidence is produced to verify its existence; if there is evidence, and under the per se rule, the SC would express a resolution or would absolve the investigated ones.

Having explained the way cartels are analyzed, the twelve cases that have been investigated since 2006 will be retaken. Seven of which were sanctioned.

The first cartel was investigated in 2007, one year before the SC started working, and after an initial process of intensive personnel training. It was an "ingenuous" cartel because the economic agents involved (agricultural commodity market), agglutinated inside an association (BOLPROES) published in one national circulated newspaper the agreement of the tariffs that would charge for its intermediation services in the bag of products and services.[6]

In 2008, the second sanctioned cartel was called the "flour cartel." The two main mills in the country were dividing the domestic market in quotas (45% y 55%). The importance of this case was not only on the sector involved (distribution of wheat flour) but the tool used for discovering it: search warrant. Through this search, the authority obtained direct evidence of the existence of the cartel. For example, managers' agendas contained notes that showed evidence of anticompetitive practices.[7]

The third sanctioned case came in 2009. As a result, from the competition advocacy efforts with the Acquisitions and Procurement Units for the public sector (UACIs, by its Spanish acronyms), certain State institutions notified the Competition Authority that four travel agencies were offering (in public procurements) the same prices in terms of service fees. Offers were identical to the cent. Additionally, testimonies obtained allowed to indirectly corroborate the collusion strategy.[8]

The fourth sanctioned case was also a "naive cartel" and took place in 2010. However, it involved telecommunications companies with international presence, aware of anti-trust law, these companies published newspaper advertisements which clearly announced that they would charge USD 0.21 per call from fixed to mobile

---

the process or procedure through the various items of evidence." Paragraph 191 de final resolution on insurance case. https://issuu.com/scompetencia/docs/resoluci__n_final_9a1662d2c2e5a1.
6. http://www.sc.gob.sv/uploads/SC-001-O-PA-R-2007_181007_1000.pdf.
7. https://issuu.com/scompetencia/docs/sc-005-o-pa-nr-2008_040908_1200_har/0.
8. http://www.sc.gob.sv/uploads/SC-001-O-PA-NR-2009_070709_0900.pdf.

networks. For this, the competition authority obtained evidence that these agents sent letters to the operators of fixed networks that had the same terms, sentence structure, even with identical grammatical and spelling errors.[9]

Later, another cartel was sanctioned in public procurements, this time in 2011 and in relation to companies providing services in the Port of Acajutla, department of Sonsonate. The two economic agents involved agreed to distort competition when the port authority summoned bids to get towing services, stevedoring, and etc.[10] Then in 2013, the SC sanctioned another cartel in a public procurement called by the National Administration of Aqueducts and Sewers (ANDA, by its Spanish acronyms), since two companies agreed to set identical prices in their services offers as well as other bidding aspects.[11]

The last sanctioned cartel case ended in 2015, a highly social relevant case. It was discovered that three insurance companies were distributing the bidding market of the two pension fund administrators in the country. The institution not only analyzed the offers and the awarding, but also analyzed the rivalry and the relation between the bidders and the administrators, as well as each executive's declarations and testimonies of the investigated agents and the sector regulator. This case was about management of the pension system affiliates' insurance and disability savings.[12]

As for the imposed fines, the cartel with the highest fine was the flour cartel because as a whole the authority of competition imposed USD 4,032,421.36, a considerable sum for the size of the Salvadoran economy. The cartel with the least amount of money was the ANDA public procurement cartel, with only USD 6,141.80.

In terms of the length of investigations, it should be noted that the competition authority of El Salvador is a small authority in terms of its material and territorial area for action; it only has fifty-two employees, three of which work solely on specialized areas. Of these, the "anti-cartels" unit, part of the investigation unit, is formed by only five economists and three lawyers; due to this, investigations cannot move fast. In the ten-year period, the longest case lasted one year and eleven months (Insurance cartel) and the fastest lasted about five months (Travel agencies and Flours cartel). The legal deadline to resolve cases is two years.[13]

Another aspect which should be highlighted is that the most common type of agreement is price-fixing, followed by market sharing. Of the sanctioned cases, five

---

9. http://www.sc.gob.sv/uploads/SC-017-O-PS-R-2010_191211_1055.pdf.
10. http://www.grupo-planb.com/sc-site/files/300811SERPORSAL.pdf.
11. http://base.crcal.org/documentos/2ef582d7-f6f4-4ce2-a6d1-0e7541875e02/El_Salvador-Cartel-2013-Gruas.pdf.
12. https://issuu.com/scompetencia/docs/resoluci__n_final_9a1662d2c2e5a1.
13. Article 45 final part "Once the file is integrated, the Superintendent shall conclude his/her investigations and send it to the Board of Directors, that shall issue a final resolution in a period no longer than twelve months, from the date the investigation started or the complaint was filed; this term may be expanded by means of a justified resolution of the Board, up to a term not exceeding twelve months, only once, and only when the circumstances so merit."

have been for price-fixing (Article 25 letters "a" and "c" of the Competition Law,[14] and only two cases for dividing market or segment shares (Article 25 letter "d "[15]).

All these cases have been challenged in court, in the Administrative Chamber of the Supreme Court; in most of cases, the competition authority obtained favorable ruling, by defending the legality of its actions with lawyers working in the investigation unit.[16]

Just as it can be seen, the cartel fight in El Salvador has been very important. Although there are few cases, cartels in the main sector of the economy have been uncovered and sanctioned, contributing to economic efficiency and consumer welfare. Just as noted previously, the wheat cartel was discovered (as a primary source of bread and sweets which are part of the country's basic nutritional basket); the phone companies' cartel, where companies did not compete on prices of landline calls ending in their respective networks, pertaining a sector growing at a large scale; the insurance provisioning cartel, among others.

Despite the success of the investigations, there is a lot to be done within this field. The Salvadoran authority cannot rest on its laurels as it must continue to progress in its fight against cartels through constant training of its personnel, using their investigative tools more efficiently, strengthening the judicial defense of its findings, encouraging citizens complaints, etc. However, cartels will always exist. The most important thing for minimizing them is awareness of competition law at all levels of society (advocacy). They can also be dissuaded by effective investigations and sanctions proportional to the harm caused to competition.

---

14. Article 25 "Anticompetitive practices among competitors are prohibited, these practices include the following, amongst others: a) Establish agreements to fix prices or other purchase or sales conditions under any form whatsoever; c) Fix or limit prices at auctions or in any other form bidding private or public, national or international, with the exception of the joint bids submitted by economic agents that are clearly identified as such in the documents submitted by the bidders."
15. Article 25 "Anticompetitive practices among competitors are prohibited, these practices include the following, amongst others: d) Market allocation; either by territory, volume of sales or purchases, by type of good sold, customer or seller, or by any other means."
16. http://app.sc.gob.sv.

CHAPTER 14
The Use of Indirect Evidences in the Fight Against Cartels in Brazil

Paulo Burnier da Silveira & Pablo Reja Sánchez

§14.01 INTRODUCTION

The fight against cartels has become a top priority to many governments. Indeed, when companies agree on price fixing or market allocation, they injure customers through higher prices and lack of innovation. According to the Organisation for Economic Co-operation and Development (OECD), cartels may increase prices in average 10%–20% of a given product or service, when compared to its normal price. In case of public procurement cartels, the price increase can be even higher. As it is the most severe infringement of competition laws, different techniques were developed to detect and to sanction cartels, such as leniency programs that are adopted in several jurisdictions, including Brazil and other Latin American countries.

In this context, this paper addresses a particular strategy of competition authorities in the fight against anticompetitive practices, which may become a trend in Latin American countries: the use of indirect evidences to sanction cartels. The indirect evidence, also named circumstantial evidence, includes both economic evidence and communication among competitors that do not explicitly proof the existence of an illegal arrangement.

The use of this instrument is backed by the fact that cartels are secret arrangements by nature. In this sense, if a given jurisdiction is required to rely on a clean and direct evidence of the infringement, it means that this country will likely leave unpunished many cartels that do not produce explicit traces of the wrongdoing. It may also create incentives to the development of even more sophisticated cartels, which will avoid producing any sort of evidence considered as a minimum standard for condemnation by local authorities.

This is precisely the reason why competition authorities and international organizations have invested time, energy and resources to discuss the use of indirect evidences in the fight against cartels around the world, particularly in the area of bid rigging. Of course, the debate is delicate as it also concerns the standard of proof that should apply to companies involved in economic infringements (vis-à-vis the standard of proof applied to individuals).[1]

This paper will analyze an important case tried by the Brazilian Competition Authority (CADE) in September 2015, in which a local bid-rigging cartel was sanctioned by CADE based solely on indirect evidences. Although it exists other cartel condemnations in Brazil that strongly relied on circumstantial evidences,[2] this may be considered the first case in which a cartel was sanctioned exclusively on indirect evidences. The chapter will follow this structure: first, the different types of bid-rigging will be briefly presented; then the Brazilian case itself will be analyzed; followed by a comparative study in order to demonstrate that the Brazilian recent experience is not innovating in this field, but it is rather in line with other countries and recommended practices; and, finally, some final remarks.

§14.02 TYPES OF BID-RIGGING

The bid-rigging cartels may take different forms. In a nutshell, the four main categories of the infringement are listed below:

Cover bidding: this is considered the most common situation of collusion in public tenders. Also named fake proposals or complementary bidding, it occurs when a company consciously presents a bid with a higher price than its competitor or which contains something that does not fulfill a certain need or requirement for the buyer to complete the transaction. Their real purpose is to indicate the existence of a genuine competition atmosphere in the procedure.

Bid suppression: in this situation, companies may agree to not participate in a certain tender or to withdraw its bid during the procedure, in order to refrain its participation. In this sense, one may also include in this category the non-conforming bids, which deliberately leaves a formal mistake on the proposal to be eliminated at a later stage of the bidding procedure, as well as the market-allocation when competitors divide the market and agree not to compete for certain customers or in certain geographic areas.

Bid rotation: under this scheme, companies continue to take part in the biddings, but arrange amongst themselves to alternate the winning bids (i.e., the best price

---

1. For a more conservative view of the topic: Maria João Melícias. "Did They Do It? The Interplay between the Standard of Proof and the Presumption of Innocence in EU Cartel Investigations". *World Competition Law and Economics Review*. vol. 35. n° 3. Kluwer Law International, 2012. For other academic views on the topic: Fernando Castillo de la Torre. "Evidence, Proof and Judicial Review in Cartel Cases". *World Competition*. vol. 32. n° 4. 2009; and Koki Arai. "Indirect Evidence in Japanese Cartel Control". Published online by Max Planck Institute for Innovation and Competition (DOI 10.1007/s40319-015-0332-1). Munich: Springer, 2015.
2. Amongst others, the steel cartel case, the Rio de Janeiro and São Paulo airline cartel case, and the newspaper cartel case in Rio de Janeiro. For further information, *see* the Brazilian contribution in: OECD. *Policy Roundtables*. "Prosecuting Cartels without Direct Evidence". Paris, 2006. Available at: www.oecd.org/daf/competition.

offer). It enables companies to rotate as winners and impose higher prices to perform public contracts. The rotation criteria may vary from the number of tenders to the total amount of a sum of contracts.

Subcontracting: in this case, the winner hires one of its competitors to perform a certain portion of the contract. It is a way of rewarding the company that collaborated to the final result of the tender.

The different categories of bid-rigging cartels are key to understand the *modus operandi* of the cartel of solar heaters in Brazil. In addition, the OECD recommends that competition authorities take close attention to all warning signs, such as an unusual bidding or pricing patterns, as these agreements are usually negotiated in secret.[3]

§14.03 CARTEL OF SOLAR HEATERS IN BRAZIL

In September 2015, CADE imposed heavy fines on six companies for bid rigging in the market of solar heaters. The cartel reached social housing programs, as the solar equipment was bought through public procurement by a State-owned enterprise in the State of São Paulo, responsible for building houses to low-income families.[4]

The infringement occurred in two public procurements in 2009 and 2010. Among the indirect evidences found during the investigation, there were: (i) identical offers in the first and secret phase of the bidding procedure, (ii) signs of lack of competition in the second and public phase of the bidding procedure, (iii) division of portions of the tender as the rules of the biddings enabled the existence of eleven winners in total, and (iv) sub-hiring of one competitor by another for certain part of the contract.

In addition, cartelist companies were members of a national solar heating association ("DASOL") which had the power to previously approve the participation of companies in the bidding procedure, creating a barrier to entry for smaller companies to participate in the public tender.

In practice, this case could be a classic textbook example of bid-rigging cartel, as it used all of its types: cover bidding, bid withdrawal, bid rotation and subcontracting. The companies managed to divide the eleven portions of the tender between themselves in a clear strategy of geographic market allocation and profit maximization. The circumstantial and economic evidences were considered as a whole, rather than separately as attempted by the defendants during the administrative proceeding.

The approach was also in line with OECD's recommended practices: "the better practice is to use circumstantial evidence holistically, giving it cumulative effect, rather than on an item-by-item basis".[5] In a similar way, the specialized literature refers to

---

3. OECD Recommendation on Fighting Bid Rigging in Public Procurement, approved by the Council on July 17, 2012. Available at: www.oecd.org/daf/competition.
4. Administrative Proceeding n° 08012.001273/2010-24. The total fines sum BRL 21 million, approximately EUR 5 million in 2016.
5. OCDE. *Policy Roundtables*: "Prosecuting Cartels without Direct Evidence". Paris, 2006. Available at: www.oecd.org/daf/competition.

"factor plus" elements, in order to create a larger picture of the conducted and provide stronger grounds for conviction.[6]

In the solar heater cartel, there was no reasonable explanation for the "coincidence of coincidences": (i) identical offers (including cents) in the secret phase of the tender, (ii) the absence of rivalry in the public phase of the tender, and (iii) the final result of the bidding, in which the convicted companies were each allocated one slot of the tender, the closest one to its respective headquarters.

The cartel was sanctioned by CADE's Tribunal by unanimity, with three separated – and converging – written votes, which indicates that the Commissioners were very much engaged in the case files and confident about the existence of a collusion, in despite of an absence of traditional direct evidences. In addition, both the Brazilian Federal Public Prosecutor's Office and the Attorney General's Office had reached the same conclusions.

§14.04 INTERNATIONAL TREND

The fight against bid rigging has been subject to various studies and debates by the global competition community.[7] All of them carry out a strong message to the private sector and policy makers: bid-rigging cartels have become more sophisticated and the understanding of the mechanisms of collusion is essential to both its detection and sanction.

A comparative look around the world confirms the use of indirect evidences as an important instrument to sanction cartels. In most cases, the circumstantial evidences serve as a complementary element of the judgment, but it has also been used as an exclusive and sufficient factor to sanction cartels.[8]

In Latin America, Mexico has a recent and very rich experience on this topic, as the legality in the use of indirect evidences was subject to judicial review and confirmed by the Mexican Supreme Court in April 2015.[9] At this occasion, the Supreme Court upheld the decision taken by the *Comisión Federal de Competencia* (CFC) that condemned pharmaceutical companies for bid-rigging in public procurements promoted by the government through the *Instituto Mexicano del Seguro Social* (IMSS). It

---

6. William Kovacic. "The Identification and Proof of Horizontal Agreements under the Antitrust Laws". *Antitrust Bulletin*. n° 28. Washington DC, 1993. pp. 5–81.
7. For instance, just to remain in recent references: OECD, "Guidelines for Fighting Bid Rigging in Public Procurement" (2009); OCDE, Ex-officio cartel investigations and the use of screens to detect cartels (2013), UNCTAD, Competition policy and public procurement (2012), in addition to innumerous discussions within the International Competition Network (ICN) as well as a priority topic in the BRICS competition forum.
8. Amongst the cases that indirect evidences played a strong role, either as a complementary or an exclusive element for convictions: (i) in Italy, the baby milk cartel case (I623, *Provvedimento* n.° 14.775); (ii) in Spain, the *Distribuidores Cine-FEECE* case (Decision n° 688/2005); (iii) in Indonesia, the case concerning fuel surcharge in domestic flight service (case n.° 25/KPPU-I/2009) and the bid-rigging case for drinking water network building (case n.° 12/KPPU-L/2009), in which the decision was confirmed by the Supreme Court (case n.° 906 K/Pdt.Sus/2010); (iv) in Turkey, the yeast case (Decision n.° 05-60/896/241); and (v) in India, the cement case (case n.° 29/2010).
9. Supreme Court of Mexico, Proceedings AR n° 624/2012, n° 453/2012 and n° 622/2012.

was an important victory to the Mexican competition authority and it will certainly shed light for its future enforcement actions in the field of antitrust.

In its decision, the CFC used circumstantial evidences, including economic analysis and communications among competitors, to conclude for the existence of illegal arrangement intended to coordinate offers in the public tenders.[10] For instance, there were evidences that companies attended the same meetings hosted by the sectorial association, in addition to other communications such as phone calls between commercial directors of the involved companies.

By its turn, the decision of the Supreme Court of Mexico was clear in its final phase of judicial review, in the sense of accepting the use of indirect evidences in the case:

> "no es extraño, que para estos casos, los distintos operadores del control de la competencia, acudan de manera primordial a la integración de las llamadas *pruebas indirectas o pruebas circunstanciales, cuya valoración adquiere una especificidad particular en este ámbito.* (...). Dentro de las llamadas pruebas indirectas, cobra especial relevancia *el parámetro probatorio de conductas económicas injustificadas en determinado mercado, respecto de cuya existencia no es posible extraer un motivo razonable, y en consecuencia, se presume que la explicación sólo es una concertación o acuerdo ilícito.* Junto a ello, se mencionan también de manera importante la existencia de pruebas de comunicación directa, entre los agentes económicos involucrados en los acuerdos".[11]

In addition, the same decision also clarified that the CFC's decision did not go against any fundamental right in Mexico, as it demonstrated the existence of the illegal collusion by indirect evidences.[12]

§14.05 FINAL REMARKS

The use of indirect evidences to sanction cartels has increased in the past years. It may be used as a complementary element, in addition to the more traditional direct evidence, as well as solely in certain occasions to convict companies for wrongdoing. One must always keep in mind that cartels are secret by nature, which can make it extremely difficult to detect and sanction. The recent Brazilian and Mexican experiences may shed lights to other Latin American countries in the use of indirect evidences

---

10. CFC, *Expediente* n.º IO-003-2006 and RA-019-2010.
11. Translation:

    > it is not unusual, for these situations, that those in charge of competition enforcement rely in the use of the so-called indirect or circumstantial evidences, which acquires a particular importance in this field. (...). Within the so-called indirect evidences, it is important to analyze the overall set of evidences of unjustified anticompetitive practices in a certain market, in regards to which it is not possible to extract a reasonable explanation and, therefore, its existence may only be explained by a collusion or illegal arrangement. In addition, there is proof of direct communications amongst companies that participate in the arrangement.

12. AR 624/2012, p. 223.

in the fight against cartels in the region. Whereas in Mexico its use has already received a green light from the higher instances of the Judiciary, in Brazil it must still be subject to judicial review in order to bring greater consistency to its use as an enforcement policy. In any case, this technique shall always be used with caution by competition authorities in order to respect constitutional rights and guarantees.

CHAPTER 15
Shareholders' Damage Claims Against Company Directors for Antitrust Violations? The Japanese Experience and Possible Lessons to Brazil and Latin America

Amanda Athayde

§15.01 INTRODUCTION

Hard core cartels are antitrust violations subject to strict scrutiny by the public authorities as well as by the private parties. On the one side, administrative, civil and/or criminal actions typically perform public enforcement, depending on the jurisdiction's legislation. On the other side, the private enforcement can be performed in several ways, including the private damages lawsuits against the cartelists by the consumers harmed by the anticompetitive conduct.

Recently, possibly triggered by the public disclosure of antitrust lawsuits and by the governments' enforcement actions, the shareholder derivative suits against corporate officers and directors[1] took off around the globe.[2] This type of derivative

---

1. For the purpose of this article, officers and directors are regarded as the ones appointed in the company's bylaws as responsible for carrying out the company's day-to-day business operations. They are elected by the General Shareholders' Meeting, according to Art. 122 (II) of the Brazilian Corporation Law: *"The general meeting has the exclusive authority: II – to elect or discharge corporation officers and auditors at any time, subject to the provisions of item II of Section 142"* and Art. 132 (III): *"An annual general meeting of shareholders shall be held every year during the first four months after the closing of the fiscal year in order: III – to elect the officers and the members of the statutory audit committee."* They have to act as agents and trustees for the corporation, and have the duty to act with care, loyalty, good will and diligence in all acts done on behalf of the corporation. The officers and directors may, or not, be shareholders, as provided in Art. 146:

lawsuit is brought by a shareholder of a corporation on its behalf to enforce or defend a legal right or claim which the corporation has failed to. In the antitrust context, the failure of the corporation to file the lawsuit may occur for instance if the potential defendant is someone close to the company – just as it is typically the case of the current or previous corporate officers and directors. Those individuals may face this type of lawsuit by a breach of its fiduciary duties of loyalty and diligence,[3] and if the shareholder derivative suit is successful, the triumphs go to the corporation.

Thereby, this article proposes some possible corporate causes for action of the shareholders against the corporate officers and directors in the case of antitrust violations. First, when the corporate officers and directors personally practiced the antitrust wrongdoing. Second, when the corporate officers and directors are conniving with other officers and/or directors who practiced the antitrust wrongdoing and fail to take action – for example, failing to apply for leniency or settlement. Third, when the corporate officers and directors are negligent to prevent the wrongdoing. For this purpose, section II presents the Japanese experience in shareholders derivative actions in the antitrust context. Hereupon, section III points out some ways through which those lawsuits could be implemented in Brazil, according to the Brazilian Corporation Act. Finally, section IV proposes conclusions and launches some debates.

§15.02 THE JAPANESE EXPERIENCE ON SHAREHOLDER DERIVATIVE ACTIONS AGAINST OFFICERS AND DIRECTORS IN THE ANTITRUST CONTEXT

The Japanese Companies Act[4] provides in its Article 423(1)[5] that the negligent corporate officers or directors are liable to the company for damages resulting thereof. Article 847(3)[6] gives individual shareholders the right to file a derivative action[7] in case

---

"*Individuals may be elected as members of the administrative bodies; the members of the administrative council must be shareholders, while the directors residing in Brazil may, or may not, be shareholders.*" Their appointment is regulated in Art. 149, as follows: "*Council members and directors shall take up their appointments by signing an instrument of appointment in the book of minutes of administrative council meetings or of board of directors' meetings, as the case may be.*"

2. For instance, recently a shareholder sued Google's holding company board in California State court accusing company leadership of violating European antitrust laws and breaching fiduciary duties to investors with its restrictive Android licensing terms (Case *Robert Jessup v. Larry Page* et al., case number CIV538782, in the Superior Court of the State of California, County of San Mateo).
3. FRAZÃO dedicates an important part of its book to develop on the duties of loyalty and due care of the corporate officers. FRAZÃO, Ana. *Função social da empresa: repercussões sobre a responsabilidade civil de controladores e administradores de S/As*. 2011. pp. 332–404.
4. Japan. Companies Act. Act. N. 86 of July 26, 2005.
5. Article 423(1) of the Companies Act in Japan: "*(1) If a director, accounting advisor, company auditor, executive officer or accounting auditor (hereinafter in this Section referred to as 'Officers, Etc.') neglects his/her duties, he/she shall be liable to such Stock Company for damages arising as a result thereof.*"
6. Article 847(3) of the Companies Act in Japan: "*When the Stock Company does not file an Action for Pursuing Liability, etc. within sixty days from the day of the demand under the provisions of*

the stock company does not file the appropriate action for pursuing liability against those officers and directors for their intentional or negligent acts.

According to RAMSEYER and NAKAZATO, derivative suits were uncommon in Japan, but due to changes in the filling fees that apply to those suits, they have become increasingly common.[8] In the antitrust context, KAWAI, SHIMADA and HEIKE[9] point out that the Japanese society and the legal and business community came to recognize the derivative shareholder actions as one of the measures to question the responsibility of corporations in the antitrust field. WALLE[10] describes that traditionally the shareholders have targeted officers and directors on the basis that they failed to prevent an antitrust violation from occurring. In 2010, however, for the first time, shareholders claimed that the officers and directors of a company were also negligent for not filing a timely leniency application.[11]

According to WALLE,[12] around fifteen derivative suits alleging antitrust violations have been brought in Japan, some of them being rejected by the court and others resulting in settlements.[13] The author explains that some of the typical defenses for

---

paragraph (1), the shareholder who has made such demand may file an Action for Pursuing Liability, etc. on behalf of the Stock Company."
7. A shareholder must continuously hold a corporation's shares for a period of six months in order to file a derivative shareholder action.
8. RAMSEYER, J. Mark; NAKAZATO, Minoru. *Japanese Law: An Economic Approach*. University of Chicago Press, 1999. p. 264.
9. KAWAI, Kozo; SHIMADA, Madoka; HEIKE, Masahiro. Chapter 16. Japan. *The Private Competition Enforcement Review*. 5th Ed. Law Business Research, 2012. p. 251. Available at: < http://www.jurists.co.jp/en/publication/tractate/docs/PCER_Fifth.pdf >.
10. SIMON VANDE WALLE. *Private Antitrust Litigation in the European Union and Japan: A Comparative Perspective*. Maklu, 2013. pp. 123–126.
11. The derivative shareholder action was filed against Sumitomo Denko, in the cartel on optical fiber cable case. *Apud* KAWAI, Kozo; SHIMADA, Madoka; HEIKE, Masahiro. Chapter 16. Japan. *The Private Competition Enforcement Review*. 5th Ed. Law Business Research, 2012. p. 251. Available at: < http://www.jurists.co.jp/en/publication/tractate/docs/PCER_Fifth.pdf >.
12. WALLE. *Ibid*. p. 124, footnote 10.
13. There were cases where the Japanese officers and directors decided to settle, paying non-negligible amounts (ranging from JPY 80 to JPY 230 million), such as in the bid-rigging cases on steel highway bridge construction orders, on the construction of a new subway line in Nagoya. WALLE. *Ibid*. According to WEST:

> Following a 1993 reduction of filing fees, the number of shareholder derivative suits filed in Japan has increased dramatically, creating a database from which to study litigation incentives. This chapter shows that most plaintiffs in Japan lose, few suits settle, settlement amounts are low, and, as in the United States, shareholders do not receive direct stock price benefits from suits. Most derivative suits in Japan, as in the United States, can be explained not by direct benefits to plaintiffs, but by attorney incentives. But derivative suits, like most things in life, have more than one source of causation. The residuum of suits not explained by attorney incentives is best explained by a combination of: (a) non-monetary factors such as altruism, spite, and social concerns, (b) corporate troublemakers (sokaiya), (c) insurance, and (d) close corporation fights. I also find that many derivative actions "piggyback" on government enforcement actions in Japan, which, especially given the lack of information available to shareholders and low white-collar crime enforcement rates, raises interesting questions regarding the relationship of public and private enforcement. These findings suggest that the difficult and messy issues of derivative suits are not unique to the relatively "litigious" or "attorney-centered" United States, and instead simply are endemic to the derivative suit mechanism.

those officers and directors in Japan are the following. First, that they were not aware of the conduct. Second, that they were not aware that the conduct in question constituted a violation/the unlawfulness conduct, and therefore its acts lacked of the requisite intent or negligence. Third, that they did not violate the Antimonopoly Act themselves. Fourth, that the harm suffered because of fines or surcharges was overweighed by the profits derived from the antitrust violation.

Besides those possible defenses, two important decisions on shareholder derivative actions regarding antitrust violations that took place in 2014 in Japan and resulted in settlements changed landscape of those derivative lawsuits.

In December 1, 2010, after condemnation by the JFTC of the optical fiber cable case, a derivative shareholder action was filed against the directors of Sumitomo Electric for alleged negligence.[14] The shareholder claimed that the directors had acted negligently because they: (a) had overlooked the cartels, (b) had not established truly effective compliance systems to prevent cartels beforehand, (c) had not established effective compliance systems relating to leniency applications, and (d) had not applied for leniency. The shareholders sought payment of around JPY 6.7 billion (around USD 630 million), which corresponded to the penalty imposed on the company by the JFTC.[15]

A subsequent suit was brought in 2012 by shareholders against company's officials of Sumitomo Electric in the automotive wire harnesses case. In that case, the shareholders alleged negligence of the officers and directors even though the company was successfully the leniency applicant in this case.[16] During the process, the court issued an order to produce some of the evidence the JFTC obtained during the investigation,[17] which enhanced the shareholders claim.

Finally, in 2014, the Osaka District Court combined both lawsuits and mediated a settlement. According to its terms, twenty-two ex-officials agreed to recover JPY 520 million (around USD 5 million) to the company for their negligence. This was the

---

WEST, Mark D. Why Shareholders Sue: The Evidence from Japan. *Michigan Law and Economics Research Article* No. 00-010, 2000.

14. JFTC. Optical Fiber Cable Case. *Cease and Desist Orders and Surcharge Payment Orders against Manufacturers of Optical Fiber Cable Products.* Available at: < http://www.jftc.go.jp/en/pressreleases/yearly-2010/may/individual-000021.html >.
15. In this context, the Osaka District Court even ordered the JFTC to submit documents in relation to the shareholder derivative suit. SHIMADA, Madoka; TANAKA, Nobuhiro. The Osaka District Court orders the Japan Fair Trade Commission to submit documents in relation to a shareholder derivative suit (Sumitomo Electric), June 15, 2012, *e-Competitions Bulletin Japan Antitrust*, Art. N° 72453. Available at: < http://www.concurrences.com/Bulletin/Special-Issues/Japan/A-Japanese-district-court-orders-72453?lang=en >.
16. JFTC. Wire harness and related products Case. *Cease and Desist Orders and Surcharge Payment Orders to participants in bid-rigging conspiracies for automotive wire harness and related products.* Available at: < http://www.jftc.go.jp/en/pressreleases/yearly-2012/jan/individual-000462.html >.
17. SHIMADA, Madoka. NAKANO, Sumito. Japanese Leniency Program: issues to be considered. *CPI Antitrust Chronicle*, September 2015. p. 5.

highest ever settlement amount for a shareholder derivative suit in Japan, justified by their failure to prevent and/or report the cartel activities in those two cases.[18]

Given all that, derivative suits in Japan, which target corporate directors and officers of companies for antitrust violations, started being successful, even if by means of settlements. This scenario brings light to some possible analogies and repercussions of this understanding in other jurisdictions, such as in Brazil[19] and other countries in Latin America.

§15.03 ARE SHAREHOLDER DERIVATIVE SUITS AGAINST OFFICERS AND DIRECTORS FOR ANTITRUST VIOLATIONS A POSSIBLE REALITY IN BRAZIL?

In Brazil, the Corporation Law,[20] in its Article 158 (I), provides that the officer shall be personally liable to the company for losses resulting from his acts with fault or fraud within the scope of his authority.[21] Article 158 paragraph 1st establishes that the corporate officer shall also exceptionally be liable for the unlawful acts of other officers when acting in connivance with them, when neglecting to investigate such acts or when, despite knowledge of them, fails to take action to prevent such acts.[22]

Article 159 paragraph 3rd also provides to individual shareholders the right to file a derivative action, i.e., an action on behalf of the company in case the stock company does not file the appropriate action for pursuing liability within three months.[23] This lawsuit may be brought even if the general meeting of the company decides not to institute proceedings, since any shareholder representing at least 5% of the capital may

---

18. Nikkei Asian Review. *Sumitomo Electric to Get Record Payout from Ex-officials*, May 8, 2014. Available at: < http://asia.nikkei.com/Business/Companies/Sumitomo-Electric-to-get-record-payout-from-ex-officials >.
19. Brazil currently investigates those two cartel cases which were the basis for the shareholders derivative actions in Japan. The optical fiber cable investigation: Brazil. CADE. Administrative Proceeding (PA) No. 08012.003970/2010-10 and 08700.008576/2012-81. The wire harnesses investigation: Brazil. CADE. Administrative Proceeding (PA) No. 08700.009029/2015-66).
20. Brazil. Corporation Law. Law 6.404/1976.
21. Article 186 (I) of the Corporation Law in Brazil: "*An officer shall not be personally liable for the commitments he undertakes on behalf of the corporation and by virtue of action taken in the ordinary course of business; he shall, however, be liable for any loss caused when he acts: I - within the scope of his authority, **with fault or fraud**; II - contrary to the provisions of the law or of the bylaws.*"
22. Article 158 paragraph 1st: "*An officer shall not be liable for unlawful acts of the other officers, except when acting in connivance with them, when neglecting to investigate such acts or when, despite knowledge of them, he fails to take action to prevent such acts. A dissenting officer shall be exempt from liability when he makes his dissent to be recorded in the minutes of a meeting of the administrative body, or, if this is.*"
23. Article 159 paragraph 3rd of the Corporation Law in Brazil: "*Article 159. By a resolution passed in a general meeting, the corporation may bring an action for civil liability against any officer for the losses caused to the corporation's property. Paragraph 3. Any shareholder may bring the action if proceedings are not instituted within three months from the date of the resolution of the general meeting.*"

file the derivative lawsuit, according to paragraph 4th of Article 159.[24] If the damages are finally recovered, it shall be transferred to the corporation and not to the shareholder who initiated the suit, but the expenses incurred with the lawsuit would be reimbursed, as provided in Article 159 paragraph 5th.[25]

The article proposes that in Brazil corporate officers and directors may face shareholders derivative suits claiming corporate liability for antitrust violations at least in three situations.

First situation: officers and directors who personally practiced the antitrust wrongdoing.

Assume there was a bid-rigging cartel in the construction sector in Brazil and that the Commercial Director of the company A – who is a corporate officer in the bylaws – agreed to fix prices and allocate markets with companies B, C and D. The Commercial Director personally joined the meetings and fostered the anticompetitive agreements, leading its employees to implement the wrongdoing. An investigation is initiated in the administrative sphere, by the Brazilian Competition Authority, the Administrative Council for Economic Defense ("CADE", in its Portuguese acronym). An investigation is also investigated in the criminal sphere, by the State and/or Federal Public Prosecutors ("MP," in its Portuguese acronym). Upon final judgment of the case by CADE's Tribunal,[26] assume that companies A, B, C and D are convicted, as well as all the individuals involved on behalf of the companies. Those individuals that practiced

---

24. Article 159 paragraph 4th of the Corporation Law in Brazil: *"Should the general meeting decide not to institute proceedings, they may be instituted by shareholders representing at least five per cent of the capital."*
25. Article 159 paragraph 5th of the Corporation Law in Brazil: *"Paragraph 5. Any damages recovered by proceedings instituted by a shareholder shall be transferred to the corporation, but the corporation shall reimburse him for all expenses incurred, including monetary adjustment and interest on his expenditure, up to the limit of such damages."*
26. In the administrative sphere in Brazil, Art. 37 of the Brazilian Competition Law (Law 12.529/2011) states that antitrust infringements subjects the ones responsible to the following fines, among other penalties: (i) in the case of a company, a fine of 0.1%–0% of the gross sales of the company, group or conglomerate, in the last fiscal year before the establishment of the administrative proceeding, in the field of the business activity in which the violation occurred, which will never be less than the advantage obtained, when possible the estimation thereof; (ii) in the case of the administrator, directly or indirectly responsible for the violation, when negligence or willful misconduct is proven, a fine of 1%–20% of that applied to the company or to legal entity; (iii) in the case of other individuals or public or private legal entities, as well as any association of persons or de facto or the jure legal entities, even if temporary, or unincorporated, which do not perform business activity, not being possible to use the gross sales criteria, a fine between BRL 50,000 and BRL 2 billion. Without prejudice to the penalties set forth in Art. 37 of this Law, when so required according to the seriousness of the facts or public interest, one or more of the penalties stated in Art. 38 may be imposed: publication in news articles of the extracts from the conviction; ineligibility for official financing and for participation in biddings; recommendation to the respective public agencies for compulsory license, denial of installment payment of federal taxes, company divestiture, transfer of corporate control, sale of assets or partial interruption of activity, the wrongdoer be provided from carrying on trade for a period of five years, among other penalties.

the cartel may also face criminal sanctions, possibly sentenced to jail time.[27] It is possible to understand that Company A, therefore, suffered losses resulting from the acts of its Commercial Director.

The above-mentioned Commercial Director of company A, who practiced the antitrust wrongdoing with the intent to bid rig, may be held corporate liable for his acts, notwithstanding the administrative and criminal sanctions. That is true since he personally practiced the antitrust wrongdoing with fraud or, at least, with fault, as provided in Article 158 (I) of the Brazilian Corporation Law. When the Commercial Director of company A deliberately practiced an illicit conduct, it exposed the company to damages, frontally violating the fiduciary duties established in Article 155[28] (Duty of Loyalty) of the Brazilian Corporation Law.

Pursuant to VASCONCELOS,[29] the duty of loyalty has a positive and a negative perspective. The positive perspective relates to the adoption of practices aiming to achieve company's scope through active behaviors. The negative perspective, by its turn, relates to the abstention of behaviors that would be contrary or harmful to the company's social purpose. The author's conclusion is that the negative perspective plays a greater role. This article proposes that the example of the conduct of the Commercial Director of company A represents an infringement of this negative perspective of the duty of loyalty. He did not absent to behave contrary to the company's social purpose, but instead actively performed anticompetitive acts that harmed and caused damages to it (even though it might have been targeting profits to the company).

---

27. In the criminal sphere in Brazil, Art. 4 of the Brazilian Economic Crimes Law (Law 8.137/1990) states that the individuals face a penalty in Brazil of two to five years of imprisonment and fines for cartel conduct.
28. Article 155 of the Corporation Law in Brazil: Duty of Loyalty:

    An officer shall serve the corporation with loyalty, shall treat its affairs with confidence and shall not: I - use any commercial opportunity which may come to his knowledge, by virtue of his position, for his own benefit or that of a third party, whether or not harmful to the corporation; II - fail to exercise or protect corporation rights or, in seeking to obtain advantages for himself or for a third party, fail to make use of a commercial opportunity which he knows to be of interest to the corporation; III - acquire for resale at a profit property or rights which he knows the corporation needs or which the corporation intends to acquire. Paragraph 1. An officer of a publicly held corporation shall also treat in confidence any information not yet revealed to the public, which he obtained by virtue of his position and which may significantly affect the quotation of securities, and shall not make use of such information to obtain any advantages for himself or for third parties by purchasing or selling securities. Paragraph 2. An officer shall ensure that the provisions of paragraph 1, above, are not infringed by a subordinate or third party enjoying his confidence. Paragraph 3. Any person detrimentally affected in a purchase or sale of securities contracted contrary to the provisions of paragraphs I and 2, above, may demand indemnity from the person responsible for the infringement for losses and damages, unless the person was aware of the information at the time the contract was made. Paragraph 4 Any officer who may receive any confidential information not yet revealed to the public shall not make use of such information to obtain any advantages for himself or for third parties by purchasing or selling securities.

29. VASCONCELOS, Pedro Pais de. *A participação social nas sociedades empresárias*. Coimbra: Almedina, 2006. p. 205.

This corporate liability becomes even more evident when the Commercial Director of company A, encouraged to confess – for example after a corporate whistleblower's tip – conceals its acts, destroys evidences and do not collaborate with the company's internal investigation efforts. This situation may specially be real if he is the Commercial Director of company A is in the Brazilian subsidiary and the internal investigation is conducted by the head office overseas.

The Commercial Director of company A, in this scenario, is in a strong conflict of interest with the company, potentially violating also Article 156[30] (Conflict of Interests) of the Brazilian Corporation Law. The Commercial Director's interest is to conceal the wrongdoing, while the company's A interest is "clean the house," uncover all the wrongdoings and get back to the track of the legal practices. This conflict of interests, eventually resulting in a lack of collaboration and even in the implementation of some opposition acts to impair the data gathering, may lead to the company's A failure to successfully apply for a marker and to execute a Leniency Agreement or a settlement that could have been in the course of negotiations. The duties required in a situation of conflict of interest are rolled-out from the duty of loyalty itself.[31] Hence, when the Commercial Director is overlooking the company's interests and emphasizing its own personal interests, he is in a situation of conflict of interest, which also constitutes a fraudulent breach of the duty of loyalty.

This duty of loyalty is likewise infringed since the officers and directors have complementary duties of transparency (full disclosure) and information.[32] Those duties are not fulfilled when the Commercial Director of company A conceals its anticompetitive acts and prevents the company to be granted immunity or to mitigate the damages by settling the case with the competition authority.

Therefore, in this first situation, the shareholders of company A may bring derivative lawsuits against the Commercial Director aiming his liability and the recovery of the losses caused to the company in accordance with Article 158 (1) of the Brazilian Corporation Law, due to the acts practiced with fault or fraud.

---

30. Article 156 of the Corporation Law in Brazil: Conflict of Interests:
    An officer shall not take part in any corporate transaction in which he has an interest which conflicts with an interest of the corporation, nor in the decisions made by the other officers on the matter. He shall disclose his disqualification to the other officers and shall cause the nature and extent of his interest to be recorded in the minutes of the administrative council, or board of directors' meeting. Paragraph 1. Notwithstanding compliance with the provisions of this article, an officer may only contract with the corporation under reasonable and fair conditions, identical to those which prevail in the market or under which the corporation would contract with third parties. Paragraph 2. Any business contracted otherwise than in accordance with the provisions of paragraph 1, above, is voidable and the officer concerned shall be obliged to transfer to the corporation all benefits which he may have obtained in such business.
31. FRAZÃO, Ana. *Função social da empresa: repercussões sobre a responsabilidade civil de controladores e administradores de S/As*. 2011. p. 336.
32. CARVALHOSA, Modesto. *Comentários à Lei das Sociedades Anônimas*. São Paulo: Saraiva, 2003. III. p. 331.

Second situation: officers and directors conniving with other officers and/or directors who practiced the antitrust wrongdoing and who fail to take action

Assume once again that there was a bid-rigging cartel in the construction sector in Brazil and that the Commercial Director of the company A agreed to fix prices and allocate markets with companies B, C and D. The Commercial Director personally joined the meetings and fostered the anticompetitive agreements, leading its employees to implement the wrongdoing. In a certain point, the Financial Director and the Vice President, who were not directly involved in the wrongdoing – but who are corporate officers in the bylaws – learned that the Commercial Director was practicing the anticompetitive conduct of bid rigging. However, they did not take any action. They did not either cease the Commercial Director's conduct immediately by means, for example, of a request of a general meeting with the board to inform, a temporary removal or even though the dismissal of the Commercial Director.

Those corporate officers hence implicitly allowed an antitrust violation to develop and continue, which exposed the corporation to enormous legal liability. They violated the duty of loyalty established in Article 155 of the Brazilian Corporation Law, since they privileged the Commercial Director' and not the corporation's interests. In this context, those Financial Director and Vice President of the company A may exceptionally be liable for the unlawful acts of other officers because they acted in connivance with them, as provided in Article 158 paragraph 1st of the Brazilian Corporation Law.

This situation also represents a failure of the corporate officers with the duty of loyalty, which, according to CLARK,[33] is a leftover concept, which can contain factual situations that no one could predict or categorize. This officer's corporate liability would be especially interesting if the Financial Director and the Vice President, learning the antitrust violation, fail to consider the application of the company for the Leniency[34] or the Settlement[35] Programs of the CADE. It is possible to understand that if those corporate officers had taken action immediately upon notice of the wrongdoing, company A could have reached CADE earlier and could have been granted full

---

33. CLARK, Robert Charles. *Corporate Law*. New York: Aspen Law & Business, 1986. p. 41.
34. According to Art. 86, para. 4, of the Brazilian Competition Law (Law No. 12.529/2011) combined with Art. 208 of the Internal Rules of CADE, once CADE's Tribunal declare that the Leniency Agreement has been fulfilled, the leniency recipients will benefit from: (i) administrative immunity under Law No. 12.529/2011, in cases in which the Leniency Agreement's proposal is submitted to CADE's General Superintendence when this authority was not aware of the reported violation; or (ii) a reduction by one to two-thirds of the applicable fine under Law No. 12.529/2011, in cases in which the Leniency Agreement's proposal is submitted to the SG/CADE after this authority becomes aware of the reported violation. For further information on the Brazilian Guidelines on Leniency Program: < http://www.cade.gov.br/upload/Guidelines%20CADE's%20Antitrust%20Leniency%20Program.pdf >.
35. According to Art. 85 of the Brazilian Competition Law (Law No. 12.529/2011) combined with article, For further information on the Brazilian Guidelines on Cease and Desist Agreement for cartel Cases: < http://www.cade.gov.br/upload/Guidelines_TCC.pdf >.

immunity in the Leniency Program or at least a significant file reduction depending on its arrival time to apply for a settlement.[36]

Therefore, in this second situation, the shareholders of company A may bring derivative lawsuits aiming liability and the recovery of the losses caused to the company in accordance with Article 158 paragraph 1st of the Brazilian Corporation Law. This lawsuit would be brought not only against the Commercial Director who personally performed the wrongdoing (first situation), but also against the Financial Director and the Vice President who were conniving with the Commercial Director and who did not take any action upon notice of the anticompetitive practice (second situation).

Third situation: officers and directors negligent to prevent the wrongdoing

Assume once more that there was a bid-rigging cartel in the construction sector in Brazil and that the Commercial Manager of the company A agreed to fix prices and allocate markets with companies B, C and D. The Commercial Manager personally joined the meetings and fostered the anticompetitive agreements. The Commercial Director, the Vice President and the President – who are corporate officers in the bylaws –, during the bidding process, received follow up information about the phases and results by this Commercial Manager. Even though they did not participate personally on the illegal acts nor did they specifically know about the wrongdoing, they recognized the possibility that this employee was performing anticompetitive conduct and neglected the fact. This would also be the case when, for example, of the Ombudsman Director of company A receives an anonymous complaint from an employee exposing the misconduct of the Commercial Manager and decides to turn a blind eye on the fact, without further investigation on the issue. Those corporate officers acted with negligence in finding out the misconduct and failed to prevent the antitrust violation, which expose the company to severe sanctions in the antitrust field.

In this situation, the Commercial Director, Vice President, President, or even the Ombudsman Director of the company A may exceptionally be liable for the unlawful acts of other officers because they were negligent, as provided in Article 158 paragraph 1st of the Brazilian Corporation Law.

This negligence would represent a violation of the duty of diligence, required in 153[37] (Duty of Diligence) of the Brazilian Corporation Act. In relation to the duty of diligence, the standard required from the officers are higher than the one of a *bonus pater familias*, and is intrinsically related to the social interest of the company, inclusively in what concerns the social role of the company.[38] It is clear that the

---

36. The settlement is Brazil is called TCC, which is the Portuguese acronym for "Termo de Compromisso de Cessação", i.e., Cease and Desist Agreement.
37. Article 153 of the Corporation Law in Brazil: Duty of Diligence. *"In the exercise of his duties, a corporation officer shall employ the care and diligence which an industrious and honest man customarily employs in the administration of his own affairs."*
38. DÍAZ ECHEGARAY, José Juis. *Deberes y Responsabilidad de los Administradores de Sociedades de Capital.* Elcano (Navarra): Editorial Aranzadi: 2006. p. 118. Apud FRAZÃO, Ana. *Função social da empresa: repercussões sobre a responsabilidade civil de controladores e administradores de S/As.* 2011. p. 352.

purpose of the companies is to obtain profits – and that a cartel may enhance, at least temporarily raise those profits. However, the social role of the company also determines that the officers have to balance this purpose with other interests involved in the execution of the company's activities, not causing unjustifiable or disproportionate damages. The duty of diligence, hence, is related primarily to the general duty of respect and prevention of danger, according to MENEZES CORDEIRO.[39] By fixing prices and allocating markets with its competitors, the Commercial Manager of company A offended the social role of the company and violated the duty of diligence.

Additionally, a lack of diligence would be apparent when the corporate officers of company A, after a condemnation by CADE of a bid-rigging cartel in the construction sector, fails to implement a corporate compliance program, which ends up in another cartel in the energy sector, for instance. The implementation of a surveillance, supervision and investigation system would be required by the duty of diligence of the officers, according to COUTO SILVA – which would have failed in the mentioned situation. The author also argues that the offices have to take an active attitude towards the company, monitoring the activities and the information in a way to assure that the shareholders rights are not being violated by the lower instances of the company.[40] In this path, the duty of diligence also prohibits the adoption of a "calculated infringement,"[41] which could be the defense argument that the cartel was "calculated" to bring more profits than damages. A failure to implement an adequate compliance program within company A, even after the first fine imposed by CADE and in a sector which favors collusive behaviors, resulted in losses for company A, which were a result of the officers acts with negligence.

According to POSNER, the danger of mismanagement (negligence) is less serious than that the danger that the managers will not deal fairly with the shareholders (disloyalty).[42] In a scale of gravity, a violation of the duty of loyalty would be more detrimental than a violation of the duty of diligence. Considering the situations presented of this article, this article proposes the following scale of gravity. The first and the second situations represent the lack of loyalty of the officers and directors and are the worst cases – (1) personally practicing the antitrust wrongdoing and (2) conniving and failing to take action when taking notice of the violation. The third situation represents the lack of diligence and is less painful – (3) by the negligence to prevent the anticompetitive illicit.

---

39. CORDEIRO, Antonio Menezes. A *lealdade no direito das sociedades*. 2007.
40. SILVA, Alexandre Couto. *Responsabilidade dos administradores de S/A. Business judgement rule*. Rio de Janeiro: Elsevier, 2007, 252.
41. FRAZÃO, Ana. *Função social da empresa: repercussões sobre a responsabilidade civil de controladores e administradores de S/As*. 2011. p. 358.
42. POSNER, Richard A. *Economic Analysis of Law*. New York: Aspen Law & Business, 1988. p. 452.

This lack of diligence is subject to the analysis of the "business judgment rule"[43] standard (established in Article 159[44] §6° of the Brazilian Corporation Law), which does not apply to the lack of the duty of loyalty. According to the "business judgment rule," there is a presumption that the officers take their decisions in an informed basis with good faith and in an honest belief that its acts are taken in the best interest of the company. In addition, there is the understanding that the corporate officers and directors decisions are unsusceptible of judicial review, expect if the motivation was fraud, conflict of interests, illegality and gross negligence.[45] The purpose of this "business judgment rule," therefore, is to overcome the difficulties to evaluate *ex post* the diligence in the acts of the officers. It provides a shift on the analysis from the right or wrong parameter to the reasonableness of the decision-making process, which protects decisions made based on due information and counseling. This mitigation on the duty of diligence analysis provides, hence, greater prominence to the duty of loyalty.[46]

In the view of this article, the implementation of a strong compliance program within the company may be a major asset for the loyal and diligent officers and directors to rebut claims on a derivative shareholder action arising from antitrust violations. The stronger is the adoption of a compliance program, the stronger is the argument that they were not negligent to prevent such wrongdoings. Additionally, the fact that the officers and directors had special counseling[47] when faced with a situation of an antitrust violation may appoint to the fulfillment of the duty of diligence required in the Brazilian legislation.

To the present day, there are no known precedents in Brazil of shareholders derivative actions against corporate officers and/or directors in the antitrust context, which may be inspired by the experience around the globe.

§15.04 CONCLUSION

The shareholders derivative action against officers and directors due to antitrust violations is a novel feature available for the accountability of the corporate individuals liable for the infringement. In Japan there have already been some successful cases

---

43. The BJR creates a presumption that corporate officers and directors "acted on an informed basis, in good faith and in the honest belief that the action taken was in the best interests of the company [and its shareholders]. In re Walt Disney Co. Derivative Litig., 907 A.2d 693, 747 (Del. Ch. 2005).
44. Article 159(6) of the Corporation Law in Brazil: "*By a resolution passed in a general meeting, the corporation may bring an action for civil liability against any officer for the losses caused to the corporation's property. (...) Paragraph 6. A judge may excuse the officer from liability, when convinced that he acted in good faith and in the interests of the corporation.*"
45. CLARK, Robert Charles. *Corporate Law*. New York: Aspen Law & Business, 1986. pp. 123-124.
46. The lack of the duty of loyalty is subject to a full analysis of the merits of the officer's acts. According to NUNES. NUNES, Pedro Caetano. *Responsabilidade civil dos administradores perante os accionistas*. Coimbra: Almedina, 2001. p. 24.
47. RIBEIRO, Renato Ventura. *Dever de diligência dos administradores de sociedades*. São Paulo: Quartier Latin, 2006. p. 227.

resulting in settlements. Those derivative shareholders lawsuit benefited the company through the reimbursement of the fines already paid by officers and directors.

This article proposes a *first situation in Brazil in which officers and directors may face shareholders derivative suits claiming corporate liability for antitrust violations: when they personally practiced the antitrust wrongdoing.* That would be a breach of the fiduciary duty of loyalty required by the officers, established in Article 155 of the Brazilian Corporation Act. This would be aggravated when the corporate officer fails to cooperate with the company's internal investigation, conceals documents and impairs data gathering to prove the collusive agreement, resulting, for example, in the failure for the company to execute a Leniency Agreement or a settlement with the Competition Authority. The officers and directors liability would be in accordance with Article 158 (1) of the Brazilian Corporation Act, since the acts are performed with fault or fraud.

This article proposes a *second situation in Brazil in which officers and directors may face shareholders derivative suits claiming corporate liability for antitrust violations: when they are conniving with other officers and/or directors who practiced the antitrust wrongdoing and fail to take action.* That would also be a breach of the fiduciary duty of loyalty required by the officers, established in Article 155 of the Brazilian Corporation Act. The failure to take action would be a evident when the officers who learned the anticompetitive conduct by another colleague did not take the appropriate actions. This would be aggravated if the officers, upon notice of the antitrust violation, fail to timely act and reach the Competition Authority to apply for a marker of Leniency or Settlement. If they had done so, they would had granted the company with full immunity or at least a significant reduction of the applicable fines, resulting in losses to the corporation. The officers and directors liability would be in accordance with Article 158 paragraph 1st of the Brazilian Corporation Act, since the acts are characterized as connivance and/or fail to take action.

This article proposes a *third situation in Brazil in which officers and directors may face shareholders derivative suits claiming corporate liability for antitrust violations: when they are negligent to prevent the wrongdoing.* That would be a breach of the fiduciary duty of diligence required by the officers, established in Article 153 of the Brazilian Corporation Act. The officers may have failed to take an active attitude towards the company, monitoring the activities and the information in a way to assure that the shareholders rights are not being violated by the lower instances of the company. However, this lack of diligence is subject to the analysis of the "business judgment rule," which protects decisions made bases on due information and counseling. The officers and directors liability would be in accordance with Article 158 paragraph 1st of the Brazilian Corporation Act, since the acts are characterized as negligence.

In summary, the three situations proposed can be expressed in this table 15.1.

Table 15.1 Situations in Brazil in Which Officers and Directors May Face Shareholders Derivative Suits Claiming Corporate Liability for Antitrust Violations

(i) when they personally practiced the antitrust wrongdoing	Failure on the Duty of Loyalty (Article 155)	Liability according to Article 158 (I)	
(ii) when they are conniving with other officers and/or directors who practiced the antitrust wrongdoing and fail to take action	Failure on the Duty of Loyalty (Article 155)	Liability according to Article 158 paragraph 1st	
(iii) when they are negligent to prevent the wrongdoing	Failure on the Duty of Diligence (Article 155)	Liability according to Article 158 paragraph 1st	*Subject to the "business judgment rule" standard*

Some debates may emerge when quantifying those damages claimed by the shareholders. Typically, the lawsuit could target the actual damages and the ceased profit resulting from the anticompetitive practice, as established in Articles 927,[48] 186[49] and 187[50] of the Civil Code. By demanding actual damages, the shareholders may target, for example, the reimbursement of the antitrust penalties already paid by the company to CADE. In addition, by demanding ceased profits, the shareholders may target the compensation for the profits lost during the period an eventual suspension to participate in the biddings, if that was one of the penalties imposed. This case would be especially sharp if the shareholders, pursuant to above-mentioned Article 187, allege that the officer or director violated the economic order and exceeded the limits imposed by the social function of the company,[51] embodied with the understanding that the company not only is imposed by limitations and abstentions, but also has duties and obligations due to its social independence.[52]

---

48. Article 927 of the Brazilian Civil Code. "*Art. 927. If a party, through an unlawful act (articles 186 and 187), causes a damage to another party, he is obliged to pay compensation. Sole paragraph. There will be a duty to compensate, irrespective of negligence, when specifically stated by the law, or when the activity performed by the party who caused the damage implies, by its nature, a certain risk to third parties.*"
49. Article 186 of the Brazilian Civil Code. "*He who by voluntary action or omission, negligence or recklessness, violate law and harm others, even if only moral, commits an unlawful act.*"
50. Article 187 of the Brazilian Civil Code. "*It also commits an unlawful act the holder of a right that, in practice it clearly exceeds the limits imposed by their economic or social order, good faith or in morals. To use a power, right harm someone brings legal effect as a duty to indemnify.*"
51. COMPARATO, Fábio Konder. Estado, empresa e função social. *Revista dos Tribunais*, v. 732, pp. 38–46, 1996.
52. FRAZÃO, Ana. Função social da empresa na Constituição de 1998. *Revista Direito, Estado e Sociedade*, n. 29, 2014.

Chapter 15: The Japanese Experience and Possible Lessons   §15.04

The shareholders may as well claim moral damage. According to Article 52 of the Brazilian Civil Code, the rights of personality are applicable, insofar as appropriate, to the legal entities the protection of the person. The Brazilian Superior Court of Justice ("STJ" in its Portuguese acronym) also prescribes, in the Summary Statement 227, that the legal entity may suffer moral damage. FRAZÃO argues that it is unequivocal that an act of disloyal management violates the company's credibility.[53] Considering the fact that an antitrust condemnation in Brazil made by CADE's Tribunal is public and attracts great media attention, the notice that the company was convicted and sentenced to pay severe fines represents a significant damage to the company's reputation. It would be feasible for the companies' shareholders in Brazil to target the officers and directors for the moral damages caused due to the antitrust violation.

In conclusion, corporate officers and directors in Brazil should be personally concerned with the antitrust violations in its company. Not only because of the administrative and criminal prosecution, but also due to their possible corporate liability as provided in the Brazilian Corporation Act (Law 6404/1976).

---

53. FRAZÃO, Ana. *Função social da empresa: repercussões sobre a responsabilidade civil de controladores e administradores de S/As*. 2011. p. 342.

CHAPTER 16
The Relation Between Antitrust and Intellectual Property Law on CADE's Case Law

Ana Frazão & Angelo Gamba Prata de Carvalho

§16.01 INTRODUCTION

Antitrust Law and Intellectual Property (IP), even though constantly irritating each other, are not antagonistic, but actually complement one another to fulfill constitutional mandates of innovation promotion and protection of free trade and free competition. The creation of artificial monopolies as a reward to innovation is of course an exception to Antitrust principles, since innovation is also an essential objective for Antitrust. The restrictions imposed by IP, hence, may of course set limits to competitors, but they are supposed to increase competition through dynamic efficiency gains by stimulating technological development.

The exercise of IP rights, however, may be seen by Antitrust authorities as fraudulent attempts to explore the privileges derived from exclusivity rights in order to produce serious harm to competitive markets. To identify the criteria to make this kind of differentiation, these two areas should be analyzed by more sophisticated instruments than the traditional neoclassical economic methods, demanding a constitutional reading of IP and Antitrust as means of reaching public interests.

This discussion at a great extent presents itself in the decision-making process at the Brazilian Administrative Commission of Economic Defense (CADE), the country's competition authority, especially when the Commission faces cases involving IP rights' abuse, mainly related to illegitimate enforcement of inexistent patent rights or patent abuse consisting of unlawful enforcement of these rights.

This paper intends to explore the relation established between Antitrust Law and IP Law in CADE's case law, trying to show the main parameters adopted by the competition authority to deal with these fundamental questions.

§16.02 THE COMPLEX RELATION BETWEEN IP RIGHTS AND ANTITRUST LAW

IP creates monopolies as a reward to innovation, not only to the degree of protection granted to private property in a general way, but also because of a framework of economic incentives directed to the promotion of the public good through invention, creation and technological development. Intangible goods are "non-rivalrous," since their ideal nature permits many individuals at the same time to utilize those goods. Incorporeal property has a high aggregated value to be explored, and the right to explore these resources is exclusively granted to the inventor as a means of incentive.[1]

Innovation is related to what Schumpeter[2] called "process of creative destruction," the tendency of new creations to overturn older market structures to produce more and more economic growth. Competition and innovation, according to Hovenkamp,[3] are highly sensitive to market structure, as long as the incentives of IP rights and Antitrust intervention are not miraculous remedies, because they work on certain conditions and may not work on others.[4] As also noted by Hovenkamp,[5] the promotion of innovation "is much less central to Intellectual Property Law than the promotion of price competition is to Antitrust Law." This feature of IP is actually due to a lack of perception of those rights as means of innovation rather than property rights.[6] Innovation, actually, is a limit posed by the Constitution to the absolutism of property, which cannot be applied to IP rights. IP rights, hence, need to be read under the light of the Constitution[7] to fulfill their function and also to adequately address new market structures.[8] It is also an objective for Antitrust Law to compensate the hindrances of IP

---

1. Lemley, Mark A. (2007) A new balance between IP and Antitrust. *John M. Olin Program in Law and Economics*. Working paper n. 340.
2. Schumpeter, Joseph (2014) *Capitalism, Socialism, and Democracy*. Sublime books, Floyd, VA.
3. Hovenkamp, Herbert (2013) *Competition for innovation*. University of Iowa Legal Studies Research Paper, 13–25.
4. Plenty of authors state that granting patents indefinitely not only reduces the quality of patents, but in fact inhibits innovation. For example: Bohannan, Christina; Hovenkamp, Herbert (2011) *Creation without restraint*. Promoting liberty and rivalry in innovation. Oxford University Press, Oxford; Carrier, Michael A (2009) *Innovation for the 21st Century*. Harnessing the power of Intellectual Property and Antitrust Law. Oxford University Press, Oxford. Käseberg, Thorsten (2012) *Intellectual property, Antitrust and cumulative innovation in the EU and the US*. Hart Publishing, Oxford.
5. Hovenkamp (2013).
6. Hovenkamp (2013).
7. The Brazilian Constitution, on Art. 23, since the promulgation of an amendment in 2015, establishes science, technology, research and innovation as objectives for the whole Federation. Even before this amendment the Constitution already protected Intellectual Property (Arts. 5, XXVII, XXVIII and XXIX), the social function of property and free competition (Art. 170).
8. Roberto Mangabeira Unger (2007, *Free Trade Reimagined*: The World Division of Labor and the Method of Economics. Princeton University Press, Princeton).criticizes the currently adopted regime of Intellectual Property in most of the countries, holding it cannot be adopted on a global

Chapter 16: The Relation Between Antitrust and Intellectual Property Law §16.02

Law through the protection of innovation by regulating its property-like effects over markets.

While IP excludes others from access to protected creations without the inventor's authorization, Antitrust Law, on another hand, tries to tackle the abuse of market power and predatory or exclusionary conducts, mainly when they potentially create monopoly power. Even though IP rights' exclusivity harms competition at a static perspective, it has positive effects on dynamic efficiency when it stimulates competition through innovation. Antitrust and IP, therefore, can be "multi-valued systems," because "a key goal of each is the same: consumer welfare."[9]

At a great extent, as noted by Landes and Posner,[10] IP rights are shaped by Antitrust Law, but that does not mean these two areas are rivals. The innovation requirement is not a mere motivation for a legitimate monopoly to be granted, but the condition for the prevention of the monopolistic and anticompetitive exploitation of IP rights.[11] The apparent paradox between IP and Antitrust is nevertheless easily set aside, because the two areas actually complement each other.[12] This relation was explained on a FTC report:

> Competition and patents are not inherently in conflict. Patent and Antitrust Law are actually complementary: as both are aimed at encouraging innovation, industry, and competition. Patent law plays an important role in the property rights regime essential to a well functioning competitive economy. For example, firms may compete to obtain the property rights that patents convey. Patents do not necessarily confer monopoly power on their holders, and most of business conduct with respect to patent does not unreasonably restrain or serve to monopolize markets. Even when a patent does confer monopoly power, that alone does not create an Antitrust violation. Antitrust Law recognizes that a patent's creation of monopoly power can be necessary to achieve a greater for consumers.[13]

---

trading regime hospitable to democratic experimentalism: "A global trading regime hospitable to democratic experimentalism must not wed itself to the particular system of Intellectual Property that has come to be established in the rich North Atlantic countries and that, with considerable success, those countries have since attempted to impose on the whole of humanity. It is the peculiar character of that system of Intellectual Property to turn innovations into assets. The traditional arguments in favor of that approach resemble in structure the conventional case for the hereditary transmission of property: they combine an appeal to consequentialist arguments about incentives to innovate with the rewards of invention. The frailties of each argument are remedied by resort to the other one, and the two together pretend to an authority that neither of them alone would be able to enjoy.

9. Sullivan, Lawrence; Grimes, Warren S (2006) *The Law of Antitrust*: An Integrated Handbook. Thomson/West, St. Paul.
10. Landes, William M; Posner, Richard A (2003) *The Economic Structure of Intellectual Property Law*. Harvard University Press, Cambridge.
11. Salomão Filho, Calixto (2006). Direito industrial, direito concorrencial e interesse público. *Revista CEJ*, 35, 12–19.
12. Salomão Filho (2013, *Direito Concorrencial*. Malheiros, São Paulo), on another hand, holds that relation could not even be designated as of "complementarity," because it could produce the understanding that one area would not be regulated by the other one, so the IP-produced monopoly would actually be understood as an Antitrust immunity case.
13. U.S., Federal Trade Commission (2003) *To promote innovation*: the proper balance of competition and patent law and policy. October, 2003.

The so-called new economy, characterized by innovation and high-technology, has IP as its main output, raising brand new Antitrust issues and the necessity to reshape the general understanding of IP. Landes and Posner's opinion on this question is that Antitrust is capable of coping effectively with the new problems presented by the new economy, but Antitrust enforcement would not be "well adapted to deal swiftly and surely with technically complex activities. The practices of a rapidly changing, highly technical industry such as computer software place enormous strains on the Antitrust system."[14]

Robert Pifotsky, former chairman of the U.S. Federal Trade Commission, holds that Antitrust issues found on traditional markets may also be encountered on the high-tech sector. In a network-influenced market, size is not the only issue that may cause barriers, traditionally produced by price discrimination, exclusionary contracts or intimidation tactics. The high-tech sector presents potential trouble with the so-called network effects, which "arise when the value of a network increases with the number of its users"[15] and tend to maintain loyal to a given service, also producing "lock-in" effects.

The fact that IP and Antitrust are built upon a constitutional basis in Brazil must orient the reading of those rights. Competition Law today does not presume anymore a market model of perfect competition, a concern that, according to Schumpeter,[16] has for a long time disoriented Antitrust Law from fundamental questions related to innovation. The Brazilian Constitution (Article 5º, XXIX) only allows temporary exclusivity rights to promote the country's technological and economical development (*desenvolvimento tecnológico e econômico do País*). At the same time, it adopts a free market and free competition regime based on innovation promotion.

Brazilian Competition Law has faced the phenomenon of "deconstitucionalization of Antitrust Law," named by CADE's ex-Commissioner Luis Fernando Schuartz,[17] who noted a process of methodological isolation of the competition authority's decisions from constitutional arguments, only adopting, without any reflection, consequentialist criteria of economic efficiency, as an inheritance from the Chicago School. Although it is difficult to overcome this approach, there have been many recent efforts in Brazil to recognize that abuse of economic power prevention and repression should not be conditioned only by economic criteria, but also by the constitutional values and fundamental rights, a particularly important perspective when the subject is IP.

Considering these areas' common interest to protect and stimulate innovation and also to generate welfare gains to consumers, the intersection between IP and Antitrust should be the achievement of constitutional mandates, essentially related to the harmonization of principles of free market, free competition, innovation and technological development. Actually, the Brazilian Constitution (Article 170) states the Economy is based on these liberal values in order to assure dignity for everyone,

---

14. Landes; Posner (2003).
15. Pitofsky, Robert (2001) Challenges of the New Economy: issues at the intersection of Antitrust and Intellectual Property. *Antitrust Law Journal.* 69, 913–924.
16. Schumpeter (2014).
17. Schuartz, Luis Fernando (2009) A desconstitucionalização do direito de defesa da concorrência. *Revista do IBRAC.* 16, 1, 325–351.

accordingly to what social justice precepts. Competition Law, as stated by Fox,[18] is symbiotic with democracy when it tries to balance power and equal opportunities of competition, based on private autonomy and merits. This is why it is important to dedicate some attention to the view of Brazilian competition authority on IP rights.

Fraudulently procured patents present even worse harms to competition than the natural static efficiency losses produced by the exclusivity, as long as the patent infringement claims derived from these inexistent exclusivity rights create false, illegitimate artificial monopolies. These claims, on the perspective of U.S. case law, constitute fraud when the patentee knowingly and willfully made a fraudulent omission or misrepresentation with a clear intent to deceive the patents office.[19] This kind of abuse of IP rights generates unfair advantages over competitors and consequently raises Antitrust issues, corresponding to the practice known as sham litigation. The Brazilian competition authority has already dealt with sham litigation accusations and formulated its own parameters for judging it, which will be shown in one of the following sections.

Notwithstanding fraud before patent authorities, generating unlawful exclusivity rights, one must also be concerned with forms of patent abuse resulted from legitimate patents. Licensing patents under discriminatory or unreasonable terms can generate serious barriers to entry and produce competitive advantages to a few chosen licensees, which may be aggravated on cross-licenses or patent pools that do not observe sufficient fairness standards when negotiating terms of licensing.[20] This matter, already dealt with in famous cases analyzed in U.S. case law,[21] will also be explored in a specific section to present CADE's position.

§16.03 LEGITIMACY OF ANTITRUST INTERVENTION OVER IP RIGHTS: THE ANFAPE CASE

In 2010, CADE has dealt with a very complex case in which the close relation between Antitrust Law and IP rights had to be thoroughly explored in the reporting Commissioner's opinion. The preliminary proceeding was filed by ANFAPE, the Brazilian national auto parts maker's association, presenting accusations of patent abuse perpetrated by automobile makers. Those makers (Volkswagen, Fiat and Ford) held the IP rights for industrial designs concerning to some parts of the automobiles they built.

---

18. Fox, Eleanor M. Post-Chicago, post-Seattle and the dilemma of globalization. In Cuccinota, Antonio; Pardolesi, Roberto; Bergh, Roger van dan (2002) *Post-Chicago Developments in Antitrust Law*. Edward Elgar, Cornwall.
19. Steinman, David R.; Fitzpatrick, Danielle S (2001-2002) Antitrust counterclaims in patent infringement cases: a guide to walker process and sham litigation claims. *Texas Intellectual Property Law Journal*. 10, 95-110.
20. "In this way, the holding of this case implies that a patent holder has broad rights to refuse to license or to refuse to sell a patented product and that such refusal is not likely to be condemned even in those cases where the motive of the refusal is anticompetitive" (Park, Jae Hun (2010) *Patents and Industry Standards*, Edward Elgar Publishing, Cheltenham, U.K.).
21. Independent Service Organizations Antitrust Litigation, 203 F.3d 1322 (Fed. Cir. 2000); *Eastman Kodak Co. v. Image Technical Servs., Inc.*, 504 U.S. 451 (1992).

The car makers filed injunctions to refrain independent auto parts makers from acting on the replacement parts markets, arguing that these companies were inflicting their exclusivity rights over the protected industrial designs. ANFAPE held that the injunctive measures intended to eliminate the independent makers from the replacement parts market, thus damaging competition, a constitutionally protected value. ANFAPE also argued that those IP rights could not be enforced against agents operating at secondary markets, but only against automobile makers, the real competitors for the rights' holders.

CADE's opinion on the matter, led by Commissioner Carlos Ragazzo's vote, tackled the main aspects on the constitutional protection of both IP rights and competition. IP rights are not at all absolute, which applies to industrial design, but the exclusivity right granted to inventors and innovators in a general way aims to incentivize innovation by rewarding economically the efforts on research and development. As long as IP rights stimulate differentiation between competing products and innovation inside markets, these rights are clearly complementary to Competition Law.

In contrast, IP rights may seriously obstruct access to markets where there is an exclusivity right to be enforced. The sole fact that IP creates artificial monopolies should worry Competition Law, even though the mere exclusivity is not an Antitrust infraction per se. According to Commissioner Ragazzo, there may be basically two kinds of abusive practices arising from IP: fraud or abuse on registering procedures; or anticompetitive conducts derived from the abuse on the performance of the IP right.

Fraud on registration procedures are harshly injurious to competition as it distorts the legitimate end of exclusivity rights, leveraging from an artificial monopoly power without the mandatory social compensation, namely the consumer welfare gains derived from innovation. As stated by Ariel Katz,[22] the necessary investment for the creation of intellectual assets is normally very high when compared with the low marginal cost to use or produce additional copies. There is, hence, a need for the investor to get back its efforts, even though this reward affects the availability of those good on the markets. Affecting the availability of goods and thus raising prices is a preoccupying effect when there are not any legitimate justifications, and that is why procedural correctness is a crucial aspect concerning IP rights.[23]

Even a lawfully held IP right may be abusively enforced, for example, when an economic player refuses to license its technology or imposes unreasonable terms for the socialization of those rights. It was the case on the ANFAPE proceeding, when Commissioner Ragazzo declared the socioeconomic goal that justifies IP rights was perverted. The mere achievement of a legitimate registration does not exclude potential

---

22. Katz, Ariel (2007) Making sense of non-sense: Intellectual property, Antitrust, and Market Power. *Arizona Law Review*, 39, 837–909.
23. As stated by the *Supreme Court of the United States on United States v. Line Material Co.*, 333 U.S. 287 (1948), "the possession of a valid patent or patents does not give the patentee any exemption from the provisions of the Sherman Act beyond the limits of the patent monopoly. [...] It is not the monopoly of the patent that is invalid. It is the improper use of that monopoly."

anticompetitive conduct,[24] which has to be analyzed on the concrete case through the rule of reason, looking for positive and negative effects of the injunctive orders.

CADE stated that the exclusivity rights did not grant to the automobile makers a monopoly on the replacement parts market. Otherwise consumers would be necessarily attached to the auto makers' parts also on the secondary market. Market analysis showed an information asymmetry for consumers, who would optimistically not consider the replacement parts market's conditions when buying a car. Hence, the primary market did not grant sufficient competition conditions to guarantee efficient prices, options and selling terms on the secondary market. Relaxing the enforcement of the industrial designs-related rights would mitigate exclusionary effects, since this enforcement was damaging statically the consumer as the prices went up. The potential dynamic efficiency generated from the enforcement – innovation, differentiation and raise on consumer welfare, for instance – were also not found by CADE, since the investments made on innovation were already compensated when the cars were sold, and therefore there was no reason for an enforcement of these rights on secondary markets.

In sum, CADE declared the automakers injunctions created a completely inefficient scenario, lessening economic and consumer welfare gravely without any relevant counterpart. The protection of those exclusivity rights therefore could not fulfill the constitutional justification for mitigating the competition standards. In other words, this practice was unreasonable and would not be beneficial for the country's technological and economical development, but only prejudicial to consumer's welfare.

CADE's position on the ANFAPE case established a very sophisticated and important standard of competition analysis of IP rights' effects, taking into account the convergent competences of the Brazilian competition authority and INPI, the Brazilian patent office. INPI is competent, according to Brazilian IP law (Law n. 9.279/96), to receive technology transfer agreements and, in the absence of consent on royalty prices, to arbitrate the value due by the licensee to the IP right holder. INPI's role on royalty fixing, however, cannot overrule the parties' agreement, protected by private autonomy. Controversies arising from any quarrel between parties may be handled by the judiciary system or, alternatively, through private arbitration, so INPI's role is mainly notarial, turning public those private agreements, and just exceptionally related to royalty fixing.

CADE, at the same time, is competent to previously analyze associative contracts, which in a general way may involve the licensing or sharing of IP rights. Therefore, a

---

24. Although there may be potential anticompetitive effects, there is no presumption implied. The interpreter need, actually, to look for eventual substitutes for the protected product and other possible barriers to entrance, as proposed by the FTC on its Licensing Guidelines:

> Market power is the ability to maintain prices above, or output below competitive levels for a significant period of time. The Agencies will not presume that a patent, copyright, or trade secret necessarily confers market power upon its owner. Although the Intellectual Property right confers the power to exclude with respect to the *specific* product, process or work in question, there will often be sufficient actual or potential close substitutes for such product, process, or work to prevent the exercise of market power.

clear lining of CADE's interest and competence on IP rights' effects over competition is essential not only for an effective decision-making and the predictability of these rulings, but also for maintaining other entities' prerogatives to deal with this kind of agreement.

§16.04 CADE'S VIEW ON STANDARD-ESSENTIAL PATENTS AND LICENSE AGREEMENTS

Technology transfer agreements are really powerful tools for the promotion of competition through the licensing of existing IP rights. Patent licensing, for instance, mitigates the monopolist effects of a patent and allows the protected technology to reach a larger amount of subjects, generating an increase on the welfare of consumers.

In 2015, for the first time CADE analyzed a case involving standard-essential patents on the telecommunications market[25] and its effects over competition. The preparatory proceeding n. 08700.008409/2014-00 was not even judged by CADE's Tribunal, but by its General Superintendency, an authority with a mainly prosecutory competence, but also capable of judging determinate kinds of cases, always with the possibility of appeal to the Administrative Tribunal of CADE.

The controversy was established by a representation issued by *TCT Mobile Telefones Ltda.* (TCT), which accused *Ericsson* of patent abuse, sham litigation and abusive negotiation. Ericsson owned two technology patents related to the international effort of implementing the 3GPP pattern in the mobile telephony market through an agreement with European Telecommunications Standards Institute (ETSI). ETSI is an international standard-setting organization, an entity entitled to harmonize technology patterns in order to avoid the difficulties of patent thickets that hamper the use and licensing of patented goods by competitors.

Standard-setting in the high-technology market, thus, unifies multiple complementary patents in a single basis, which is regulated by an international entity, allowing the compulsory licensing of these essential patents in *fair, reasonable and non-discriminatory* (FRAND) terms.

The representation analyzed by CADE's General Superintendency was motivated by a series of injunctions filed by Ericsson, trying to refrain TCT from using its protected patents on any of the company's devices, because the technology in question

---

25. Standard-essential patents are considered an exception to the impossibility of applying the essential facility doctrine to Intellectual Property Law. This doctrines states that the essentiality of a given good which cannot be easily accessed by its holder's competitors is a reasonable basis for the State to enforce ways by which it can be explored. Compulsory licensing is a clear example of a measure to facilitate access to essential facilities (Lipsky, A. B.; Sidak, J. G. (1999) Essential Facilities. *Stanford Law Review*, 51, 1187–1249). Since Intellectual Property is based on the creation of exclusivity rights as a reward to innovative efforts, this theory is generally not applied, but the necessity to incentivize innovation has to be flexibilized to handle the idiosyncratic aspects of innovation on a globalized and connected world. The construction of patterns can be healthy for competition as long as the so-called blocking patents (hardly licensed patents) are weakened (Shapiro, Carl (2001) Navigating the patent thicket: cross licenses, patent pools, and standard setting, in Adam Jaffe, Josh Lerner, Scott Stern (Eds.), *Innovation policy and the Economy*, MIT Press, Boston).

was not, at the time, correctly licensed to TCT. In response, TCT argued that standard-essential patents cannot be used to justify injunction orders, since the function of those patents is to harmonize technology and to facilitate access to market by products equipped with the protected technology, looking forward to stimulating a healthy competition environment and to reducing costs imposed to consumers.

The injunctions filed by Ericsson, in TCT's opinion, had to be considered abusive or, in other words, part of a sham litigation strategy perpetrated by Ericsson to set aside TCT's effort to join the market as a competitor. Ericsson responded to argue TCT was actually committing patent holdout, which consists of an agent's unjust enrichment based on the exploration of a patent without the correspondent reward to its owner. TCT, in Ericsson's view, was acting against competition while disrespecting the legitimate monopoly generated by the patent and acting as a free rider, hence producing hindrances over the incentives expected by an innovative company holding an IP right. The cited injunctions were actually filed because Ericsson has tried to negotiate with TCT without success, resulting in a pending arbitration procedure where the contractual terms would supposedly be settled.

CADE's ruling on this issue favored Ericsson, establishing, at first, that CADE was not competent to settle contractual terms related to technology transfer agreements, but only its effects over competition. Ericsson and TCT were not competitors, since Ericsson, at the time, was not acting at the Brazilian mobile phone market, which led to CADE's conclusions that there was not any economical rationality of an eventual imposition of barriers to entrance, because the avoidance of a new competitor would not favor the patent-holder at all. Furthermore, CADE stated that the competition authority should only intervene on the matter if the patent-holder were trying to impose restrictive terms – instead of FRAND terms –, intending to block an agent's entrance to the market. Since the negotiation was in course, given the existence of a pending arbitration procedure, CADE concluded there was no abuse at all and neither an attempt of sham litigation, considering TCT could not be allowed to explore the protected technology before obtaining the license.

In previous rulings, CADE has shown the importance of dealing with technology transferring even in mergers and acquisitions. As noted by Cueva[26], the main IP issue concerning mergers on technology-guided sectors is the exclusivity of licensing.

As noted by Commissioner Abraham Sicsú in a merger involving Monsanto and Syngenta,[27] patent licensing is socially beneficial when it helps to propagate technology. However, special caution must be observed in order to prevent the risk of market restrictions caused by exclusivity clauses imposed to the licensees, who can find themselves confined to the previously settled terms and therefore to the previous technology. In a strongly innovative market, many technological alternatives may emerge in a short period of time, and the existence of such a clause may seriously harm competition and weaken incentives for innovation. That is the reason, as a matter of

---

26. Cueva, Ricardo Villas Bôas (2009). A proteação da propriedade intelectual e a defesa da concorrência. *Revista do IBRAC*, 16, 1, 121-147.
27. CADE, AC n. 08012.005135/98-01, Comm. Roberto Pfeiffer, judged on July 23, 1998.

fact, why the ruling on the merger prohibited exclusivity clauses in the license agreements made by the company.

The verification and control of contractual terms, hence, is not CADE's task in a general way, since the competent authority for analyzing those agreements is the Brazilian National Institute of IP. CADE's task on this matter is to identify eventual negative effects of contractual terms over competition, analyzing also the possible efficiencies derived from the celebration of the agreement. In sum, having into account the rulings hereby narrated, CADE's analysis needs to consider the context of innovation in which the discussion of IP and technology transfer is inserted, since the level of welfare generated by a given contract and the market's competition conditions are strongly influenced by it.

The matter of standard-essential patent abuse was already presented to CADE in two occasions[28] beyond this one about telecommunications and the 3GPP standard. Both of the cases involved suspects of abusive royalty pricing, and in both of them CADE denied the claims of patent abuse, since the Commission was not competent do deal directly with pricing but in a residual way, related to the effects of anticompetitive conduct over pricing. The cases were, overall, contractual controversies, and the case files did not show sufficient evidence of Antitrust infractions.

§16.05 SHAM LITIGATION AND INTELLECTUAL PROPERTY

"Sham litigation" stands for the abusive pursuing of lawsuits in order to achieve an anticompetitive goal.[29] Although the right to petition to public powers is a constitutionally guaranteed right also in Brazil, this right may be abused.[30] There will be sham litigation, hence, when someone repeatedly files lawsuits with the intent of obtaining anticompetitive advantages just for the fact those suits were filed, not necessarily intending to get a favorable decision. This conduct directly relates to the costs derived simply from the litigation, and not from its results.[31]

Sham litigation may be either intentional or not, and may produce relevant effects even when the misfeasor does not hold great market power. The non-intentional kind of sham litigation is based on the lack of due care by a given agent, whose conduct may observe high standards when faced with IP rights, since its effects are naturally exclusionary when legitimate and, thus, even worse when falsely enforced. The benefits derived from IP need to be interpreted carefully in order to prevent even more serious competition restrictions, as stated by CADE.[32]

---

28. CADE, AP n. 08012.001315/2007-21, Comm. Olavo Zago Chinaglia, judged on May 13, 2009; CADE, AP n. 08012.005181/2006-37, Comm. Paulo Furquim de Azevedo, judged on April 29, 2009.
29. Klein, Christopher C (2007) Anticompetitive Litigation and Antitrust Liability. *Department of Economics and Finance Working Papers Series*, August 2007.
30. Sham litigation was developed on the United States case law as an exception to the Noerr-Pennington doctrine, which guarantees the right to petition government, mainly the Legislative power, even if the law for which someone is advocating may have anticompetitive effects.
31. Klein, 2007.
32. CADE, PA n. 08012.007189/2008-08, Comm. Ana Frazão, judged on October 1, 2014.

Chapter 16: The Relation Between Antitrust and Intellectual Property Law §16.05

Successfully registering a patent is also not sufficient basis to set aside sham litigation accusations, since patent abuse does not only occur when a patent office wrongfully grants an IP right but also when the right is wrongfully used to attack rivals.

United States' case law, including some important Supreme Court rulings, established some parameters to identify sham litigation. On *Professional Real Estate (PRE) Investors v. Columbia Pictures Industries*, the Supreme Court ruled that sham litigation has to be identified by a double test: first, an objective one, i.e., the formal wrongfulness of the lawsuit; and second, a subjective one, when strategic lawsuit filing intent – looking to obtain advantages over competitors – will be analyzed. In another case (*USS POSCO Industries v. Construction Trades Council*), the Supreme Court also stated that if some of the lawsuits filed by the misfeasor are granted, the anticompetitive intent is not set aside, since its results arises from the orchestrated series of lawsuits systematically presented to judicial or quasi-judicial authorities to unlawfully obtain advantages over competitors.

CADE has also dealt with sham litigation cases, establishing its own parameters based on American case law and on the abuse of rights thesis, more common in civil law-based systems, such as those from continental Europe and Brazil.[33] In one of the first sham litigation cases analyzed by CADE,[34] the Commission took into account the plausibility of right the party was pursuing, the reliability of information, adequacy and reasonableness of the adopted means, and the chance of success of the lawsuit. Acting in bad faith while filing lawsuits claiming something the plaintiff beforehand knew was precarious, looking to harm competitors, would then represent sham litigation.

In another ruling,[35] CADE stated that even though a given lawsuit could be considered opportunistic, not necessarily it would be abusive. Specific conducts, then, are not enough for the Commission to condemn anyone for sham litigation, but CADE is capable of analyzing the picture in a holistic view, trying to identify if that conduct fits in an anticompetitive strategy.

The ability of competition authorities to look to the larger picture when judging a sham litigation case was part of CADE's ruling on a case involving the pharmaceutics industry Eli Lilly. Eli Lilly tried, in 1993, to register a patent on a process to produce cancer drug formula before INPI, the Brazilian patents office. INPI's final ruling concluded that Eli Lilly's patent was not able for protection, so the company pursued the invalidation of that ruling through a judicial suit. This behavior is not unlawful at all, since it is rightful to believe one's claim is right, even against the opinion of an authority, so it is normal to pursue the judiciary system to correct any flaws on the process.

---

33. According to Jorge Americano (1932, *Do Abuso do Direito no Exercício da Demanda*. Casa Vanorden, São Paulo), a classical and prominent Brazilian law scholar, one cannot deny that, in a series of unlawful misconducts, someone may invoke a right as ground to something illicit, thus abusing this right.
34. CADE, AP n. 08012.006076/2003-72, Comm. Luiz Carlos Thadeu Delorme Prado, judged on September 4, 2007.
35. CADE, PA n. 08012.004484/2005-51, Comm. Fernando de Magalhães Furlan, judged on August 18, 2010.

At the same time, however, the company modified the scope of the patent register files to reach not only a process, but also a pharmaceutical product. This part of the company's strategy built the basis for another suit that was moved on another jurisdiction, claiming a special exclusive marketing rights (based on TRIPS agreement) that could only be granted to a product patent. INPI, because of a decision that prohibited the administrative process to follow on, could not even officially say if the modified patent could be granted. Eli Lilly got the temporary exclusive marketing rights, hence, without any legal basis, for eight months, by omitting relevant information to different jurisdictions, thus incurring also in abusive forum shopping.

Commissioner Ana Frazão's leading opinion on Eli Lilly's case stated that unlawfully claiming patent protection brings meaningful damages to competition, since it creates an artificial monopoly without granting the social counterpart of innovation to consumers. There were, in the eight months in which competitors were set aside, not only potential, but concrete damages to the market. After the end of the exclusive marketing right, the price of the protected medicine went down to a third of the price exercised while the monopoly was on. The lawsuit was considered baseless and unreasonable on the Antitrust point of view, and even the suits where the company won were doubtful, since crucial information was omitted from the judges or shown in an obscure way.

Eli Lilly's case is a clear example of an IP-related Antitrust infraction arising from the enforcement of a baseless and inexistent exclusivity right. Of course, one cannot simply understand the whole bunch of the acts involved on the sham litigation accusation were rationally architected, and neither cannot state the individual acts were legitimate and thus the company was innocent. Sham litigation lies on the border between lawful and unlawful conduct, which is why an authority capable of connecting isolated facts in order to picture the perpetrated strategy must thoroughly and carefully analyze this claim.

§16.06 FINAL REMARKS

The relation between IP and Antitrust Law is not yet sufficiently well explored on Brazilian law. This may be explained not even by the recentness of many of the questions related to new technologies and the rapidness of its developing, but also by a crucial aspect of Brazilian Antitrust Law: its difficulty to constitutional debate and its tendency to be confined to economic methods and parameters, setting great difficulties to establishing an effective dialogue with other institutions and other legitimate interests. This criticism may be extended to Brazilian IP Law, which just rarely opens dialogue with other areas.

CADE's case law on IP rights shows a large variety of subjects of public interest, reflecting the main tendencies of technological development – the standard-essential patents, for example – and also the most sensitive issues concerning the framework of patent protection, like the legal treatment of pharmaceuticals. Obscurity and uncertainty in the discipline of IP law are utterly prejudicial even to innovation, which is why the relating legal directives need to be clear and contextually adapted to digital modernity.

Brazilian law shows also many difficulties to harmonize competences between different authorities, such as CADE, the competition authority, and INPI, the patent office – institutions with very different proceedings but with some convergent interests. These institutions, mainly INPI, need to work together to stimulate innovation and fulfill their constitutionally established missions of protecting the public interest and the economy. In spite of these hitches, CADE has been working to play its role by improving the parameters for decision-making on Antitrust Law, remarkably maintaining high standards of quality and rationality in many complex and publicly relevant cases.

Antitrust must act when IP's function of protecting innovation through the grant of artificial monopolies as exclusivity rights and the prevention of free riding fails, then it cannot intervene to hamper those objectives, but only to assure there will be no more restrictions beyond the legally acceptable. Under this perspective, Antitrust helps to define and to shape IP and the limits of its exercise. CADE's case law shows, even though in an inceptive way, great examples of cases in which this preoccupation with the effects of IP over competition are explored to build reasonable parameters of conduct evaluation, looking to protect competition and also to stimulate innovation.

CHAPTER 17
Merger Control in Mexico: Development and Outlook

Francisco Javier Núñez Melgoza

§17.01 GENERAL OVERVIEW

The aim of the Federal Law of Economic Competition (FLEC) is to preserve and promote the process of free competition. This process requires the existence of measures that allow maximum competition among the economic agents within the market. This competition compels the competing entities to strive to improve, by implementing efficient procedures and to reduce costs. This rivalry among competitors allows the consumer to benefit from better prices, supply, variety and quality. The Federal Economic Competition Commission (COFECE) protects this process through a range of different procedures. First, there is a sanctioning process, for investigations of monopolistic practices (abuse of dominant position), absolute monopolistic practices (collusion) and improper mergers. These procedures set penalties, when conduct harms the competitive process. Second, there are special procedures such as declarations on the existence of competition conditions and two new concepts which come from the 2013 constitutional reform: access to essential input and assessment of barriers to competition. Finally, preventive procedures exist, such as merger control and assessment of tendering procedures.

Through preventive measures, the authority seeks to avoid mergers that lead to a deterioration of competition. They are preventive because their aim is to prevent situations where mergers can lead to unwanted conduct in economic terms.[1] The preventive nature of the provisions on competition has been analyzed by the Supreme Court, which has stated that the purpose of the FLEC has been to fight preventively,

---
1. Although the procedure provides for the application of sanctions on issues such as submission of false information or failure to comply with conditions.

conducts that can cause damaging consequences for society.[2] By requiring prior notification of certain concentrations, COFECE prevents conducting mergers, acquisitions and other acts that once carried out, would be complex to reverse.

In 2013, the Constitution was amended to allow the creation of the COFECE (which replaced the former antitrust agency, the CFC) and the Federal Telecommunications Institute (IFT), as autonomous bodies responsible for implementing competition policy in Mexico. The aim of this paper is to briefly outline the evolution of merger control in Mexico, by changes in the law and through a brief summary of some relevant cases. At the end some of the aspects that should work to maintain the merger control system updated in analytical and procedural terms will be outlined.

§17.02 EVOLUTION OF THE REGULATORY FRAMEWORK, 1993–2014

[A] Merger Control in the 1993 FLEC

The key elements in the analysis of mergers and acquisitions were introduced by the FLEC and came into force in 1993. In terms of definitions the law defined a merger as a concentration, acquisition of controlling interest or any other act whereby a concentration between operators takes place, where companies, partnerships, shares, stocks, equity instruments or assets in general are joined. The term allows the analysis not only of situations where a formal change of control occurs, but also situations where acquisitions of minority positions take place, which could affect the strategic performance of economic agents and affect competition.

The 1993 FLEC contained the key elements to define the relevant market and market power. Regarding the first point, it stated that to define the relevant market, demand and consumer perspective must be taken into account, this is the substitutability of goods and services and related aspects such as distribution costs, access to goods and services, as well as inputs and the costs of accessing other markets and those generated by regulatory restrictions.

Regarding market power, the spirit of the Act indicates that it is the unilateral ability to raise prices or restrict supply without competitors or consumers being permitted to counter this unilateral action. To determine market power, the FLEC established the need to assess barriers to entry and positioning of competitors, among other things. For the specific case of mergers, the FLEC also noted the need to consider the degree of market concentration. For purposes of not authorizing or allowing a transaction, it is necessary to consider whether as a result of the act, the resulting economic agent could obtain market power or have the ability to exclude competitors, restrict access to the market or engage in monopolistic practices.

---

2. Executory fifteen of May 2000 in 2617/96 under review, Grupo Warner Lambert Mexico, S.A. de C.V. *Semanario Judicial de la Federación y su Gaceta* Volume XII, July 2000, page 278.

In terms of procedure, the law established that prior notification be required where concentrations reached certain monetary thresholds.[3] Thus, the law opted for a compulsory scheme, unlike other jurisdictions where a voluntary scheme applies or where it is the authority that determines whether it is necessary to conduct an investigation. However, the Act did not include provisions to prevent individuals from being able to close the transaction at their own risk, when notified. In case of dispute, individuals must proceed to undo the effects of the concentration or to modify it, although in reality it was difficult to reverse the legal and economic effects once the act was introduced.

The law opted to use monetary thresholds to determine the obligation to notify. These thresholds refer to the transaction amount, assets, sales and capital of the parties. This information is available to businesses. On the other hand, the thresholds are updated according to a unit of reference (prior to 2016, the reference was the minimum wage in the country's capital) The Act established a procedure that counted terms in calendar days, causing various operational complications which compromised the effectiveness of the commission's work.

[B] Changes to the FLEC in 2006

The reform in 2006 did not change the substantive conceptual issues, mainly how to define the relevant market, market power and the concept of concentration. However, two significant procedural modifications were introduced.

First, it established that the time limits for procedures be counted in working days. This enabled greater certainty in review periods and facilitated the operation of the agency. In addition the time to resolve changed, it went from forty-five calendar days with the option to extend by sixty calendar days, to thirty-five working days with the option to extend by forty additional working days.

Second, it was established that ten days following a notification being filed, it was possible to issue an order not to carry out the concentration until it was authorized.

Furthermore, to determine whether a merger should be challenged or sanctioned, the need to consider the effects of the transaction in respect to other competitors and consumers of goods and services, as well as other operating agents or related markets were included. Also, analysis of cross participation of those involved in the concentration in other economic agents, participants in the relevant market or in related markets were included. Finally, the opportunity for parties to submit elements to prove that the transaction would achieve greater efficiency in the market was included.

Another feature to highlight was the adjustment of monetary thresholds, which increased from 50 to 75%. This change was made to limit the number of notifications,

---

3. The Law was remiss about the possibility of voluntary reporting, so that the criterion to accept and resolve such notifications was adopted. It also established the option to challenge concentrations which had no obligation to notify, until one year after made.

which exceeded the institution's capacity to perform adequate analysis.[4] The Act included a new simplified procedure for treatment of notifications of concentrations. This procedure considered the possibility of individuals submitting elements to prove the concentration would have no effect on competition. Once regulated, the procedure established specific circumstances under which it complied with clearly not hindering, damaging or impeding free market access and economic competition.

Initially, the procedure was widely used; however, the difficulty of conclusively proving it complied with clearly not hindering, damaging or impeding free market access and economic competition led to the mechanism being rarely used.

The reform was characterized by a tightening of penalties for submitting false information, performing a prohibited concentration and for a extemporaneous notification submission. New penalties were also introduced for violating the conditions under which concentration was authorized and individuals who participate in or contribute to the establishment of a prohibited concentration. Unfortunately no penalty was introduced for not obeying the non-execution order.

Finally, the Act was amended to include provisions on transparency, classification and access to information.

[C] Changes to the FLEC in 2011

The authorities' power was substantially extended to situations where market power could be unlawfully jointly held, in order to include in competition analysis, scenarios where coordination among competing agents occurs.

As for the simplified procedure, the FLEC foresaw the cases where criteria of not hindering, damaging or impeding free market access and economic competition would be fulfilled, which were: (i) that it is the first time the buyer participates in the relevant market and the buyer has no presence in related markets; (ii) the buyer already owns a minority stake and does not gain control from the concentration increase; and (iii) the acquirer already has control and through the transaction, it consolidates.

The most notable aspect of the reform was the introduction of a set of exemptions from the obligation to notify operations that hardly affect competition, including: corporate restructuring; increases in controlling interest; management or security trusts; operations abroad with no impact on national territory; acquisitions in the stock market that does not allow the opportunity to influence the management of the acquired and not permitting accumulation of more than 10% of stock ownership; and operations of investment funds for purely speculative purposes.

Finally, the reform established penalties for submitting false information, performing a prohibited concentration, extemporaneous notification, breaching the conditions under which a concentration was authorized and individuals who participate or contribute in the execution of a prohibited concentration. It also established penalties for disobeying non-execution orders.

---

4. It is important to mention that to reduce the notification burden of corporate restructuring, a mechanism for the submission of notices of restructuring was created in the regulation of the FLEC.

[D] The Current Legal Framework

On July 7, 2014 the new FLEC which replaced that of 1993 came into force. The changes included in the new system on mergers, cannot be understood without referring to the 2013 constitutional amendments. The constitutional reform led to the creation of two bodies with constitutional, independent autonomy in their decisions and operations: COFECE and the Federal Institute of Communications. The later from 2013 is responsible for applying the competition provisions in the telecommunication and broadcasting market, including merger control.

The Constitution established: (i) the creation of rules for the Commissioners interaction with representatives of regulated operators; (ii) the obligation of Commissioners to refrain from participating in investigation procedures; (iii) obligation of transparency of plenary sessions; (iv) the means of challenging acts of the COFECE is the indirect appeal proceeding only where proceedings are ended so that the right for review by the agency was abandoned; and (iv) the establishment of specialized courts for Economic Competition, Broadcasting and Telecommunications.

The new FLEC maintained, with respect to the above, the main concepts, such as relevant market, market power and the handling of barriers to entry. The concept of concentration remains, but with a minor drafting change. The compulsory prior notification of concentrations to update the monetary thresholds was also maintained, which did not change and only an adjustment made to clarify that the sum of sales or assets of the economic agents involved in the merger is in national territory. Provisions about the simplified procedure and the exemptions from the obligation to notify, which were introduced in Law in 2011 also prevailed. Unlike the conceptual framework, there were significant changes in the procedure. The most notable is the disappearance of the non-execution order. Now, in all cases the parties must wait to obtain authorization to proceed with the merger. Thus the opportunity to circumvent the decisions of the authority narrows.

Another important change relates to the extension of deadlines to meet. Indeed, the term the authority has to issue its decision, after receiving the information required is sixty working days, which may be extended by forty days. This means an increase of twenty-five days, which is very important in allowing the opportunity to perform the analysis in complex cases. This increase in term is inconsequential to most cases, which are resolved at a lower average term of twenty days. Moreover, this extension of the term will be important because it will allow the flexibility to operate the new mechanism for submission of proposals of remedies. In terms of time, the term to request basic information also extended from five to ten days, the same term applies for individuals to present requested information. To give greater flexibility to the procedure, the law now provides for the possibility to reiterate the warning and the request for basic information.

The new FLEC gives certainty about the possibility of requesting information from third parties and public bodies to better assess the transaction. To preserve the powers of gathering information and clarification of same, the Law and the Regulatory Provisions allow the operating staff to hold meetings with individuals.

Because COFECE proceedings are challenged by indirect appeal proceedings and the right to appeal for reconsideration before the agency was abandoned, it became necessary to create an instance in the procedure to allow interaction between the authority and the parties, in cases where the COFECE believes that there are potential risks to the process of free competition. The procedure laid down in Article 90 provides that the Commission shall inform the notifiers, at least ten days prior to the date on which the file is listed for resolution, in order that they are able to offer remedies which allow the identified risks to be corrected.

Moreover, the LFEC includes several provisions that were in the regulations. This means that the law is now a much more extensive and detailed document than what it was. The evolving practice has been required to be more specific in several aspects, which may be achieved by the use of the new powers that the Constitution gives the agency to issue regulatory provisions.

The Act now points to the possibility that the exchange of information between competitors is considered an absolute monopolistic practice. This has raised concerns about the potential for exchanges of information occurring in the context of acquisition audits of mergers and other situations which may be considered improper.

§17.03 BRIEF REVIEW OF SOME RELEVANT CASES

This section recounts various landmark cases resolved by the old CFC and some corresponding to the COFECE are presented. It is not the purpose whatsoever to evaluate decisions, the goal is to present the way various concepts of economic nature have been applied and interpreted, in the context of a legal framework that has been changing.

[A] Mexicana/Aeromexico

Without doubt, air passenger transport has been the industry in which the CFC participated most prominently in its twenty years of existence on mergers. The institution assessed allowing a potential merger between Aeromexico and Mexicana in 1995, when as a result of deteriorating business the holding company Cintra was created; in 2000, when it was asked an opinion on the possibility of joint sale of both airlines; in 2004 when asked about the merger of the companies, subject to the divestiture of a package of regional airlines and routes to mitigate the effects of the merger; and in 2007, when Mexicana raised the possibility of acquiring control of AeroMexico through a public offering. In all cases, the CFC ruled that the airlines should remain separate and as competitors.[5]

---

5. See resolutions of records CNT-25-95 and CNT-101-2007.

Chapter 17: Merger Control in Mexico: Development and Outlook   §17.03[A]

The decisions of the CFC were important because they represented a systematic effort to define the relevant market, by applying the principles of demand from consumers, as well as by measuring the market concentration of the relevant markets.[6]

According to various analyzes carried out by the authority, the industry is characterized by the existence of barriers to entry, mainly access to supplies provided by takeoff and landing rights (slots); airline alliances; the introduction of loyalty schemes; and regulatory barriers, among other elements. When analyzing the evolution of the airline industry, it was seen that the joint market share of Aeromexico and Mexicana and its affiliates nationwide, on domestic routes, was decreasing from levels close to 90% in 1993 to reach just over 50% 2007.

In the context of this evolution of market share, in 2007 the last analysis on the possibility of allowing the integration of the companies was made. Overall, it was found that new companies had emerged which had a favorable outcome in a relatively short time. And Toluca International Airport (TIA) had been formed as a base of operations that apparently rivaled Mexico City International Airport (AICM).

The CFC reiterated that the relevant markets were those of each city pairing, because from the point of view of the consumer, a journey between two given points, say A and B, cannot be replaced by a trip between different points. Therefore, the relevant market was not national, in which total shares of the airlines had actually decreased, but there were twenty-five relevant domestic markets and fifteen international, in which the parties were competitors and because of the merger they would cease to be. The conclusion was that the merger generated significant risks to competition in various markets, most of them linked to operations in AICM.

Regarding the substitutability of operations between AICM and AIT, the CFC analyzed the development of demand for both from a set of destinations where there were overlapping operations from both airports. No statistical behavior was found that indicated a shift from AICM to the AIT. Moreover, it was shown that the AICM was a key airport for the airlines, due to the capabilities of networking operations that AIT airport did not have. Due to its saturation, the AICM limited expansion opportunities or entry of new competitors.

In its various analysis, CFC linked a number of elements in addition to the shares and concentration indices, such as access to slots, saturation at AICM, configuration of network services and regulatory barriers, among others, to conclude that the operation would be a risk to competition and be in detriment to consumers.

---

6. In 1993, the Federal Government allowed the controlling group of Aeromexico take control of Mexican. The then Commissioner Pascual García Alba conducted an econometric study that found evidence of the relationship between the changes in the concentration of markets at the route level measured by the indices of Herfindahl and Dominance, with variations in prices observed after change of control. See García Alba Iduñate, Pascual, "Índice de dominancia y el análisis de competencia de las líneas aéreas mexicanas," *Gaceta de Competencia Económica*, year 1, number 1, March–August 1998.

[B] Coca-Cola/Jugos del Valle

In 2007, the CFC examined the acquisition by Coca-Cola Femsa and The Coca-Cola Export Corporation, of the Jugos del Valle corporation. The corresponding markets for these parties were carbonated drinks, juices and nectars and non-carbonated soft drinks, all of which were analyzed on a national scale.[7]

The analysis of the operation is interesting, because the transaction meant a relatively minor increase in levels of market concentration. Indeed, the Herfindahl index increased marginally in the case of carbonated beverages; juices and nectars; and refreshing non-carbonated beverages. A merger in each of the markets separately, would probably not have been challenged. Although, in some cases the degree of market concentration was already high, the transaction modified little to the competitive structure of each market.

However, the Commission determined that the merger would increase the barriers to market entry in terms of brand recognition of the products produced by Jugos del Valle, as well as providing privileged access of companies connected to the purchaser's distribution channels.

The authority determined that the market power of the buyer in the market for carbonated beverages would be strengthened, but also, and this is the new aspect of the decision, this could be used to transfer said power to the market of juices and nectars. Thus, the conclusion was that the transaction would give buyers market power that would, among other things, substantially prevent competitors access to the distribution channel outlets. The use of the transfer of power from one market to another is the distinctive element of this resolution and was the first practical use of the idea of a relationship between two markets, in a case of mergers. This possibility was given because: (i) both types of products are non-perishable and may require refrigeration; (ii) the purchaser was a major supplier of refrigeration equipment on loan and supported other traditional channel outlets; (iii) due to the nature of the products, their distribution systems could be coordinated; (iv) the creation of a broader portfolio of products and brands, targeting the same consumers.

The operation was authorized by offering remedies in the instance of appeal for reconsideration and on presentation of efficiency arguments during the examination of the merger.

[C] Mexichem

The CFC analyzed various transactions carried out by Mexichem, a Mexican company that operates various businesses related to the petrochemical industry. In particular, the group participates in activities associated with the production chains of caustic soda and chlorine. In the latter case, the company had made various mergers in the markets of PVC resin, PVC piping and vinyl chloride monomer.

---

7. Record CNT-12-2007.

The group, which had participated in the production of PVC resin in the country, acquired Grupo Primex in 2005, which meant that the number of participants of the market were reduced to two.

In 2007 it acquired the Amanco PVC piping business in several countries in Latin America, which represented vertical integration in the resin business. In 2008, the group reported two acquisitions related to Cydsa group, in the resin and PVC piping businesses.[8]

Both concentrations represented a new development in the way in which the analysis was conducted, in particular by the way that relevant markets were defined. In the case of PVC resin,[9] the parties argued that the market was open to imports and that the resin had substitutes, mainly PVC compounds. Resin imports from the U.S. were subject to a compensatory duty that severely limited trade, and the CFC also found that imports as a share of apparent consumption were reduced and consumers did not import from other regions. On the other hand, no practical evidence of substitutability between resins and compounds was found, because to develop compounds, users had to invest in infrastructure. So for those who had not made such investments, the opportunity to develop their own compounds did not exist.

In regards to piping it was also argued that the market had a dimension of at least the NAFTA region and that there were various substitutes, mainly piping made of other plastic materials such as polyethylene and polypropylene.

The analysis was innovative due to the use of econometric techniques to analyze the available pricing information, to verify the existence of a long-term structural relationship between the prices of various products. Thus, in the case of resins, in addition to analyzing the relationship between the prices of PVC resins at national level concerning the reference prices of the same product in the U.S. market for export, the CFC analyzed the possible connection between the prices of PVC resins in the domestic market and compound prices for rigid and flexible products, both the domestic and imported product. In all cases the existence of a possible structural relationship was statistically dismissed.

In economic terms, for two products to co-exist in the same market, they are required to have similar prices or maintain parallel behavior. Neither situation was verified through statistical analysis, which strengthened the evidence that the relevant market proposal submitted by the parties was inadequate.

That said, the CFC determined that the mass/suspension PVC resin market had a national geographical dimension which meant that the merger would create a monopoly, so it was not authorized. The transaction was notified again, in 2009, once the countervailing duty was abolished. The CFC verified that market conditions had changed enough to consider that the relevant market should include the NAFTA region.

---

8. The analysis of these two operations is in the resolutions of the CNT-91-2008, CNT-93-2008, CNT-088-2009, RA-27-2009 and RA-28-2009 files.
9. There are several types of PVC resins. The analysis was conducted in the suspension/mass type market.

In the piping case, they ruled out the general plastic piping market, as polyethylene and polypropylene products have different uses, resistance and physical characteristics to the PVC pipe. As for the geographical dimension, it was found that imports of PVC pipe were marginal in relation to domestic consumption and mainly close to the border, so they were insufficient to generate any kind of competitive pressure in most of the National territory. As in the other case, the concentration was not authorized in the first instance because the high market share buyer would obtain and the risk of vertical foreclosure of competitors, requiring access to PVC resin. The concentration was authorized subsequently by submitting remedies that included the divestiture of assets for the production of PVC pipe to third parties.

[D]   Televisa/GSF Telecom Holdings

In 2012, the CFC ruled on the concentration through which Grupo Televisa acquired 50% of the shares of GSF Telecom Holdings, which controlled businesses in mobile and cellular telephony, internet and cable television networks through Iusacell and Total Play Tele-communications. In the resolution of the file, the CFC decided not to authorize the operation.[10] In an appeal, the authority authorized it but with various conditions.

The issue involved the analysis of various markets. However, there are two aspects that are relevant and which are worth further examination in this chapter.

First, one of the reasons for the authority not approving in the first instance and imposing conditions subsequently was the possible involvement of related markets. The resolution on the concentration indicated that the transaction was risky, which meant a partnership in equal parts of Grupo Televisa and Grupo Salinas in GSF Telecom Holdings, in the context that these groups held the 95% of the licenses to operate broadcast television stations and together controlled a large percentage of the audience. The operation gave incentives to the groups to act in a coordinated manner in the relevant markets related to the concentration, in particular the content/programing and advertising for broadcast television. In this regard, the parties argued that the CFC incorrectly used the term related market and noted that there was no productive relationship between the defined relevant markets and related markets allegedly affected.

The other important aspect which dealt with the discussion was the concept of economic efficiency. The parties argued that the operation was favorable for consumers, it allowed the opportunity to improve the competitive intensity in the markets for fixed and mobile telephony as well as the Internet. In the worst case, if there were an impact on the market related to content/programing and advertising for broadcast television, the magnitude of the alleged harm was, as the parties argued, well below the potential benefits that could be obtained in the markets where competition would improve.

---

10. See resolution of the case CNT-031-2011.

[E] Nestle/Pfizer

In 2013, the CFC ruled on an acquisition of Pfizer's different products including infant formulas by Nestle. This case is emblematic for several reasons: the wealth of information on file, including market research to which the authority had access, which allowed an in depth analysis of the determinants of demand; because of the use of techniques never formally employed to determine the possible effects of the concentration; and the meticulous detail in the drafting of the remedies to which the concentration was subject to.[11]

The operation was not authorized in the first instance, but it was, in the appeal and by submitting remedies. The approval was made subject to remedies that in fact made it impossible for Nestle to maintain control of acquired assets, i.e., the CFC authorized a temporary concentration solely to the effect that the parties could conclude the transaction at the international level.

Initially, the parties argued that the market had a geographic dimension of at least the NAFTA region, specialty formulas were routine formula substitutes and that there were no significant barriers to entry, particularly for private labels. The CFC analysis paid special attention to these arguments. Thanks to the abundance of information gathered, which included varied kinds of market studies, it was determined that physicians play a decisive role in the demand for products, the consumer is not willing to replace the use of milk formulas for other products and that brand recognition plays an important role, so there are few cases of successful private brands.

Uncertain whether the products of the parties belonged to the same market, by price difference, the authority had access to elasticities of demand calculations, that enabled a merger simulation exercise using the technique of diversion rates applicable to the study of mergers in markets of differentiated goods, from which it was established the reaction consumers may have to price changes of various products on the market.[12] Thus, there was evidence that indicated that where there were price increases to Pfizer products, a significant proportion of consumers would be willing to purchase Nestlé products. Thus, the consolidation of a broader portfolio of brands by Nestle, would have created the means and incentives to apply differentiated price increases.

Moreover, the analysis concluded that specialty formulas are not substitute for routine formulas, so as the former are prescription products, as opposed to the later which are only from a doctor's recommendation. Thus, it was concluded that a significant part of the imports concerned specialty formulas and that competitors' behavior in the market cannot be disciplined.

As for the remedies offered in the motion for reconsideration, the authority accepted them since it verified that they were submitted in accordance with best practices in the field applied in other jurisdictions and that were suitable to: (i) ensure

---

11. See resolutions of the records CNT-035-2012 and RA-002-2013.
12. An overview of this technique can be found in Oxera, "Best of Both Worlds? Innovative Approaches to Modelling Merger Price Rises," May 2010. Available at http://www.oxera.com/Latest-Thinking/Agenda/2010/Best-of-both-worlds-Innovative-approaches-to-mode.aspx.

the transfer of assets in a short period minimizing the risk of business damage; (ii) achieve acquisition by a buyer with the ability to properly operate in the market; and (iii) include in the package to divest not only physical assets but also the rights for use of trademarks and formulations over a sufficiently long period to ensure the success of the transferred business.

[F]   Cinemex/Cinemark

The CFC analyzed various concentrations in the film exhibition market. To do this, it applied a similar methodology employed in other jurisdictions, particularly the United Kingdom, consisting mainly in determining the effects on competition on areas of influence.[13] In the British case equal timing methods have been used to define radios; Mexico has used information from the databases of registered frequent customers who have established radios 5 kilometers in Mexico City and 6 kilometers in other locations, within which market concentration is measured.

The purchase of Cinemark by Cinemex in 2013 was a peculiar case, because in the first instance, it was not authorized by the CFC and the decision was reversed by the COFECE in the appeal for reconsideration.[14] The reason for the initial objection was not connected to possible unilateral effects that would result from the analysis of horizontal concentration by areas of influence, but with the potential for exercising joint dominance in these local markets and related real estate leases and procurement markets acquiring distribution rights. This decision probably represented the only time the Mexican competition authority has employed the concept of joint dominance in a concentration and its use was mainly based on the concern that with the elimination of a competitor only two main exhibiting chains would remain in the market.

The COFECE reversed, by a majority the refusal of the concentration considering that the CFC decision was based solely on the reduction in the number of competitors and did not analyze various market characteristics which suggested that it was unlikely to have a joint dominance behavior.

[G]   Comex/Sherwin Williams

Like the Cinemex / Cinemark case, the Comex / Sherwin Williams merger was challenged by the CFC and corresponded to the COFECE ruling on the motion for reconsideration. Unlike the first, this time the COFECE upheld the decision of the CFC.

The analysis concluded that the acquisition would be risky for competition because the resulting company would hold a significant market share and would be several times the size of its closest competitor in the relevant market of decorative

---

13. See Competition Commission, Vue Entertainment Holdings (U.K.) Ltd and A3 Cinema Limited. A Report on the Completed Acquisition of A3 Cinema Limited by Vue Entertainment Holdings (U.K.) Ltd, February 24, 2006.
14. See resolutions of the records CNT-010-2013 and RA-029-2013.

coatings. Similarly, authorities determined the existence of significant barriers to entry, which would be reinforced as a result of the merger.[15]

The most distinctive element of the resolution was the claim that Sherwin Williams would acquire an operator, Comex, which already held market power in the relevant market of coatings, which would be strengthened with concentration. The decision was supported by evidence presented by the parties, according to which in a context of significant growth in prices of major raw materials, Comex had been able, in recent years, to maintain it's gross margins and even make a higher profit than those of its main competitors.

§17.04 CONCLUSIONS

While the Mexican authority has moved away from the exclusive use of structural evidence to build economic cases that support their decisions of non-authorization or conditioning, there are several things that must work in order to incorporate international best practice in analytical terms and procedure. Some of them are as follows:

(i) A greater emphasis should be placed on the use of theories and economic techniques to identify complex cases, in order to expedite review of cases that pose no risk to competition and devote most of their resources to the analysis of cases that generate risks to competition.
(ii) It is important to make an effort to clarify the legitimate areas for cooperation between competitors and exchange of information between them in the context of negotiating a merger.
(iii) The Law sets or leads to various economic concepts of increasingly frequent use, which could be clarified through criteria or guidelines. This is the case of concepts such as a joint dominance and related market.
(iv) Probably the greatest challenge lies in refining the procedure to report risks to the economic agents involved in a concentration, the key issue for the submission of remedies and effective negotiations between the authority and the parties.

---

15. See resolutions to records CNT-95-2012 y RA-027-2013.

Part III International Cooperation

CHAPTER 18
Regional Coordination in Cartel Investigations: The Liquid Oxygen Case

Pierre Horna[*]

> International cooperation in tackling global cartels has progressively become more intense: while the same level of cooperation is developing within and between some regions, the challenge increasingly will be to impart the same intensity of cooperation to all regional cartels"[1]

§18.01 INTRODUCTION

The question of performance and outcome of relevant competition authorities such as the U.S. Department of Justice or the Federal Trade Commission, and the Directorate General for Competition of the European Commission, is a recurrent aspect that enforcers and practitioners discuss when they meet at international conferences. This is not only true with respect to the assessment of the results of long-standing competition regimes, but strangely enough questions in this respect are raised by young agencies all over the world and directly referred to decisions and strategies that may amount to determine their short and long-term achievements. The questions and the expected accountability that newer agencies have to address –when an "important" case has not been handled yet or ruled upon may constitute a source of a healthful initial stress for the agency but irredeemably will lead to decisions on how to investigate more efficiently and make effective use of the toolbox provided by Congress or government to the new or established authority.

---

[*] The views hereby expressed are exclusively of the author and do not necessarily reflect those of UNCTAD Secretariat and its Member States.
1. Pages 274-275 ICN at Ten launched at the 10th ICN Annual Conference in The Hague.

Nevertheless, it seems that raising the issue of how to strengthen coordination between competition authorities when investigating multi-jurisdictional practices such as price-fixing cartels, in the case of Latin America, could be regarded *prima facie* as not a priority for competition authorities as there are other important domestic topics that shape the daily agenda of their interventions. In addition, in regard to cartels, there are constraints to foster domestic enforcement in Latin America due to the relatively lack of financial and human resources where competition authorities are relatively young and internal markets less contestable with a non-significant competition culture.

Therefore, it should be first reckoned the importance to design a strategy to boost domestic competition law enforcement against local cartelization in Latin American markets and thereafter starting to assess the impact of regional cartels that have also a great impact on domestic markets.[2]

Nonetheless, there are special circumstances when a series of similar "domestic" cartels involving the same group of multinational corporations can be formed and operated across several jurisdictions. Since each of the cartels only affects one country and there is no common or unifying scheme to characterize an international cartel, the cartels are, by definition, domestic cartels. Despite the qualification of "domestic" cartel, these types of cartels surely contain, to some extent, international dimensions. Multinational companies have their businesses in several countries, allowing them multi-market contact, and this frequent contact in turn facilitates the formation and operation of cartels across the region, thereby forming intra-regional cartels.

In Latin America, multinational companies supplying medical liquid oxygen to hospitals formed bid-rigging *domestic* cartels in several jurisdictions, in which the subsidiaries of these multinational companies operated. These multinational companies closely observe the developments and capabilities of cartel enforcement activity at local level in different Latin American civil law jurisdictions and act in accordance to these capabilities.[3]

---

2. In fact, one of the UNCTAD recommendations in the way forward to increase cooperation between competition authorities in developing countries is to build reputation and capabilities so as to attract leniency applications from international cartelists. UNCTAD's worldwide capacity building programs assist younger authorities to level up their anti-cartel enforcement effort probably into domestic cartels, from which they may build up their capabilities and reputations on their anti-cartel enforcement in general "Cross-Border Anticompetitive Practices: The Challenges for Developing Countries and Economies in Transition". Note by the UNCTAD secretariat, 2011. See also latest UNCTAD note on Modalities and procedures for international cooperation in competition cases involving more than one country (2013).
3. Local enforcement of competition rules in Latin America have taken place particularly in essential goods and services sectors by relatively advanced competition authorities of well-established competition authorities in Brazil, Mexico and Chile. A special situation arose in Argentina and Venezuela's authorities, which had good case law development during the 1990s and part of the 2000s. Other countries, such as Costa Rica, Colombia and Peru, have rapidly strengthened their enforcement actions in response to their rapid economic development during last decade. Another set of countries, including Ecuador (2011), Bolivia (2008), Nicaragua (2007), El Salvador (2004), Honduras (2006), Dominican Republic (2008) and Uruguay (2009), have recently adopted competition rules for their domestic markets, primarily enforcing cases concerning sensitive sectors. Two Spanish speaking countries remain with no competition law at the time of drafting this document: Guatemala and Paraguay.

When looking at the Latin American regional dynamics, it is also clear that multinational companies have not seen progress or any serious effort to find new instruments for competition authorities to coordinate, cooperate and converge in its actions, a fact that clashes with the increase of trade flows. This is probably due to the great number of Regional Trade Agreements and bilateral agreements between Latin American countries and the particularities of regional integration taking place in Central America, where conversely enough, companies have a special motive to foster regional business alliances.

There are two phenomena that could be drawn from these facts:

(i) That, resulting from international business firm integration and regional vertical integration to act "glocally" by adjusting their self-corporate governance rules to domestic competition rules but act differently when it comes to cross-border business patterns (similarly to international transfer pricing activities to avoid double taxation). This could be fostered by those companies that do not adopt policies and programs that amount to a "race to the top", in the sense of considering the laws applied by the most active and sophisticated enforcement agencies as the basis for their corporate compliance policy, applied everywhere regardless of jurisdiction and cross-border effects.

(ii) That in this sort of "duality" of business behavior, depending whether the firm operates only at a domestic or cross-border level, there could be incentives to collude between firms of the same industry and therefore enter into the realm of international price-fixing or export/import cartels and committing offenses with an impact in different local markets.

These two facts are known to the competition authorities and indeed in different Latin American regional fora (such as the Central American Group of Competition, the Andean Community of Nations and MERCOSUR) and international fora ranging from the International Competition Network (ICN), OECD to UNCTAD, such that competition authorities gathered to agree on certain soft-rules concerning cross-border effect of cartels that may help in the future, particularly in Latin American countries.[4]

Despite this awareness of the threat of international and regional cartels that harm local consumers in domestic markets, there are several challenges concerning the enforcement of competition rules at the regional level in Latin America. These range from sharing information (non-confidential and publicly available), when competition authorities are investigating cases of cross-border nature, to recognition and inclusion of internationally gathered evidence in local cases.

This paper is organized into four parts. First, it deals with assessing the case law of the seven jurisdictions and similarities, as well as divergences, are identified. Second, it looks at the overall panorama of cooperation agreements signed by some of

---

4. See ICN Working Group on Cartels; OECD's Competition Committee and UNCTAD's Intergovernmental Group of Experts, available at www.internationalcompetitionnetwork.org, www.oecd.org/competition, www.unctad.org/competition, respectively.

the jurisdictions under scrutiny. Third, it identifies the difficulties of sharing information under the specific domestic regulations of these jurisdictions. Lastly, it provides some ideas for further discussion for the improvement of the level of coordination and cooperation between enforcers when investigating recurrent and similar cartels in Latin America.

§18.02 REVIEWING THE FACTS OF LIQUID OXYGEN CARTEL CASES IN PANAMA (2001), ARGENTINA (2005), CHILE (2007), PERU, BRAZIL AND COLOMBIA (2010) AND MEXICO (2011)[5]

During the last decade, seven jurisdictions have administratively, and in some cases judicially, sanctioned domestic cartels in the liquid oxygen market. One of these seven jurisdictions (Mexico) did not sanction the anticompetitive practice due to the lack of strength in the evidence presented, according to the Federal Competition Commission (CFC). With the exceptions of Colombia and Mexico, all cases were related to bid-rigging activities concerning the procurement of liquid oxygen for public hospitals or industrial activities.

Let us briefly review the facts of each of these cases.

First, we describe the two cases in which judicial reviews took place (closed cases) under Panamanian and Chilean competition laws:

(i) *Panama (2008)*: The Panamanian Competition Authority at the time (CLICAC), now called ACODECO, established that the defendant firms colluded to organize sales of industrial oxygen. The collusive agreement consisted in distributing the rows (provinces) of the bid between two offer bidders. The row of the winning bidder showed a competitive offer of USD 0.01 in tanks of 12 and 14 cubic feet. In the rows of the losing bidder, a higher price offer was shown in tanks of 12 and 14 cubic feet. The rows were awarded by adding the prices of tanks of 12, 24 and 200 cubic feet. In tanks of 200 cubic feet the price offered was the real one. CLICAC based its statements on report tests made in the Social Security Administration, documents obtained in an exhibitory diligence and statistical expertise. In the statistical report, a probability (close to zero) that the two investigated companies had not agreed to submit a competitive proposal in any row of the bid, was calculated. In this case, both the Court of First Instance (Court) in 2004 and the court of second instance (High Court) in 2008, awarded the decision to CLICAC based on the statistical analysis used as circumstantial evidence of the existence of the collusive practice because of the lack of direct evidence. The Court imposed the maximum fine allowed in 2008, by Act 29 of 1996, of

---

5. UNCTAD co-organized together with the Ecuadorian Competition authority (Superintendence for the control of Market Power) an International Workshop on International Bid-rigging in Latin America in Ecuador in March 2013. The case handlers from Brazil, Chile, Mexico, Panama and Peru gathered to discuss the ways they investigate their domestic cartels. More information can be found at http://www.programacompal.org/5-Seminario-Internacional.html.

USD 100,000 to each of the two economic agents involved in the attempt to divide the national medical oxygen market.[6]

This investigation began when a third player presented a claim in December 1997 asserting that the prospective bidding process had technical requirements that amounted to the imposition of anticompetitive barriers that favored the other two companies that were finally sanctioned. It is important to mention as a particularity of the case, that officers of CLICAC were present at the opening of the bids, so a conclusion that could be drawn is that regardless of the close "surveillance" of the authority of the bidding procedure circumstantial evidence to support the existence of a concerted practice was detected.

It has to be considered that CLICAC did not have powers to raid premises and Panama does not have an immunity and leniency program for cartel detection. This kind of "surveillance" when relevant bidding procedures are in course is seen also in other countries such as Chile (bidding process for TV transmission of soccer matches) but today is not a standard procedure in this country.

(ii) *Chile (2007)*: After an investigation, the National Economic Prosecutor (FNE) brought a complaint against four oxygen providers (Aga S.A., Air Liquid Chile S.A., Indura S.A. and Praxair Chile Ltda.), arguing that they had engaged in coordinated behavior aimed at dividing the market, particularly in public hospitals. The Chilean Competition Tribunal (TDLC), after the legal procedure was conducted and considering the arguments, accepted the application made by FNE. The Tribunal found that the four enterprises had interfered with the procurement process conducted by the health procurement entity, CENABAST, to provide liquid oxygen to public hospitals in 2004. The collusive tendering action by the four enterprises was construed in order to eliminate competition from the procurement process. The Tribunal fined the oxygen providers – Aga, Air Liquid, Indura and Praxair – more than USD 2 million. On appeal, the Supreme Court overruled the Tribunal's decision, concluding that the collusive behavior was not proved because the evidence presented for the allegation was circumstantial and the results of the bidding process derived from probable behavior of the enterprises facing the tender and the structure of the industry.[7]

FNE did not have strong powers to investigate cartels in the period of the enforcement proceedings -conduct dawn raids or wiretapping-; only in 2009 did Congress expand the FNE' toolbox, including a provision for leniency. The case was opened after the health procurement entity, which succeeded

---

6. For the full-text of the two rulings, see: www.acodeco.gob.pa.
7. In this sense, the indirect evidence and economic analysis made by the first instance Competition Tribunal was not recognized by the court on appeal (Supreme Court in Chile) and therefore, only hard-core evidence was the preference of the judicial reviewers in this case. See also "The case of Liquid Oxygen". Romero et al. 2010.

in implementing a strategy in order to reduce the effects of possible coordinated behavior by incumbent oxygen providers, nevertheless detected interferences in its 2004 process.[8] FNE during the investigation was informed of a similar ongoing case in Argentina and CNDC's decision, -that was handed a month before the FNE presented its case to the TDLC, in August 2005-, included information on e-mails of discussions of activities in Chile by firms that operated in both countries.

The second set of jurisdictions is still pending confirmation by the courts. Only administrative rulings took place and these are composed of:

(i) *Argentina (2005):* CNDC fined the Argentine subsidiaries of Praxair, Air Liquide, AGA and Indura a total of USD 24.3 million in July 2005. The investigation was launched in 2001 when hospitals were unable to secure contracts for liquid oxygen from competing suppliers. Usually they received bids from only their incumbent supplier. Otherwise, when competing bids were submitted, the incumbent was usually the lowest bidder. The hospitals' complaints caused the Secretariat for Competition, Deregulation, and Consumers Defense (the predecessor to the Secretariat for Technical Coordination) to instruct CNDC to begin an investigation. The market for this product was highly concentrated, entry was difficult and there were effectively only four suppliers. The CNDC conducted raids on the four companies, which were highly effective in producing strong documentary and electronic evidence of customer allocation and price-fixing over a five-year period.[9]

Remarkably, Argentina was one of the first jurisdictions in the region to enact powers to raid premises; consequently, in this case, CNDC was the first agency to conduct non-voluntary inspections. The analysis made in CNDC's decision of the documents and e-mails found depicts, in this case, the level of information exchange and communication industry wide.

(ii) *Peru (2010):* The Peruvian Competition Authority, INDECOPI, fined the Peruvian subsidiaries of Praxair, AGA and Messer for having organized a market allocation cartel in Peru in the bid processes in the market of medical liquid oxygen, essential for hospitals in the country. INDECOPI sanctioned companies with a fine of almost USD 8 million that provided this product to Peru's public health system, between 1999 and 2004, these companies had geographically distributed the bids for the sale of medical liquid oxygen.[10] One of the results of the investigation, that began after a complaint was presented in 2003 by the public health insurance service of Peru (ESSALUD)

---

8. CENABAST aggregated the demand of liquid oxygen of all hospitals in Chile for this bid, based on an economic report by experts specially retained to present a strategy to confront possible coordinated behavior of incumbent liquid oxygen providers.
9. The case is still under revision of the Judicial Power in Argentina. There is a chance that the administrative decision by the CNDC will be overturned.
10. See at http://www.indecopi.gob.pe/RepositorioAPS/0/2/par/RES_051_2010_CLC/Res051-2010.pdf.

based on the results of the different bidding processes, established that the firms engaged in a concerted strategy of "self-dismissal" by means of presenting bids that were higher than the maximum acceptable price established by ESSALUD, resulting in its disqualification. INDECOPI assessed all the counterarguments from the firms concluding that there were no alternative explanations as to why the market allocation took place and the coincidental ways that the offers were made in different bids nationwide.[11]

(iii) *Brazil (2010)*: CADE issued a landmark decision fining medical and industrial gases producers Air Liquide, Air Products, IBG, Linde and White Martins more than USD 1.4 billion for price-fixing, customer allocation and bid rigging. White Martins was fined approximately USD 1.1 billion for recidivism, the largest fine ever in the history of antitrust enforcement in Brazil, and the third largest in the world at the time. CADE found that the cartel had been active since at least 1998 and that it had harmed the health-care industry and several other businesses. CADE also levied substantial fines on seven executives. The CADE decision led to a significant number of private actions for damages, including a collective action filed by more than 250 hospitals, in which a preliminary injunction was issued in order to displace the collusive price equilibrium.[12]

CADE's investigation involved the production of relevant communications and documents seized after inspections and also obtained from telephone interceptions. CADE's core analysis refers to the different rules implemented to stage the allocation of clients and markets by the defendants. The use of these powers resulted in extensive litigation due to the fact they were exercised in the context of parallel criminal proceedings against individuals implicated.

(iv) *Colombia (2010):* Following a five-year investigation of Fábrica Nacional de Oxigeno S.A. (Linde Colombia S.A.), Oxígenos de Colombia Ltda. (Oxicol) y Gases Industriales de Colombia S.A. (Cryogas), Superintendence of Industry and Commerce (SIC) issued a ruling against the companies for having entered into concerted practices in the distribution and trading of liquid oxygen, which were aimed at obstructing or impeding the entry of other firms in the Colombian market and trading channels.[13]

(v) *Mexico (2011)*: The Mexican authorities decided not issue sanctions relating to any liquid oxygen cartel, although there were allegations of hard-core evidence obtained by testimonies (hearings), requests for information and other economic evidence. Mexico's CFC initiated a formal proceeding in 2006

---

11. INDECOPI in December 2006 made a voluntary inspection of the premises of the firms involved and in January 2008 opened a formal proceeding that reviewed several bidding processes from 1998 to 2006.
12. Decision of reporting Commissioner and acting Chairman of CADE Fernando Furlan in *Pocesso Admnistrativo* n° 08012.009888/2003-70 against AGA S.A. et al.; affirmed by the plenary of CADE, Commissioners Marquez de Carvalho, Joppert Regazzo, Costa Alves de Mattos, Machado Ruiz, September 1, 2010, 474th ordinary session.
13. Resolution No. 65477, November 25, 2010, issued by Superintendent De la Calle.

and the scope of the investigation included practices that began in 1983. According to the testimony of former employees, the firms had an agreement that included cover denominations through different colors (red for AGA, blue for Infra Group, black for Praxair). The investigation also produced evidence of bid rigging behavior in detriment of the government petroleum producer, PEMEX. In 2009 a statement of objections was presented to the CFC but finally all accusations were dismissed and the case was closed.[14]

Table 18.1 Investigated Firms in the Cartel of Liquid Oxygen in Latin America

Country	Multinational Firms Involved				Local Firms
	Air Liquide	AGA	Praxair	Messer	
Argentina	AL Argentina	✓	✓	✓	INDURA Argentina
Brazil	AL Brazil	✓	White Martins		Air Products Brazil, Industria Brasileria de Gases (IBG)
Chile	✓	✓	✓		INDURA Chile
Colombia			Oxigenos de Colombia (Praxair)		Fábrica Nacional de Oxigenos (LINDE) Colombia
Mexico	✓ (not relevant market share)	✓	✓ (Ahora Praxair absorbió a AGA)		INFRA Mexico
Panama			?		Aceti-Oxigento & Distribuidora de Gases Industriales
Peru		✓	✓	✓	

Source: UNCTAD presentation at the International Bid Rigging Workshop, Ecuador March 2013.

Final comment on this section

It seems that jurisdictions that followed the lead struck by Argentina did not have serious problems in obtaining key evidence to prove the practices. This could be partially explained by the nature of the cartels: they were local cartels but not parts of an international cartel.

---

14. File No. DE-022-2006, August 9, 2011; a minority vote was issued against the dismissal by commissioners Perez Motta and Morales Elcoro.

Chapter 18: Regional Coordination in Cartel Investigations   §18.03

The competition authorities did not have any relevant coordination in the investigations even though they have signed memorandum of understanding. On the other hand, the multinationals seem to have not given a full attention to the investigations done in other jurisdictions. In this regard, they were not coordinated either, to the advantage of competition authorities.

The nature of the cartels may explain the lack of coordination or cooperation between the agencies, to some extent:

(i) They might not have seen any scheme of an international cartel, so that they did not bother to report the investigation to others or investigate together.

(ii) Normally an agreement or memorandum requires a communication or notification from a party to the other when its investigation targets the other's companies. But international comity is the basis for these understandings and it may probably be that did not find any reason to inform their investigations to other counterparts since the firms under investigation were not U.S. and EU-based companies but multinationals, or otherwise their own local firms.

§18.03 REVIEWING COOPERATION AGREEMENTS IN SOME OF THE JURISDICTIONS OF THE LIQUID OXYGEN CARTEL CASES: BRAZIL, CHILE, COLOMBIA AND PERU

Basics on cooperation when enforcing cartel cases[15]

Cooperation between competition agencies in cartel investigations is crucial in the fight against international, regional and even domestic cartels. A domestic cartel can be discovered simply by two agencies talking to each other, or when only one agency has cognizance of its occurrence. In the case of international cartels, coordination of investigatory measures may be necessary in order to avoid the risk of detriment to the proceedings and even destruction of evidence if one agency moves before other agencies.[16]

In the case of the seven jurisdictions under scrutiny, efforts were made by its competition agencies to achieve certain types of cooperation schemes that emphasized different phases of an investigation (pre-investigatory, investigatory or even post-investigatory phases)[17]

---

15. Information based on the Document "Cooperation between Competition Agencies in Cartel Investigations". International Competition Network (ICN), 2007.
16. See: Best practices for the formal exchange of information between competition authorities in hard-core cartel investigations. OECD, Competition Commission, October 2005.
17. For example, at the pre-investigatory phase (before evidence gathering) agencies can cooperate regarding markets to be investigated, companies to be targeted which operate regionally where non-confirmed allegations exists, the location of evidence and the avoidance of destruction of evidence. In turn, at the investigatory phase, during which evidence is gathered and analyzed and the case built up, they may coordinate investigatory measures. This could include the organization of simultaneous searches, raids or inspections, issuing of subpoenas or other

In all of these phases, aspects relating to exchanging information can cover the following types of information: (i) public information,[18] (ii) agency information,[19] (iii) information from the parties already in the possession of one agency[20] and (iv) information obtained from the parties at the request of another agency.[21] It is clear that the last type of information represents the peak of a very deep and close cooperation between agencies that may result from *second generation* agreements, such as that recently negotiated between the European Union (EU) and Switzerland (see *infra*).

Information exchange in general

The core element of any effective cooperation agreement is the intended exchange of specific, case-related information between the competition authorities. Thus, the competition authorities can share views and exchange information related to the application of their respective competition laws if certain requirements are met. They may discuss any information, including information obtained during the investigative process, insofar as necessary to carry out cooperation and coordination.

The exchange of agency information (information obtained during the investigative process) might be possible even if the competition authorities have not opened a formal investigation but merely a preliminary investigation. At this stage of the procedure, the parties may have no access to the files yet and cannot even judge what kind of information could be transmitted abroad.

Brief overview of the provisions of the seven jurisdictions under analysis

In what follows, a brief review of whether the seven jurisdictions involved have signed cooperation agreements with each other and the coverage provided by these agreements.

Brazil: The agency (CADE) established cooperation agreements and protocols with Argentina (October 2003) and Chile (October 2008), which allow for cooperation

---

requests for information, or interviewing of witnesses. Finally, at the post-investigatory phase, which concerns prosecution, adjudication and sanctioning, agencies may exchange evidence and other information that they have obtained, and they may cooperate via general case discussions between the investigators. See ICN. *Ibid.* at page.

18. In this case, one agency simply helps another agency to gain time by providing information that is already in the public domain (perhaps a hard-to-find market report, information about the market arising from studies carried out by the agency or decision and reports that are not easily available).
19. This is information which is not necessarily in the public domain, but that is generated within the agency itself, rather than provided by parties to the investigation (although it may be based on information supplied by the parties). Such "agency information" may concern, for example, the stage that the investigation has reached, the planned timing of further steps, the provisional orientation of the investigation, conclusions reached about the nature of the market and so forth.
20. This kind of material can be evidence of an infringement, background information on the market or the activities of the parties (such as turnover figures). The information may have been provided voluntarily (by an immunity/amnesty applicant, for example) or under compulsion (in an inspection, under subpoena etc.)
21. Where two agencies have a highly developed cooperative relationship, it may be possible for one of them to request the other to obtain information from parties in its jurisdiction, which is not already in its possession.

between agencies on the form of notifications with respect to enforcement activities that may affect the other agency's interests, consultations, technical cooperation, exchange of information (subject to the laws of each jurisdiction protecting confidential information), regular meetings and the granting of negative or positive comity considerations. In this regard, it could be said that the intention was to cover the first and second types of information mentioned above (public and agency information) but with a very important caveat related to the full protection of confidential information. As a result, basically only information regarding the launching of enforcement activities -through a notification the respective agency deems appropriate in the particular case- may end up being exchanged. In practice, this scheme has proven not to be a very effective form of cooperation.[22]

Recently Brazil has stated that its cooperation is usually based on the exchange of non-confidential information and general views on the case.[23] In the majority of cases, investigators obtained information through public vehicles, such as agencies' websites, which is regarded as information in public domain and may serve as evidence in the Brazilian proceeding.[24]

Finally, confidential information obtained from a defendant or foreign agency may also serve as evidence within Brazilian proceedings but must be kept confidential within Brazil. Confidential information is treated as such until a final decision is rendered or, depending of its content, may be kept confidential even after a final decision is rendered.

Chile: Of the seven jurisdictions under scrutiny, FNE has signed cooperation agreements with Brazil (October 2008), Peru (August 2006) and Mexico (June 2004). Overall, the areas covered by these agreements, similarly to the Brazilian framework, are related to notification, information sharing and consultation, whenever it is possible and domestic regulations of each party allow it.[25]

---

22. At the post-investigatory phase but at the level of countries, Brazil signed MLATs with Colombia, Peru and Uruguay. Pursuant to a MLAT it is possible to execute a request, for example, for providing confidential and non-confidential information, searches, as well as lifting of (banking, fiscal, telecom and communication) secrecies, and seizure, confiscation, and repatriation of assets. See Brazil's contribution to the OECD World Competition Forum of 2012 at www.oecd.org.
23. Sometimes informal discussions about practical aspects of the investigation are held, such as the difficulties with the service of process abroad and how to overcome bureaucratic hurdles. This cooperation takes place usually by e-mail or telephone (face to face meetings are less frequent because of the long distances usually implicated). The rate of success has varied a lot depending not only of the agency involved but also the particular circumstances of the case. Some cases favor more intense cooperation than others. One successful example of cooperation with the DOJ and DG Comp happened in the course of the investigations of a case relating to the compressors market, in which the three agencies managed to conduct a joint dawn raid. See Brazil's contribution to the OECD World Competition Forum of 2012 at www.oecd.org.
24. It is important to clarify that, pursuant to the principle of free motivated convincement, the Brazilian Courts and the antitrust agency is free to weight evidence and reach a final judgment based on its motivated convincement. Therefore, the decision as to the extent to which both the Courts and the agency will rely on information produced in another jurisdiction falls entirely upon them and is made on a case-by-case basis.
25. See Chile's contribution to the OECD World Competition Forum of 2012 at www.oecd.org.

Chile has recently reported that cooperation initiatives in cartel investigations are not frequent. Unfortunately, FNE has not been requested to cooperate in specific cases of cartel enforcement activities and it has only been informally requested to report on a transnational cartel case once it was made public.[26]

Colombia: The SIC has signed agreements with four of the seven jurisdictions under scrutiny: Ecuador,[27] Panama,[28] Peru and Mexico.

Peru: INDECOPI has signed cooperation agreements[29] with three of the seven jurisdictions under scrutiny: Chile, Colombia and Panama.

Preliminary observations of the way these Latin American cooperation agreements have been implemented

- As some of these seven jurisdictions are relatively young authorities, they are currently developing bonds with other competition agencies and expect to engage in cooperation in the near future. Hence, the majority of these cooperation agreements have not yet been implemented and used in practice.[30]
- Some authorities have said that these agreements have really not been used as the request for cooperation in cartel enforcement has addressed mainly

---

26. FNE participates in regional networks of competition authorities such as the Inter-American Alliance and the *Red Iberoamericana de Competencia*. Even though these networks are useful for the general exchange of views about current developments on competition policy and law across countries, they do not yet play a significant role in the case of cooperation in law enforcement purposes. This is mostly because the latter usually occurs among smaller numbers of authorities (most frequently in a bilateral context) and when, in addition, specific characteristics of sectors investigated are common as well as when trust relationships between agencies are already built.
27. The MoU signed with Ecuador's Ministry of Industries and Productivity covers the following topics: (i) exchange information and documentation, (ii) Execute courses, conferences and workshops in competition and consumer protection issues, (iii) Provide information related to studies and plans especially designed by the parts to optimize the promotion of competition and consumer protection.
28. (ACODECO) (1) Determine general bases for institutional coordination for the establishment of permanent mechanisms of cooperation to ensure economic liberty, promote cooperation among competition authorities, help prevent and identify possible anticompetitive practices, as well as to exchange perspectives, institutional policies, knowledge and experiences. (2) Exchange information and documentation for the efficient compliance of the object of the covenant subject to its reserved nature. (3) Subject to agreement among the Parties, offer courses and conferences in order to publicize the programs developed and disseminate the rights granted by law. (4) Provide information regarding studies, plans and programs especially designed by the Parties, in an individual manner to optimize the defense and promotion of the economic competition. (5) Appoint the personnel responsible for the planning of the promotion and diffusion of each one of the objectives of the Covenant. (6) Report, in case of having any knowledge, the existence of anticompetitive practices among economic agents that can have effects in the markets of the country with which the Covenant is subscribed.
29. Inter-institutional Cooperation Agreements (ICA).
30. Only recently, Indecopi has had the opportunity to identify a possible cross-border cartel and is currently investigating that case. Indecopi expects that the near future will show how international cooperation could be useful in such cases.

authorities investigating the same sector worldwide but not necessarily located geographically in Latin America but elsewhere.[31]
- Authorities have claimed that one of the main obstacles to cooperation is how to handle confidential information due to strict restrictions of civil law jurisdictions (all of the seven are[32]) and the lack of a common definition of confidential information. Indeed, none of these cooperation agreements attempts to define this term. Moreover, there are many cases where the obtained information is not owned by the regulatory body but belongs to the economic agents involved in a particular case, so authorities may need agents' consent for disclosure (waiver). The issue of confidentiality of information gathered in the course of investigation that must be respected by a given competition authority is even more salient when it comes to a civil law jurisdiction, where this definition is not very well defined (particularly in this seven jurisdictions that sanctioned the Oxygen Cases in Latin America). To err on the side of caution, competition authorities tend to define everything that comes from an open investigation as confidential information.[33]
- Another obstacle to cooperation is the asymmetry in antitrust procedures in the countries involved in this exchange. In the case of Mexico, for example, the antitrust procedure is considered to be administrative, with the option of turning into a judicial procedure in case of review, in comparison to other jurisdictions, like the United States or Chile, where the system is prosecutorial. In this way cooperation may be obstructed due to differing information treatment depending on each jurisdiction.

---

31. See the case of Chile in its first participation in an international cartel in 2010, where the Chilean competition system has proven effective in dealing with international cartels. Indeed the first immunity application was submitted by a participant in a transnational cartel case in 2010. The immunity applicant in this case received total immunity and during the procedure before the Competition Tribunal, issues of extraterritorial application of the law have been raised. The Supreme Court's ruling on this case is about to be issued. This experience illustrates very well what is mentioned above. Several jurisdictions were investigating the case at the time proceedings began in Chile, where the case was motivated by a leniency program applicant. Once foreign authorities had taken notice that they were facing an international cartel with probable effects in different jurisdictions, good practice may have suggested that these authorities promoted the initiation of joint investigation. Nevertheless these initiatives depend on the stage of the investigation, the need to preserve confidentiality with respect to the investigative measures to be taken, the existence of an immunity and leniency program and the assurances of the level of protection of the confidential nature of the information and evidence that could be provided. The success of coordinated enforcement against transnational cartels depends on the leading role by some competition authorities more than on anything else.
32. Undoubtedly, civil law jurisdictions (basically Latin American countries) are very cautious in observing strictly procedural rules when ruling on cases. That is to say, the absence of the observance of these rules will mean that when this case is reviewed judicially the whole administrative procedure could be invalidated.
33. Looking beyond Latin America and EU Competition Law enforcement, where the European Competition Network (ECN) is entitled to share information on open cases amongst EU competition authorities, a similar structure can be seen only with Nordic Regional Cooperation, where competition authorities are cooperating in gathering evidence in one country and sharing it with requesting authorities. Attempts to transpose this experience to Latin America have been unsuccessful due to the lack of ad-hoc bilateral cooperation agreements between competition authorities.

- Finally it has to be considered that there is a lack of experience in effectively applying these agreements and, apparently, they have not been tested as to the extent the information exchanged and if it could amount to be considered evidence to be used in court or before a decision making body.[34]

§18.04 CHALLENGES IN STRENGTHENING COOPERATION IN CARTEL CASES FOR THE SELECTED JURISDICTIONS

Despite a number of efforts to strengthen cooperation and the signing of agreements that the seven competition authorities have undertaken, there are important challenges that cause cooperation to remain sub-optimal. Transnational cartel prosecution often refers to jurisdictional issues due to the cross-border character of anticompetitive effects and the problems arising when evidence is located abroad. To be more specific, in investigating cross-border international cartels, competition authorities will have to cooperate more extensively in the process of gathering evidence and establishing the different components of a "regional analysis" of the relevant market as part of the competition analysis that should be always pursued when assessing the impact of anticompetitive practices.[35] The result can be under-enforcement and under-sanctioning of cartels.[36]

[A] Low Levels of Cooperation Between Competition Agencies

There are certain kinds of cooperation that can only take place between certain agencies, depending on the nature of the agreements between their jurisdictions or the substantive standing of the cartel infringement. In this sense, as procedures may be long and cumbersome and vary according to the cooperation instrument involved, insufficient cooperation between agencies may allow some cartels to escape detection completely.

---

34. The Competition Tribunal (TDLC) and the Supreme Court of Chile reasoned on the value of information submitted by the CNDC of Argentina, regarding the earliest case brought against liquid oxygen producers in 2001. The CNDC's decision made references to e-mails that ascertained the fact that executives also discussed activities in Chile. The Supreme Court overturned the TDLC's 2006 condemnatory ruling and asserted that the documents referred to different facts, occurred in an other country, forbidding use of analogy to sustain a similar behavior in Chile.
35. However, one could say that by establishing the infringement of a cartel, being a rule per se, there would be no requirement to assess the effect of that practice and therefore the discussion will rely on the existence of the practice, that is to say, the standard of proof and the law of evidence must be observed in this sense. Further, it should be noted that the definition of "relevant market" in the context of the cartel analysis is based mainly on the "volume of consumption" rather than studying the difference in price, quality and use of products; terms that could create confusion at the moment of defining the relevant market.
36. A priori we have witnessed a relative under-enforcement of domestic competition rules in Latin America, which has also been closely followed by a lack of regional enforcement of competition laws. This is despite efforts at the sub-regional level, such as the case of the Andean Community of Nations and Central American countries.

Several reasons have been identified to explain the lack of regional cooperation between competition authorities, particularly in developing countries. These include, the limited experience and institutional capacity of authorities specially regarding cartel enforcement[37] (most of the agencies in the seven jurisdictions are relatively young), lack of monitoring of the activities of cartels and other anticompetitive practices, formally or informally, and lack of bilateral or multilateral agreements related to other jurisdictions. Added to this, the analysis of information vis-à-vis the legal requirements of each country are a complex and expensive task, especially for countries deficient in strong administrative structures and experiences.

The following is a reality check, throughout the three stages of any investigation, as to whether cooperation of any sort took place between the seven jurisdictions under scrutiny

Preliminary reports suggest that, during the *pre-investigatory phase*, none of these authorities shared leads and background information about the industry and relevant actors, or notified initial investigative actions that could have facilitated later specific investigative requests for assistance. Needless to say, because of the limited scope of their cooperation agreements, there was no coordination of searches, raids, inspections, interviews or any travel by officials to foreign jurisdictions to conduct interviews.

Likewise, at the *investigative phase* of these investigations, with the exception of Argentina and Chile, there was no sharing of critical topics of this phase, such as the state of play of the procedure and the general assessment of the case. Even so, the ICN manual has highlighted that in some investigations of matured agencies, there has been reported travel by officials to foreign jurisdictions to conduct interviews of foreign parties relevant to the investigation and even orders requiring a company to produce certain documents in the possession of its foreign affiliates.[38]

Finally at the *post-investigative phase*, as the court rulings of Chile and Panama became available in 2007 and 2008 respectively, and although these court rulings were contradictory in essence, they were issued at the time when investigations in Peru and Brazil started to take place. To this end, it has been preliminarily reported that none of these jurisdictions, on the one hand, Panama and Chile; and on the other, Peru and Brazil, shared information. For instance, at this stage of post-investigative phase, Panama/Chile Judge rulings could have been part of the pre-investigative phase of Peru's and Brazil's investigations, by formally providing copies of public court filings, even with specific access to non-public information that is not statutorily protected or otherwise entitled to confidential treatment or similar. One positive aspect of the

---

37. Asymmetry in the processes of institutional development: Another important issue to note is that while some authorities apply competition rules with considerable success and experience, other agencies are in a development phase in drafting legislation and establishing effective practices (as in the case of Guatemala). The questionnaire prepared by UNCTAD revealed that the authorities were unable to respond positively to requests for cooperation from other agencies for this reason. Source: "Substantive analysis and case studies of national laws of Costa Rica, Honduras, Nicaragua, El Salvador and Guatemala." UNCTAD Questionnaire for the start of the first phase of the project.
38. "Cooperation between Competition Agencies in Cartel Investigations". International Competition Network (ICN), 2007.

rulings of Panama and Chile resulted in an implicit coordination with other agencies on the filing of charges.

Additional issues regarding the extended scope of application and consequences of these ruling could constitute notifications to foreign agencies of guilty pleas and convictions of foreign corporations as, in the case of the Liquid Oxygen, multinational companies are the issue here. Finally, the aspect related to adoptions of decisions in cases that are also under investigation in other jurisdictions, a quick reality check exercise draws that this was not straightforward.

Issues for further research on the seven cases

Without prejudice of the preliminary ideas established above, it would be desirable to delve into specific items of each jurisdiction in order to rightly assess the viability of each of the challenges presented here. These items may be:

- Investigation powers of each national competition authority involved in the case (exercise of powers to raid premises): The comparison of legal sequencing of the enforcement tools of the authorities that were involved in the cases.
- Existence of immunity or leniency programs during the investigation of the case in the jurisdictions.
- Standard of proof and treatment of evidence at the administrative and judicial levels: the kind of proof that can be exchanged between different agencies in order for judges and administrative bodies involved to assert the existence of cartel conduct.
- Diverse judicial recognition and treatment of indirect evidence (cfr. Cases in Panama and Chile): differences that could be detected between the analysis conducted in the decision making process of judges with regard to the evidence presented or assessed.

[B] Prohibition to Exchange Information in Open Cartel Investigations

The issue of exchanging information has become one of the main obstacles in moving forward to deal with cross-border cartelization. Even in the presence of competition cooperation agreements between authorities, they often refrain from including any provision that can address the problems arising with confidentiality of information.[39] There are a number of factors that may contribute to this fact:

---

39. This is the case in Central American countries where difficulties in implementing agreements between agencies were prescribed to the complete prohibition of exchanging confidential information. For example, the authority of Costa Rica has signed institutional cooperation agreements in competition matters with the Commission for the Defence and Promotion of Competition of the Republic of Honduras, the Institute for Promotion of Competition (Pro Competition) of the Republic of Nicaragua, the Superintendence of Competition of El Salvador and the Authority for Consumer Protection and Competition in Panama, among others. While these agreements are intended to promote free competition in the region, these efforts have been overshadowed by the lack of agreements on the exchange of confidential information between authorities, mainly due to the limitations of their domestic laws on the subject.

- Variations in the definition of "confidential information" between jurisdictions -because of their different legal framework or internal practice of the agency[40]- may mean that similar pieces of information can be shared by some agencies but not others. This has created significant limitations on what type of information may be exchanged (e.g., "agency" information). A vicious circle may also happen: as there is no common definition on confidential information, one agency cannot be aware that another agency is or may be dealing with the same case.[41]
- Apparent lack of engagement in the confidential information exchange. This affects the overall outcome from the beginning when agencies are not willing to consider others' experience and decisions when they have to decide preliminary on the merits of an investigation. And for this decision information exchange is of the essence. The lack of engagement can also be explained by the fact that the agreements between these countries are fairly recent and since their enactment, there have not been cases in which the exchange of confidential information has been needed to solve cross-border anticompetitive practices. This does not explain the fact that agencies seldom engage even informally in order to coordinate its activities not to mention information exchange.
- Confidentiality not only affects the development of investigations but disclosure of confidential information could also harm legitimate interests and rights of defendants, persons or companies under investigation, such as the professional and business secrecy clauses.
- Lack of mutual confidence and trust between the authorities.

Legal viability on exchange of confidential information resulting from Trade agreements?

An important case to note is the Free Trade Agreement (FTA) signed between the Republic of Costa Rica and Canada. This treaty includes a section on competition, which also establishes powers in the exchange of confidential information between authorities when it comes to investigating cases of competition. A possible explanation for this is the nature of the agreement. On the one hand, the FTA is an agreement that includes provisions for promoting trade but also includes provisions regarding tax, budgetary and competition policies. Due to this, both Canada and Costa Rica have an obligation to disclose confidential information, even if the exchange of confidential information is not provided or permitted by national legislation. This same situation has occurred in the signing of bilateral agreements between Central American countries and other nations, applying the national laws of each country on the

---

40. The level of trust with the counterpart and the experience in exchanging confidential information determines the willingness of the authority to engage and cooperate.
41. As one agency states: "this situation is most likely to occur in cases where a company has made leniency applications in both jurisdictions and informed one or the other of this." This may also occur when an informant or whistleblower is willing to let the agencies share the information provided amongst them.

authorization, permit or refusal of the exchange of confidential information between competition authorities in specific cases under investigation.

[C] Modest Developments in Implementing Leniency Programs in the Seven Jurisdictions, with the Exception of Brazil and Chile

With a lack of international cartel enforcement mechanisms to deal with multi-jurisdictional investigations, coupled with the lack of effective domestic leniency programs in Latin American jurisdictions with correspondent and reciprocal immunity between authorities, the international discovery and prosecution of these practices is virtually impossible.[42] In the recent amendments of competition laws in Peru (2008), Mexico (2011) and Brazil (2012), the provisions on leniency programs are more detailed and in line with international standards, common practices and local circumstances. For instance, although Peru's competition Authority (INDECOPI) has not yet had the opportunity to exchange information with other jurisdictions in the framework of a leniency program, the Peruvian Competition Act contains provisions regarding waivers for effective cooperation in the framework of a leniency program that could eventually be applicable to cross-border investigations.[43]

[D] Proper Recognition of the Evidence Gathered Abroad

Often the evidence in open cartel investigations of cross-border nature is located overseas. However, because of a low-level cooperation scheme between agencies and an outright statutory prohibition to reveal confidential information, the case handlers may not have access to evidence located outside their own jurisdiction. Further, there will be very little, if any, general discussion and comparison of notes between investigators of the same cartel in different agencies, thereby undermining the smooth progression of the case and an ideal rebutting of the arguments of the parties.

In addition, if authorities are calculating sanctions, at present the information on turnover that is relevant cannot be exchanged. Between jurisdictions with sanctions against individuals, such as the case of Brazil and Mexico, extradition proceedings are not be possible. If the evidence required for conviction is scattered in different jurisdictions, which cannot share it for legal reasons, or even if one agency has adequate information to carry out a successful prosecution, other jurisdictions that

---

42. Brazil and Chile, notably, have displayed substantive efforts in implementing their novel tools in industries were consumers have been widely affected (e.g., retail fuel distribution and retail pharmacies).
43. Specifically, according to the Peruvian Competition Act (Legislative decree 1034), the first economic agent (person or company) that provides evidence of the existence of an anticompetitive behavior will benefit from an exemption of punishment. The subsequent agents that provide such evidence could benefit by a reduction of their fines if their collaboration is in some way useful. Nevertheless, those provisions have not yet been applied. These provisions do not exclude the applicability of the benefits within the framework of a joint investigation with agencies abroad. See Peru's contribution to the OECD World Competition Forum of 2012.

have also been harmed by the cartel may find themselves unable to impose sanctions because of an inability to obtain the necessary information from other agencies.

If all of these hurdles are solved and authorities can obtain information gathered outside of their respective national borders, this information may not be used and referred to in the case file. Other associated problems are related to witness evidence, due process, the variety of legal standing (civil vs. criminal prosecution of cartels) and the deficient role of the courts.

§18.05 SOME RECOMMENDATIONS TO IMPROVE COORDINATION BETWEEN CARTEL ENFORCERS IN LATIN AMERICA

The following sections look at the different options that competition authorities may take in order to overcome, with relatively good success, the challenges posed in section §18.03.

[A] Improving the Level of Cooperation and Coordination Between Agencies

Having reviewed the specific situation of each of the seven jurisdictions above, the following will examine feasible options to strengthen cooperation between authorities by using the provisions of the cooperation agreements in force and informal coordination and exchange of information:

- *At pre-investigatory phase:* All cooperation agreements that have been signed by the seven jurisdictions do not impede the exchange of public information between the parties. Based on this general, common and cross-cutting feature, a useful recommendation should aim at *"studying possible markets or sectors in which cross-border cartels may be more plausible, making it imperative for cooperating agencies to exchange information as for the elaboration of regional studies to assess the condition of competition"*.[44] The latter will result in

---

44. See Colombia's contribution to the OECD World Competition Forum in 2012. The Colombian delegation suggested that an important step towards joint investigations with another country in order to discover and/or to sanction a cross-border cartel is the launch sectoral regional studies. Colombia suggests that the start of any cooperation activity directed to investigate international cartels should start from the identification of relevant markets susceptible to be subject of anticompetitive conducts. For this to happen, it would be crucial to subscribe to Memorandums of Understanding with neighboring countries, aiming to perform sectoral studies that are geographically expanded to the territory of the countries involved. This mechanism would allow the cooperating countries to have a general knowledge of the agents, their participation and their behavior in the market. The process of gathering information on companies under a certain country's control and surveillance would be the charge of each country, but the parameters of such a process and the analysis of the results would be carried out jointly by the parties. To this end, the regional component of the COMPAL Program, an UNCTAD led initiative, has undertaken a number of activities to strengthen ties between Colombia and Peru.

agencies sharing background information and possibly leads about the industry and relevant actors[45] in order to support investigative actions. These efforts could also facilitate later specific investigative requests for assistance.

Another aspect that has to be strengthened in this preliminary stage is the assessment of information which can be provided by an agency with respect to its ongoing investigations, or decisions already handed, before an other agency decides to formally open a case. The practices involved may have certain commonalities and in this sense it will be very helpful for agencies to discuss, share views and exchange information before formally opening a proceeding. For instance, some cases may need to be disregarded in order to efficiently use the agency's resources if there is difficulty in obtaining the evidence needed in light of the experience of other counterparts. There is a possibility also that discussions with other agencies may lead to the conclusion that the practice sought is not meritorious to initiate enforcement proceedings.

– *At the investigative phase:* The majority of the cooperation agreements mentioned above refer, to some extent, to different degrees of notification of enforcement activities that may affect the other authorities' interests.[46]

Let us assume that the lowest degree of exchange of information this notification could amount to is the public information that is available but not necessarily known to the other agency. However, this type of information may

---

45. The quality of the information these studies can obtain will be determined by the powers the agencies can exercise to obtain industry data.
46. The level of *coordination of enforcement activities* can determine whether a cooperation agreement can be deemed as "1st generation" or "2nd generation". For instance, EU has already concluded so-called "first generation" bilateral cooperation agreements with the United States of America, Canada, Japan and South Korea. The Cooperation Agreement with Switzerland may be qualified as a "second generation" cooperation agreement due to the fact that the scope of the information exchange is broader and information can be exchanged even against the will of the concerned companies and in some cases, outside of a formal investigation. The future agreement between EU-Switzerland (soon to be ratified by the Swiss Parliament) constitutes a new effort in the fight against international cartels and the way the Swiss Competition Commission can be involved in open cartel investigations with its main trading partner, EU. In this regard, under the Cooperation Agreement, the Swiss and the European competition authorities are required to notify each other with respect to their enforcement activities (any application of competition laws by way of investigation or proceedings) if these may affect important interests of the other party of the Cooperation Agreement. In particular, a notification of the other competition authority will occur if undertakings in the jurisdiction of the other authority are involved, if a significant part of the activities took place in the territory of the other party, or if the activities in question involve conduct believed to have been encouraged, required or approved by the other party. To avoid possible conflicts between the parties, the Cooperation Agreement contains non-binding provisions on conflict avoidance (negative comity) and the possibility of requests to initiate enforcement activities (positive comity); see Arts. V and VI of the Cooperation Agreement. The Cooperation Agreement also allows the Swiss and European competition authorities to coordinate their enforcement activities when they pursue enforcement activities in related matters. Particularly, the Cooperation Agreement enables the authorities to coordinate dawn raids and they no longer have to rely on a waiver of a leniency applicant. However, the Cooperation Agreement does not serve as a basis for the Swiss competition authorities to conduct dawn raids on behalf of the European competition authorities and vice-versa. See: "Competition Law Cooperation Agreement EU/Switzerland" David Mamane, Schellenberg Wittmer.

not sufficiently provide a completely detailed "state of play of the procedure or case" and instead provide a "general assessment" of it. It will be necessary, as a result, to increase the leverage to "agency information". In this sense, Brazil's cooperation agreement refers to exchanging information provided that laws on confidential information of each jurisdiction are respected. As general as it appears, it might be possible to have specific domestic laws on Intellectual Property that protect information such as industrial secrets. However, even in this type of legislation, the majority of the jurisdictions under scrutiny provide for the possibility of sharing information overseas, as long as the recipient country has similar measures to protect sensitive information. A priori it seems that if Brazil and Peru have similar provisions in this regard, it may be possible to exchange sensitive information and there will be no violation of any domestic laws.[47] Other items related to contact between agencies through consultations, technical cooperation, regular meetings and also the application of negative or positive comity considerations throughout their enforcement activity can be also fall within this assumption.

- At the post-investigative phase: Besides stressing the importance of formally providing copies of its court filings and of the public information of the official case file to other jurisdictions, they could enter into a specific task-force of uploading, onto a virtual platform, the description of the case, and imposed sanctions and also, whenever possible, the decisions regarding the commencement of ongoing investigation, through points of contact in each country (officials of each agency). The idea being to further determine if an initiated investigation in one country can have a direct and/or indirect impact on a neighboring country (that will also be in connection to the second phase that would trigger specific provisions of the relevant cooperation agreement). In the future, one could foresee an actual cooperation between agencies and eventually the exchange of evidence gathered in each country. Nevertheless, this phase can only be reached once the abovementioned steps are consolidated.[48]

§18.06 STEPS TOWARDS EFFECTIVE EXCHANGE OF INFORMATION IN PARALLEL INVESTIGATIONS

Experience shows that parallel but uncoordinated investigations on concurrent business patterns and actors can be harmful to the effective enforcement and deterrence of

---

47. A recently enacted IP law in Peru named "Personal Data Protection Act" (Act 29733) explicitly provides that cross-border flow of information is conditional on the recipient country having similar measures to those provided in the Act in order to ensure the protection of the information exchanged (Art. 15). This is a minimum guarantee to the owners of the information and to persons or companies under investigation, and therefore it does not constitute a strong constraint to the development of joint activities of cooperation and investigation.
48. Colombia's suggestion before the OECD World Competition Forum and the IGE on Competition Law and Policy of UNCTAD in 2012.

cross-border cartels. The case study between EU and Switzerland is a good example of how detrimental it can be not to have strong cooperation between two economies that are extremely connected, where parties and trade flows are outstanding.

As recent case law shows, if Switzerland had a formal cooperation with the EU, this would have benefited the two parallel investigations carried out separately. This was the case with the Water Management Cartel,[49] where both investigations separately revealed indications and documents suggesting the existence of price-fixing cartels in the EU. There were clear indications and documents concerning the cartels established in Switzerland are to be found in the European investigation. The exchange or transmission of indications and documents concerning the other inquiry would no doubt have facilitated and even accelerated the proceedings[50]

The first "second generation" cooperation agreement on competition cases recently concluded between the EU and Switzerland (pending ratification of their Parliaments) will have far-reaching consequences. The fact that under this agreement it will be possible to exchange information and transmit documents even in cases when the companies concerned do not agree, without a right to appeal, and even outside of a formal investigation, is of significance. Of course, this type of ahead-of-the-curve provision is designed for preparing dawn raid situations, as well as the assessment of multi-jurisdictional leniency applications (i.e., whether to include Switzerland). This is a major change compared to the present status, as well as an extension in comparison with similar cooperation agreements concluded by EU.[51]

Let us examine how the transmission of information without the consent of the undertakings will work under this agreement. The *sine qua non* is that both competition authorities must investigate the same or related conduct or transaction. If this assumption is fulfilled, the following conditions apply to the exchange:

---

49. On December 16, 2008, Comco opened an investigation against several firms active internationally in markets of components for sanitary installations (water management), heating and air-conditioning. The investigation was concluded on May 10, 2010; Comco imposed a penalty of fr.169,000. The decision was not appealed. The parallel procedure was opened in EU but closed in June 2012. See EU Press release at www.europa.eu/rapid/press-release_IP-12-704_en.htm.
50. Two investigations, those concerning air freight and transportation services, are still suspended in Switzerland, while the airfreight investigation in EU has been closed. One may ask why the Swiss proceeding is taking so long and why it could not be wrapped up at more or less the same time as the European Commission's investigation. The reason lies essentially in the impossibility of cooperating with that institution (...). Moreover, when a parallel proceeding is conducted by the European Commission, the Swiss competition authorities, in the absence of formal cooperation, have no way of knowing before that investigation is completed what conduct the EU is going to prosecute and punish (...). Under these conditions, the Swiss competition authorities must await the EU decision in order to determine clearly their jurisdiction and the facts in question, which inevitably makes for lengthy and unsatisfactory proceedings for the companies. Without a cooperation agreement with the EU, there can be no discussion or decision on these key questions, at the beginning or during the course of the procedure. Nor is it possible to coordinate the scheduling of the procedure.
51. For the details of the cooperation agreement, please check the following link: http://eur-lex.europa.eu/LexUriServ/LexUriServ.do?uri=COM:2012:0245:FIN:EN:PDF.

Chapter 18: Regional Coordination in Cartel Investigations   §18.06

- Information already in possession of the competition authority[52]
- Information that contains personal data: Personal data may only be transmitted if the European and Swiss competition authorities investigate the same or related conduct or transaction.[53]
- Information concerning leniency applicants and parties to settlement agreements: The transmission of information is not permitted with regard to information provided by leniency applicants or by parties to a settlement agreement, unless a written consent exists.[54]
- Procedural rights and legal privilege: Information shall not be discussed or transmitted if using the information in question would be prohibited according to the procedural rights and privileges guaranteed under the respective laws of Switzerland or the EU.[55]

A final remark to this agreement is that the Cooperation Agreement does not foresee any additional recourse or right to appeal any of the decisions to transmit information if there is no consent. Nevertheless, the agreement does include limitations with regard to the use of discussed and transmitted information[56] and the sacrosanct

---

52. The exchange is limited to information already in possession of the respective authority. This limitation underlines that the Cooperation Agreement is not a basis for the collection of information solely on behalf of the other foreign authority. Rather, the information qualifying for being shared with the foreign authority must have been collected within the framework and for purposes of domestic proceedings.
53. This limitation also applies if the company concerned consents to the transmission of the information. Swiss law on data protection goes further than some data protection laws of EU Member States, as it also applies to companies and not only to natural persons. The Cooperation Agreement does not regulate this aspect. It must therefore be feared that data provided to the European competition authorities may not be granted the level of personal data protection that meets the standards of the Swiss data protection law.
54. Several uncertainties remain, however. First, a settlement can occur at many stages of a procedure and there seem to be no rules in the Cooperation Agreement on what should happen to information that has been discussed and/or exchanged prior to the settlement. Second, it is unclear whether the initiation of settlement talks itself blocks the discussion or transmission of information, or whether only the signature of the settlement agreement, which may occur much later in the process, will block the information exchange. Third, it also remains unclear whether the information already discussed or transmitted may be used by the competition authorities if, at a later stage of the procedure, the parties conclude a settlement agreement and refuse to consent to an information exchange between the authorities. See: "Competition Law Cooperation Agreement EU/Switzerland" David Mamane, Schellenberg Wittmer.
55. Accordingly, an exchange of information protected by legal professional privilege or affecting a person's right against self-incrimination is not permissible if these rights have not been validly waived. However, the Cooperation Agreement does not seem to preclude the transfer of information subject to specific Swiss blocking statutes, such as the banking secrecy. The question arises whether the data of bank customers qualifies as personal data and thus whether the data transmission should be allowed as long as the competition authorities of the parties are investigating the same or related conduct or transaction. However, in light of the far-reaching consequences such a data transfer may have, a clear and therefore reliable regulation would certainly be necessary.
56. (Article VIII of the Agreement): If a company explicitly consents to the information exchange, the discussed or transmitted information may be used for the purpose of generally enforcing the receiving party's competition laws by its competition authority. If an explicit consent has not been issued, the exchanged information may only be used for the enforcement of the receiving party's competition laws with regard to the same or related conduct or transaction and for the

protection of the exchanged information, which must be kept confidential by the receiving competition authority based on its respective legislation.[57]

§18.07 IMPROVING THE REQUEST OF EVIDENCE ABROAD AND RECOGNITION: ESTABLISHING IDEAS FOR A VICTIM OF AN INTERNATIONAL/REGIONAL CARTEL TO CLAIM PRIVATE/CIVIL DAMAGES LOCALLY

When one competition authority decides to launch an investigation of a cartel already being investigated and needs to gather some evidence abroad, it must trigger specific provisions of already adopted cooperation agreements. Here we are facing an issue called "access to evidence in a truly international context".[58]

Therefore, there could be a scenario where a private actor (claimant) needs to access to files, documents and evidence held by a foreign competition authority in order to claim damages before a domestic civil court. This situation could be the victim of an international cartel with recurrent business pattern in different jurisdictions, such as the liquid oxygen case. Access to evidence may be the deciding element on the question whether the action has any chance of success. In most of the cases, civil

---

purpose defined in the request. Furthermore, no information discussed or transmitted shall be used to impose sanctions on natural persons (Art. VIII paragraph 4 of the Cooperation Agreement). However, it cannot be excluded that the transmitted information, which is used to establish the unlawful behavior, would also result in indirect effects on an individual.

57. In general, the respective information shall not be disclosed to a third party or another authority. However, the confidentiality of the information is by no means granted in an absolute manner: (1) The authorities may, inter alia, disclose information necessary for other companies under investigation to defend themselves within the investigation or insofar as it is indispensable for the exercise of the right of access to documents (Art. IX paragraph 1(b) and (d) of the Cooperation Agreement); and (2) The European Commission may disclose information transmitted by the Swiss competition authority to the competent authorities of the Member States and to the EFTA Surveillance Authority in order to fulfill its information obligations (Art. X paragraph 1 of the Cooperation Agreement).

58. A first aspect is specific to competition law. In Europe, the distinction between *public enforcement and private enforcement* is fundamental because it is based on another distinction, between the role of the specialized authorities and that of the ordinary courts. This difference, however, may be blurred in third States where the ordinary courts intervene in two ways. The American example is the most topical one. Confronted with an international situation, and in order to verify their international jurisdiction, the American courts reason similarly whether confronted with a case brought by the Department of Justice or in a triple-damages action. They consider their substantive jurisdiction under the Sherman Act and, potentially, their personal jurisdiction, exactly as an administrative authority in Europe would do. On the other hand, in Europe, an ordinary court must first verify its international jurisdiction having regard to the solutions of private international law before, in a second stage, considering the applicable law for the substantive issues, which may be a foreign law. This divergence in competition law actions is finally a mere reflection of a *fundamental difference in the conception of private international law*. The European conception, deeply marked by Savigny's influence in the nineteenth century, is not universally recognized. Even though the theory of conflicts of laws has evolved considerably in Europe over the last few decades, the distinction between the court's international jurisdiction and the designation of the applicable law, with the corollary of being able to apply a law other than the law of the forum, remains fundamental. See BASEDOW, Jürgen, FRANCQ, Stéphanie and Laurence IDOT. "International Antitrust Litigation. Conflict of Laws and Coordination". Oxford and Portland, 2012, pp. 279 and 280.

Chapter 18: Regional Coordination in Cartel Investigations §18.07

proceedings will follow a condemnation by a public authority (follow-on action) and might raise the following coordination issues:

- Recognition of the decision of a foreign competition authority by a domestic civil judge. If recognized, what would be the impact of the administrative decision if it is limited according to the territorial reach of the foreign competition authority's power? For determining the exact amount of damages, access to files, documents and evidence held by the foreign competition authority would be needed. In this regard, the administrative decision itself might be sufficient.
- The identification of the applicable law as in international private law rules. However, competition law would demand not only the identification of the law applicable to the damage claims but also a determination of the law applicable to the assessment of the legality of an anticompetitive practice affecting various jurisdictions.[59]

As a result, applicable Law under this reasoning would imply the application of domestic rules for cross-border litigation cases in different stages at the administrative level and judicial level. When referring to the application of domestic rule for international activity, the word "extra territorialism" comes into the discussion. Traditionally, the issue of extraterritoriality application of competition rules has been viewed as a struggle to find the right balance between deterring anticompetitive conduct abroad and the respect for foreign sovereignty.

It would make sense for a country to apply their domestic competition rules to foreign conduct if this conduct has effects in their domestic markets. The question would be how to enforce the foreign activity if the firm is located outside the jurisdiction of the competition authority. In this particular scheme, the competition authority of the incumbent country needs the cooperation and support of the competition authority where the firm is located.

In a world of more convergent competition rules thanks to international "soft law" coming from ICN, OECD and UNCTAD, worldwide competition networks,

---

59. Traditionally, private international law techniques and instruments have been developed separately from the path made by competition authorities to deal with cross-border antitrust investigations against transnational cartels. For instance in Europe, thanks to Regulation 1/2003 and the establishment of the European Competition Network, exchanges of information are well covered. Here, the distinction between public enforcement and private enforcement of competition rules is based on another distinction, between the role of the specialized authorities and that of the ordinary courts. Nonetheless, in a true international cartel investigation beyond EU borders, the distinction between public and private enforcement may be blurred where the ordinary courts often intervene in two ways and the question of access to the file in a public enforcement context challenges the system of exchanges of information among the various competition authorities. Therefore, in dealing with international price-fixing in different jurisdictions, issues such as the rules on jurisdiction or the applicable law and the recognition of decisions at administrative or judicial level are commonly taking place. Hence, it is useful to examine whether certain private international law techniques can be useful to solve issues typically resulting from the international nature of private relationships. The latter may shed light as regards how to improve levels of coordination and sharing of evidence as well as the protection of business secrets and the interplay between administrative and judicial procedures.

jurisdiction problems may be solved by States applying cartel laws extraterritorially. As these States tend to have similar substantive competition laws where all hard-core cartels are punished (although it may vary between administrative and criminal sanctions), extra-territorialism may not be opposed.[60]

For the time being, competition authorities should be coordinating more in terms of being aware the types of cartel case investigations neighboring countries are carrying out. For instance, in the case of oxygen for medical use, major Latin American competition authorities were enforcing locally bid-rigging activities separately, without coordinative enforcement actions. The signal sent to the international bid rigger was clear: *"you could continue performing your collusion in public bidding in a more sophisticated way and you will not be detected in other countries"*.

Limits of international cooperation[61]

In putting in place the recommendations suggested in this section, one should also be aware of the limits of this cooperation. The following summarizes some of them:

- The Uranium Cartel Case was the first time that the Hague Convention was used in the 1970s. However it was a failure when the UK House of Lords and the Canadian Supreme Court refused to provide evidence to the U.S. Rogatory Letters.[62] Nevertheless in 1987, in cases beyond competition law area, such as the Aérospatiale Case of 1987, the Supreme Court judged that use of the procedure put in place by the Commission was merely a possibility and not an exclusive means for ordinarily legal proceedings.
- As a result, international cooperation based on the Hague Convention has not been effective, at least in transatlantic relations. Hence, U.S. courts have

---

60. A problem connected to the application of extraterritorial rules is the different nature (administrative/prosecutorial) of proceedings used by the agencies involved as well as the degrees of progress, at each given point in time, for each of these enforcement systems. The outcomes of judicial and administrative procedures may be different in terms of facts, duration and other features of the cartel conduct. The burden of avoiding potential differences is on the parties collaborating to the investigation, who should not behave strategically before different authorities.
61. See BASEDOW, Jürgen, FRANCQ, Stéphanie and Laurence IDOT. "International Antitrust Litigation. Conflict of Laws and Coordination". Oxford and Portland, 2012, p. 281 and the following.
62. The Hague convention on the taking of evidence abroad in civil or commercial matters of March 18, 1970 (October 1972) was initially intended to overcome differences in conception between the civil law countries and common law countries concerning the collecting of evidence. Under this scheme, two techniques of this convention can be used: (i) letters of Request; and (ii) Diplomatic or consular agents and commissioners (However, Art. 23 makes it possible NOT to respond to pre-trial discovery if the Contracting State makes such a reserve. This reserve, which has been widely used, has greatly contributed to making the United States lose much of its interest in the Convention. See B. ANCEL Le transfer international des informations necessaries a la administrtation de la preuve in L'internationalisat du droit: Melanges en l'honneur de Y Loussoarn (Paris, Dalloz, 1994), L.Collins The Hague Evidence Convention and Discovery: A Serious Misunderstanding, in Essays in International Litigation Oxford, Clarendon Press, 1994 289.

preferred to apply their competition provisions of domestic law unilaterally as they did before the ratification of the Hague Convention.[63]
- When it comes to the recognition and enforcement of foreign judgments around the world,[64] the trend is to allow more recognition and enforcement. (i.e., France has eliminated obstacles to recognize foreign judgments coming from Third countries). However, there are still major differences concerning which model to follow between the U.S. and EU Model.
- Finally, there are open topics that remain for further research. First, the issue related to punitive damages deserves important attention, particularly when these damages are ordered in a number of legal regimes, what would be the implication? Second, there is the relationship between the imposition of administrative penalties ordered by competition authorities and the civil damages ordered by courts.

§18.08 FINAL REMARKS

In Latin America, competition authorities have only limited possibilities to coordinate their enforcement activities, even in the case of parallel cartel investigations with an international reach. Coordination is currently possible only on an informal basis and exceptionally also through the use of waivers issued by leniency applicants coming from Brazilian, Mexican or Chilean jurisdictions. Otherwise, cooperation is strictly limited to the exchange of non-confidential, public information.

The cartel cases prosecuted in the Liquid Oxygen market in several jurisdictions in Latin America have shown how business patterns can be recurrent when competition authorities do not coordinate between each other to tackle these types of cross-border anticompetitive practices and mitigate their impact on local consumers.

It is important to highlight that, despite the importance of informal contacts between enforcers, in none of these cases did formal -or, presumably, even informal- coordination between competition authorities take place. It is unfortunate that effective coordination of enforcement actions and cooperation with respect to sharing of non-confidential information did not occur when Latin American competition authorities were investigating these recurrent, anticompetitive business patterns. Had it been otherwise, when the Argentine authorities detected a problem in this market in 2001

---

63. The only real change lies in the fact that it is more the development of leniency programs and the will of competition authorities to preserve these tools, rather than blocking statues, which cause problems. The recent Rubber Chemicals case, as developed by Maurice Stucke, is most interesting in this respect, illustrating how after the commission decided against a cartel disclosed in a leniency request, the question of access to the leniency applicant's declarations arose in an action for damages in the U.S. The claimant in the triple-damages action was finally refused access to the leniency declarations, after the court proceeded with balancing the competing interests in accordance with the criteria of paragraph 442 Third Restatement.
64. See for instance in U.S.: *Hilton v. Guyot* (1895): good law and often cited as the source of federal law) and EU: 1968 Brussels Convention (replaced by Regulation 44/2001) and Lugano Convention of 1988. See also 1970 Hague Convention and at the recognition and enforcement chapter of the 2005 Hague Convention on choice of Court.

and raided the premises of the companies involved, perhaps some of the actions of these multinational liquid oxygen companies also would have been detected and prevented in other jurisdictions, well before the other competition authorities intervened.

In an ideal world, following the lead by Argentina and Panama, competition authorities in Peru, Chile, Colombia, Brazil could have launched an international investigation on a presumably domestic cartel with regional dimensions. As the above experience shows, this type of cartel investigation has several advantages. Multinational companies have a physical presence, which allows authorities in affected countries to employ traditional investigative instruments, including dawn raids. There is no issue of the service of documents. Exchange of informal information may be enough to trigger follow-on investigations. These enforcement actions may in time be successfully coordinated in different countries and could lead to secure evidence that otherwise could be destroyed. Another great advantage, especially for developing countries, is that it allows them to build up reputation as active anti-cartel enforcers among multinational companies who are normally members of global cartels.

In order to overcome these challenges, younger agencies need more experience in dealing with international cartels. With some exceptions, the prosecution of international cartels is a task undertaken by competition authorities in developed countries because scarcity of resources is a relatively less significant problem. The authorities from these jurisdictions should take a leading role in fighting international cartels, inviting younger authorities to participate, coordinating efforts in joint investigations and enforcement activities.

Recommendations were made in order to improve the level of coordination between authorities. For this, it would need the following actions:

At the enforcing level:

- At the pre-investigatory phase: exchange public information not easily accessible and if trust is fostered, including some types of agency information. There should be mechanisms to be implemented by neighboring agencies such as the creation of a notification system or databases.[65]
- At the investigatory phase: If concurrent business practices are identified thanks to the successful transmission of public and agency information, agencies may be able to discuss and exchange strategies on how to approach the case and eventually coordinate dawn raids in order to avoid the destruction of evidence as such. The experience of EU-Swiss Cooperation Agreement could be the model for this cooperation.

---

65. See Peru's proposal to South American neighboring competition agencies to sign a framework agreement on cartel investigations that includes the setting up of a task-force and the creation of a virtual platform to register competition cases and investigations (Lima Declaration – June 17, 2013). UNCTAD has launched an initiative dedicated to information exchange between competition agencies, as part of its ongoing work on capacity building and international cooperation. The new information platform will facilitate exchange of non-confidential information and serve, in particular, to enhance and aggregate the enforcement capacity of young and developing competition regimes. See: http://www.concurrences.com/Journal/Issues/No-4-2012/UNCTAD-s-collaborative-information?lang=fr.

- At the post-investigatory phase, all administrative rulings should be able to be publishable in the network database.

At the policy level:

- Greater convergence in investigative powers and comparable fines between administrative and criminal sanctions for cartelists.
- Creating and improving the application of leniency programs in Latin American jurisdictions.
- Possible assessment whether some domestic rules could be applicable for cross-border litigation cases in different stages at the administrative level and judicial level.
- Converging the definition of confidential information gathered in open competition cases.
- Cooperation between competition authorities in foreign evidence gathering and striving for a framework for legal recognition as valid evidence in open cases.
- Recognition of administrative rulings in other countries by applying judicial cooperation and international law jurisprudence.

Finally, it all comes to one problem that has impeded competition authorities to investigate cross-border cartels in Latin America: how to handle "public and agency information" when two or more competition authorities decide to investigate the impact of regional or international cartels in their domestic markets?

BIBLIOGRAPHY

Jürgen Basedow, Stéphanie Francq and Laurence Idot, "International Antitrust Litigation Conflict of Laws and Coordination" (Hart Publishing Ltd., 2012).

Maher Dabbah, "International and Comparative Competition Law" (Cambridge University Press, 2010).

Einer Elhauge and Damien Geradin, "Global Competition Law and Economics" (Hart Publishing Ltd., 2011).

Ariel Ezrachi, Hassan Qaqaya, UNCTAD's collaborative information platform (Concurrences N° 4-2012 art. N° 49298, pp. 204-207)

David Gerber, "Global Competition: Law, Markets and Globalization" (Oxford University Press, 2010).

Scott Hammond and Ann O'Brien, "The Evolution of Cartel Enforcement over the last two decades: The US Perspective," in Changes in Competition Policy Over the Last Two Decades, ed. Malgorzata Krasnodebska-Tomkiel (2010).

Mark Le Clair, "Cartelization, Antitrust and Globalization in the US and Europe" (Routledge, 2011).

Chris Noonan, "The Emerging Principles of International Competition Law" (Oxford University Press, 2008).

Anestis Papadopoulos, "The International Dimension of EU Competition Law and Policy" (Cambridge University Press, 2010).

Brendan Sweeney, "The Internationalization of Competition Rules" (Taylor & Francis, 2010).

"Cooperation between Competition Agencies in Cartel Investigations". International Competition Network (ICN), 2007

Best practices for the formal exchange of information between competition authorities in hard-core cartel investigations. OECD, Competition Commission, October 2005

Cross-Border Anticompetitive Practices: The Challenges for Developing Countries and Economies in Transition. Note by the UNCTAD secretariat, 2011

"Modalities and procedures for international cooperation in competition cases involving more than one country". Note by the UNCTAD secretariat, 2013

CHAPTER 19
The Defense of Competition in Mercosur

Eugênia Cristina Nilsen Ribeiro Barza & Marcelo Cesar Guimarães*

§19.01 INTRODUCTION

Regional trade agreements have proliferated since the 1990s, among and between developed and developing countries. MERCOSUR – the Common Market of the South (*Mercado Común del Sur* in Spanish and *Mercado Comum do Sul* in Portuguese) is one of the world's leading economic blocs, representing 72% of South America's land area, 70% of its population and 80% of its gross domestic product.

MERCOSUR was established by the Treaty of Asunción, signed on March 26, 1991, by Argentina, Brazil, Paraguay and Uruguay. On August 12, 2012, Venezuela was officially admitted as full member. The bloc aims to create a common market, which shall involve free movement of goods, services and factors of production between its members, the adoption of a common external tariff and a common trade policy in relation to third States, as well as the coordination of economic and commercial positions in regional and international fora. However, despite some advances, MERCOSUR has so far only reached the stage of an imperfect customs union.

Just as several other regional arrangements, MERCOSUR has also introduced provisions encompassing competition issues, in order to adopt a regional antitrust policy within the bloc. The purpose is to deepen the regional integration, as well as to provide the national antitrust authorities with tools to deal with transnational anticompetitive practices.

This paper aims to analyze the evolution of the antitrust policy in MERCOSUR, from the Treaty of Asunción to the Agreement for the Defense of Competition, highlighting the latest innovations introduced by the latter and the challenges the bloc must face to ensure a regional competition.

---

* The views hereby expressed are exclusively of the author and do not necessarily reflect those of the organizations involved.

§19.02 THE TREATY OF ASUNCIÓN AND THE PROVISIONAL REGULATION OF COMPETITION LAW

The Treaty of Asunción does not state any concrete rule on the defense of competition,[1] although Article 1 refers to the assurance of proper competition between the States Parties as a need to achieve the common market.[2] Besides, the same article requires the commitment by the States to harmonize their legislation in the relevant areas, which is the case of competition, albeit the Treaty does not assert how such harmonization should be made.[3]

Furthermore, the defense of competition is mentioned in Article 4, even though it only indicates general notions on the subject when it disposes of antitrust protection in international trade and within the bloc. It asserts that the States shall ensure equitable trade terms in their relations with third countries through the application of their domestic legislation to punish practices that distort the normal course of trade. In relation to anticompetitive practices within MERCOSUR, there is only a commitment of the States to coordinate their national policies with a view to drafting common rules for trade competition.[4]

Therefore, the Treaty of Asunción has not established general principles or drew the basic lines of competition policy in the bloc, stating that the matter should be treated subsequently by secondary norms of MERCOSUR Law.[5]

The starting point was the Decision of the Council of the Common Market (CCM) No. 01/92, which included on the agenda of the Working Subgroup No. 10 of the Common Market Group (CMG), responsible for the coordination of macroeconomic policies, the comparison between the antitrust legislation of the then four States Parties and the formulation of a proposal for the harmonization of antitrust rules. This led to the Decision CCM No. 21/94, which established the provisional regulation of competition law applicable to companies, ruling the general prohibition of agreements, concerted practices and abuse of dominant position, not encompassing, however, the government monopolies and subsidies. This Decision has also fixed harmonization guidelines, with criteria for defining common rules.[6]

In 1995, the Technical Committee No. 5 was installed, with the function of drafting the legal instruments that are required for the achievement of an antitrust

---

1. MELO, Murilo Otávio Lubambo de. *Defesa da Concorrência no MERCOSUL: Entraves e Soluções Normativas*. Boletim Latino-Americano de Concorrência, n.º 23, September 2007. p. 20.
2. MARQUES, Frederico do Valle Magalhães. *Direito Internacional da Concorrência*. Rio de Janeiro: Renovar, 2006. p. 290.
3. BAGNOLI, Vicente. *Introdução ao Direito da Concorrência: Brasil, Globalização, União Europeia, MERCOSUL, ALCA*. São Paulo: Singular, 2005. p. 214.
4. CUNHA, Ricardo Thomazinho da. *Direito de Defesa da Concorrência: Mercosul e União Europeia*. Barueri: Manole, 2003. p. 182.
5. MARQUES, Frederico do Valle Magalhães. *Supra* p. 291; BAGNOLI, Vicente. *Supra* p. 215.
6. MELO, Murilo Otávio Lubambo de. *Supra* p. 20; CUNHA, Ricardo Thomazinho da. *Supra* p. 185/187.

system within the bloc. Subordinate to the MERCOSUR Trade Commission (MTC), the Technical Committee is composed of a technical body of the States Parties.[7]

Then, given the need to consolidate a competitive environment in the territory of MERCOSUR and to ensure the free market access and the balanced distribution of the economic integration process, the CCM adopted the Decision No. 18/96, which approved the Protocol for the Defense of Competition of MERCOSUR, the so-called Fortaleza Protocol.

§19.03 THE PROTOCOL FOR THE DEFENSE OF COMPETITION OF MERCOSUR (FORTALEZA PROTOCOL)

The Protocol for the Defense of Competition of MERCOSUR established a common antitrust statute, which points out the outlines of the anticompetitive conducts in the integrated space, assuring competitive conditions in the market, and harmonizes the treatment of this matter.[8]

According to the Protocol, the implementation of its provisions should be carried out by the CCM and the Committee for the Defense of Competition (CDC), both having the legal authority to impose, at the administrative level, the antitrust rules. Instituted by the Protocol, the aforementioned Committee is an intergovernmental institution composed of the national antitrust authorities. In addition, those national authorities should also work together with the CCM and the CDC through the application of their respective legislation, the participation in the procedures set out in the Protocol for the investigation of illicit practices and the execution of the penalties imposed by the regional institutions.[9]

The rules of the Fortaleza Protocol are applicable to acts committed by individuals or juridical persons, public or private, or other entities, which have as their object or effect, regardless of fault, the limitation, restriction, falsification or distortion of competition within MERCOSUR and which affect trade between States Parties. Therefore, two conditions are required for the application of the Protocol: the intention or the production of anticompetitive effects and the damage caused to the market.[10] On the other hand, each State Party has exclusive competence in applying its own antitrust law when the anticompetitive practices are located only in its territory and whose effects are restricted to it.

The Fortaleza Protocol defines the illicit conducts and establishes the procedure for the investigation and the repression of the anticompetitive practices. Besides, it sets out the sanctions, the possibility of adopting commitment decisions and the dispute settlement mechanisms.

---

7. OLIVEIRA, Gesner; RODAS, João Grandino. *Direito e Economia da Concorrência*. São Paulo: Revista dos Tribunais, 2013. p. 351; MELO, Murilo Otávio Lubambo de. *Supra* p. 20.
8. OLIVEIRA, Gesner; RODAS, João Grandino. *Supra* p. 351/352.
9. CUNHA, Ricardo Thomazinho da. *Supra* p. 207/210; BAGNOLI, Vicente. *Supra* p. 216.
10. It should be noted that, unlike what the European Antitrust Law states, it is not enough that the act is potentially onerous to the market, regardless of the results produced (ANDRADE, Maria Cecília. *A Defesa da Concorrência no MERCOSUL e o Protocolo de Fortaleza*. Boletim Latino-Americano de Concorrência, n.° 12, July 2001. p. 46).

However, despite being a milestone in the establishment of an antitrust protection within MERCOSUR, only Paraguay and Brazil ratified the Protocol. It only entered into force between those countries, although it has never been applied. Thus, the Fortaleza Protocol represents another example of the "normative hypertrophy" which characterizes MERCOSUR, where several acts have been adopted over the years, but few of them have actually entered into force.[11]

Moreover, the Protocol has numerous limitations. For example, it was silent on two key issues for a regional antitrust system: the control of concentrations between undertakings and the State aid control.[12]

Another point that prevented the success of the Fortaleza Protocol was the lack of a stabilized antitrust culture in the region. The emergence of a competition law is new in the States Parties of MERCOSUR, particularly Uruguay and Paraguay, which only adopted an antitrust legislation after the Protocol was signed (in 2007 and 2013, respectively).[13]

Finally, the difficulties involved in the consolidation of MERCOSUL constituted a major obstacle to the implementation of a regional competition law. The institutional framework of MERCOSUR hinders the establishment of a regional antitrust system, given the absence of supranational authorities to effectively apply an antitrust policy and the non-existence of the precedence of the regional norms over the national ones. In this sense, the distribution of competences stated by the Fortaleza Protocol was always criticized, since it would only have been compatible with a supranational arrangement, where some powers are transferred from the States to a community institution, such as in the European Union. In an intergovernmental integration, however, a cooperative and consensual institution (in the case of MERCOSUR, the CDC) is entrusted with the application of the antitrust rules, which encumbers the enforcement of the regional competition law.[14]

---

11. BOTTA, Marco. *The Cooperation between the Competition Authorities of the Developing Countries: Why it does not Work? Case Study on Argentina and Brazil*. Competition Law Review, volume 5, issue 2, July 2009. p. 169.
12. The protocol only mentions each of these subjects in programmatic norms, which impose on the States Parties the commitment to adopt common standards on these matters within two years. However, this has never been fulfilled (JAEGER JÚNIOR, Augusto. *Direito Internacional da Concorrência: Entre Perspectivas Unilaterais, Multilaterais, Bilaterais e Regionais*. Curitiba: Juruá, 2008. p. 363/364).
13. OLIVEIRA, Gesner; RODAS, João Grandino. *Supra* p. 353; NAVEGA, Antonio Poli; SOUZA, Luciano Inácio de; SILVEIRA, Paulo Burnier da. *Direito da Concorrência*. In RIBEIRO, Elisa de Sousa (ed.). Direito do MERCOSUL. Curtiba: Appris, 2013. p. 311/314. Nevertheless, this argument is not unanimously accepted as a problem for the success of the Fortaleza Protocol. According to some scholars, regional antitrust may contribute to the establishment and the effectiveness of the national systems (CUNHA, Ricardo Thomazinho da. *Supra* p. 163). Besides, regional competition authorities may be more effective in imposing remedies in comparison to the national ones (FOX, Eleanor. *Competition, Development and Regional Integration: in Search of a Competition Law Fit for Developing Countries*. In DREXL, Josef et al. (ed.). Competition Policy and Regional Integration in Developing Countries. Cheltenham: Edward Elgar, 2012. p. 288).
14. AMARO, Zoraide Sabaini dos Santos. *A Estrutura Orgânica do Mercosul: Direito de Concorrência no Processo de Integração*. Rev. Jur., Brasília, v. 9, n. 85, jun./jul. 2007. p. 33; NAVEGA, Antonio Poli; SOUZA, Luciano Inácio de; SILVEIRA, Paulo Burnier da. *Supra* p. 307, 314/315; MARQUES, Frederico do Valle Magalhães. *Supra* p. 296.

Therefore, despite the adoption of the Fortaleza Protocol seemed to indicate that MERCOSUR would institutionalize a regional antitrust system, the years following its adoption were marked by inactivity, both by the States Parties and the regional institutions. In addition to the aforementioned issues, it contributed significantly to this scenario the economic situation in the region, greatly affected by the global crisis of the period, in particular the Asian financial crisis of 1997–1998 and the subprime mortgage crisis of 2007–2010. Thus, during the period, the States Parties changed their objectives and priorities and intensified protectionism, putting regional antitrust in second place.[15]

§19.04 NEW DIRECTIONS FOR THE MERCOSUR ANTITRUST POLICY

[A] The Antecedents

Despite the failure in the implementation of the Fortaleza Protocol, the process to ensure the defense of competition in MERCOSUR has continued to move forward, albeit slowly, but in a different way from that originally established by the Protocol. The vertical top-down regulation, stated by the Protocol, has been replaced by a process characterized by the horizontal and the vertical bottom-up flows, in which subnational authorities have been recognized by the States Parties as legitimate initiatives beyond the traditional diplomatic channels. Hence, the competition policy has been carried out by subnational agents (the national antitrust authorities), instead of the usual ones (the state diplomatic structures).[16] Besides, MERCOSUR starts following the current international trends in the regulation of cross-border anticompetitive practices, which is the improvement of international cooperation.[17]

This new direction in the MERCOSUR antitrust policy began with the bilateral cooperation agreement, signed by Argentina and Brazil in October 2003,[18] with the objective to exchange non-confidential information, but also technical cooperation, between their national competition authorities.[19]

Subsequently, the standard introduced by the abovementioned agreement has been extended to MERCOSUR, in order to overcome the shortcomings of the Fortaleza Protocol. In this sense, the Decisions CCM Nos. 4/2004 and 15/2006 were adopted,

---

15. CREUZ, Luis Rodolfo Cruz e. *A Construção da Defesa da Concorrência no MERCOSUL*. Univ. Rel. Int., Brasília, v. 9, n. 1, jan./jun. 2011. p. 88.
16. CREUZ, Luis Rodolfo Cruz e. *A Construção da Defesa da Concorrência no MERCOSUL: Uma Perspectiva Construtivista – Cooperação e Interesses nas Relações Internacionais*. Master's Thesis, UNICAMP, Campinas, 2010. p. 155/156. Retrieved February 17, 2016, from < http://www.bibliotecadigital.unicamp.br/document/?code=000774937 >.
17. HEINEMANN, Andreas. *La Nécessité d'um Droit Mondial de la Concurrence*. Revue Internationale de Droit Économique, 3/2004, t. XVIII, 3. p. 293/324. p. 299; ARANOVICH, Tatiana de Campos. *Inovações na Cooperação Jurídica Internacional para o CADE*. Revista de Defesa da Concorrência, n.° 1, May 2013. p. 125/126; JAEGER JÚNIOR, Augusto. *Supra* p. 48/49, 247; OLIVEIRA, Gesner; RODAS, João Grandino. *Supra* p. 345.
18. The agreement is in full force, since both Argentina and Brazil have ratified it, in 2010 and 2014, respectively.
19. CREUZ, Luis Rodolfo Cruz e. *Supra* p. 149/150; BOTTA, Marco. *The Role of Competition Policy in the Latin American Regional Integration: A Comparative Analysis of Caricom, Andean*

concerning the cooperation between the States Parties' national antitrust authorities, which marks a turning point in the defense of competition in MERCOSUR.

The Decision CCM No. 4/2004 approved the Memorandum of Understanding (MOU) on Cooperation between the Antitrust Authorities of the States Parties of MERCOSUR for the enforcement of their national competition laws. This instrument sets out the basic guidelines for cooperation between the States Parties' competition authorities, taking for granted that cooperation and coordination can be much more effective than individual actions taken by each authority individually.[20]

The main purpose of the MOU is to promote cooperation (both enforcement and technical) between the antitrust authorities of the States Parties and to ensure that they give careful consideration to one another's important interests in the application of their competition laws.

In this way, each State Party shall notify the other State(s) Party(ies) with respect to the enforcement activities of the MOU (specified in Article II.2), identifying the nature of the practices under investigation and the legal provisions concerned. Besides, the States Parties may share information that will facilitate the effective detection of anticompetitive practices and the enforcement of their antitrust laws. In addition, if a State Party believes that anticompetitive practices carried out in the territory of another State Party adversely affect its important interests, the first may request that the second's competition authority initiate the cooperation procedures provided by the MOU.

However, neither State Party is required to communicate information to the other States Parties if such communication is prohibited by the laws of the State possessing the information or would be incompatible with that State's important interests. Thus, the MOU is limited to the exchange of non-confidential information.

Two years later, the Decision CCM No. 15/2006 approved the MOU on Cooperation between the Antitrust Authorities of the States Parties of MERCOSUR for the control of concentrations between undertakings at the regional level. Adapting the provisions of the 2004 MOU to the cross-border control, the instrument established a system of exchange of information and consultation in that field, with the aim of preventing anticompetitive effects in the region, implementing a more efficient procedure and promoting legal certainty for the parties involved.

Both MOU entered into force in June 2012, after its incorporation into the States Parties' legal orders.[21] Despite seeking to achieve the general objectives of cooperation already stated by Article 30 of the Fortaleza Protocol, the MOU's went beyond, since the Protocol emphasizes technical cooperation and yet in a merely superficial manner.

Community and Mercosur. IX Annual Conference of the Euro-Latin Study Network on Integration and Trade (ELSNIT). "Revisiting Regionalism", St. Gallen, October 21–22, 2011. p. 10. Retrieved February 17, 2016, from < http://www10.iadb.org/intal/intalcdi/PE/2012/09801a05.pdf >.

20. NAVEGA, Antonio Poli; SOUZA, Luciano Inácio de; SILVEIRA, Paulo Burnier da. *Supra* p. 310.
21. Retrieved February 20, 2016, from MERCOSUR website < http://gd.mercosur.int/SAM/GestDoc/pubweb.nsf/Normativa?ReadForm&lang = ESP&id = 8B6A494E760DF229032576 0F0048B4CC >; < http://www.mercosur.int/innovaportal/v/1038/2/innova.front/decisiones_2006 >.

The MOU's, for their part, focus precisely on cooperation, concerning both technical and enforcement, representing a breakthrough in the defense of competition in MERCOSUR.[22]

[B] The Agreement for the Defense of Competition of MERCOSUR

Consolidating the aforementioned trend in the enhancement of international competition cooperation between the national antitrust authorities, the CCM adopted the Decision No. 43/2010, which approved the Agreement for the Defense of Competition of MERCOSUR and repealed the Fortaleza Protocol.

Therefore, the project to create a regional antitrust system, with an intergovernmental institution (the CDC), competent to identify anticompetitive practices and to determine the appropriate sanctions, was left behind.[23]

Instead, a more realistic plan was adopted, focusing on the establishment of a network between the national antitrust authorities to improve the cooperation on investigations concerning cross-border anticompetitive practices. In this sense, the mechanisms set up by the former MOU were institutionalized and strengthened.

The rules which defined the illicit conducts and established the procedure for the investigation and the repression of the regional anticompetitive practices, stated by the Fortaleza Protocol, were replaced by a more direct and coherent consultation model. Furthermore, it was included a chapter on the coordination of enforcement activities related to a specific case and another on the joint activities of technical assistance for the development, adoption, implementation and enforcement of competition laws and policies.[24]

Regarding the provisions of the MOU's, besides the mechanisms of notification, technical assistance and exchange of non-confidential information, the Agreement has introduced a framework of consultation, which represents a significant advance compared to the previous system. Indeed, while under the system of the MOU's the duty of notification was on the national competition authority conducting an investigation which could affect the jurisdiction of other State Party, under the new system of consultation the procedure is triggered by the authority whose State Party is affected by the investigation conducted outside its jurisdiction. Therefore, unlike the previous system, which was rarely carried out due to the indifference of the national authorities conducting the investigation to transmit information to the other States Parties, the mechanism of consultation should be more successful, given that the State Party

---

22. UNIÃO. Procuradoria Federal Especializada junto ao CADE. Nota Técnica GTI/002/2010, August 10, 2010. *Comentários à Proposta de Alteração do Protocolo de Fortaleza*. Draftsmen: Maria Rosa Guimarães Loula (CADE's Federal Attorney) and Tatiana de Campos Aranovich (Senior Executive Service). p. 4; CREUZ, Luis Rodolfo Cruz e. *A Construção da Defesa da Concorrência no MERCOSUL: Uma Perspectiva Construtivista – Cooperação e Interesses nas Relações Internacionais*. p. 154.
23. UNIÃO. Procuradoria Federal Especializada junto ao CADE. *Supra* p. 3, 6.
24. CREUZ, Luis Rodolfo Cruz e. *Há Novos Ventos na Defesa da Concorrência no Mercosul.* Revista Consultor Jurídico, September 15, 2011. Retrieved February 22, 2016, from < http://www.conjur.com.br/2011-set-15/novos-ventos-defesa-concorrencia-ambito-mercosul >.

directly affected by an anticompetitive practice investigated outside its jurisdiction has the competence to initiate the procedure.[25]

In this light, the Agreement recognizes the exclusive competence of the national antitrust agencies for the defense of competition in MERCOSUL and foresees the elimination of cross-border anticompetitive practices through the enforcement of national antitrust regulations. Although it does not define the prohibiting behaviors, such as the Fortaleza Protocol, the Agreement enounces them in a general way, stating that these conducts must be qualified in accordance with the national antitrust norms (Article 2, "c" and "d").[26]

Article 3 of the Agreement provides that each State Party has exclusive competence to regulate not only the anticompetitive practices carried out in whole or in substantial part in its territory, but also those practices performed in the territory of another State Party which produce or may produce effects on its competition. Thus, besides the territorial principle, the Agreement incorporates the extraterritorial application of the antitrust laws, in accordance with the international trends in this matter, as well as with the States Parties' national legislation (except the Venezuelan one).[27]

However, despite the aforementioned exclusive competence of national antitrust authorities, it should be noted that the Technical Committee No. 5, installed in 1995, was retained as an active body in the new procedure, being competent to interpose an offer or request for consultation, to make notifications and to intervene in different matters of interpretation or execution of the Agreement.[28]

Concerning the procedures, Article 6 provides that either national antitrust authority may request for consultations regarding any matter relating to the Agreement, regardless of prior notification, through the form sets out in the Annex to the Agreement, in which the party shall indicate the object and the reasons for the request. In addition, each competition authority shall consult within ninety days, although this period may be reduced in case of urgency or deadline for the use of information. Despite the fact that the consultation procedure does not limit its discretion, the requested authority shall give careful consideration to the views expressed by the other authority, in accordance with the purposes of the Agreement, especially the promotion of international cooperation and the respect for negative and positive comity.[29]

---

25. BOTTA, Marco. *The Role of Competition Policy in the Latin American Regional Integration: A Comparative Analysis of Caricom, Andean Community and Mercosur.* p. 11/12.
26. SUÑÉ, Natasha. *Mercosur Competition Defence Rule.* ZEI Regional Integration Observer, vlume 5, issue 3, December 2011. p. 5.
27. In Brazil, Art. 2 of Law No. 12.529/2011; in Argentina, Art. 1 of Law No. 25.156/1999; in Uruguay, Art. 2 of Law No. 18.159/2007; in Paraguay, Art. 3 of Law No. 4.956/2013. Venezuela incorporates only the territorial principle, as provided by Art. 4 of its antitrust act (*Ley para Promover y Proteger el Ejercicio de la Libre Competencia*, from 1992).
28. SUÑÉ, Natasha. *Supra.*
29. INTER-AMERICAN DEVELOPMENT BANK. *Latin American and Caribbean Regional Competition Agreements.* Document written for Inter-American Development Bank by consultant Luis Diez Canseco, under the supervision of Mario A. Umaña and Ignacio de Leon, for use in discussions at the 11th meeting of the OECD-EDB Latin American and Caribbean Competition Forum, held on September 3–4, 2013, in Lima, Peru. p. 7. Retrieved February 22, 2016, from < http://www.oecd.org/officialdocuments/publicdisplaydocumentpdf/?cote = DAF/COMP/LA CF(2013)5&docLanguage = En > .

Moreover, the antitrust authority of a State Party may express interest to another State Party's competition authority in the coordination of their enforcement activities in a specific case, subject to the competition laws of both jurisdictions (Article 14). In this context, when they identify that their enforcement activities may generate conflicting decisions, the States Parties shall use its best efforts to provide a solution to the problems arising therefrom, albeit such coordination does not limit the discretion of the Parties (and therefore does not eliminate legal uncertainty).

The Agreement also provides that the States Parties must work together in technical assistance related to competition law enforcement and policy. These activities include knowledge and information sharing, training purposes at one another's competition agencies, participation of competition agency personnel as lecturers or consultants at events relating to antitrust and exchanges of competition agency personnel. It is also stated that States Parties' competition authorities shall exchange legal doctrine, case law and public market studies, information on antitrust enforcement and any possible reform related to competition issues. The objective of these activities is to facilitate the effectiveness of competition law enforcement and to promote a better understanding of the legal system of the States Parties, in order to establish a regional culture of competition.

It should be noted that the technical cooperation must be carried out by Brazil, whose system of defense of competition is the most advanced among the members of MERCOSUR. As previously mentioned, the other States Parties' antitrust systems are incipient, with laws which often still serve as government instruments to control the distribution and prices.[30]

On the other hand, the Brazilian system has developed greatly in the last years. The Brazilian antitrust authority (CADE) has speeded up the time of merger review in order to focus on cartel investigations and demonstrated independence from the executive branch in several important cases,[31] assuming a prominent role among antitrust agencies worldwide.[32] Therefore, Brazilian experience should be shared with the other States Parties to help them to also advance in this matter.

Furthermore, Article 20 of the Agreement states that each national antitrust authority shall endeavor to notify the other States Parties' competition agencies with respect to enforcement activities that: (a) are relevant to enforcement activities of another Party; (b) may adversely affect another Party's important interest; (c) involve restrictions on competition which are liable to have a direct and substantial effect in the territory of another party; or (d) concerns anticompetitive acts or concentrations between undertakings taking place principally in the territory of another party. Insofar as possible, such notification should be made at the early stages of the process, in order that the notified Party may give its opinion.

---

30. CUNHA, Ricardo Thomazinho da. *Supra* p. 127; INTER-AMERICAN DEVELOPMENT BANK. *Supra* p. 8.
31. BOTTA, Marco. *The Cooperation between the Competition Authorities of the Developing Countries: Why it does not Work? Case Study on Argentina and Brazil.* p. 172, 176.
32. CARVALHO, Vinícius Marques de; RAGAZZO, Carlos Emmanuel Joppert (ed.). *Defesa da Concorrência no Brasil: 50 Anos.* Brasília: Conselho Administrativo de Defesa Econômica – CADE, 2013. p. 171/178.

Nevertheless, neither national competition authority is required to communicate information and confidential data to the other Parties if such communication is prohibited by the laws of the Party possessing the information or would be incompatible with that Party's important interests or governmental policies. Besides, any information provided under the Agreement is considered confidential and will only be used by the receiving competition authority for the purpose of the effective enforcement of the antitrust law, unless otherwise specified.

Additionally, Article 29 states that nothing in the Agreement shall prevent the States Parties from seeking or providing mutual assistance under the terms of other agreements, treaties, arrangements or practices between them or other States or regional arrangements. Thus, in parallel with the treatment of the matter at the regional level, the States Parties and MERCOSUR itself may conclude cooperation agreements with other States or regional arrangements, which could even contribute to ensure the competition in the bloc.

Finally, Article 30 provides that the Agreement shall enter into force thirty days after the date of deposit of the last instrument of ratification by the States Parties of MERCOSUR. Since only Argentina and Uruguay have ratified the Agreement (in 2011 and 2014 respectively), the new competition framework within MERCOSUR is not yet into force.[33] However, both in Brazil and in Paraguay the ratification process is already under way[34] and it is expected therefore that the Agreement will soon be an effective instrument for the defense of competition in MERCOSUR.[35]

[C]   **A Review of the Agreement for the Defense of Competition of MERCOSUR and the Challenges of Cooperation Within the Bloc**

Despite the innovations introduced by the Agreement for the Defense of Competition, some scholars are criticizing it. In this way, they argue that, repealing the Fortaleza Protocol, the new instrument hinders the establishment of an antitrust protection within MERCOSUR. Even though the Technical Committee No. 5 has been retained, important provisions from the Protocol were suppressed, such as the programmatic norm which imposed the commitment to the adoption of common standards on control of concentrations between undertakings. Thus, being shorter and simpler than the

---

33. Retrieved February 26, 2016, from MERCOSUR website < http://www.mercosur.int/t_ligaenmarco.jsp?contentid = 4824&site = 1&channel = secretaria > .
34. Retrieved February 26, 2016, from the Chamber of Deputies of Brazil website (< http://www.camara.gov.br/proposicoesWeb/fichadetramitacao?idProposicao = 947629 >) and from the Chamber of Senators of Paraguay website (< http://sil2py.senado.gov.py/formulario/VerDetalleTramitacion.pmf?q = VerDetalleTramitacion%2F105026 >).
35. Regarding Venezuela, in accordance with Art. 3 of the Protocol of its accession to MERCOSUR, the absence of ratification by that State Party will not prevent the Agreement from entering into force between the other four Parties of the bloc. In consulting the Venezuelan National Assembly website, nothing has been found on the ratification of the Agreement by that country (< http://www.asambleanacional.gob.ve/ > , February 26, 2016).

Protocol, the Agreement is limited to settle a framework for cooperation and coordination between the States Parties' competition authorities and does not seek to harmonize the national antitrust laws.[36]

However, one major argument against this criticism is that the failure in the implementation of the Fortaleza Protocol was mainly due to the complex procedure it established. As previously stated, the framework intended by the Protocol was not suitable to an intergovernmental arrangement, as is the case with MERCOSUR. Indeed, the Protocol would only become effective if the bloc was endowed with a supranational authority. Thus, the adoption of the Agreement was beneficial, since it only sets out a cooperation network between the national antitrust authorities, in order to overcome the political and cultural barriers and to reduce the structural and organizational obstacles.[37]

The Agreement, then, adopts a more pragmatic view and introduces a system less ambitious and more consistent with the reality of the bloc. It is assumed that the challenges MERCOSUR must face to ensure a regional competition should be dealt with gradualism, flexibility and equilibrium.[38] Hence, although a deeper antitrust regional system, such as provided by the Fortaleza Protocol, would be very desirable, it is believed that the Agreement is more appropriate for the current reality of the bloc.

However, indeed, the Agreement fails not to introduce mechanisms for the harmonization of national antitrust legislation and policies, which is paramount to the safeguard of competition within MERCOSUR. To achieve this goal, it is suggested, for example, a systematic review of the national competition legislation and case law, in order to identify the basic principles and the degree of convergence and divergence between them.[39]

Furthermore, it is undeniable that the achievement of the cooperation under the Agreement will be an arduous task, and many challenges must be overcome. As already mentioned, the absence of a stabilized antitrust culture in the region and the asymmetries between the States Parties' competition laws lead to a lack of mutual confidence between the authorities, which greatly hinders the cooperation.[40]

Besides, the lack of contacts between the officers of the national competition authorities is another problem. In fact, the meetings within the international conferences concerning antitrust law are often the only opportunity for that dialogue, and yet only a few number of commissioners participate in these events. To make matters worse, some States Parties do not have an officer competent to keep international

---

36. SILVEIRA, Paulo Burnier da. *Le Contrôle des Concentrations Transnationales*. Paris: l'Harmattan, 2013. p. 166/167.
37. CREUZ, Luis Rodolfo Cruz e. *Regulação da Defesa da Concorrência no Mercosul*. Instituto Brasileiro de Estudos de Concorrência, Consumo e Comércio Internacional (IBRAC), October 18, 2011. Retrieved February 27, 2016, from < http://www.ibrac.org.br/Noticias.aspx?id = 1089 >.
38. SUÑÉ, Natasha. *Supra*.
39. MELO, Murilo Otávio Lubambo de. *Supra* p. 31/32.
40. BOTTA, Marco. *The Cooperation between the Competition Authorities of the Developing Countries: Why it does not Work? Case Study on Argentina and Brazil*. p. 172/173. The author discusses the relationship between Argentina and Brazil, arguing that despite their antitrust authorities did establish an informal and sporadic cooperation, these contacts have never been crucial for the resolution of a case investigated by both States.

relations with other authorities (such is the case of CADE's International Unit, in Brazil).[41]

In this context, the Agreement provides for technical cooperation to solve these very kinds of problems. Thus, it aims to stimulate an exchange of knowledge and experiences between the States Parties' antitrust authorities to strengthen the confidence and the dialogue within the bloc.

Moreover, the role of the Technical Committee No. 5 as an intermediary between the parties in the consultation and notification procedures should also be criticized. Actually, the Agreement only introduces a bureaucratic mediator in the dialogue between the States Parties' antitrust authorities, which is contrary to the aims of expediting and simplifying the cooperation in the region. Instead, the Committee should have been entrusted with the task of organizing and convening regular meetings of the national competition authorities, in order to improve the institutional dialogue within MERCOSUR.[42]

Lastly, it should be emphasized the limitations of the Agreement, particularly relating to the restriction of the exchange of confidential information. In fact, as previously mentioned, the exceptions are so numerous and so vague (prohibition by national law or incompatibility with the State Party's relevant interests or governmental policies) that the only exchangeable information is that already public. In this context, it is argued that even in criminal procedure, in which there is a more extensive list of individual rights, there are already agreements for exchange of confidential information.[43] Thus, a great opportunity was lost to deepen even further the antitrust cooperation in the bloc.

§19.05 CONCLUSION

In the context of the defense of competition in MERCOSUR, the Agreement for the Defense of Competition, adopted by the Decision CCM No. 43/2010, consolidates the trends that were taking shape during the 2000s. Therefore, the system provided by the Fortaleza Protocol was replaced with a scheme in which the States Parties' antitrust authorities were recognized as the legitimate agents to carry out the competition policy within the bloc. In this sense, the Agreement adopts a more pragmatic view and introduces a system less ambitious and more consistent with the reality of the bloc, focusing on strengthening cooperation mechanisms.

Thus, despite its imperfections and all the challenges MERCOSUR must face to establish an effective cooperation between the States Parties, the Agreement will surely promote an enhancement of the competition in the bloc. In fact, it may even be an intermediate tool to create an environment where a deeper antitrust system is feasible.

Ultimately, the Agreement may increase the productivity, the efficiency and the competitiveness of the States Parties of MERCOSUR, which will contribute to the

---

41. BOTTA, Marco. *The Cooperation between the Competition Authorities of the Developing Countries: Why it does not Work? Case Study on Argentina and Brazil.* p. 173/175.
42. UNIÃO. Procuradoria Federal Especializada junto ao CADE. *Supra* p. 10.
43. *Ibid.* p. 11.

region's integration into the world economy and to the improvement of economic and social development.

BIBLIOGRAPHY

Amaro, Zoraide Sabaini dos Santos. *A Estrutura Orgânica do Mercosul: Direito de Concorrência no Processo de Integração.* Rev. Jur., Brasília, v. 9, n. 85, pp. 20–39, jun./jul. 2007.

Andrade, Maria Cecília. *A Defesa da Concorrência no MERCOSUL e o Protocolo de Fortaleza.* Boletim Latino-Americano de Concorrência, n.° 12, July 2001. p. 45/55.

Aranovich, Tatiana de Campos. *Inovações na Cooperação Jurídica Internacional para o CADE.* Revista de Defesa da Concorrência, n.° 1, May 2013. p. 124/148.

Bagnoli, Vicente. *Introdução ao Direito da Concorrência: Brasil, Globalização, União Europeia, MERCOSUL, ALCA.* São Paulo: Singular, 2005.

Botta, Marco. *The Cooperation between the Competition Authorities of the Developing Countries: Why it does not Work? Case Study on Argentina and Brazil.* Competition Law Review, volume 5, issue 2, July 2009. p. 153/178.

Botta, Marco. *The Role of Competition Policy in the Latin American Regional Integration: A Comparative Analysis of Caricom, Andean Community and Mercosur.* IX Annual Conference of the Euro-Latin Study Network on Integration and Trade (ELSNIT). "Revisiting Regionalism", St. Gallen, October 21–22, 2011. Retrieved February 17, 2016, from < http://www10.iadb.org/intal/intalcdi/PE/2012/0980 1a05.pdf > .

Carvalho, Vinicius Marques de; Ragazzo, Carlos Emmanuel Joppert (ed.). *Defesa da Concorrência no Brasil: 50 Anos.* Brasília: Conselho Administrativo de Defesa Econômica – CADE, 2013.

Creuz, Luis Rodolfo Cruz e. *A Construção da Defesa da Concorrência no MERCOSUL.* Univ. Rel. Int., Brasília, v. 9, n. 1, pp. 73–102, jan./jun. 2011.

Creuz, Luis Rodolfo Cruz e. *A Construção da Defesa da Concorrência no MERCOSUL: Uma Perspectiva Construtivista – Cooperação e Interesses nas Relações Internacionais.* Master's Thesis, UNICAMP, Campinas, 2010. Retrieved February 17, 2016, from < http://www.bibliotecadigital.unicamp.br/document/?code = 0007749 37 > .

Creuz, Luis Rodolfo Cruz e. *Há Novos Ventos na Defesa da Concorrência no Mercosul.* Revista Consultor Jurídico, September 15, 2011. Retrieved February 22, 2016, from < http://www.conjur.com.br/2011-set-15/novos-ventos-defesa-concorrencia-ambito-mercosul > .

Creuz, Luis Rodolfo Cruz e. *Regulação da Defesa da Concorrência no Mercosul.* Instituto Brasileiro de Estudos de Concorrência, Consumo e Comércio Internacional (IBRAC), October 18, 2011. Retrieved February 27, 2016, from < http://www.ibrac.org.br/Noticias.aspx?id = 1089 > .

Cunha, Ricardo Thomazinho da. *Direito de Defesa da Concorrência: Mercosul e União Europeia.* Barueri: Manole, 2003.

Fox, Eleanor. *Competition, Development and Regional Integration: in Search of a Competition Law Fit for Developing Countries.* In DREXL, Josef et al. (ed.). Competition Policy and Regional Integration in Developing Countries. Cheltenham: Edward Elgar, 2012. p. 273/290.

Heinemann, Andreas. *La Nécessité d'um Droit Mondial de la Concurrence.* Revue Internationale de Droit Économique, 3/2004, t. XVIII, 3. p. 293/324.

Inter-American Development Bank. *Latin American and Caribbean Regional Competition Agreements.* Document written for Inter-American Development Bank by consultant Luis Diez Canseco, under the supervision of Mario A. Umaña and Ignacio de Leon, for use in discussions at the 11th meeting of the OECD-EDB Latin American and Caribbean Competition Forum, held on September 3-4, 2013, in Lima, Peru. Retrieved February 22, 2016, from < http://www.oecd.org/officialdocuments/publicdisplaydocumentpdf/?cote = DAF/COMP/LACF(2013)5&docLanguage = En > .

Jaeger Júnior, Augusto. *Direito Internacional da Concorrência: Entre Perspectivas Unilaterais, Multilaterais, Bilaterais e Regionais.* Curitiba: Juruá, 2008.

Marques, Frederico do Valle Magalhães. *Direito Internacional da Concorrência.* Rio de Janeiro: Renovar, 2006.

Melo, Murilo Otávio Lubambo de. *Defesa da Concorrência no MERCOSUL: Entraves e Soluções Normativas.* Boletim Latino-Americano de Concorrência, n.º 23, September 2007. pp. 19/34.

Navega, Antonio Poli; Souza, Luciano Inácio de; Silveira, Paulo Burnier da. *Direito da Concorrência.* In Ribeiro, Elisa de Sousa (ed.). Direito do MERCOSUL. Curtiba: Appris, 2013. p. 305/316.

Oliveira, Gesner; Rodas, João Grandino. *Direito e Economia da Concorrência.* São Paulo: Revista dos Tribunais, 2013.

Silveira, Paulo Burnier da. *Le Contrôle des Concentrations Transnationales.* Paris: l'Harmattan, 2013.

Suñé, Natasha. *Mercosur Competition Defence Rule.* ZEI Regional Integration Observer. Vol. 5, n.º 3, December 2011. p. 5.

UNIÃO. Procuradoria Federal Especializada junto ao CADE. Nota Técnica GTI/002/2010, August 10, 2010. *Comentários à Proposta de Alteração do Protocolo de Fortaleza.* Draftsmen: Maria Rosa Guimarães Loula (CADE's Federal Attorney) and Tatiana de Campos Aranovich (Senior Executive Service).

CHAPTER 20
Implications of the Trans-Pacific Partnership for Competition Policy

Martha Martínez Licetti, Graciela Miralles Murciego & Guilherme de Aguiar Falco[1]

§20.01 INTRODUCTION

The short answer is yes.

The long answer, developed throughout this chapter, will allow us to elaborate on *"why yes"* and, most importantly, *"how to achieve this yes"* by: (1) prosing a comprehensive reading of the Trans-Pacific Partnership (TPP) competition policy related obligations, and (2) maximizing the synergies among the different chapters of the agreement. This approach supports the role of the TPP as a key tool to foster competition on the merits in key sectors as well as economy-wide in Latin America, the Pacific Rim and beyond.

The TPP, signed on February 4, 2016 after several years of negotiations, constitutes an explicit recognition that effective implementation of trade-related commitments demands a pro-competitive environment that fosters open markets and penalizes anticompetitive behavior.[2] International experience confirms the value of this approach. The European Union, for instance, advanced its goal of regional integration by promoting the establishment and enforcement of national competition policies that run in harmony with the Union's objectives of reducing market distortions towards a more integrated economy.

---

1. The chapter builds on the general framework for TPP Competition Policy related commitments prepared by the WBG Competition Policy Cluster of the Trade and Competitiveness Global Practice. However, the views expressed in this chapter are those of the authors and do not necessarily represent or reflect those of the World Bank Group.
2. Twelve countries signed the agreement: Australia, Canada, Japan, Malaysia, Mexico, Peru, United States, Vietnam, Chile, Brunei, Singapore, New Zealand. See the full text of the agreement made available by the Office of the United States Trade Representative at https://ustr.gov/tpp/.

The agreement requires parties not only to establish and enforce a procedurally fair and transparent competition law framework (Chapter 16) but also to level the playing field between public and private operators (Chapter 17), advising for measures able to implement competition throughout all economic sectors. At the same time, the TPP requires parties to promote pro-competition regulatory environments in key sectors for the economy such as telecommunications (Chapter 13), financial services (Chapter 11) and public procurement (Chapter 15). In this sense, The TPP presents itself as an opportunity to foster effective national competition policies covering both horizontal and vertical perspectives.

Chile, Mexico and Peru, three key regional players in Antitrust, are already part of the TPP while Colombia,[3] among others, expressed their interest in joining. Moreover, the membership of the U.S. and Canada only makes the whole idea of a single competition policy framework for the continent more desirable since the TPP was conceived as a tool for economic advancement of the region through increased trade.

This chapter offers a discussion on the scope and implications of competition-related commitments of the TPP. Consistent with international best practice, the article covers the TPP competition-related commitments that correspond to the main pillars of an effective competition policy framework: fostering pro-competition regulations and government interventions; measures to guarantee competitive neutrality in markets and effective economy-wide enforcement of competition law. These pillars, summarized by Figure 20.1, rely on an effective institutional set up that is able to foster and guarantee healthy market conduct.[4]

---

3. In a recent official visit to the United States, the Colombian President Juan Manuel Santos has reaffirmed the country's intention to join the TPP. See "Colombia President: Interested in Joining TPP", news from the MNI, Deutsche Borse Group (February 3, 2016), available at https://mninews.marketnews.com/content/colombia-president-interested-joining-tpp.
4. The purpose of the note is to provide *ex ante* guidance on the scope of application of TPP commitments and the potential risks associated with non-compliance. The note is based only on data publicly available through desk research and therefore is an initial assessment of compliance. Authoritative interpretation of the text of the TPP can only be provided by the dispute resolution panel set up and consulted following the legal means provided by the treaty itself as complemented by the principles of International Public Law.

Figure 20.1 A Comprehensive Competition Policy Framework

FOSTERING COMPETITION IN MARKETS		
PRO-COMPETITION REGULATIONS AND GOVERNMENT INTERVENTIONS: OPENING MARKETS AND REMOVING ANTICOMPETITIVE SECTORAL REGULATION	**COMPETITIVE NEUTRALITY AND NON-DISTORTIVE PUBLIC AID SUPPORT**	**EFFECTIVE COMPETITION LAW AND ANTITRUST ENFORCEMENT**
Reform policies and regulations that strengthen dominance: restrictions to the number of firms, statutory monopolies, bans towards private investment, lack of access regulation for essential facilities.	Control state aid to avoid favoritism and minimize distortions on competition	Tackle cartel agreements that raise the costs of key inputs and final products and reduce access to a broader variety of products
Eliminate government interventions that are conducive to collusive outcomes or increase the costs of competing: controls on prices and other market variables that increase business risk	Ensure competitive neutrality including vis-a vis SOEs	Prevent anticompetitive mergers
Reform government interventions that discriminate and harm competition on the merits: frameworks that distort the level playing field or grant high levels of discretion		Strengthen the general antitrust and institutional framework to combat anticompetitive conduct and abuse of dominance

Source: WBG-OECD (2016). Adapted from Kitzmuller M. and M. Licetti, "Competition Policy: Encouraging Thriving Markets for Development" Viewpoint Note Number 331, World Bank Group, August 2012.

In order to account for how TPP obligations interact with the different dimensions of an effective competition policy framework, this chapter is divided in three sections. The first section addresses the horizontal commitments under the Competition Chapter, focusing on how they affect the establishment of comprehensive national competition policies in Latin American parties to the TPP. The second section explores the horizontal commitments under the Chapter on State Owned Enterprises (SOE) and Designated Monopolies by developing an analytical framework to assess the scope of its obligations and identify how they intend to promote competitive neutrality. Finally, the third section addresses the vertical commitments of competition-related obligations of the TPP, particularly under the Telecommunication, Public Procurement and Financial Service Chapters, assessing how the agreement builds on obligations from several chapters in order to foster pro-competition regulation that open markets and remove anticompetitive sectoral regulation.

Read in conjunction, horizontal chapters like the ones on Competition and SOEs together with vertical chapters on Telecommunications and Financial Services offer the basic elements to build comprehensive competition policy frameworks that account for the necessary interplay between antitrust and regulation. In this sense, the sector-specific chapters reinforce the promotion of competition by setting regulatory frameworks that eliminate entry barriers and foster a level playing field between public and private operators as well as between national incumbents and firms from other TPP parties.

In practice, the TPP Competition Policy Related Commitments present a vision that is consistent with a comprehensive implementation of competition policy: fostering competitive neutrality principles[5] across economic and public policies of the TPP parties. From a domestic perspective, the case of Australia, in particular, offers an interesting example for Latin American TPP parties. In 1990, as the country was undertaking a major microeconomic reform program, it became obvious that the effects of the reforms would be severely limited if the existing rules that shape market outcomes were not reviewed and modified. In April 1995, the Australian State and Territory Governments agreed to implement a National Competition Policy (NCP).[6] The guiding principles of this NCP, much along the lines of the TPP itself, was that legislations and regulations should not restrict competition unless: (i) the benefits of the competition restriction to the public as a whole outweighed the costs and (ii) the objectives of the legislation could only be achieved by restricting competition. Public bodies had to show that new legislation that restricts competition is consistent with the guiding principle.

---

5. The principle of competitive neutrality which, as first proposed in Australia, requires that government business activities do not enjoy net competitive advantages over their private sector competitors simply by virtue of their public ownership. For a detailed discussion, see generally 2011 OECD Working Paper on "Competitive Neutrality and State-Owned Enterprises."
6. Based on a blueprint from the earlier independent review (the so-called Hilmer Review), available at http://ncp.ncc.gov.au/docs/National%20Competition%20Policy%20Review%20report,%20 The%20Hilmer%20Report,%20August%201993.pdf; see also the Competition Principles Agreement from April 11, 1995, available at http://ncp.ncc.gov.au/docs/Competition%20Principles%20Agreement,%2011%20April%201995%20as%20amended%202007.pdf.

In practice, the NCP process triggered: *(i) legal and regulatory reforms*: revision and amendments of national and subnational legislation that restricted competition, *(ii) competitive neutrality reforms*: national and subnational governments had to ensure that their publicly owned businesses did not enjoy any net competitive advantage simply because they are publicly owned and *(iii) structural reforms*: national and subnational governments had to implement measures to guarantee competition in the market before privatization or market liberalization, including non-discriminatory access to infrastructure services and separation of regulatory and commercial function. As a result, competition policy reforms boosted Australia's GDP by at least 2.5%, due to their effect on increased productivity and lower prices during the 1990s.[7] As it will be shown in this chapter, the TPP Competition Policy Commitments are embedding this approach with the objective of achieving similar results on the ground.

Box 20.1 Australia's Comprehensive Competition Policy Framework

Acknowledging the complementary nature of sectoral and economy-wide competition policies was key to Australia's successful reform path toward a competitive level playing field. More detailed analysis of the Australian experience reveals that four factors in particular facilitated the success of the competition reforms: recognition of the need for reforms at all levels of the government; agreement on priority areas; a solid conceptual framework and information base; and effective procedural and institutional mechanisms to carry out the reforms.

To address sector-level competition issues, the Legislative Review Program was introduced to review regulatory restrictions on competition in number of sectors, including professional services. The goal of the program was to review whether regulatory restrictions on competition were in the public interest and if not, to amend the appropriate provisions. As the result, improvements in competition were pursued in a number of areas. For example, competition in the market for conveyancing services – the transfer of legal title of property from one person to another, or the granting of an encumbrance such as a mortgage -increased in Victoria, the regional government reported, once fee scale regulation was removed, fee advertising was permitted, and restrictions on entry into the market were reduced. Similarly, the number of providers of conveyancing services increased and service fees decreased by 17% from 1994 to 1996 in New South Wales, the regional government reported, due to the elimination of the legal profession's monopoly on this type of services.

From an economy-wide perspective, a major step toward competitive markets and competitive neutrality between competing private and public sector firms was to abolish exemptions for state-owned enterprises (SOEs) from competition law. Anticompetitive conduct provisions of the major legislative instrument of competition law in Australia

---

7. This conservative estimate does not consider the effects of dynamic efficiency gains from more competitive markets. See Australian Government, Productivity Commission Inquiry Report (2005), "Review of National Competition Policy Reforms", No. 33, p. XIX, available at http://ncp.ncc.gov.au/docs/PC%20report%202005.pdf and Sims, Rod (2013), "Driving prosperity through effective competition", THE MEXICO FORUM, page 11, available at https://www.accc.gov.au/system/files/The%20Mexico%20Forum%202013%20-%20Driving%20prosperity%20through%20effective%20competition_0.pdf.

the Trade Practices Act 1974, were extended to government businesses. SOEs adopted a corporatization model where appropriate. Government guarantee both regulatory (applying same regulations to the private sector) and tax neutrality (imposing on the SOEs full taxes or tax equivalents and debt guarantee fees to offset advantages from government guarantees). Structural reforms were also undertaken, including the creation of independent authorities to set, administer or oversee prices for monopoly service providers, and requirement to provide third-party access to essential infrastructure services. As a result, the financial performance of SOEs has improved significantly since the early 1980s.

Source: NCP (1995); Capobianco and Christiansen (2011); Rennie and Lindsay (2011).

§20.02 THE COMPETITION CHAPTER

The key elements of Chapter 16 of the TPP on Competition Policy commitments can be grouped around three pillars:

(A) *Competition Policy as an overarching tool to promote economic efficiency and consumer welfare.* The TPP requires parties to adopt the basic building blocks for antitrust enforcement including national competition laws that promote economic efficiency and consumer welfare, an authority entrusted with its enforcement and a number of specific obligations to ensure due process.[8] In particular, before imposing sanctions or remedies, the affected (legal/natural) person shall be duly informed about the authority's competition concerns and have a reasonable opportunity to speak and be represented by counsel.[9] Affected persons shall also have the right of appeal, the option to settle with the competition authority and the ability to seek private damage compensation.[10] Competition authorities bear the burden of proof of anticompetitive conducts.[11] They shall protect confidential information and endeavor to apply its national competition laws to all commercial activities in their territory.[12] In practice, these obligations strengthen the antitrust enforcement and institutional framework to combat anticompetitive conduct throughout all sectors of the economy.

(B) *International cooperation and Transparency as the backbone for regional implementation of competition-related obligations.* The Chapter provides for cooperation and coordination among competition authorities on the development of competition policy and enforcement, including notifications, consultations and information exchanges as testament of the

---

8. See Art. 16.1.1, Chapter 16, TPP: "Each Party shall adopt or maintain national competition laws that proscribe anticompetitive business conduct, with the objective of promoting economic efficiency and consumer welfare, and shall take appropriate action with respect to that conduct".
9. See Art. 16.2.1, Chapter 16, TPP.
10. See Art. 16.2.4; 16.2.5 and 16.3, Chapter 16, TPP.
11. See Art. 16.2.7, Chapter 16, TPP.
12. See Art. 16.2.8 and 16.1.2, Chapter 16, TPP.

increasing importance of cross-border cases.[13] The TPP parties are also encouraged to enhance technical cooperation among authorities as means to promote dynamic communication and awareness among them. This type of cooperation might be enacted through the exchange of officials (twinnings), sharing experiences on competition advocacy and assisting other parties to implement their competition laws.[14] As a necessary complement to the cooperation objective, the Parties also recognize the value of making their competition enforcement policies as transparent as possible, especially by making available information concerning its competition law enforcement policies and practices, exemptions and immunities.[15] Parties shall also ensure that final decisions finding a violation of their national competition law are made in writing and set out, in non-criminal matters, findings of fact as well as the reasoning, including the legal and, if applicable, the economic analysis, on which the decision is based.[16]

(C) *Consumer protection as a necessary complement of antitrust policies to regulate firm behavior.* The inclusion of consumer protection obligations within the competition policy chapter constitutes a recognition of the role of consumer protection policy and enforcement as a key complementary tool to create efficient and competitive markets and enhance consumer welfare.[17] In this sense, the TPP parties have committed to adopt the necessary laws to prosecute fraudulent and deceptive commercial activities.[18] These practices are specifically defined in the text of the TPP as commercial practices that cause actual or imminent harm to consumers, including (i) misrepresentation of material fact, (ii) failure to deliver products or provide services after consumers are charged and (iii) charge or debit consumers' accounts without authorization.[19]

However, the Competition policy chapter itself offers limited mechanisms of direct enforcement– the Chapter is excluded from the Dispute Settlement mechanism established by the TPP (Chapter 28) and also fails to create an ad hoc committee to oversee the implementation of commitments. Instead, Chapter 16 only establishes the right to enter into consultations at the request of another party. Therefore, enforcement will be based on the institutional tools established to oversee the implementation of domestic competition policies. Finally, parties may exclude some activities from the competition law provided that these exclusions are transparent and based on public policy or public interest grounds.[20]

---

13. See Art. 16.4.1 Chapter 16, TPP.
14. See Art. 16.5, Chapter 16, TPP.
15. See Art. 16.7.1 and 16.7.3, Chapter 16, TPP.
16. See Art. 16.7.4, Chapter 16, TPP.
17. See Art. 16.6.1, Chapter 16, TPP.
18. See Art. 16.6.3, Chapter 16, TPP.
19. See Art. 16.6.2, Chapter 16, TPP.
20. Brunei, that by 2015 did not have a competition law, will not be subject to the obligations under the competition policy chapter until it establishes a competition authority or for a maximum period of ten years after the entering into force of the TPP.

Like the TPP, a large number of multilateral trade agreements include some reference to competition policy. In general terms, the stronger the vocation to achieve economic integration, the more detailed the competition related provisions.[21]

However, to a large extent, the efforts to develop global convergence of competition law and policy in substantive terms have been somewhat futile. Obvious difficulties to define one-fit-all solutions to firm behavior within different economic paradigms have prevented, not without reason, further analytical convergence until the moment. An example is the Working Group on the interaction between Trade and Competition Policy (WGTCP) established by the World Trade Organization (WTO) in 1996 to develop multilateral solutions to the matter, an effort interrupted in 2001 as consequence of disagreements around the Doha Round.[22]

Instead, rather than promoting substantive convergence by defining the notion of anticompetitive practices,[23] the Competition chapter of the TPP focuses on formal commitments necessary to ensure procedural fairness and thus further support transparency and enhanced collaboration among authorities. Interestingly, this is not the case on consumer protection matters where the parties define what conduct will be considered fraudulent or deceptive.[24]

What some considered a missed opportunity to foster a (somewhat utopic) substantive convergence might become the secret of the TPP success. The focus on procedural convergence might be instrumental to emphasize the importance of

---

21. The TPP's core obligations are contained in several other international agreements. For example, Art. 41(i) of the ASEAN Economic Blueprint requires members to endeavor to introduce competition policy by 2015, while Art. 1501 of NAFTA requires parties to adopt or maintain measures to proscribe anticompetitive business conduct. Furthermore, Art. 170(2) of the CARICOM treaty requires Member States to establish and maintain national competition authorities. Lastly, Art. 170(3)(c) of the CARICOM treaty obligates national competition authorities to cooperate on enforcement and exchange information for such purposes. Consequently, the TPP's competition provisions contain obligations stronger than traditional free trade agreements, which merely require the adoption of competition laws, but weaker than customs unions, which require the close coordination of competition policies. An example of the later is the Protocol for the Defense of Competition of MERCOSUR signed in 1996 which covers substantive and procedural issues and has direct applicability for Member States. Unfortunately, this instrument has hardly ever been applied due to the particular reasons surrounding the institutional evolution of MERCOSUR in the past few years.
22. See World Trade Organization (2004):

   Relationship between Trade and Investment, Interaction between Trade and Competition Policy and Transparency in Government Procurement: the Council agrees that these issues, mentioned in the Doha Ministerial Declaration in paragraphs 20-22, 23-25 and 26 respectively, will not form part of the Work Program set out in that Declaration and therefore no work towards negotiations on any of these issues will take place within the WTO during the Doha Round.

   Doha Work Program. Decision Adopted by the General Council, WT/L/579, page 4, available at https://www.wto.org/english/tratop_e/dda_e/ddadraft_31jul04_e.pdf.
23. For instance, Art. X-01.5 of the Comprehensive Economic and Trade Agreement (CETA) between the EU and Canada, an instrument that has significantly influenced the drafting of Chapter 17 of the TPP does provide guidance in terms of substance by defining "anti-competitive business conduct" as means anti-competitive agreements, concerted practices or arrangements by competitors; anticompetitive practices by an enterprise that is dominant in a market; and mergers with substantial anticompetitive effects.
24. See Art. 16.6, Chapter 16, TPP.

procedural fairness as a minimum common denominator for workable competition policy frameworks not only among TPP parties themselves but within the region. This approach is confirmed by the significant efforts of the International Competition Network (ICN) to encapsulate and promote procedural fairness in antitrust investigations.[25] In addition, these obligations are *conditio sine qua non* to implement the cooperation commitments under Article 16.4 of the Chapter. Effective cooperation between two competition authorities in the framework of an international antitrust investigation will hardly be possible absent minimum standards that ensure a similar treatment of procedural parties or confidential information.[26]

Given this procedural focus, all three Latin American parties of the TPP seem to be fairly aligned with the competition related commitments under Chapter 16, at least on paper. It shall be noted that when it comes to procedural fairness actual implementation can only be assessed on a case-by-case basis and even the most advanced competition authorities often face breach of due process allegations.[27] On the one hand, a first look indicates that Latin American TPP parties will derive net benefits from other TPP members implementing the procedural obligations already in place in their national frameworks. On the other hand, the TPP can be leveraged as a tool to enhance international cooperation which might require the existence of specific agreements.

For instance, in Peru, international cooperation among antitrust authorities can only happen in the context of international agreements.[28] To this end, the national competition authority of Peru, the *Instituto Nacional de Defensa de la Competencia y de la Protección de la Propiedad Intelectual* (INDECOPI) has signed cooperation

---

25. See the introductory statement of the ICN Guidance on Investigative Process:

    > Fair and effective investigative process is essential to sound competition law enforcement; this includes availability and use of effective agency investigative tools, transparency and engagement with the parties during an investigation, and protection of confidential information. Effective enforcement tools, procedural safeguards, and consistency of process and procedures within an agency contribute to efficient, effective, accurate and predictable enforcement by competition agencies. Cooperation and engagement from parties and third parties are key contributing factors to an agency's ability to pursue fair and effective investigations. The credibility of a competition agency and, more broadly, of the overall mission of competition enforcement are closely tied to the integrity of the agency's investigative process and public understanding of such process.

    Text available at http://www.internationalcompetitionnetwork.org/uploads/library/doc1028.pdf.

26. On the importance to settle common rules about the exchange of confidential information in order to foster cooperation among Antitrust enforcement agencies, see OECD (2014), "Recommendation of the OECD Council concerning International Co-operation on Competition Investigations and Proceedings", [C(2014)108], pp. 6–10, available at http://www.oecd.org/daf/competition/2014-rec-internat-coop-competition.pdf.
27. See Anne MacGregor and Bogdan Gecic (2012), "Due Process in EU Competition Cases Following the Introduction of the New Best Practices Guidelines on Antitrust Proceedings" Journal of European Competition Law & Practice, Vol. 3, No. 5, pp. 425 and 437; Douglas H Ginsburg and Taylor M Owings (2015), "Due Process in Competition Proceedings", Competition Law International, Vol 11 No. 1, pp. 40–41.
28. See 3rd Final Complementary Disposition of the Peruvian Competition Law, added by Legislative Decree n. 1034/2015, available at https://www.indecopi.gob.pe/documents/51771/196578/Decreto_Legislativo1205.pdf/5167539c-8184-4a3c-959a-5b1e5f793d81.

agreements of different nature with a number of countries, including Chile.[29] Given the increasing number of cross-border cases within the region and beyond, closer cooperation and timely exchange of information among competition agencies is becoming a key factor to assess multijurisdictional mergers or destabilize multinational cartels.[30] The important role acquired in the past few years by the Regional Competition Center for Latin America constitutes a testament to this trend. This regional network of Authorities was established in 2011 with the support of the World Bank Group and the Inter-American Development Bank as a tool to counteract the low levels of cooperation within the region.[31] Recent cases, notably in regards to anti-cartel enforcement, confirm the benefits of enhanced cross-border collaboration among competition authorities.[32]

Even more so, substantive aspects of competition obligations under Chapter 16 could potentially be drawn from the text of the TPP itself since the commitment under the TPP goes beyond simply having a competition law and requires the objective of this law to be the promotion of economic efficiency and consumer welfare.[33] In this sense, substantive provisions offering broad exclusions from the scope of application of the law, potentially prohibiting pro-competitive practices on the basis of a structural definition of dominance[34] or allowing for non-efficiency based exemptions might raise concerns regarding compliance with Article 16.1.2[35] of the TPP.

---

29. Convenio de Cooperación Interinstitucional entre el Instituto Nacional de Defensa de la Competencia y de la Protección de la Propiedad Intelectual de Perú y la Fiscalía Nacional de Economía, August 26, 2010 http://www.fne.gob.cl/wp-content/uploads/2013/10/acco_xx_20 10.pdf.
30. The investigation of a cartel in the toilet paper market in Chile led to the investigation of the same market in Peru, attended by the same multinational company, as developed by Reuters in an article from December 15, 2015, available at http://www.reuters.com/article/peru-regulator-idUSL1N1441M220151215.
31. See the written agreement that created the Regional Competition Center for Latin America made available by the Center's official website at http://www.crcal.org/quienes-somos-acta-constitutiva.
32. *Ibid.* at footnote 28. Also, see Licetti and Goodwin (2016), Anti-Cartel Enforcement Database for Developing Countries: An application to Latin American Countries. World Bank Policy Research Working Paper. Forthcoming.
33. See Art. 16.1.1, Chapter 16, TPP: "Each Party shall adopt or maintain national competition laws that proscribe anticompetitive business conduct, with the objective of promoting economic efficiency and consumer welfare, and shall take appropriate action with respect to that conduct".
34. According to the International Competition Network, dominance may be defined in behavioral, structural and/or durability terms. The behavioral definition of dominance, commonly used across the EU, Canada, the United States and Australia, most of Latin American countries, among others, takes into account the ability of firms to act independently from the competitive constraints of the market. A structural definition takes into account market shares as the core issue to establish the existence of dominance. Finally, some jurisdictions including the U.S., the EU, Canada and New Zealand, include some analysis regarding market dynamics and require firms to maintain their position over a given period of time. Establishing a market share above which companies might be considered dominant might deter investment and competition on the merits and therefore hinder economic efficiency since dominant companies are prevented from engaging in normal business conducts, such as undercutting price to the consumers' benefit that would otherwise be perfectly pro-competitive if performed by non-dominant firms. See ICN (2007) "Report on the Objectives of Unilateral Conduct Laws, Assessment of Dominance/Substantial Market Power, and State-Created Monopolies." At pp. 40 et seq. Available at http://www.internationalcompetitionnetwork.org/uploads/library/doc353.pdf.
35. Text of Art. 16.1.2: "Each Party shall endeavor to apply its national competition laws to all commercial activities in its territory".

§20.03 THE SOE CHAPTER

The TPP is the first Free Trade Agreement (FTA) that seeks to address comprehensively the commercial activities of SOEs competing with private companies in international trade and investment. Even though the chapter's commitments build on principles from the WTO and previous U.S. FTAs, notably the Canada-EU Comprehensive Economic and Trade Agreement (CETA), the TPP significantly expands the scope of commercial consideration and non-discrimination commitments as it advances on the control of distortive public support and subsidies through non-commercial assistance (NCA) obligations. In other words, the Chapter works to promote competitive neutrality and non- distortive public aid support.

More specifically, under Chapter 17 of the TPP, SOEs and designated monopolies should be bound to compete on the basis of quality and price rather than benefitting from discriminatory regulation and distortive subsidies. Basically, the obligations established by the Chapter on SOE and designated monopolies tap on three main commitments by TPP parties: (i) avoiding discrimination and applying commercial considerations by SOEs, including a limitation for designated monopolies to engage on anticompetitive practices; (ii) parties must NOT concede NCA[36] capable of causing adverse effects or injury to the interests of another Party, meaning to economically support SOEs in terms more favorable than those commercially available;[37] (iii) parties must offer an impartial regulatory and institutional framework for SOEs, yet making them accountable for their actions in other TPP countries. Figure 20.2 below details the Chapter's framework.

---

36. Assistance meaning "direct transfers of funds or potential direct transfers of funds or liabilities, such as: grants or debt forgiveness; loans, loan guarantees or other types of financing on terms more favorable than those commercially available to that enterprise; equity capital inconsistent with the usual investment practice (including for the provision of risk capital) of private investors; goods or services other than general infrastructure on terms more favorable than those commercially available to that enterprise." (Art. 17.1)
37. Non-commercial assistance includes (1) direct transfers of funds or potential direct transfers of funds or liabilities and (2) goods or services other than general infrastructure on terms more favorable than those commercially available to that enterprise (definitions p. 17-2). The TPP excludes non-commercial assistance measures taken prior to the TPP entering into force and/or enacted within three years of it, if based upon a decision taken prior to its entering into force (Art. 17.7.5).

Figure 20.2   TPP Obligations Based on the SOE Chapter[38]

Non-discrimination and commercial considerations	Prohibition of non-commercial assistance	Impartial regulator/access to civil courts
• SOE shall apply commercial considerations except when fullfiling public service mandate. • SOEs/designated monopolies cannot discriminate, i.e. accord worse terms and conditions to firms from other TPP parties, unless differentiated tratment is based on commercial considerations. • Designated monopolies cannot use its monopolistic position to engage in anticompetitive practices.	• Non-commercial assistance includes (1) direct transfers of funds or potential direct transfers of funds or liabilities and (2) goods or services other than general infrastructure on terms more favourable than those commercially available to that enterprise. • In order to be prohibited, non-commercial assistance needs to cause adverse effects or injury to another TPP party.	• Regulators of markets with SOE presence shall be impartial vis a vis SOE or private operators from other TPP parties • Foreign SOEs shall be accountable to the commercial courts of the TPP party where they engage in commercial activities. • TPP parties need to puiblic a list of SOEs and provide additional information on their activities upon request.

From an institutional perspective, the parties agree to participate in a Committee on SOEs and Designated Monopolies undertaking, among other functions, the promotion of the principles underlying the disciplines contained in Chapter 17 as well as to foster technical cooperation among authorities to share best practices on public policies that level the playing field between state-owned and private enterprises, including competitive neutrality. The obligations of Chapter 17 can be claimed before the Dispute Settlement Body to be established under the TPP.

The TPP obligations of the SOE Chapter focus on guaranteeing that SOEs compete on an even playing field and therefore are to a large extent behavioral. The SOE Chapter sets obligations aimed at developing a level playing field for direct government participation in the economy based on the respect of commercial considerations, non-discriminatory market practices and promotion of equal regulatory treatment. This framework leverages the experience of the implementation of the competitive neutrality principle[39] by some of the TPP parties, notably, Australia and the U.S.

Figure 20.3 identifies potential competition distortions and negative market effects that each main obligation under the SOE chapter intends to prevent.

---

38. See Annex one with a box summarizing obligations and exceptions under the Chapter.
39. The principle of competitive neutrality which, as first proposed in Australia, requires that government business activities do not enjoy net competitive advantages over their private sector competitors simply by virtue of their public ownership. For a detailed discussion, see generally 2011 OECD Working Paper on "Competitive Neutrality and State-Owned Enterprises."

Chapter 20: Implications of the Trans-Pacific Partnership §20.03

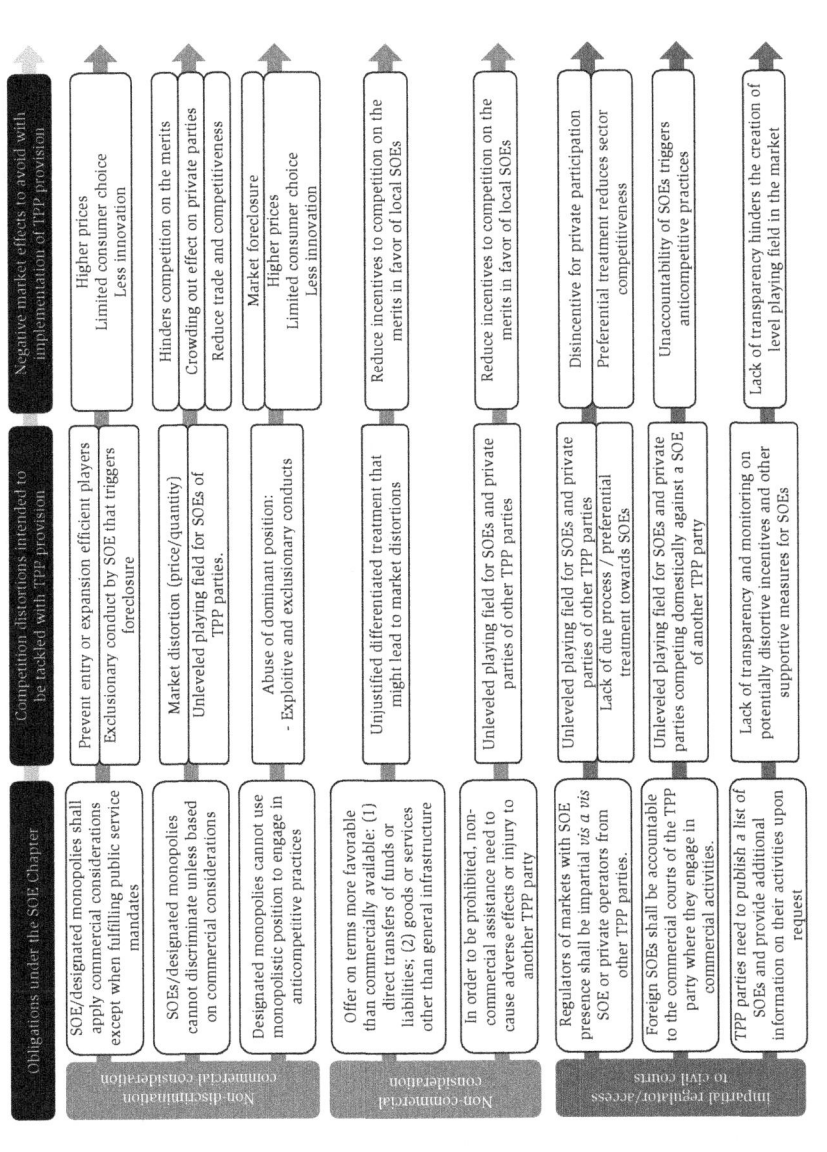

Figure 20.3 Competition Distortions Intended to Be Prevented with TPP Commitments

Source: Developed by the World Bank Group Competition Policy Team based on the SOE Chapter.

The TPP obligations crystalize basic concerns of TPP parties regarding the threat and potential market distortions that heavily subsidized national public champions may bring about when competing internationally. To that end, these obligations shall be read in a broader regional and international framework that the TPP itself since they will affect other trading partners having a significant number of SOEs competing in the markets of TPP parties, both from the region, notably the case of Brazil, as well as beyond such as China, India or Russia.

First, these benefits can become a sort of standard to influence and be replicated across international trade agreements currently under negotiation. This influence can already be seen in the talks on the EU-US Transatlantic Trade and Investment partnership (TTIP)[40] as well as the EU-China Bilateral Investment Treaty (BIT) with similar demands expressed by the EU in relation to the need to curb non-commercial benefits for SOEs.[41]

Second, while direct claims on non-discrimination and commercial considerations (first set of obligations on Figure 20.2) can only be made by TPP parties, the other two (NCA and impartial regulator) will indirectly benefit any (private/public) firm from a non-TPP party competing in a market covered by TPP obligations:

- *Prohibition of distortive non-commercial assistance*: On the one hand, preventing the grant of any distortive NCA to SOEs will level the playing field for any company competing with that SOE. Therefore, as a hypothetical example, by disciplining the access to distortive non-commercial support for a Vietnamese SOE competing in Peru, a Brazilian or Chinese competitor entering the same market will equally benefit. The problem is, however, that companies from non-TPP countries will not be bound by similar obligations and thus might end up posing a bigger threat in the recipient market. Even more so giving that foreign SOEs from non-TPP countries will not need to be accountable under the commercial courts of the country of destination.
- *Regulatory transparency and impartial regulation*. On the other hand, the transparency and impartiality obligations captured under the TPP have a strong potential to leveling the playing field including with firms from other countries.

---

40. See information about the EU-US T-TIP negotiations (summary of U.S. objectives, negotiating round and public forum information, fact sheets and reports) made available by the Office of the United States Trade Representative official website, available at https://ustr.gov/ttip.
41. About Chinese SOEs and the lack of a level playing field for prospective and existing European investors in China and concerns regarding the level of Chinese Investment in the EU, see European Parliament's Committee on International Trade, Ex-Ante Impact Assessment Unit (2013), "European Commission proposal on EU-China Investment Relations. Initial appraisal of a European Commission Impact Assessment", Impact Assessment (SWD (2013) 185, SWD (2013), available at http://www.europarl.europa.eu/RegData/etudes/note/join/2013/514077/IPOL-JOIN_NT(2013)514077_EN.pdf.

Chapter 20: Implications of the Trans-Pacific Partnership §20.03

> **Box 20.2 Chilean SOEs**
>
> Even though the SOE sector can be considered relatively small in Chile, it includes large companies in key markets and accounts for non-trivial portion of the government's revenue:
>
> - SOEs employ around 49,000 people (0.7% of total employment); aggregate expenditures account for approximately 9.4% of GDP; revenues generated amount to 12.8% of GDP and total investment amounts to 1.2%.
> - There are thirty-three SOEs linked to the central government; twenty-seven are entirely state-owned and the rest has private participation. They operate in both competitive and non-competitive markets, and their activities spread across different sectors.
> - SOEs are particularly important in the mining and financial sectors, where SOE revenues represent 11% and 1.1%% of Chile's GDP, respectively. *The figure below summarizes SOEs participation by sector.*
>
>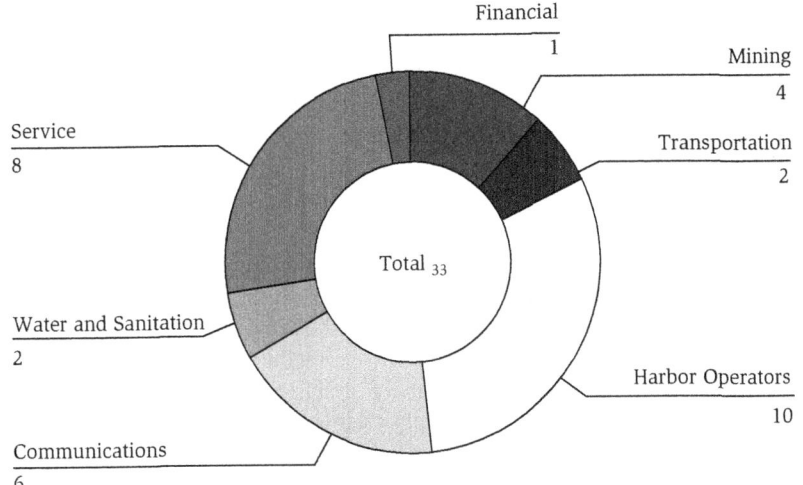
>
> The World Bank Group (2014), "Corporate Governance of State-Owned Enterprises in Latin America Current Trends and Country Cases", Governance Global Practice, Latin America and the Caribbean Region, page 87.

However, the application of the SOE commitments under to TPP SOE Chapter is triggered only when certain conditions are met. The TPP applies to the corporate entity as a whole, not to selected business or product lines.[42] In practice, the scope of application of the SOE Chapter is limited to *activities of state-owned enterprises*[43] and *designated monopolies* of a Party that *affect trade or investment between Parties within*

---

42. Article 17-4 of the TPP states "Each Party shall ensure that each of its state-owned enterprises, when engaging in commercial activities (...)", in other words, the whole entity despite the fact that some parts of the SOE might be involved in commercial activities and some others not.
43. The scope also includes "designated monopolies" which are defined by Art. 17.1 as "a privately owned monopoly that is designated after the date of entry into force of this Agreement and any government monopoly that a Party designates or has designated".

the free trade area of the TPP.[44] Therefore, in order to identify whether a company falls under the mandate of Chapter 17 it will be necessary to understand the definitions given to each of these aspects.

While the definition of designated monopolies is quite straight forward, the difficulty lies in understanding which monopolistic companies hold a protected status in each TPP party. Designated monopolies are entities (either public or private) designated as the sole provider or purchaser of a good or service within the territory of a TPP party. Generally, there are no specific (policy/legal) instruments identifying all designated monopolies within a country. Therefore, it is necessary to carry a case-by-case analysis in order to understand whether monopolistic markets/market segments are the result of specific rights granted by the TPP party to a public/private company or just the result of market dynamics.

In Mexico, for example, there are designated monopolies in some segments within several sectors, such as hydrocarbons and electricity.[45] Regarding the meaning of "activities of SOEs", the TPP leaves out situations where the public enterprise *principally* performs public services. While these exclusions can be socially and economically justified and even desirable, it is also important to limit their potential to distort markets. In Europe, for instance, Member States are allowed to grant special or exclusive rights to public or private undertakings to perform *services of general economic interest (SGEI)*, typically related to liberalized sectors of the economy, i.e., energy, telecoms, postal services, transport, waste disposal, and tentatively in the social sphere.[46] However, undertakings entrusted with the provision of SGEI are exempted from the application of general competition and state aid rules *only to the extent* that the application of such rules obstructs the provision of the service.[47] In Peru, this notion is aligned with the subsidiarity principle entrusted in the country's constitution limiting the government's intervention in the economy to situations where the private sector cannot effectively supply products and services.[48]

---

44. As per exact wording of Art. 17.2.1.
45. See Art. 28, Political Constitution of the United States of Mexico:

    No constituirán monopolios las funciones que el Estado ejerza de manera exclusiva en las siguientes áreas estratégicas: correos, telégrafos y radiotelegrafía; minerales radiactivos y generación de energía nuclear; la planeación y el control del sistema eléctrico nacional, así como el servicio público de transmisión y distribución de energía eléctrica, y la exploración y extracción del petróleo y de los demás hidrocarburos.

    Available at http://www.diputados.gob.mx/LeyesBiblio/htm/1.htm.
46. See for a general discussion: Wolf Sauter (2008), "Services of General Economic Interest and Universal Service in EU Law", European Law Review 33: 167–193.
47. The freedom of the state in granting the provision of SGEI to a particular undertaking is limited by objective criteria, such as that the general service mission has to be clearly defined and explicitly entrusted and the parameters for calculating compensation for the provision of the service should be objective and transparent. See Art. 106 (2) of the Treaty on the Functioning of the European Union.
48. See Art. 60, Political Constitution of Peru:

    El Estado reconoce el pluralismo económico. La economía nacional se sustenta en la coexistencia de diversas formas de propiedad y de empresa. Sólo autorizado por ley expresa, el Estado puede realizar subsidiariamente actividad empresarial, directa o

Notwithstanding the necessary alignment among TPP and national laws towards the limits of government participation in the economy, enforcement might be another challenge. In Peru, where the Constitution reserves for the State a subsidiary role in the provision of economic activities, INDECOPI's analysis confirms if the government oversteps the limits of its mandate to intervene directly in the economy.[49] The mandate of the Peruvian Competition Authority includes the ability to enforce the principle of subsidiarity by sanctioning SOEs for engaging in non-subsidiary business activities.[50] The economic activity (directly or indirectly) of the State is constitutionally legitimate only when the following circumstances are met: (1) the State business activity has been expressly authorized by law; (2) the State activity in a certain market takes place due to the absence and potential of private initiative to meet the demand; and (3) the State business activity is of high public interest or national convenience.[51]

The definition of the public services mandate of SOEs is also relevant for the enforcement of Antitrust. It is not uncommon that Competition Laws exclude companies either providing public services or linked to government monopolized activities.[52] Overly broad exclusions might harm the effectiveness of national competition policies,

---

    indirecta, por razón de alto interés público o de manifiesta conveniencia nacional. La actividad empresarial, pública o no pública, recibe el mismo tratamiento legal.

    Available at http://www4.congreso.gob.pe/ntley/Imagenes/Constitu/Cons1993.pdf.

49. According to the Comision de Libre Competencia of INDECOPI, from 115 separate activities of 13 different SOEs, at least 41 would have failed to meet the subsidiary requirement. See this and other detailed information about the Peruvian experience on Gonzalo Ruiz, Martha Martínez and Eduardo Quintana (2006), "El Carácter Subsidiario de la Actividad Empresarial del Estado desde una Perspectiva de Políticas de Competencia", In Boletin Latinoamericano De Competencia, Page 123–124, available at http://ec.europa.eu/competition/publications/blc/boletin_22.pdf.

50. See Art. 14.3 of Decreto Ley 1044/2008: "La actividad empresarial desarrollada por una entidad pública o empresa estatal con infracción al artículo 60° de la Constitución Política del Perú configura un acto de violación de normas que será determinado por las autoridades que aplican la presente Ley. En este caso, no se requerirá acreditar la adquisición de una ventaja significativa por quien desarrolle dicha actividad empresarial", available at http://www.wipo.int/wipolex/es/text.jsp?file_id=202203.

51. For a detailed explanation of the criteria used by INDECOPI to assess subsidiarity, see the Precedente de observancia obligatoria (Resolución 3134-2010/SC1-INDECOPI. Expediente 201-2008/CCD) that interprets the application of Art. 14.3. of Decreto Ley 1044, available at http://www2.congreso.gob.pe/sicr/cendocbib/con3_uibd.nsf/DF9984646295D99E052578EE005BD72B/$FILE/Re3134.pdf.

52. See OECD (2015):

    Regarding SOEs in particular, the International Competition Network (ICN)'s 2014 special project examined 'State-owned enterprises (SOEs) and competition law'. A background report was prepared following a questionnaire which was answered by competition authorities from 35 jurisdictions. They reveal some of the reasons for granting competition laws exemptions to SOEs, which could apply to non-SOE actors similarly: 34% of the responding jurisdictions do not recognize any exemption for SOEs, 34% exempt SOEs not engaged in an economic activity and 34% grant exemptions to SOEs entrusted with public service obligations; a few jurisdictions also exempt SOEs exercising their activity in a regulated sector (17%) or in strategic sectors (6%).

    Roundtable on Competition Neutrality, DAF/COMP(2015)5, page 14, available at http://www.oecd.org/officialdocuments/publicdisplaydocumentpdf/?cote=DAF/COMP(2015)5&docLanguage=En.

reduce competitive neutrality and could potentially violate TPP obligations under Chapter 16.[53] Mexico, for example, has taken the approach to balance general public interests with competition principles. The Constitution protects the exercise of public functions by the government for which it holds exclusive jurisdiction due to strategic reasons, such as those functions assigned in electricity transmission and distribution or oil perforation and extraction. In these cases, the action of the government will not be considered a monopoly in the sense of the Competition law which specifically prohibits monopolies as well as monopolization activities that harm competition.[54] This public mandate has not precluded the Mexican Antitrust Authority, *Comision Federal de Competencia Economica*, (COFECE) from taking action against SOEs in those markets when violating the competition law in those markets where they do not hold a legal monopoly. For instance, in 2013, COFECE imposed a USD 50 million fine to Pemex, the incumbent in one of these sectors, for abuse of market power in tying arrangements with gas stations.[55]

---

53. Chapter 16, Art. 16.1.2 demands that each Party shall endeavor to apply its national competition laws to all commercial activities in its territory.
54. See Art. 52 of the Competition Law of Mexico: "Están prohibidos los monopolios, las prácticas monopólicas, las concentraciones ilícitas y las barreras que, en términos de esta Ley, disminuyan, dañen, impidan o condicionen de cualquier forma la libre concurrencia o la competencia económica en la producción, procesamiento, distribución o comercialización de bienes o servicios."
55. See news from Forbes, August 23, 2013, "CFC multa a Pemex con 653 mdp por prácticas monopólicas", available at http://www.forbes.com.mx/cfc-multa-a-pemex-con-653-mdp-por-practicas-monopolicas/.

Chapter 20: Implications of the Trans-Pacific Partnership §20.03

> **Box 20.3   Peruvian SOEs**
>
> In 2012, SOEs in Peru employed around 22,000 people (0.3% of total employment); aggregate operating expenditures were around 3% of GDP and total investments reached around 0.33% of GDP.
>
> - Thirty-one SOEs are overseen by the centralized ownership agency National Fund for Financing State Business Activity (Fondo Nacional de Financiamiento de la Actividad Empresarial del Estado – FONAFE). The central government of Peru is owner of at least 87% of each SOE.
> - Despite the relative small amount of SOEs in the country, public companies are key players in backbone sectors as electricity generation and distribution, water and sanitation, transportation, Oil & Gas and Financial services. The Figure below summarizes the presence of SOEs in Peru by sector.
>
>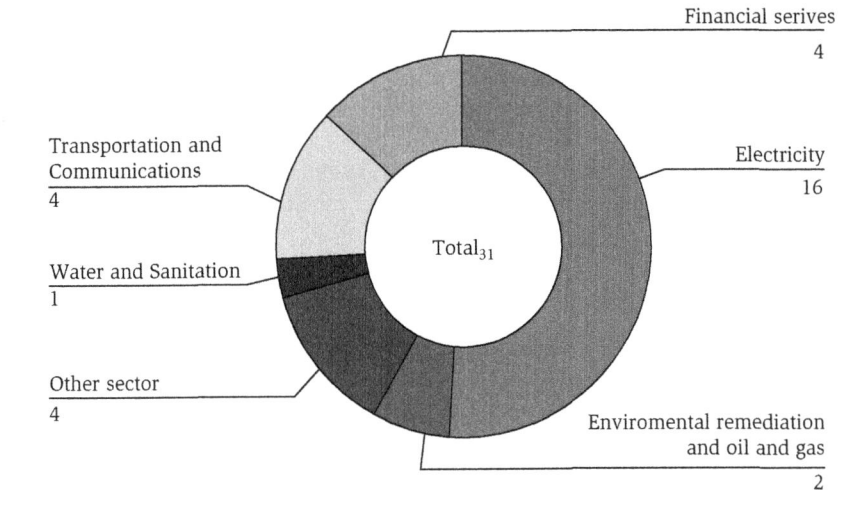

Source: The World Bank Group (2014), "Corporate Governance of State-Owned Enterprises in Latin America Current Trends and Country Cases", Governance Global Practice, Latin America and the Caribbean Region, pages 112–113.

The SOE Chapter of the TPP mostly cares about leveling the playing field in relation to profit maximizing SOEs taking their own commercial decisions since these are more likely to be in true competition with other firms. In this sense, companies performing non-for profit activities (even when these involve the supply of good/services to consumers) as well as those profit-based activities where the price/conditions are not set by the SOE itself but by the TPP Party are excluded from the scope of application of the Chapter. In other words, it is possible that SOEs where the intervention of the government might be more distortive end up out of the SOE Chapter scope. This can be the case of line ministries that establish the commercial conditions of national champions of industry, for instance within the framework of industrial policy goals.[56] To this end, while the TPP constitutes a platform to promote a more level playing field for the benefit of the private sector, a truly effective competitive neutrality policy should necessary go beyond the text of the agreement itself and rather focused on achieving its overall goals of economic integration.

The TPP also demands that a government controls either the majority of (i) total capital, (ii) voting rights or (iii) rights to appoint board members in order to characterize a firm as SOE. These requirements exclude situations in which governments holding minority shares (having less than 50% share of capital or voting rights) still have a decisive influence in the running of the company, as in the case of SOEs having golden shares, a common feature of a number of privatization processes across countries.[57]

Regarding the meaning of "affecting trade and investment within the free trade area of the TPP", relevant guidance to apply this notion might be found on other TPP provisions as well as other regional integration experiences. While Article 17.2 of the TPP chapter limits its scope of application to activities that affect trade and investment between parties within the free trade area, it does not offer guidance on the expected interpretation of this requirement. This gap is to some extent addressed later in the provision by stating that measures having "adverse effects" within the territory of a TPP party as those described under Article 17.7 of the SOE chapter will generally fall within the TPP.

---

56. In Chile, for example, this might be the case of smaller SOEs under control and supervision of the State-Owned Enterprises System (Sistema de Empresas Públicas – SEP) – in 2014, SEP controlled twenty-three out of thirty-three SOEs in Chile. According to the WBG (2014), "The SEP's main functions include nominating and appointing SOEs' directors, approving strategic plans, establishing annual goals and controlling the management of the SOEs under its supervision". "The largest Chilean SOEs are not under SEP control and supervision, but operate in a decentralized and autonomous way. In particular, the National Copper Corporation (Corporación Nacional de Cobre - CODELCO), the national oil company (Empresa Nacional del Petróleo - ENAP), the Chilean State Bank, the companies active in the communications sector, and all defense-related state companies are subject to separate institutional arrangements. Many of these companies have a regulatory framework specifically developed for their operations and approved by special laws." Corporate Governance of State-Owned Enterprises in Latin America. Current Trends and Country Cases, Governance Global Practice, Latin America and the Caribbean Region, pages 88, available at http://www-wds.worldbank.org/external/default/WDSContentServer/WDSP/IB/2014/09/08/000470435_20140908091500/Rendered/PDF/894680WP00P1260orate0Governance0LAC.pdf.
57. A golden share is a nominal share which is able to outvote all other shares in certain specified circumstances, often held by a government organization, in a government company undergoing the process of privatization and transformation into a stock-company.

Chapter 20: Implications of the Trans-Pacific Partnership §20.03

> **Box 20.4 Article 17.7: Adverse Effects**
>
> 1. For the purposes of NCA, adverse effects arise where:
>
> (a) the effect of the NCA is that the production and sale of a good by a Party's SOE that has received the NCA displaces or impedes from the Party's market imports of a like good of another Party or sales of a like good produced by an enterprise that is a covered investment in the territory of the Party;
>
> (b) the effect of the NCA is that the production and sale of a good by a Party's SOE that has received the NCA displaces or impedes:
>
>   (i) from the market of another Party sales of a like good produced by an enterprise that is a covered investment in the territory of that other Party, or imports of a like good of another Party; or
>
>   (ii) from the market of a non-Party imports of a like good of another Party;
>
> (c) the effect of the NCA is a significant price undercutting by a good produced by a Party's SOE that has received the NCA and sold by the enterprise:
>
>   (i) in the market of a Party as compared with the price in the same market of imports of a like good of another Party or a like good that is produced by an enterprise that is a covered investment in the territory of the Party, or significant price suppression, price depression or lost sales in the same market; or
>
>   (ii) in the market of a non-Party as compared with the price in the same market of imports of a like good of another Party, or significant price suppression, price depression or lost sales in the same market;
>
> (d) the effect of the NCA is that services supplied by a Party's SOE that has received the NCA displace or impede from the market of another Party a like service supplied by a service supplier of that other Party or a third Party; or
>
> (e) the effect of the NCA is a significant price undercutting by a service supplied in the market of another Party by a Party's SOE that has received the NCA as compared with the price in the same market of a like service supplied by a service supplier of that other Party or a third Party, or significant price suppression, price depression or lost sales in the same market.
>
> *Source:* Text of the SOE Chapter

The foreign element of the concept of *adverse effects* sheds light on the meaning of "affecting trade within the TPP area." The TPP dimension of "adverse effects" is based on a foreign element: either on the presence of a (private/public) firm from another TPP party in a domestic market where the SOE participates or on the internationalization of an SOE that participates in the market of another TPP party. This would exclude from the application of the TPP purely domestic situations. It shall be noted that the TPP dimension exists whether there is a horizontal or a vertical relationship between the SOE and the firm/s from other TPP party.

Additional guidance on the meaning of "affecting trade and investment" can be found on other regional economic integration organizations such as the European Union. In this sense, in 2004, the European Commission issued Guidelines on the Effect of Trade Concept. This instrument is built around the notion of *appreciability* which incorporates a quantitative element to the concept of having an effect on trade. To this end, *appreciability* can be appraised in particular by reference to the position and the importance of the relevant undertakings on the market for the products concerned.

This quantitative approach is in line with the general exception of the TPP to SOEs with an annual turnover below the threshold of 200 million Special Drawing Rights (SDRs).[58]

Only after passing all these filters can the actual distortive impact of a measure be evaluated against the TPP obligations of the SOE Chapter. Thus, this final evaluation should not be applied *ex ante* to all SOEs, in all markets, but only to those that might have an actual effect –positive or negative-within the TPP area.

Potential market distortions related to SOE treatment/behavior under Chapter 17 are linked to (1) the provision of NCA by the government of the TPP party to the SOE/designated monopoly as well as (2) the discriminatory treatment or non-commercial behavior of the SOE/designated monopoly towards its commercial partners:

(1) NCA in the sense of the TPP requires identifying those measures that favor SOEs *vis a vis* other competitors (either private or even public).[59] Ultimately, NCA can unlevel playing field by (i) having an adverse effect on trade – impeding, displacing or undercutting prices of imports and sales of a like product or the provision of services within the TPP area; or (ii) causing injury to a domestic industry of another TPP Party.[60]

(2) At the same time, Chapter 17 demands from covered SOEs the respect of commercial considerations[61] in the purchase or sale of a good/service, as well as the implementation of the Most Favored Nation (MFN) principle, i.e., non-discrimination obligation.[62] Moreover, this Article also requires designated monopolies to refrain from using their position to engage in anticompetitive practices in non-monopolized markets within their territory.[63]

Figure 20.4 below summarizes the key steps to identify which companies are considered SOEs falling under the scrutiny of Chapter 17 obligations and how to evaluate whether the SOE treatment/behavior fosters competitive neutrality.

---

58. Average SDR for April 2016 was SDR = USD 1.408. Therefore, the threshold would amount to around USD 280 million for April 2016. Data from the International Monetary Fund, SDR valuation, available at https://www.imf.org/external/np/fin/data/rms_sdrv.aspx.
59. See Art. 17.1, Definition of non-commercial assistance, Chapter 17, TPP.
60. Injury includes material injury, threat of material injury or material retardation of the establishment of a domestic industry. For rules of adverse effect on trade, see Art. 17.7, Chapter 17; for rules on injury to domestic industries, see Art. 17.8, Chapter 17, TPP.
61. According to Art. 17.1, Chapter 17 of the TPP: "Commercial considerations means price, quality, availability, marketability, transportation, and other terms and conditions of purchase or sale, or other factors that would normally be taken into account in the commercial decisions of a privately owned enterprise in the relevant business or industry."
62. See Art. 17.4.1 and 17.4.2, Chapter 17, TPP.
63. See Art. 17.4.2.(d), Chapter 17, TPP.

Figure 20.4 Scope of Application of the SOE Chapter: Consolidated Criteria

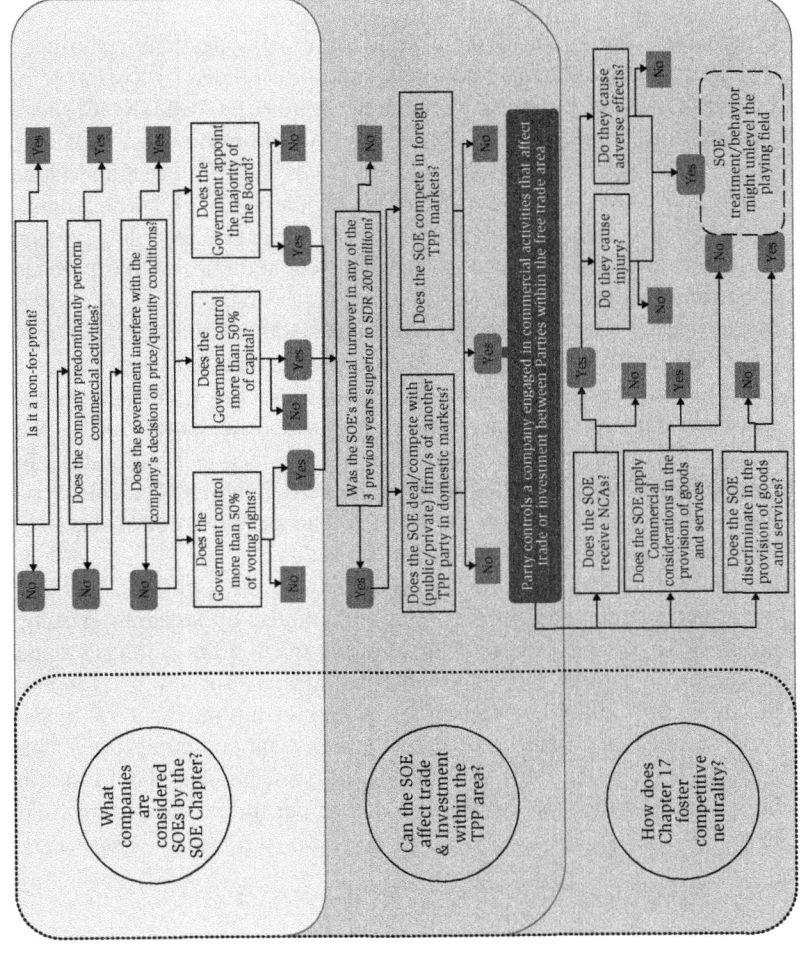

Source: World Bank elaboration;
Note: the word "No" implies non-application of the SOE Chapter.

In practice, however, some of the potential benefits of the application of the SOE Chapter are limited by extensive general and country specific carve outs. The SOE Chapter already excludes, to all Parties, the application of its obligations regarding: (i) public procurement, (ii) sovereign wealth funds, (iii) independent pension funds, (iv) measures to deal with failing financial institutions, (v) monetary or credit policies enabled by Central Banks, (vi) regulatory functions for financial institutions and (vii) SOEs dependent from regional or local governments. On top of that, each TPP party adopted an Annex IV Schedule detailing specific exclusions, for example:

- Chile carved out six of its main SOEs from key obligations regarding non-discrimination, commercial consideration and commercial assistance under Chapter 17: ENAP (Empresa Nacional del Petróleo), CODELCO (Corporación Nacional del Cobre, ENAMI (Empresa Nacional de Minería), METRO (Empresa de Transporte de Pasajeros Metro S.A.), TVN (Televisión Nacional de Chile) and BANCOESTADO (Banco del Estado de Chile).[64] The Annex also allows for discriminatory treatment by any Chilean SOE regarding preferential treatment to Indigenous people and their communities in the purchase of goods and services.[65]
- Mexico carved out three energy players and six financial institutions from key obligations regarding non-discrimination, commercial consideration and commercial assistances under Chapter 17, namely, the Comisión Federal de Electricidad, Petróleos Mexicanos, Centro Nacional de Control del Gas Natural and the development bank institutions (as classified by the Country) Banco Nacional de Obras y Servicios Públicos, Banco del Ahorro Nacional y Servicios Financieros, Banco Nacional del Ejército, Fuerza Aérea y Armada, Nacional Financiera, and la Sociedad Hipotecaria Federal.[66]
- Peru carved out Petróleos del Perú (PETROPERU S.A.) from NCA obligations in case of restructuring process. Moreover, it also excluded all existing and future SOEs at the central level of government from non-discriminatory obligations regarding more favorable treatment to socially or economically disadvantaged minorities and ethnic groups in the purchase of goods and services (meaning indigenous, native and peasant communities).[67] This exemption is consistent with the subsidiarity principle that should inform the intervention of the state in the economy as per the Political Constitution of Peru.[68]

---

64. See Annex IV, Schedule of Chile, pp. 1–6, available at http://www.treasury.gov.my/pdf/TPPA/AnnexIV_Chile.pdf.
65. See Annex IV, Schedule of Chile, p. 7, available at http://www.treasury.gov.my/pdf/TPPA/AnnexIV_Chile.pdf.
66. See Annex IV, Schedule of Mexico, available at http://www.treasury.gov.my/pdf/TPPA/AnnexIV_Mexico.pdf.
67. See Annex IV, Schedule of Peru, available at http://dfat.gov.au/trade/agreements/tpp/official-documents/Documents/annex-iv-peru.pdf.
68. See footnote 50.

These specific exclusions further support the need for an integrated reading of the different competition-related obligations of the TPP. Moving forward, the spirit of the TPP as a tool to increase economic integration in the region should be the guiding principle in designing policy options that will enable signatory countries to fully leverage the benefits of enhanced trade and investment. In other words, the *economic rationale* of the horizontal and vertical chapters of the TPP read in conjunction aims at opening markets for the benefit of trade by eliminating either behavioral or regulatory constraints to competition and removing privileges either for public or private operators thus fostering effective NCP frameworks. This idea is further explored in the next section.

§20.04 VERTICAL DIMENSION OF COMPETITION-RELATED COMMITMENTS

As presented by Figure 20.1 at the beginning of this chapter, a comprehensive NCP demands (i) effective economy-wide enforcement of competition law, (ii) measures to guarantee competitive neutrality in markets and (iii) pro-competition regulations and government interventions. Chapter 16 of the TPP addresses the first pillar of a NCP by requiring parties to adopt national competition laws that promote economic efficiency and consumer welfare, an authority entrusted with its enforcement and a number of specific obligations to ensure due process. Chapter 17 addresses competitive neutrality, controlling state aid to avoid favoritism and minimize distortions on competition, by regulating NCA and market behavior of SOEs and designated monopolies as well as limiting discrimination and non-commercial considerations. In order to tackle the third and last pillar of an effective NCP, the TPP makes use of several chapters that intervene on different sectors under the common denominator of promoting a pro-competitive environment to open markets and remove anticompetitive sectoral regulation.

The TPP specifically promotes pro-competition regulatory environments in key sectors of the economy, including financial services (Chapter 11); telecommunications (Chapter 13); and government procurement (Chapter 15). These vertical obligations are essential to guarantee a comprehensive competition approach to trade in the context of significant carve outs in horizontal commitments exemplified by the extensive exceptions applied to the SOE Chapter and some strategic activities eventually exempted from the scrutiny of national competition laws. Therefore, even those firms escaping the scrutiny of the SOE or the Competition Policy Chapter of the TPP, may be caught by the obligations established under the sector-specific chapters.

In this context, the Financial Service Chapter of the TPP peruses the facilitation of cross-border services through the implementation of market access rules[69] and classic international trade principles of MFNs[70] and national treatment.[71] The Chapter particularly limits regulatory barriers to entry of foreigner companies – Article 11.5,

---

69. See Art. 11.5, Chapter 11, TPP.
70. See Art. 11.4, Chapter 11, TPP.
71. See Art. 11.3, Chapter 11, TPP.

Chapter 11 of the TPP states that no Party shall adopt or maintain with respect to financial institutions of another Party or investors of another Party limitations on:

(i) the number of financial institutions whether in the form of numerical quotas, monopolies, exclusive service suppliers or the requirement of an economic needs test;

(ii) the total value of financial service transactions or assets in the form of numerical quotas or the requirement of an economic needs test;

(iii) the total number of financial service operations or the total quantity of financial services output expressed in terms of designated numerical units in the form of quotas or the requirement of an economic needs test; or

(iv) the total number of natural persons that may be employed in a particular financial service sector or that a financial institution may employ and who are necessary for, and directly related to, the supply of a specific financial service in the form of numerical quotas or the requirement of an economic needs test.

The Latin American Parties of the TPP, Chile, Mexico and Peru, already enjoy relatively open markets when it comes to competition from international players in financial markets. In this setup, they could be among those TPP parties to benefit the most from other TPP parties establishing similar standards. In Chile, foreign banks may already establish themselves by opening a subsidiary, by holding shares in an existing Chilean bank, or by setting up a branch with separate capital. There are no restrictions regarding the amount of branches that can be open up. Foreign insurance companies enjoy the same facilitate access to domestic markets.[72] Mexico has significantly liberalized access to its financial sector after implementing NAFTA and in 2015 had 70% of its banking assets held by foreign institutions.[73] However, the participation of foreign investment in other financial institutions such as leasing, factoring, insurance and foreign exchange brokers is still limited to 49% of the paid-up capital.[74] With a specific nationality prohibition for non-Mexican firms to invest into Credit Unions.[75] Peru enjoys similar level of market oppeness, with the majority of its banks being foreign owned.[76] Although foreign banks have to follow specific regulation that take their origine into account, in general there are no restrictions on foreign involvement in the financial and insurance markets.[77]

The telecommunication commitments[78] of Chapter 13 are also intended to guarantee a pro-competition framework able of enhancing sector performance and consumer welfare by eliminating policies and regulations that strengthen dominance through statutory monopolies, limited access to essential facilities and discriminatory

---

72. See WTO Secretariat, Trade Policy Review of Chile (2015), pp. 126–127, 129.
73. See USDS, Mexico Investment Climate Statement (2015), p. 15.
74. See WTO Secretariat, Trade Policy Review of Mexico (2013), pp. 141, 144, 148.
75. See Art. 6 of the Law for Foreign Investment. Available at http://dof.gob.mx/nota_detalle.php?codigo=4817271&fecha=27/12/1993.
76. See USDS, Investment Climate Statement (2015), pp. 20–21.
77. See WTO Secretariat, Trade Policy Report of Peru (2014), pp. 83–84.
78. Article 13.2 restricts the scope of the Chapter only over telephone and data transmission.

behavior of incumbent companies. Key obligations of the telecommunication Chapter are based on: (i) competition for the supply of services and equipment, (ii) non-discriminatory market conditions and (iii) market-oriented regulatory solutions. The goal is to create positive externalities to sectors that depend on telecommunication services by addressing issues on fair access to government resources, transparency in rule making, fair procedures and rule of law.

General principles[79] and rules on accessibility and non-discrimination[80] within the telecom Chapter ensure the right to access networks on reasonable and non-discriminatory bases, establishing portability, number access and fair international roaming rules for firms from other TPP parties. The Chapter expands on accessibility and non-discrimination rules when it comes to dealing with entities with market power,[81] establishing obligations for interconnection, non-discrimination, unbundling requirements, co-location and access to poles, ducts, conduits, international submarine cable systems and rights-of-way owned or controlled by major suppliers.

Here again the position of Chile, Mexico and Peru, that in the past years have developed sector-specific regulatory frameworks that promote competition principles by fostering equal access, non-discrimination and even prevent anticompetitive behavior such as margin squeeze through *ex ante* regulation, is strengthened by the commitments of the TPP that should enable similar regulatory framework in other TPP parties. However, there is scope to enhance the current sector performance and further leverage the overall benefits of the TPP in the sector; particularly regarding guaranteeing competitive neutrality for wholesale public networks on broadband and refining regulations of telecommunication wholesale services for financial end–users.

Finally, also in the case of public procurement, the TPP commitments are set to foster more open and competitive public procurement markets. According to the World Bank "the public procurement market is massive. In developing countries, governments spend an estimated USD 820 billion a year, about 50% of their budgets, on procuring goods and services. Public procurement is large in high-income countries as well, reaching about 29% of total general government expenditure. In the past decade, public procurement has increased ten-fold. And this growth trajectory is expected to continue."[82] TPP Parties share an interest in accessing each other's large government procurement through transparent, predictable, and non-discriminatory rules. In the Government Procurement chapter, TPP Parties commit to core disciplines of national treatment and non-discrimination, to treat tenders fairly and impartially, to award contracts based solely on the evaluation criteria specified in the notices and tender documentation, and to establish due process procedures to question or review complaints about an award.

Along these obligations, the existing public procurement laws in Chile, Mexico and Peru set pro-competition regulatory frameworks that generally promote efficiency

---

79. Articles 13.1, 13.2, 13.3, 13.17.
80. Articles 13.4, 13.5, 13.6, 13.8, 13.9.
81. Articles 13.7, 13.10, 13.11, 13.12, 13.13, 13.14, 13.15.
82. See WBG (2016), "Benchmarking Public Procurement 2016: Assessing Public Procurement Systems in 77 Economies", page iv, available at http://bpp.worldbank.org/~/media/WBG/BPP/Documents/Reports/Benchmarking-Public-Procurement-2016.pdf.

and transparency. Again, the TPP commitments could also allow to introduce competition principles in tender design more explicitly and prevent bid-rigging behavior *ex post*.

Interestingly, the rationale behind sector-specific commitments of the TPP is to foster the removal of policies and rules that are harmful to the development of competition. Using the World Bank Group's Market and Competition Policy Assessment Toolkit (MCPAT) framework, Figure 20.5 shows how sectoral commitments on the financial services, telecommunications and procurement sectors have been designed to eliminate rules that (i) reinforce dominance or limit entry, (ii) are conducive to collusive outcomes or increase costs to compete in the market and (iii) discriminate and protect vested interests. In this sense, e the TPP explicitly advance on a comprehensive approach to competition by setting rules that intend to eliminate those regulations having harmful effects on competition.

Specifically, and as example, following the Financial Services Chapter, each Party shall not limit market entry by adopting or maintaining quotas about number of institutions, number or value of transactions or require economic need tests.[83] In other words, the TPP commitments are avoiding that Parties impose conditions that constitute either an *absolute or a relative ban for market entry* which in turn will have the general effect of *reinforcing dominance or limiting entry*. Similarly, the Telecommunication Chapter demands from each Party independent and impartial telecommunications regulatory bodies that do not hold financial interests or operating/management roles in any supplier of public telecommunications services.[84] Such commitment addresses potential *lack of competitive neutrality vis-a-vis government entities*. Therefore this commitment intends to mitigate the anticompetitive effects of those *rules that discriminate or protect vested interests* as identified by the WBG MCPAT. Finally, the Government procurement Chapter requires Parties to adopt measures that fight corruption and fraudulent behavior in public procurement process, which, by nature, implies a prohibition of bid rigging.[85] This type of commitment is intended to counteract *rules that facilitate agreements among competitors* in the sense of the MCPAT and therefore have the general effect of being *conducive to collusive outcomes or increase the costs to compete in the market*.

---

83. See Art. 11.5, Chapter 11, TPP.
84. See Art. 13.6.1, Chapter 13, TPP.
85. See Art. 15.18, Chapter 15, TPP.

Chapter 20: Implications of the Trans-Pacific Partnership §20.04

Figure 20.5   How TPP Sector Specific Obligations Foster the Removal of Government Interventions That Harm Competition

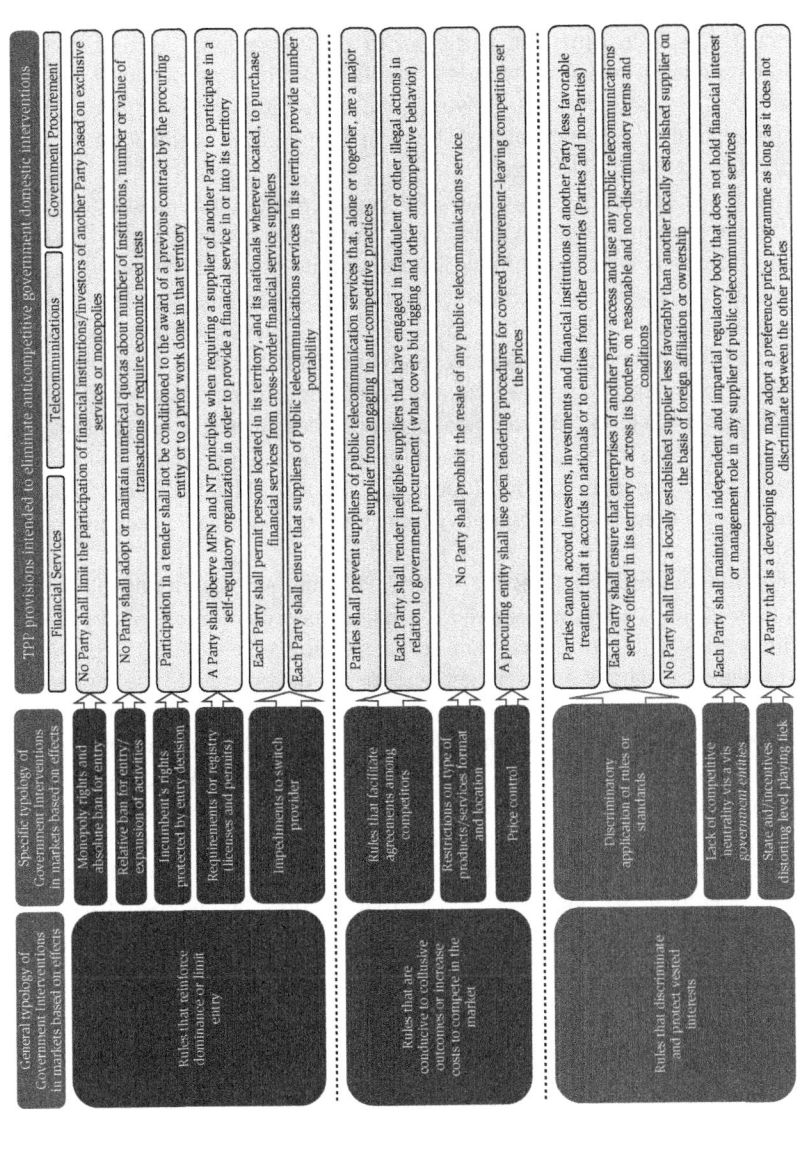

Source: Developed by the authors based on the Markets and Competition Policy Assessment Tool,-World Bank Competition Policy Team and the text of the TPP.

§20.05 FINAL REMARKS

How to capitalize the TPP-Competition Policy Provisions to shape market outcomes in Latin America?

As expected, the Latin American parties of the TPP – regional leaders in antitrust regulation – are fairly compliant with the establishment of fair procedural rules in the enforcement of competition laws. However, the competition policy implication of the TPP go far beyond this chapter: indeed the competition policy implications of the TPP go beyond the text of the TPP itself.

From a general perspective, the TPP captures the key elements of effective competition policy frameworks by connecting economy-wide (horizontal) and sectoral (vertical) obligations affecting both public and private firms. In this sense, it offers a platform that could be used to elevate competition to a national policy as some of the TPP parties have done in the past, notably Australia. However, further developing this notion would require a much larger engagement of TPP members.

From a more specific perspective, the implications of the different chapters are also significant for their potential to foster better policies, incentivize all market players to behave competitively and shape market outcomes both domestically and regionally.

International Cooperation and Procedural Fairness obligations could contribute to address cross-border anticompetitive behavior that seems to be affecting key markets for consumers and business in the region.

First, the competition Chapter of the TPP aims at guarantying that relevant international trade partners will share the same standards in terms of application of competition rules. This represents a non-trivial step towards leveling the playing field among providers of goods and services within the region, regardless ownership or nationality that can especially support enforcement in cross-border antitrust cases. For instance, recent cartel investigations in the region such as Liquid Oxygen or Hygiene products show strong links between cartelized markets across LAC countries.[86] In this setup, a framework that enables collaboration among competition authorities to consult on procedural matters or share evidence and confidential information could be extremely important to enable enforcement and even foster deterrence. It also gives a platform to operationalize national strategies that prioritize potential antitrust enforcement on markets prone to collusive behavior – particularly for relatively young agencies.

Competitive neutrality commitments could foster more effective and less distortive public support measures to SOEs

SOE Commitments provide a platform for the development of an analytical framework to help identifying and removing distortive non-commercial support for SOEs. In fact,

---

86. Licetti and Goodwin (2016), Anti-Cartel Enforcement Database for Developing Countries: An application to Latin American Countries. World Bank Policy Research Working Paper. Forthcoming.

the TPP provides the foundations for the establishment of a regulatory framework similar to state aid control applied in the EU. In practical matters, this could include:

- Increasing transparency of public aid supported granted to SOEs and designated monopolies.
- Implementation of inventories of non-commercial support measures to SOEs.
- Assessment of the effects of granted non-commercial support measures to SOEs.
- Identification of competition distortions stemming from non-commercial support measures to SOEs.
- Evaluation of the proportionality of support measures and alternatives to minimize distortions on competition.
- Design of strategies to phase out recurrent non-commercial support measures to SOEs in order to minimize distortions on competition.
- Design of mechanisms to prevent designated monopolies from engaging in anticompetitive practices and to foster compliance with Competition related commitments under the TPP.

A key tool for the implementation of the notion of competitive neutrality build on the peer experience of Peru is the analysis of subsidiarity applied to the participation of the TPP party in the economy through SOEs. This analysis would be based on the implementation of the subsidiarity principle according to which the Government has a subsidiary duty to perform only those tasks where private supply is not feasible. In this sense, SOEs should not replace or interfere in any manner with private businesses when they are fully capable to meet a particular demand.

Pro-competition sectoral commitments could promote regulatory and structural reforms that embed competition principles in key sectors of the economy

At the same time, the competition-related commitments embedded in the sectoral chapters of the TPP will reinforce trade and investment among TPP parties in regulated sectors such as telecommunications, financial services and public procurement. An option for regional TPP parties to leverage the benefits of this agreement could be to focus their competition advocacy efforts on key markets for international competitiveness within the TPP area. In this sense, special attention could be given to support the implementation of pro-competition regulations in those markets covered by the TPP sectoral chapters. Initial measures in those markets could include:

- Systematically assess and identify existing regulatory and behavioral constraints to competition in resulting in market distortions.
- Defining the role of the competition agency and promoting inter-institutional collaboration with other sector regulators.
- Introduce, design and implement *ex ante* assessment of regulations that include competition analysis for new policies and regulations.

Governments can continue their efforts to enhance cooperation between Competition authorities and sector regulators to foster regulatory neutrality in markets with SOE presence as well as to ensure application of competition principles in regulated sectors. They can also start implementing subnational strategies, with involvement of several level of governments by providing incentives to eliminate and reduce anticompetitive government interventions. These measures will constitute building blocks of a more comprehensive analytical framework for the governments' participation and intervention in the economy that aims at leveling the playing field among market players.

All of these measures, if carried out effectively constitute building blocks to elevate competition policy into a national policy – and eventually, Latin American countries could potentially see the benefits achieved by other TPP parties with the implementation of comprehensive competition policy reforms such as Australia.

Index

A

Abuse
  dominant position, Paraguay, 47, 49–55, 57
  exclusionary, 151–154
  interconnection services, 10
  market power, 24, 37, 42
  price predation, 155, 157
Accountability
  corporate individuals, Japan, 250
  newer agencies, Cartel Investigations, 285
  obligations, 19–20
  and transparency, Mexico, 21
Advocacy
  and antitrust enforcement, 69
  COFECE, 33–34
  competition, 39, 42, 58, 71, 74, 76, 85–110, 129, 334, 359
  document for foreign companies, 28
  efforts, 229
Agency
  CADE, 60, 294
  CNDC, 290
  competent, 22
  competition, 18, 23, 24, 85–86, 88, 95, 97–99, 101, 105, 108, 323, 359
  creativity, 109
  design, 27
  federal regulatory, 5, 12
  foreign, 295
  government, 181
  independent, 41
  information, 294, 295, 301, 305, 312, 313
  international, 27
  investigative and decision-making powers, 18
  movement, 293
  national, 15, 143
  operation of, 271
  privatizations, 93
  regulatory provisions, 274
  resorces, 304
  review, 273
AJUFE. *See* Association of Federal Judges (AJUFE)
Anticompetitive agreement
  and abuse of dominant position procedure, 55
  bid rigging in Ecuador, 191
  competitors, 228, 229
  CRCAL, 127
  illegal conducts, Law No. 4956, 48
  indirect effects, 53
  officers and directors, 244, 247, 248
  sanctions, 45
Anticorruption
  and antitrust, 59, 62–66
  compliance, 66, 68, 81
  regulation, 60
Antitrust compliance
  Brazil (*see* Compliance Program, Brazil)
  Chile, 69–70
  Mexico, 70–71
Appointment

Index

Commissioners, 12, 16, 53
  internal comptroller, 17
Argentina
  automotive market, special customs
      area
    Cámara Federal de Apelaciones de
        Comodoro Rivadavia, 202–203
    fine, 201–202
    Law 19.640, 198
    legal frame of investigation,
        200–201
  new competition policy
    advocacy, 42
    description, 37–38
    enforcement, 38–39, 42–43
    international approach, 40
    new draft bill, 40–41
    state intervention, 37
    strengthening of the CNDC, 39–40
Assessment
  COFECE's, 96
  competition, 96, 103, 110, 121–131
  COMSAT International (2010) case,
      145
  concentrations and merger control, 55
  CORMAGDALENA case, 147
  ex ante impact, 110, 359
  legality, anticompetitive practice, 309
  markets, 22
  MCPAT, 356
  and merger control, 269
  pro-competitive regulatory, 111–131
  regulatory impact assessment, 95
  SOEs, 359
Association
  admission, 54
  AJUFE, 62
  American Bar Association (ABA), 40,
      65
  anticompetitive agreements, 48
  BOLPROES, 229
  civil, 40, 65, 73–84
  DASOL, 235

dissemination of the competition
    culture
  economists, 33
  farmers, 127
  functions, 213
  guidelines, 94, 209, 223, 224
  International Bar Association (IBA),
      40, 65
  national auto parts maker's, 259
  pharmacist, 105
  practices, 29
  private real estate, 191
  producer, 127
  professional and trade, 29
  sectorial, 237
  trade and business, 87, 90, 105, 212,
      213, 221, 222
Association of Federal Judges (AJUFE),
    62
Australian Competition & Consumer
    Commission (ACCC), 193
Authority
  competition, 3, 5, 9, 15, 26, 30, 45,
      51–54, 85–87, 93, 95–97, 102,
      103, 105–108, 122–126, 136,
      138, 140, 145, 149, 150, 169,
      170, 187, 190, 193, 197, 203,
      229–231, 234, 237, 244, 246,
      251, 255, 256, 258, 259, 261,
      263, 267, 280, 288, 290, 297,
      300, 302, 304, 307–309, 320–
      324, 334, 337, 345
  national, 41
Autonomy
  and constitutional independence, CO-
      FECE, 15
  Federal Competition Commission, 5, 6
  independent, 273
  investigative and the decision-making
      authorities, 17–19
  private, 259, 261
  transparency and accountability
      obligations, 19

B

Best practice
  advocacy, 33, 107, 108
  competition agencies, 26
  Compliance Program, 83
  governmental bodies, 79
  international, 13, 23, 34, 119, 281, 330
  Nestle/Pfizer, 279
  public policies, 340
  regulation, 117
Bid-rigging
  activities, 288, 310
  area, 234
  behavior, 356
  CADE, 234
  cartel of, 235, 236, 244, 247–249, 286
  Colombia (*see* Public procurement)
  Ecuador (*see* Ecuador)
  investigations, SIC, 143
  multimarket contacts, 215
  pharmaceutical sector, 9
  prohibition, 356
  public procurement, 96
  public tenders, 215
  risk, 96
  types, 234–235
  and of unilateral violations, 68
Bill of law, 40–42
Brazil
  advocacy strategies, 107
  antitrust compliance
    initiatives, 75–76
    programs (*see* Compliance program)
  antitrust deterrence and enforcement efforts, 56
  below and above-cost predation standard, 182
  Brazilian Competition Law, 258
  Brazilian Corporation Act, 240, 251, 253
  CADE, 75–76, 122, 124, 129, 253, 255, 265

cartels
  bid-rigging (*see* Bid-rigging)
  CADE, 234
  economic analysis and communications, 236
  judicial review, 237
  mechanisms of collusion, 236
  pharmaceutical companies, 236
  sanctions, 237–238
  solar heaters, 235–236
civil associations and non-governmental organizations, 73
CNDC, 199
competition authority, 259, 261
competition law
  administrative proceedings, 77
  antitrust and anti-corruption, 77
  antitrust compliance, 76
  bankruptcy and arbitration, 78
  IBRAC's objectives, 79–83
  private actions, anticompetitive practices, 78
  rophylactic-guidance, 83
  values, 78–79
competition restrictions, 116
constitution, 258
cooperation agreement, 305
enforcement of criminal penalties, 30
illegal per se predatory pricing, 169–171
implemention, Leniency programs, 302
leniency program, 58
Liquid Oxygen cases, 291–295
market regulation, 118
Mercosur antitrust policy, 315, 318, 319, 323, 324, 326
patents office, 265
rule-of-reason approach to predatory pricing, 171

Index

shareholder derivative suits, antitrust
  violations, 243–250
strengthening, 74
Superior Court of Justice, 253
TPP, 342
Brazilian competition authority (CADE),
  60, 66–67, 75, 234, 236, 244,
  253, 255, 262–264
Burden of proof
  anticompetitive conducts, 334
  CEBB, 98
  competition authorities, 179
  high regulatory,
    Latin America, 118–119
  macro-economic performance, 110
  private parties, 68, 181

C

Cartel
  Brazil (see Brazil)
  challenges and New Competition
    Framework, 27–30
  El Salvador case
    anti-trust regulation, 227
    economic efficiency, 227, 231
    consumer welfare, 231
    "flour cartel", 229
    jurisprodence, SC, 228–229
    "naive cartel", 229–230
    price-fixing, 230–231
    public procurements, 230
  exchanges of information
    multimarket contacts, 215
    prices, 214–215
    quantity, 213
  monopolistic practices, 5
  regional coordination, Liquid Oxygen
    case (see Liquid Oxygen case)
Challenges
  analysis, remedies, 10
  bid rigging, Colombia (see Public procurement)
  CFC's resolution, 9
  Cinemex/Cinemark case, 280

CNDC, 203
COFECE proceedings, 274
competition advocacy, 110
economy, 109
FLEC, 271
judicial, 20
MERCOSUR, 324–326
new competition framework
  advocacy, 33–34
  cartels, 27–30
  COFECE, 23–25, 31–32, 34
  coordination with the IFT, 30–31
  identification, 22
  institutional arrangements, 26–27
  investigation, 25–26
  market studies, 32–33
  mergers, 33
  Mexico, 26
perceptions of competition law,
  Brazil, 77–83
policymakers, 129
strengthening cooperation, cartel
  competition agencies, 298–300
  implementation, Leniency Programs,
    302
  prohibition to exchange
    information, 300–302
  recognition of the evidence,
    302–303
COFECE. See Commissioner of the
  Federal Economic Competition
  Commission (COFECE)
Colombia
  bid rigging in public procurement (see
    Bid-rigging)
  competition advocacy, 101–102
  reviewing cooperation agreements,
    296
Commission
  ACCC, 193
  Argentinean Competition, 173
  attributions, 11
  CADE, 255, 258, 265
  CEB, 125
  CEBB, 98, 99

364

Index

CFC, 3, 5–6, 8, 9, 40, 285, 288
CNDC, 39, 40
COFECE, 15, 70, 96, 269
Commissioners' appointment procedure, 12, 16
competition, 55, 98–100
CONACOM, 52–53, 57, 58
CRC, 102
designation, 12
European, 40, 55, 349
FECE, 95
FTC, 192
guidelines, 29
interaction, 273
interim measures, 13
Mexican Competition, 170, 172
monopolistic practices, 22, 29
MTC, 317
performance, 17
Peruvian Competition, 175
powers, 11, 20
restriction, 42
SCPM, 195
structure, 19
successes and limitations, 11
Transition Commission of Guayas, 193
Commissioner, 6, 12, 16, 20, 26, 39, 41, 46, 52–54, 57, 58, 236, 259, 260, 263, 266, 273
Commissioner of the Federal Economic Competition Commission (COFECE), 15, 19, 21, 23–25, 31–34, 96, 270, 274
Competition policy
  Argentina (*see* Argentina)
  Mexico
    advocacy, 33–34
    cartels, 27–30
    cases, 8–11
    COFECE, 23–24
    competition authority, 3
    competition law, 3
    constitutional reform 2013, 14–21
    coordination with IFT, 30–31
    creation of the CFC, 5–6
    first competition provisions, 4
    institutional arrangements, 26–27
    legal reform 2006, 11–13
    legal reform 2011, 13–14
    market studies, 32–33
    mergers, 33
    new federal law of economic competition, 21–22
    new powers of COFECE to conduct market investigations, 31–32
    public opinion, 6–7
  Paraguay
    abuse of dominant position, 49–50
    anticompetitive agreements, 48
    CONACOM, 52–54
    laws, 45
    legal framework, 47–48
    merger control, 50–51
    procedure to investigate and punish illegal acts, 54–57
    recommendations, 57–58
    state aid, 51–52
    unfair competition, 51
  TPP (*see* Trans-Pacific partnership (TPP))
Competitiveness, 4–7, 13, 24, 42, 124, 127, 213, 326, 359
Compliance
  antitrust compliance programs, 59–72
  competition legislation, 82
  corporate, 249, 287
  facilitate, 13, 33
  guidelines, 106, 209
  initiatives, 75–76
  and market, 90
  non-compliance, 131
  Program (*see* Compliance Program)
  public procurement, 90
  recognition, 24
  strict, 34
  supervisors of, 143
Compliance Program
  Brazil
    antitrust and anticorruption, 63–66

Index

antitrust compliance, BCDS, 60–63
BCDS, 59
CADE's Guidelines, 66–67
HSBC/Bradesco, 68–69
jurisdictions, 71
mitigating circumstances, 67
PPI, 66
corporate, 249
effective, 82
IBRAC, 83
implementation, 215, 250
The Competition Regional Centre for Latin America (CRCAL), 127
Concentration
concept of, 271, 273
control, 320, 324
degree of, 206
effects, 279
ex post control, 57
first competition provisions, 4
high, 26
market, 13, 50, 153, 155, 178, 184, 207, 275, 276, 280
and merger control, 52, 55, 60, 270, 271
pre-concentration activities, 29
prevention, 39
prohibition, 272
treatment of notifications, 272
Congress, 11, 12, 19–21, 26, 32, 38, 41, 45–47, 53, 54, 60, 96, 98, 102, 124, 285, 289
Constitution
absolutism of property, 256
Argentina, 38
Brazil, 63, 258, 264
collective rights, 135
Colombia, 136
2013 Constitutional Reform, Mexico
amendment, 273
autonomy, investigative and decision-making authorities, 17–19
COFECE, 270
creation, new autonomous agencies, 15–16
economic competition, 15
incremental powers, 17
The New Federal Law, economic competition, 21–22
political context, 14
specialized courts, 20–21
transparency and accountability obligations, 19–20
economic competition, 24
Ecuador, 189, 190
functions, 98
justification, 261
modification, Mexican Constitution, 70
Paraguay, 46, 47
Peru, 345, 352
protection, 260, 346
rights and guarantees, 237
subsidiarity principle, 93, 97
terms, 24
Consumer
ACCC, 193
Argentina, 39, 42
benefits, 90, 106, 108, 111, 113–114, 121, 129, 131, 167, 216, 258, 269
Brazil, 73, 77–81, 83
and businesses, 111
choices and information, 120, 122–123
and competition, 124
concept of agreement, 211
damages, 239, 261
digital economy innovations, 130
dominance, 180
and economy, 188
and firms, 154, 158
fuel stations, 129
goods and services, 271, 279, 347
group, 192, 219
innovation, 266
international and regional cartels, 287

intervention, 96
limitations, 128
local, 311
markets, 128, 358
Mexico, 5, 21, 26, 27, 32, 33
mobile communications, 102
Paraguay, 46, 48, 49, 51, 53, 57, 58
perspectives, 121, 270
prices, 105
pro-consumer, 162
productivity, 113, 126
protection, 103, 112, 125, 335–338
reforms, 110
welfare, 112, 120, 127, 129, 159, 171, 195, 231, 257, 260–262, 334, 353, 354

Coordination
anticompetitive, 215, 217, 218
deficiencies, 123
exchanges of information on quantity, 213
with IFT, 30–31
impact, 219–220, 224–225
Mercosur, 315, 316, 320, 321, 323, 325
oligopolistic, 216
regional, cartel investigations (*See* Liquid Oxygen case)
sustainability, 218

Corporate
Brazilian Corporation Act, 240, 251, 253
Brazilian Corporation Law, 245–248, 250
compliance, 59, 60, 65, 69
  Brazil, 59, 60
  policy, 287
  program, 249
convictions of foreign corporations, 300
culture, 70, 143, 150
directors and officers, 239, 240, 243, 244, 247, 249–251
engineering and transactions, 77
entity, 343
environment, 83
governance, 347
integrity, 66
international firms and corporate bodies, 5
law, 77, 243, 244
liability, 244, 246, 251, 253
responsibility, 241
restructuring, 272
self-corporate governance rules, 287
shareholder, 240, 244
state aid, Paraguay, 51
voluntary adoption of integrity and corruption prevention measures, 83

Court
Argentina, 197, 198, 201, 202
Australia, 193
Canada, 310
Chile, 208, 210
commercial, 342
creation of specialized courts, Mexico, 20–21, 30, 273
decisions, 67
El Salvador, 231
European, 159, 163, 167, 175, 203
Mexico, 236, 237, 269
National Antitrust Court of Appeals, Argentina, 41
SC, Mexico, 9, 12, 13, 18
US, 265

CRCAL. *See* The Competition Regional Centre for Latin America (CRCAL)

Criminal
and administrative theories, 141
confession of, 141
consequences, 135, 139, 140
decisions on, 143
enforcement of criminal penalties, 29–30
exercise of criminal action, 141
Federal Criminal Code, 29
investigations, 139, 140, 244

Index

offense, competition restrictive agreements, 139
"opportunity principle", 141
penalties for cartels, 22
proceedings, 291, 326
prosecution, 253, 303
prosecutor, 195
records, 124
sanctions, 245, 310, 313

D

Damage
　actions, 41
　compensation, 334
　consumers, 27
　fine, 201
　predatory pricing, 171
　private/civil, 308-311
　quantification, 78
　risk of business, 280
　Shareholders (*see* Shareholders' damage claims, antitrust violations)
Decision-making
　antitrust law, 267
　authorities, 17-19
　mechanisms, 127
　process, 163, 178, 184, 250, 255
Defense of Competition, Mercosur
　antitrust policy
　　agreement, 321-324
　　antecedents, 319-321
　　challenges of cooperation, 324-326
　　Fortaleza Protocol, 325
　protocol, 317-319
　provisional regulation of competition law, 316-317
　treaty of Asunción, 316-317
Development
　cartel enforcement activity, 286
　communication, 33
　competition advocacy, Latin America, 85-110

economic, 7, 12, 26, 115, 124, 258, 261
free competition regime, 79
institutional, 3
international, 64
Leniency Programs, 302
merger control in Mexico, 269-285
national, 14
networks of competing airlines, 25
new competition policy in Argentina, 38-42
OECD, 63, 187, 233
SECOFI, 5
social, 327
technical, 48, 200, 215, 255, 258, 266
Dominance
　abuse of, 10, 49
　collective, 13
　joint, 280, 281
　market, 154
　price predation, 180
　reinforces, 90, 356
　structural definition, 338

E

Ecuador
　anticompetitive agreements, 191
　Cirrus and others, UK, 192
　competition legislation, 190
　CRONIX case, 194-195
　marine hoses, Australia, 192-193
　Multiple Listing Service, Inc. (MLS), US, 191-192
　public procurement
　　and competition law, 191
　　legislation, 189
　TUBOS case, 193-194
Emerging economy
　below and above-cost predation, 182-183
　decision-making process, 178-179
　effects-based approach
　　dominance, 180

pro-competitive effects, 180
profits sacrifice, 180–181
Enforcement
BCDS, 60–62
competition policy, 14
political priority, 38–39
predatory pricing, 176–183
subsidiarity principle, 97–98
Ex officio, 18, 24, 53, 96, 98, 99, 107, 142, 209, 228

F

Fairness, 189, 259, 336, 337, 358
Federal Economic Competition Commission (COFECE), 269
Free market
COFECE, 21
FLEC, 272

G

Guidelines
CADE's, 66
COFECE, 21
FNE, 70
IBRAC, 83
trade association, 209

I

Illegality, 12, 144, 160, 161, 200, 214, 250
Illicit, 71, 206, 245, 249, 265, 317, 321
Indirect evidence
bid-rigging cartels, 234–235
international trend, 236–237
solar heater cartel, 235–236
Industrial, 90, 152, 207, 259, 260, 288, 291, 347–348
Information exchange, 28–29, 205–207, 216, 226, 294, 334
Institutional
arrangements, 26–27

checks and balances
accountability obligations, 19–20
creation of specialized courts, 20–21
investigation and decision-making authorities, 17–19
and substantive framework
in Chilean competition law, 211–212
institutional framework, 208–210
provisions, 210–211
Intellectual property (IP)
ANFAPE, 259–262
antitrust law, 256–259
CADE, 262–264
Sham litigation, 264–266
International competition network (ICN)
competition advocacy, 86
INDECOPI, 100
International cooperation, 28, 310–311, 319, 322, 334–335, 337, 358
International Monetary Fund (IMF), 5, 7, 118
Investigation
CNDC, 39, 42, 197, 199–203
COFECE, 31–32
CONACOM, 52
FNE, 209
IBRAC, 80
prohibition to exchange information, 300–302
Telcel, 10

J

Judicial review, 22, 41, 236–238, 250, 288

L

Liquid Oxygen case
bid-rigging domestic cartels, 286

competition authorities, competition authorities, 285–286
cooperation agreements, 293–298
coordination, 308–309
effective exchange of information, 305–308
implementing Leniency Programs, 302
limits of international cooperation, 310–311
low levels of cooperation, Competition Agencies, 298–300
prohibition, exchange information in open cartel investigations, 300–302
recognition of the Evidence Gathered Abroad, 302–303
recommendations, 303–305
regional trade agreements and bilateral agreements, 287
review, 288–293

M

Mandate
 advocacy and enforcement activity, 100
 competition
  agency's advocacy, 88, 93, 94, 101
  authorities, 88, 210
 economic competition, 24
 INDECOPI, 99–100
 innovation promotion, 255
 legal, 88, 94, 97, 98, 107
 Peruvian competition authority, 345
 remedies, 26
 SOEs, 345
Market studies, 32–33, 93, 95, 100, 104, 107, 109, 279
Merger control, Mexico
 cases
  Cinemex/Cinemark, 280
  Coca-Cola/Jugos del Valle, 276
  Comex/Sherwin Williams, 280–281
  Mexicana/Aeromexico, 274–275
  Mexichem, 276–278

Nestle/Pfizer, 279–280
Televisa/GSF Telecom Holdings, 278
COFECE, 270
evolution, regulatory framework
 1993 FLEC, 270–271
 2006 FLEC, 271–272
 2011 FLEC, 272
Mexico
 competition
  policy (see Competition policy)
  specific impact assessment, 95
 compliance
  antitrust, 70–71
 federal public administration programs and policies, 96–97
 liquid oxygen cartel cases, 291–292
 merger control (see Merger control, Mexico)
 regulatory policies, markets and disruptive innovations, 96
Ministry of Development, Industry and Trade (MIFIC), 54
Ministry of Economy, 12, 21
Ministry of Finance, 60, 106
Ministry of Foreign Affairs, 103
Ministry of Industry and Commerce (MIC), 52
Ministry of Industry and Productivity (MIPRO), 190, 193–194
Ministry of Information Technology (MinTIC), 102
Ministry of Justice, 66
Ministry of Planning, 65
Ministry of Public Works, 127
Ministry of Trade and Industrial Development, 5
Ministry of Transport and Communications, 125
Monopolistic
 anticompetitive agreements, 191
 competition, 156
 economics, 156
 Mexico, 7

practices, 4, 5, 8

N

National Public Procurement System (SNCP), 189
National Public Procurement System Act (LOSNCP), 189

O

Organisation for Economic Co-operation and Development (OECD)
competition assessment
Greece, 121
toolkit, 111, 120–122
competition benefit, 113–114
economics, 116, 117
fast-growing emerging economies, 114
fighting bid rigging, Colombia, 143
international business transactions, 63
product market regulation (PMR), 87
product market regulation indicator, 115
public procurement & fighting bid rigging, 66
WBG-OECD PMR Indicators, 87

P

Paraguay. See Competition policy
Paraguay's Ministry of Finance, 46
Per se
hard core cartels, 41
illegal price predation
above-cost predation, 165–168
below average variable cost predation, 162–165
below marginal cost predation, 161, 182
Brazilian Secretaria de Direito Econômico, 170, 171
CFC v. Warner Lambert, 169
Colombian and the Brazilian policies, 171
Latin American countries, 169
SIC v. Cadbury Adams, 169
legal and illegal behavior, 157
legal below cost selling, 158–160
rule, collusions and price fixing, 48
violations, 5, 49
Policy-makers, 90, 94, 109, 111, 236
Predatory pricing policy
approach justification, emerging Latin American economies
administrability, below and above-cost predation standard, 181–183
effect-based price predation standard, 179–181
economics
exclusionary pricing and abusive pricing policy, 152–154
market power, exclusionary behavior and price predation, 154–157
per se illegal price predation
above-cost predation, 165–168
below average variable cost predation, 162–165
below marginal cost predation, 161
Brazilian Secretaria de Direito Econômico, 170, 171
Colombian and the Mexican competition authorities, 169, 170
Mexican Commission, 170
price–cost analysis, 171
per se legal below cost selling, 158–160
rule-of-reason approach
Areeda-Turner test, 172
Argentine Chamber of Stationer's Shops v. Supermercados Makro, 173
Chilean and Peruvian statutes, 171
Chilean Telecommunications Company (CTC), 173, 174
Chilean Tribunal, 173, 174
Mexican Commission, 172

Peruvian Competition Commission, 175
Tagua-Tagua Chamber of Commerce, 174
Pro-competitive regulatory assessment
  burden, 118–119
  competition enhances productivity, 114–115
  competition policy, 111–112
  consumers benefits, 113–114
  emerging opportunities
    digital economy innovations, 130–131
    ex post assessment, 128–130
  identification, 122–123
  limitations
    ability of suppliers, 126
    choices and information available to consumers, 128
    incentives of suppliers, 126–127
    range of suppliers, 123–125
  OECD competition assessment toolkit, 120–121
  restrictions, competition harm growth, 115–118
Public procurement
  advantages, 66
  Argentina, 40
  bid rigging, Colombia
    anticompetitive conducts, 135
    competition authorities, 135
    Comsat international (2010) case, 145
    CORMAGDALENA (2013) case, 147
    historical review prior to law 1340 of 2009, 136–138
    IDIPRON (2013) case, 148–149
    INPEC (2012) case, 145–146
    modernization, 138–144
    NULE BIENESTARINA GROUP (2013) case, 147–148
    NULE HOGARES (2013) case, 148
    PAVIGAS (2014) case, 149
    RAPISCAN (2012) case, 146
  VALME (2016) case, 146–147
  VIGILANCIA (2015) case, 149
  Brazil, 233, 235, 236
  Ecuador, 187, 189, 191, 194, 195
  Mexico, 9
  process, 96
  promote compliance, 90
  TPP, 352, 355, 359

R

Reform
  building productive relationships, public stakeholders, 110
  bureaucratic barriers system, 99
  Chile, 64
  CNDC, 39
  COFEMER's, 96
  competition law, 96, 100
  institutional framework, 41, 63
  Latin America, 87
  legislative, 182, 183
  Mexico
    COFECE, 33, 34
    2013 constitutional, 14–16, 21, 34, 269
    financial, 32
    innovative institutional, 4
    2006 legal reform, 11–13, 28
    2011 legal reform, 13–14, 28
  pro-competitive, 88, 110, 117
  regulatory, 87, 114, 119, 333
  structural, 112, 117, 333
Regional cooperation, 299
Regulatory
  barriers, 106
  CNDC Report, 42
  framework (*see* Regulatory framework)
  measures, 87
  policies
    emerging markets, 101–102
    markets and disruptive innovations, 96–97

pro-competitive (*see* Pro-competitive regulatory assessment)
provisions, 34
reform, 90
transparency, antitrust matter proceedings, 52
Regulatory framework
  digital and disruptive innovations, 87
  evolution, Mexico
    FLEC in 2006, 271–272
    FLEC in 2011, 272
    legal framework, 273–274
    merger control, 1993 FLEC, 270–271
  Mexican, 15
  pro-competitive, Latin America
    beneficial to consumers, 113–114
    competition enhances productivity, 114–115
    harms growth and productivity, 115–118
    regulatory burden, 118–119
Restriction
  barrier to competition, 17, 23, 98
  civil law jurisdictions, 297
  COFECE (Mexico), 124
  competition harm growth, 115–118
  financial institutions and compliance., 68
  foreign involvement, financial and insurance markets, 354
  market, 263
  procompetitive, 162
  protect domestic producers, 126
  regulatory, 119, 128, 270
  road-freight sector in Mexico, 113
  types, 121

S

Shareholders' damage claims, antitrust violations
  derivative suits against officers and directors, Brazil
    antitrust wrongdoing, 244–250

Article 158 (I), 243
Japanese experience, shareholder derivative actions
  Antimonopoly Act, 242
  antitrust violations, 241, 242
  legal and business community, 241
  RAMSEYER and NAKAZATO, 241
  Sumitomo Electric, 242
State aid, 51–52, 58, 318, 344, 353, 359
Superintendence of Control of Market Power (SCPM), 190
Supreme Court
  administrative chamber, 231
  Amparo Proceeding 554/2011, 18
  Brooke, 167
  Canadian, 310
  Commission's economic analysis, 9
  Mexico, 236, 237
  predatory bidding, 159
  TDLC, 210
  Tribunal's decision, 289
  Unconstitutional Action 33/2006, 12
  U.S., 159, 163, 164, 214, 265

T

Trans-Pacific partnership (TPP)
  adverse effects, 349–350
  control, 348
  framework, 330–331
  FTA, 339
  government participation, 345–346
  National Competition Policy (NCP) process, 332–333
  negotiations, 329
  obligations, 332, 340
  potential market distortions, 350–353
  pro-competition regulatory, 353–356
  pro-competition sectoral commitments, 359–360
  promote economic efficiency and consumer welfare, 334–338
  provisions, 358
  regulatory framework, 359
  SOEs, 332, 339–344, 347

Transparency
  anticompetitive coordination, 218
  CFC, 13
  CNDC, 42
  COFECE and IFT, 19
  competition-related obligations, 334
  complementary duties, 246
  Conarroz's decision-making mechanisms, 127
  market, 29, 224
  obligations, 20
  public procurement, 189
  Secretariat of, 142
Transportation
  market, 26, 123, 172
  Mexico, 9, 25, 97
  passenger air, 25, 106
  price fixing and predating, Chilean, 172
  TNCs, 97
  U.S., 25
Tribunal
  administrative, 60, 68
  Brazilian, 171
  CADE's, Brazil, 75, 236, 244, 253, 262
  Chilean, 172–174
  INDECOPI's, 97–98
  TDLC, 208

U

UNCTAD
  international bid rigging workshop, 292
  international organizations, 40
  OECD, 287, 309
Unfair competition, 49, 51, 57, 58, 98, 183, 211
Unjustified, 48, 49, 54, 182

W

World Bank, 40, 85, 108, 118, 129, 338, 355
World Trade Organization (WTO), 81, 336, 339